Jesus' Words Only

Or Was Paul the Apostle
Jesus Condemns in Rev. 2:2?

Second Edition (March 2007)

ISBN 0-7414-2965-9
Published by:

INFINITY
PUBLISHING.COM

1094 New DeHaven Street, Suite 100
West Conshohocken, PA 19428-2713
Info@buybooksontheweb.com
www.buybooksontheweb.com
Toll-free (877) BUY BOOK
Local phone (610) 941-9999
Fax (610) 941-9959

TABLE OF CONTENTS

VERSE DEDICATIONS

If you claim that ***he said something that he never said***, he will reprimand you and show that ***you are a liar***. (Proverbs 30:6.)

Verily, verily, I say unto you, If a man ***obey my teaching***, he should never see death. (John 8:51.)

Jesus said unto them, Verily, verily, I say unto you, ***Before Abraham*** was born, ***I am***. (John 8:58)

Thus shalt thou say unto the children of Israel, ***I AM*** hath sent me unto you. (Exodus 3:14.)

And Jesus said....You [*i.e.*, the twelve apostles] also shall sit upon ***twelve thrones***, judging the ***twelve tribes of Israel***. (Matt. 19:28.)

And they prayed, and said, Thou, Lord...show of these two the one whom thou hast chosen, to take the... ***apostleship from which Judas fell away***... and the lot fell upon Matthias; and ***he was numbered with the eleven apostles***. (Acts 1:24-26.)

[A]nd the wall of the city [of the New Jerusalem] had twelve foundations, and in them names of the ***twelve apostles*** of the Lamb. (Rev 21:14.)

If I ***bear witness of myself***, my witness is ***not true***. (John 5:31.)

Yea and in your law it is written, that the witness of ***two*** men is ***true***. (John 8:17.)

Paul, an ***apostle*** of Christ Jesus through the will of God, to the saints that are at ***Ephesus***....(Eph 1:1.)

To the ***Ephesian*** Assembly... I have known thy works, and thy labour, and thy endurance, and that thou art not able to bear evil ones, and that thou hast tried those ***saying themselves to be apostles*** and are not, and hast found them ***liars***. (Rev 2:1-2.)

Passage Dedication

If someone who has been a true prophet tells you later that God now permits what God prophetically ***previously*** prohibited, what are you to think?

> 1 Kings 13:1-26 (1) At the LORD's command a prophet from Judah went to Bethel..... (6) King Jeroboam... said to the prophet, "Come home with me and have something to eat. I will reward you for what you have done [*i.e.*, a healing]." (8) The prophet answered, "Even if you gave me half of your wealth, I would not go with you or eat or drink anything with you. (9) ***The LORD has commanded me not to eat or drink a thing, and not to return home the same way I came.***" (10) So he did not go back the same way he had come, but by another road. (11) At that time there was ***an old prophet*** living in Bethel....(14) "Are you the prophet from Judah?" he asked. "I am," the man answered. (15) "Come home and have a meal with me," [the old prophet] said. (16) But the prophet from Judah answered, ***"I can't go home with you or accept your hospitality. And I won't eat or drink anything with you here,*** (17) ***because the LORD has commanded me not to eat or drink a thing, and not to return home the same way I came."*** (18) Then the old prophet from Bethel said to him, "***I, too, am a prophet just like you, and at the LORD's command an angel told me to take you home with me and offer you my hospitality.***" But **the old prophet** was ***lying***. (19) So the prophet from Judah went home with the old prophet and had a meal with him. (20) As they were sitting at the table, ***the word of the LORD came to the old prophet***, (21) and he cried out to the prophet from Judah, "***The LORD says that you disobeyed him and did not do what he commanded.*** (22) Instead, you returned and ate a meal in a place ***he had ordered you not to eat in.*** Because of this ***you will be killed, and your body will not be buried in your family grave***." (23) After they had finished eating, the old prophet saddled the donkey for the prophet from Judah, (24) who rode off. On the way a lion met him and killed him. His body lay on the road, and the donkey and the lion stood beside it.... (26) When the old prophet heard about it, he said, "That is the prophet ***who disobeyed the LORD's command***! And so ***the LORD sent the lion to attack and kill him, just as the LORD said he would***."

Book Reviews of Jesus' Words Only

Bookwire[1] Review May 30, 2006

Is Paul the Apostle really who he claimed to be? Or is he a false prophet whose writings should be excluded from the New Testament? Attorney Douglas J. Del Tondo deftly argues his case in the book *Jesus' Words Only – Or Was Paul the Apostle Jesus Condemns in Revelation 2:2?*

A self-proclaimed "evangelical Christian" since age 15, Del Tondo informs readers in the book's introduction that his soul-searching began as a result of questioning the Baptist doctrine of eternal security and the Calvinist doctrine of perseverance of the saints. After searching for answers, Del Tondo was frustrated to find that although these teachings always originated with Paul, Jesus' words seemed to contradict Paul's. Irritated at what appeared to be an "incessant marginalization of Jesus in preference for Paul," Del Tondo asks and seeks to answer the controversial question: "Why not Jesus' words alone?"

A practicing attorney, Del Tondo's obvious skill for in-depth research and proficient prosecution is evident, as he lays down argument after argument to support his verdict: Paul is guilty of being a false prophet, and therefore, his writings should not be included in the New Testament.

First, Del Tondo says, Paul never made a valid prophecy, which is the only way a true prophet could add text to the Bible (Deut. 18:15). Second, the writings of Paul negate the law, which Del Tondo says is clear evidence that he was a false prophet (Deut. 13:5). Third, Del Tondo points out that Jesus' mention of Balaam in Revelation 2:14 points to Paul as the Balaam-type figure in the New Testament church.

1. Bookwire, a Bowkers company, provides professional reviews. This particular review was made available to bookstores nationwide as their introduction to the text.

(Balaam was an Old Testament prophet who taught that eating meat sacrificed to idols is permissible, as did Paul.)

Del Tondo uses evidence from both early Church History and scripture to weave a convincing case against Paul, although Paulinists would argue that there are numerous holes in his theory. The majority of evangelical Christians will most likely find Del Tondo's charges heresy, saying that God would not allow his Word to be tainted in such a manner (Del Tondo even offers an answer for this). For Del Tondo and his claims, however, the jury is still out, and his book is food for thought for those who are serious students of the Bible.

BookWire Review
www.bookwire.com/PDF/deltondo.pdf
May 30, 2006

Amazon-Posted Book Reviews

A classic! A most enlightening, comprehensive, educative, courageous and brilliant book! (M. Aluouchier 5/21/06.)

It is the very next book that everyone should read right after reading the Bible. (S. Nelson, 4/21/06.)

And while many luminaries...have criticized Paul, none have ever laid out a case against Paul as Douglas Del Tondo. (T. Moran, 3/28/06.)

The author of *Jesus' Words Only* has written a comprehensive review of the two competing gospels in the Bible, that of the Messiah and his Apostles versus that of the 'Apostle' Paul....Mr. Del Tondo points Christians clearly to the Messiah.... (C. Felland, 3/28/2006.)

Author Biography

Currently, I am an attorney in California, and have been one for twenty-five years. In school, I studied Classical Greek and Latin at an East Coast preparatory school. I received special recognition there as a Classic Language Scholar. I can speak Spanish and Italian.

I have been an evangelical Christian since age 15. It began thirty-three years ago while on a vacation to Florida. I became a Christian on a camp out sponsored by a Baptist Faith Bible Church. I then attended a Baptist church in New York City where I was soon water-baptized. Once in California, I joined Westwood Hills Christian Church in about 1983. Beginning in approximately 1987, I joined a conservative-reformed Calvinist Presbyterian church in Calabasas, California. There for several years, I led the high school class in Bible studies after church as well as frequently taught adult Sunday School classes. In 1998, my wife and I moved to Costa Rica to do missionary work for five years. Our ministry was at Las Tablas. It was one of the poorest *precarios* of San Jose. We worked with another couple in sponsoring weekly Bible lessons. Over several years, approximately 350 children visited the Las Tablas' make-shift soup kitchen and board-and-cement church. God led many of these children and their parents to accept Jesus as their Lord and Savior.

It was during my time abroad as a missionary *without portfolio* (self-funded) that I took time to study some doctrines of the Presbyterian church. In particular, I was troubled by Calvin's teaching about God's role in evil. This led me to question Calvinist predestination doctrine, perseverance of the saints and finally eternal security (its Baptist counterpart).

I endeavored to find the origin of these teachings. It always came back to Paul. Yet, Jesus' words always appeared to differ. I became irritated at what appeared to be an incessant marginalization of Jesus in preference for Paul. This book is the result of asking the question: why not Jesus' words alone?

I did not start this investigation with any revolutionary agenda. For over twenty-five years of my Christian walk, I have been at home among evangelicals and Calvinists. I never had any reason to doubt standard doctrines.

However, one day my Calvinist pastor taught me what the "reformed" believe about God's role in evil.[1] What he taught forced me to stop in my tracks. I began to doubt for the first time the trustworthiness of the doctrine held by the church I attended. As to this doctrine of evil, I then realized the pastor and elders had been using a euphemism all along which obscured their doctrine which a more stark term might have revealed. They hid their doctrine under the innocuous label of the 'sovereignty-of-God-doctrine.' I later learned this doctrine was first clearly formulated by Calvin. With further digging, I found Paul was always regarded as the most important source for these teachings.[2] However, I felt no pressure on earth could make me accept God as the deliberate author of evil, both of the evil thought and the evil outcome. Then and there, for the first time, I resolved not to compromise my loyalty for Jesus Christ in favor of any tradition of the church.

Then it struck me: 'What other doctrines could be wrong?' I soon turned my attention upon my most cherished belief in eternal security. I saw Paul was both friend and an enemy to Jesus' words in Mark 9:42-47. Paul was a friend to Jesus' words in Galatians 5:19 but an enemy to them in Romans 8:1. Why this contradictory message from a single mouth? Frustrated, one day it dawned on me: why are we dealing with Paul? Since God came down to earth, who can compare anyway. Wouldn't the best way to honor and love Jesus be to simply follow His words alone? And thus was born this book, whose sole aim is for you to trust and obey solely the words of the Lord Jesus, unfettered by anyone else's doctrine. There is only one Teacher. And one Way.

---

1. See page 433 *et seq.*
2. See Footnote 60, page 512.

1 *Introduction*

If A Later Prophet Diminishes A Prior Prophet, He Is A False Prophet

The Bible commands us in Deuteronomy 4:2 to not "diminish" any of the words of prior Prophets. Thus, this prohibits adding prophets who contradict *earlier* prophets.

For example, because Jesus and Moses came before Paul, the principle of *priority* applies so that Jesus' and Moses' words are to be used to test the *validity* of Paul's words for inspiration.

The Bible also tells us to ignore prophets with signs and wonders that "come to pass" but whose words contradict or "diminish" the earlier validated prophets. If they "seduce us from following" the commands of God through His earlier prophets, God commands us to treat them as false prophets despite true "signs and wonders." (Deut. 13:1-5.) (For more detailed discussion, see the chapter entitled "Must We Apply The Bible's Tests For a True Prophet to Paul?" on page 37.)

Jesus was frequently concerned about the "signs and wonders" prophets to come who would mislead Christians. (Matt. 7:15-23, *viz.*, v. 22; 24:11, 24.) Jesus warns of these false prophets again in Mark 13:22-23. They "shall show signs and wonders to ***seduce***, if possible, even the elect." Jesus' words are quoting Deuteronomy 13:1-5, and thus He intended us to apply that passage to discern true from false prophets.

Jesus in Matthew 7:15-24 refers again to these same "signs and wonders" prophets. Jesus says He will deny He ever knew them even though on Judgment Day they are able to say they did "marvelous works in Your name," and many "prophecies in Your name." (Matt. 7:22.) Jesus rejects them because they are workers of "*anomia.*" (Matt. 7:23.) The correct translation choice for the Greek word *anomia* is not *lawlessness*. These signs and wonders prophets obviously come with the appearance of an angel of light, doing amazing signs and wonders, and even true prophecy. They are not going to be notorious workers of *lawlessness*. Such sinners could not deceive "if possible, the elect." Rather, Jesus' real meaning could only be the second Greek dictionary definition of *anomia* which is "negator of the Law (of Moses)."[1] The false prophet who will do many miracles and signs and wonders *in Jesus' name* will be one who is a "negator of the Law (of Moses)." Jesus is warning us that this false prophet to come is one who says he is a Christian, has sign and wonders, and preaches Christ, but he will be a "negator of the Law of Moses."

Thus, for example, even if Paul came with true signs and wonders, this does not make him a true prophet if his words *diminish the Law of Moses*, or otherwise contradict earlier validated prophets, such as Moses.

These are not radical propositions. What is radical is *looking in the direction of Paul* to see whether he can be validated Biblically. Mainstream Christian commentators say, for example, that the prophetic words of Moses and Jesus must be used to validate any 'holy book' or person. For example, Muncaster states:

> Importance of prophecy is stressed in the Bible with commands to:
>
> 1. *Test everything*...including 'holy books' and people.
>
> 2. *Use prophecy*...to determine if something is from God.[2]

1. See "Why Anomia Means Negator of Mosaic Law" on page 60.
2. Ralph O. Muncaster, *The Bible Prophecy Miracles: Investigation of the Evidence* (Mission Viejo: Strong Basis to Believe, 1996) at 5.

However, Mr. Muncaster would likely object that the Bible's test can ever be applied to test Paul's validity. In effect, most Christians operate on the assumption that the Bible's prophetic words can only test those with whom we disagree. Most Christians appear to believe if we like someone's doctrine and we assume it is Holy and from God, we do not apply the Bible's test to validate them as a new prophet. Yet, this practice of Christians is itself a violation of God's command to test everything by the word of God. We must compare what Paul said to the words of every verified prophet that *preceded* Paul. To survive God's tests, Paul must not only have true prophecy in God's name of unlikely events, he must never seduce us not to follow a single command God gave previously. God commands us to be able to defend Paul's inclusion in the Bible as much as any other writer.

Canon History: Additions to Scripture Have Not Been Scrutinized

We often take for granted that every book in the New Testament has been scrutinized by some responsible council or group to satisfy a Bible-based test for inspiration. Yet, it is mere presupposition with no basis in history.

The first *recognized* semi-***official*** New Testament list of books assembled by anyone took place in 397 A.D.[3] That year, three African bishops agreed on a list identical to our current list. (See Appendix B: *How the Canon Was Formed.*) The list was expressly stated to be tentative. The bishops

3. Neither Catholics nor Protestants agree the list from the Council of Laodicea of 363 A.D. is authentic. The evidence is that it was authentic, in my view. (See www.jesuswordsonly.com.) However, if you go by the traditional view, then the first church-wide council of any denomination to determine a list and promulgate it was not until the Roman Catholic Council of Trent in the mid-1500s.

wanted to consult with the bishop across the sea (*i.e.*, apparently Rome). These three bishops did not tell us the criteria they used to form their list. It is a mystery. They did not purport to say this list was true for all of Christendom.

Moreover, there was no long tradition that accepted their list of 397 A.D. The prior *informal* lists and even the earliest printed canon (Codex Sinaiticus, late 300s) included Christian writings that were inexplicably dropped in 397 A.D. In particular, this is true regarding the book entitled the *Shepherd of Hermas*. It previously had been identified closely with canon for 200 years. It was dropped in 397 A.D. (This is not to suggest it is canon. It lacks any *legitimizing* prophecy.) Thus, the 397 A.D. list suddenly *dropped* previously accepted books, but without any explanation.

The 397 A.D. list also *added* items previously routinely ignored. In particular, most of the 'canon' lists prior to 397 A.D. excluded Second Peter as an obvious *pseudograph*. For some unexplained reason, these three bishops in 397 A.D. suddenly accepted Second Peter. Second Peter still appears in our common New Testament despite its extremely unlikely authenticity. Even Calvin (a Reformation leader from the 1500s) said it was a forgery. Calvin provided a very elaborate analysis to prove this.[4]

The next attempt to determine canon was in 1522. Luther published a version of the New Testament (NT) with a commentary introducing the entire set. Even though Luther's NT list simply adopted the list from 397 A.D., Luther declared two books uninspired. This was explained in his 1522 *Preface to the New Testament*. These two supposedly uninspired works were the Book of Revelation and the Epistle of James. His reasons had a lot to do with his adherence to Pauline doctrine. (For discussion on James, see "Luther's Admission of James' Direct Conflict with Paul" on page 247. For detailed discussion on Luther's view of Revelation, see page 370.)

4. "The Special Question of Second Peter" on page xix of Appendix B.

In response, the Roman Catholic Church (RCC) gave its first publicly official list in the mid-1500s at the Council of Trent. It based this list on tradition, citing the expressly *tentative* list of 397 A.D. from the three bishops of North Africa. At the Council of Trent (1545-1563), the Council endorsed our current 27 books of the New Testament. They are the same as in the Protestant New Testament. The fact there actually was never a church-wide decision earlier may be surprising, but this is undisputed fact. In "The Canon," the *New Catholic Encyclopedia* even admits:

> According to Catholic doctrine, the proximate criterion of the biblical canon is the infallible decision of the Church. ***This decision was not given until rather late in the history of the Church at the Council of Trent.***

Soon thereafter, a false impression was given to Christians that our New Testament had been as rigorously tested as had the works in the Hebrew Scriptures. This misleading impression was given by the simple step of printing as one volume the New Testament with the Hebrew Scriptures labelled as the 'Old Testament.'

Accordingly, it was just assumed that our New Testament was also long ago rigorously tested by the same Biblical standard that Jews used to add new prophetic works. All of us assume someone sat down to ensure each work in the New Testament satisfies the Biblical criteria for canon. Those criteria are predictive prophecy in the name of the Lord combined with the fact nothing that preceded it has been negated. (Deuteronomy chs. 12, 13 &18.) Yet it is a totally unsupportable idea. It is an exercise that one can never find has been performed in a systematic analysis by any person, council, or church in Christian history.

This is also obvious from history. First, the criteria used to compile the list of 397 A.D. was never explained. Second, when Roman Catholicism in the 1545-1563 Council of Trent finally affirmed this 397 A.D. list as the 'official' list, it likewise gave no justification other than tradition and its own authority.

Thus, there has never been any responsible voice that employed Biblically-mandated criteria to discern why *should* any book of the New Testament be included. When we examine the lists leading up to 397 A.D., this is even more evident. Books are attached one day and excluded the next. There is neither rhyme nor reason. As Ludlow notes in *The Unity of Scripture* (2003):

> With regard to most books it was a question of [the church] explaining why it had what it had, rather than deciding on what it ***should*** have. No council sat down to choose the texts according to ***some pre-established set of criteria***, just as a selection committee might decide on the sort of person they want to fill a post, before interviewing the candidates. Rather, there is some sense in which the canon chose (or formed) the Church, rather than the Church chose (or formed) the canon....[W]hat seems to be happening...is that the Church is ***formulating reason or explanations for why it has what it had, not criteria for choosing what it should have in the future***.[5]

This is how we ended up today with the notion that the sole basis for what we decide is Scripture is *how* it sounds to us. Here is the official *Orthodox Presbyterian Church's* (OPC) sole explanation of how we know something is Scripture from God.

5. Morwenna Ludlow, "Criteria of Canonicity and the Early Church" in John Barton and Michael Wolter (eds.), *The Unity of the Scripture and the Diversity of the Canon* (Berlin and New York: Walter de Gruyter, 2003) at 69-93.

> Q. 4. How doth it appear that the Scriptures are the Word of God?
>
> A. The Scriptures manifest themselves to be the Word of God, by their majesty and purity; by the consent of all the parts, and the scope of the whole, which is to give all glory to God; by their light and power to convince and convert sinners, to comfort and build up believers unto salvation: but the Spirit of God bearing witness by and with the Scriptures in the heart of man, is alone able fully to persuade it that they are the very word of God.[6]

This is a completely impoverished explanation. This Catechism lesson on how to determine Scripture offers no Bible-based justification for adding to God's words. It is all how it sounds to us, *e.g.*, it appears to us to have power to 'convert sinners.' In the next section, we will see the reason for this weak explanation. We will discover why no Christian can say prophetic inspiration was ever the sole grounds for *everything* we included in the New Testament. This embarrassing fact is what led to this above deficient explanation of how Scripture is determined.

What the Lists Prove About Criteria for Canon

The history of canon formation, detailed in Appendix B, demonstrates clearly that no coherent criteria was ever being used to assess *what is* and *what is not* approved reading in churches. Up through 397 A.D., texts come and go without explanation. Some are discarded for wrong reasons at various

6. *The Larger Catechism of the Orthodox Presbyterian Church* (68th General Assembly of the OPC) at http://www.opc.org/documents/wlc1-50.html (accessed in 2005).

points. Completely erroneous letters, such as Second Peter, somehow worm their way into our current canon. Works such as The Epistle to the Hebrews are ascribed to no one, then to Paul, then not to Paul. It is ignored, then accepted, then ignored again, but then finally accepted.

Applying the Biblical-test for inspiration is never explicitly done in the period leading up to 397 A.D. The focus is on genuineness—whether the author identified truly authored the work. Yet, no test of whether the work passes the Biblical-test of the prophetic is ever considered.

With genuineness the key issue, we then find some books are rejected as non-genuine on flimsy arguments.

For example, politics seem to enter the fray regarding Revelation by John. It is easily accepted as genuine in the first three lists beginning from 170 A.D. to 325 A.D. However, then Eusebius raises doubts sometime around 325 A.D. The Book of Revelation is dropped at the Council of Laodicea in 363 A.D. (assuming the records are accurate), only to be re-attached in 397 A.D. without any explanation.

Proof of the lack of any consistent criteria of acceptance is also evident from looking at the early list from the *Muratorian Fragment* (170 A.D.?-350 A.D.). This list included the *Apocalypse of Peter*. No one considered that work afterward as canon. Another example is that in 380 A.D., the Syrian Apostolic Canon adopted a blatant forgery—the *Constitution of the Apostles*. No one else gives it any credibility then or now. Why do they come and go? No one knows.

Furthermore, the lack of institutional memory affected the evaluation of various books' genuineness. For example, the Epistle of Jude was included in the very early Muratorian list of 170/350 A.D., but then is repeatedly disputed in the 300s period on grounds that Jude was not cited earlier. Yet now we know it was in the early Muratorian list itself. *James* was disputed on the same ground, but we find the ancient presbyters did cite it early on. Thus, books are being discarded for brief periods as non-genuine for wrong reasons, showing a lack of institutional record-keeping.

From this history of canon-formation in Appendix B, it is abundantly and shamefully evident there is a lack of diligence about determining what is genuine. Nor is anyone paying any attention to the issue of inspiration. They are preoccupied with determining what is genuine, and not doing a very good job on that score either.

This failure to focus on the question of inspiration is even more evident when lists are set forth in council rulings, such as Laodicea in 363 A.D. or Carthage in 397 A.D. Despite their semi-official nature, no explanation is attached to the otherwise long council records purporting to explain why the list is true. There is never any defense to justify the decision.

How Can The Question of Inspiration Be Ignored?

It is hard to imagine how this issue of inspiration has been ignored for Paul's letters. It is easy to understand for John and Peter who do not claim inspiration in their letters. Likewise, Jude does not make any claim to inspiration. Nor does James make such a claim in his epistle. Nor does Barnabas who authored Hebrews claim inspiration. Luke, for his part, disavows affirmatively he is writing under inspiration. Instead, Luke affirms he has investigated like an historian the events involving Jesus. (Luke 1:1-4.) As the *Catholic Encyclopedia*'s article on "Canon of the New Testament" states, the New Testament lacks "a strong self-witness to Divine inspiration."[7] That is to put it mildly.

7. http://www.newadvent.org/cathen/03274a.htm (last accessed 8/27/05).

However, Paul is a different case. He certainly repeatedly stakes out a claim that the *Lord directly gave him a message.* (*E.g.*, 1 Cor. 14:37; 1 Tim. 2:11; 1 Cor. 2:13; 1 Thess.4:1-2,8; 1 Thess. 2:13; Eph. 4:17. *cf.* 1 Cor. 7:25, 40.)

If the intent in putting the NT together early on was simply as a ***reading list***, then we can understand why the issue of inspiration was not being addressed. That appears to be the ***real explanation*** for the origin of the canon: it was a reading list. However, Paulinist[8] scholars insist there was something more implied in the lists other than that they were to be read in church. Yet, is there any evidence that the issue of the Biblical-test for inspiration was addressed *ever* in the history of *any* Christian denomination?

No Scholarly Discussion Anywhere of Inspiration

With the exception of Eusebius around 325 A.D. saying Jesus' words on the fall of the temple of Jerusalem prove Jesus was a Prophet, there is never any discussion why we should believe anyone else in the NT is inspired. Never once will you find a discussion based on the Bible-test of inspiration (Deut. ch. 12-13, 18) why Paul, James, Jude, the author of Hebrews, Peter or John in their Epistles would be treated as *inspired* (as opposed to edifying). No one thinks it is worth a moment's attention to ask for prophetic credentials.

Thus, Battifol, a Catholic scholar, correctly recognizes "the Judaic notion of inspiration did not at first enter into the selection of the Christian Scriptures." Later, he explains the NT writings which we accept today were merely

8. A Paulinist does not mean every Christian who believes Paul is inspired. Rather, a Paulinist is someone whose doctrines conform to Paul, not Jesus, when there is an apparent conflict.

"assimilated" as "Scripture" with the 'Old Testament,' without any explanation.[9] Thus, the most fundamental question of all has never been addressed anywhere in church history!

This error is then perpetuated today by scholars who realize one can never find any early or later analysis for the lists being developed.[10] They resort to claims that the books of the New Testament are somehow self-authenticating. These works' own existence allegedly forced themselves upon us by some magical power. This is the view of Metzger, whose book on canon formation is regarded as the modern standard of how to defend the formation of the Christian canon. Yet this is his ultimate reasoning:

> In the most basic sense neither individuals nor councils created the canon; instead they came to perceive and acknowledge the ***self-authenticating quality of these writings***, which imposed themselves as canonical upon the church.[11]

---

9. "Canon of the New Testament," in the *Catholic Encyclopedia* (http://www.newadvent.org/cathen/03274a.htm)(last accessed 8/27/05).

10. The article "Canon of the New Testament," in the *Catholic Encyclopedia* is most illuminating in this regard. One can see various theories put forth *today* why a work was accepted as New Testament canon. Some say it is because the work can be linked to an apostle as the voice behind the writing. But this is not true in Jude's case, nor in Barnabas' work (*Hebrews*), nor of Luke. In light of this, we are left concluding the criterion must have been a work's "evangelical character." We are thus reduced to a completely subjective criterion: does it fit the evangelistic message we prefer? This is the worst reason to accept something as canon. The only thing never considered is to ask whether a Biblical standard for inspiration was applied. If we asked the proper question, the answer comes back in the negative. Everyone knows several NT works *on their face* must no longer be regarded as inspired because they lack any validating prophecy.

11. Metzger, *The New Testament: Its Background, Growth and Content* (New York: Abingdon Press, 1965) at 276.

Thus, Metzger says the New Testament works "imposed themselves" upon the community as authentic without any testing.

However, the Bible teaches us that books do not impose themselves on us as authentic. We are duty bound to test them, under Deuteronomy 4:2 and chs. 12 & 13. There is a complete absence in Christian history of even once such a rigorous testing ever being applied to explain the selection of any current NT book.

What Metzger regards as the books imposing themselves on us, as if they had a life and force of their own, is simply one way to describe a credulous church's shameful behavior of accepting works without testing their prophetic authority.

Books do not authenticate or impose themselves. Rather, a community decides, by testing or by laziness, that books are accepted. Our Christian history has all the earmarks of a lazy church who disobeyed Jesus' warnings to beware of false prophets to come. We were duty bound to authenticate the works being submitted for canon approval using the Biblical-tests of Deuteronomy chapters 4, 12, 13, and 18. Metzger's statement thus becomes an excuse for the most fundamental omission of all by the early church: testing what is canon by the Bible's own test.

Jesus' Words Alone Pass the Test of Canonicity

However, if we apply the test we were supposed to apply, it turns out that Jesus alone passes the rigorous test of Deuteronomy ch. 12, 13, and 18. Jesus' prophecy of the fall of the Temple of Jerusalem (Matt. 24:2; Luke 21:33)[12] and of

12.For reasons explained elsewhere, the Hebrew Matthew was likely written before 65 A.D. See page ix of Appendix B.

His own resurrection (John 13:19) make His words that of a prophet satisfying the tests of Deuteronomy. This is true whether His words are in the gospels or the book of Revelation. All Jesus' words are therefore inspired. (And more so because of *who* He truly was.) We trust the Holy Spirit then inspired the twelve apostles to recollect Jesus' words accurately, as Jesus told them the Spirit would do. (John 14:26.) Thus, the apostolic gospels are all reliable Scripture.

However, no other New Testament figure than Jesus uttered fulfilled prophecy "in the name of the Lord" of highly unlikely events. That includes Paul.

Yet, when someone proposes to treat Jesus' Words Only as the inspired part of the New Testament, they receive resistance. Why?

No one would mind treating Jesus as the sole inspired prophet of canon if it meant pushing aside writings other than Paul. None of the epistles of John or Peter suggest new doctrines that would be lost if they were eliminated *as inspired canon*. So the resistance has a different explanation.

The Authority of the Twelve Apostles (Of Which Paul Is Not Numbered in the Bible).

Let me pause to note here the authority retained by the ***epistles*** of John and Peter, and the bishop-***letters*** of James and Jude. First, Jesus taught us to heed the ***twelve*** apostles' words as authoritative messengers (*apostoli* means *messenger*) rather than as teachers. He would not even let them call themselves *teachers*. (Matt. 23:8-11.) But they carried a very important message. Jesus, speaking to the ***twelve***, warned that whoever would not "receive you, nor hear you" shall be in danger of judgment. (Matt. 10:14-15.) The message they carried was so important that if rejected, the listener would be in danger of judgment. Jesus said the message they were to deliver was to teach the nations "to observe (*tereo*) all things whatsoever I commanded you." (Matt. 28:19-20.) Thus, we heed the twelve apostles not because every word from them is *as* an inspired prophet. Rather, it is because they are putting forth the teachings and commandments of *the* inspired Prophet.

Then this command of Jesus to heed the twelve applies to their appointed bishops, such as James and Jude when they too carried the teachings of Jesus.

The twelve apostles had a second role given by Jesus: they were judges. In this capacity, their judicial decisions are binding in heaven. (Matt. 16:19.) This did not extend to the twelve apostles a constant prophetic authority. Their every word did not become thereby *inspired* legislation from God. We would say a judge who starts to legislate is an activist judge violating the scope of his office's authority. Likewise, the twelve apostles did not have authority to *legislate* merely because they had judicial authority to 'bind and loose.'

Let's review this with some care because it has been a source of misunderstanding by Catholics and Protestants.

The twelve apostles had authority from Jesus to "bind and loose." (Matt. 16:19.) This is a clear reference to the power of a judge. In court, a judge could let go of a criminal defendant by ordering the "loosing" of a leather strap. A judge could also order his arrest and condemnation by "binding" him with such a strap. This fits exactly the role Jesus said the apostle would have in the regeneration: the ***twelve*** apostles would be the "***twelve*** judges" sitting on "***twelve*** thrones" over the "***twelve*** tribes." (Matt.19:28.)

Thus, when the eleven adjudicated Judas's transgression, they remedied this by having Matthias replace Judas. Matthias would become the twelfth. This finding and remedy were in the nature of a judicial decision that would be binding in heaven. (Acts 1:26.) Such a decision was not as a law-giver whatsoever. It was a judicial determination of transgression and its remedy of replacing Judas. (John 20:22-23.)

Thus, it is very important to realize Jesus never told us the apostles' personal writings are on par with inspired canon. The apostles like elders in Jesus' day had authority over God's people, but like elders in Jesus' day, they were to be tested by prophetic inspired canon. When a conflict arose, we were to obey the inspired canon, not the elders. (Matt. 15:6.) Thus, the Epistles of John, Peter, Jude and James stay, but if they contradict Scriptures *provable as prophetic*, then Jesus commands us to follow the higher authority of *inspired* Scripture. In the case of these four authors, I know of nothing they ever said that contradicts the words of a *validated prophet.*

Paul Alone Must Be Tested by Deuteronomy's Test for False Prophets.

Returning to the point at issue, what motivates the resistance to the proposition of using Jesus' Words Only (JWO) as the test of orthodoxy? It principally comes from a desire to protect Paul. There is no concern to protect the *inspired* status of the Epistles of John, Peter, James or Jude. This is true because none of these writers ever claimed inspired status for their own epistles. If we denied inspired status to them now, we would not be taking away anything the authors of those writings claimed for their epistles.

By contrast, Paul repeatedly made the claim that *thus sayeth the Lord* belonged on his lips. (*E.g.*, 1 Cor. 14:37; 1 Tim. 2:11; 1 Cor. 2:13; 1 Thess.4:1-2,8; 1 Thess. 2:13; Eph. 4:17. *cf.* 1 Cor. 7:25, 40.) It is Paul alone who made statements that he was, in effect, speaking as a prophet. This is why we are duty-bound to apply to Paul the test for a true prophet under Deuteronomy chapters 12, 13 & 18.

Why do so many find protecting Paul so important? Because if we accept Jesus as the sole prophetic authority in the New Testament, we have a dilemma. Paul had many *novel* and *unusual lessons of what the gospel represents.* If Paul is no longer on par with Jesus, then Pauline salvation doctrine would lose its grip and legitimacy. A different salvation doctrine would emerge.[13] If we only had Jesus, then Jesus' message on initial justification by repentance from sin would emerge unmolested. (Luke 18:10 *et seq.*; Mark 9:42 *et seq.*) If

Jesus' message had sole emphasis, salvation would be a process that requires ongoing repentance from sin to stay justified with God and be saved. (1 John 1:9; John 15:1-6.) We would no longer have the freedom to sin without losing salvation, contrary to what Paul is viewed to teach. (Rom. 8:1; 10:9; Eph. 2:8-9.)

Instead, if we relied upon Jesus' words without any constraint to make them fit Paul's doctrines, we would have to trust Jesus' promise of salvation for endurance and obedience in keeping His words. (John 8:51; Matt. 10:22.) If we had Jesus' words alone, then Jesus' doctrine would emerge that we have only two choices: we can go to heaven maimed (*i.e.*, having repented from sin) or hell whole (*i.e.*, not having repented from sin). (Mark 9:42 *et seq.*) Jesus' message is not comforting at all to those engaging in sin after becoming a Christian. We will lose the assurance we are still saved despite our unrepentant sinning. To some, this assurance is the essence of saving faith. If we lose Paul, then we lose the very gospel that comforts us. We would then be forced to accept Jesus' very different and uncomfortable gospel.

Jesus' Words Only *Is A Valid New Testament Test for Canonicity*

Some people respond to the JWO proposition by saying you cannot test Paul by the standard for a true prophet in the *'Old Testament.'* It is old. We are under the new. They do not see this is based on a fallacious presupposition that Paul is inspired. The very notion that the old is nullified and no longer valid comes from Paul. We cannot rely upon a teaching of Paul that discards the very source for testing him. ***This is precisely what a false prophet would love to do***: come with

13.For a thorough comparison of Jesus' versus Paul's salvation doctrine, see the chapter entitled "Does It Matter If We Rely Only Upon Jesus?" on page 447 *et seq.*

a false message and then ***give you a reason to disregard the Bible's standard for determining whether he or she is a true prophet***. Thus, this idea that we cannot use the 'Old Testament' to measure Paul rests on a fallacious presupposition that we can rely upon Paul's doctrine. (He alone declared the Law abolished and defunct. See Chapter 5.) Such a response fallaciously assumes the validity of Paul, which is the very question at issue.

Regardless, even if Paul could conflict with the 'Old Testament' and still be a true prophet, Paul could not be valid if he conflicts with Jesus. There are three passages that set this up as an *additional standard* that Paul must pass to be *truly* canonical. This New Testament standard requires consistency with Jesus' words.

The following New Testament (NT) passages support the proposition that (a) we need only teach Jesus' Words in the NT era and (b) any author who contradicts Jesus' words is uninspired.

First, Jesus commands us to teach His teachings. He did not authorize us to come with Paul's *distinct* teachings. In Matthew 28:19-20, Jesus says we are to "make disciples of all the nations... ***teaching them to obey*** (*tereo*) ***all things whatsoever I commanded you.***"

Jesus thus commanded us to teach "whatsoever I commanded," not anyone else's teachings. Jesus also said He was to be our sole teacher; we should not call anyone else our teacher. (Matt. 23:8-11.) Clarke explains this means "To him [Jesus] ***alone*** it belongs to guide and lead his Church....Jesus is the ***sole teacher*** of righteousness. It is he ***alone***...that can illuminate every created mind." Thus, Jesus' words are the sole source of NT teaching. No one else can share this honor:.

Apostle John explains this principle. He says if we go "beyond" Jesus' teachings, we *do not have God* when so speaking. John writes in 2 John 1:8-11 (Websters' Bible):

> (8) Watch yourselves, that we [*i.e.*, the twelve apostles] don't lose the things which we have accomplished, but that we receive a full reward.

> (9) Whoever ***transgresses*** [*or* ***goes beyond***][14] and ***doesn't remain in the teaching of Christ, doesn't have God***. He who ***remains in the teaching [of Jesus Christ]***, the same has both the Father and the Son.

The phrase "teaching of Christ" in the Greek means clearly "Christ's doctrine." It does not mean teachings *about* Christ.[15] Canon is to be tested by the *words of* Jesus, not whether we like your *words about* Jesus. Any teacher who contradicts Jesus offers 'no light' at all.

Apostle John therefore is warning that if you ***go beyond*** or ***overstep*** those teachings from Jesus, John can lose his reward. You are following doctrines of men, not God. You are following those who do not *have* God, *i.e.*, they lack the Holy Spirit when so teaching. You can become lost and, if so, John will lose his reward. To go *beyond* the teachings of Christ, *transgressing* them, includes teaching something that *contradicts* Jesus. Anyone who blatantly contradicts Jesus and disobeys Him lies when he says he "knows" Jesus.[16] Thus, everyone claiming to be a prophet who came after

---

14.The *Textus Receptus* has *proagwn,* but the UBS GNT has *parabainwn.* The word *proagwn* in the TR means *go before* or *lead forth.* It doesn't make much sense. Thus, some translate this as *run ahead* to fit the context. It appears the UBS GNT variant is more accurate while still similar in meaning. The word *parabaino* means "to go aside" or "to go beyond." Judas fell because he *parabaino*-ed (Acts 1:25.) A good paraphrase would be *overstepping, exceeding* or *going beyond the bounds*.

15.Some try to claim Paul can contradict Jesus and still be canonical as long as Paul's teaching *about* Christ is correct. However, the verse is talking about *the teachings of Christ* in a way that means *by Jesus*, not about Him. The Greek format is identical to all similar references to *teachings by someone* yet in these other contexts we would never misconstrue it means *teachings* ***about*** *these people*, *e.g.*, "doctrine of the Pharisees" (Matt. 16:6, 12); "the apostle's doctrine" (Acts 2:42); "doctrines of men" (Matt. 15:9); "doctrine of the Nicolaitans" (Rev. 2:15); etc.

16.John explains: "He that saith, I know him, and does not keep on obeying (*tereo*) His commandments, is a liar, and the truth is not in him." (1 John 2:4.) Here, *tereo* is in the present participle active.

Jesus must therefore be subject to the test of 2 John 1:9. If Paul teaches contrary to Jesus, Apostle John says Paul does not "know" Him and Paul is a "liar."

Accordingly, if Paul goes beyond the teaching of Christ, and contradicts Him, then if we follow Paul, not Jesus' words, we are at great risk. If it causes us to break fellowship with God, our Lord will deny we know Him. Adhering to Paul's word, if contrary to Jesus, runs a *terrible risk.* These principles also prove that Paul is as much subject to this test of 2 John 1:9 as anyone. Hence, even if Paul can explain away the *Hebrew Scriptures* as the *Old Testament* and entirely eliminated (he cannot), Paul has to prove he does not transgress Our Lord's words.

To discharge our duty under Matthew 23:8-11 and 2 John 1:8-11, the examination must be thoroughly objective and neutral. If anything, we need to err on the side of favoring protecting Jesus' words over Paul's words. The reason is that Jesus tells us to love Him above any human being.[17] Also, we receive a special assurance of "eternal life" if we should have "obeyed" (*tereo*) Jesus' words. (John 8:51.)

How are we to apply the "Sole Teacher" test to Paul and remain objective, unaffected by a presupposition that Paul is valid? Here is a test true to the "Sole Teacher" test:

- The Christian must resist the temptation to bring two texts into harmony when their affirmations do not agree, if he or she is convinced that such a synthesis is incompatible with the word meaning and historical context of each competing passage. If you disobey this, be careful that you are not putting your love for Paul above your love for Jesus Christ. (Matt. 10:37.)
- The Christian must do this no matter how painful it may be to admit a contradiction by Jesus of something Paul says. If you disobey this, be careful you are not again putting your love for Paul above your love for Jesus Christ.

17.Matthew 10:37 says: "He that loveth father or mother more than me is not worthy of me; and he that loveth son or daughter more than me is not worthy of me."

- In case you are unsure, err on the side of excluding Paul precisely because Jesus told you to have a priority of love for Him anyway. (Matt. 10:37.)
- Remember always there is never any risk following Jesus' words only. There is only risk in not following Jesus' words and accepting contradictory notions.

Is It Too Radical To Be A Strict Fundamentalist?

The key to being a conservative fundamentalist is to *know* and to *be able to prove* what is Scripture. It is not established by tradition. It is not established by presuppositions. Rather, it is established by testing each book we affix to Scripture by the revealed word of God that came before. It must fit the prior Prophetic words before it is accepted as Scripture.

The premature and presuppositional addition of Scripture is what the Bible prohibits. That is spiritual liberalism. The gullible addition to God's word is spiritual liberalism at it worst. Such a liberal textual approach does not depend on Biblical-tests for additions. It depends rather on how *nice it sounds*, or how long it has been accepted. However, one cannot presuppose inspiration because *you like the writer's thoughts*. That is the *worst reason* to accep*t* something as inspired. Man was snared in the garden by *new and seductive words* from the serpent who by subtle commentary *changed* and *added to God's words*. This led to taking the fruit of the forbidden tree of knowledge. Adam and Eve had a liberal understanding on how to test *new* messages.

So the questions presented here are the most *fundamental* and *conservative* questions you can possibly ask. And the most important. Fundamentalism is not something we should just preach to the Mormons. We must look at the beam in our own eye before we try to remove the speck from their eye. We need to test our own assumptions within the evangelical Protestant community by the same rigor we want others to examine their own history and additions to canon.

Didn't The Twelve Apostles Already Make This Determination?

Many respond to JWO by asking: 'didn't the twelve apostles accept Paul?' In Acts 9:28 and 15:4, they received Paul. They counted him a beloved brother. (Acts 15:5.)

Yet, this evidence is inadequate to prove they accepted Paul as either a thirteenth apostle or as a prophet. In fact, in that encounter with the twelve apostles in Acts chapter 15, Paul is not proclaiming any inspiration or even apostleship. Not once will you find such a statement in the Acts account. Rather, Paul comes with a question from the church of Antioch. He wanted to find out what the twelve apostles would decide about the issue of circumcision.

Had Paul in Acts chapter 15 been saying instead that he had a revelation from Jesus that answered the question, we would have a different situation. The twelve would have needed to examine whether Paul had a prophetic office. If they did, then we would have some basis to conclude their acceptance of Paul was *after* applying the Deuteronomy test. But that is not what is going on at all. Paul is a mere messenger of a question. In presenting the question, Paul never suggests he has an authority *on par* with the apostles to give an *answer*. Paul, like the twelve apostles are doing, waits for James, the Lord's brother, to reach a final decision. (See "James Is the Head Bishop of the Church" on page 242.)

In fact, the issue of Paul's possible apostasy (*i.e.*, contradicting the Law of Moses) does not arise in Acts until later, but the investigation is not completed. This is clearly presented in Acts 21:18-26. This passage is probably the most overlooked significant passage in the New Testament.

In Acts 21:18-26, Luke describes James' encounter with Paul a couple of years after the Jerusalem council. James says he has heard rumors that Paul is teaching the law is no longer binding on Jews who come to Christ. James then reassures Paul that he knows Paul would never teach such a thing. In that context, James says he wants Paul to prove in the eyes of others that Paul is not teaching this. Paul can do this by going through the public gestures required to fulfill the Nazirite vow from the book of Numbers chapter six. James then reiterates that his decision in the earlier Jerusalem council—circumcision was not for Gentiles—only applied to Gentiles. James explains this earlier ruling was not meant to imply that Christian Jews did not have to circumcise their children. Paul then complies, and does the public acts to keep the vow from Numbers. Paul never once suggested that indeed he held the view that the Law of Moses was no longer binding on Jews who come to Christ. Yet, we all know that Paul's letters precisely teach this. Paul does so in particular in Romans chapter 7. (For proof of this, read the chapter entitled: "Did Paul Negate the Law's Further Applicability?" on page 73 *et seq*.)

Thus, the New Testament leaves the validity of Paul's teachings as an unresolved issue as of Acts chapter 21. It was being examined. However, James had insufficient data. The Jerusalem Bishop, James, must never yet have seen any of Paul's letters. For clearly, Paul's letters directly affirm that Jews in Christ are "released" from the Law of Moses. (Romans 7:2.) In Acts chapter 21, James assumed the rumor to this effect was false. We are left wondering what will be the outcome when James and the twelve find out what Paul was truly teaching.

If Paul Is Like Balaam, It Matters Little If the Apostles Approved of Him Initially

Furthermore, even if the apostles knew and approved of Paul as a true prophet of God, this does not mean Paul could not change and become like Balaam. Who is Balaam?

In the lifetime of Moses, Balaam was a diviner who was converted to a prophet of God by his meeting an angel on the Road to Moab. Later, Balaam is filled with the Holy Spirit and utters prophetic messages direct from God, according to Moses' account in the Book of Numbers. Yet *later* Balaam apostasizes by teaching the Israelites that it was permissible to eat meat sacrificed to idols. Because Balaam seduced the Israelites from following the Law, he became a "false prophet" under the standards of Deuteronomy 4:2 and 13:5. In other words, Balaam apostasized against the Law of Moses, and hence became a false prophet.

Jesus Himself in Revelation 2:14 said His church was threatened from within by a New Testament "Balaam." Thus, it was a realized risk within the early New Testament church.

Furthermore, there is strong reason to believe Jesus was identifying Paul as Balaam in Revelation 2:14. Jesus said this NT Balaam says it is permissible to eat meat sacrificed to idols. It is an undisputed fact that Paul three times teaches it is permissible to eat meat sacrificed to idols.[18]

Therefore, even if early on the apostles accepted Paul, this does not end the analysis. You still have the possibility a true prophet turned false, like Balaam (or like the old prophet in 1 Kings 13:1-26), using the standards in Deuteronomy 4:2.

Our Core Duty Remains To Test Paul

The possibility that Paul is like Balaam brings us, of course, back to our core duty. We have to be able to prove Paul passes the test of Deuteronomy chapters 12, 13 and 18 because *we are commanded to do this.* We cannot rely upon supposition or conjecture about what the apostles did or did not do. We must see the proof in the writings of Paul that he can pass this Biblical test before we can *add* to Scripture anything Paul wrote. Jesus' words can be scrutinized to this very

18.See the chapter "Why Does Jesus Mention Balaam in Rev. 2:14?" on page 131.

day, and Jesus can be proven to pass Deuteronomy's tests with flying colors. (This includes Jesus' prophecy on the fall of the Temple and on His own resurrection). Then why should we not be able to test Paul the same way?

Historical Note: What Was Defective In The Pharisees' Teaching?

—Was It Legalism? Or Anomia (Negation of the Law)?—

Jesus excoriated the Pharisees for shallow teaching which undermined the Law of Moses, including: (1) teaching selectively from the Law only the lesser commands (such as tithing), leaving the more weighty matters of the Law untaught (Matt. 23:23); (2) teaching traditions which if followed led to the violation of the Law of Moses (Matthew 15:2-9)(certain korban payment negating duty to honor your parents); and (3) expressly teaching that certain wrongs under the Law were acceptable behavior (*e.g.*, adulterous lust was permissible if no adulterous act followed).(Matt. 5:27-28.)[19]

Josephus in 93 A.D. said the Sadducees likewise faulted the Pharisees for taking people's focus ***off*** the Law of Moses:

> What I would now explain is this, that the Pharisees have delivered to the people a great many observances by succession from their fathers, which are ***not written in the Law of Moses***; and it is ***for this reason that the Sadducees reject them***, and say we are to esteem those observances that are ***in the written word***, but are ***not to observe what are derived from the tradition of our forefathers***. (Josephus Flavius, *Antiquities of the Jews* 13.10.6 (13.297)

19. "People had come to believe that one could lust after a [married] woman, as long as the act of fornication was not committed. But Jesus showed that this understanding was foreign to the actual command by Moses." Robert A. Hawkins, "Covenant Relations of the Sermon on the Mount," *Restoration Quarterly* Vol. 12, No. 1 (explaining Matt. 5:27-28).

2 *Does Paul's Long Acceptance in NT Prove God's Will?*

Hasn't God Implicitly Approved Our NT List?

> "I have to believe God has protected His word throughout time from being tainted by fraud. Is God not powerful enough to preserve the sanctity of His word?"
> Felgar, Calgary, Canada Nov. 9, 2004

Some raise an intriguing response to the entire notion of testing Paul's canonicity. If God intended for us to exclude Paul, why has it taken this long to address the issue? Would not God have corrected us earlier? If God is truly sovereign, then He would not have allowed this to happen. As Felgar says in the side-bar quote, "Is God not powerful enough to preserve the sanctity of His word?"

This has superficial appeal, but it is at odds with the Bible itself.

For example, if a correct argument, then no true book of the Bible could long be separate from the Bible. God would have to supernaturally intervene promptly to re-affix the lost book to where it belongs.

Yet, the story in 2 Kings 22:8 *et seq*. refutes that God's sovereignty works this way. The Book of Deuteronomy was originally part of the inspired writings of Moses. He wrote it by hand. Yet, it was put in a corner of the Temple. It was then forgotten and lost. No one had made a copy. For 300 years Temple practices deteriorated. These practices bore no resemblance to what Deuteronomy required. Then Deuteronomy was found in a corner of the Temple. King Josiah had it read aloud. He realized how far Temple practices had fallen below the Bible standard. He tore his clothes in repentance. Deuteronomy was re-affixed to canon. Reformation began.

Thus, the inspired book of Deuteronomy was lost for hundreds of years at great damage to the community. If God's sovereignty means He must act as we suppose, then how could He not have acted sooner in supernatural ways to preserve His word? Why would generations lack His revealed word? Apparently, God's sovereignty does not work in the way we assume. Rather, the Israelites had a responsibility not to "diminish" the Law given to them (Deut. 4:2). This meant, among other things, they had to preserve it properly *in back-up print copies*.

Furthermore, the Bible even tells us that inspired writings have been permanently lost. In 1 Chronicles 29:29, we read of three *inspired* writings which have been lost: "Now the acts of David the king, first and last, behold, they are written [in] a *Book of Samuel* the Seer, and in the *Book of Nathan* the Prophet, and in the *Book of Gad* the Seer...." Adam Clarke admits these books are "now lost."

The Bible tells us the word *Seer* was the word used at one time to mean *Prophet*. (1 Samuel 9:9, "Beforetime in Israel...he that is now called a Prophet was beforetime called a Seer" ASV.)

The way these three books are described, Chronicles intends for us to understand they are all written by true prophets. Clarke resolves the dilemma of how any prophetic work could be lost by asserting these were all uninspired, and not true prophets. Yet, that can only be based on (a) a willingness to deny the Bible's express claim that these were prophetic works and (b) a willingness to make an unsubstantiated presupposition about how God's sovereignty works. For the Bible says they are prophets/seers.

Thus, Clarke is obviously assuming that works described by the Bible as written by prophets nevertheless must be uninspired simply because these works are now lost.

Clarke is grounding this upon a presupposition that God's sovereignty would not allow a truly inspired work to be lost. This is pure supposition used to negate the plain meaning of the Bible itself. Chronicles clearly points to Nathan as a Prophet, and Gad and Samuel as Seers. To repeat, 1 Sam. 9:9 say the word *seer* has the same meaning as Prophet. The clear reading of Chronicles is that these *prophetic* titles were accurate. Thus, these three lost works were inspired by God because written by *true* Prophets. Otherwise the Bible would not have referred to them as such. Despite these works being prophetic, everyone must concede these three prophetic works have been lost. God's sovereignty did not protect us as we assume *it should.* Humans have *personal responsibility* to guard His word from loss.

What About the Dilemma Caused by the Ethiopian Christians' Inclusion of the Book of Enoch?

Furthermore, if we hold to the view that God's failure to block Paul's inclusion in canon means God approves Paul, we have a dilemma posed by the Book of Enoch. This is a book that has been included for 2000 years as inspired canon of the Ethiopian Christian Orthodox church. Ethiopia went through long periods of being run by Christian Kings. Its church body consists today of 20,000 churches in a land of 58 million. The Book of Enoch was also part of universal Christianity's canon until 363 A.D. It was actually quoted by Jude in our New Testament as the words of true prophecy (Jude 17). This gives strong support for the Ethiopian Christians' claim that the Book of Enoch belongs in canon.[1] However, in 363 at the Council of Laodicea, the Book of Enoch was dropped by the Roman Catholic Church from the canon list for the 'Old Testament.' No explanation was offered. It then disappeared in the Western Church while it remained canon in the Eastern church.

If God's sovereignty works the way Paulinists suppose, and they reject the Book of Enoch as non-canonical (as they frequently do by saying 'canon is closed'), then they have a problem. They have to insist the Ethiopian Christians for 2000 years wrongly have *added* to Scripture. Likewise, the early universal Christian Church must have wrongfully treated the Book of Enoch as canon for over 300 years. Then if their position is that Christians in the early church and in Ethiopia have for long periods wrongfully *added* to Scripture, why cannot the Paulinists consider it possible that Paul's writings for 1,970 years were *added* wrongly to canon?[2] If you assume Enoch is non-canonical, God in His sovereignty allowed large communities (*i.e.*, Ethiopia & early universal Christianity) wrongfully to add the Book of Enoch for very long periods of time. So if Enoch was wrongly added, then God for 2000 years has not yet intervened to correct the Ethiopians. Accordingly, the Paulinist must concede it is equally possible that a mistake was made about adding Paul to canon. If God did not prevent the Ethiopians from adding the Book of Enoch, there is no reason to believe God always prevents *human error* in assembling canon lists. Paulinists cannot infer our decisions on canon have God's sanction by the mere lapse of time or God's failure to act supernaturally.

1. Indeed, an argument exists that the Book of Enoch was wrongfully excluded in the West after 363 A.D. It is a book filled with Messianic prophecies that Jesus fulfilled. For discussion, see *What About the Canonicity of the Book of Enoch?* (2005) available on-line at www.jesuswordsonly.com.
2. This number of 1,970 years reflects the evidence that the earliest apostolic church known as The Poor (Ebionites) rejected Paul's writings from the 40s though 70 A.D. See Appendix B: *How the Canon Was Formed.*

If, on the other hand, Paulinists try to shift positions, and claim they now admit the Book of Enoch is canonical because Jude quotes it as prophetic, then they still have a similar dilemma. They would have to explain how God allowed the church of the West from 363 A.D. to the present era to *diminish* God's word by wrongfully excluding the Book of Enoch. God did not protect us in the West from a wrongful subtraction of the Book of Enoch from Scripture, contrary to how some suppose that God's sovereignty works.

Thus, regardless of how the Paulinist tries to escape the dilemma posed by the Book of Enoch, it defeats their position. The sovereignty of God does not dictate that He would prevent wrongful *addition* or wrongful *diminishment* of Scripture even for as long as 2000 years. God has left the question of canonicity in our hands. We can obey Him by *testing* claims that something is prophetic or we can *disobey* God and not test each book we add to His word. The history of the Book of Enoch proves God does not intervene to fix our errors. The fact we have a book that our Western tradition calls the New Testament does not prove God's agreement with our list.

Thus, we cannot infer a long presence of Paul in canon makes it *God's choice* rather than our own.

What About the Additions to the End of Mark's Gospel?

It is now recognized among most evangelical Christians that the verses after Mark 16:8 were improperly added. The last page of the folio in Greek was lost. In *The Westminster Study Edition of the Holy Bible* (Philadelphia: Westminster Press, 1948), the authors explain regarding this passage:

> [T]his section is a later addition. The original ending appears to be lost. The best and oldest manuscripts of Mark end with ch. 16:8.

Beginning in the 400s, two different endings were employed after Mark 16:8. One is called the Longer Ending, which appears in the KJV. This includes a verse often used as a proof text that baptism is vital for salvation. We read in Mark 16:16: "He that believes and is baptized shall be saved; but he that believes not shall be condemned." Catholic authorities believe this section is canonical but admit the "vocabulary and style indicate it was written by someone other than Mark."

The other ending to Mark is known as the Shorter Ending. It exists in many other manuscripts and goes back in its tradition to the 400s as well, having been known to Jerome.[3]

Thus, from approximately 400 A.D. to our 20th Century, we have had an addition to Scripture that has gone undetected and treated as canon even though it was certainly written three hundred years after Mark died.

If God's sovereignty works the way we suppose, God would not have permitted this addition to Scripture all these centuries. If God's sovereignty must protect us as we assume, God certainly would not allow an addition on a point so crucial as salvation, misleading numerous souls that water baptism was essential for salvation. However, obviously God's sovereignty does not work in the way we suppose. A long period of our tradition to include something as canon does not prove it belongs in inspired canon.

3. For this background, see Notes to *New American Bible* at http://www.usccb.org/nab/bible/mark/mark16.htm (last accessed 2005).

Tradition Is Invalid Grounds To Justify A Canon List

This inference of canonicity from long acceptance, furthermore, violates Scripture itself. It is a lazy man's way to permit ongoing violation of God's commands. The fact is that the Bible presumes we can make mistakes in joining wrong books to canon. The Bible's command to not do so *assumes we can add a non-prophetic work to Scripture*. That is why God *imposes on us* the rigid tests to determine valid prophecy. Why else would such verses even exist in Deuteronomy chapters 4, 12-13 and 18 unless God intended for us to *exercise the decision of what to add to canon*? If God were going to do this work for us, He would not give us tests to do it ourselves. The commands would be pointless if we did not have to worry about them because God would anyway protect His word.

In fact, if God protected His word supernaturally, it would defeat God's purpose in allowing false prophets to even exist. God explains why He left it up to us to sift the true prophets from the false: it tests whether we love Him with our whole heart and mind. (Deut. 13:3.) If God sovereignly intervened, and prevented mistakes regarding false prophets, God would thereby avoid the tests of our faith that God expressly says is His intention. God uses such tests and trials to *strengthen*, not weaken, our faith. (James 1:3.)

We should also remember this Sovereignty of God argument was speciously used to resist the Reformation. The papacy argued, in effect: how could the church be so wrong on indulgences if for so long God permitted it to err? Luther in his *Epistle on Galatians* (1535) put his opponent's arguments this way: "Do you suppose that God would have left His Church floundering in error all these centuries?" Luther called this sophistry. Luther said it fundamentally misunderstands the correcting nature of Scripture itself *if applied*. Tradition means nothing. The true Bible text means everything, Luther replied.

Luther was correct. The false teacher will set up his teaching as a tradition that you must not allow others to contradict. To protect themselves, they will tell you to "avoid" or "stay away" from those who might bring correction to their doctrine. False teachers are afraid you will use Scripture to examine their teaching, claiming it is divisive and destructive of the faith of many. Of course it would be, because Scripture's correcting nature is destructive of false faiths. Rather than avoid others who come with doctrines contrary to what you believe, Apostle John tells you to try them whether they are from God (*i.e.*, compare them to God's word):

> Beloved, believe not every spirit, but ***prove the spirits, whether they are of God***; because many false prophets are gone out into the world. (1 John 4:1.)

You are to remain engaged in a dialogue with those whom you share disagreement. You can never know you have the truth if your teacher/leader frightens you to "avoid" or "stay away" from others who have different teachings. Only false prophets/teachers can benefit from instilling such fear among Christians.

Thus, tradition means nothing. The Sovereignty of God idea that makes tradition into dogma rests upon a false assumption of how God *should* protect His canon supernaturally. The Bible only supports that God expects us to protect and guard His word after delivered to us. We cannot avoid applying the tests of Deuteronomy chapters 4, 12-13 and 18 of what constitutes a false prophet on the assumption that God will always intervene to prevent erroneous inclusion of books into canon. A long period of acceptance by a large group of Christians proves nothing about God's divine plan. The history attached to the Book of Enoch for 2000 years stands as a constant reminder of the folly of such a notion, whether one believes Enoch is canonical or not.

Luther & Calvin Both Rejected the Sovereignty of God Argument on Canon Inclusion

Finally, both Luther and Calvin would reject the idea God's sovereignty has protected the New Testament canon for all these thousands of years. They both claimed various books that now have been attached for 2000 years to the NT canon were erroneously included. Thus, nothing put forth in the JWO proposition runs afoul of the Sovereignty of God, even as Luther and Calvin understood that doctrine.

First, Luther in his 1522 *Preface to the New Testament* clearly said two books do not belong in the New Testament canon: the Book of Revelation and the Epistle of James. Luther said he could not see "the Holy Spirit" in the Book of Revelation. (See *infra* page 370.) As to James' Epistle, because it "contradicts Paul," Luther said it could not possibly be inspired. (See page 248 *infra.*) Luther printed both books as part of his New Testament simply for historical reasons. Thus, Luther did not regard almost 2000 years of inclusion *ipso facto* proves inspiration. Luther rejected the idea that God's sovereignty implies approval of our New Testament list on the assumption God would not have delayed so long to fix things.

Likewise, Calvin insisted that Second Peter was wrongfully included in canon. (See *infra* page xix of Appendix B.) The Second Epistle of Peter has a verse that troubled Calvin's doctrine of predestination. This probably motivated Calvin's antagonistic viewpoint. Regardless of Calvin's motives, Calvin's position is valid. The inclusion of Second Peter is one of the most universally recognized flaws in the New Testament. This epistle was never recognized fully in any canon list until 367 A.D. It was expressly rejected by Eusebius in 325 A.D. as a pseudograph. It has several internal evidences of its pseudograph nature. Thus, Calvin's view was legitimate.

More important, Calvin's view proves Calvin did not regard almost 2000 years of inclusion *ipso facto* proves inspiration. God's sovereignty does not imply approval merely by God not having supernaturally intervened for 2000 years to reassemble the canon list.

Thus, even though Calvin and Luther surely would not want Paul excluded from canon, both Calvin and Luther would concede it is correct to test Paul's canonicity. There is no presumption that Paul belongs in the NT list merely by passage of time and a long tradition. The Bible demands testing Paul's inclusion by *humans*. The Bible sets forth those tests we *humans* are to apply. However, we *humans* love to shirk responsibility by attributing all events that support our errors to God. However, our Lord does not tolerate such a lazy servant. Let's get to work now and do the job that God commanded us to do: test Paul.

Regardless, The Earliest Tradition Excluded Paul as Inspired Canon

Furthermore, the actual history of canon formation suggests God did tell the early Church that Paul was uninspired. The Ebionites of 65 A.D. asserted Paul was an apostate because of his position on the Law of Moses. The Ebionites insisted Paul's writings must be deemed heretical. Only the Hebrew version of Matthew's Gospel should be canon. (No other NT writing yet existed in 65 A.D.) The evidence strongly suggests that *Ebionites* was a term used for the Apostolic Jerusalem Church under James. The word *Ebionites* is an Hebraism meaning *The Poor.* Paul twice refers to collecting funds for *The Poor* at Jerusalem. However, this link between *The Poor* at Jerusalem and the *Ebionites* was obscured in our New Testament by printing *the poor* in lowercase letters and not transliterating it to Hebrew as *Ebionites*.[4]

Next, Paul was expressly identified by recognized Christian leaders as uninspired when Marcion caused a crisis in 144 A.D. Marcion insisted Paul alone had the true gospel, not the *twelve apostles*. In response, the early universal Christian church said Paul is ***not*** an inspired author. This is clearly set forth in Tertullian's *Against Marcion* from 207 A.D.[5]

Thus, from 65 A.D. to 207 A.D., God apparently did tell the church through James and Tertullian to reject Paul as lacking inspiration. God did not leave us ignorant. We may have simply chosen to ignore God's early messages through His agents. However, there is no time like the present to make amends for errors in our past. We must stop trying to shift responsibility to God for our decisions when we fail to obey God's commands to test the words of alleged prophets.

Historical Note: Has Adding An Edifying Work To Canon Ever Been Mistaken As Proof of Inspiration?

Tertullian in *Against Marcion* (207 A.D.) thought Paul's words should be treated as edifying rather than as inspired material. Unfortunately, this original purpose for reading Paul along with the Gospels was forgotten in the ensuing centuries. Has the notion of *inspired* canon ever been shaped by a misunderstanding of the original intent in joinder? Yes. A similar oversight led Catholics in 1546 to decree the Apocrypha was inspired. However, when it was added to canon eleven centuries earlier, it was solely as *edifying but non-inspired* material. Catholic scholars now recognize that the original purpose of adding the Apocrypha to canon was forgotten over time. Its joinder originally did not mean to imply it was *inspired* material. Yet, confusion set in and now it is regarded as inspired material by Catholic authorities.[6]

4. See *infra page 298* (evidence why Ebionites were the Jerusalem Church under James).
5. For extensive quotations from Tertullian, see *page 408 et seq.*

6. Has overlooking Tertullian's writings on Paul led to a crucial misunderstanding on Paul's supposed inspiration? A similar lapse in memory happened among Catholics regarding Jerome's view of the Apocrypha which he combined with the inspired Bible text. The Apocrypha represented seven books within the Vulgate Bible prepared by Jerome in 411 A.D. Why did Jerome include this section? Jerome in a commentary on Solomon explained the Apocrypha was "for the edification of the people, not for the authoritative confirmation of doctrine." However, ***the memory of Jerome's original purpose faded in time***. In 1546, the Catholic Council of Trent affirmed the Apocrypha as sacred, and it belonged to the Bible. The Apocrypha still is considered an official inspired portion of the Catholic Bible. Thus, the memory of the purpose of joining a *noninspired* writing to *inspired* texts was, after eleven centuries, forgotten. However, the scholars who wrote the "Canon" article for the *New Catholic Encyclopedia* concede what really happened: "The latter [*i.e.*, the Apocrypha] he [Jerome] judged were circulated by the Church as ***good spiritual reading*** but were not recognized as authoritative Scripture. The situation remained unclear in the ensuing centuries...." Thus, in other words, such ***close association*** between *edifying* material and *inspired* material ***caused confusion*** among Catholic authorities over the centuries. Meanwhile, Catholics later adopted doctrines about Purgatory that solely had support in the Apocrypha. Hence, it became embarrassing for Catholicism to later eject this section as *noninspired.* And thus it stands. A joinder to edify the reader became conclusive proof the writing was inspired! Yet, we cannot judge the Catholics too harshly for this error. ***It appears identical to what we did with Paul***. If Tertullian was a voice of orthodoxy on Paul, as it appears he most certainly was, then as of approximately 200 A.D., the church which *first* added Paul to canon close in time must have done so with Tertullian's views in mind. This would mean that such close association of Paul with *inspired* canon later caused us confusion. The early church's original purpose became "unclear [to us] in the ensuing centuries...." Then we, like the Catholics, superimposed our belief system about what *canon* means today on a prior era which viewed canon quite differently. This is apparently how Paul went from an edifying writer who had virtually no impact on doctrine in both the Eastern and Western church for fifteen centuries (see page 425 *et seq.*) to a figure today whose every word is now hung upon by many as inspired text. Also, this episode of how the Apocrypha went from edifying material to inspired writ should remind us that ***the concept of canon has varied over time***. We must not regard the mere fact something was joined as *canon* for centuries as proof that the item is anything more than *reading material* in church. Only if a writing is objectively prophetic material can it stand on its own and be deemed validly inspired.

3 *Must We Apply The Bible's Tests For a True Prophet to Paul?*

Test for Valid Prophets

> *Deuteronomy* 12:32 says: **"Whatsoever thing I command you, shall you observe to do: thou shall not add to it, nor diminish from it."**

Only a true prophet from God can add text to the Bible. (Deut. 18:15.) The Bible itself lays out the tests for such authorized additions to the Bible. These tests are spelled out in Deuteronomy chs. 4, 12, 13 & 18. A key test is that no prophet could be legitimate who tried to "diminish" (subtract) any command previously given. (Deut. 4:2; 12:32 (quoted in inset).) This was true even if they had "sign and wonders that came to pass." (Deut.13:1-5.) This is reiterated in Isaiah 8:20.

However, no Christian council or scholar has ever systematically applied the Bible's tests for false prophets to any writing in our New Testament. This is especially true when Paul's teachings are in question. Of course, this is partly because other than for Paul, there is no need to be concerned about canonicity. The apostles John and Peter along with bishops Jude and James never say anything remotely contradictory of Jesus. Yet, Paul is in a different category. Paul makes statements at apparent odds with Jesus. For example, Paul says the law is abolished while Jesus says this will not happen until heaven and earth pass away. Matt. 5:18.

If the issue of a conflict between Paul and Jesus is raised, one frequently hears a knee-jerk response. There is consternation that anyone would want to test the canonicity of Paul's writings. 'How can we even consider throwing out half the New Testament!' There are murmurs of shocked dismay. Yet, such a response presupposes an affirmative answer to the very question posed: does Paul belong in the New Testament?

My answer to such a response is simple: if Paul truly belongs, then *prove it!* Simply use the Bible's test for adding to Scripture and show everyone that Paul passes its tests. Is this asking too much?

The Bible insists that a Christian demand an answer. We are duty bound to ask our Christian brothers: where is the proof that Paul is to be treated as an inspired prophet? Where is the case Paul has ever been tested and proven a true spokesperson of God by the rigorous demands of Deuteronomy chapters 12, 13 & 18? No one wants to go there but the *Bible commands it!*

> "The flock is supposed to be on the lookout for wolves in *sheep's clothing.*"
> John F. Mac Arthur, Jr.
> *The Gospel According to Jesus* (1994) at 135.

If these tests are to be ignored as to Paul in particular, then ***why do you think a decade prior to Paul's entry into Christian circles that Jesus emphasized repeatedly that false prophets were to come?*** (Matt. 7:15, 24:11, 24.) Why do you think Jesus warned us these false prophets would come with true signs and wonders? So we would lower our guard and never apply Biblical tests for false prophets? Why would Jesus warn us these false prophets would come *in His name*? (Mark 13:22-23). Wasn't Jesus trying to encourage distrust of *Christians* who claimed to have a prophetic office? How could we obey Jesus by refusing to apply the Biblical tests of a true versus a false prophet to Paul? Did Jesus provide us tests of orthodoxy so we would blindly accept someone like Paul who came with signs and wonders (*i.e.*, healings, jails opening in earthquakes, etc.)? Of course not. Jesus made no exception for Paul.

The Bereans in Acts 17:10-15 knew this. They tested a sermon by Paul against Scripture. Yet, they had little written material available to them. By comparison, today we are privileged to examine all of Paul's letters. The Bereans only had a single sermon whose contents are unknown. But if Luke presents the Bereans as doing something appropriate, then why would we think we don't have to test Paul in the same manner? We cannot just trust the Bereans' one-time test resolved the issue for all time. Paul could become a Balaam: an evil man converted into a true prophet who later apostasizes. (For further discussion on the Balaam issue, see page 52 below.) Just because Balaam passed the test for a true prophet initially does not guarantee he remained forever a true prophet. Balaam apostasized later and became a false prophet. Accordingly, the Bereans' conclusion about Paul proves nothing. Rather, we need to follow their example of testing Paul to see whether he seduces us from following the commands from prior Scripture and known Prophets (including Jesus).

We thus have an inescapable command from God to test Paul.

Moreover, we shall see Jesus reiterated these tests almost verbatim from Deuteronomy. He intended us specifically to use them to test the writings of anyone which the community wanted to add as inspired canon.

The first test of a valid prophet is they must make a specific prophecy using the *name of the Lord*. (Deut. 18:20-22.) If the speaker will not say God told them this secret about the future, the alleged prophetic statement is insufficient to validate the speaker as a true prophet even if it came true. The reason for such strictness is the test has both a positive and negative side. On the positive, if valid, we treat such a speaker's words as from God. Thus, the speaker's words must squarely come within God's *definition* of valid prophecy. On the negative side, we must impose the death penalty if the speaker used God's name for a prophecy and it did not come true.

Therefore, if the speaker attributed as his source someone other than God, *e.g.*, an angel *alone* was his source, we cannot impose the death penalty on the speaker for false prophecy. We must follow Scripture strictly. In this example, the speaker did nothing worthy of death because he claimed his prophecy came from an angel alone, without God's voice confirming it. Thus, unless the would-be prophet says *thus sayeth the Lord* at some meaningful point as his source in conjunction with his prediction, he cannot be a prophet in the Biblical sense if his prediction *just so happens* to come true. For the same reason, if what he said proves false and he did not ascribe his source to God personally, we cannot kill him. Because he did not dare make the prophecy in the Lord's name, he suffers no penalty. No risk, no gain. No risk, no loss.

Likewise, if the event is easily predictable, such as the sun will come up or a plane will safely weather a storm, there is nothing highly improbable in such an outcome. The predicted outcome, while not guaranteed, is predictable. It has a significant probability it would have happened anyway. The Bible says such predictions are not *prophetic* material. Jeremiah chapter 28 tells us that predictable events are no basis to regard their prediction as true prophecy.[1]

In summary, *divine prophecy* implies necessarily that the prediction must be something specific and highly improbable that only God would know. If it does not happen, the false prophet is to be killed. Of course, to repeat, the would-be prophet had to first use the words *thus sayeth the Lord* or an equivalent, *e.g.*, Jesus claimed to speak as I AM Himself

1. *See*, Jer. 28:8-9. As Knudd Jepperson (D.D., University Lecturer) points out on this verse: "The prophet who in the name of the Lord foretold misery and misfortune, however, would sooner or later be right. If the time had not yet come, one could rest assured that eventually there would be so much evil, that misery necessarily had to come." (Jepperson, *On False And True Prophets in the Old Testament*, at http://www.theonet.dk/spirituality/spirit95-6/prophesy.html (last visited 2005.)

(John 8:58). The speaker must clearly claim divine inspiration from *God Himself* for a highly specific and unlikely prediction. Otherwise, imposing a death penalty would be unjust. (Deuteronomy 18:20-22.) However, once exposed as false prophecy, God says: "Thou shalt not be afraid of him." (Deut. 18:22.) The necessity to follow this testing of their words comes from the command to *not add to canon* (Deut. 4:2) unless it passes the Bible's test for valid prophecy.

Second Level Test: False Despite True Prophecy and Signs

The Bible then has a second level test. Jesus clearly repeats this test. (Matt. 7:15, 24:11, 24.) It is set forth in Deuteronomy 4:2 and 13:1-5. A false prophet can include someone who tries to "diminish" the words of a prior validated prophet. (Deut. 4:2.) While a valid prophet can add to Scripture (Deut. 18:15), he is invalid if he "diminishes" from prior Scripture. (Deut. 4:2.) Thus, the Bible warns that even if someone comes with what otherwise appears to be valid true prophecy, they are invalid if they "diminish" the words of a prior valid prophet. Deuteronomy 13:1-5 teaches if they come with true "signs and wonders" which "come to pass," they are still a false prophet if they thereafter try to "**seduce you from the way in which the Lord your God commanded you to walk**." (Deut. 13:5.) This is reiterated in Isaiah 8:20, which states: "To the Law [of Moses] and to the testimony: if they speak not according to this word, it is because there is no light in them." (KJV). Thus, God tells us one who teaches contrary to the commands in the Law is a false prophet despite his having true prophecy and real signs and wonders. As Barnes comments on Isaiah 8:20: "By this standard all doctrines are still to be tried."

Balaam is an example of this type of prophet. At one point he provides true prophecy that indeed came from God. He was filled by the Holy Spirit during those times. (Numbers 24:1-2.) However, later he teaches people it is permissible to do acts which the Law flatly prohibits. He tells them they can eat meat sacrificed to idols and they can commit fornication. (Numbers 31:16; Rev. 2:14.) Thus, he is a false prophet under the Deuteronomy 4:2 and 13:1-5 test. Despite this kind of prophet being inspired for a time, you must ignore everything he thereafter said. You must brand him a false prophet once he ever tries to "seduce you from the way in which the Lord your God commanded you to walk." (Deut. 13:5.) (For a full discussion on Balaam, see page 133 *et seq.*)

Thus, Balaam went from a true prophet to a false prophet solely by the *content of his teachings*.

God explains *why* he allows such men to speak prophetically and have signs and wonders "that come true." God allows them to come to seduce you as a *test of your Love for God*. The Lord explains this precisely in Deuteronomy 12:32-13:5:

> Whatever I command you, you shall be careful to do; ***you shall not add to nor take away from it***. If a prophet or a dreamer of dreams arises among you and ***gives you a sign or a wonder, and the sign or the wonder comes true***, concerning which he spoke to you, saying, 'Let us go after other gods (whom you have not known) and let us serve them,' you shall not listen to the words of that prophet or that dreamer of dreams; for ***the Lord your God is testing you to find out if you love the Lord your God with all your heart and with all your soul.*** You shall follow the Lord your God and fear Him; and you shall keep His commandments, listen to His voice, serve Him, and cling to Him. But that prophet or that dreamer of dreams shall be put to death, because he has counseled rebellion against the Lord your God who brought you from the land of Egypt and redeemed you from the house of slavery, ***to seduce you from the way in which the Lord***

> ***your God commanded you to walk***. So you shall purge the evil from among you. (ASV.)[2]

If some would-be prophet seeks to "seduce" us "from the way in which the Lord your God commanded you to walk," you must reject him. His *god* cannot be the true God. His *god* must be an idol even if he calls on *Yahweh*. This is true even if he comes with signs and wonders. God tells us to ignore such a prophet's words or otherwise we are joining his rebellion. Isaiah instructs us to apply a similar *content*-oriented test to determine a true prophet.

> [Compare teachers] [t]o the Law and the Testimony [and], if they **speak not according to *this* Word**, it is because there is no light in them. (Isaiah 8:20).

Norman Geisler, a conservative Christian scholar and President of the Southern Evangelical Seminary in Charlotte, concurs on the essential meaning of Deuteronomy. He agrees that if Paul seduces us from following what God already commanded in previous Scripture, he must be rejected:

> [A]ny teaching about God contrary to what the people already knew to be true was to be rejected....If the teaching of the apostle [Paul] did ***not accord*** *with the teaching of the Old Testament*, it could not be of God. (Norman Gei-

2. In context, Deuteronomy 13:1-5 does speak of the false prophet trying to lead them to 'other gods.' Some assert this passage could never invalidate a person who uses Yahweh's name and teaches against the Law's validity. This view argues that using Yahweh's name for Lawless teaching somehow insulates the person from being viewed as a false prophet. This is erroneous. A seduction to disobey God's commands and to listen to the signs-and-wonder prophet is the same as trying to lead you to other gods—the prophet himself. He becomes a demi-god. His god, even if called Yahweh, cannot be the true Yahweh. In accord, Isaiah 8:20 demonstrates that the alleged prophet's validity turns on consistency with prior valid Scripture, starting with the Law of Moses and moving forward.

sler, "The Canonicity of the Bible, Part One," *Baker Encyclopedia of Christian Apologetics* (Baker Book House: 1999).)

Thus, if any New Testament writer tries to seduce us from the way in which God commanded us to walk in the Hebrew Scriptures, the Bible *brands* him a false prophet. Geisler, a conservative defender of Scripture, agrees that Paul must be measured by whether his words ***accord*** with what God commanded in the original Hebrew Scripture.

Jesus says so likewise in Matthew 7:15-23 and 24:11, 24. So does Deuteronomy 4:2 and 13:5.

As to Paul, the Bereans were on the right path. They compared Paul to Scripture. (Acts 17:11.) The Bereans simply did not have the later words of Paul. They did not have access to Paul's letters that we do. Paul's later words must be tested by Scripture that God delivered by the prophets before him. Paul's words must also be tested by the words of Jesus who is both Prophet and Lord.

Before we examine this Deuteronomy test, let's see what test is commonly used instead.

Does Paul Get A Free Pass Because of His Fiery Spirit, Zeal, and Long Acceptance?

When it comes to the question why was the canon put together to include Paul, Paulinists typically give unbiblical justifications. They retreat to a justification of inclusion based on our *feelings, our perception of a good purpose*, and long *tradition*. These grounds are set forth as an independent test which can validate something as canon despite the writing not otherwise satisfying the proper Biblical test.

For example, Josh McDowell in his famous *Evidence that Demands a Verdict* says the criteria for New Testament canon are: "Is it authoritative.... prophetic.... authentic.... dynamic? Was it received, collected, read and used...?"[3]

However, the only proper test in the Bible is whether the prophecy:

- Was a predictive prophecy of an unlikely event;
- Was made *in the name of the Lord*;
- Came true; and
- The would-be prophet's teachings at all subsequent times are 100% consistent with prior *tested* and *tried* Scripture, and do not negate any commands in such Scripture.

The Origin of McDowell's Test

Where did the Josh McDowell test come from? Such a criteria to assess canon clearly first appears in a work called the *Shepherd of Hermas*. This work was written near 125 A.D. The *Shepherd* was part of Christian canon for about two hundred years thereafter. In the Codex Sinaiticus from the late 300 A.D. period, the *Shepherd* was printed right after the book of Revelation. Numerous church leaders said it was "divinely inspired."

The *Shepherd* taught in what it calls the *Eleventh Commandment* that "a true prophet" is someone who changes their hearers for the better, whose message is lofty, and who is meek and peaceable himself. By contrast, the false prophet will "shun" teaching the righteous. His listeners will be as empty as before they heard their message.[4] Under this loose test of the prophetic, the *Shepherd* itself was allowed to pass into the NT canon for two hundred years of early Christianity.

However, then in the late 300s, the *Shepherd* began to be dropped from canon productions. It was removed apparently because it said adultery could be forgiven. Tertullian

3. Josh McDowell, *Evidence that Demands a Verdict* (San Bernardino: Here's Life, 1979) Vol. 2 at 29.
4. See the *Eleventh Commandment* at http://www.earlychristianwritings.com/text/shepherd.html (last accessed 2005).

had in the 200s insisted the book should be removed from canon for this reason. He said its position on adultery being a pardonable sin was impious. The *Shepherd* then disappears from Christian canons beginning in the 300s. It never returns.

This adultery-as-unpardonable principle may seem an odd criteria to determine canon. However, it is the very same reason why pious Christians in the 300s tampered with Jesus' words in John 7:53-8:11. This is the passage where Jesus pardons the woman accused of adultery. Most versions of John's Gospel in the era of the 300s removed this passage. Augustine in 430 A.D. skewers them for deleting the text. Augustine mentions his contemporaries wrongly thought Jesus could not forgive the woman charged with adultery.[5] As a result of this deletion, most of us have read the NIV's note which says the most "reliable" manuscripts of that era omit the passage.

5. The NIV footnote reads: "The earliest and most reliable manuscripts and other ancient witnesses do not have John 7:53-8:11." This makes it appear this is a forgery. However, the NIV comment is misleading by lacking context. It is also patently false as to the claim "ancient witnesses" do not have the passage. First, the passage is in numerous uncials, including Codex D (Bazae Cantabrigiensis), G, H, K, M, U, and G. It also is in early translations such as the Bohairic Coptic version, the Syriac Palestinian version and the Ethiopic version, all of which date from the second to the sixth centuries. It is also in the Latin Vulgate (404 A.D.) by Jerome. Further, the passage is cited by a number of the patristic writers. Among them are *Didascalia* (third century), Ambrosiaster (fourth century), and Ambrose (fourth century). It is also in *Apostolic Constitutions*, which is a collections of writings from Antioch Syria that is dated between 220 A.D. and 380 AD. Augustine (430 AD) reveals that the reason some were deleting this passage in later manuscripts was because of its message that adultery could be forgiven. Augustine writes: "This proceeding, however, shocks the minds of some weak believers, or rather unbelievers and enemies of the Christian faith: inasmuch that, after (I suppose) of its giving their wives impunity of sinning, ***they struck out from their copies of the Gospel this that our Lord did in pardoning the woman taken in adultery***: as if He granted leave of sinning, Who said, Go and sin no more!" (Saint Augustine, *De Conjug. Adult.*, II:6.). Thus, one can see in Augustine's day, there was a sentiment that Jesus' pardoning this woman of adultery was a wrong teaching. Augustine says this is why it was edited out of various copies of John's gospel.

While the manuscripts that delete this are generally reliable, this particular deletion is not itself reliable. What this demonstrates is the removal of the adultery passage in John coincides with the departure of the *Shepherd* from canon. The reasoning behind both changes are identical. A false Christian piety grew up in the 300s which not only threw out the *Shepherd*, but also deleted words of our Lord.

This history is important on the issue of canon formation. While the *Shepherd* properly was excluded from canon in the 300s, it was removed for the *wrong reason*. The right reason is that it was not prophetic. It lacked a predictive prophecy to validate it. Also, it contradicted Deuteronomy on how to define and recognize a prophetic statement. The *Shepherd* was a false prophetic work. Yet, the *Shepherd* was rejected on the wrong-headed notion that adultery was an unpardonable sin. The same wrong-headed thinking caused Jesus' words in John 7:53-8:11 to be cast off in the 300s by sincere well-meaning but misdirected Christians.

As a result, when the *Shepherd* was ejected, it already had spread its erroneous notion about what is prophetic. During those two-hundred early years (125-325 A.D.), the *Shepherd* was accepted as a *divinely inspired message*. It redefined the test of what is prophetic canon. Then when the *Shepherd* was ejected, it unfortunately did not cause anyone to re-evaluate the notion of how to define valid prophetic canon.

The *Shepherd*'s test of canon is the same as Josh McDowell's test quoted above. Under this test, we use our subjective impression of how authoritative it *feels* to us. We look to see if it has a positive *effect*, as we subjectively evaluate it.

If presence in canon implied early-on that a book was 'inspired', then the clearest proof of the effect of the *Shepherd* on early canon lists is the presence of the Epistle to the Hebrews. It actually was written by Barnabas.[6] Then what

6. Tertullian in about 207 A.D. points out that Barnabas is the author. Origen twenty years later claimed that the author is unknown.

explains its presence in the NT canon of that era even down to the present time? There is no prophecy in *Hebrews*. There is not even apostolic authority involved. The only test that justifies its inclusion comes from the *Shepherd*'s loose canon test. The Epistle to the Hebrews is inspiring, lofty, and can change its hearers. Otherwise, it has nothing to justify any kind of inclusion in the NT canon. It passes the *Shepherd*'s test of prophetic. However, nothing from the word of God endorses the inclusion of the Epistle to the Hebrews in our NT canon.

Did Paul Have A Predictive Prophecy in The Lord's Name Come True?

This leads us back to our main point. Under Deuteronomy, if we examine what belongs in the New Testament, there is no case to add anyone to canon except Jesus. He alone made a significant prophecy that came true, *i.e.*, the fall of the Temple at Jerusalem and His own resurrection.

Paul, by contrast, has merely one arguable prophecy that came true. However, the claim for it is weak. In the middle of a terrible storm, Paul claimed an angel, *without God simultaneously present in the vision,* told him that no one would lose their life in a ship crash. However, he predicted the ship would be lost. (Acts 27:22-25.) Paulinists never cite this as an example of Paul's predictive prowess. This is because in the same context, Paul's lack of *constant inspiration* is also exposed. Why? Because when Paul brought the warning initially, he said the opposite.

Historical Note: Early Adherents of Faith Alone
—'Faith Despite Disobedience Saves'—

Marcion, ***Antitheses*** (144 A.D.) said:
18...our Christ was commissioned by the good God [of the NT] to liberate all mankind.
19...the Creator [of the OT] promises salvation only to those who are obedient. The Good [God of the NT] redeems those who believe in him, but he does not judge those who are disobedient to him.

See Table 1 below.

TABLE 1. Paul's Words Are Not Always Prescient

Paul Predicts Loss of Life	Paul Predicts No Loss of Life
Acts 27:10	Acts 27:22-24
[A]nd said unto them, Sirs, I perceive (*theoreo*, perceive with the eyes, discern) that the voyage ***will be*** with injury and much loss, not only of the lading and the ship, but ***also of our lives.***	(22) And now I exhort you to be of good cheer; for there ***shall be no loss of life*** among you, but only of the ship. (23) For there stood by me this night an angel of the God whose I am, whom also I serve, (24) saying, Fear not, Paul; thou must stand before Caesar: and lo, God hath granted thee all them that sail with thee.

More important, Paul claims the source of this second contradictory prediction is an *angel* who relays God's decision to save all on board. This takes away from it any claim that it is a *prophecy* at all. To be a prophecy that *can* be valid, *it must take a risk of being a prophecy that is invalid*. To be a prophecy of such kind, it had to be *In the Name of God (Yah-*

weh or 'I am')[7] Somewhere, there must be a claim God was present giving confirmation of the angel's words. We read in Deuteronomy 18:20-22:

> (20) But the prophet, that shall speak a word presumptuously ***in my name***, which I have not commanded him to speak, or that shall speak in the name of other gods, that same prophet shall die.
>
> (21) And if thou say in thy heart, How shall we know the word which Jehovah hath not spoken?
>
> (22) when a prophet speaketh ***in the name of Jehovah***, if the thing follow not, nor come to pass, that is the thing which Jehovah hath not spoken: the prophet hath spoken it presumptuously, thou shalt not be afraid of him.

Thus, had Paul's prediction been false, Paul could not fall under the false prophecy penalty of death in the Mosaic Testament. This is because the prophet must claim *the prophecy is going to come true in God's name:* "Thus speaketh Yahweh...." or some equivalent.[8] If it is attributed directly to an angel without God simultaneously present in the encounter, it does not qualify. By claiming instead it will come true and you

---

7. God actually identifies Himself by *two names* and variations on the name. The first is *Yahweh* (and variants) and the second is "I am." *See*, Exodus 3:14 ("And God said unto Moses, I AM THAT I AM: and he said, Thus shalt thou say unto the children of Israel, I AM hath sent me unto you.") Jesus used this name for Himself. In John 8:58: "Jesus said unto them, Verily, verily, I say unto you, Before Abraham was born, I am." Thus, everything Jesus predicts *is in the name of the Lord* since He was claiming to be I Am.

8. An example of a false prophecy in Scripture is Hananiah in Jeremiah 28:2, battling Jeremiah, the true prophet. In Jeremiah 28:2, Hananiah begins, "***Thus speaketh Jehovah of hosts, the God of Israel***, saying, I have broken the yoke of the king of Babylon." Thus, by invoking God's name as the direct source of the prophecy, Hananiah was taking the risk of being found a false prophet if he was wrong. Otherwise, Hananiah could not be taken seriously if a prophecy happened to come true.

use God's name, the prophet-claimant thereby takes the risk that if his words do not come true, then he can be regarded as a false prophet and be put to death. That's obviously why the old prophet in 1 Kings 13 carefully attributed his false prophecy to an angel alone. It spared his life.

This requirement of using God's name arises from practical reasons. If the 'prophecy' had *not* come true, Paul would have been able to say 'some darker angel' must have given him the message that proved untrue. 'The angel deceived me.' There is wiggle room to avoid the death penalty if his prediction had proven untrue. Thus, to make a valid prophecy, one must by definition not only have a prophecy that *comes true*, but one must in advance say the message is *directly from God*. You cannot receive the reward of recognition as God's prophet unless one is willing to use His name initially in giving the prophecy. "No pain, no gain" embodies the principle. Thus, if one claims an angel gave it, and you do not claim it came with God's direct presence, it cannot be treated as a valid prophecy *ab initio* even if it later happens to come true.

This brings up a second problem with Paul's prediction about the storm as prophecy. Angels in the Hebrew Scripture make birth announcements and explain visions of the future with God present. They are heralds of a very limited nature. For example, in Daniel, they show and explain visions of the future with the "Son of Man" (Jesus) present. They speak God's words only when God is described as simultaneously present.[9] Paul's attribution of *predictive* words to an angel without God present in the vision is therefore most peculiar.

9. When an angel appears to Gideon, God is present talking; the angel makes no prediction. (Judges 6:21-23.) An angel tells Manoah and his wife about their son Samson to be born. (Judges 13:9-21.) In Daniel, the prophet sees the "son of man" who receives kingdoms, and then a "man's voice" tells Gabriel to "make this man understand the vision." (Dan. 8:15-16.) The angel then explains the vision of the future.

In sum, the prediction Paul makes in Acts chapter 27 suffers from several defects:

- It does not predict an outcome that is so highly unlikely that absent God's foresight it would be unimaginable.
- It is not in the name of Yahweh or an equivalent expression. It is attributed to an angel without God present.
- It attributes to an angel a predictive statement that angels did not make in the Hebrew Scripture outside of birth announcements or in vision presentations with God simultaneously present.

Yet, even if we grant this one prophecy as validating Paul as a prophet, he could still become like Balaam who prophesied with the Holy Spirit but later apostasized. Thus, one cannot rest Paul's validity solely upon the claim this 'angel-vision' mentioned in Acts chapter 27 is prophecy.

Paul Could Still Be A Balaam Who Initially Has True Prophecy

To be a true prophet, Paul must prove also not to offer teachings that negate what came before. (Deut. 4:2; 13:1-5.)

Jesus was completely consistent with what came before. Jesus upheld every jot and letter of the Law, and insisted upon an ongoing necessity to teach and follow the Law. (Matt. 5:18.)

Consequently, Jesus' words qualify as (a) prophetic (*i.e.*, predictive and confirmed); (b) valid (*i.e.*, consistent with and never negating what preceded); and (c) in the name of *I am* because Jesus claimed to be *I am*. (John 8:58.)

By contrast, Paul's predictive statement is certainly not invoking *Yahweh's* name. Instead, Paul relied upon an angel alone. Even if Paul had a prophecy in God's name, there is a substantial question whether Paul's words were also valid, *i.e.*, consistent with and not negating what preceded. Paul must be examined to determine if he started true, turned false and apostasized later. The example from history that proves this is a correct test of Paul is the story of Balaam. Despite Balaam prophesying with the Holy Spirit (Numbers 24:1-2) and believing in the Coming Messiah (Christ) to rule the world (Numbers 24:17), Balaam later apostasized and was lost!

Balaam's Star Prophecy of Messiah (1290 B.C.)

Most Christian commentators acknowledge the false prophet Balaam did originally give true Messianic prophecy in the Star Prophecy. (See *Treasury of Scriptural Knowledge*, Wesley, Henry, JFB, and Gill.) This is why Matthew identifies the Magi following the star to Bethlehem. (Matt. 2:1, *magos*.)

Let's see how amazing is Balaam's prophecy of Numbers 24:17 to realize how Balaam was a true prophet of Christ *at one time* but who later turned false. In Numbers 24:17, we read Balaam's words:

> I see him, but not now; I behold him, but not nigh; there shall ***step forth a star out of Jacob***, and a ***scepter*** shall rise out of Israel, and shall smite through the corners of Moab, and break down all the sons of tumult. (ASV).

Friedman, in the modern Jewish translation, renders the first key part "a star has ***stepped from*** Jacob...." (*Commentary on the Torah*, *supra*, at 511.) The "scepter" implied this star would identify a new king. The last part on someone ruling the "sons of tumult" was interpreted by ancient Jews as meaning "rule the world." The *Targum of Onkelos* from circa 150 A.D.—the Aramaic interpretation of the Law—restates this passage to have a Messianic application: "a king shall arise from the house of Jacob, and be anointed the Messiah out of Israel." Clearly, Numbers 24:17 was deemed a Messianic prophecy by Jews long before Jesus appeared.[10]

10. The oracle of Balaam is quoted four times in the Dead Sea scrolls in conjunction with Messianic prophecies: the War Scroll (1QM 11.6-17); Damascus Document (CD 7.19-21); Messianic Testimonia (4Q175 1:9-13), and Priestly Blessings for the Last Days (1QSb 5:27). (See Wise, Abegg, & Cook, *The Dead Sea Scrolls: A New Translation*.)

Balaam Was Not Saved Despite Believing in Messiah To Come

The fact Balaam uttered a Messianic prophecy has important meaning in salvation doctrine. It answers the question whether believing in a Messianic prophecy and knowing about Christ, as did Balaam, saves you. Balaam's destruction at Moses' request proves such belief alone did not save Balaam. Yet, indisputably, Balaam was one of the first *under inspiration of the Holy Spirit* to believe in and prophesy specifically about the *Messiah*. He saw Christ and ***believed in Him***. Yet, Balaam later apostasized by teaching Jews that they could eat meat sacrificed to idols and they could fornicate. (Num. 31:8, 16; Rev. 2:14.) (See also page 135 for detailed discussion.) Balaam clearly became lost. (Rev. 2:14.)

Why Do Paulinists Ignore Balaam's Prophecy?

Why would Paulinists not want to focus upon this amazing Messianic prophecy in Numbers 24:17? You rarely hear any discussion of it in Paulinist-oriented congregations. It actually is necessary to know about this story to make sense of why the Magi arrived at Bethlehem and why they were following a star. There is no excuse to not help people understand the Star of Bethlehem and its key role in the nativity.

This prophecy is ignored for three reasons. First, it shows how one of the most amazing *inspired* prophecies of Messiah came from a man who *later apostasizes* and is certainly *lost*. Such a possibility is denied by eternal security advocates, relying principally on Paul for their teaching. Thus, any mention of Balaam's prophecy causes embarrassment to proponents of eternal security.

Second, the background on the Star Prophecy shows that people steeped in error and pagan practices, like the Magi, could still hold onto true Messianic prophecy of the Bible. Yet, believing in Messianic prophecy did not make them saved Christians. It likewise does not make someone a Christian who thinks they can believe *the intellectual side of a prophecy* with no change in the heart. The Magi's doctrines (Zoroastrianism) taught them they were saved if they used the right verbal formula for belief, known as a *mantra*. They also believed they could pray to those in the afterlife. (Lucian, *Mennipus* 6-9.) Their teachings about mantras thereby violated the Law given to Moses, which preached salvation by repentance from sin, atonement, and faithfulness. Moreover, the Magi's teachings about talking to the dead also violated the Law given to Moses. (Deut. 18:11; *cf.* Isaiah 8:19; 19:3.) Thus, for those steeped in eternal security, it is difficult to mention the Magi were unsaved people who believed in Messianic Prophecies.

Lastly, the Magi (from Babylon) in Matthew 2:1 make us uncomfortable for another reason. Their presence proves how Jesus wanted us to understand the ***symbolism of Babylon in the Book of Revelation***. The Magi of Babylon came from a culture steeped in a *certain type* of doctrinal error. They must have ***correctly worshipped*** the God of Daniel. First, Nebuchadnezzar acknowledged Yahweh. Lastly, King Darius also later specifically decreed that "the God of Daniel" was the true God and that his entire vast empire had to acknowledge this. (Dan. 4:34-37; 6:26). Thereafter, Daniel obviously had ample opportunity as the chief officer over the Magi to inculcate faith in the true God among the Magi. (Dan. 6:1-2.) Based on Matthew 2:1's mention of the *magos* (Greek for *magi*), there is every reason to be believe this Jewish component of Babylonian religion continued. Babylonian religion must have absorbed this as part of Zoroastrianism—a monotheistic religion. In it, Daniel's God must have continued to be *their one true God* for some significant period.

So what does Babylon represent? A pagan religion? No! Babylon represents a faith with the right emphasis on the *true God* and the *true Christ* but ***adulteration*** by adding salvation and legal principles at odds with God's Law.

How do we know the Magi had the right emphasis on the true Christ? That they were waiting for Messiah's birth?

Because Babylon's spiritual & political leaders (the Magi) were clearly aware of Daniel's prophecy of Messiah's date for being cut-off (*i.e.*, killed). (Dan. 9:25-26.) Daniel was the ***chief of the Magi***, by appointment of the king (Dan. 6:1-2). Thus, Daniel's prophecy would be well-known by the Magi. This prophecy, uttered in 604 B.C., said the Messiah shall come and be cut-off after sixty-nine "periods of sevens" (*viz.*, a sabbath cycle of seven years)[11]— 483 years — from the "order to restore and to build Jerusalem." (Dan. 9:25-26.)

The *Jewish Encyclopedia* says this order went forth in 444 B.C. Nehemiah "arrived in Jerusalem in 444 BCE with an appointment as governor of Judah... [and his] first action was to rebuild... Jerusalem [including the temple]." ("Nehemiah," *The Jewish Encyclopedia of Judaism* (1989) at 520.)

What year could the Magi deduce Messiah's being cut-off?

The year ***33 A.D.*** The Jewish calendar year is a lunar-based year. There are only 360 days in the "year" of which Daniel is prophesying. Daniel's prophecy of 483 *lunar* years thus represents 173,880 days (483 x 360). This equates to 476 solar years in our calendar. If you subtract 476 years from 444 B.C., you hit square on ***33 A.D***. How amazing!

Thus, from Daniel's prophecy, the Magi would know the date of the Messiah's being cut-off is 33 A.D. The Magi then could piece this together with the Star Prophecy of Balaam to determine his approximate time of birth.

How did the Magi know of the Star Prophecy?

Again, the Magi no doubt were also trained by Daniel in the Messianic Star Prophecy from Numbers 24:16-19. Daniel mentions his continued use of the Law of Moses while living in Babylon. (Dan. 9:11-13.) Daniel would then have shared this Star Prophecy in the Law of Moses with his Magi.

---

11. This is often mistranslated as *weeks*. The word is *shebu'im*. In the feminine form, it means a "period of seven days." However, in the masculine, as is present here, it means simply "a time period of seven units" (*e.g.*, month, year, sabbath cycle of seven years). *See, Theological Workbook of the Old Testament* (G.L. Archer, R.L. Harris, & B.K. Waltke, eds.) (Chicago: Moody Press, 1992) (2 Vols.) at 2:899; G.L. Archer, "Daniel," *The Expositor's Bible Commentary* (Gabalein, Ed.)(Grand Rapids) Vol. 7 at 112.

Why would this Star Prophecy tell the Magi that a star's rising would mark the *birth* of the Messiah? After all, the word *birth* is not mentioned in Numbers 24:16-19?

For two reasons. First, a star rising (which for ancients included planetary conjunctions) was ordinarily claimed by the ancients to mark the birth of important future rulers. This is why the Romans understood the Star Prophecy in the First Century A.D. to signal such a birth. For example, Suetonius tried claiming a star in that period augured the birth of one of their own emperors who would rule the world in fulfillment of the Star Prophecy from the East.[12]

Second, history proves the Magi understood the Star Prophecy as a birth augur. Christian historians have traced the prophecy of Balaam after 600 B.C. within the Babylonian religion. Abulfaragius (1226-1286) in his *Historia Dynastarium*[13] says that Zoroaster[14] was a student of Daniel, and that Zoroaster taught the Magi that a new star would one day signal the ***birth*** of a mysterious child whom they were to adore.[15]

Thus, the Magi would understand the Star Prophecy to be talking of the *birth* of the same person who is *cut-off* in 33 A.D. in Daniel's Prophecy. Therefore, the Magi of Babylon would be naturally looking backwards one adult life-time (40 years approximately) prior to 33 A.D. This would identify the birth-time for this Messiah to be approximately 7 B.C. Thus, the Magi were on the look-out for this star precisely at about the time Jesus was born in about 3 B.C.

---

12. Suetonius in *Lives of the Twelve Emperors* says: "There had spread over all the Orient an old and established belief that it was fated at that time for a man coming from Judaea to rule the world. This prediction, referring to the emperor of Rome, as it turned out, the Jews took to themselves, and they revolted accordingly [in 66 A.D.]." (Suetonius, *Vespasian* 4.5.)
13. This is recorded by Oxford Professor, Thomas Hyde, in his masterpiece of 1700 A.D. entitled *Historia religionis veterum Persarum.*
14. Zoroaster, according to traditional and conservative modern practitioners of Zoroastrianism, lived around 580 B.C. He founded the Magi.
15. George Stanley Faber (1773-1854)(Anglican theologian), *The Origin of Pagan Idolatry Ascertained from Historical Testimony and Circumstantial Evidence* ([London] F & C. Rivingtons, 1816) Vol. 2 at 92.

The Magi of Matthew 2:1 are thus following Balaam's Star Prophecy and Daniel's Messianic Prophecy to the letter. This is what squarely allows them to arrive at the right time in Bethlehem to give presents to the infant Jesus.

Yet, throughout Revelation, Babylon is synonymous with the harlot. What does this mean? God is telling us that Babylon, led by its *Magi* rulers, was a nation whose faith is like that of Balaam: ***it knew the true God and His Christ but it taught its people to violate God's commands***. It taught salvation by mere mantras (*i.e.*, verbal formulas). Furthermore, it was a nation built on *legal* apostasy. In other words, Babylon had the correct faith in the true God and ***waited for the true Messiah*** and ***even rejoiced at finding Him.*** Otherwise, it had the wrong salvation principles and all its behaviors were contrary to God's Law. Babylon is thus depicted in Revelation as a *harlot*—prostituting itself to base desires.

Consequently, the lessons of Balaam for us are many. We need to examine how important it is that we can alone say the right mantra of faith, and be sincere, and want to know Christ, like the Magi did. But what happens if we trust a mantra (like the Magi did) to save us despite our rejection of the Law which "I Am" (Jesus) gave Moses?

Conclusion

Balaam was a true prophet who was later convicted as a false prophet under Deuteronomy 4:2 and 13:1-5. Balaam truly had the Holy Spirit when he blessed Israel and gave the Star Prophecy of Messiah. Moses *expressly says so.* Yet, Balaam is an apostate and lost. The Bible, through Moses and Jesus, tells us this too. Balaam's error was later telling Israel they could eat meat sacrificed to idols and they could commit fornication. (Rev. 2:14.) He ***diminished*** the Law. (Deut. 4:2.)

The story of Balaam is proof that we cannot just assume that if someone like Paul gave a true prophecy one time that he has passed every test or that he can never apostasize later.

4 *Did Jesus Warn of False Prophets Who Would Negate the Law?*

Introduction

Jesus was concerned about the "signs and wonders" prophets misleading Christians. (Matt. 7:15-23, *viz.*, v. 22; 24:11, 24.) Jesus warns of the false prophets in Mark 13:22. They "shall show signs and wonders to ***seduce***, if possible, even the elect."

In Deuteronomy, these signs-and-wonders prophets are false not because their prophecies are untrue. Rather, their signs and wonders are extraordinary. Indeed, ***their prophecy comes true***. (Deut. 13:2, "the sign or the wonder ***come to pass***, whereof he spake unto thee.") Rather, the proof they are false is in ***the content of their message as subversive of the Torah*** (*i.e.*, the Five Books of Moses). These prophets try to "draw thee aside out of the way which Jehovah thy God commanded thee to walk in." (Deut. 13:5. *Cf.* Deut. 4:2.)

When Deuteronomy was written, all there was of Scripture was Genesis, Exodus, Leviticus, Numbers, and Deuteronomy. Thus, even a prophet with true prophecy must be rejected if he seduces you to "draw aside" from the commandments in them. The supposed prophet's validity turns on whether, contrary to Deuteronomy 4:2, he *diminishes* the Law God has already given. Balaam is an example from the Bible of someone who was once a true prophet who later was found false based solely on these principles. Thus, even though Balaam ***believed in Christ*** and ***truly prophesied of Him*** with the Holy Spirit (so says Moses), Balaam ***later*** became a ***false*** prophet. This fall was merely because he diminished the Law by teaching certain violations of it were permissible. (Numbers 24:1 *et seq*; Rev. 2:14.) (See page 41 *et seq*. for further discussion.)

Jesus in Matthew 7:15-24 is clearly alluding to these same "signs and wonders" prophets. Jesus says they are lost. He will deny He ever knew them even though on Judgment Day they are able to say they did "marvelous works in Your name," and many "prophecies in Your name." (Matt. 7:22.) Jesus tells us He will reject them. It is not because they lacked true prophecy or marvelous wonders. Rather, the sole reason to reject them is they are workers of "*anomia.*" (Matt. 7:23.)

This Greek word *anomia* here means "negators of the Law (of Moses)." This is one of its two lexicon definitions. In choosing this definition over *lawless*, we do so primarily because Jesus' warning was obviously paralleling Deuteronomy 13:1-5. See discussion in the next section.

If you agree on choosing this dictionary definition, then we can easily anticipate that Paul is not going to fare well. Paul's doctrine that the Law of Moses was abolished by Jesus' coming is well known. See chapter five.

Why Anomia Means Negator of Mosaic Law

Jesus tells us we can identify the false prophets because they are workers of "*anomia.*" (Matt. 7:23.) What does this Greek word *anomia* mean?

In Greek, *anomia* is a feminine noun, related to the adjective *a-nomos. Nomos* is the Greek word to identify the Law or Torah, *i.e.*, the Five Books of Moses. (Strong's #3551.) The prefix *a* is a negative particle in Greek. Putting the parts together, it should mean *negation of the Law (Torah)*.

Do the lexicons agree? What does *anomia* precisely mean in Matthew 7:23? The best lexicon of ancient Greek (which is free online) is Henry George Liddell's and Robert Scott's *A Greek-English Lexicon.*[1] It defines *anomia*[2] as one of two meanings:

- "the negation of the law"
- "lawlessness, lawless conduct."

The common rendering of Matthew 7:23 opts for the second meaning. (See ALT, KJV, and ASV translations.) These texts ignore entirely the first option. These translations do not reveal these workers practiced the "negation of the Law." Yet, this is the meaning Jesus' intended in this context.

Jesus is talking about workers of the *negation of the Law* because He is paraphrasing Deuteronomy 13:1-5. Let's see how by comparing the concepts in Matthew 7:15-23 with Deuteronomy 13:1-5. When put side by side, we find *lawlessness* is an incongruent break from the paraphrase by Jesus of Deuteronomy. However, "negation of the Law" would be in line if Jesus' intended a paraphrase of Deuteronomy.

---

1. *Logos Software* describes LSJ (its acronym) as "the world's ***most comprehensive and authoritative dictionary*** of ancient Greek...." http://www.logos.com/products/details/1772 (visited 2005). It explains the 1940 edition is the core of the 1996 edition. As to the 1940 edition, *Logos* explains LSJ is the "***central reference work*** for all scholars of ancient Greek authors and texts discovered up to 1940...." *Id.*
2. The least expensive way to verify this is online. To do so, go to Tuft University's online version of the Westcott-Hort Greek New Testament at http://www.perseus.tufts.edu/cgi-bin/ptext?doc=Perseus%3Atext%3A1999.01.0155&layout=&loc=Matthew+7.1 Then find Matthew 7:23, and the last word is *anomian*. Click *anomian* and then select the LSJ link for this lexicon. Or you can purchase this lexicon in book and computer form from *Logos* at www.logos.com.

Deuteronomy 13:1-5	Matthew 7:15-23
"prophet...give thee a sign or wonder" (v. 1)	"Beware of false prophets.... (v. 15)
"and the ***sign or wonder*** come to pass, whereof he spake unto thee" (v.2)	"Many will say to me in that day, 'Lord, Lord, did we not ***prophesy*** by thy name? and by thy name cast out demons? and by thy name do ***mighty works***?" (v. 22) cf. Mark 13:21 ("false prophets will arise and will make ***signs and wonders*** in order to ***seduce***, if possible, the elect.")
"that prophet...has spoken....to ***seduce you from the way which*** Jehovah thy ***God commanded*** thee to walk in" (v. 5)	"And then will I profess unto them, I never knew you: depart from me, ye that work ***ANOMIA***." (v. 23)
"thou shall not hearken unto the words of the prophet...." (v. 3)	"I never knew you: depart from me, ye that work ANOMIA." (v. 23)
Match "seducing you from the way which Jehovah thy God commanded thee to walk in...." (Deut. 13:5.)	Match *Anomia* def#2 = negation of the Law (Torah). It matches a parallel to Deuteronomy 13:5, and is thus the correct meaning between two definitions of *anomia*.

Thus, if you read Matthew 7:23 as *workers of the negation of the Law (of Moses),* then it parallels Deuteronomy 13:1-5. Both involve true prophets with true signs and wonders. Yet, they are still false. Why? Because their preaching seduces you from following the Law (of Moses). (Deut. 13:1-5.) Their preaching works *negation of the Law* (of Moses). (Matt. 7:23.)

Furthermore, the alternative reading makes the test so broad that Jesus' words are potentially meaningless. In fact, the translation as *lawless* or *iniquity* would make any human prophet a false prophet by definition. How so?

> ***Signs & Wonders***
>
> **"Indeed the *signs* of the apostle *were worked* among you in all patience, *in signs and wonders*, and in powers." *Paul*, 2 Cor.12:12 (talking about what proved his validity).**

If the test is whether these people are *workers of iniquity* or *lawlessness*, then since all of us sin, there would never be a true prophet you could trust as long as he is human. Thus, if you accept Paul's truism that "all have sinned, and fall short of the glory of God..." (Rom. 3:23), then Paul and all prophets are workers of iniquity merely by being human.

Thus, everyone is a worker of iniquity at some point. If we apply *iniquity* as the meaning of *anomia* in Matthew 7:15-23, as it commonly is translated, it ends up making Jesus give a meaningless warning. That is, the verse becomes pointless because we all work iniquity. There could never be true prophecy we trust if a true human prophet is rendered false merely because he is like us who sins from time-to-time. *Iniquity* never was the proper translation of *anomia*. Only *workers of negation of the Law (of Moses)* fits Jesus' intended meaning.

What If Anomia Did Mean Iniquity? Was Paul a Worker of Iniquity?

However, if one insists the traditional translation of *anomia* as *iniquity* is correct, Paul is encompassed by the verse anyway.

Paul's letters reveal very egregious behavior. He even flaunts this in front of Christian congregations. Paul did not leave his sins for private evaluation. Paul shamelessly put them on public display.

For example, Luther admits that Paul's letter to the Galatians includes curses on others (Gal. 1:9).[3] Furthermore, Paul also tells us he "condemned" Apostle Peter in front of a big crowd of people. (Gal. 2:11.) Paul also called the "brethren" of Galatia "foolish" ones. (Gal. 3:1.) Another time Paul listed off a series of accomplishments, confessing repeatedly he was "boasting." (2 Cor. 11:16-18.)

Yet, Jesus and the Bible prohibit such curses, condemnations of others without private personal confrontation first, labelling brothers as fools, and boasting. (See the Table below for Bible references.)

Therefore, if one insists Jesus' words in Matthew 7:23 require proof someone was a worker of *iniquity,* Paul is caught again. The list in the table below is not only long, but also appears in teaching letters to a spiritual community! As James 3:1 says, *teachers* will receive a "heavier judgment" for their errors.

Paul's Letters	Violation of God's Commands?
Cursing Others. Galatians 1:8, 9: "Anathema" (cursed) is anyone or angel if preaches "a different gospel" than Paul preaches. See also, 1 Cor. 16:22: "anathema" (cursed) is "anyone who does not love the Lord Jesus."	James 3:10: "Out of the same mouth comes forth praise and cursing; my brothers [and sisters], these [things] ought not to be happening in this way" — emphatic "It's wrong!" Prov. 10:7 "[Evil man's] mouth is full of cursing..." *Cf.* Nu 23:8
Calling Others Fools. Gal. 3:1: "O foolish Galatians...." Paul calls them "brethren." (Gal. 1:11; 3:15.)	Matthew 5:22 "whosoever shall say to his brother, Thou fool, shall be in danger of the hell of fire."

3. Luther admits Paul's cursing in Luther's lecture on Galatians in 1531. In commenting on Galatians 1:9, Luther says: "Paul repeats the curse, directing it now upon other persons. Before, he cursed himself, his brethren, and an angel from heaven."

Paul's Letters	Violation of God's Commands?
Boasting. 2 Cor. 11: "(16) let no man think me foolish; but if ye do, yet as foolish receive me, that *I also may boast a little.* (17) That which I speak, I speak not after the Lord, but as in foolishness, in this confidence of boasting.(18) Seeing that many *boast* after the flesh, I will *boast* also." (ALT). [Greek *kauchaomai* = boasting.][a]	James 4:16: "But now you boast in your pretentious pride; all such boasting is evil." (ALT) [Greek *kauchaomai* = boasting.]; 1 John James 2:16: "the boasting (*alazoneia*)[b] of life is not of the Father but of the world." Prov. 29:23 "pride/arrogance" (*gauth*) shall bring a man low." Prov.27:2 "Let another man praise you, and not your own mouth; A stranger and not your own lips."
Condemning Others. Galatians 2:11: "But when Peter came to Antioch, I opposed him to [his] face, because he had been condemned [by me]." v. 12 (text of the outspoken condemnation of Peter in front of audience). (*kataginosko* = condemned).	Matthew 7:1 "Stop judging [*i.e.*, condemning], so that you shall not be judged...." (*krino* = condemn or judge)[c] Matthew 18:15: "if they brother sin against thee, go, show him his fault between thee and him alone."

a. Paul goes on and makes boasts of his background and achievements: 1 Cor. 11: "(22) Are they Hebrews? *so am I.* Are they Israelites? *so am I.* Are they the seed of Abraham? *so am I.* (23) Are they ministers of Christ?... *I more*; in labors *more abundantly,* in prisons *more abundantly,* in stripes above measure, in deaths oft."

b. The Greek word *alazoneia* is often incorrectly translated as *pride.* (ASV, ALT, KJV, GSB.) However, the meaning of the Greek is *boasting* or a synonym, not *pride*. The definition *pride* is not even listed by Liddell Scott. The Liddell Scott Lexicon defines it solely as "boastfulness" "false pretension" or "imposture."

c. Jesus orders us to evaluate whether someone is a false prophet (Matthew 7:11-23). Jesus commends the Ephesians for finding someone to be a "liar" who said he was an apostle but was not. (Rev. 2:2.) Thus unless Paul was accusing Peter of being a false prophet/apostle, Paul is violating Jesus' prohibition against condemning others publicly without first having a private confrontation. (Matt. 18:15.) Such findings (False Prophet/ False Apostle) are not, in fact, 'condemnations' *per se*. They are necessary findings to fulfill our duty to "not harken unto the words of that [false] prophet" (Deut. 13:3). The findings are not intended to condemn such a person without a private confrontation, but rather to distinguish true Scripture from false.

*Paul Admits He Is **Anomos***

There is a more significant reason why Jesus' words against wonder workers of *anomia* are not translated correctly in Matthew 7:23. It is because Paul admits he practiced *anomos* in 1 Cor. 9:20-21. Thus, if Jesus' word *anomia* were correctly translated in Matthew 7:23, it would lead to an instantaneous proof of Paul's invalidity *by Paul's own admission.*

What does *anomos* mean in 1 Cor. 9:20-21?

Anomos is the adjective form of the noun *anomia.* (The word *anomia* is the word at issue in Matthew 7:23.) *Nomos* is the word one would use to indicate the *Torah* of Moses. (Strong's #3551.) The particle *a* in Greek is the negation of whatever follows. *A-Nomos* should mean *negation of Torah/Law/law.* Without looking at a lexicon, one can anticipate *anomos* might have some meaning bearing on the *Torah.* Strong's Lexicon says *anomos* has two meanings: either a violator of the Law/law or "one destitute of the (Mosaic) Law." Liddell Scott likewise say *anomos* means either "lawless, impious" or "without the (Mosaic) Law." It specifically cites the latter meaning as what Paul means in 1 Cor. 9:21.

Indeed, when you read Paul's remarks, it is clear he means he practices to be "without the *Mosaic* Law." Paul says the following in 1 Cor. 9:20-21:

> (20) And to the Jews I became as a Jew, that I might gain Jews; to them that are ***under the law*** [*i.e., Nomos*], as under the law, ***not being myself under the law*** [*i.e. Nomos*], that I might gain them that are under the law; (21) to them that are without law, [I became] ***as without law*** [Greek ***anomos***], not being without law to God, but under law to Christ, that I might gain them that are without law. (ASV)

In verse 20, Paul is clearly using *Nomos* to mean *Torah*, *i.e.*, the books of Moses. He equates becoming as a Jew as practicing being under *Nomos*. His usage of *Nomos* thus starts out clearly meaning *Torah*. He practiced being *Torah* submissive as an evangelical tool.

Then, still in verse 20, Paul says he behaves as if under the Mosaic law even though he is "not...myself under the [Mosaic] Law..." His expression in Greek is expressly "not being under the Law"— *me on autos hupo numon*. The word *me* in Greek means *not*. It serves an equivalent function as the prefix *a* in front of *Nomos*. Paul is plainly saying therefore he is *not under the Law* that applies to Jews. Paul accordingly is announcing he is *Not under Nomos*.

Paul then emphasizes this by saying in verse 21 that to those who are not under the *Nomos*—here he uses the word *anomos*, Paul "becomes"[4] as one "not under *Nomos*"—again using the word *anomos*. Paul thus not only says in verse 20 he is *not under Nomos*, but also says he ***works*** to appear this way, *i.e.*, *Anomos*, as a tool of evangelism.

Matthew 7:23	1 Cor. 9:21
ergozomai anomia	***ginomai anomos***
workers of negating the Law	[I, Paul] work to become without (Mosaic) Law

What about verse 21 where Paul does assert that he is under the *Law of Christ?* It is clear Paul does not mean he is under *the Law of Moses*. In verse 20 he just said he is not under *Nomos* (*i.e.*, the Torah). We will explore in the next chapter precisely what Paul means by the *Law of Christ*. Briefly, he means he is under a new moral system. It is not

4. The Greek is *ginomai*. It also means *make*. Paul *made himself as one not under the Law, i.e., anomos*. This entire expression parallels "workers of negation of the Law" in Matthew 7:23 which is *ergozomai anomia, i.e., work anomia*.

based on *Torah.* It is based on other principles that Paul explains are guided by conscience. See the discussion in the next chapter entitled: "The New Morality In Its Place" on page 80.

Yet, what Paul is admitting in 1 Cor. 9:20-21 is what Jesus is warning about in Matthew 7:23. Jesus is warning about those who will come in His name, and come with true signs and wonders. Yet they are workers of *A-nomia*. This is the noun form of the related word *A-Nomos*, an adjective, that appears in 1 Cor. 9:20-21. Jesus is warning of someone who will uproot the *Torah*. This someone will replace the *Torah* with what is in essence merely the commandments of men. *See*, Matt. 15:6 ("thus have ye made the commandment of God of none effect by your tradition.")

How Jesus' View of Mosaic Law Aids Translation of Matthew 7:23

Jesus by Paul's own admission is on a different page than Paul. Jesus made it clear that His use of the term *anomia* in Matthew 7:23 is to identify those who will *negate the Law* (of Moses). In Matthew 5:18-29, Jesus expels any idea that He intends to introduce any new morality that would supplant the *Torah* (Law of Moses). In Matthew 5:18-19, Jesus explains that anyone who "shall teach" others not to follow the least command of the Law of Moses will be least in the kingdom of heaven:

> (18) For verily I say unto you, Till heaven and earth pass away, one jot or one tittle shall in no wise pass away from the Law [*i.e.*, *Nomos*], till all things be accomplished. (19) ***Whosoever therefore shall break one of these least commandments, and shall teach men so, shall be called least in the kingdom of heaven***: but whosoever shall do and teach them, he shall be called great in the kingdom of heaven. (ASV)

One would be hard pressed to find a more direct way of saying a Christian must teach and keep the Law of Moses. We should clearly see Jesus had every intention that the Law continued in the New Testament community. This passage is not isolated.

Jesus emphasized repeatedly keeping the letter of the Law, while not exaggerating it. Law-keeping was a constant theme of His teachings. Besides Matthew 5:18-19, Jesus taught that traditions of men should not be accepted which supplant the Law. (Matt. 15:3-6.) He emphasized keeping the Ten Commandments as part of His gospel of salvation. (Matt. 19:17.) In Revelation 2:14, Jesus is upset with those teaching contrary to Exodus that you are permitted to eat meat sacrificed to idols. If you read with care Jesus' correction of the Pharisees, it is always about their exaggerated or misguided interpretations of the Law. Jesus never faults their desire to obey the Law. They set aside the "weightier" matters of the Law to follow the less "weighty" matters of the Law. Jesus wanted them to follow *both* aspects of the Law. (Matt. 23:23.)

Those who glibly have tried to make Jesus out to attack keeping the Law have failed to weigh the consequences of their argument. While they shield Paul, they end up making Jesus a false messiah. For any prophet who would seduce Israel from keeping the Law would be, even if he had miracles and signs, a false prophet. (Deut. 4:2,13:5.)

These Law-keeping passages should impel a Christian to come to grips with the question of ***where Jesus would have stood in the debate over the Law*** in the early church. ***Jesus was insistent on conformity with the Law which Paulinists have ignored.*** Such a conclusion, if recognized, would have ***revolutionary implications*** on modern Christian doctrine. When we think about the hue and cry if we should quote Jesus to answer the question, we must remember Jesus' pro-Law keeping view is a truth staring back at us from the pages of Scripture. We cannot lightly dismiss it. The revolutionary implication is that Jesus' warning of the false prophet to come who would negate the Law means He was warning us about Paul.

Now one can see why the translators of Matthew 7:23 who assume Paul's validity elected to use a nonsensical translation of *anomia* as *lawlessness* or *iniquity*. If *lawless* or *lawlessness* were the test of a prophet who comes with signs and wonders to deceive Christians, everyone is suspect. Jesus' warning would then be so broad that it is rendered meaningless. This makes it nonthreatening to Paul's validity. However *anomia*'s other meaning, according to Liddell-Scott, is *negation of the law* (of Moses). That meaning parallels Deuteronomy 4:2 & 13:1-5. Those with true signs and wonders but whose purpose is to seduce us from following the *Torah* are false prophets. (Deut. 13:1-5.) Paul is instantly in the hot seat. He even admits in 1 Cor. 9:20-21 of practicing to be *anomos*, *i.e.*, one who *negates the Law (of Moses)* by dismissing it.

Given Jesus' repeated emphasis on keeping the Law, Jesus must have intended us to understand those who would undermine His emphasis on keeping the Law of Moses were going to be the mark of the false prophet to come. Jesus intended *anomia* in Matthew 7:23 to mean *negator of the Law of Moses.*

However, let's keep an open mind. Did Paul actually ever teach that the 'least commandment' in the Law of Moses was abrogated for a follower of Jesus? If so, then Jesus tells us Paul is a false prophet by Jesus' very blunt words in Matthew 7:15-23. To follow Paul would mean we are disobeying Christ. To follow Paul in such a circumstance would also mean we are violating God's command in Deuteronomy 4:2 against *diminishing* from God's word. To follow Paul would also mean we are violating Deuteronomy 13:1-5 wherein God tells you to not fear or listen to the prophet who tries to seduce you from following God's commands in the Law. God specifically commands us to not add such a prophet to *inspired* canon. Or is there even the slightest chance Paul did not negate the Law of Moses?

A Passage to Meditate Upon: What Causes Empty Worship?

Jesus on Negation of The Law by Traditional Religious Doctrine. Says Leads to Vain Worship.

(1) Then there come to Jesus from Jerusalem Pharisees and scribes, saying, (2) Why do thy disciples ***transgress*** [*i.e., parabaino*, go contrary to] the tradition of the elders? for they wash not their hands when they eat bread. (3) And he answered and said unto them, ***Why do ye also transgress the commandment of God because of your tradition***? (4) For God said, Honor thy father and thy mother: and, He that speaketh evil of father or mother, let him die the death. (5) But ye say, whosoever shall say to his father or his mother, That wherewith thou mightest have been profited by me is given to God [*i.e.*, the korban payment to the Temple created by the religious leaders as a substitution for directly supporting destitute parents]; (6) he shall not honor his father. ***And ye have made void*** [*i.e., akuroo*, invalidate, make of none effect] ***the word of God because of your tradition***. (7) Ye hypocrites, well did Isaiah prophesy of you, saying, (8) This people honoreth me with their lips; But their heart is far from me. (9) But ***in vain do they worship me, Teaching as their doctrines the precepts of men***. (Matt 15:1-9, ASV)

Jesus in this passage says that the Pharisees were teaching "for doctrines [about God] the commandments of men." (Matt. 15:9, KJV.) The Greek version of Matthew is a paraphrase of Isaiah 29:13, which Jesus is in substance quoting. In Isaiah, what Jesus describes as *men's doctrines* is called in Hebrew *mitzvat anashim melumada.* According to Hebrew scholar Nehemiah Gordon, it means "a learned commandment of men." (N. Gordon, *Hebrew Yeshua v. Greek Jesus* (2006) at 23-24.) Gordon further explains this means a commandment of men that is recognized as law by performing it over and over again. This is reflected in the RSV and JPS versions that translate Isaiah as saying, "commandment of men learned by rote." What is Jesus' point?

This passage in Isaiah was commented upon by later Karaite Jews in the ninth century. Their application of Isaiah appears to be identical to Jesus' point.

First, who were the Karaites? Nehemiah Gordon is a modern Karaite Jew. This is a Jew who rejects man-made accretions to the Law of Moses. Karaites represent a movement founded in the ninth century within Judaism. When Nehemiah Gordon read Jesus' words in Matthew 15, he was both "impressed and surprised." For Gordon explains Isaiah 29:13 became the "battle cry of the Karaites against Rabbinic innovations and this phrase appears countless times in medieval Karaite writings." (N. Gordon, *Hebrew Yeshua v. Greek Jesus* (2006) at 24.) Thus, Jesus brought this message first!

Finally, Nehemiah Gordon quotes the ninth century Karaite commentary on Isaiah 29:13. It sounds familiar.

> Abandon the learned commandments of men that are ***not from the Torah***; do not accept anything from anyone except that which is written in the Torah of the Lord alone. (Daniel al-Kumisi, *Epistle to the Dispersion*.)

Jesus had the same explanation of Isaiah. Jesus took it one step further. He explained when you teach the *learned commandments of men* so as to *diminish* from the Law given to Moses, you have "empty worship." Thus, by violating Deuteronomy 4:2, which prohibits diminishing the Law, Jesus said you violate the Second Commandment — you are now taking the "Lord's name in vain." Your worship is now *in vain*. Thus, Jesus said that when the Pharisees taught God's personal command to *honor your mother and father* could be substituted with a special payment to the temple (Matt. 15:5 *supra*), they were *negating* the Fourth Commandment. They caused the worshipper who used God's name to now be worshipping in vain, thus violating the Second Commandment. The consequence? Jesus later explained in Matthew 23:23 that the Pharisees' teachings which diminished the "weightier matters of the Law" thereby made their pupils become "twice the sons of hell" as their teachers. (Matt. 23:15.)

5 *Did Paul Negate the Law's Further Applicability?*

Applying the Consistency Test

No one ever seriously claims Paul made any qualifying prophecy. Certainly nothing he predicted of a highly improbable nature has yet come true. Thus, the addition of Paul to canon immediately has a wobbly foundation. It appears to violate Deuteronomy 4:2.

Assuming for argument sake that Paul made some qualifying prediction, we next must apply the Bible's second level test. Even if they come with "signs and wonders" that come true, the Bible says they are still a false prophet if they simultaneously try to "***seduce you from the way in which the Lord your God commanded you to walk***." (Deut. 13:5.) If they "diminish the Law," they violate God's word and must be false. (Deut. 4:2.) Jesus in the same vein warns of those with true "signs and wonders" but who are workers of *A-Nomia*, *i.e.*, negators of *Nomos*—the word for *Torah* in Greek. (Matt. 7:15, 24:11, 24.)[1] As a result, even though Paul insists his "signs and wonders" validated his message (Romans 15:19), we need to examine whether Paul' teachings are consistent with the Scripture that preceded Paul. We will thereby follow the example of the Bereans who used Scripture to test Paul's validity. (Acts 17:11.)

1. See "Did Jesus Warn of False Prophets Who Would Negate the Law?" on page 59 *et seq*.

Did Paul Abrogate the Law for Everyone?

Paul has many statements that appear to abrogate the Law *in its entirety*. Paul does not merely say that Jesus fulfilled the law of sacrifice, making actual sacrifices *moot*. (This is Barnabas' reasonable approach in *Hebrews*.) Paul does not merely say the sacrificial ceremonies within the Law are gone. Rather, it appears Paul says Jesus removed the Law in its entirety as a code.

Luther believed Paul unequivocally declared that all aspects of the Law were abolished. Paul even abolished the moral components of the Law. Luther wrote:

> The scholastics think that the judicial and ceremonial laws of Moses were ***abolished*** by the coming of Christ, but not the moral law. They are blind. When Paul declares that we are delivered from the curse of the Law ***he means the whole Law***, particularly the moral law which more than the other laws accuses, curses, and condemns the conscience. The Ten Commandments have no right to condemn that conscience in which Jesus dwells, for Jesus has taken from the Ten Commandments the ***right*** and power to curse us.[2]

We can find handy one-line proofs in Ephesians 2:15 and Colossians 2:14. Paul declares the Law is abolished for Christians.

Ephesians 2:15

Let us start with Ephesians 2:15. We will quote its wider context to be sure of its meaning.

---

2. Martin Luther, *Epistle on Galatians* 4:25 (1535), reprint at http://www.biblehelpsonline.com/martinluther/galatians/galatians4.htm (last accessed 2005).

> (14) For he is our peace, who hath made both one, and hath broken down the middle wall of partition [at the Temple of Jerusalem]; (15) **Having abolished in his flesh the enmity, [even] the law of commandments [contained] in ordinances;** for to make in himself of twain one new man, so making peace; (16) And that he might reconcile both unto God in one body by the cross, having slain the enmity thereby: (Ephesians 2:14-16, ASV)(bracketed text added by ASV to make flow better)

Most reputable commentators agree that Paul says here that Jesus abrogated the *entire* Law of Moses. Gill clearly says it is the Law given at Mount Sinai. Gill says Sinai means "hatred" in Hebrew. Thus, Paul is engaging in word-play with its synonym in Greek—*enmity.* Gill then explains Paul means that from Sinai "descended 'hatred' or 'enmity' to the nations of the world: now this Christ abolished." Jamieson likewise says Paul means Jesus abrogated the entire Law of Moses. Jesus supposedly replaced it with the "law of Love." Henry hedges a bit. He says Paul means the "ceremonial law" was abrogated.

Colossians 2:14

Second, Paul rewords Ephesians 2:14-16 in Colossians 2:14. The abrogation of the Law is crystal clear in Colossians. *All the Law* including the commandment to rest on the Sabbath *is abolished*:

> (14) **Blotting out the handwriting of ordinances that was against us, which was contrary to us, and took it out of the way,** nailing it to his cross; (15) And having spoiled principalities and powers, he made a shew of them openly, triumphing over them in it. (16) **Let no man therefore judge you** in meat, or in drink, or in respect of an **holyday**, or of the new moon, or of the **sabbath days**: (17) Which are **a shadow of things to come**; but the body is of Christ. (Colossians 2:14-17, ASV)

Here the commentators have no disagreement. Paul means by ordinances blotted away "primarily...the Mosaic Law." (*Vincent Word Studies*.) This is not merely the ceremonial law. Paul picks out one of the Ten Commandments—the Sabbath command. Then Paul sweeps it away. As Martin Luther in a sermon entitled *How Christians Should Regard Moses* given August 27, 1525[3] says of this passage:

> Again one can prove it from the third commandment that Moses does not pertain to Gentiles and Christians. ***For Paul*** [Col. 2:16]...***abolish[ed] the sabbath***, to show us that the sabbath was given to the Jews alone, for whom it is a stern commandment. [4]

Paul will repeat this abolition of Sabbath in Romans 14:5-6. Paul writes: "One man considers one day more sacred than another; another man considers every day alike. Each one should be fully convinced in his own mind." Christian commentators explain this means regarding Sabbath: "Christians are permitted to make up their own minds about a special day."[5] You can take it or leave it. It is up to you.

Paul also wipes out all the food laws and festival days. (*See also*, 1 Tim. 4:4, 'all food is clean.') Paul clearly is teaching against any obedience to the Law of Moses *per se*.

"I am the Lord. I change not."
Mal. 3:6

In Colossians, we have a clearer idea of the "enmity" spoken about in Ephesians 2:15. *All* the ordinances of God in the Law of Moses are "against us." (Col. 2:14.) Vincent says Paul's meaning is that the Law of Moses had the "hostile character of a bond" or debt. In Christ, Paul clearly is saying we (Jew and Gentile) are free from this debt. The proof is in the pudding. Paul says in verse sixteen that no one can judge you any

3. Martin Luther, "How Christians Should Regard Moses," *Luther's Works: Word and Sacrament I* (Philadelphia: Muhlenberg Press, 1960) Vol. 35 at 161-174.

longer for not obeying the Sabbath. The command for a Seventh Day-Sabbath rest is clearly not a ceremonial law about sacrifice. It is one of the Ten Commandments.

Furthermore, Paul makes it clear that there is no distinction between Jew or Gentile who are so liberated from the Law. In both Ephesians 2:15 and Col. 2:14-17, Paul emphasizes how "one new man" emerges (Eph. 2:15). He explains this is so because the Temple wall that barred Gentiles from sacred parts of the Temple has been spiritually abolished. *Id.*

Did Jesus Say We are to Obey the Pharisees or Moses?

"The Pharisees and sages sit on Moses' seat. Therefore, all that he* [*i.e.*, Moses] says to you, diligently do, but according to their reforms [*i.e.*, additions] and their precedents [*i.e.*, examples used to justify conduct], do not do because they talk but they do not do [Torah]." Hebrew Matt. 23:2-3, as Jewish scholar Nehemiah Gordon translates in ***Hebrew Yeshua.***

*In the Greek Matthew, it says 'all that they say, do."

4. In the ellipsis of this quote, Luther claims the following passages also abolish the sabbath: Matt. 12:1-12; John 5:16; 7:22-23; 9:14-16. Luther does not realize this, but if Jesus abolished the Sabbath, Jesus would be *an apostate and false prophet* under Deuteronomy 13:5. So Luther had better be correct. In fact, these passages do not stand for this proposition. Rather, in Matthew 12:1-12, Jesus says it was taught the priests are permitted to work in the temple on the Sabbath and "are guiltless." If this were true for priests, Jesus says this is true for Himself for one greater than the Temple is before them. The remaining three passages likewise do not support Luther's claim: John 7:22-23 (if the Jews keep the command to circumcise a certain number of days after birth even if it takes place on the Sabbath, then they should permit Jesus to heal on Sabbath); John 9:14-16 (Jesus healing on sabbath); John 5:16 (Jesus told a man to pick up his mat, interpreted by Jewish leaders to be a *work, but Jesus disapproves this understanding,* saying there is no command against *doing good* on the Sabbath). *Cfr.* Jer. 17:21-24 ("be careful to not carry ***a load*** on Sabbath.") *See also*, "Sabbath" in *Anchor Bible Dictionary* (ed. David N. Freedman) Vol. 5 at 855-56 (Jesus misunderstood as disaffirming Sabbath, but rather reaffirmed it universally for all men in Mark 2:27. Jesus' criticisms were against the man-made teachings that violated the true spirit of the Sabbath command); *cf.* Matt. 12:12 (lawful to do good).

The Abolished Law Was A Ministry Of Death

Paul has a section of Second Corinthians that totally demeans the Ten Commandments. He then unequivocally says they have "passed away." Once more, Paul demonstrates certainly that he is teaching Jews and Gentiles to no longer follow the Law of Moses.

In this passage from Second Corinthians, Paul calls Moses' ministry one of "death" and "condemnation." Paul calls Christianity a ministry of Spirit and liberty. The Law of Moses kills. Christianity gives life. (Incidentally, Paul's reasoning is dubious at best.)[6] The Law of Moses is "done away with." Its "glory was to be done away with." It is "done away." Finally, it is "that which is abolished." All these quotes are found in 2 Corinthians 3:6-17:

> (6) Who also hath made us able ministers of the new testament; not of the letter, but of the spirit: for **the letter killeth**, but the spirit giveth life. (7) But if **the ministration of death**, written and **engraven in stones**, was glorious, so that the children of Israel could not stedfastly behold the face of **Moses** for the glory of his countenance; which **glory was to be done away**: (8) How shall not the ministration of the

5. Dan Corner, *Six Facts For Saturday Sabbatarians To Ponder* at http://www.evangelicaloutreach.org/sabbath.htm (last accessed 2005).

6. In saying the earlier covenant is *death* and the second *life*, Paul demonstrates a lack of understanding of what Jesus' atonement represents. Jesus is the atonement satisfying once for all the atonement-requirements in the Law, as Paul should admit. If so, then Jesus' sacrifice provides the same grace that was provided by the sacrificial system in the Law of Moses. The only difference is Jesus' payment is *one-time* rather than *repetitive*. Thus, the Levitical atonement-system cannot minister death while Jesus' death ministers life. The outcome of both is identical: forgiveness by God's mercy through atonement. Grace was in both systems. In both, the penitent does not suffer the blood-atonement which pays the price for sin.

> spirit be rather glorious? (9) For if the **ministration of condemnation** be glory, much more doth the ministration of righteousness exceed in glory. (10) For even that which was made glorious had no glory in this respect, by reason of the glory that excelleth. (11) For if **that which is done away was glorious**, much more that which remaineth is glorious. (12) Seeing then that we have such hope, we use great plainness of speech: (13) And not as Moses, which put a vail over his face, that the children of Israel could not stedfastly look **to the end of that which is abolished**: (14) But their minds were blinded: for until this day remaineth the same vail untaken away in the reading of the old testament; **which vail is done away in Christ**. (15) But even unto this day, when Moses is read, the vail is upon their heart. (16) Nevertheless when it shall turn to the Lord, the vail shall be taken away. (17) Now the **Lord is that Spirit**: and where the Spirit of the Lord is, **there is liberty**. (ASV)

There is nothing unclear in this passage. Paul says the Law of Moses is done away with. The glory that fell upon Moses' face has faded away. This fading away was a foreshadowing that the Ten Commandments would be done away with later. Paul says this time is now. We are entirely free of any and all of the Law's commands.

Gill in his famous commentary is blunt. This passage of 2 Cor. 3:11-17 means that the "law is the Old Testament, or covenant, which is vanished away."

Barnes concurs. He says "the former [*i.e.*, the Law] was to be done away...." Barnes comments on Paul's explanation that when we turn to the gospel, we simultaneously turn away from the Law. It was merely a veil blocking our view of God. Barnes concludes: "When that people should turn again to the Lord, it [*i.e.*, the Law] should be taken away, 2 Cor. 3:16."

Romans Chapter Seven Says the Jews Are Released From the Law

Paul makes his views clear again in Romans 7:1 *et seq*. Paul says he is addressing those who *know the Law*. Paul then teaches that the Jews under the Law are the same as if Israel were a wife of God. When Jesus died, the husband died. This then ***"releases"*** the bride (Jews) from the Law. (Rom. 7:2.) The Jews are now free to remarry another. In this instance, they can now join with the resurrected Jesus who no longer offers the Law to follow. The Law instead, Paul says, is a bond to the dead husband-God, applying Paul's analogy.

There is no doubt on Paul's meaning in Romans 7:2. The word translated as "releases" is from the Greek *katarge*. Paul uses the same Greek word in Romans 6:6. There he prays the body of sin "may be *destroyed*," and uses the word *katarge* to mean *destroyed*, *abolished*, etc. *Katarge* means in Greek *bring to nothing* or *do away with*. It is the same word Paul uses in Ephesians 2:15 to say the Law was "abolished."

Thus, Paul clearly taught in Romans 7:2 again that the Law was abolished. He made this truth specific to Jews too.

The New Morality In Its Place

One of the proofs that Paul declared the Law abolished is how Paul explains a new morality exists for Christians. If Paul intended us to view the Law of Moses as abolished, then we would expect Paul to utter a new standard to guide us in our ethical conduct. We find that Paul does provide a replacement ethical system. Paul teaches a new morality based on what is "obvious" as wrong to a person led by the Spirit. (Gal. 5:19.) The general test is: "All things are lawful but not all things are necessarily expedient." (1 Cor. 6:12, ASV). "All things are lawful for me." (1 Cor. 10:23.) "Happy is he who does not condemn himself in that thing which he allows." (Rom. 14:22.) Issues of whether to observe Sabbath at all are reduced to sentiment of what feels best to you: "Let every man be fully persuaded in his own mind." (Rom. 14:5.)

This new morality is another proof that the Law is done away with. As one commentator notes:

> As we have said, one of the three aspects of our 'liberty in Christ' is our freedom from the Law of Moses. So, when Paul says 'all things are lawful for me' he is simply referring to the fact that we are free FROM the Law of Moses.[7]

Thus, if you are in Christ, Paul teaches anything is allowed that conscience permits. The Torah no longer applies. If your conscience allows you to think something is permissible, it is permissible. It is as Bob George—a modern Christian radio personality and author of numerous books—said one day in response to whether fornication was prohibited:

> And as Paul said, "All things are permissible, but not all things are profitable." So is committing fornication permissible? Yes. Is it profitable? No, it is not.[8]

Accordingly, Paul's repeated axiom "all things are lawful for me" was not some pagan truth that Paul was mocking, as some prefer to think. It arose from Paul abolishing the strict letter of the Mosaic Law "which kills."

The proof that this is Paul's viewpoint is how Paul analyzed actual issues. He repeatedly used an expediency test to resolve what is right and wrong. For example, this expediency principle had its clearest application in Paul's reinterpretation of the command not to eat meat sacrificed to idols. He says he is free from that command. Paul knows an idol is

---

7. "Liberty, 1 Corinthians 10, and Idolatry," *Christian Bible Studies,* at http://www.geocities.com/biblestudying/liberty14.html (accessed 2005).
8. Bob George, *People to People* (Radio Talk Show) November 16, 1993.

nothing. However, it is not necessarily expedient to eat such meat if someone else you are with thinks it is wrong. So when in the company of this "weaker" brother, Paul will not eat meat sacrificed to idols. The test depends upon *who may be benefited or harmed by your behavior.* In a word, the test is its *expediency.*[9]

Paul's expediency test is evident again in his lack of concern for the letter of the original Law of the Sabbath. This was God's command to rest on the "seventh day" of the week—sunset Friday to sunset Saturday. (Ex. 20:10.) On this point, Paul says in Romans 14:5: "One man esteemeth one day above another: another esteemeth every day alike. Let every man be fully persuaded in his own mind." It's all relative to *how you feel about it.*

Paul thus clearly identifies a new moral law *divorced* from the written precepts of the Law. Paul made the new morality depend on the circumstances. It also depended on its expediency. There are no strict moral rules to follow.

Paul's doctrines are what traditionally we would call *antinomianism.* If your conscience "led by the Spirit" is your guide, and you reject the Law of Moses in its ***express*** moral precepts, then you are *antinomian.* You are using your own decisions "led by the Spirit" of when and how to comply, if at all, with any of the express commands in the Law of Moses.

This aspect of Paul is what makes him so attractive to the world. Paul gave flexible guidelines about what is sin. Paul also established a system where a believer is allowed to sin without risk of eternal damnation (Rom. 8:1) as long as you follow some simple steps. You are eternally secure if you confessed Jesus and believed in the resurrection. (Romans 10:9.)

Jesus' teachings are not so attractive as Paul's teachings in this regard. Jesus required you live a good life according to the commandments in the Law. Anyone who taught

9. For a full discussion on this, see "Paul Permits Eating Meat Sacrificed to Idols" on page 118 *et seq*.

against the validity of the Law given Moses by God was least in the kingdom of heaven. Not one jot or tittle from the Mosaic Law would pass away until heaven and earth pass away. (Matt. 5:18.) Jesus told the rich young man that if you would "enter life," obey the Ten Commandments. (Matthew 19:16-26; Mark 10:17-31; Luke 18:18-26.)[10] If you violate the commandments, Jesus required severe repentance from such sin to avoid being sent to hell. (Matthew 5:29, Matthew 18:8, and Mark 9:42-48.) Jesus described the repentance needed as 'cutting off the body part ensnaring you to sin.'

Paul is much easier, and far more attractive. For Paul, by contrast, when you sin against the Law, the issue is whether your conscience can allow you to live with it. "Happy is he who does not condemn himself in that thing which he allows." (Rom. 14:22.)

Most of those in the world coming to Christ opt to follow the message of Paul. They can even boast of their lack of perfection and bask in the feeling of being forgiven. Based on Paul, they are confident they are destined for heaven regardless of never truly *repenting* from their sin against the Law. They are sure they are heading for heaven despite blatant disobedience to the Law of God, *e.g.*, the duty to rest on the true Sabbath. Paul has become a magnet for the modern Christian. Jesus' message of righteousness *in action, obedience to the Law, and severe repentance after failure* has lost all its appeal.

Denigration of the Law as Given by the Angels

The most troubling aspect of Paul's writings on the Law is his attribution of the Law to angels. As we will discuss next in depth, Paul in Galatians says the Law was given by angels to Moses as a mediator. If we want to go back to

10. Some think it is significant that the Sabbath command is not repeated in this same context. Christians have developed an odd hermeneutic that if a recap of applicable law in the NT omits a single command, it is abolished. Why? Jesus said all the Law, to the least command, remains. (Matt. 5:13.)

following the Law, Paul says we are desiring to submit to those who "are no gods." We want to submit to the "weak and beggarly elements (angels)." (Gal. 3:19; 4:8-9.) Thus, Paul clearly says the Law was not given by God.

This is also evident in how Paul derides submitting to the Law, because given by angels. We contrast this with how Paul insists we must submit for conscience sake to government officials as "ministers of God." (Romans 13:1, 4.) Yet, we must not submit to the Law because given by angels. We come up with a troubling deduction. Paul must be understood to be saying that we do not have to submit to the Law because angels *alone* gave it. Unlike government officials, the angels must not have been ministers of God when giving the Law. This is why the angels are not even on par with government officials whose decrees (Paul says) must be followed as God's ministers.

These statements are extremely troubling because Paul contradicts the Bible on two points: (a) his claim the Law was given by angels; and (b) the Law given to Moses by angels was not worthy of submission, implying the angels acted without God's authority. To the contrary, the Bible is clear that the Law was given directly by God to Moses. Furthermore, even if given by angels, Jesus says the angels of heaven are always obeying God.[11] We would still obey a set of decrees if we only knew angels of heaven were its author.

Have you ever looked carefully at Paul's remarks? They require strict scrutiny in light of the obvious heresy behind them.

11. The Lord's Prayer asks that God's will be done on earth "as it is done in heaven." This implies the angels of heaven are in perfect obedience. The angels of which Jesus speaks are depicted as *in heaven. See*, Matt. 18:10 (the guardian angels of children "do always behold the face of my Father who is in heaven"); Luke 15:10 (joy among angels for one sinner saved).

Paul Says the Law Was Ordained through Angels

Starting with Galatians 3:19-29, we read:

> (19) What then is the law? It was added because of transgressions, ***till*** the seed should come to whom the promise hath been made; and ***it was ordained***[12] ***through angels by the hand of a mediator.*** (20) Now a mediator is not a mediator of one; but God is one. (21) Is the law then against the promises of God? God forbid: for if there had been a law given which could make alive, verily righteousness would have been of the law. (22) But the scriptures ***shut up*** all things under sin, that the promise by faith in Jesus Christ might be given to them that believe. (23) But ***before*** faith came, we were ***kept in ward under the law***, shut up unto the faith which should afterwards be revealed. (24) So that the law is become ***our tutor to bring us unto Christ***, that we might be justified by faith. (25) But now faith that is come, ***we are no longer under a tutor.*** (26) For ye are all sons of God, through faith, in Christ Jesus. (27) For as many of you as were baptized into Christ did put on Christ. (28) There can be ***neither Jew nor Greek***, there can be neither bond nor free, there can be no male and female; for ye all are one man in Christ Jesus. (29) And if ye are Christ's, then are ye Abraham's seed, heirs according to promise. (ASV)

Above, Paul starts out his attack on obeying the Law by saying it was "ordained by angels through the hands of a mediator," *i.e.*, Moses. (Galatians 3:19.)

---

12. The Greek word Paul uses for the angels' activity is *diageteis*. It means *arrange, set in order,* often *instruct* or *command*. It refers back to *ho Nomos*, the Law. The *Nomos* was commanded *dia* (through) *aggelos*—the angels.

This attack fits precisely into Paul's message. He says the Law is no longer binding on us. Paul is saying the same thing he said in Ephesians 2:15 and Colossians 2:14. He tells you the reason: the Law was "ordained by angels," not God the Father. (Gal. 3:19.) Paul will repeat this idea again twice—in Galatians 4:8 and 4:9. (We will discuss these verses next.) There is no mistaking Paul's point is to demean the Law so we will accept his teaching it has been abolished.

Why Be Subject to Those Who Are Not Gods (*i.e., Angels*)?

Paul has more to say about the angels. In chapter 4 of Galatians, Paul will say that because the Law was given by angels, why do we want to be subject to those who are not gods? (Gal. 4:8.)

In this portion of Galatians, Paul speaks of the Law as bondage. Rather than the Law being a positive thing, Paul recasts the nature of the entire Hebrew Scriptures to make this a very bad thing.

Paul does this by a fanciful re-telling of the Bible story of Abraham. Paul says the bondage of the Law now belongs to the son Ishmael produced by Abraham and Hagar. The Law thus carries a curse on Hagar's child Ishmael. Paul's ideas were a total invention, having no basis in the Scripture itself. Then Paul says Hagar's son Ishmael corresponds with Israel of Paul's day. This likewise was pure fiction. Paul then reasons those Jews under the Law at Mount Sinai are now "by an allegory" represented by Ishmael, the son of Hagar. Paul next says Israel, which now corresponds to Ishmael, is cursed to have to follow the Law of Moses. (***This is what I call The Great Inversion.***) Mixed in with this, Paul brings up again that the Law was given by angels to a mediator (Moses), not by God himself. So here Paul wonders why any-one wants to submit to those who are "not gods?" *i.e.*, the angels.

As you read these statements from Galatians below, please focus on two things. First, does Paul truly invert Israel and Ishmael? Second, does Paul intend to denigrate the Law by mentioning it came from the angels? If you agree Paul makes either claim, then realize ***both claims are completely contradictory of the Bible.*** Why? Because the Law was given to the Sons of Israel on Mount Sinai by God's own voice (***not angels***) through the mediator Moses. (Exodus 20:22.)[13] The son of Abraham and Hagar is Ishmael. (Gen. 15:16). The son of Abraham and Sarah is Isaac. (Gen. 17:19.) It is with Isaac's "seed" that God will fulfill an "everlasting covenant." (Gen. 17:19.)[14] Isaac's son with Rebekah was Jacob. (Gen. 25:26.) **Israel was the new name God gave Jacob**. (Gen. 32:28.) Ishmael was never given the Law. Instead, he and his mother were cast out by Abraham into the desert. (Gen. 21:14.) The Law was given to the sons of Sarah (Israel), not the sons of Hagar. (Ex. 20.)

TABLE 2. The Great Inversion

Paul's "Allegory"	Bible's View
Hagar's son is "born after the flesh." (Gal. 4:23.)	Hagar's son is Ishmael. (Gen. 15:16.)
Hagar bore sons "unto bondage" (Gal. 4:24.)	Hagar & Ishmael were cast out into the desert. (Gen.21:14.)
This son (Ishmael) has a "covenant" of bondage at Sinai. (Gal. 4:24.) "Jerusalem... is in bondage with her children." (Gal.4:25.)	The covenant at Sinai was with the sons of Israel, **not** Ishmael. (Ex. 20:22.) The Law was given at Sinai to the sons of Israel. (Exodus 20.)
Sarah's children are children of the "freewoman." (Gal. 4:22.) "Jerusalem that is above is free." (Gal. 4:26.) Christians are children of the freewoman. (Gal. 4:31.) *Sarah's children are not bound to the Law*; only the sons of Hagar are bound to the Law.	Sarah's son was Isaac, whose son Jacob had his name changed by God to Israel. (Gen. 17:19, 32:28.) The Law was given to the Sons of Sarah, not Hagar. *The children of Sarah were bound by God to the Law.* (Exodus 20).

13."And Jehovah said unto Moses, Thus thou shalt say unto the **children of Israel**, Ye yourselves have seen that **I have talked with you from heaven.**" (Exodus 20:22, ASV.)

14."I will establish my covenant with him for **an everlasting covenant** for his seed after him." (Gen. 17:19, ASV.)

Paul thereby provides an "allegory" that is totally at odds with the Biblical record. It is a 100% inversion of Scripture. ***No one has liberty to break God's promise to Israel by redefining to whom the promise was given.*** Paul has redefined Israel to be Ishmael. He thereby claims that Christians can inherit the promise to Isaac (father to Israel) apart from the true seed of Isaac who Paul, in effect, puts under a curse. Paul therefore says we are free to ignore the Bible-story that Israel (son of Isaac) was later given the Law. Paul invites us to accept that instead the Law should now be seen as given to Ishmael as a curse. It never happened. This is *rewriting the Bible* with an *agenda in hand.* I can come to any outcome I want if I can rewrite the passages. That is not Bible exegisis. This is Bible-contradiction.

Not even a Prophet of God is given the power to make up stories—calling them *analogies*—that contradict Scripture to spin the Bible to fit a desired outcome. As the Bible itself says:

> [Compare teachers] [t]o the Law and the Testimony [and], if they speak not according to *this* Word, it is because there is no light in them. (Isaiah 8:20).

Yet in Galatians 4:1-11 and 20-31, we read Paul not speaking at all according to this Word:

> (1) But I say that so long as the heir is a child, he differeth nothing from ***a bondservant*** though he is lord of all; (2) but is ***under guardians and stewards*** until the day appointed of the father. (3) So we also, when we were children, ***were held in bondage*** under the rudiments of the world: (4) but when the fulness of the time came, God sent forth his Son, born of a woman, born under the law, (5) that he might redeem them that ***were under the law,*** that we might receive the adoption of sons. (6) And because ye are sons, God sent forth the Spirit of his Son into our hearts, crying, Abba, Father.

(7) So that thou art ***no longer a bondservant,*** but a son; and if a son, then an heir through God. (8) Howbeit at that time, not knowing God, ***ye were in bondage to them that by nature are no gods***: (9) but now that ye have come to know God, or rather to be known by God, how turn ye back again to ***the weak and beggarly elements,***[15] ***whereunto ye desire to be in bondage over again***? (10) Ye ***observe days, and months, and seasons, and year***s. (11) I am afraid of you, lest by any means I have bestowed labor upon you in vain. **** (20) but I could wish to be present with you now, and to change my tone; for I am perplexed about you. (21) Tell me, ***ye that desire to be under the law***, do ye not hear the law? (22) For it is written, that Abraham had two sons, one by the handmaid [*i.e.*, a bondservant], and one by the freewoman [*i.e.*, Sarah]. (23) Howbeit the son by the handmaid is born after the flesh; but the son by the freewoman is born through promise. (24) ***Which things contain an allegory***: for these women are two covenants; one from mount Sinai, bearing ***children unto bondage, which is Hagar***. (25) Now this Hagar is mount Sinai in Arabia and answereth to the Jerusalem that now is: for ***she is in bondage with her children.*** (26) But the Jerusalem that is above is free, which is our mother. (27) For it is written, Rejoice, thou barren that bearest not; Break forth and cry, thou that travailest not: For more are the children of the desolate than of her that hath the husband. (28) Now we, brethren, as Isaac was, ***are children of promise***. (29) But as then he that was born after the flesh persecuted him that was ***born after the Spirit***, so

15. The word is *elements*, but the ASV changes this to *rudiments*, as if a *principle* were involved. The correct translation is *elements*. (See Lat. Vulgate "elementa"; KJV, YLT, Webster "elements".)

> also it is now. (30) Howbeit what saith the scripture? ***Cast out the handmaid and her son: for the son of the handmaid shall not inherit with the son of the freewoman.*** (31) Wherefore, brethren, ***we are not children of a handmaid, but of the freewoman***. (ASV with change in verse 8 as noted in fn 15.)

Paul clearly is referring to the angels in verse 8. He says 'you' desire to be in bondage to them who are "not gods." This is because Paul mentions that returning to obey the Law is being in "bondage again." So when Paul says being in bondage again to the Law is the same as bondage to them who are "not gods," there is only one conceivable explanation. Paul is harkening back to Galatians 3:19. There he says the Law was ordained by angels. They are "no gods." Paul thus means the Galatians' desire to be in 'bondage' to the Law is a desire to be in bondage to those who are "not gods."

Paulinists such as Fowler concur this is Paul's meaning in 4:8. However, they fail to note Paul is contradicting Scripture. Commentators agree Paul's point in Galatians 4:8 is to emphasize once more that the Law of Moses is "secondary" because of its "indirect transmission" through angels rather than coming directly from God.[16]

What makes the point unmistakable is that Paul repeats this idea in the very next verse. It is *not readily apparent* in our common English translations. Paul says in Galatians 4:9 that the Galatians desire to be subject again to the "weak and beggarly *elements* of the world." What or *who* are *elements* of the world? Paul equates this desire to submit to the Law as being in "bondage again" to these "elements." Previously, this was equated with submitting to angels

16.James Fowler, *The Precedence of God's Promises* (1999) reprinted at http://www.christinyou.net/pages/galpgp.html (last accessed 2005).

because they ordained the Law. Here, Paul means by *elements* the same thing: *angels*. This is true in both Greek and Jewish thought.

One commentator points out that in Greek thought, the reference to "elements of the world...likely [means] celestial beings..."[17] Likewise, in Jewish thought, *elements of the world* means *angels*. In *Vincent's Word Studies* on this verse, we read:

> The **elements** of the world are the personal, elemental spirits. **This seems to be the preferable explanation,** both here and in Col 2:8. According to Jewish ideas, all things had their special angels. In the Book of Jubilees, chapter 2, appear, the angel of the presence (comp. Isa 63:9); the angel of adoration; the spirits of the wind, the clouds, darkness, hail, frost, thunder and lightning, winter and spring, cold and heat.

Thus, Galatians 4:8 and 4:9 are both evoking Galatians 3:19's message that the Law was ordained by angels, not God himself. Paul is chiding them for wanting to be subject to

> **"We want the crown without the cross. We want the gain without the pain. We want the words of Christian salvation to be easy....But that gospel is a false gospel, a treacherous lie. That easy access gate doesn't go to heaven. It says 'Heaven' but it ends up in hell."**
>
> J. MacArthur, ***Hard to Believe*** (2003) at 12, 14

17.Comment on Gal. 4:9, from *New American Bible* (Confraternity of Christian Doctrine), reprinted at http://www.usccb.org/nab/bible/galatians/galatians4.htm

a Law that did not come from God. Hence they want to be in "bondage over again" to the weak and beggarly "celestial beings."[18]

TABLE 3. Who Are "no gods" and "elements" in Gal. 4:8, 9? *Angels*

Galatians' intended Lawkeeping is bondage to whom? (Gal. 4:8)	Galatians' intended keeping of Law given Moses is "bondage again" to "elements." (Gal. 4:9) Who are "elements"?	How do we know Paul intends *No Gods & Angelic Elements* are the true source of the Law of Moses?
Those who are "no gods." (Gal. 4:8.)	"Elements" are ***angels*** in Greek & Hebrew thought.	Because Paul says so in Galatians 3:19. He says the Law of Moses was "ordained" by angels through Moses as a Mediator. (Gal. 3:19.) Thus, continuing to obey the Law is bondage again to those who are "no gods" and "weak and beggarly elements."

There is no misreading of Paul involved here. Luke, a companion of Paul, repeats this in the words of Stephen in Acts 7:53. Stephen says: "You received the Law as ***ordained by angels*** and did not keep it." Barnabas, a companion of Paul, and author of Hebrews, refers likewise to the "word spoken ***through angels***." (Heb. 2:2.) Both Stephen and Barnabas are making a misapplication of Scripture. It is correct to say as Stephen does in Acts 7:35 "the angel... appeared to him

18. The most troublesome of all solutions to save Paul from contradicting Scripture is by Gill. He says the Law was given by "the angel of the divine presence, the second person of the trinity." (Comment on Acts 7:38.) Gill means Jesus. However, if you follow Paul's logic that the Law is inferior by having come from angels, and submitting to it means you are subjecting yourself to those "who are no gods" (Gal. 4:8), then if Gill is right, you have Paul affirming Jesus was not God. If you accept Gill's effort to save Paul, you have Paul clearly being an apostate.

(Moses) in the bush." (See Exodus 3:2.) But it is incorrect to say that Hebrew Scripture indicate the Law was given by angels. Such a view contradicts Exodus chapter 20, and specifically Ex. 25:16, 21-22. This passage says God Himself gave the Law.

Paul's claim also directly contradicts Jesus. Our Lord said that "in the bush,... God spake unto him." (Mark 12:26; Luke 20:37.)

In sum, Paul's unmistakable point is that because the Law was ordained through angels, it is secondary. It does not deserve our submission. Paul is asking the Galatians why do they want to be subject to those who are "not gods." They are "weak and beggarly elements."

However, we cannot ignore Paul's view on the angels *contradicts* the account in Exodus. There is no conceivable gap in Exodus chapter 20 that can ever justify Paul's claim, as some Paulinists suggest to avoid the dilemma. Exodus chapter 20 directly quotes God giving the Ten Commandments. Paul is flatly wrong.

Does Paul Imply The Angels Lacked God's Authority in Issuing the Law?

When you examine other letters of Paul, it is clear Paul means in Galatians that *the angels lacked God's authority in giving the Law.* You can deduce this by looking at Paul's comments in Romans 13:1 about our duty to submit to Roman authorities. Paul says they are God's ministers. By contrast, in Galatians chapters 3 & 4, we have no duty to submit to the Law "ordained by angels." In other words, Paul gives the Roman governors a higher *spiritual authority than angels.*

In Romans 13:1, Paul says "Everyone must submit himself to the governing authorities...." Paul explains why. The Roman rulers are "the ***minister of God*** for your own good." (Rom. 13:4, repeated twice.)

Next, look at Galatians 3:19, 4:8-9. Paul says you should not submit to the Law of Moses. It was merely ordained by angels. Paul says 'do not submit to those who are not gods.' (Gal. 4:8.) However, when we look at Romans chapter 13, Paul says you should submit to the "governing" (Roman) authorities as the "minister(s) of God."

The implication arises that the angels must *not* have been acting as God's ministers when they gave the Law. If they were, Paul would tell you to submit to the spiritual authority of these angels. They would be at least on par with the Roman rulers. Paul said such rulers were "the ministers of God." You owe them obedience for "conscience sake."

So why instead are Roman rulers deserving of submission but angels are not? Why does Paul fault a desire to submit to the Law as seeking to submit to those who are "not gods"—the angels? It must be Paul thought the angels acted without God's authority in giving the Law. That's the only explanation why you must submit to Roman rulers who are "ministers of God" but not to the angels who supposedly gave the Law of Moses. Paul must be understood as saying the angels gave the Law without God' authorization. In saying this, Paul certainly contradicts the Bible.

Jude Finds Paul's Ideas Heretical

Paul calls angels "weak and beggarly elements" (Gal. 4:8). He is severely putting them down. Paul also implicitly slights the angels for acting without authorization in bringing the Law of Moses to us. (Gal. 3:19; 4:7-8.)

Paul's statements bring to mind Jude's condemnation of those who make "grace a license for immorality." (Jude 4.) Jude was also a brother of Jesus. He mentions modestly his heritage in Jude 1 by saying he was a brother of James.

In warning us of teachers of a *dangerous grace,* Jude gives us a clue to identify such teachers. Jude says these same grace-teachers are also those who "rail at dignities." (Jude 8.) The word *dignities* is literally *glories* in Greek. (JFB). Commentators concur Jude's meaning is *angels*. (Gill.) Thus, some translations say these "grace" teachers "slander celestial beings." (WEB). By Paul telling us that angels issued the Law, not God, and that they are "weak and beggarly," Paul is "railing at the glories." He is railing at the *angels*. Jude's letter appears directed at Paul on this point. This is especially evident when Jude describes the message of *dangerous grace*.

Jude's Criticism of A Dangerous Pauline Grace Teaching

Jude warned of wolves in sheep clothing who "have secretly slipped in among you." (Jude 4.) They are putting down the angels—slandering them. (Jude 8.) These false teachers are the same who teach "grace is a license to immorality." (Jude 4.) Jude then defines this as a teaching that once you are a Christian we do not risk "eternal fire" (Jude 7) if we engage in "immorality" (Jude 4, 7).

We can further deduce what this teaching was by studying the warnings Jude gave. Jude warns us from the example of Israel whom God "saved" initially from Egypt, but when they were afraid to enter the promised land, all but two "not having believed" became lost (Jude 5).[19] Jude warns us again from the example of the angels who "did not keep their appropriate habitation" in heaven, but fell away by disobedience. (Jude 6.) The examples which Jude gives us are meant to identify an initial salvation, even presence with God in heaven, that is brought to nothing by sin/having lost faith. Thus, being initially saved and even being in heaven itself is not a guarantee one will be finally saved and not enter "eternal fire." Those who teach to the contrary, and guarantee salvation no matter what sin you commit after initially being

19. The Greek is *active aorist participle* of *pisteuo.* In context, it means "having not trusted/believed." *See* http://abacus.bates.edu/~hwalker/Syntax/PartAor.html (accessed 2005)(the aorist active participle for *have* means "having released.")

saved, Jude says are false teachers who are "twice dead"—meaning they were dead in sin, then born again, and died once more by virtue of their apostasy. (Jude 12.)

As a solution, Jude urges the reader to "keep yourselves..." (Jude 21). This reminds us of Jesus' words that those who "keep on listening" and "keep on following" cannot be snatched from Jesus' hand. (John 10:27-29.) Your security initially depends upon your faithfulness to God. *cf.* 1 Peter 1:5 ("kept by the power of God through faith/trust.")

Jude explains your *keeping yourself* is to be an active effort at "contending earnestly"—a form of the word *agonize*—for the "faith" delivered "one time for all time." (Jude 3.) By contrast, these false teachers "*disown* our only master, God, and Lord, Jesus Christ." (Jude 4.) The Greek meaning is *disown* (Greek *ameomai*). (Weymouth New Testament.) It means they were rejecting the *authority* of God's word, delivered "one time for all time." It was not that they denied the existence of God or Jesus, as some translations suggest. This is underscored in Jude 8 where it says they "despise authority." Instead, in disrespect of God's authority, these false teachers "speak proud things" about themselves (Jude 16) and disown the authority of God and the Lord Jesus Christ. (Jude 4.)

In summary, Jude says we must not stray from the words of God and our Lord Jesus by listening to these false teachers who rail at dignities (angels), deny God's authority (in giving the Law) and contradict Jesus' teachings, boast of their own accomplishments, and who give us an assurance that God's grace will protect us from any sin we commit after our initial salvation. (See website www.jesuswordsonly. com for further discussion "Of Whom Did Jude Speak?")

Unless Stanley's position in *Eternal Security: Can You Be Sure?* (1990) is wrong, Paul taught precisely what Jude condemns. Stanley insists Paul teaches that once you confess Jesus and believe He resurrected, you are saved (Romans 10:9), and now there is "no condemnation" ever possible again of such a Christian (Romans 8:1), no matter what sin you commit. No sin that you commit can ever separate you from God again. Your inheritance in heaven is guaranteed. *See* 2 Cor. 5:19; Eph. 1:13-14; 4:29-32; Col. 2:13-14; Phil. 1:6; 2 Tim. 1:12; 1 Thess. 5:24; Rom. 5:1,9-10; 6:1, 8-11, 23; 8:28-30, 39.

Paul otherwise fits the characteristics of which Jude speaks. We have already seen elsewhere that Paul denies God's authority in giving the Law (ascribing it to weak and beggarly angels), that Paul boasts unabashedly of his own accomplishments and that Paul routinely contradicts the message of Jesus on salvation (*e.g.*, the need to repent from sin). Jude appears to be certainly talking about Paul and his followers.

Jesus Himself Condemns Paul's Undermining of Moses' Inspiration

If you accept Paul's views, then you have undermined the very authority necessary to trust in Christ. If one discredited the source of Moses' writings as delivered by "weak and beggarly" angels who are "no gods," Jesus said it is impossible to truly trust in Him. "If they hear not Moses...neither will they be persuaded if one rises from the dead." (Luke 16:31.) Trust in Moses' words is the way to truly know Jesus was Messiah. Jesus says this. Jesus says again "if you believed Moses, you would believe me, for he wrote of me." (John 5:46.)

If Paul were correct about the angels and the Law, then how do Jesus' words make sense that ***trust in Moses' writings as inspired from God is essential to faith in Jesus***? Jesus' words make no sense if Paul is correct. Paul takes away the key that Jesus says is necessary to *truly know and trust in Jesus*. Something is seriously wrong in our tradition that includes Paul.

Paul Contradicts Jesus Too

Jesus also emphasized the validity of the Law up through the passing away of Heaven and Earth, thus confirming its inspiration and ongoing validity. In Matthew 5:17-19 we read:

> (17) Think not that I came to destroy the law or the prophets: I came not to destroy, but to fulfil. (18) For verily I say unto you, ***Till heaven and earth pass away***, one jot or one tittle shall in no wise pass away from the law, till all things be accomplished [*i.e.*, ***all things predicted appear on the stage of history***].[20] (19) Whosoever therefore shall break one of these least commandments, and shall teach men so, ***shall be called least in the kingdom of heaven:*** but whosoever ***shall do and teach them***, he shall be called great in the kingdom of heaven. (ASV)

Thus, Jesus can never be accused of seducing any Christian from following the Law. Jesus cannot be a false prophet under Deuteronomy 13:5. Jesus said it remained valid until the Heavens and Earth pass away. This passing of

20. The Greek word is *ginomai.* Strong's 1096 defines it as "to become" *i.e.*, "come to pass"; "to arise" *i.e.*, "appear in history"; "to be made, finish." Some prefer to understand Jesus "finished" (which they read as 'completed') "all things" required by the Law. What Jesus means is until all things prophesied in the Law and prophets appear in history, *i.e.*, they come to pass, the Law remains in effect. This is evident from verse 17 where Jesus says He came to "fulfill" the "law and the prophets." The word there is *pieroo.* It means "to make complete in every particular," "fulfil" or "carry through to the end." (Thayer's.) Thus, in context, Jesus first says He came to fulfill the prophesies (verse 17) and the Law and Prophecies remain in effect until "all things" prophesied "come to pass" or "appear in history." For more explanation, see the discussion in the text.

heaven and earth occurs at the end of the Millennium. This is 1000 years after Christ's Second Coming, according to the Book of Revelation.

Some Paulinists respond by saying Jesus fulfilled *all* of the Law's demands at Calvary. They insist all the Law was dead letter thereafter. There are several fundamental impossibilities with this claim.

First, there are *two* "untils" in the same sentence: the Law shall not pass away "***until*** the heaven and earth pass away...***until*** all things be accomplished." One cannot ignore the first *until*, preferring to think instead the second *until* means the Law ends in just two more years at the cross.

Second, this Pauline spin ignores the Law contains a Messianic prophecy in Genesis 3:15 which will only be fulfilled at the point that the heavens and earth will pass away. This predicts a death blow to Satan's head by Messiah. However, this remains unfulfilled until the end of the Millennium which point happens to also coincide with the passing of the heavens and the earth. (Rev. 20:7-10.) Thus, this Messianic prophecy of Genesis 3:15 remains unfulfilled until the heavens and earth pass away. Thus, the Law remains in effect until all things prophesied, including Satan's final death blow, come to pass which is far off in our future.

This then proves the two *until* clauses were intended to identify the identical point. There is no less time signified by Jesus' adding the second *until* ("until all things be accomplished") as the Paulinist tries to spin the passage.

Third, Jesus clearly intended the commands in the Law to remain valid *in toto* until a point *after Calvary.* He combined His promise that not one jot or tittle will pass with His insistence that whoever teaches ***against*** following the least of the commandments in the Law would be least in the kingdom of heaven (Matt. 5:19)—the Christian epoch.

Thus, Jesus did not envision the Law expired a couple of years later at Calvary. Rather Jesus saw it continuing until the passing of the heavens and the earth. And doing His will on earth as in heaven meant keeping the Law.

Martin Luther Defends Paul's Attribution of the Law to Angels & Its Abolished Nature

If you believe I have stretched things, I am in good company in concluding Paul taught: (1) the Law originated with the angels; (2) God did not intend to bless Jews with the Law; and (3) we are free to treat the Law as simply from Moses and disregard it entirely. Martin Luther goes so far as to say these are valid reasons why Christians do not have to obey the Law. I thus enjoy the very best of company in understanding Paul's words. The only problem is my companion so thoroughly rejects Moses that he does not see how what he is saying makes himself an apostate, tripped up by Paul's teachings. (Thankfully, Luther later repented. See page 106.)

In a sermon entitled *How Christians Should Regard Moses* given August 27, 1525,[21] Martin Luther simply assumes Paul's words are *authoritative* on who truly spoke at Sinai. While Moses said it was God, and Scripture calls this person God, Luther says it really meant *angels* because Paul says this is who truly gave the Law. Listen how a man caught in a contradiction reasons this out. Luther says:

> Now the words which are here written [in the Law of Moses] were ***spoken through an angel***. This is not to say that only one angel was there, for there was a great multitude there serving God and preaching to the people of Israel at Mount Sinai. ***The angel***, however, who spoke here and did the talking, ***spoke just as if God himself were speaking and saying***, "I am your God, who brought you out of the land of Egypt," etc. [Exod. 20:1], as if Peter or Paul were speaking in God's stead and saying, "I am your God," etc. In his letter to the Galatians [3:19],

21. Martin Luther, "How Christians Should Regard Moses," *Luther's Works: Word and Sacrament I* (Philadelphia: Muhlenberg Press, 1960) Vol. 35 at 161-174.

> Paul says that the law was ordained by angels. That is, ***angels were assigned***, in God's behalf, ***to give the law of God***; and Moses, as an intermediary, received it from the angels. ***I say this so that you might know who gave the law.*** He did this to them, however, because he wanted thereby to compel, burden, and press the Jews.

Luther is distancing God from the Law of Moses, just as Paul had done. It was delivered by angels, not God personally. Luther is ignoring that Jesus Himself said that God was the *direct* deliverer of the Law from the burning bush.[22] Having planted a false seed to distance God from the Law, Luther next begins talking as if God *did not give the Law.* Because Jesus is God, Luther's next remark has all the earmarks of someone who has not thought through the implications of his statement:

> We would rather not preach again for the rest of our life than to let Moses return and to let Christ be torn out of our hearts. We will not have Moses as ruler or lawgiver any longer.

But it is not Moses who gave the Law. Nor did angels. It was Jesus who is the "I AM" who gave the Law. (Ex. 3:14, "tell them ***I AM*** sent you"; John 8:58, "before Abraham was, ***I AM***.") Rewrite this and you can see how incongruous Luther's statement now appears:

> We would rather not preach again for the rest of our life than to let [Jesus's words to Moses] return and to let Christ [preached by Paul] be torn out of our hearts. ***We will not have [I AM who is Jesus who gave the Law] as ruler or lawgiver any longer.***

Martin Luther then announces proudly his total rejection of the Law.

22. Mark 12:26; Luke 20:37.

> So, then, we will neither observe nor accept Moses. Moses is dead. His rule ended when Christ came. He is of no further service....***[E]ven the Ten Commandments do not pertain to us***.

If this is true, then why did Jesus teach to the contrary that whoever taught the smallest commandment of the Law should no longer be followed would be *least* in the kingdom of heaven? (Matt. 5:19.)

Luther Was Sometimes On the Right Track In This Sermon

In fairness to Luther, at other times in the same sermon, Luther's answer on whether the Law applies to us is to examine whether the passage is addressed to Jews alone. ***This is the only correct limitation***. For example, if a command is solely to Jews, such as the law of circumcision (Gen. 17:11; Lev. 12:3, Josh. 5:2),[23] then it obviously does not apply to Gentiles. In the Jerusalem council in Acts chapter 15, James ruled this command does not apply to Gentiles. (Acts 15:19.) James said this not because the Law was abrogated in its entirety,[24] but rather because the circumcision command was

23.However, if a Gentile chose to enter the Temple *proper* of Jerusalem, Ezekiel says even "strangers" must be circumcised. (Ez. 44:9.)

24.The KJV atypically accepts one late textual corruption. This is in James' mouth in Acts 15:24. This makes it appear James said the Law does not apply at all to Gentiles. The KJV has it that James says some have tried "subverting your souls, saying, ***Ye must be circumcised***, and ***keep the law***: to whom we gave no such commandment." (Act 15:24.) However, the ASV & NIV correctly omits "ye must be circumcised and keep the law," saying instead some tried "subverting your souls; to whom we gave no commandment." Why did the KJV add the above bolded words? The UBS' *Greek New Testament* (4th Ed) says this *entire* phrase first appears in the miniscule 1175 (pg. 476), which dates from the Tenth Century A.D. (pg. 17). The phrase "keep the Law" first appears in quotations of Acts 15:24 in the *Apostolic Constitutions* and in the writings of Amphilochius (pg. 467). Amphilochius died "after 394," and this copy of the *Apostolic Constitutions* is dated to "about 380" (pg. 31.) All the earlier texts omit both changes to Acts 15:24.

limited to Jews whom James later told Paul must still, as converts to Christ, follow the circumcision command. (Acts 21:21, 25.)

That James was following this principle is evident again when he imposed on Gentiles prohibitions on eating certain animals with their blood still in it (Acts 15:20).The Law of Moses said this food-rule applied not only to Israelites but also to 'strangers' in the land. (Leviticus 17:10,12 (food with blood).) James likewise adds that Gentiles must refrain from fornication. James no doubt had the Hebrew meaning of that word in mind, which meant adultery.[25] Once again, we find this command against adultery was stated in Leviticus to apply not only to Jews, but also to "strangers that sojourn in Israel." (Lev. 20:2, 10.)[26]

Was James following Scripture in making this distinction? Yes, indeed. The Law of Moses had an example that a command for a son of Israel not to eat meat of an animal that died naturally did not apply to non-Israelite sojourners who were permitted to each such meat. (Deut. 14:21.) Thus, this proves that commands to Israelites do not automatically apply to the non-Israelite. James simply applied this principle to interpret the scope of other commands in the Law of Moses.

If you apply the Israel-sojourner distinction which James employed, then of the Law of Moses which applies to non-Jews it would ***primarily*** be the open-ended Ten Commandments[27] as well as sojourner-specific provisions in Leviticus chapters 19 & 20 & 24:13-24, and Exodus 12:19 (prohibition on leaven during feast of unleavened bread)[28] which Jesus alludes to many times. These are commands that do not introduce themselves as commands to only Israelites. If James' approach is valid, then all the fuss about *the Law* as some terrible burden is a non-starter. The burden on Gentiles is

25.See page 138 *et seq*.

26.On why the idol-food command that James also gives was a deduction as applicable to both Jew and Gentile, see Footnote 1 on page 118.

quite insignificant if we follow the distinction in the Law of Moses *itself* between "sons of Israel" and "sojourners" as James was obviously doing. The alleged burdensome nature of the Law on Gentiles was a *red herring* all along.

James thus did not *add* to the Law. Instead, he refused to apply Israel-only principles to Gentiles. ***He kept to the strict letter of the Law.*** James says the reason to maintain this distinction of Jew versus Gentile in the New Covenant is so that "we trouble not them that from among the Gentiles turn to God." (Acts 15:19.) His ruling also complied with Deuteronomy 4:2.

So if James is right, when Jesus says "Whosoever therefore shall break one of these least commandments, and shall teach ***men*** so, shall be called least in the kingdom of heaven" (Matt. 5:19), Jesus meant us to understand as to Gentiles, that no obedience would be required as to Israel-only commands (unless Jesus extended them). And if James is right, when Jesus says whoever teaches you to obey the least command in the Law would be the greatest in the kingdom, Jesus meant as to Gentiles that if you taught them to obey open-ended commands and commands directed at sojourners in the Law then you would be the greatest in the kingdom. (Matt. 5:19.) But if you go beyond this, and add Israel-only commands on Gentiles which God (including Jesus) never imposed on them, you are unduly burdening their entry into the kingdom of God. You are violating Deuteronomy 4:2 by *adding* burdens nowhere in the Law itself (unless a prophet, such as Jesus, *added* the command, pursuant to Deut. 18:15).

27. Some argue that the Ten Commandments (Decalogue) are not open-ended, implied from Exodus 20:2 which says "I...brought you out of the Land of Egypt." This is largely irrelevant. You can find specific mention of most of the Ten Commandments imposed on sojourners: blasphemy — using God's name in vain (Lev. 24:16; Num 15:30); murder (Lev. 24:17); Sabbath-breaking (Deut. 5:12-15; Lev. 25:6; Exo 23:12); adultery (Lev. 20:2, 10), etc. Even if the Decalogue as a whole does not apply, Bonhoeffer says Jesus extended the Decalogue to all in the New Covenant when He spoke to the young rich man. (Matthew 19:16-26; Mark 10:17-31; Luke 18:18-26.) See Bonhoeffer. *Cost of Discipleship* (1937) at 72-84.

Did Jesus ever speak this way Himself? Yes, this is one of the obvious applications of the principle behind the lessons about the *old and new cloth* and the *old and new wineskin*. (Matt. 9:16-17.) Combining the two items in each case makes things worse, and fails to preserve the *old* side-by-side with the *new*. The *new cloth* put on *old clothing* causes a "worse rent." *New wine* in an *old wineskin* causes the wine to be "spilled and the skins perish."

James similarly speaks that putting the Israel-only commands upon Gentiles is "trouble" for those "turning to God." You cause more problems that you solve by doing so. The *new cloth* is not of the same inherent material as the *old cloth*, and lacks the same elasticity. It cannot be stretched as far as the *old*. The Jew can be pushed further in commands than a Gentile. It is inherent in their *culture*, as God molded the Jews. The *new wine* in an *old wineskin* will swell up from pressure trying to stay within the bounds of the *old wineskin*. The *new wine* will *spill out* (*i.e.*, become lost) if you try to make the *new* fit the *stiffness* and *boundaries* of the *old wineskin*. Gentiles cannot be pressed to follow the Israel-only provisions; the pressure will force them out of the wineskin.[29]

---

28. Passover dinner, which precedes the feast of unleavened bread, is optional for the Sojourner. However, if he "will keep it," then the Sojourner has to be circumcised. (Exo 12:48; Nu 9:14.) Thus, Passover was an honor for a non-Jew sojourner to celebrate. If he chose to do so, he must be circumcised. As discussed in Appendix C, Jesus contemplated His Jewish apostles would keep Passover, and amended the Passover remembrances to include His anticipated work on the Cross. If Gentile Christians observe Passover, it is an honor. When we do so, we were to do the remembrances that Jesus outlined in the last passover. This explains why the early apostolic church was anxious to and did keep Passover; and this is why Passover is a feast worldwide in all forms of Christianity (Protestant, Catholic, and Orthodox) except in English-speaking nations where it is known as Easter. Why the different nomenclature? Because Catholicism could not root out the English/Germanic preference to call that season by the name of the goddess Eastre. As a result, English-speaking Christians have lost memory of what festival they are attempting to celebrate while Christians of all denominations and faiths in non-English speaking countries keep Passover under its proper name. For more discussion, see Appendix C: The Easter Error.

29. Yet, bear in mind, Jesus as Prophet can add a command to the Law of Moses.

Unfortunately, Luther in this sermon did not consistently maintain this valid Israel-Sojourner distinction. Luther ends the sermon by throwing off of the Gentiles *all* the Old Law, even the *sojourner* commands. He put the *New* beyond any testing for its validity against the Law given Moses. Luther says:

> The sectarian spirits want to saddle us with Moses and all the commandments. We will just skip that. We will regard Moses as a teacher, ***but we will not regard him as our lawgiver — unless he agrees with both the New Testament and the natural law.***[30]

Here you see how one falls into apostasy. No longer do you accept the Law given to Moses to define what is a false prophet. Thus, you have accepted a set of new teachings that are beyond the reach of God's prior revelation to test its validity. Luther thereby became in 1525 totally *antinomian*—making the validity of principles in the Mosaic Law turn on the superior validity of what Luther regarded as New Testament writings but only if also confirmed by natural law.

Please note, however, that later from 1532 to 1537 Luther reversed his position on the Law. He denounced antinomianism in the *Antinomian Theses* (1537).[31] He said a Christian can spiritually die and become like a non-Christian. To revive, they must examine themselves by the Ten Commandments, and repent from sin. Luther's *Catechisms* of late 1531-1532 (which the Lutheran church uses to this day) state Jesus' doctrine on salvation and the Law ***while ignoring Paul's doctrines*** (except on how to treat government officials, wives, etc.) For this reason, evangelicals condemn

30. Luther repeats this statement later in his 1525 sermon: "In the first place I dismiss the commandments given to the people of Israel. They neither urge nor compel me. ***They are dead and gone***, except insofar as I gladly and willingly accept something from Moses, as if I said, 'This is how Moses ruled, and it seems fine to me, so I will follow him in this or that particular.'"

31. Martin Luther, *Don't Tell Me That! From Martin Luther's Antinomian Theses* (Lutheran Press: 2004).

Luther's *Catechisms*. Miles Stanford said the "Lutheran Church" turned into "legalism" by adopting an "unscriptural application of 'the law as the rule of life' for the believer."[32] Likewise, Pastor Dwight Oswald regards Luther's *Catechism* as making Luther so at odds with Paul's doctrines that even Luther must be deemed lost and responsible for having led countless numbers to perish in hell.[33] Similarly, Calvinists at Calvin College skewer Luther's 1531 edition of his catechism for departing from the faith he previously taught so boldly.[34]

However, prior to this radical switch, Luther was willing to endorse everything Paul said. Luther inspired by Paul said the angels gave the Law; the Law was a curse on Jews; Jesus never intended the Law applies to non-Jews who follow Him; and the Law is dead and we only follow those aspects that coincide with reason ('natural law') if re-affirmed in the New Testament. Accordingly, unless Luther in 1525 misread Paul, Paul must be understood to have thrown off the entire Law by denigrating its origin and purpose. I therefore enjoy the very best of company in my reading Paul the same way.

But we can take heart from the fact that Luther later made a radical separation from his own earlier antinomianism. Luther must have finally seen the error of the doctrine Luther deduced from *Galatians*. In fact, it appears no coincidence that Luther's switch quickly followed his lecture on *Galatians*. For in that epistle, we have Paul's most virulent anti-Law writings, with Paul's rationale clearly exposed in Galatians 4:22 *ff.* With such new conviction, Luther had the courage to reform himself. That's the best explanation for

32.Quoted in Bob Nyberg's *Covenant Theology Versus Dispensationalism A Matter of Law Versus Grace,* reprinted online at http://4himnet.com/bnyberg/dispensationalism01.html.

33.See Pastor Dwight Oswald, "Martin Luther's Sacramental Gospel," *Earnestly Contending For The Faith* (Nov-Dec. 1997). See also, *Lutheran Heresy* at http://www.jesus-is-savior.com.

34.Calvinists thereby find the 1531 *Catechism* defective spiritually. See Calvin College at http://www.ccel.org/s/schaff/hcc7/htm/ii.v.xiv.htm.

why we find ***Jesus' Words Only emerging*** in Luther's *Catechisms.* Luther made one more radical revolution, once more willing to face the charge of being a heretic. This time, however, it was for basing his ***core*** doctrine on Jesus' words only.

What About Pro-Law Comments by Paul?

Messianic Christians hallow the Law today. They regard the Law of sacrifice completed in Yeshua (Jesus). They have a variety of verses they like to cite from Paul to prove he did not abrogate the entire Law. Their view on the Law's ongoing validity is certainly a minority view. Messianics are regarded in this respect as borderline-heretical by many other Christians. However, Messianics are not deemed un-Christian. The Messianics are thus tolerated by mainstream Christianity. I suspect when Paulinist Christians realize they are about to lose Paul's validity, they might cite these Pauline pro-Law verses (which Messianics cite) as a last gasp to save Paul. So let us examine these verses which the Messianics cherish.

First, Paul said that by faith we "establish the Law." (Rom. 3:31.) Elsewhere, Paul says "Wherefore the Law is holy, and the Commandment is holy, and just and good." (Rom.7:12.) The Messianics even cite the self-contradictory verse: "Circumcision is nothing and uncircumcision is nothing, but ***the keeping of the Commandments of God*** [is what matters]." (1 Cor. 7:19).[35] Lastly, Paul is also quoted by Luke as saying: "I worship the God of my ancestors, ***retaining my belief in all points of the Law....*** " (Acts 24:14).

However, to lift these snippets from Paul's writings, and say this explains all of Paul's thought, is to mislead the listener. It allows self-deception too. It would be like taking Paul's statement in Romans 3:23 that "all have sinned" and say that Paul means Jesus sinned too. Paul clearly regarded

35.It is self-contradictory because circumcising Jewish children was a command of God. (Lev. 12:3.)

Jesus as sinless. To take out-of-context Romans 3:23, and apply it to Jesus, would be perverse. Likewise, to use these snippets to say Paul endorsed the Law's ongoing validity is just as perverse a lie as saying Romans 3:23 proves Jesus was a sinner. If you cannot take Paul out-of-context in Romans 3:23, you cannot take him out of context in Romans 3:31 or Romans 7:21.

Also, Paul's compliments about the Law's good nature in Romans 3:31 do not mean much. We can all speak kindly of the dead. It is only by agreeing that those principles are more than dead letter would Paul's words have any bearing. Such words are absent in Paul.

Furthermore, in 1 Corinthians 7:19, Paul is clearly self-contradictory. He says being circumcised is nothing. Paul then says keeping God's commands is everything. Since being circumcised is a command of God for Jews, these are two logically incoherent statements. But this self-contradiction is purposeful. What Paul is doing is using the word *commands* as a *neologism* (*i.e.*, a word that the speaker privately holds an opposite understanding than what his listener would suppose) to lead the pro-Law listener to think he is on their side. It still works on the Messianics to this day.

How Acts 24:14 Unravels Paul's Authority

Finally, to prove Paul upheld the Law, Messianics cite to Luke's quoting Paul in a tribunal (Acts 24:14). Paul tells Felix that he "retains all my belief in all points of the Law." If Paul truly made this statement, it has no weight. It cannot overcome Paul's view on the Law's nullification. Those anti-Law views are absolutely clear-cut, repeated in numerous letters with long picturesque explanations.

Rather, the quote of Paul in Acts 24:14 brings up the question of Paul's *honesty*, not his consistency with the Law. If Luke is telling the truth, then Paul perjured himself before Felix. To prevent the casual Christian from seeing this, Acts 24:14 is usually translated as vaguely as possible.

However, pro-Paul Greek commentaries know Paul's meaning. They try to defend Paul's apparent lack of ethics. They insist Paul was not out to trick Governor Felix. For example, Robertson in *Word Pictures* makes it clear that Paul deflects the charge that he heretically seeks to subvert the Law by asserting he believes in all of it:

> Paul has not stretched the truth at all....He reasserts his faith in all the Law....A curious heretic surely!

Robertson realizes that Paul disproves to Felix any heresy of seeking to turn people from further obedience to the Law by affirming "his faith in all the Law....," as Robertson rephrases it. Yet, Paul's statement (if Luke is recording accurately) was a preposterous falsehood. He did not believe in "all" points of the Law *at all*. Robertson pretends this is not stretching the truth "at all." The reality is there is *absolutely no truth* in Paul's statement. Paul did not retain his "belief in all points of the Law," as he claimed to Felix.

This account of Luke represents Paul making such an outrageous falsehood that a growing segment of Paulinists (such as John Knox) ***believe Luke was out to embarrass Paul in Acts***.[36]

If we must believe Luke is a malicious liar in order to dismiss that Acts 24:14 proves Paul is guilty of perjury, then this also undercuts the reliability of all of the Book of Acts. If so, then where does Paul's authority come from any more?

36.John Knox recently suggested Luke-Acts was written to bring Paul down and thereby counteract Marcion. (Knox, *Marcion*, *supra*, at 114-39.) If so, then it was Paul's own friend Luke who saw problems with Paul and presented them in a fair neutral manner. On their friendship, see 2 Cor. 8:18; Col. 4:14; 2 Tim. 4:11.

Luke alone in Acts preserves the accounts of Paul's vision of Jesus. That is the sole source for what most agree is Paul's only authority to be a teacher within the church. The vision-experience *nowhere appears in Paul's letters*. If Luke is a liar in Acts 24:14, why should we trust him in any of the three vision accounts which alone provide some authority for Paul to be a 'witness' of Jesus?

As a result, the Paulinists are caught in a dilemma. If Paul actually said this in Acts 24:14, he is a liar. If Paul did not say this, then Luke is a liar. But then Paul's sole source of *confirmation* is destroyed. Either way, Paul loses any validity.

Escapes from this dilemma have been offered, but when analyzed they are unavailing. If Paul made this statement, he clearly was lying to Felix.[37]

Thus, Acts 24:14 cannot be cited to prove the truth of what Paul asserted. Instead, it raises an unsolvable dilemma. Either Luke is lying or Paul is lying. This means Acts 24:14 proves the impossibility of accepting Paul's legitimacy *whichever way you answer the dilemma*. If Luke is lying here, it undermines all of Acts, upon which Paul's authority as a witness rests. If Paul is lying (and Luke is telling the

37. The literal Greek means: "I worship the God of our Fathers, continuing to believe [present participle active] in all things which are according [*kata*] to the Law and in the prophets." The ASV follows this translation. Some Paulinists emphasize the word *according* in the verse. They argue Paul means to reject anything that is no longer in *agreement* with the Law. Thus, Paul is read to mean that he only affirms agreement with the part of the Law with which he can still agree. (Given O. Blakely, *A Commentary on Paul's Defense Before Felix* at http://wotruth.com/pauldef.htm.) This argument fails because Paul believes in nothing from the Law except that it was pregnant with its own abolition. Paul was still being deceptive. Paul was in effect saying, he believes still in everything in the Law that is valid today, but since this is nothing, the statement is empty patronizing. Blakely commends Paul for his shrewd way of saying this. Paul made it appear he was affirming all the Law was valid when instead Paul meant to affirm its entirely fulfilled nature, and hence its defunct nature. Whether a shrewd way of expressing this or not, the literal words are still a falsehood in how Felix would understand the statement *in a court of Law*.

story truthfully), then Paul is disqualified *ipso facto* because he is committing perjury. Acts 24:14 proves to be a passage that unravels Paul's authority any way you try to resolve it.

Bless the Messianics. They cited Acts 24:14 to insist Paul was upholding Torah. What they did is bring to everyone's attention a verse whose very existence destroys viewing Paul as a legitimate teacher.

Did God Ever Respond To Paul's Teachings on the Law's Abrogation?

We already saw, Paul says that "***Circumcision is nothing*** and ***uncircumcision is nothing****....*" (1 Cor. 7:19.)

Then consider thee following command in Ezekiel: if one "uncircumcised in flesh [is caused] to be in my sanctuary, to profane it," then it is an "abomination." (Ezekiel 44:9.) If uncircumcision became *nothing* after the Cross, then a Gentile was free to ignore this command and enter the Temple.

Did a Gentile friend of Paul ever trust this principle to the point of violating the middle wall of the Temple, which kept the Gentiles outside the Temple? We will see that this is precisely what took place in 58 A.D. We will also see how God responded, proving God's legal principles on what abominates had not evaporated at the Cross in 33 A.D.

What happened is that in 58 A.D., Trophimus, an uncircumcised Gentile from Ephesus, entered the prohibited area of the Temple. (Acts 21:28-29.) Neither Luke nor Paul ever deny Trophimus profaned the Temple. Instead, both Luke and Paul merely try to deny there was ***proof*** that Paul had brought Trophimus into the prohibited area. (Acts 21:29, 24:6, 13, 18; 25:7-8.) Luke says the Jews ***supposed*** Paul had done so because they earlier saw Paul together with Trophimus in Jerusalem. (Acts 21:28-29.) Trophimus was indeed a close companion of Paul. (Acts 20:4; 2 Tim.4:20.) Yet, Paul said his accusers merely found him (Paul) purifying himself in the temple. (Acts 24:18.)[38] This was the only inadequacy Paul cited to the charge that he (Paul) was responsible for

Trophimus' profaning the Temple. Paul did not make any stronger refutation such as that Trophimus had not breached the middle wall of the Temple, evidently because Paul knew that charge was true.

Why did Trophimus breach the middle wall that had warning signs declaring that no uncircumcised Gentile could pass into the Temple without facing a death penalty? Trophimus must have been convinced of a ***new principle*** that was ***superior to the principle*** God gave the prophet Ezekiel. Where did Trophimus learn such new principle that could give him such liberty?

There is little doubt that Trophimus, a travelling companion of Paul, must have relied upon Paul's doctrine. First, Paul said that "circumcision is nothing and uncircumcision is nothing." (1 Cor. 7:19.) Lastly and most important, Trophimus, an ***Ephesian***, must have been convinced he could pass this middle barrier because of Paul's letter to the ***Ephesians.*** In it, Paul taught God "has broken down the *middle wall of partition*" at the Temple, "having abolished in his flesh... the law of commandments [contained] in ordinances...." (Eph. 2:14-15.) The true "habitation of God" is now the church, built upon the "apostles and prophets." (Eph.2:20-22.)

Yet, was this middle wall abolished in God's eyes? Or were the Prophetic words of Ezekiel still in place after the Cross of 33 A.D.? In other words, would an uncircumcised Gentile ***inside*** the temple still be an abomination ***standing in the Holy Place***? The answer is *yes.* First, Jesus said that He did not come to do away with the "Law or the Prophets" (Matt. 5:17). Also, Jesus said not until "heavens and earth pass away will one little jot or tittle of the Law pass away...." (Matt. 5:18.) In the Law, we read God promises that if we "walk contrary to Me," then "I will bring your sanctuaries unto ***desolation***." (Lev. 26:27,31.)

38.Incidentally, this was the charge that Paul appealed to Caesar, which caused his being taken to Rome. (Acts 25:8-11.)

Thus, if the Law and Prophets were still in effect after the Cross, then one would expect God would respond by desolating His own Temple for Trophimus' act. God's word appears to require He desolate it in response to such a crime.

Indeed, history proves this took place. God did desolate His temple in 70 A.D. Every stone of the Temple was torn down. Thus, the Law did not expire at the Cross. Instead, thirty-seven years later it was vigorously enforced.

If Paul's teachings misled Trophimus, look then at the horrible consequences of trusting Paul's views. Let's learn from Trophimus' mistake and only trust Jesus' view on the Law's continuing validity until heaven and earth pass away. (Matt. 5:18.)

Conclusion

Paul is blunt in Ephesians 2:15, Colossians 2:14, 2 Cor. 3:11-17, Romans 7:13 *et seq*, and Galatians 3:19 *et seq*. The Law is abolished, done away with, nailed to a tree, has faded away, and was only ordained by angels who are no gods. If we were to cite Paul's condemnations of the Law in one string, the point is self-evident that Paul abrogated the Law for everyone. *See* 2 Cor. 2:14 ("old covenant"); Gal. 5:1 ("yoke of bondage"); Rom. 10:4 ("Christ is end of the law"); 2 Cor. 3:7 ("law of death"); Gal. 5:1 ("entangles"); Col. 2:14-17 ("a shadow"); Rom. 3:27 ("law of works"); Rom. 4:15 ("works wrath"); 2 Cor. 3:9 (ministration of condemnation); Gal. 2:16 ("cannot justify"); Gal. 3:21 (cannot give life); Col. 2:14 ("wiped out" *exaleipsas*); Gal. 3:19, 4:8-9 ("given by angels...who are no gods [and are] weak and beggarly celestial beings/elements").

To save Paul from being a heretic, some claim Paul is talking against *false interpretations of the Law.*[39] But this ignores that Paul tears away at the heart and soul of the Torah.

39.Martin Abegg, "Paul, 'Works of the Law,' and MMT," *Biblical Archaeological Review* (November/December 1994) at 52-53.

He disputes it was given by God. He claims instead it was given by angels. Paul says no one can judge you any longer for not keeping the Sabbath. This is one of the Ten Commandments. Paul, as Luther said, clearly *abolished* the Sabbath. All efforts to save Paul that do not grapple with these difficult passages are simply attempts at self-delusion.

Rather, Calvin was correct when he said "this Gospel [of Paul] ***does not impose any commands,*** but rather reveals God's goodness, His mercy and His benefits."

To Paul, faith was everything and a permanent guarantee of salvation. There was no code to break. There was supposedly no consequence of doing so for Abraham. We are Abraham's sons. We enjoy this same liberty, so Paul teaches.

Then how do we understand the Bible's promise that the time of the New Covenant would involve putting the "Torah" on our hearts? (Jeremiah 31:31 *et seq*.) How do we understand God's promise that when His Servant (Messiah) comes, God "will magnify the Law (Torah), and make it honorable"? (Isaiah 42:21 ASV/KJV.)

You have no answer if you follow Paul. He says you no longer have to observe all God's Law given Moses. You just choose to do what is expedient. You do not worry about the letter of the Law. You can, instead, follow your own conscience. Whatever it can bear is permissible.

How are the contrary verses about the Law in the New Covenant Age then explained? It is seriously asserted by commentators that when Christ returns, the Law of Moses will be re-established. Thus, prior to Paul, there was Law. After Paul but before Christ comes again, there is no Law. When Christ returns, the Law of Moses is restored. (See Footnote 20 on page 393.) So it is: Law—No Law—Law. God is schizophrenic! It is amazing what people can believe!

Consequently, one cannot escape a simple fact: Paul's validity as a teacher is 100% dependent on accepting his *antinomian* principles. Then what of Deuteronomy 13:5 which says someone with true signs and wonders must be ignored if he would seduce us from following the Law?

Paul even anticipated how to defend from this verse. Paul has shielded himself from this verse by ripping away all of the Law. He would not even acknowledge that we can measure him by Deuteronomy 13:5. This is part of the Law of Moses. Paul claims it was given by angels (Gal. 3:19). Paul says you are not to believe even an angel from heaven if it should contradict "my gospel" (Gal. 1:8). Hence, Paul would reject the test from Deuteronomy 13:5.

Yet, Paul has not escaped thereby. For Jesus in Matthew 7:23 reiterated Deuteronomy 13:1-5. In doing so, Jesus specifically warned of false prophets to follow Him that would teach *anomia.* They would come with true signs and wonders. However, they are false because they taught *anomia.* As discussed earlier, they would be workers of *negation of the Law.* This is a legitimate *dictionary definition* of the word *anomia* in the world's best Greek lexicon—the Liddell-Scott Lexicon. For a full discussion, see page 60 *et seq*.

Now Christians must ask themselves this question: do you really believe Jesus made all those warnings about false prophets who come with *true* signs and wonders yet who are workers of *anomia* (*negation of Law*) (Matt. 7:23) so we would disregard the protective principle of Deuteronomy 13:5? So we would disregard even Jesus' words in Matthew 7:23?

You can only believe this if you are willing to disregard Jesus. You can only believe this if you then disregard the Law of Moses was given by God Himself. The Bible clearly says God delivered it *personally* in Exodus chapters 19-20, 25. Jesus likewise says it was God in the bush speaking to Moses. (Mark 12:26; Luke 20:37.)

Or will you allow Paul to convince you that the Law was given by angels (Gal. 3:19) and thus Paul's words are higher than of angels (Gal. 1:8)? Will you be seduced to believe you are thus free to disregard Deuteronomy 13:5? And have you also somehow rationalized away Matthew 7:23, and its warnings of false prophets who bring *anomia*?

Your eternal destiny may depend on how you analyze these simple questions.

6 *Paul Contradicts Jesus About Idol Meat*

Introduction

Jesus in Revelation 2:6, 14 takes on those persons teaching the Ephesians that it was acceptable to eat meat sacrificed to idols. Among them Jesus says were the Nicolaitans. The Nicolaitans were an actual historical group. They taught Paul's doctrine of grace permitted them to eat meat sacrificed to idols. Jesus commends the Ephesians for refusing to listen to the Nicolaitans on the issue of eating meat sacrificed to idols.

Yet the Nicolaitans were not merely deducing it was permissible to eat such meat from Paul's doctrine of grace. Paul, in fact, clearly teaches *three times* that there is nothing wrong *per se* in eating meat sacrificed to idols. (Romans 14:21;1 Corinthians 8:4-13, and 1 Corinthians 10:19-29.)

However, Jesus, as we will see, three times in Revelation says it is flatly wrong. The Bible says when God commands something, we are not free to "diminish" it by articulating our own exceptions. "What thing soever I command you, that shall ye observe to do: thou shalt not add thereto, ***nor diminish from it***." (Deut. 12:32, ASV.)

Let's explore thoroughly the origin of this command against eating meat sacrificed to idols. Let's see also the starkness of the contradiction between Paul and Jesus.

Jerusalem Council Ruling on Meat Sacrificed to Idols

Acts chapter 15 recounts James' ruling at the Jerusalem Council. The issue presented was whether circumcision was necessary for salvation. The outcome was a decision involving what behaviors Gentiles had to follow as Christians. The first decision was to prohibit Gentiles who wanted to become Christians from committing fornication. The second decision was to prohibit eating meat sacrificed to idols. This principle is drawn from Exodus 34:13-16.[1]

Paulinists claim that this prohibition on eating meat sacrificed to idols (which was sold in meat markets) was not an absolute command. It was flexible enough to fit Paul's approach. Paul taught idol meat was perfectly acceptable unless someone else thought it was wrong. Paulinists argue that the Jerusalem Council only meant to prohibit eating such meat if it would undermine a weaker brother who thought it was wrong, as Paul teaches.

---

1. Exodus 34:13 says Jews were to tear down the altars of the Gentiles rather than make a covenant (*i.e.*, a peace treaty). In Exo 34:15-16, God says if you prefer making a covenant and allow their pagan altars, you risk "one call thee [to eat with him] and thou eat of his sacrifice." The command to destroy the pagan altars was so that Jews would avoid eating meat sacrificed to idols even *inadvertently at a meal at a Gentile home*. This altar-destruction command also had the indirect affect of preventing a Gentile from eating idol meat. For this apparent reason, James in Acts 15:20, 25 and 21:25 prohibits Gentiles from eating idol meat. (On how James construed when the Law applies to Gentiles, see page 102.) It is ludicrous to argue, as some do, that God was concerned only that one *knowingly* ate such meat. If true, the Bible could have just prohibited such food as it did with other foods. However, idol meat cannot be identified by appearance. Thus, merely prohibiting eating such meat would not be enough if God was displeased by you eating it *unknowingly*. Hence, to prevent *unknowing* eating of such meat, God commands the destruction of pagan altars. Thus, Paul's allowance of eating such meat by not asking questions is precisely what the Bible *does not countenance*. Rather, if a Jew lived in a society where pagan altars operated and idol meat was sold in the market, the Law intended the Jew not to eat meat whose origin he/she could not be sure about.

However, there is no basis to believe the prohibition in Acts chapter 15 is merely a prohibition on undermining someone else, causing him to violate his conscience. It is clear that eating meat sacrificed to idols is simply wrong *in itself*. It is also no less absolute a prohibition than the prohibition on fornication. Had the Jerusalem Council ruling intended the eating-idol-meat rule to be only a command to follow during social intercourse, then the council used the wrong words to convey such an interpretation.

In fact, the prohibition on eating meat sacrificed to idols was stated three times in Acts. It was never once stated with an exception or qualification. There is no hint that eating such meat was permissible in your private meals. In fact, when we later look at Jesus' words in Revelation absolutely condemning such practice, Jesus is talking *after Paul's words are written down*. Had Jesus intended to affirm Paul's view that eating such meat is permissible, Jesus' absolute directives against *ever* eating such meat were the wrong way to communicate this. Jesus left no room to find hairsplitting exceptions.

This absolute prescription first appears at the Jerusalem Council in Acts 15:20. Initially, James decided that "we write unto them, that they abstain from the pollutions of idols...." (Acts 15:20.) Second, Luke then quotes James' letter to the Gentiles as saying one of the "necessary things" is "you abstain from things sacrificed to idols." (Acts 15:29.) James reiterates this for a third and final time in Acts chapter 21. James is reminding Paul what the ruling was at the Jerusalem Council. He tells Paul that previously "we wrote giving judgment that they [*i.e.*, the Gentiles] should keep themselves from things sacrificed to idols...." (Acts 21:25.)

James restates the principle *unequivocally*. It is a flat prohibition like any food law or the prohibition on fornication. As James states the rule, it has nothing to do with rules only at social gatherings. It has no limited application. There is no exception to permit eating idol meat at home.

Jesus' Confirmation of Jerusalem Council Ruling

Jesus in Revelation 2:14 faults the churches at Pergamum for tolerating those who teach it is acceptable to eat meat sacrificed to idols and commit fornication. Jesus says "some... hold the teaching of Balaam, who taught Balak to cast a stumblingblock (*skandalon)* before the children of Israel, ***to eat things sacrificed to idols***, and to commit fornication." Jesus does not say the error was eating meat sacrificed to idols only if you believed an idol was real. Nor did Jesus say it was wrong only if the person involved thought eating such meat was wrong. Jesus simply laid down a prohibition. Nothing more. Nothing less. Deuteronomy 4:2 prohibits "diminishing" from God's *true inspired words* by making up exceptions.

In this Revelation 2:14 passage, the use of the word *skandalon* is important. In Matthew 13:41-43, Jesus warned that on judgement day all those *ensnared* (*skandalizo*-ed) will be gathered by the angels and sent to the "fiery furnace." Hence, Jesus was telling us in Revelation 2:14 that eating meat sacrificed to idols was a serious sin. He called it a *skandalon*—a trap. It was a salvation-ending trap.

Jesus reiterates the prohibition on eating meat sacrificed to idols in Revelation 2:20. Jesus faults the church at Thyatira for listening to a false *Jezebel* who "teaches my servants to commit fornication, and ***to eat things sacrificed to idols***."

> **"You have people there who hold to the teaching of Balaam, who taught Balak to entice the Israelites to sin by eating meat sacrificed to idols."**
> **Jesus in Revelation 2:14**

The church at Ephesus, by contrast, is commended by Jesus on this issue. The Ephesians were the ones who tried those who claimed to be an "apostle and are not, but [are] a liar" (Rev. 2:2.)[2] The Ephesians were also commended for rejecting the Nicolaitans' teaching on idol meat. (Rev. 2:6.)

The Nicolaitans, Jesus notes, taught that a Christian could "eat things sacrificed to idols...." (Rev. 2:14-15.) Jesus thus has commended the church at Ephesus for not only having identified the person who falsely claimed to be an apostle, but also for its having rejected the teaching that it was permissible to eat meat sacrificed to idols. It is no coincidence. The Ephesians' rejection of someone who said he was an apostle but could not be in Rev. 2:2, if this were Paul (see Chapter Ten), would have to go hand-in-hand with the Ephesian's rejection of Paul's doctrine that idol meats were permissible.

Furthermore, the Nicolaitans' true historical background reveal whose underlying teaching that Jesus is truly criticizing. Robertson (a Paulinist) in *Word Pictures* confesses the Nicolaitans defended eating such meat based on Paul's gospel:

> These early Gnostics practiced licentiousness since they were not under law, but under grace. (*Robertson's Word Pictures* on Rev. 2:14.)[3]

---

2. Later, we will examine whether Jesus was identifying Paul in Rev.2:2 as a false apostle. See "Did Jesus Applaud the Ephesians for Exposing Paul as a False Apostle?" on page 215 *et seq*.
3. Irenaeus around 180 A.D. wrote that Nicolas, their founder "departed from sound doctrine, and was in the habit of inculcating *indifference* of both life and *food*." (*Refutation of All Heresies*, 7.24.)

> **"To the pure, all things are pure."**
> **Paul in Titus 1:15**

Therefore, we see Jesus extols those who hate the Nicolaitan's grace teaching which says Christians can eat meat sacrificed to idols. Jesus then condemns twice those who teach a Christian may eat meat sacrificed to idols. Jesus is just as ***absolute*** and ***unwavering*** on this prohibition as James is in Acts. When Jesus says it, we are not free to "diminish" it by making up exceptions. (Deut. 12:32.)

Notice too how three times James in Acts repeats the point. Then three times Jesus repeats the point in the Book of Revelation. (Rev. 2:6, 14 (Ephesus); Rev. 2:14-15 (Pergamum); Revelation 2:20 (Thyatira).) In the New Testament, there is no command emphasized more frequently than the command against eating meat sacrificed to idols.

This *three-times* principle, incidentally, is not without its own significance. For Paul says *three times* that it is permissible to eat meat sacrificed to idols, as discussed next. God wanted us to *know for a fact* He is responding to Paul.

Paul Permits Eating Meat Sacrificed To Idols

> **"The first sin committed by man was not murder or adultery or stealing; it was eating something they were told not to eat."**
> **Gordon Tessler, Ph.D. *The Genesis Diet* (1996) at 14.**

Paul clearly teaches *three times* that there is nothing wrong in itself eating meat sacrificed to idols. (Romans 14:21;1 Corinthians 8:4-13, and 1 Corinthians 10:19-29.) The first time Paul addresses the question of "eating meat sacrificed to idols," Paul answers: "But food will not commend us to God; neither if we eat not...." (1 Cor. 8:8.) Paul then explained it is only necessary to abstain from eating such meat if you are around a "weaker" brother who thinks an idol is something. (1 Cor. 8:7, 8:10, 9:22.) Then, and only then, must you abstain. The reason is that then a brother might be emboldened to do something he thinks is sinful. The brother is *weak* for believing eating meat sacrificed to an idol is wrong. This is thus a sin for him to eat, even though you know *it is **not** sinful* to eat meat sacrificed to idols. Thus, even though you know better than your weaker brother that it is *no sin to do so*, it is better to abstain *in his presence* than cause him to sin against his weak conscience and be "destroyed." (1 Cor. 8:11.) [4]

Paul is essentially laying down a principle on how to be considerate of others who *think it is wrong to eat meat sacrificed to idols.* At the same time, Paul insists as a matter of principle, *there is nothing wrong eating such meat.* If you were instead the *weaker brother*, and read Paul's epistles on this topic, you certainly would walk away knowing Paul teaches it is *permissible to eat meat sacrificed to idols.* You would even think your *weak-mindedness* on this issue should be abandoned. You should no longer burden your conscience on your brother who refrains due to your overly sensitive conscience. With Paul's instructions in hand, you would certainly *know* that it is permissible to eat meat sacrificed to idols. You can now get over your undue and ill-founded concern about eating such meat.

4. Paul is thought to teach you should not take communion if one was eating idol meat at a pagan service. In 1 Cor. 10:20-21, Paul says you cannot be partaker of the Lord's table and the "table of devils." This was thus not a flat prohibition on eating idol meat. Most commentators reconcile Paul to Paul by saying Paul means you cannot go to a pagan sacrifice and eat the meat during a pagan service and still partake of communion. There is still thus nothing inherently wrong in eating such meat. In the context in which Paul says this, Paul also repeats his famous axiom, "all things are lawful, but not all things are expedient." (1 Cor. 10:23.) Then Paul says when you buy food or eat a stranger's home, "ask no question for sake of your conscience." (1 Cor. 10:25,27.) Thus, Paul says it is best you *not know* what you are eating. Don't let your *conscience* dictate questions about what you are eating. In a sense, Paul believes it is better you not know the meat's origin rather than try to scrupulously avoid eating such meat.

In teaching this, Paul is clearly contradicting James and Jesus. He thereby is "diminishing" Jesus' words by contradicting Him. Paul is prohibiting eating such meat only if someone else is foolish enough to think eating such meat is wrong. Paul has turned Jesus' words on their head. Paul developed a relativistic approach that swallowed the rule. He made the prohibition of none effect. Paul's words clearly violate Deuteronomy 4:2 and 12:32. James and Jesus both say eating meat sacrificed to idols is flatly prohibited and *wrong*. There are no excuses, hairsplitting qualifications, situational-ethics, or easy outs in deciding whether *to obey God*. It is *wrong* and prohibited.

Paul Clearly Teaches It is Permissible to Eat Idol Meat

Yet, Paul teaches it is permissible to eat idol meat. This is transparent enough that Pauline Christians admit Paul is saying meat sacrificed to idols is clean and permissible. They make these admissions apparently unaware that Jesus in Revelation reconfirmed the prohibition on meat sacrificed to idols.[5] A Presbyterian pastor unwittingly admits:

> Paul says to his readers that ***even though there is no ontological or theological basis for refusing to eat meat that has been sacrificed to an idol***, nevertheless out of consideration for brothers and sisters in Christ for whom it

5. Kenneth Loy, Jr. in *My Body His Temple: The Prophet Daniel's Guide to Nutrition* (Aroh Publishing: 2001) at 69 writes: "***Idol Meat Is Clean*** (Romans 14 and 1 Corinthians 8): God had forbidden idol meat originally because it caused the children of Israel to go 'whoring after' the gods of other nations. (Exodus 34:15-16.) Since the Gentiles were now equal in the sight of God, this ***restriction was no longer necessary.*** Jewish Christians even preferred idol meat since it was usually less expensive in the market place....**Paul stipulates another reason why idol meat is *permitted***: 'As concerning therefore the eating of those things that are offered in sacrifice unto idols, we know that an idol is nothing in the world, and that there is none other God but one....' (1 Corinthians 8:4-6)."

> was a great problem and in an effort to be sensitive to their struggles, a Christian should be willing to abstain [from idol meat].[6]

This pastor unwittingly destroys Paul's validity for a person who wants to obey Jesus Christ.

Paul's Antinomianism on Idol Meat Issue versus Jesus

What do we do then with such absolute commands as Jesus gave against eating meat sacrificed to idols? Jesus clearly threatens spewing out of His mouth those committing such deeds.

Modern Paulinists find no problem. First, they apparently share the young Luther's view that the Book of Revelation is noncanonical. Thus, they do not regard Jesus' prohibition on eating meat sacrificed to idols as a hurdle for Paul to overcome. Then what of Exodus' commands (Ex. 34:13-16) designed to prevent eating idol meat? Paulinists defend Paul's position that eating idol meat is permissible by saying the Law was abolished. They then insist this means that any legalistic notion to not eat meat sacrificed to idols was abolished. In fact, these same Paulinists ridicule any first century Christian who would have tried to enforce the command against eating such meats. The Law has been utterly abolished, they explain.

Dan Hill, Pastor of Southwood Bible Church in Tulsa, Oklahoma, shows you that if you came to the conclusion in the first century that you should not eat idol meat, you were

6. Dr. Peter Barnes (Senior Pastor, First Presbyterian Church, Boulder, Colorado), *The Question About Christian Freedom (1 Corinthians 8:1-13)* (2002) reprinted at http://www.fpcboulder.org/Sermons/Sermon1-27-02.htm

in serious error. You were violating Paul's *antinomian* morality based on expediency. Pastor Hill describes the error of such a first century crusader against eating such meat:

> So you start a crusade, you get a banner, get others to march, you picket the temple and the shambles, you chant, you sing, you light candles, you campaign against the ***sin of eating the idol's meat.***
>
> And remember, you have some ***pretty good verses to use on this matter.*** You can pull them out and get very dogmatic about what God thinks (or what you think He thinks).
>
> Then you go to Bible Class one day and there the Pastor is reading ***Paul's first epistle to the Corinthians***. And you find out that... you... have liberty [because Paul teaches]:
>
> 'All things are lawful for me, but not all things are expedient [*i.e.*, Paul's axiom].'
>
> ***You were wrong***, especially in trying to force your decision upon others.
>
> But you would have even been more wrong in thinking that ***you had to figure out what God thinks... that is part of the fatal assumption of the Law.***[7]

Thus, Pastor Hill affirms antinomianism as why Paul said it was permissible to eat meat sacrificed to idols. There is no law. There are no absolute principles. ***Your first mistake was to think there are any laws.*** There is just a question of what is expedient. Eating idol meat is only wrong if it is ***in***ex-

7. Pastor Dan Hill, *Romans 6:14* (Grace Notes) (reprinted at http://www.realtime.net/~wdoud/romans/rom26.html)

pedient to do so. Eating such meat might set you back in evangelism or offend another Christian. It might become *inexpedient* temporarily. Otherwise, there are no absolute rules against eating such meat.[8]

What Pastor Hill is saying is that had he been alive in the first century, he would admonish the 'trouble-maker' Christian. 'Stop trying to make people avoid eating meat sacrificed to idols!' Pastor Hill would not admonish the one eating the meat. They are OK. He would scold you if you said it was wrong to eat such meat.

Unwittingly, Pastor Hill helps us prove how to interpret Jesus' response. Jesus is looking at Paul's entire outlook on the Law. Paul's broader message is because there is no Law any longer, it is permissible to eat such meat. Paul, in fact, says James' command in Acts 15:20 against eating such meat is not binding. The Laws of Exodus are not directed to God's people. You apply an expediency test whether to follow it or not. Jesus was the end of the Law, as Paul says. (Rom. 10:4.)

Jesus' remarks prove Pastor Hill's notion cannot possibly be true. Jesus is angry to the hilt in Revelation 2:6, 14. He is upset that Christians are being told they can commit fornication. He is furious they are told they can eat meat sacrificed to idols. If there is no more strict Law for Christians, and just expediency is the test, then Jesus' words are pointless. We are covered. There is no condemnation for those in Christ Jesus. (Romans 8:1.) Jesus apparently had not read that passage. He didn't 'learn' its truth. Instead, Jesus is full of condemnation for Christians who violate *laws*!

---

8. If you live by Paul's principles, it is totally acceptable to outwardly behave in a manner that does not offend others, while inwardly you do not have to live and believe those principles. What did Jesus repeatedly say to the Pharisees who reasoned to the same conclusion as Paul? Jesus' response is in Mat 23:28: "Even so you also ***outwardly appear righteous to men***, but ***inwardly*** you are full of ***hypocrisy*** and iniquity." (WEB)

In truth, Jesus in Revelation chapter 2 is clearly attacking *antinomianism*. He is laying down absolutes on fornication and eating meat sacrificed to idols. Jesus is highlighting the error of the Nicolaitans. They were known from Irenaeus' writings to be antinomians. Irenaeus said they believed they could eat any foods. The Nicolaitans taught the Law was abrogated and they lived under grace instead.[9]

Jesus' attack on antinomianism is also obvious from Jesus' condemnation of the permissiveness on the issue of fornication. Jesus is not only prohibiting fornication at idol worship ceremonies, as a few Paulinists contend. To save Paul's validity, some seriously contend Jesus meant to prohibit fornication only at idolatrous ceremonies. However, no such limitation can be found in the text. The fornication prohibition is stated just as absolutely as the prohibition on eating meat sacrificed to idols. There are no exceptions. There are no plausible hairsplitting arguments that can construe Jesus as only prohibiting fornicating at a pagan ceremony. (If true, it would imply Jesus permitted fornication otherwise.) This spin to save Paul leads to absurdities.

Thus, one cannot read into Jesus' words any expediency-test on eating meat sacrificed to idols any more than you could read such a test into Jesus' words condemning fornication.

Apostle John, who is the human hand of Revelation, took Jesus' attack on antinomianism to heart. He later wrote likewise that those who say they know Jesus but disobey His commands are liars. John's attack on antinomianism appears in 1 John:

> 2:4 He that saith, I know him, and ***keepeth not his commandments, is a liar,*** and the truth is not in him.***3:10...whosoever doeth not righteousness is not of God.... (ASV)

9. See text and footnote on page 121.

John and Jesus are encouraging strictly following Jesus' commands. This includes His command to not eat meat sacrificed to idols. Apostle John has a harsh message for those ***who claim to know Jesus but who refute His commands***. You are a liar when you say you know Jesus. Who else is called a *liar* by John's pen? The one who told the Ephesians falsely he was an apostle of Jesus. (Rev. 2:2.) We shall see that it is no accident 1 John 2:4 would affix the label *liar* to Paul for his contradiction of Jesus' command on idol meat. Revelation 2:2 affixes the same label of *liar* to someone the Ephesians put on trial for claiming to be an apostle and found he was not one. (See the chapter entitled "Did Jesus Applaud the Ephesians for Exposing Paul as a False Apostle?" on page 215 *et seq.*)

Conclusion

In light of the foregoing blatant contradiction by Paul of Jesus, who seriously can hold onto Paul any longer as an inspired person? Who can really believe he is a true apostle?

Jesus is pointing his arrow at Paul who is long gone when the book of Revelation is written. Unquestionably, Paul had been teaching others to violate Jesus' commands and the commands of the twelve apostles. It is blatant. Jesus takes Paul's teaching to task.

This brings to mind Jesus' 'fruit' test for a false prophet. In Matthew 7:15-20, Jesus says:

> (15) Beware of false prophets, who come to you in ***sheep's clothing***, but inwardly are ravening wolves. (16) ***By their fruits ye shall know them***. Do men gather grapes of thorns, or figs of thistles? (17) Even so every good tree bringeth forth good fruit; but the corrupt tree bringeth forth ***evil fruit***.

Thus, when Paul teaches someone to violate Jesus' commands to not eat meat sacrificed to idols, is this good fruit or evil fruit? Obviously evil fruit. Jesus says "beware those who come in sheep's clothing." (Matt. 7:15.) What is a *sheep* in that verse? A Christian. Beware those who come claiming to be a Christian but who have *evil fruit*. Paul fits both criteria. Jesus then continues, saying even if they come with signs and wonders, He will tell those who work *anomia* (negation of Mosaic Law) that He never knew them. (Matt. 7:23.)

How many ways must Jesus say it before we recognize He is talking about Paul?

7 *Why Does Jesus Mention Balaam in Revelation 2:14?*

How Jesus' Reference to Balaam Applies to Paul

If we dig a little deeper into the eating of idol-meat issue, we find Jesus mentions Balaam in Revelation 2:14.[1] Jesus says the source of this heretical idol meat doctrine is a "teaching of Balaam." Jesus says Balaam taught one can eat meat sacrificed to idols, among other things. Why is Jesus mentioning *Balaam*, a figure from the era of Moses? Evidently because Balaam is a *figure* who resembles the one who in the New Testament era teaches eating meat sacrificed to idols is permissible.

What do we know about Balaam that would help us identify who was the Balaam-type figure in the New Testament church?

The Biblical story of Balaam in the book of Numbers does not reveal the precise nature of the teachings of Balaam. Jesus alone tells us that Balaam taught the Israelites they could eat meat sacrificed to idols and commit fornication. (Rev. 2:14.) Thus, with these additional facts, let's make a synopsis of the story of Balaam. Then we can see whether anyone appears similar in the New Testament era.

- Balaam was a Prophet in the Hebrew Scriptures who was changed from an enemy to a friend by an angelic vision on a Road.

1. Revelation 2:14: "But I have a few things against thee, because thou hast there some that hold ***the teaching of Balaam***, who taught Balak to cast a stumblingblock before the children of Israel, to eat things sacrificed to idols, and to commit fornication." (ASV)

- Balaam, after properly serving the Lord for a time, changed back into being an enemy.
- This inspired prophet is deemed to be an enemy of God because he taught it was permissible to eat meat sacrificed to idols and to commit fornication. This part of the story was omitted in Moses' account. Jesus alone reveals this.

Who else is a prophet of God who was changed from an enemy to a friend by an angelic-type vision on a Road, but then later taught it was permissible to eat meat sacrificed to idols? Who likewise taught an act of fornication condemned by Jesus (*i.e.*, remarriage after divorce if certain circumstances were lacking) was perfectly permissible? (See page 138.) Who likewise is interpreted by most Paulinists as saying fornication is no longer strictly prohibited and no longer leads to spiritual death but instead the propriety of fornication is examined solely based on its expediency? On those key points, we shall see in this chapter that Balaam identically matches Paul.

Jesus is putting a thin veil over the fact He is talking about Paul. Jesus reveals His purpose by referring to Balaam in Revelation 2:14.

By citing the example of Balaam, Jesus reminds us that a true prophet who is turned from evil to good then could turn back and completely apostasize. Jesus' citation to Balaam in this context destroys our assumptions that Paul could never apostasize. By referencing Balaam, Jesus is telling us, at the very least, that Paul *could* turn and apostasize after his Road to Damascus experience. Paul could be just like Balaam who did so after his Road to Moab experience.

Is Revelation 2:14 A Type of Parable?

Did Jesus mention the "teaching of Balaam" as a parable to identify Paul?

It appears Revelation 2:14 is a type of parable. Jesus identifies the false teaching as the "teaching of Balaam." Yet Balaam is dead. Someone in the apostolic era is like Balaam. To know whom Jesus meant, one has to find someone who matches Balaam's historically-known qualities.

Furthermore, we have a second reason to believe a parable is intended in Revelation 2:14. At the end of Revelation chapter 2, Jesus says: "He that hath an ear, let him hear what the Spirit saith to the churches." (Rev. 2:29.) This is Jesus' standard catch-phrase when He wanted you to know there are symbolic meanings in His words.

Let's next try to identify who was the Balaam-like figure in the New Testament apostolic era by studying the life of the original Balaam.

Balaam Was Changed to A True Prophet By A Vision on A Road

In the book of Numbers (written by Moses), Balaam begins as a soothsayer intent on accepting money from Moab's King Balak. He was offered payment to travel to Moab to curse Israel. As such, he begins as an enemy of the true God.

God then appeared to Balaam and told him not to curse Israel. (Numbers 22:5-12.) King Balak then called on Balaam again to come to Moab. However, God appeared to Balaam and allowed him to go on condition Balaam did only what the Lord told him to do. (Numbers 22:20.) Apparently after starting on his trip, Balaam decided to still curse Israel. On route to Moab, Balaam (on a donkey) and his two companions are stopped on a road by an unseen angel of the Lord. (Some commentators think Numbers 22:35 proves this was actually Jesus, the "eternal" angel of His presence—Gill.) Then the famous incident takes place where Balaam's donkey talks back to him. The donkey complains that Balaam is goading him by smiting him with his staff: "What have I done unto thee, that thou hast smitten me these three times?" (Numbers 22:28.) At first Balaam cannot see the angel which is blocking the donkey. (Numbers 22:25-27.) Balaam is in a sense blinded. However, then God "opened the eyes of Balaam" and he could see the angel. (Numbers 22:31-33.)

Balaam then confesses to the angel that he sinned. (Numbers 22:34.) He offers to go home. The angel tells Balaam to continue onto Moab, but repeats the command that Balaam must only bless the Israelites. (Numbers 22:35.) Then Balaam proceeded to Moab. (Numbers 22:36.)

Next when Balaam arrived in Moab, he warned King Balak that he could only do what the Lord allowed him to say. (Numbers 22:36-38.) Balaam's famous oracles of blessings over Israel then followed. (Numbers 23:1-29.)

While giving the blessing, God through Moses says Balaam was directly led by the Holy Spirit. Balaam simultaneously turned away from his prior practice of using omens. Moses writes in Numbers 24:1-2:

> (1) And when Balaam ***saw that it pleased Jehovah to bless Israel***, he went not, as at the other times, to meet with enchantments, but he set his face toward the wilderness. (2) And Balaam lifted up his eyes, and he saw Israel dwelling according to their tribes; and ***the Spirit of God came upon him***. [Then Balaam blesses Israel.]

Thus Balaam had become a true prophet whom Moses reveals was having true communications from Yahweh God. Balaam is indwelt by the Holy Spirit and repeats precisely what God wants him to say. God wants us to know through Moses that Balaam begins as a ***truly inspired prophet*** of God Almighty. The last we see of Balaam in action, he is acting as a good prophet. His words of blessings end up as part of standard synagogue services to this very day, known as the *Mah Tovu*.

How Balaam Fell: His Idol Meat & Fornication Teaching

Then something negative happens that Moses only cryptically revealed. In Numbers 31:16, Moses writes: "Behold, these caused the children of Israel, ***through the counsel of Balaam, to commit trespass against Jehovah*** in the matter of Peor, and so the plague was among the congregation of Jehovah." Balaam had counseled the Israelites that they could sin in some unspecified manner. This cryptic statement is the only explanation why later in Numbers 31:8 that the Israelites, during their slaying of the Midianites, also kill Balaam.

Rabbinic tradition tries to fill in the missing information. It attributed to Balaam the lapse of Israel into the immorality we find in Numbers 25:1-9.[2]

Jesus, however, gives us an inspired message on what was missing in the Biblical account. Jesus says Balaam misled the Israelites by teaching them they can eat meat sacrificed to idols and they can commit fornication. Jesus is the only inspired source of this information. Jesus says:

> But I have a few things against thee, because thou hast there some that hold the teaching of Balaam, ***who taught*** Balak to cast a stumbling-block before the children of Israel, ***to eat things sacrificed to idols***, and to commit fornication. (Rev. 2:14, ASV.)

The Rabbinic tradition in Judaism supports what Jesus said, but only in general terms.

---

2. Morris Jastrow Jr., "Balaam," *Encyclopedia of Judaism* (online at *http://www.jewishencyclopedia.com/view.jsp?artid=161&letter=B&search=balaam.*) If we look at Numbers 25:2, we will see the Israelites were invited to the sacrifices to idols, and ate the idol meat. (Numbers 25:2, "for they called the people unto the sacrifices of their gods; and ***the people did eat***, and bowed down to their gods.")

So Who is Balaam in the New Testament Era?

The prophet Balaam was a person whose life mirrors apostle Paul's life to an extraordinary degree. Absent Jesus telling us that Balaam taught it was permissible to eat meat sacrificed to idols, we would never have known *how virtually identical are the two lives*. Yet when Jesus filled in the missing detail, it made the parallel between Balaam and Paul become extraordinarily uncanny.

In particular, Balaam's Road to Moab experience has many striking parallels to Paul's Road to Damascus experience. In fact, how it affects both Paul and Balaam is identical. Balaam is on his road with the wrong intent to curse God's people. This is true for Paul too, aiming to imprison God's people. (Acts 22:5.) Balaam is on the road with two companions. Paul likewise has companions with him. (Acts 22:9.)

Next, Balaam is given a message by the angel that converts his way to the true God. Gill even says this 'angel' is the "eternal angel" (non-created) of the Lord's presence—Jesus—because of the unique wording of Numbers 22:35. Likewise, Paul gets a message from Jesus that converts his way to the true God. (Acts 22:8.) Both Balaam and Paul follow God *for a time*. Both apostasize when they teach it is permissible to eat meat sacrificed to idols.

There is another odd parallel between Balaam and Paul. After Balaam strikes his donkey to make him move, Balaam's donkey asks: "What have I done unto thee, that thou hast smitten me these three times?" (Numbers 22:28.) The donkey in effect asks *Why are you persecuting me*? Balaam then learns that an angel of God was itself stopping the donkey from moving. Balaam learns it is hard for the donkey to keep on kicking (moving ahead) against the goads of God's angel. *It is hard to keep on kicking against divine goads.*

Now compare this to Paul and his vision. Paul is likewise confronted by Jesus with a similar question: "Saul, Saul, why persecutest thou me?" (Acts 22:7.) And most telling, Jesus adds in the "Hebrew" tongue: "it is hard for thee ***to kick against the goad***." (Acts 26:14.)

When Jesus spoke to Paul on the road in the Book of Acts, He was speaking in a manner that would allow us to invoke the memory of the story of Balaam. In Acts, Jesus laid the seeds for us to later identify Paul as the apostolic era Balaam. To repeat, first Jesus asks Paul why Paul is persecuting Jesus. The donkey asked Balaam the same question. He asked why was Balaam persecuting him. Second, Jesus said to Paul that it is hard for Paul to keep moving forward against God's goads. Likewise, Balaam's donkey was up against the goads of God's angel. Jesus' words in the vision experience with Paul were well chosen to invoke a *precise* parallel to the story of Balaam. Thus, we could never miss the point in Revelation 2:14. We thereby could identify the NT Balaam.

What Does It all Mean?

Paulinists apparently sense a problem if Balaam's story were ever told in detail. They always identify Balaam as merely a false teacher or someone who prophesied for money. But this misses Jesus' point.

Balaam is precisely the example, unique in Hebrew Scriptures, of an enemy converted by a vision on a road, turned into a true spokesperson of God, but who later *apostasizes* by saying it is permissible to eat meat sacrificed to idols. ***Balaam precisely matches Paul in an uncanny way despite millennia separating them***.

Thus, in Paul's vision experience, God laid the groundwork for a comparison to events two millennia earlier. What an amazing God we have! Jesus specifically made sure the encounter with Paul would have all the earmarks of the Balaam encounter:

- It would be on a road.
- There would be a divine vision.
- Jesus would ask why is Paul persecuting Him.
- Jesus would let Paul know it is hard to go up against the goads of God.
- The experience would turn Paul around to be a true spokesperson of God *for a time.*
- Finally, Paul would fall like Balaam did by teaching it was permissible to eat meat sacrificed to idols.

Of course, to understand this, you have to have ears to hear. (Rev. 2:29.)

In other words, God set in motion what happened on the Road to Moab, just as He did on the Road to Damascus. Paul apparently indeed had the experience he claims. That's why Jesus could cite the teaching of Balaam as repeating itself in the apostolic era. Yet, to cement the similarity, Jesus had to give us a crucial new similarity between Balaam and Paul. By disclosing Balaam's idol meat teaching, Jesus in Revelation 2:14 suddenly made appear an extraordinary parallel between Paul and Balaam that otherwise remained hidden.

Just as Jesus said Elijah was John the Baptist, "if you are willing to receive it" (Matt. 11:14), Jesus is saying the teaching of Balaam that deceives Christians is the teaching of Paul, "if you are willing to receive it."

What About Permission to Commit Fornication?

Jesus in Revelation 2:14 says the Balaam of the apostolic era also taught *Christians* that it is permissible "to commit fornication."

In the Hebrew Scripture, the word *fornication* meant primarily adultery. In English, it has evolved into almost exclusively the meaning of unwed sexual intercourse. The reason for this change in meaning is because Paul used the synonym for this word in 1 Corinthians 7:2 apparently to mean unwed sexual intercourse.[3] However, in the Hebrew, *fornication*'s meaning differs from our own usage.

Brown-Driver-Brigg's Hebrew Dictionary defines the contexts for *fornication* (Hebrew *zanah*) as:

> 1a1) to be a harlot, act as a harlot.
>
> 1a2) to commit ***adultery***
>
> 1a3) to be a cult prostitute
>
> 1a4) to be unfaithful (to God)

Thus, fornication in Hebrew is synonymous with adultery. (Out of this arises metaphorical meanings such as 1a1, 1a3 and 1a4 above.) In turn, adultery was sex with another man's wife. (Lev. 20:10.) There is no concept within *zanah* of 'to have sex among unwed partners.' One can also see in context of Matthew 5:32 that the Greek word for *fornication*, as Jesus intended it, had to have the underlying Hebrew meaning of only *adultery*. Jesus says you can only put your wife away if she committed *zanah*, translated in Greek as *fornication* but which must mean she committed *adultery*. Thus, because the word *fornication* in Hebrew here did not mean sexual relations among unwed people which meaning mismatches the context, we know Jesus' original spoken language only meant *adultery*. This then was innocently translated as *fornication* but is too broad in meaning.

3. The debate has raged whether the New Testament word *porneia* had the primary meaning of *unwed sexual intercourse*, or the more limited meaning of *sexual intercourse with a cultic or commercial prostitute*. It seems clear that Paul's usage was intended to mean *unwed sexual intercourse*. Jesus' usage in Matthew 5:32 can only mean *adultery*. The word has many broad meanings in Greek, but the corresponding word in Hebrew (*zanah)* meant *adultery* and metaphorically *prostitution*.

So if we rely upon the primary Hebrew meaning of the word *fornication—adultery*, let's ask whether Paul ever permitted an act of adultery which Jesus specifically prohibited? The answer is yes. It is a most disturbing contradiction.

This involves Paul's statement on remarriage. Paul says a wife whose "unbelieving [husband] leaves (*chorizo*)"[4] her is "not under bondage." (1 Cor. 7:15.) No divorce certificate was issued, yet she is not under bondage to her departing husband. Almost every commentator agrees the context means she is free to remarry without committing *adultery*. (Calvin, Clarke, Gill, etc.) Yet, as Paul describes the situation, the Christian woman was not abandoned because she committed adultery. Nor had she received a certificate of divorce.

However, Jesus said in the Greek version of Matthew 5:32 the husband who unjustifiably leaves the wife "causes her to commit adultery" if she remarries. In the Hebrew version of the same verse, Jesus says instead that a husband who leaves a wife without giving a certificate of divorce causes the wife, if she remarries, to commit adultery.[5]

Whether you accept the Greek or Hebrew version of Matthew, Paul says the Christian woman who both was *unjustifiably* abandoned and abandoned *without a divorce*

---

4. This was not the word used for *divorce* in the NT: *apoluo*. *Chorizo* means *to place room between, depart,* or *separate.* (Strong's # 5563.)
5. There is an apparent corruption of the Greek version of Matthew in this verse. In the Hebrew version, what Jesus is saying is when a man leaves a wife *without a bill of divorcement*, and the woman remarries, she commits adultery as does the one who marries her. In *The Hebrew Gospel of Matthew* by Howard, Matthew 5:32 reads in part: "And I say to you that everyone who leaves his wife is to give her a bill of divorce." Then it goes on to treat the violation of this principle as the cause of adultery, both by the man leaving and the wife who remarries another. The Hebrew appears more correct because Deuteronomy 24:2 allows a woman who receives a certificate of divorce to remarry. However, even if the Greek version of 5:32 were correct, Jesus is merely saying that if the certificate were improperly delivered to the wife, without her being guilty of an *unseemly thing* as required by Deut. 24:1, the divorce was invalid and the right of remarriage under Deut. 24:2 does not exist. This makes sense even if Jesus never said it.

certificate does not commit adultery by remarrying. However, Jesus says she *absolutely* does commit adultery under either of those circumstances. Since adultery is synonymous with fornication in Jesus' original vernacular, Paul permits the very act of fornication which Jesus prohibits.

Incidentally, if the Greek text were correct, Jesus would be resolving a dispute under the divorce Law on what *unseemly* thing was necessary to justify a bill of divorce.[6] Yet, if the Hebrew version of Matthew 5:32 were correct, Jesus was re-invigorating the requirement of using a bill of divorce, which apparently had fallen into disuse. Men apparently were abandoning their wives and simply remarrying with impunity. Whether the Greek or Hebrew text is correct, Jesus was reinvigorating the Law of Moses, and as Campenhausen explains, Jesus "reaffirmed" it.[7] (For more on the fact that Matthew was originally written in Hebrew and then translated into Greek, see page xiii of Appendix B.)

Regardless, what remains the problem is that under either text tradition, Paul permits the very act of fornication/adultery that Jesus prohibits.

What About Paul's Anti-Fornication Statements?

If we ignore the prior example, could Paul ever possibly be faulted for permitting fornication? Didn't Paul oppose fornication, as he says in Galatians 5:19 that those who "practice fornication" shall not "inherit the kingdom of God"?[8]

6. The Bible required "some unseemly thing" for divorce. (Deut. 24:1.) Hillel thought any trivial reason qualified, while Shammai believed adultery alone justified divorce. ("Adultery," *International Standard Bible Encyclopedia.*) In the Greek version of Matthew 5:32, Jesus would be siding with Shammai's view.
7. Hans van Campenhausen, *The Formation of the Christian Bible* (J. A. Baker, trans.) (Philadelphia: Fortress Press, 1972) at 13.

Yes, Revelation 2:14 still could apply to Paul. First, most Paulinist commentators dispute Paul means to threaten Christians in Galatians 5:19. (Clarke, Barnes, Gill.) Because of Paul's other teachings of eternal security, these commentators claim Galatians 5:19 means only unsaved persons who engage in fornication are threatened with exclusion. Thus, they contend Galatians 5:19 is not a message to Christians. Hence this verse does not prove what Paul taught Christians about the consequences of fornication.

---

8. This is Paul's strongest anti-fornication statement. His other negative statements are weaker. For example, Paul in 1 Cor. 6:18 says "Flee fornication...he that commits fornication sins against his own body." This is not very strong because Paul did not say you sin against God; you sin against yourself. This means it affects only yourself, giving you room to permit it. Again Paul in 1 Cor. 7:1 says it is "good for a man not to touch a woman." In context, the concern is it can lead to fornication. Yet, again, Paul is not strong. He does not make the prohibition direct or threaten a serious loss. Again in 1 Thess. 4:3 (ASV), Paul says "the will of God" is that "you abstain from fornication." Paul goes on to say that if you "reject this" (*i.e.*, 'annul this'), you "reject God who gives His Holy Spirit to you." (1 Thess. 4:8.) This appears strong—to threaten loss of salvation for fornication by a Christian. However, the Pauline commentators explain the context does not justify this is talking about fornication in its broad sense. The *New American Standard* (Protestant-Lockman Foundation) commentary in the footnotes says that the word translated "fornication" or "immorality" here really only means "unlawful marriage." It explains "many [incorrectly] think that this passage deals with a variety of moral regulations (fornication, adultery...)." It then explains this passage deals *in this context* instead with "a specific problem, namely marriage within degrees of consanguinity...." (See reprint of this commentary at http://www.usccb.org/ nab/ bible/ 1thessalonians/ 1thessalonians 4.htm.) Furthermore, most Paulinists find Paul's doctrine of eternal security trumps this verse. Because this verse threatens God will deny you for the sin of "fornication" (as translated), this must be directed at a non-believer. It does not say the person has *received the Holy Spirit yet*. Otherwise, Paul would be contradicting himself that salvation does not depend on what you do. (Romans 4:4.) Thus, this is read to be a warning to a non-believer, not a believer. As a result, while 1 Thess. 4:3, 8 at first appears strongly against fornication, Paulinists interpret it so it does not apply to anything but to a very specific consanguinity issue or not to a Christian at all.

However, this view is unsatisfactory because clearly Paul's warning in Galatians 5:19 is intended for Christians. The Book of Galatians is addressed to genuine believers (Gal 1:8-9). In Galatians 5:13, Paul refers to those addressed in Galatians 5:13-26 as *brethren*. Furthermore, in Galatians 6:1, Paul again refers to those being warned as *brethren*.

This has led other Paulinists to admit that Paul is warning Christians in Galatians 5:19-21. However, they still have a response that permits a Christian to commit fornication without losing their inheritance in heaven. They claim Paul means that fornicating Christians (a) only are at risk if they *practice* fornication and (b) if so, they only risk losing a reward (*i.e.*, sharing ruling authority in heaven.)

They point to Paul's use of the term "practice" in Gal. 5:21. They insist Paul means that occasional *fornication by a Christian* is permissible.[9] Paul's words are "they who ***practice*** such things [*e.g.*, fornication] shall not inherit the kingdom of God." Paul's threat does not intend to warn a Christian who engages in *occasional* fornication that they should fear the loss of salvation.[10]

John MacArthur is a major voice of modern evangelical Christianity. His position reflects this.

> Some people wonder if that verse means a Christian can lose his salvation if he has ever done any of those things. Although the Authorized Version says 'they who do such things shall not inherit the kingdom of God,' the Greek word for *do* is *prasso,* which means 'to practice.' It is a verb that speaks of ***habitual practice*** rather than occasional doing. Thus, the verse refers to those who habitually practice such things as an expression of their char-

9. James, by contrast, says a single act breaks all the law. (James 2:13.)

10. Paul's *occasional-practice* distinction is at variance to the Hebrew Scriptures. The Law says it only takes one act of adultery or murder to be deemed worthy of death. (Lev. 20:10, Numbers 35:16; Ezek. 33:18.)

> acters. The word of God bases its evaluation of a person's character ***not on his infrequent actions,*** but on his habitual actions, for they demonstrate his true character. The people who habitually perform the works of the flesh will not inherit the Kingdom because they are not God's people.
>
> Some ***Christians may do some of those things infrequently, but that doesn't mean they will forfeit the full salvation of the Kingdom of God.*** Rather they will receive divine discipline now and forfeit some of their heavenly rewards.[11]

MacArthur thus concedes Paul's threat in Galatians 5:19 is only for a person who *practices* fornication. MacArthur says a true Christian will never practice this, and thus is never threatened *actually* with loss of salvation. A true Christian at most will *occasionally* commit fornication. The Christian who does so has an eternal destiny as safe and secure as the Christian who resists *all* acts of fornication.

In the quote above, MacArthur then adds to Paul's words to make Paul appear to say fornication is not entirely permissible for a Christian. Paul does not ever say anything anywhere about Christian fornicators receiving divine disciple. That is John MacArthur's hopeful addition.

Putting this unfounded addition to one side, what is still clear is MacArthur admits Paul does not intend to alarm Christians who "infrequently" commit fornication that they have anything serious to concern themselves about. Paul's warning in Galatians 5:19 does not apply to warn a Christian who occasionally fornicates. Thus, MacArthur can reassure such Christians that heaven awaits them despite committing

11.John MacArthur, *Liberty in Christ*, reprinted at http://www.biblebb.com/files/MAC/sg1669.htm.

unrepentant occasional fornication. MacArthur says God would never condemn you for occasional *fornication*, citing Paul's words in Galatians 5:21.

Furthermore, Dillow insists that even if a Christian practices fornication, Paul does not mean to threaten anything more than loss of rewards. Dillow argues that Galatians 5:19 and the comparable 1 Corinthians 6:9 mean by threatening the loss of an inheritance of the kingdom to threaten only a loss of rewards. The argument is a forced-one, stretching over chapters 3-5 of Dillow, *Reign of the Servant Kings*. Yet, if this is how Paulinists construe Paul to keep him squared with his *faith-alone* doctrine, then I can rely upon Dillow to conclude Paul never puts a serious threat over the Christian who *practices* fornication. And when I combine MacArthur's distinction with Dillow's views, I can say Paul never threatens ***at all*** a Christian who *occasionally* commits fornication.

Paul Is Boldly Claimed To Teach Fornication Is Permissible

Now that we see how Paulinists dismiss the threats in Galatians 5:19-21, it should come as no surprise that mainstream Christians declare Paul says a Christian can commit fornication, not repent, and expect to be saved. Galatians 5:19-21 never enters their analysis.

They argue strenuously that Paul permits fornication, apparently to make their point more blatant about Paul's doctrine of grace. To prove Paul permits fornication, they rely upon three independent proofs.

1. Paul's Says Fornication is Permissible But It Might Be Unprofitable

First, Paulinists say Paul declared the Law abolished, and that in its place the new criteria is: "all things are lawful but not all things are expedient" (1 Cor. 6:12). Paul thereby implied it was permissible you could commit fornication. The test is expediency; it is no longer whether it is absolutely prohibited.

This reasoning is bluntly stated by Bob George. Mr. George is an author of numerous mainstream theological books on eternal security. Over the past several years, he has been a national radio talk host whose daily topic is often eternal security. You have been able to hear him on the radio in Los Angeles every week day. He bluntly said in a 1993 broadcast that Paul says it is permissible to commit fornication:

> And as Paul said, 'All things are permissible, but not all things are profitable.' ***So is committing fornication permissible? YES.*** Is it profitable? No, it isn't.[12]

George is not alone. John MacArthur, a giant of modern evangelical Christianity, says the same thing. In addressing whether fornication is permissible in the article quoted on page 143, MacArthur never once cites any absolute prohibition on acts of fornication from the Hebrew Scriptures. Instead, he quotes Paul's axiom "all things are lawful...." Then MacArthur tries to prove fornication is not expedient. Fornication harms you, it enslaves you, etc. He tries to squeeze out a negative answer using Paul's principle, "All things are permissible, but not all things are profitable."[13] Thus, the starting point is that fornication is not wrong *per se*. You have to look at its *expediency, i.e.*, its costs versus its benefits. Then if the costs outweigh the benefits, it is wrong.

Thus, George and MacArthur reflect Paul's paradigm shift. The Law is gone. In its place a new analysis is applied. Under it, fornication is permissible but not necessarily profit-

---

12.Bob George, *People to People* (Radio Talk Show), 11/16/93.

13.John MacArthur, *Back to Basics: The Presentation of My Life: Sacrifice* at http://www.biblebb.com/files/MAC/1390.htm (last accessed 2005).

able. A strong case can be made about its unhealthy results, etc. Therefore George and MacArthur say 'don't do it.' This is an *antinomian* (anti-Law) shift away from simply knowing that the Law says it is wrong. In its place, we now have a cost-benefit analysis whether fornication *works* for you.

Under Paul's balancing test, we can see the result just as easily could be that fornication is more beneficial for me. As long as the guilt from violating the Law is erased, then I do no wrong if I think "fornication" works for me. As long as I applied a cost-benefit analysis of what is more expedient, and I reasonably justify it, it is no sin. For example, if I love someone and commit "fornication" with her, and it suits our mutual needs to ignore the legalities of the situation, then in a very cogent way, I have justified fornication in a manner that passes the cost-benefit analysis Paul offers. "All things are lawful" and in this scenario it is more "expedient" to not be hyper-technical about our behavior.

This example raises the dilemma the church faces today: it desperately wants to give a cost-benefit analysis for this scenario to steer people away from such fornication because Paul ***removed the ability to cite the Law itself as reason enough***. Consequently, the modern Pauline-Christian analysis of right-and-wrong starts from "all things are permissible," including fornication. Then by applying the *costs versus the benefits test*, their analysis tries to steer people to an outcome parallel to the Law.

Thus, clearly Paul's saying all things are permissible includes fornication. It is only to be abandoned if the costs outweigh the benefits. However, there are going to be times where the benefits of fornication will outweigh the costs. That is why Paul is still the leading candidate to be the Balaam figure of the New Testament era mentioned in Revelation 2:14.

2. Paul's Doctrine of Grace Means Fornication is Permissible

Other Paulinists defend that Paul teaches fornication is permissible with no significant penalty for a Christian on another ground. This is Paul's doctrine of grace. All your future acts of fornication are already forgiven when you became a Christian, they insist. Such a sin might cause the loss of rewards, but there is no loss of something you cannot afford to lose. Luther defends this idea:

> [N]o sin will separate us from the Lamb, ***even though we commit fornication*** and murder a thousand times a day.[14]

Zane Hodges, a leading evangelical writer, similarly says:

> Paul does not say...his readers should question their salvation if they become involved in ***sexual impurity.***[15]

Unless these mainstream writers are wrong, Paul is teaching a grace that permits sexual immorality with no serious loss. At least there is no penalty.

What about loss of rewards? Paul never says expressly you lose a reward for fornication. But assuming he did say this, if anyone loses a reward that does not affect salvation, it is certainly not a penalty. It is not even a set back. You simply do not move ahead. In fact, you will have eternity to overcome the loss of initial rewards. It is no problem at all. How many would not trade a few lost rewards you can live without to take today the delectable pleasures of fornication?

---

14. Martin Luther, *Luther Works, I Letters* (American Ed.) Vol. 48 at 282.

15. Zane Hodges, *Absolutely Free!* (Dallas, TX: Redencion Viva, 1989) at 94.

In sum, Paul's grace doctrines are read to permit fornication with no serious consequence or penalties. This second proof reconfirms that Revelation 2:14 is Jesus' direct identification of Paul as the one bringing the "teaching of Balaam."

3. The Sexually Immoral Man in 1 Cor. 5 Was Never Lost

As the third and final proof that Paul says fornication is permissible, Paulinists actually cite 1 Corinthians 5:5. They insist this passage proves that a sexually immoral Christian is never at risk of losing salvation.

In that passage, Paul deals with a sexually immoral member of the Corinthian church who lives with his father's wife, his step-mother. If the father is alive, this is *incest.* Paul decrees: "deliver such a one unto Satan for the destruction of the flesh, that the spirit may be saved in the day of the Lord Jesus." (1 Cor. 5:5.)

Dillow contends Paul ordered the man was to be expelled and then killed. Paul's wording therefore proves that if the man were killed in his unrepentant state that Paul meant this carnal Christian was still saved. Dillow, whose book is now treated as required reading at many evangelical seminaries, explains:

> An extreme example of the '***consistently carnal Christian***' seems to be found in 1 Cor. 5:5....Paul hands this carnal Christian over to physical death, but ***he notes that he will be saved at the day of the Lord Jesus***.[16]

Thus, Dillow means that Paul wants the man killed immediately. (Paul's conduct shows disregard for the civil rights protected in the Law of the accused.)[17] Dillow understands Paul's other words as assuring us that the man's death

16.Dillow, *Reign of the Servant Kings* (1993) at 321.

in this situation means the man will enjoy salvation despite his unrepentant and consistent sin. Thus, this verse proves eternal security, Dillow claims.

Dillow is not an aberrant view of this passage. The mainstream idea of *once saved always saved* boldly proclaims this passage teaches a Christian is free to commit repetitive unrepentant fornication without the slightest threat to their salvation.

> The man who had 'his father's wife'—a terrible sin—didn't lose his salvation thereby. (Dave Hunt.)[18]
>
> Some have regarded 1 Corinthians 5:5 as ***the strongest verse in the Bible for once saved, always saved and I would not disagree.*** (R.T.

17.Many commentators try to avoid what Dillow so gladly affirms. They argue Paul did not mean the person should be killed. However, the early church fathers correctly understood Paul's command was to kill the man. Tertullian said Paul was invoking the Hebrew Scripture's familiar "judicial process" whereby a "wicked person being put out of their midst" was done by the "destruction of the flesh." (Tertullian, *Against Marcion*, Book 5, ch. VII.) This is evident in Paul's language about *purging*. It was taken directly from the death penalty laws in the Mosaic Law, *e.g.*, Deut. 17:7, 21:21, 22:21. Furthermore, Paul uses the language of a judicial officer rendering a verdict in 1 Cor.5:3, which a death sentence would require. This incident reveals a flaw in Paul's ideas that *all* the Law was abrogated, even its civil rights to protect the accused. Under the Law, a hearing was necessary where two eye witnesses tell the judge the persons were caught in the very sexual act prohibited in the Law. No inference was permitted in capital cases. (Deut. 17:7; *cf.* John 8:4.) Second, the witnesses in an incest case with a stepmother had to confirm the father was alive at the time of the act. Otherwise, as some Rabbis pointed out, the act was not *precisely* prohibited by the Law. Then, in strict compliance with the Law, Paul should have required the two witnesses to be the ***first*** to throw stones. (Deut. 17:7; John 8:4 *et seq*.) Paul instead presumptuously declares the death penalty over an accused without hearing testimony and questioning the circumstances. Paul's abrogation of the Law thus cut out barriers against precipitous actions by those in authority. Paul took full-advantage of a freedom he gave himself from the Law of Moses to *ignore civil rights* protected in the Law.

> Kendall, *Once Saved Always Saved* (Chicago: Moody Press, 1985) at 156.)
>
> In spite of the sin of fornication, Paul still regarded the person as a saved man. (Gromacki, *Salvation is Forever* (Chicago: Moody Press, 1976) at 138.)

If Dillow and these writers are correct (and they are accepted as correct by mainstream evangelical Christianity which Moody Press typifies), then Paul taught a carnal sexually immoral and unrepentant fornicating Christian has nothing significant to lose. Paul is supposedly saying a Christian can commit even incest with his step-mother and be saved all the while. Thus, of course, the same must be true of "consistently unrepentant fornicating Christians."

Recap: How Mainstream Christianity Proves Paul Teaches A Christian May Fornicate

Accordingly, mainstream Christianity offers several proofs that Paul teaches it is permissible for a Christian to commit fornication although it may not be expedient:

- The Law is abrogated.
- If one said fornication were strictly impermissible, that is not only Legalism, but also it implies a works-salvation.
- Paul only warns loss of rewards in Galatians 5:19 if a Christian *practices* fornication. (Dillow.) Thus, no rewards nor salvation are lost for occasional fornication; and
- Paul's language in 1 Corinthians 5:5 implies consistent acts of unrepentant incest do not even threaten loss of salvation, so practicing unrepentant fornication cannot possibly pose such a threat.

18. Dave Hunt, *CIB Bulletin* (Camarillo, CA: Christian Information Bureau) (June 1989) at 1.

Why Paul Must Be The Figure Who Permitted Fornication

Consequently, Paul permitted an act of adultery that Jesus prohibited. Paul permitted a Christian woman who was unjustly abandoned without a divorce certificate to remarry. However, Jesus said absent there being grounds she committed adultery and/or a certificate, if she remarried, she committed adultery. Paul thus permitted fornication in the sense that Jesus was condemning fornication in Revelation 2:14. Paul's doctrine on remarriage and *fornication* evoked Jesus' harsh response in Revelation 2:14.

Furthermore, if we look to verses where Paul uses the term *fornication* (where he usually means unwed sex), mainstream Christianity today teaches Paul's other lessons mean either (1) fornication is clearly occasionally permissible for a Christian with not even loss of rewards or (2) if the fornication is repetitive and unrepentant, it poses no threat to a Christian's salvation, citing 1 Corinthians 5:5. In either case, fornication is subject only to the expediency test. This has opened the doors to all kinds of immorality condemned in the Law of Moses. In fact, if we cite the Law and we insist salvation must be threatened if you commit sexual sins because of Jesus' words in Mark 9:42-47 (better heaven maimed than hell whole), we are labelled a heretic. We are seen as undermining Paul's doctrine of salvation by faith without works.

Thus, the Paulinist spin on Galatians 5:19 as threatening loss of *rewards*, not salvation, for *practicing* fornication (Dillow) is the only rational view that squares Paul with Paul. If you disagree, and you claim Paul means to threaten a Christian with losing salvation (and thus he teaches what Jesus teaches in Mark 9:42-47), Stanley accuses you of being a dangerous heretic attacking the core of Christianity:

> The very gospel [*i.e.*, of Paul] itself comes under attack when the eternal security of the believer is questioned.[19]

Consequently, if Paulinists have won the day that Galatians 5:19 does not teach any loss of salvation for an occasionally or repetitiously fornicating Christian, no one can cite Galatians 5:19 to prove Paul 'prohibited' fornication either for such a Christian. If Paulinists also construe it as permitting *occasional* fornication by a Christian *with no threat* (as most do), I then can cite this verse to prove Paul at minimum permits *occasional* fornication by a Christian with no negative consequences whatsoever, *not even loss of rewards!* Such a limited loss of rewards is only reserved for those who *practice* fornication!

This brings us right back to our conclusion that Revelation 2:14 is talking about Paul. He injected a moral ambiguity into Christianity by abrogation of the Law. He changed Biblical morality into the principle "all things are permissible, but not all things are expedient." Paul implied in 1 Corinthians 5:5 that the member who engaged in a persistent and unrepentant incest relationship was still saved. This led others such as Luther to conclude Paul taught a Christian was *permitted* to commit fornication. While it might not be always *expedient,* fornication was permissible. This formula was identical to Paul's teaching that it was *permissible* to eat meat sacrificed to idols, even though it was not always *expedient* to do so. Only if by eating such meat you would harm the conscience of another should you refrain. With that same principle, Paul is understood in the Modern Gospel to permit Christians to fornicate *occasionally* without any fear and even commit repetitious unrepentant fornication while remaining saved all the while.

19. Charles Stanley, *Eternal Security: Can You Be Sure?* (Thomas Nelson Publishers: 1990) at 192.

Recapitulation of The Meaning of Revelation 2:14

To repeat, Revelation 2:14 states:

> But I have a few things against thee, because ***thou hast there some that hold the teaching of Balaam***, who taught Balak to cast a stumblingblock before the children of Israel, ***to eat things sacrificed to idols,*** and ***to commit fornication***.

The Christians at Pergamum were being criticized by Jesus for some members holding to the "teaching of Balaam." Who was Balaam? He was a figure who precisely prefigures Paul.

The only missing pieces were *first* whether Paul taught it was permissible to eat meat sacrificed to idols. We saw in the prior chapter that Paul taught it is permissible to eat meat sacrificed to idols. (See page 117.)

The *second* missing piece was whether Paul also taught it was permissible to commit fornication. We saw first that in Jesus' day, adultery and fornication were synonymous in the underlying vernacular in which Jesus spoke. We also saw that Paul permitted an act of adultery that Jesus squarely prohibited, *i.e.*, remarriage by a wife whose husband had no grounds for divorce or where a certificate of divorce had not been used at all.

Or, if we instead look at merely passages where Paul talks about fornication (which for Paul usually means unwed sex), Paul fares no better. While Paul has one, perhaps three verses, that disparage fornication, there is no verse clear-cut saying fornication is *impermissible*. Indeed, Paul's teachings lead Paulinists to insist Paul says fornication is permissible. All things are permissible, they quote Paul. Yet, not all things are expedient. So they insist, fornication may not be expedient, but it is not *per se* wrong. The Law is abrogated. To claim it is wrong *per se* is heretical legalism. Even if one performs fornication a thousand times a day, the young Luther says

Paul's grace teaching means we remain saved. Luther's youthful view is corroborated by every other mainstream interpreter of Paul's gospel. They appear to be correct because if you can lose your salvation for fornication then you keep it by obeying God, which would be a works-contingent salvation. Paul calls that heresy, plain and certain.

When you add up all the facts that parallel Paul to Revelation 2:14, the conclusion is overwhelming. Paul is certainly the intended author of the "teaching of Balaam" that Jesus identified in Revelation 2:14. He matches Balaam's life almost identically. He teaches it is permissible to eat meat sacrificed to idols. Finally, he also teaches it is permissible to commit fornication (*i.e.*, adultery in remarriage). Paul is also understood by leading commentators to have taught fornication as he used the term (*i.e.*, unwed sex) was (a) occasionally permissible, although it was not necessarily expedient to fornicate, with utterly no *negative* consequence; and (b) able to be committed repetitiously and without repentance with no repurcussion on salvation. There is therefore no ground to distinguish Paul from the teacher of Balaam's doctrine in Revelation 2:14. Thus, Jesus was identifying Paul in Revelation 2:14 by referring to Balaam.

Conclusion

When the early church leader Irenaeus in 180 A.D. defended Paul's authenticity from opponents of Paul *within the church*, Irenaeus argued that if you accept Luke's Gospel, then you must accept Luke's account in Acts that Jesus revealed himself to Paul. For Irenaeus, this vision experience sealed the case in favor of Paul. Thus for Irenaeus, once Paul has a vision of Jesus on a road, the case in favor of Paul is settled.[20] However, not once did the story of Balaam's experience on the road and temporary conversion into a true prophet cause Irenaeus to see the error in this argument. Here is Irenaeus' argument from circa 180 A.D. in defense of Paul:

> But again, we allege the same ***against those who do not recognize Paul as an apostle***: that they should either reject the other words of the Gospel which we have come to know through ***Luke alone,*** and not make use of them; or else, if they do receive all these, ***they must necessarily admit also that testimony concerning Paul,*** when he (Luke) tells us that the Lord spoke at first to him from heaven: 'Saul, Saul, why persecutest thou Me? I am Jesus Christ, whom thou persecutest.' [Acts 26:15]. (Irenaeus, *Against Heresies* Book III: 257.)[21]

However, Irenaeus missed the point. Paul could be a Balaam. He could be converted on a road ***for a time***, but later apostasize. Irenaeus' argument simply overlooks that clear example from Scripture. Thus, I accept Luke's Gospel and I accept Paul's account in Acts 22 of having a direct encounter with Jesus. However, it does not resolve the issue. Paul could still have been a Balaam later. Revelation 2:14 is Jesus telling me that Paul indeed was the modern Balaam of the New Testament church.

20.Please note that Paul's position in the New Testament church was still being disputed into 180 A.D. This was a dissent from good Christians whom Irenaeus presupposed accepted Luke's gospel, and would thereby be persuaded to accept Luke's account in Acts.

21.Irenaeus in this quote also made an incorrect supposition that Jesus in the three vision accounts in Acts 9, 22, and 26 appointed Paul an apostle. Jesus never does so. Instead, Jesus says Paul is to be a *martus*, a witness. For further discussion on that, see page 215 *et seq.* Even had Jesus appointed Paul an apostle, Irenaeus would also have been overlooking the case of Judas. The fact Judas was an apostle did not prevent his fall later. Thus, whether a true prophet or apostle, God gives us abundant examples that one can fall from such status.

8 *Does Jesus Share Salvation Doctrine with Paul?*

Introduction

Did Jesus and Paul have any doctrine in common on salvation? Some cite Luke 7:47 and others John 3:16. The Lucan passage is infrequently cited as compared to John 3:16. Luke's passage is viewed as potentially being consistent with Paul while John's passage is widely thought to be the same as Paul's gospel message. However, on close scrutiny, even these two passages of Jesus are indeed in conflict with Paul's salvation theology. Let's see why.

Luke 7:47

Jesus encountered a woman who loved Him much, washing His feet with her tears. Jesus declares her sins forgiven. He tells us why in ways that when Paulinists look closely at the passage, they cringe. Can Jesus forgive someone because they love much, and not on faith alone? Nevertheless, we read in Luke 7:47:

> Wherefore I say unto thee, Her sins, which are many, are forgiven; ***for she loved much***: but to whom little is forgiven, the same loveth little. (ASV).

The word-for-word translation of the literal Greek of the key phrase is: "released are her many sins ***because*** she loved much."[1]

Commentators on the Greek who accept Paul's view of salvation are fraught with dismay. Adam Clarke states:

> In the common translation her forgiveness is represented to be ***the consequence of her loving much***, which is causing the tree to produce the root, and not the root the tree [*i.e.*, it would contradict Paul's views]. I have considered *ioe* here as having the sense of *aeioe*, therefore;... we must suppose her love was the effect of her being pardoned, not the cause of it.

However, to arrive at Adam Clarke's solution, you have to suppose a completely different Greek word is used to erase the causation between her *love* and Jesus' *forgiveness of sins*. Clarke *confesses* this by suggesting a different Greek word would convey the meaning that *fits Pauline doctrine.*

Moreover, on close examination, the Greek is clear. The Greek conjunction underlying "***for*** she loved much" is *hoti*. Strong's #3754 says it means "causatively *because*" or can mean *that.* In this context, all the translations into English realize it has a *causative sense*. They render it *for.* Its more concrete synonym in English is *because*. The word *hoti* means *because* here, especially due to its clear placement in the sentence. To repeat, the literal Greek is: "released are her many sins ***because*** she loved much." Only the meaning *because* makes sense. The alternative meaning *that* would render the second part unintelligible.

Other commentators are so fraught with dismay they simply assert Jesus cannot mean what He says in Luke 7:47. Based on the presupposition of Paul's validity, they assert her great love was the "proof, not the reason for her forgiveness." (Robertson's *Word Pictures*.)

1. A more literal translation would also render the introductory *charin* as "for this reason" rather than use the vague term *wherefore*: "For this reason I am saying to you released are her many sins because she loved [*aorist tense*] much; to whom few [sins] are being forgiven [present indicative] they love [present indicative] little."

Somewhere along the way, commentators learned the power of repetition. They realized that if you repeat often enough an alleged truth of Christianity from Paul that is actually contrary to what Jesus says, you can create a social pressure to affix Paul's teaching upon Christ's teaching. This works because the listener recognizes Paul's teaching. The Christian is trained to ignore, however, that there is a mismatch between the words of Paul and Jesus. The repetition of Paul's doctrine serves to thwart Jesus' teachings every time. This wears down the Christian's critical sense to *understand the clear meaning of words.* The Christian who is barraged by the drum-beat of *salvation by faith alone* no longer senses the contradiction by Paul of Jesus. Any person free from this barrage can easily read Jesus' words and see the linguistic impossibility that both Paul and Jesus are saying the same thing. Thus, this galvanizing thumping on Paul's salvation themes has glued in place an adherence to Pauline teachings that actually contradict Jesus. Any slight questioning of the paradigm leads to firm and loud accusation that one is *returning to Rome.* The poor soul who holds up Jesus' words against Paul's is to be branded a heretic. Thus, repetition and social pressure has nullified our sense of a loyalty to Christ that should trump our loyalty to Paul. For these Paulinists, questioning Paul's validity has become non-sense. They assume the scholars and theologians have worked out what they themselves take no time to study. Social conditioning thereby has made Paul's doctrine, not Jesus' teachings, something that must be protected *at all costs*! It is like brainwashing. You can hear it over and over, like a mantra.

The commentators' approach to solving the dilemma of Luke 7:47 is just one more example of this mantra. The Pauline commentators vigorously utter the textually-unsupportable notion that Jesus does not mean the love she had was the "cause of her remission" of sins. This would be *works* in addition to faith, they admit. *It just cannot be viewed that way, they insist.* Yet, the very reason they must insist this is what Jesus means is because what Jesus says plainly is that her great love was part of the *causative* reasons her sins were forgiven. Jesus contradicts Paul. The only way to save Paul is to repetitiously insist Jesus' words do not mean what they literally mean.

As a result of this torture of Jesus' words, the Pauline interpretation of this passage is that Jesus meant she was forgiven for no particular reason other than faith. Of course, Jesus gave faith a role too in her salvation. "Thy faith has saved you." (Luke 7:50.) However, seeing *faith* as the sole reason for her forgiveness is wilful self-delusion. One is squeezing out of the passage only the one part that sounds like Paul. You are ignoring the *causative* statement glaring back at you that contradicts Pauline doctrine: "Released are her many sins *because* (hoti) she loved much." (Luke 7:47.)

The Uniqueness of Luke 7:50 in the Synoptics

What is most interesting is that in all of the Synoptic Gospels (Matthew, Mark and Luke), this is ***the only passage where Jesus goes on to say someone is saved by faith.*** Jesus next says to the woman (Luke 7:50):

> And he said unto the woman, ***Thy faith hath saved thee***; go in peace.

Yet, to repeat, the Greek is unmistakable that her love mixed with faith were the *causative* elements in "forgiveness" and "salvation." Jesus says she was forgiven and saved ***because*** "she loved much" and had "faith." Faith alone did not save this young woman!

We have more to say below on the strange fact that this is the ***only time in the Synoptic Gospels*** that faith is mentioned as having any *positive* role in salvation. As you can see, however, in this one example, it is faith and love in mixture that Jesus says leads to her forgiveness and being saved.

What About Faith in the Synoptics?

Faith is barely mentioned in Matthew, Mark and Luke. They are also known as the *Synoptic Gospels*. The special purpose of John's Gospel and why *believing* is so often mentioned awaits discussion below.

One Paulinist confesses the Synoptics are anti-Paul, but then provides an odd explanation:

> Ever notice that the first three gospels (the synoptic gospels) ***never explicitly speak of salvation through faith in Christ*** (except for [the non-canonical] Mark 16:16).[2] In fact in those gospels when Jesus is asked the question, 'What must I do to have eternal life?' he responds with the Law—***a performance based concept of righteousness.*** [It is not] the gospel of grace which is a faith based righteousness, which is...found in Paul's writings [such] as in Romans. Why the difference?
>
> I infer that the synoptic gospels were primarily to prepare people to hear the gospel of grace, ***rather than actually presenting the gospel message explicitly.*** [3]

There is a much more likely reason the Synoptics are antagonistic to Paul's doctrines than the reason this Paulinist suggests. It is so self-evident that it is startling it is never considered: the Synoptics were written *specifically* to counter the message of Paul!

The fact nothing in them confirms Paul's gospel of grace is startling *in its historical context*. Paul's many letters certainly were in circulation for at least 10-20 years continu-

2. For a discussion on the erroneous addition of Mark 16:16, see page 29.
3. *The Message:Attitudes of Faith* (Boston Christian Bible Study Resources: 2004) at http://www.bcbsr.com/topics/fj7.html (last accessed 2005).

ously *prior* to Matthew, Mark and Luke having been written. Standard dating of Mark is as early as 65 A.D. The Hebrew Matthew could be in the same vicinity. Luke was written between 64 and 85 A.D.[4] By comparison, Paul's letters date from the 40s through the 60s. Paul's writings were clearly in circulation for as much as twenty years when the Synoptics were written.

Yet, how strange that Matthew and Mark provide absolutely no confirmation of Paul's salvation-by-faith message! There is not a single passage in Matthew or Mark that links faith to salvation in a causal sense. This is true too of Luke, Paul's own companion.[5] The only half-exception is in Luke where the woman who bathes Jesus' feet in tears. Jesus says her "faith has saved her." However, as already noted, even there Luke's research led him to a passage that Jesus links both her "great love" and "faith" to salvation and forgiveness, not faith alone. (See Luke 17:47-50, and discussion page 157 *et seq.*)

Thus, as surprising as this may sound, if you look only at the Synoptic Gospels (*i.e.*, Matthew, Mark & Luke), ***Jesus actually never says that you obtain eternal life by faith alone.*** The only time faith is given a causal role, the

---

4. For a defense of early dating and discussion of standard dates, see John A.T. Robinson, *Redating the New Testament* (SCM Press: 1976).
5. Faith plays almost no role to mention in the synoptics. The only time it is described causing something is when Jesus heals people. He says "your faith has made you whole." (Matt. 9:22; Mark 5:34, 10:52, Luke 8:48, 17:19, 18:42.) We read what this means when Jesus says: "according to your faith let it be done unto you." (Matt. 9:29.) Otherwise, faith is not linked causally to anything. See Matt. 8:10, Luke 7:9 ("I have not found so great faith"); Matt. 8:26, 14:31, 16:8, 17:20, Luke 12:28 ("Oh ye of little faith"); Matt. 9:2, Mark 2:5, Luke 5:20, ("seeing their faith"); Matt. 15:28 ("great is thy faith"); Matt. 21:21, Luke 17:6 ("If you have faith and doubt not...." "if you had faith..."); Matt. 23:23 ("weightier matters... faith"); Mark 4:40, Luke 8:25 ("have you not faith?" "where is your faith?" (storm on the Galilee); Mark 11:22 ("have faith in God" in relation to prayer); Luke 17:5 ("increase our faith"); Luke 18:8 ("shall he find faith"); Luke 22:32 (prayed "your faith fail not").

young woman is forgiven and saved "for she loved much" ***and*** had "faith." (Luke 7:47-50.) Faith and love are mixed. They were the causative elements in her forgiveness and salvation, according to Jesus. Thus, rarely, if ever, does anyone look at the Synoptics for support of Paul's doctrine of salvation by faith, let alone his ideas of salvation by faith alone.

The Synoptics' Doctrine on Works Proves Its Agenda on Paul

What demonstrates beyond doubt that the Synoptics were designed to prove Paul as a false apostle is their strong emphasis on salvation by works beyond mere faith. As one author puts it, in the Synoptics, the "main path to salvation that [Jesus] described is based on good works and attitudes."[6]

In fact, in the Synoptics, the point is that mere faith without works is useless. There is no countervailing Pauline concept that if you *once believed* this somehow excuses or satisfies the requirement of repentance from sin, good works, and obedience to the Ten Commandments to enter "eternal life." For example:

- See Matthew 25:31-46 (the sheep who do charity go to heaven; those goats who refuse go to hell).
- See Matt. 19:17 and Luke 10:25-27 (Jesus' answer how to have eternal life starts with keeping the Law, quoting Deuteronomy 6:5 and Leviticus 19:18).
- See Matt. 5:20 (your righteousness must exceed the Pharisees to enter the kingdom of heaven which Jesus then defines as not cursing, lusting, etc.).
- See Matt. 16:2 (Son of Man will come and "reward each according to his works").
- See Mark 9:42-48 (better to cut off a body part causing you to sin and enter heaven maimed than to not repent of sin and go to hell whole).

---

6. *SALVATION: According to the synoptic gospels* reprinted at http://www.religioustolerance.org/chr_savj1.htm (last visited 2005).

- See Matt. 25:14-30 (servants who produce fruit are saved; the servant who produced no fruit is "unprofitable" and thrown outside where there is weeping and gnashing of teeth; *cf.* Matt. 13:42 the ensnared are thrown into the "fiery furnace" where there is weeping and gnashing).
- See Matt. 13:3-23 & Luke 8:5-15 (those who "believe for a while" but in time of temptation fall away or who are choked and bring no fruit to completion are lost, but the one who in a good and noble heart brings forth fruit to completion in patient endurance is saved).

What About John's Gospel?

If we look at the context of John's very different recollections than those in the Synoptics, we will see the Apostle John had the same secondary objective as the Synoptics: to address the question of Paul.

What About Faith in John's Gospel?

Luther once said that the "science of theology is nothing else but Grammar exercised on the words of the Holy Spirit."[7] Luther is correct that deciphering the Bible's meaning must start with the grammar of each particular verse. If you have the wrong grammatical construction, you do not have the *intended meaning*. Thus, for example, the correct meaning of John 3:16 is dependent on having the correct grammatical understanding of the verse.

If you look at John 3:16, when properly translated, it is not about salvation by faith. It is about endurance. It is about Matthew 10:22: "He who endures to the end shall be

7. Johann Brecht Bengel, *Gnomon of the New Testament* (ed. A. Fausset) (trans. J. Bandinel, J. Bryce, W. Fletcher)(Edinburgh: T&T Clark, 1866) at 1.44 (quoting Luther), as quoted in Alan J. Thompson, "The Pietist Critique of Inerrancy? J.A. Bengel's *Gnomon* as a Test Case," *JETS* (March 2004) at 79.

saved." In fact, all of John's Gospel uses the Greek present active verb tense for *pisteuo*, meaning he who *continues to believe/trust*. The theme of John is that trust must endure for salvation to be realized, not that a one-time faith saves.

One can easily see this by reading *Young's Literal Translation* of John's Gospel. Young renders each Greek present active participle of *believe* as "is believing." (John 1:12; 3:15,16,18,36; 5:24; 6:35,40,47; 7:38; 11:25-26; 12:11, 37, 44, 46; 14:12; 17:20.)[8] The form *is believing* is known as the English Present Continuous Tense of *believe*.

For an extensive explanation why *Young's Literal* reads this way, it is in Appendix A: *Greek Issues*. (A short synopsis will appear below.)

Thus, all these verses in John's Gospel have been mistranslated in the KJV and NIV to be talking about salvation caused by a one-time verbal or mental acknowledgment (*believes*) of Jesus as savior. This translation matched Paul's salvation formula in Romans 10:9. Paul used the Greek *aorist* tense for *believes* in Romans 10:9, which corresponds to a one-time faith. However, John's literal words in the continuous tense—the Greek *present active tense*—have nothing to do with a one-time action—the Greek *aorist tense*. The meaning of John 3:16 is in the true translation of the verb tense: *continues to believe* or *trust*. All who keep on trusting in Jesus "should" be saved, says John 3:16.[9] It is about endurance in trust, not salvation by faith.

In fact, one could interpret John's gospel as being intentionally anti-Pauline.

For consider that when you compare John to the Synoptics (*i.e.*, Matthew, Mark & Luke), Jesus never utters any statement in the Synoptics comparable to John about *faith*. Why was John summoning this message about *pisteuo* from

---

8. To verify the Greek verb's grammatical usage, download the *Interlinear Scripture Analyzer* free on the Internet.
9. For the explanation why the KJV "should," and not the NIV "shall have eternal life" is correct, see Footnote 15 on page 383.

his memory with the inspiration of the Holy Spirit? Precisely because Paul had made such a big focus on faith. Paul's influence was growing although not as significant as we all assume.[10] The Synoptics had not enough impact on the budding church to expose the stark difference between Paul and Jesus. Some Christians were still persuaded that Paul had the true gospel. Thus, John's gospel was the Holy Spirit's inspiration to John to fix this, by showing Jesus' true doctrines on faith and believing.

In other words, John was remembering all the times Jesus used the word *pistis* or its relative *pisteuo* (the verb form, *to believe* or *trust*) when *linked* somehow to eternal life. (Of course, Jesus spoke in Aramaic or Hebrew, but John was translating to Greek.) This way we could make a comparison between Jesus and how Paul uses the similar word in relation to salvation. No one has offered a more reasonable explanation why John reads so differently than the Synoptics. There was something pressuring John. It was the question of Paul.

Thus, John must have asked the Holy Spirit to call to his mind every instance Jesus mentioned faith as somehow causally related to salvation. This way we could examine Paul's teaching in this regard. This produced a Gospel with a very different set of recollections which were not as ***important*** to the original Gospel writers.

How John's Gospel Addresses the Issue of Faith & Salvation

So how does John answer the key question whether a one-time faith or a one-time confession saves as Paul teaches in Romans 10:9? Does John back Paul up? Or does John expose Paul as a false teacher?

10.See *Paul or James' Church: Who Was The Most Successful Evangelist?* (Available exclusively online at www.jesuswordsonly.com.)

The answer is amazing. Everywhere that *faith/trust* is mentioned as causally connected to eternal life in the Gospel of John, it is in a verb form of the present active in Greek. (See John 3:16, 5:24, 6:35, 37, 40, 47 *etc.*) Every time!

Thus, John's Gospel is repetitious on the issue of salvation. This is for emphasis by John. He could not recall it once said *any other way*. What does this imply?

A short synopsis follows which summarizes the discussion in Appendix A. Greek grammar makes John's point unmistakable.

Synopsis of Appendix A on the Greek Present Active

First, unlike English, Greek has a specific verb tense for a one-time action. It is known as the *aorist* tense. This can be rendered in English by use of the English Simple Present Tense, *e.g.*, "believes." We can read "believes" in English to mean a one time expression of faith.[11] English Simple Present Tense thus can ***correspond to the aorist participle*** in Greek.

Paul in Romans 10:9 uses the *aorist* tense to signify salvation is by one time events: "if ever (*ean*) you confess (*aorist active subjunctive*) by your mouth that Jesus is Lord and [if] you [ever] believe (*aorist active subjunctive*) that God raised Him from the dead, you shall be saved." (This is my literal word-for-word translation.) Thus, Paul is using the Greek *aorist* verb tense. He means you are saved if you ever once confess and believe. No continuity is implied in verse nine.

11.For this reason, Charles Stanley, the head of the Baptists, says "believes" in John 3:16 (which is the KJV and NIV translation) means a one-time faith. Stanley explains "believes"—the English simple present tense of *to believe*—can mean a one-time event that does not have to continue. From this, Stanley deduces a one-time faith saves. (Charles Stanley, *Eternal Security of the Believer* (Nelson: 1990) at 95.)

By contrast, in Greek, the ***exact opposite*** meaning from the *aorist* tense is conveyed by the Greek *present indicative active* or *present participle active.* In Greek, these two forms of the present active tense mean the action is continuing. It is best translated into English using "continues to" or "keeps on" in front of the English gerund.[12] For example, "he who continues to believe" or "he who keeps on trusting" is the better translation.

This distinction is confessed by leading Calvinists who are staunch Paulinists. Dr. James White is a well-respected Calvinist. He writes about the verb tense in John 6:35-45 in his book *Drawn by the Father: A Summary of John 6:35-45* (Reformation Press: 1999) at pages 10-11:

> Throughout this passage an important truth is presented that again ***might be missed by many English translations.*** When Jesus describes the one who comes to him and who ***believes*** in him [3:16, 5:24, 6:35, 37, 40, 47, etc.], he uses the ***present tense*** to describe this coming, ***believing***, or, in other passages, hearing or seeing. The present tense refers to a ***continuous, on-going action***. The Greek contrasts this kind of action against the ***aorist tense***, which is ***a point action***, a single action in time that is ***not on-going***.... The wonderful promises that are provided by Christ are ***not for those who do not truly and continuously believe***. The faith that saves is a living faith, a faith that ***always looks*** to Christ as Lord and Savior.

12.See Appendix A: *Greek Issues* for a full discussion. Young's Literal Translation always renders the Greek present indicative active or the present participle active with "is...ing" (the gerund form of the verb). This is the English present continuous tense. It is a satisfactory rendering. However, to catch the nuance of the Greek, the NIV was correct to use "keeps on" or "continues to..." as it did so often. However, only *Young's Literal* translation has had the courage so far to fix John 3:16 to read more accurately.

However, this is news to most Christians. The King James Version of the Bible (KJV) was primarily a production of Calvinist Puritans. The KJV always rendered the Greek present active tense with the English Simple Present Tense (*i.e.*, "believes") rather than the English Continuous Present (*i.e.*, "is believing" or "keeps on believing"). The KJV thus conveyed a completely *opposite* meaning than John intended. The KJV English translation corresponds to the Greek *aorist* tense of Romans 10:9, not the Greek *present active tense* of Apostle John. The KJV corresponds to a teaching of a one-time faith should save rather than an ongoing trust doing so.

The KJV was either protecting Paul from the implication of John's gospel or committed a gross blunder. The New International Version (NIV) fixed the KJV translation of the Greek present active in over seventeen instances by adding to the verb clause "keeps on" or "continues to" each time. The only principal time the NIV would not correct the translation of the Greek present active was when the Greek word for *believes* was involved.[13] The NIV left us still in the dark on the most important doctrine of all: salvation. There is no defense for this inconsistency.

The NIV thereby held back the true meaning of John 3:16 is *keeps on* or *continues to believe/trust.* The NIV was unwilling to inform us that John *contradicts* Paul. We are actually being misled by the NIV to believe John was agreeing with Paul that a one-time faith saves! If this were true, John in John 3:16 would have used the *aorist* tense just as Paul does in Romans 10:9. It did not happen.

When the translation is repaired, other verses in John take on diametrically different meanings as well. For example, another Paulinist favorite is John 5:24. Instead of a one-time faith causing you to have passed from death to life, it now depends on *continuous* trust on your part. John 5:24 correctly translated reads:

13.See Appendix A: *Greek Issues* for a full discussion at page v.

> I keep telling you (*present active indicative*) the one who keeps on listening (*present participle active*) to my teaching and keeps on believing (*present participle active*) in the one who sent me (*aorist active participle*) keeps on having (*present active indicative*) eternal life and does not come (*present middle deponent*) into condemnation but has departed (*perfect active indicative*) out of death into life.

You can verify the verb tenses by downloading the free *Interlinear Scripture Analyzer.*

Thus, while Paul says a one-time (*aorist*) belief in certain facts saves you (Romans 10:9) and now there is no condemnation (Romans 8:1), a contrary meaning arises from John 5:24. There is no *condemnation* for those who *keep on* listening to Jesus and who *keep on* trusting/believing in the Father. In other words, John is remembering words of Jesus *at total odds* with Paul. Yet, our KJV and NIV lead us to believe there is agreement between Paul and Jesus by using in John 5:24 *hears* and *believes.* These are in the English Simple Present form. They are not in the English Continuous Present. Both the KJV and NIV translations use a tense that corresponds to Paul's *aorist* tense in Romans 10:9, not John's actual *present active* tense. It is completely obvious when you peak under the covers and look at the verb tenses. Now anyone can do this by using the *Interlinear Scripture Analyzer* free for download. The emperor has no clothes any more.

If you are tempted to throw out John's Gospel now that you know its intent is anti-Pauline, it is pointless to do so. You would also have to get rid of Luke. For the verb *pisteuo* was used in the same manner as John in Luke's account of the Parable of the Sower. Jesus in this account uses *believing* in the identical manner as in John's Gospel. For in Luke, Jesus identifies a *believing* that continues for a time but then stops. Jesus indicates this person becomes withered, apostate and lost. Luke, like John, viewed a faith/trust that continues as essential to salvation. We discuss this next.

What The Parable of the Sower Confirms About Faith in John's Gospel

The Parable of the Sower is the only other passage in the Synoptics that talks about faith and salvation, but does so in a *negative manner.* The Parable of the Sower teaches that the failure to continue in *faith* or *trust* leads to becoming lost. It never says faith that later fails saves. In fact, the only person saved among the seeds is the one who *produces fruit to completion.* Thus, in this parable Jesus addresses faith and works in a way totally at odds with Paul. Now please note this is not a parable that Paulinists can avoid by claiming its meaning remains a mystery. Jesus explained its symbolic meaning in *excruciating detail.*

Let's analyze with care the Parable of the Sower.

The first seed never believes because Satan snatches the word from his heart before he can believe "and be saved." (Luke 8:12.) Unlike the first seed, the second seed (*i.e.*, the seed on rocky soil) (Luke 8:6) "sprouted." Jesus explains this means the second seed "received the word with joy" and "***believes for a while***." (Luke 8:13.)

In Luke 8:13, the Greek tense for "believes" is the present indicative active of *pisteuo.* Jesus is saying the seed on rocky ground "***keeps*** on believing." Jesus then adds an adverb meaning "for a while." In this context, the present indicative is indistinguishable from the present participle active of *pisteuo* which is used uniformly in John's Gospel.[14]

14. The Greek word for *believes* in Luke 8:13 is *pisteuosin.* This is one form of the present participle active when a masculine dative is involved. *Pisteuosin* is also a present indicative active if the subject is a third person plural. (Walcott-Hort online at *Perseus.com.*) The subject pronoun in 8:13 is *hoi*, a masculine plural noun. Thus, *believes* in Luke 8:13 is the present indicative active. By comparison, *believe* in John 3:16 is *pisteuon*, which is the present participle active because the subject is a masculine nominative. This difference in *believes* between Luke 8:13 and John 3:16 is not substantive. Both correspond to a continuous tense. See Appendix A: *Greek Issues.*

Logically, if the first seed would have been "saved" had Satan not prevented faith from forming, this second seed must be "saved." Thus, Jesus is saying the second seed is "saved" for a while because it believed for a while yet the first seed is never saved because it never believed.

Jesus goes on to say the second seed then "withered away" (*i.e.*, shriveled up). (Luke 8:6). Jesus explains this means it fell into "temptation" (sinned) and "fell away." (Luke 8:13, *aphistami.*) Why did it fall away? It shriveled up "because it lacked moisture." (Luke 8:6.) The Greek of this verb was present active as well, meaning "it did not continue to have moisture." Jesus explains again why, saying the seed "did not have root." (Luke 8:13.) The verb, however, is again present active in Greek (*ecousin*) and means "it ***did not keep holding*** on to the Root."

TABLE 4. **Parable of the Sower: Second Seed**

Second Seed Metaphor	Jesus' Explanation
sprouted	received the word with joy
	continued to believe for a while
did not continue to have moisture	did not keep holding to the root
withered away (shriveled up)	tempted, fell away

Thus, Jesus is saying that someone who received the word with Joy, "continued to ***believe*** for a while," and thus "sprouted," then fell into temptation. This person ends up withered away (dead). Dead means no life. No life means no eternal life. The reason is they "did not keep holding to the Root" and so they "fell away." This was a lesson about faith lacking endurance and being destroyed by sin (temptation). Thus, it is a negative message about faith. ***It is not an example of faith saving, but how faith can be brought to naught by sin.***

What was the warning Jesus intended in this parable? Keep holding on to the Root. Jesus is the Root. Hold to Jesus' words and you will not fall into temptation (sin). Let go and you are opposite of the saints who "keep the commandments of God, and the faith of Jesus." (Rev. 14:12.) By falling into temptation you fail to "keep...the commandments...and faith of Jesus" and become lost.

There is no missing this point if you see the precise parallel to Revelation 2:4-5.

There Jesus tells the Ephesians they have "left your first love," and "art fallen," so "repent" and do your "first works."

Compare this then to the second seed in the Parable of the Sower. The second seed had "joy" in the word at first, like the Ephesians had "love at first." The second seed "sprouted" and thus had "first works," just like the Ephesians. The second seed then sinned and "fell away," just as the Ephesians "art fallen." The solution, as always, is "repent," as Jesus told the Ephesians in Revelation 2:4-5 and do your "first works."

Now who is the only saved person in the Parable of the Sower? It is the fourth seed, which is the only one who brings forth *fruit* or...dare I use the synonym...works.

The fourth seed is the good and noble heart that is saved. To understand the fourth seed, we must see the contrast to the third seed. The KJV says the third seed "brings no fruit to perfection." (Luke 8:14, KJV.) However, the translation is lacking. The third seed is choked by thorns (*i.e.*, the worries of this world) and so does not *telesphorousin*. This Greek word combines *teleos*, which means *end*, with *phore*, which means *to produce, bring forth*. Together, the two words literally mean "to complete" or "bring to a finish." *Telesphore* is often used with regard to fruit, pregnant women or animals. (*Robertson's Word Pictures*.) *Telesphorousin* is the present active form in Greek. So it means "did not keep on producing to the end" or "did not continue to the finish." The idea of "bringing fruit to *perfection*" is incorrect. The word "fruit" is also not actually in this verse. Completion, not perfection, is in view. They did not *telephorousin*, *i.e.*, they did not keep on producing to completion. They were choked off. This is reminiscent of the Sardisians whom Jesus tells in Revelation 3:3

that their works are "not fulfilled," *i.e.*, incomplete. (*Cfr.* KJV "works not perfect"). Failure to complete your works leads to a loss of salvation.

Knowing the flaws of the third seed opens our understanding of the fourth seed's reason for being saved. The fourth seed, by contrast, "fell into good ground, and grew, and brought forth fruit a hundredfold." (Luke 8:8.) Listen to Jesus' explanation of why this person alone among the four is ultimately saved:

> And that in the good ground, these are such as in an honest and good heart, having heard the word, hold it fast, and ***bring forth fruit with patience***. (Luke 8:15 ASV).

The Greek verb for "hold it fast" is in the Greek present active again. It means "keep on holding down." It is not hold "fast," but hold "down." (*Robertson's Word Pictures.*) This is a significant point. As Jesus tells the parable, the devil swooped down and stole the word from the first sewn seed, depriving it of salvation. By continuing to hold down the word, the fourth seed is guarding itself. It is doing everything possible to keep Satan from snatching the word away. It is the same meaning behind John 8:51. He who has "kept guard" over Jesus' word "should never [ever] taste death." (John 8:51, ASV.)

Finally, what does it mean that the only saved person in this parable "brings forth fruit with patience." (Luke 8:15, ASV)? Salvation depends on completing works to the end.

Luke 8:15 really means: "who keep carrying on producing fruit with endurance." The Greek verb this time is *karpos* (carrying) combined with *phore* (produce, bear) in the Greek present indicative. So it has a continuous meaning. This is followed by *hupomeno* in Greek. In most translations of this verse, *hupomeno* is rendered as *patience.* However, almost everywhere else *hupomeno* appears in the NT it is translated as *endurance,* which is the more likely intended meaning of Jesus. The combination of *karpos* and *phore* implies fruit-bearing by definition. This parallels Luke 8:8 which mentions "fruit a hundredfold." Thus, literally, Jesus is saying the saved seed "keeps carrying on producing fruit with endurance." This is in sharp contrast with the third seed which was lost because it did not "continue to the finish" or "produce to completion." (Luke 8:14.)

So let's build a diagram of the saved person in the Parable of the Sower.

TABLE 5. **Parable of the Sower: Fourth Seed**

Fourth Seed (The Saved)	Jesus' Explanation
good ground	noble and good heart
seed sewn	heard the word
grew	kept holding the word down (protecting it)
keeps on producing fruit a hundredfold	keeps on carrying on producing fruit with endurance. *Cfr.* third seed fails to produce to the finish

Here is Jesus' salvation formula in a nutshell. Producing fruit is never optional. Fruitlessness and being choked are pictures of the lost, even including those who "kept on believing for a while" and who "received" the word with joy at first. In fact, Jesus' point is even more adamant than just that: Jesus is saying partial fruitfulness is not enough. Jesus portends gloom for the one who has growth and then is choked off by thorns. Your initial good works are forgotten if you do not finish and complete well. Instead, you must endure to the end to be saved. This is an echo of Matthew 10:22 once more. It is reminiscent of Ezekiel 33:12. Salvation by faith alone is clearly refuted. Salvation by works alone is not approved either. However, salvation by endurance in good works to the end is crucial besides faith. So says the Lord Jesus Christ.

To hold onto Pauline 'faith alone' doctrine, one has to do many twists and turns with this parable. Jesus explained it, so you cannot say it is a parable *hard to understand*. Jesus already explained it!

Luther Could Not Come Up With A Gloss To Solve the Parable of the Sower

In fact, no one has ever properly explained how Jesus' Parable of the Sower can even remotely line up consistent with Paul. Luther's effort is so untenable that it proves how absolutely impossible it is to reconcile the two. Luther must have realized Jesus contradicts Paul. Thus, he injects Paul's doctrine of faith, not works, into what saves the second seed. Luther then ignores how this mismatches the rest of what the parable means.

Luther begins his commentary properly. The first type who has their seed snatched are those who "hear the word" but do not understand it. (*Sermons of Martin Luther*, Vol. II, at 114.)[15] These "never believe" and never become saved. (*Id.*, at 115.)

Luther then says the second seed knows the correct doctrine of salvation, *i.e.*, "they know the real truth" that they are saved by "faith without works" (Paul's Gospel). However, "they do not persevere." He adds: "when it comes to the test that they must suffer harm, disgrace and loss of life or property, then they fall and deny it....in times of persecution they deny or keep silence about the Word."

Luther in essence is saying that they lose their salvation because under pressure they deny this truth that salvation is by faith alone. This is a bizarre self-contradiction. If you

15.Martin Luther, "The Parable of the Sower," *The Precious and Sacred Writings of Martin Luther* (Minneapolis, MN: Lutherans in All Lands, 1906) Vol. 11 reprinted as *The Sermons of Martin Luther* (Grand Rapids, Michigan: Baker Book House) (1983) Vol. II at 113 *et seq*.

can lose your salvation by losing faith in the principle of faith alone, then faith alone does not save you. You must *endure* or *persevere* in the doctrine of faith alone or be lost. This is a self-contradiction, because then faith alone did not save you. Faith and ***perseverance in faith alone*** saves you. These two ideas are self-contradictory: if you must persist in faith to be saved, then *persistence*, not the faith alone, is necessary for salvation. Hence, Luther's solution is nonsensical. (Anyone who has read eternal security arguments know that they reject Luther's argument precisely because salvation then depends on more than a one-time faith. Luther is actually contradicting Paul to save Paul from the Parable of the Sower.)

Luther's comments on the third group are enlightening as well. This group of seeds "always possess the absolutely pure Word...." (*Id.*, at 116.) Their fault is "they do not ***earnestly*** give themselves to the Word, but become ***indifferent*** and sink in the cares, riches and pleasures of this life...." (*Id.*, at 117.) They are thus apparently initially saved. Luther says "these have all in the Word that is needed for their salvation, but they do not make any use of it, and they rot in this life in carnal pleasures." Luther seems to understand Jesus is saying their problem is sin, not lack of proper faith. Luther says that despite the proper knowledge of the Gospel, "they do not bring under subjection their flesh." (*Id.*)

This leads Luther to the correct conclusion why the fourth seed is saved. Luther says they "bring forth fruit with patience, those who hear the Word and *steadfastly retain it*, meditate upon it and *act in harmony with it*." This leads to as true a statement as you will ever hear by Luther:

> Here we see why it is no wonder there are so few true Christians, for all the seed does not fall into good ground, but only the fourth and small part; and that they are ***not to be trusted who boast they are Christians*** and praise the teaching of the Gospel. *Id.* at 118.

Luther realizes that salvation depends in the Parable, as Jesus depicts it, on *YOU!* It depends on the earnestness of *your response and productivity!*

This is the end of Luther's substantive commentary. What did he do? He explained Jesus' parable correctly. Yet, he pretended it was consistent with Paul by injecting Paul's gospel as what saved the second and third seeds initially. Luther did so without acknowledging it was self-contradictory nonsense. How can a seed that is saved by faith alone have to persevere and not succumb to sin? How can it lose salvation by being overcome by the thorns (pleasures) of this life? Nor did Luther try to ever explain away why the saved fourth seed alone had completed works.

Luther's response is a perfect example of how people retain Paul even when he contradicts Jesus. Luther is conceding certain unavoidable aspects of this parable are at direct odds with Paul. Yet by injecting Paul's wording in the middle, Luther makes it appear that Jesus' words are compatible with Paul's words. In this manner, Luther has somehow rationalized away that a conflict exists.

It is as Isaiah prophesied: "the wisdom of their wise men shall perish, and the understanding of their prudent men shall be hid." (Isaiah 29:14.)

Comparing the Parable of the Sower to John's Gospel

Finally, now we can make a comparison between the Parable of the Sower and John's Gospel.

John and Luke use *pisteuo* in the present active verb form to make the same point about faith. In Luke, saving faith cannot be a seed that fails to "keep holding onto the Root." Thus, the Parable of the Sower and John have the identical concept of faith that pertains to salvation: it must continue. It must endure. If the believer fails to keep enduring to the end, he or she will become lost. ***Faith in the gospels is thus frequently portrayed as tenuous:*** as something that is insufficient alone, can fail, is ruined by sin, and that exhortations are necessary to remind us to endure in bringing forth fruit *to the end.*

Conclusion

The Parable of the Sower is an amazing nugget of Jesus' doctrine. For here is the whole *true* gospel of salvation from Jesus' lips. It is all contained in a very unassuming Parable of the Sower. Jesus tells you how to be saved and what is necessary to complete your salvation. Jesus tells you also how to be lost even after you have faith and accepted His word with joy and experience initial growth ("sprouted").

Accordingly, the Parable of the Sower puts an end to the salvation by faith alone idea. It puts an end to the idea that producing fruit is not essential. It shows the folly of thinking you can get to heaven having believed and withered, or having grown significantly and then having been choked, never bringing your works to completion.

Thus Jesus in this parable shows the error of Paul's starkly different doctrine. If you read Paul, ***it is all over once the seed is successfully sown***, no matter what happens next. Paul's main salvation verses at odds with this Parable of the Sower are well-known:

- Romans 3:28 ("man is justified by faith apart from observing the law").
- Romans 4:5 ("To the man who does not work, but trusts God who justifies the wicked, his faith is credited as righteousness").
- Gal. 5:4 ("You who are trying to be justified by law have been alienated from Christ; you have fallen away from grace").
- Romans 7:6 ("Now, by dying to what once bound us, we have been released from the law, so that we serve in a new way of the Spirit, and not in the old way of the written code").
- Gal. 2:16 ("A man is not justified by observing the law, but by faith in Jesus Christ, because by observing the law no one will be justified").

- Ephesians 2:8-9 ("For it is by grace that you have been saved, through faith, this not from yourselves, it is the gift of God, not by works, so that no one can boast.")

Paul has a *different voice* than our Lord Jesus. Paul's themes are *alien* to Jesus's message of salvation. They undercut, if not destroy, the message of Jesus. The true sheep of Jesus *recognize* His voice, and will not follow another. (John 10:27-29.) Who are you following?

Thus, how many times must Jesus make the same points about repentance from sin and productivity at odds with Paul's *different message* before we will listen? If we think the Parable of the Sower is some distorted addition to Scripture, then think again. It appears in all three Synoptic gospels. (Matt. 13:3 *et seq*; Luke 8:5 *et seq*; Mark 4:3 *et seq*.) There is no lineage of any early manuscript that ever omitted it. You have to deal with Jesus' Words alone versus Paul's different message.

The fact we cannot find Paul's gospel in Jesus' words brings us back to the fundamental questions presented in this book:

- When will we finally make a commitment to keeping Jesus' words only?
- What is our *Biblical* justification for adding Paul to Scripture?
- What fulfilled prophecy did Paul give?
- Even if Paul gave a valid prophecy, does Paul seek to seduce us from following the Law and thus is disqualified from being added to Scripture by virtue of the Law's strict *disqualification* rule in Deuteronomy 4:2 and 13:1-5 and Isaiah 8:20?

9 *Is Jesus' Salvation Doctrine in Revelation A Rebuttal to Paul?*

Revelation Is A Post-Pauline Writing of an Apostle

Key features of the Book of Revelation are that:

- It is written long *after* Paul's writings.
- It was written by one of the twelve apostles.
- It was written in a region where Paul's writings were available to Apostle John.
- The churches addressed are in Gentile lands, thus potentially under the influence of Paul.
- Only one church of the seven churches mentioned was one that Paul visited (according to the Bible): the church at Ephesus.
- ***Jesus*** is the ***actual speaker*** in much of Revelation.

Thus, Jesus could address the key issue about Paul's ministry: is Paul correct that salvation is by grace through faith alone without works (Eph. 2:8-9; Rom. 4:4)?

Jesus in the Book of Revelation is speaking after Paul's ministry. Jesus has every opportunity to confirm or disaffirm Paul. Jesus has every opportunity to skewer Paul on doctrine or confirm Paul. Jesus has the opportunity to identify Paul as a thirteenth apostle or restate the number of apostles as only twelve. What does Jesus do?

First, *grace* is mentioned only twice in Revelation. The word is used as part of greetings and farewells. (Rev. 1:4; 22:21.) *Grace* is never mentioned as part of salvation statements. Nor are *faith* and *believing* ever mentioned as saving doctrines *anywhere* in the Book of Revelation.

"Grace and peace to you." Rev. 1:4

"The grace of the Lord Jesus Christ be with the saints." Rev. 21:22

Yet, salvation themes from James, the Parable of the Sower, and the Parable of the Ten Virgins are evoked repeatedly: repentance, the spirit flickering out, faith becoming dead due to incomplete works, casting out those with lukewarm works, and giving the crown of life to those who resist apostasizing. Jesus is backing up James' salvation theology to the hilt!

Also, Jesus never mentions a thirteenth apostle. Instead, Jesus portrays there are only twelve apostles for eternity. The New Jerusalem is built on the twelve foundation stones which the twelve apostles represent. Paul is left out completely.

This emphasis on works and ignoring grace doctrine appears to be no accident from even a superficial examination of Revelation. Despite Paul's supposed popularity and alleged approval by Jesus and the twelve, there is not the slightest approving mention of Paul in Revelation even though it post-dates Paul's ministry and death. Instead, the doctrinal contradiction between Jesus and Paul is repeatedly exposed in the Book of Revelation.

Paulinists Admit Revelation is Anti-Pauline

Paulinists are completely aware of the anti-Pauline nature of the Book of Revelation. Most of the time, they avoid mentioning it. Luther was willing to say he could not see the 'Holy Spirit' in the book. He insisted the Book of

Revelation must be non-canonical. (See page 370.) Calvin did a commentary on every book in the New Testament other than the Book of Revelation. The Calvinist Westminster Confession of 1647 initially excluded the Book of Revelation from inspired canon.[1]

Other Paulinists openly recognize the problem and boldly decry the Book of Revelation. These Paulinists do so apparently unaware that Revelation can *truly* be linked to Apostle John based on the witness of his friend Papias. Thinking they can prove it is non-apostolic, they let down their guard on the Book of Revelation. They boldly proclaim the Jesus presented in the book of Revelation is *heretical* because this Jesus *contradicts* Paul on salvation issues.

In an article entitled *Why the Book of Revelation is Heresy*, Dr. Weakly—a Methodist Minister with a Masters in Theology—unwittingly lays out a case against Paul while he thinks he is debunking the Book of Revelation as heresy. We read:

> Would Jesus vomit you and me out of the Kingdom of heaven for being only luke warm?
>
> Would Jesus change salvation by faith back to salvation by works?
>
> ****
>
> Pergamum (2: 12) is in Satan's territory. It held fast and did not deny Jesus during persecutions. But [John of] Patmos' Jesus ***rebukes them for eating food sacrificed to idols*** (2: 14). Here Patmos' ***Jesus contrasts with Paul who said this is permitted*** (1 Cor. 8).

1. See "Reformation Doubts About the Canonicity of Revelation" on page 9 of my article *The Authenticity of the Book of Revelation* available online at http://www.jesuswordsonly.com.

Sardis (3: 1) is judged by Patmos' Jesus as being dead for lacking works. If their works do not improve, Patmos' Jesus will come undetected and save only those in Sardis who have good works. ***Contradicting [Paul's] Gospel, Jesus, Patmos' salvation is by works and not by faith.***

Philadelphia (3: 7) has done everything right according to Patmos' Jesus. They have endured patiently. If they will just keep on enduring, they will receive their reward. ***Reward here is based on enduring rather than believing.*** It is ***these who endure that Patmos' Jesus will save.*** Those who cannot handle persecutions are outside the blessings. [Patmos'] Jesus is entirely different [from Pauline doctrine].****

Laodice (3: 14) is neither hot nor cold so Patmos Jesus will ***vomit the lukewarm Christians out of his mouth*** expel them from the body of Christ (3: 15,16)....Patmos' Jesus qualifies who he will bless by their works, ***their endurance being the measure by which they are judged worthy to be saved and remain saved.***

Works are the basis salvation for Patmos' Jesus. That doctrine is specifically stated in *Revelation*'s twentieth chapter (20: 12,13).

****

John Patmos' Jesus salvation by works takes away this 'blessed assurance.' The result of Revelation's doctrines is that no one can know their status with God until they are raised from the dead and judged (20: 12,13).

John Patmos' Jesus is that of the Old Testament God, holding grudges, ruling with an 'iron rod,'

> ***judging our works,*** and viciously punishing. His is not the loving Abba Heavenly Father of Apostle John's Jesus.
>
> ***'Revelation' continues the ancient argument about 'works' (James' Letter) versus 'faith' alone (Paul) that is explained in Paul's letters***, (Romans 10, esp. 10:4).[2]

These are excellent points. Dr. Weakley agrees Paul permits eating meat sacrificed to idols. However, he also agrees Jesus in Revelation prohibits it. Paul says salvation is by faith (alone), without works, but Dr. Weakley say Jesus in Revelation repeatedly contradicts this.

Thus, we have a flat contradiction of Paul by Jesus *after* Paul's writings were published and well-known. These passages in Revelation contradict Paul's salvation formula that excludes works. The message of Revelation is that instead of us being judged by faith, we are judged and justified by works. As one commentator writes:

> Jesus says in the book of Revelation also that we are justified by our works.
>
> It reads: 'Behold, I come quickly, and my reward is with me, ***to give every man according to his WORK shall be.*** ' Revelation 22: 12.
>
> 'And death and hell delivered up the dead that were in them, and they were ***judge every man according to their WORKS.*** ' Revelation 20: 12.
>
> So now we have Jesus and his disciple...John ***are different than Paul's teaching.***

2. Clare G. Weakley, Jr., *Why the Book of Revelation is Heresy* reprinted at http://www.christian-community.org/library/revelheresy.html (last visited 2005.) Dr. Weakley is a licensed Methodist minister with a Masters in Theology.

> To justify and to judge a sinner or a believer, God shall ***analyze them by their works according to the law.***[3]

There is never any assurance given in Revelation that *without works* you are seen as perfect based upon a one-time belief in Jesus. There is never any suggestion in Revelation that works are not your *personal* responsibility and now you can lean back and relax and expect God to perform in you or attribute to you based on faith. Let's review what Jesus tells us about salvation and test whether Paul lines up with Jesus' words.

Faith and Works in Revelation

Jesus in Revelation aims a dagger right at Paul's teaching on faith and works. Jesus is going to strike hard again and again. In Revelation, salvation is under constant threat for members of seven churches. Jesus gives several warnings on how to overcome, and how ***not to be blotted out from the book of life.*** In the salvation message in Revelation dating to 90 A.D., ***grace*** is never mentioned although it was Paul's banner slogan from 45-62 A.D. Faith in the sense of a mental assent is likewise ignored. Jesus does so despite *faith* being the lynch-pin of the salvation doctrine from Paul 25-45 years *earlier*. (Eph. 2:8-9; Rom. 10:9; Rom. 4:4.) Rather, in Jesus' Book of Revelation, faithfulness is promised the crown of life: "Be thou ***faithful*** unto death, and I will give thee a crown of life." (Rev. 2:10.)[4]

3. *Judgment According to Our Works* (2003) available at http://www.captelco.qc.ca/churchofjesus/_disc1/00000154.htm (last visited 2005).

Rather than salvation by grace without works (Eph. 2:8-9), Jesus tells us in Revelation those whose works are "not complete" are "dead." They must repent because otherwise something living in them is about to die. (Rev. 3:1-3.) James 2:14-21 is ringing in our ears.

In a threatening context (not a promise of happy rewards), Jesus likewise says He judges by works. "And I will kill her children with death; and all the churches shall know that I am he which searcheth the reins and hearts: and ***I will give unto every one of you according to your works***." (Rev. 2:23.) Jesus promises again later that on Judgment day "every man" is "judged...according to their works." (Rev.20:13.)[5] *Cf.* Matt. 12:36-37 ("every idle word that men shall speak, they shall give account thereof in the day of judgment. For by thy words thou shalt be justified, and by thy words thou shalt be condemned.")

"We are saved by faith, but we will be judged by our works! The final Judgment will be based on our works of obedience." Pastor Reimar Schultz (on Rev. 20:13)

4. Paulinists are loathe to admit this is synonymous with eternal life. The only other reference to the "crown of life" in the New Testament is in James. "Blessed is the man that endureth temptation; for when he hath been approved, he shall receive the ***crown of life***, which the Lord promised to them that love him." (James 1:12.) This verse stands in contrast to Luke 8:13 where the seed "believes for a while" but in "time of temptation" falls away and is lost. This seed does not endure in obedience. Thus, James is holding up the fate of the fourth seed against the second seed. The *crown of life* must be *eternal life.* Gill and Henry claim James means eternal *happiness*, not *life*, while Jamieson admits James means *eternal life* by the term *crown of life.*

5. In Rev. 20:11-15, the *final* criterion for salvation is works. All are judged by works, without distinction. It is not merely wicked people who are judged by works. Rather, Jesus says the distinction at the judgment between the finaly saved and unsaved is based on works.

Then Jesus emphasizes to members of particular churches that holding fast is the way to avoid being *blotted out of the book of life.* Contrary to the Paulinist spin of these passages, Jesus is addressing *individuals* on their personal salvation within a church. Jesus is not measuring the value of the corporate body's activity. For a church can neither be written in nor blotted out *as a body* from the *book of life*.

> (3) ***Remember therefore how thou hast received and heard***, and ***hold fast***, and ***repent.*** If therefore thou shalt not watch, I will come on thee as a thief...(5) He that overcometh, the same shall be clothed in white raiment; and **I will not blot out his name out of the book of life**, but I will confess his name before my Father, and before his angels. (Rev. 3:3-5, KJV.)

To those who will not hold fast the word and do not repent, Jesus has a warning. To the Christians at Laodicea, Jesus writes:

> (15) I know thy ***works***, that ***thou art neither cold nor hot***: I would thou wert cold or hot. (16) So then ***because thou art lukewarm***, and neither cold nor hot, ***I will spue thee out of my mouth.*** (Rev. 3:15-16, KJV.)

Jesus is declaring clearly that those who have not zealously pursued works of some sort will be rejected. The lukewarm in that regard will be spewed out.

Thus, Jesus in Revelation issued a salvation theology identical to that of James in James chapter two. It was the same message Jesus gave in His own earthly ministry. Jesus thereby let it be known in a thinly veiled manner that Paul was a false apostle. Paul's view of salvation is diametrically different, as everyone knows. (Eph. 2:8-9.)

In fact, Jesus' monologue in Revelation is filled with allusions to the Parable of the Sower and the Ten Virgins. In Revelation 3:1-3, Jesus will be talking of the spirit that is flickering out as equal to works that are incomplete and makes these Christians "dead." Jesus will talk of works that are neither hot nor cold. Jesus will spew out of His mouth Christians who are guilty of such incomplete works. Jesus' solution is a call to repent and obey and do the works they did at first. Otherwise, they will be blotted out of the book of life. *What message further from Paul, and more confirming of James 2:14-21 can you find*? He who has ears to hear, let him hear.

Yet, Paul hinged everything on his doctrine of salvation on faith alone without works. (Ephesians 2:8-9; Rom. 4:4.) This was his entire gospel. Every word quoted from Revelation's different message is cringed at by Paulinists because they know if they lose this battle then they lose everything. Their domination over Jesus Christ with Paul as their most revered apostle will be exposed. They have banked everything on Paul's doctrine. Now it is time for Jesus to speak!

To do this, we must start with the Parable of the Ten Virgins, for Jesus definitely alludes to it in Revelation as the means to rebuff Paul. Thus, to understand Revelation fully, we need to go back to Jesus' earthly preaching.

Parable of the Ten Virgins & Revelation 3:1-3

In Matthew 25:1 *et seq*., there were ten virgins waiting for the bridegroom to come. Five still had oil for their lamps when the groom came. The other five were running out, and their lamps were beginning to go out just before the groom came. Thus, the second five were not prepared as the crucial time approached. They had the oil for a time, but then they ran out ("their lamps were going out"). So these five determined just before the groom came that they would try to get more oil. To their shock and dismay, the groom came when their oil was barren and they were hoping to get more. The door is then shut and they are excluded from the wedding feast.

The moral of the story is it was then too late. Their *good intentions were not enough*. They postponed getting the extra oil too long. The door was shut. When the second five heard the groom arriving, they turned back from their shopping trip. These five tried knocking on the door for entry. However, they found they were excluded from the banquet. They suffer weeping and gnashing of teeth outside. Jesus then says this should teach us "you will not know the day nor hour." So the lesson is we must always be ready for our Lord's return. *We cannot rest on our good intentions to someday get the oil we need.* Instead, God will *absolutely* require sufficient oil burning when that time comes.

To whom is this parable directed? A Christian or a non-Christian?

Oil in Scripture typically represents the Holy Spirit.

A *virgin* in Scripture usually symbolizes a blameless person. A saved person. The term *virgin* is never used elsewhere to describe the lost. It also makes no sense to refer to a lost person as a *virgin*.

Jesus closes this parable saying we must be ready and watch for when He returns because you know not the day nor hour of His return. (Matt. 25:13.)

Could Jesus' parable be a warning to a non-Christian to be watching and ready for when Jesus returns? That makes no sense. First, a non-Christian having *oil* makes no sense. Second, the label *virgin* for a non-Christian makes no sense. Lastly, the warning to be ready makes more sense for a Christian than a non-Christian. Everything points to them being a Christian.

However, there is an exception—the NIV says the five foolish ones did not bring "any" oil. That translation implies they did not even have oil in their lamps. Thus, these virgins lacked any oil, according to the NIV. Hence, they are non-Christians who do not have the Holy Spirit, if you trust the NIV.

Therefore, the NIV asks us to believe Jesus would incongruously call someone a virgin who *entirely* lacks the Holy Spirit. Something does not make sense in the NIV version.

It turns out the NIV is a mistranslation. The original Greek does not say they did not bring *any* oil, nor they brought *no* oil with them. The original Greek simply says the five foolish virgins did "not bring oil." By contrast, the wise virgins brought "extra oil in jars." Yet, the Greek also clearly reflects the unwise virgins had oil for a time burning in their lamps. Even the Calvinist *The Expositor's Bible Commentary* points out the Greek says their "lamps were going out," implying a flickering out process as the oil burned away. It notes the Greek is the "present tense" of the verb "*are going out,*" and not as the KJV has it: 'are gone out.'[6] Something in their lamps is burning, but is going out. They had oil in their lamps, but they did not carry extra oil with them like the wise had done.

Thus, most commentators acknowledge the foolish virgins must have initially had oil in their lamps, but unlike the wise, they did not bring ***extra*** oil in separate jars. Otherwise, there is no way of explaining how the five foolish virgins had lamps that were burning for a while. They complain later that their "lamps are being quenched," implying they were burning but going out. The *Amplified Bible* realizes this and translates the passage to say the five foolish ones did not bring "extra oil in jars."

So there are several clear indicators that the five foolish virgins were Christians.

What is happening with them? While they are pure virgins, they also have very little oil in their lamps and the light is about to flicker out in them. When the oil is

6. *The Expositor's Bible Commentary* (1989), *supra*, Vol. VIII at 513.

exhausted, they will suffer weeping and gnashing of teeth in darkness outside the kingdom of God. They foolishly did not pack extra oil prior to the Lord's arrival. What does the Parable of the Ten Virgins mean?

Paulinists Preempt The Parable's Application by Denying Any Parabolic Meaning

Paulinists attempt to deflect this parable before it can influence doctrine. What they do is astonishing. They can see what is coming if the obvious parabolic meaning is used. Keeping one's *oil* burning focuses on some *work.* The line between foolish and wise is drawn between *two kinds of initially justified and innocent persons* (*i.e.*, virgins). If a Christian can be foolish and later become lost, then some kind of personal irresponsibility becomes relevant to salvation. Paul's contrary message would be exposed if *any kind of spiritual interpretation is applied to a Christian* from this parable.

Thus, the Paulinist simply denies the Parable of the Ten Virgins has any parabolic meaning. This approach is clearly set forth in the Calvinist *The Expositor's Bible Commentary* (1989):

> There is ***no point*** in seeing hidden meanings in the *oil*...
>
> The oil ***cannot easily apply*** to...the Holy Spirit. It is merely an element in the narrative showing that the foolish virgins were unprepared for the delay...
>
> The ***point is not*** these girls' *virginity,* but simply that ten...*maidens* [were] invited to the wedding. (Vol. VIII at 512, 513).

So the Paulinist cannot permit any secondary meaning to the word *oil* or the word *virgin*. They try to recast the *virgins* as simply *maidens*. The reason is that *The Expositor's Bible Commentary* states it is aware that otherwise a condition exists upon the virgin being accepted in the kingdom: "there must be behavior acceptable to the master, the discharge of allotted responsibilities." *Id.*, Vol. VIII at 512.

If we accepted the obvious that the *virgin* represents a Christian, and the *oil* represents the Holy Spirit, we would have a dilemma. The Paulinist would have to accept that Jesus expressly taught that a Christian will not go to Heaven absent "behavior acceptable to the master, the discharge of allotted responsibilities." Jesus would contradict Paul. ***Rather than ever question their paradigm thinking that assumes Paul is an inspired writer, these Paulinists would prefer taking the outrageous step of saying Jesus had no parabolic intent in a parable.*** This, of course, leaves the parable utterly meaningless. This is frankly shocking.

In fact, it is deplorable that a Bible commentary would insist that there is no "need" to see "hidden meaning" to the significant objects of this parable such as the *oil* and the *virgins*. A parable precisely calls an aware Christian to meditate on a symbolic meaning. We could respect the commentary if it suggested other symbolic meanings. However, to suggest that we should not try to imagine there is any symbolic meaning is shocking. *Yet, it helps us see the lengths to which reputable Paulinists must go to resist letting their paradigm viewpoint be challenged by the words of Jesus*. The Paulinist is forever jumping into foxholes to dodge Jesus' challenges to his system of thinking.

The solution in this parable is easy: *oil* is the Holy Spirit and the word *virgins* means cleansed and washed Christians.

Now let's explore the meaning behind the fact five had their *lamps going out*.

How Revelation 3:1-3 and James 2 Relate to the Parable of the Ten Virgins

What does the fact five have their lamps going out mean? Do they face spiritual death despite having been a virgin? Yes, especially when you compare this to Revelation 3:1-3.

Somehow commentators have missed a precise parallel between the Parable of the Ten Virgins and what is contained in Revelation 3:1-3. Jesus tells the church at Sardis:

> (1) I know your deeds; you have a reputation for being alive, but you are **dead.** Wake up! Strengthen what remains and **is about to die**, (2) for ***I have not found your deeds complete*** in the sight of God. (3) Remember, therefore, what you have received and heard; obey it and repent. But if you do not wake up, I will come like a thief, and you will not know at what time I will come. (ASV)

These three verses exactly parallel the Parable of the Ten Virgins:

- The lamps of five virgins are about to flicker out and die due to lack of oil. The Sardisians likewise have something in them "about to die."
- The foolish virgins failed to watch and be ready. The lesson Jesus draws is that "Watch, for you will not know the day nor hour" (Matt. 25:13). This is likewise the precise lesson to the Sardisians. "I will come like a thief, and you will not know at what time I will come." (Rev. 3:3.)

It is obvious in both situations that the Spirit is present, but in both cases the Spirit is going out. In the Book of Revelation, this is explained. What is bringing about the Sardisians' spiritual death is their works ***were not complete in God's sight.*** In fact, Jesus says they have a reputation for being alive, but they are "**dead**."

The picture of the Sardisians is very interesting:

- They are dead.
- Something still flickering in them is about to be quenched.
- Their works are not complete.

Let's make a reasonable inference on what these points mean. The first point means their faith is dead. The second point means the Holy Spirit is about to be quenched and depart. The third point means they have no completed works or mature fruit to show.

The threat is implicit that damnation will follow unless they "repent" and "obey." We know this explicitly from the parallel Parable of the Ten Virgins. It tells us that when the spirit departs—their lamps were finally quenched—that damnation results. They suffer weeping and gnashing, left outside. Jesus elsewhere explains this is hell itself. *See* Matt. 13:42 ("and shall cast them into the furnace of fire: there shall be the weeping and the gnashing of teeth").

So Revelation 3:1-3 sounds a lot like a ***dead faith*** without completed ***works*** does not ***save***. Where have we ever read that before?

Jesus' Confirmation of James' Doctrines & Rejection of Paul's

Where else does the Bible say a Christian without deeds has a faith that is dead and such faith cannot save? Yes, the often resisted James 2:14-25 passage. James 2:17 reads: "Even so faith, if it hath not works, is dead, being alone." James asks rhetorically "can such faith save?" which calls for a negative answer. Thus, faith without works, James says, cannot save.[7]

7. Greek scholars admit that James' meaning is that faith without completed works cannot save, *i.e.*, works are not merely a forensic proof of your already saved condition. James means works (besides faith) are indispensable for you to be saved. See page 261 *et seq*.

In Revelation 3:1-3, what must those with a faith that has become dead and who lack completed works do to awaken spiritually?

Revelation 3:3 says they must "remember what you have received and heard; ***obey*** it and ***repent***." A non-Christian does not have anything to remember. They never have been a Christian. Nor does a non-Christian receive a spark which then is later dying out in them. Non-Christians are not judged for incomplete works, but sin. Only a Christian can be in view in Jesus' words in Revelation 3:3.

Thus, because the Parable of the Ten Virgins parallels the warning of Revelation 3:3, we know the foolish virgins are Christians like those warned in Revelation 3:1-3.

Accordingly, Jesus is teaching in the Parable of the Ten Virgins that faith without works is dead. You are spiritually dying and about to have the Spirit quenched. How do we know this? Because Jesus gives a precisely parallel message in Revelation 3:1-3 that duplicates the Ten Virgins Parable in declarative statements. While in the parable we are not sure what it means to have the spirit flickering out, Revelation 3:3 tells us precisely: the ***Sardisians are lacking completed works.***

Incidentally, the Sardisians' spiritual condition identically matches the third seed in the Parable of the Sower. This seed has thorns choke them. Jesus says they did not *telesphourin.* (Luke 8:14.) This means the third seed fails to produce to the end, or fails to bring its fruit to completion. (For more discussion, see "What The Parable of the Sower Confirms About Faith in John's Gospel" on page 171.)

Finally, those statements in Revelation 3:1-3 about not completing your works contain one more piece of crucial information. It says that despite their reputation for being alive they are ***dead.*** They have incomplete works. Something is flickering out in them. These additional facts let us see a precise overlap to James 2:17. The Epistle of James says such faith without completed works is dead. Therefore, we realize the Parable of the Ten Virgins is the same as Revelation 3:1-3 which is the same as James 2:17.

So what do these three passages mean? They boil down to James' message that *faith alone...cannot save.* If you do not add works of charity which James mentions, your faith is dead. The Spirit is about to leave you. Quicken what little remains. If not, you will suffer spiritual death and be sent to a place of weeping and gnashing, being left outside. Jesus tells us this is the fiery furnace—hell itself. (Matt. 13:42.) Jesus' warning is to repent and obey, and bring the works assigned to you to "completion."

Why? Because Jesus can come as a thief anytime, and you will find yourself, once a pure virgin with the oil of the Holy Spirit burning, so dead and the spirit so lacking (flickering out) that it will be too late when Jesus returns. You will find yourself left outside weeping and gnashing your teeth. This is precisely the meaning of the warning of the Parable of the Ten Virgins. Jesus makes works absolutely *vital* to add to *faith* so we are ready when He returns.

What kind of works? They might primarily or exclusively be works of charity if James' illustration is a definitive application of Revelation 3:1-3. We shall later see that Jesus ***confirms it at least means works of charity*** in his Parable of the Sheep and the Goats. We will discuss that parable in the next section.

So we see that Jesus is approving James' position. Revelation 3:1-3 mentions "incomplete works" and "dead." Jesus is stepping into the debate between James and Paul. Jesus is coming down on the side of James. Jesus did this elsewhere in Revelation 2:14 on the issue of meat sacrificed to idols. Jesus does it again here. This time Jesus is resolving the faith-alone versus faith-plus-works debate.

No one wants to see this. Almost everyone prefers thinking that "incomplete works" (Rev. 3:2) has something to do with *corporate worship* practices. The mention of salvation and being blotted out of the book of life rule out such *corporate* interpretations. The parallel between Revelation and James chapter 2 and Jesus' Parable of the Ten Virgins likewise proves Revelation speaks to *individuals* in churches. The Book of Revelation is not simply addressing churches who happen to have individuals.

To understand the works that Jesus is referring to in Revelation 3:1-3 that one must complete, we need to look at one more parable of Jesus. It is a parable often overlooked and ignored but focuses on works of charity. As you read this, ask yourself are such works optional for salvation as Jesus tells the Parable of the Sheep and the Goats.

The Parable of the Sheep and The Goats Proves Faith Alone Does Not Save

Jesus tells a parable known as the Parable of the Sheep and the Goats. (Matthew 25:30-46.) Jesus says that one group who calls Him Lord serves Jesus' brothers in need with food and clothing. This group goes to heaven. Another group who calls Him Lord but who fails to do likewise are sent to hell.

Jesus is commanding charity to his brothers on threat of going to hell if you do not do it. Jesus is promising eternal life to those who do it. Faith that is alone does not save.

As we shall see below, Jesus' statement that charity *is crucial for salvation* is exactly repeated by his brother James. We read in James' Epistle chapter two a discussion of ***precisely these same works*** that a dead faith fails to do—if you see a brother in need, and you do not feed him or clothe him. James asks of such a person, "Can such a faith save him?" (James 2:14 NIV.) The rhetorical form of the question calls for a negative answer. Jesus gives a big negative to the same question in this parable.

Let's break this parable down to better understand what it promises and threatens. Does faith alone save?

- There are two types in view: the sheep v. the goats.

- The sheep are called the "righteous." (25:37.)
- The sheep receive as an "inheritance...the kingdom." (25:34.)
- The goats are called "cursed" and are sent "into the ***eternal fire*** prepared for the devil and his angels." (25:41.)

Why the different ends? Is it because one believed and the other did not? Or rather is it because among those who knew the Lord some served Him by clothing, feeding and visiting the "brothers" of the King while others did not?

Or another way of asking this is to inquire why do the sheep inherit the kingdom. Is it because they are believers who are saved despite failing to do works of charity? Was their faith alone enough? *No.*

Jesus says:

> (35) For I was hungry and you gave me something to eat, I was thirsty and you gave me something to drink, I was a stranger and you invited me in, (36) I needed clothes and you clothed me, I was sick and you looked after me, I was in prison and you came to visit me.

The sheep confess they do not remember doing it for the Lord himself. The King explains: 'I tell you the truth, whatever you did for one of the least of these brothers of mine, you did for me.'

Why are the goats sent to "eternal fire"? Did they lack ever having faith? No, rather Jesus says:

> (42) For I was hungry and you gave me nothing to eat, I was thirsty and you gave me nothing to drink, (43) I was a stranger and you did not invite me in, I needed clothes and you did not clothe me, I was sick and in prison and you did not look after me.

The goats confess the same error, not ever having seen the Lord in need. And the King replies:

> I tell you the truth, whatever you did not do for one of the least of these, you did not do for me. (Mat. 25:45.)

The answer is that one group serves the brothers of the King and the others do not, by works of charity. ***One has works of charity and one doesn't.*** That is the dividing line in being finally saved, as told in this parable. ***Both the sheep and goats call him Lord, so both had faith.*** One was dead and one was alive.[8]

If, instead, you reject this interpretation, and believe only the sheep had faith, then you have the incongruous lesson that Jesus is warning people already lost (the goats) that they better do works of charity for His brothers or face hell.

---

8. On the significance that both groups call Jesus *Lord*, Paulinists deny it any significance. In doing so, they merely engage in *ad hoc* denial that the lost were at one time Christians. They cite no adequate proof for this reading. *The Expositor's Bible Commentary*—an evangelical text—states: "There is ***no significance*** in the fact that the goats address him as Lord... for at this point there is no exception whatever to confessing Jesus as Lord." (Vol. 8, at 522.) What does this mean? The argument appears to be that this event occurs on judgment day when *according to their interpretation of Paul* everyone must confess Jesus as Lord. However, Paul *never* said this. It is a pure *myth* he did so, by amalgamating two disparate verses together. The first is Philippians 2:11. Paul says God exalted Jesus so that "every tongue *should* confess Jesus is the Lord." Nothing is said about this actually occurring universally at the judgment seat. The second is Romans 14:11-12 where Paul says God will examine each person at the judgment seat. There "every knee shall bow and every tongue shall confess to God. So that every one of us shall give account of himself to God." There confession of *sins*, not of Jesus, is in view. Some amalgamate the two verses to mean "every tongue *shall* confess Jesus is Lord" when "every tongue shall confess" at the judgment seat. Yet, the two verses cannot be combined without violence to the original *context* of each verse. Thus, the *Expositor's* is relying upon a commonly heard amalgamation of two distinct verses. This common axiom says every tongue *must* confess Jesus as Lord at the judgment seat. However, in relying upon this, the *Expositor's* is relying on a *myth.* There is no basis to suppose non-Christians are going to confess Jesus on judgment day. The truth is Jesus in the parable wants us to know not only that the sheep and the goats are both *believers* but also that mere *belief* does not seal your salvation.

The incongruity is further aggravated by the fact Jesus would be letting the saved know they are saved by doing those works *alone*. Jesus clearly says this is the dividing line between the two groups. Jesus would be making salvation depend *only* on works (of charity). Thus, it follows that Jesus wants us to understand the goats were already Christians (*i.e.*, had accepted him as Lord and Savior) but they failed to serve Him by works of charity to his followers. The formula is faith *and* works (of charity). This charitable service then becomes the dividing line in terms of who is and who is not ultimately saved among people who have faith in Jesus.

Comparison of the Parable of the Sheep & Goats to James Chapter 2

The fact that Matthew 25:30-46 appears similar to James chapter two is not in one's imagination. They are virtually ***verbatim copies*** of each other. Again, I have not seen a single commentator noticing this.

James writes:

> (14) What doth it profit, my brethren, if a man say he hath faith, but have not works? ***can that faith save him?*** (15) If a brother or sister be naked and in lack of daily food, (16) and one of you say unto them, Go in peace, be ye warmed and filled; and yet ye give them not the things needful to the body; what doth it profit? (17) Even so ***faith, if it have not works [ergon], is dead in itself*** [*i.e.*, if alone]. (James 2:14-17, ASV.)

Now compare this faith that is not completed because it lacks works of charity and thus cannot save in *James* with Jesus' words in the Parable of the Sheep and the Goats. In that parable, Jesus threatens damnation for lacking charity. The parallels are striking:

Parallelism of James 2:14-17 & Parable of the Sheep & the Goats

TABLE 6.

James	Jesus
"brother or sister without clothes..." (James 2:15.)	"I needed clothes and you did not clothe me."(Matt. 25:36.)
"brother or sister without... daily food..." (James 2:15.)	"For I was hungry and you gave me nothing to eat." (Matt. 25:42.)
"faith without works...." (James 2:14.)	"Lord...when did we see you hungering...or naked....?" (Matt. 25:44.)
"is dead [and] can[not] save." (James 2:14.)	"Be going...into the eternal fire prepared for the devil and his angels." (Matt. 25: 41.)

Thus, we see Matthew 25:30-46—the Parable of the Sheep and the Goats—is identical in message and content to James 2:14-17. It resolves any doubt that James' mention of works was to merely *prove* you have faith. The parable prevents any attempt to say we are seen as righteous by God by faith alone without having to do any of the crucial deeds of Matthew 25:30-46. Good intentions to one day have such works is not enough. (This was also the point of the Parable of the Ten Virgins.)

In response to such clarity, Paulinists attempt to marginalize Jesus and James. Their goal is simply to save Paul. They say James is merely a *forensic* test of works to show an inward completely-sufficient reality. Paulinists claim James really means that works only *prove* we are already saved. However, James makes it just as clear as Jesus' parable that faith alone without ***these identical deeds of charity*** does not save. Works are part of the salvation formula, not a forensic proof of an earlier salvation that was permanently sufficient without adding charitable works.

Thus, face the fact even as Luther did: James contradicts Paul. (See page 247.) And thus so does Jesus contradict Paul in the Parable of the Sheep and the Goats.

What makes the contradiction by James of Paul intentional and self-evident is James goes on to say faith plus deeds *justifies*. And *yes*, James uses the same Greek word Paul uses for *justifies*. James also uses the very same figure, Abraham, as Paul does, to give this lesson.[9]

Thus, it is false to teach that we "prove" we are saved through faith by works of charity, but we could still be saved by faith and be derelict in works of charity. Rather, we are saved by (among other things) doing works of charity to ***complete*** our faith. That is how Jesus and James wanted us to see the risk and the requirement. Works of charity are not optional, nor mere proof of faith. Faith alone does not save. James says it is "faith... working with [our] works" (*synergei tois ergois*) that saves us. (See Footnote 22, page 261.) Those works are dependent on our prayer relationship to Jesus (John 15:1-6), but they are not thereby no longer our personal responsibility.

Why Is Charity So Central in God's Word?

Why would charity toward others be so crucial to salvation, as Jesus says? We could do an entire Bible study on this. It appears that charity toward others is the most significant way you mark departure from your old life of sin. Daniel can tell the king "break off (discontinue) your sins...by showing mercy to the poor." (Dan. 4:27.)

Charity in the Hebrew Scriptures was frankly one of the most elevated commands to obey. One might even say it is central to Torah. It reflects obedience to God's command to *love thy neighbor* in a concrete way. Thus, the Law of Moses said if a brother of God's people is in your midst who is

9. See page 258 *et seq.*

"needy" then "thou shalt surely open thy hand unto him, and shalt surely lend him sufficient for his need in that which he wanteth." (Deut. 15:7-8.) Thirty-six times the Bible then commands the same charity must be shown to the "stranger" in your midst for "you were once strangers in the Land of Egypt." (*E.g.*, Deut. 10:19.)

The charity-principle is one of the most characteristic ways of doing justice in God's eyes. God desires it more than any blood sacrifice. (Prov. 21:3; Mark 12:33.) In Isaiah 58:7 *et seq*. (NLT), God promises "***salvation*** shall come like the dawn" if you bring the poor into your home, give him clothes, etc. If you are charitable, God promises if you call on Him, then "the Lord will answer." (Isaiah 58:9.) Thus, even the issue of whether God will speed an answer to prayer depends on how charitable you are being to the poor.

Furthermore, if you are charitable, God will guide you "continually" and make you like a watered garden. (Isaiah 58:11.) God promises special blessings to those who give charity to the poor.

Thus, there is no end of verses that elevate charity above almost every other command except to Love the Lord thy God with your whole mind, heart and soul.

Jesus Says Charity Is An Essential Break From Your Life of Sin

As already noted, charity in Daniel was also linked to the end of sinning in your life. (Dan. 4:27.) As Jesus tells it, charity has this function. After repentance from sin, then you need to be charitable to enter into eternal life. At least this is what Jesus told the young rich man is how to "enter eternal life." (Matthew 19:16-26; Mark 10:17-31; Luke 18:18-26.) While it may not match Pauline doctrine, Jesus was consistent about this. When Zaccheus repented of his sin and gave his wealth to the poor, Jesus assured him that "salvation has come to this house." (Luke 19:9.)

One might say charity is a work worthy of repentance. As Jesus explains it, it is not optional. It *completes* your faith. Hence, faith plus works of charity are *essential* in Jesus' doctrine.

Paulinist Interpretation of the Parable of the Sheep & Goats

Most of the time, Paulinist congregations ignore this parable. One Christian expresses my own experience, and perhaps your own:

> In my Baptist upbringing, and even after becoming a Christian, Matthew 25[:31 *et seq.*] was NEVER touched on, mentioned, taught, etc. And you'd be surprised how easy it is to gloss over it in your own studies when your own denomination, pastor, teachers, and friends don't give it any notice, either.[10]

Whenever the Parable of the Sheep and the Goats is actually examined, because it is James 2:14-17 stated as a parable, Paulinists lose all semblance of reasonable interpretation.

Dillow endorses the view that the sheep are Christians who ministered with food and clothing and visited in prison ***Jews***, Jesus' "brothers." However, they are not just simply any Jew of every generation, but only Jews living in the great tribulation period. (Dillow, *Reign of the Servant Kings, supra*, at 73.) Dillow explains that if we do not choose this interpretation which imposes 'faith plus works saves' as true for a very small future historical group, then the present *standard* 'gospel' is ruined for the rest of us. Dillow says that but for

10. http://onefortruth.blogspot.com/2005/09/sheep-and-goats-parable-or-prophecy.html (Ninjanun comment to 9-29-05 blog).

this explanation, Matthew 25:34 means "that inheriting the kingdom is conditioned on obedience and service to the King, a condition far removed from the New Testament [*i.e.,* Pauline] teaching of justification by faith ***alone*** for entrance into heaven." (*Id.*)

Thus, this spin of the parable defers Jesus' teaching on salvation by works to only those trapped in the tribulation who were never Christians pre-tribulation. Dillow believes Paul's "faith alone" doctrine remains the valid salvation formula for us pre-tribulation.

However, James said "faith alone" does not save. In fact, the words "faith alone" only appear in the entire Bible in one passage: James 2:17. And he says "faith alone" does not justify you.

Furthermore, consider how absurd it is to interpret a parable as having a distinct salvation message for only the tribulation period. Why would it change just for those in this seven year period?

So the Pauline spin of this passage ends up teaching there is a separate salvation message for a small historical group that does require works of charity plus faith. Therefore, we today are comforted that we do not have to change Paul's gospel message until the tribulation is upon us. In this view, reconciling Paul to Jesus is not necessary because Jesus' teaching applies when Christians 'are gone anyway.'

In this manner, this parable is neatly swept under the rug to be dusted off when the time is right for non-Christians to find it. (Please note this recognizes that faith-plus-works will one day be a non-heretical doctrine; it just does not fit our time, according to Paulinists.)

This tribulation-only solution can be dismissed with just one Bible verse. Christ's 'brethren' does not mean ethnic Jews, let alone only Jews of a seven year future period. Jesus asked once "who are my brothers?" Jesus answered that His brothers and sisters should be those "doing the will of God." (Matthew 12:48-50.)

If one must escape this parable with such a nonsensical notion that Jesus' brothers are non-Christian Jews of the tribulation period, Paulinism is not being held even loosely based on Jesus' words. The Paulinist view of salvation is being held *in spite* of whatever Jesus teaches.

Another example of this is Calvin's even weaker explanation of this Parable of the Sheep and the Goats. Calvin claimed that when Jesus says to one group who performed charity that they will "inherit"[11] the kingdom, the word *inherit* means they did not receive it by works, but by a gift.[12] This is a non-sequitur. It does not follow. Jesus says the crucial difference in salvation was that some did works of charity while others did not do so. Thus, an essential factor in salvation, as told by Jesus, is *charitable works*. The concept of *inheritance* cannot erase this fact.

Furthermore, Calvin mistakenly spun this to suggest the word *inherit* implies somehow salvation is contingent on God's donative intent—His intent to make a gift. However, an *inheritance* in the Law does not rely upon donative intent. Rather, one inherits based on family relationship, without any donative intent at all. (Numbers 27:7-11.) The only relevance of intent is that a parent could always disinherit a son for disobedience. God declares He can do so in Numbers 14:12 toward us. God says to the disobedient "I will disinherit them." A son under the Law who had proven disobedient despite chastening was obviously disinherited by denying you ever knew him. This was the only way to spare the son of the Law's only other option of a death penalty. Deut. 21:18-21. The First Century legal fiction was you would say the

11.This is not necessarily a correct translation. The Greek word also means *receive* or *share*.

12.Calvin, *Institutes*, 20, 822 (III, xviii, 2) Calvin wrote: "even in these very passages [Matt 25:34-46 and Col. 3:23-24] where the Holy Spirit promises ***everlasting glory as a reward for works***, [yet] by expressly terming it an 'inheritance' he is showing that it comes to us from another source [than works]."

son's disobedience meant he "denied" his parent, allowing the parent to "deny" he ever knew the son.[13] Thus, a parent's intent only had relevance to prove the grounds to deny inheritance. An inheritance was otherwise required by Law with no intent to make a gift being involved.

Thus, the Parable of the Sheep and the Goats was an example of a disinheritance warning. Do charitable works, and you will safely inherit eternal life. Fail to do them, and be forewarned—God will disinherit you. Thus, the dividing line in the Parable is clearly *works*. There is nothing in the word *inheritance* that suggests even remotely that salvation is a no-strings attached *gift,* and that Jesus is somehow suggesting salvation never turns *at all* on works.

How did Calvin reach the wrong conclusion? Calvin was confusing the law of wills and trusts (which does depend upon donative intent) with the law of *inheritance*. Calvin erred when he construed the word *inherit* to necessarily imply God was giving salvation as a gift to the sheep. Then with this error in hand, Calvin then somehow viewed the word *inherit* as overpowering Jesus' meaning that charity was crucial to salvation. For Calvin, making Jesus sound like Paul was the only priority that mattered. Letting Jesus correct Paul's doctrine was an inconceivable option for Calvin.

---

13. Jesus spoke of those who did many miracles and prophecies in His name but worked *anomia* that He will tell them "I never knew you." (Matt. 7:23.) Paul refers to how this works: "if we endure, we shall also reign with him: ***if we shall deny him, he also will deny us***." 2Ti 2:12 ASV. Obviously, in both Paul's and Jesus' statements, the people who are denied were *one-time* believers. They are true sons. Otherwise, how could they have done miracles and prophecies in Jesus' name? Paul likewise refers to a collective *we* which includes himself. How do these passages help explain the legal practice of that era to disinherit a son? In the earlier time of the Code of Hammurabi, a son who was disobedient was said to have "denied his father." *The Code of Hammurabi* (2500 BC) (Translated by L. W. King)(With commentary from Charles F. Horne, Ph.D. (1915), reprinted at http://www.ancienttexts.org/library/mesopotamian/hammurabi.html. It does not take much deduction to realize that parents under the Law given Moses who were compelled by Deut. 21:18-21 to put their son to death for wilful disobedience would rather accept the legal fiction of denying they ever knew their son rather than see their son killed. This declaration would spare his ***earthly life***, but ***cut off his inheritance***. Thus, both Paul and Jesus are referring to giving warnings of disinheritance of eternal life based on disobedience/*anomia*. (Incidentally, Paul in 2 Tim. 2:13 then undermines his own warning, which Charles Stanley has accepted as more true.)

Furthermore, while the Greek word *kleronomeo* in Matthew 25:34 ("*inherit* the kingdom prepared for you") can mean one receives property by the *right of inheritance*, it has other meanings. These other meanings are legitimate and arguably preferable translations. The word *kleronomeo* in Matthew 25:34 means also simply *receive, share* or *obtain.* (*Strongs* # 2816 "getting by apportionment"; "receive as one's own or as a possession; to become partaker of, to obtain.") These are completely satisfactory alternative renderings. Thus, Jesus says you shall *share in*, *receive*, or *obtain eternal life* if you do these charitable works. If you fail to do so, you are sent to hell's fire. Even if Calvin's argument about *inheritance* were possible, it is not necessarily an accurate translation. Either way you look at this, Calvin's point is irrelevant.

In sum, anyone can see *inherit* does not imply a *gift*. In fact, an inheritance is obtained by right of sonship and lost by disobedience. No donative intent is implied. God can make your sonship and right of inheritance depend on your behavior and attitudes. *See.* Ps. 39:9-11 & Matt. 5:5 ("the meek shall *inherit* the earth"); Matt. 19:29 ("every one that hath left houses, or brethren, or sisters, or father, or mother, or children, or lands, for my name's sake, shall....*inherit* eternal life"); Rev. 21:7-8 ("he that overcometh shall *inherit* all things, and I will be His God and he shall be my son, but the fearful and unbelieving...and all liars shall have their part in the lake which burneth with fire.") *Cf.* Ps. 149:4 ("he will beautify the meek with salvation").

Thus, Calvin's spin was clearly erroneous. Nothing in the Parable of the Sheep and the Goats suggests the saved sheep receive salvation based solely on grace without works.

Finally, others like Bob Wilkin who cannot reconcile the parable to Paul insist we are forced to do so regardless of the language.

> [I]t follows from the discussion above that the basis of 'inheriting the kingdom' ([Matt.] 25:34) is good works. Since Scripture cannot contra-

> dict itself, we know from a host of other passages that cannot mean that these people will gain entrance to the kingdom because they were faithful.[14]

Thus, the final foxhole is the *ad hoc* denial that Jesus can mean what He says because we know what Paul teaches *must* remain true.

The Meaning of the Parable of the Sheep & The Goats

We see in the Parable of the Sheep and the Goats, Jesus clearly teaches here the message of James chapter 2. You must do works of charity (feed and clothe) to Jesus' brothers—those who do the will of God. However, if you fail to do works of charity for those who needed food and clothing when you had the means—you will be sent to hell. Like James says, if you do not feed and clothe your spiritual brothers when you can, such faith is dead. Such faith cannot save you. ***There are perhaps no two more alike passages in all of Scriptures,*** outside of Synoptic parallels.

Because James chapter 2 is a thorn by itself to the "faith alone" view, none of the major commentators has ever drawn the parallel to Matthew 25:30-46. The latter makes it that much harder to explain away James chapter 2.

Daniel Fuller encourages us to assess this Parable of the Sheep and the Goats without any preconceived ideas. He exhorts us to allow Jesus to challenge our core Pauline doctrines:

> To the objection that...Matthew 25 and Colossians 3:23-24[15] lead us right back to Rome and ***salvation by works***, my answer is twofold.

14. Bob Wilkin, *Has This Passage Ever Bothered You? Matthew 25:31-46 - Works Salvation?* http://www.faithalone.org/news/y1988/88march1.html (last accessed 11/05).

> First, we must determine, ***regardless of consequences***, what the intended meaning of each of the biblical writers is. We must let each one speak for himself and ***avoid construing him by recourse to what another writer said***. Otherwise ***there is no escape from subjectivism in biblical interpretation***. (Fuller, *supra*, "Biblical Theology" fn. 22.)

Thus, reading Jesus through the overlay of Paul is wrong. You cannot press Jesus' words down so they fit Paul. Such conduct is reprehensible. In fact, the duty to construe Jesus free from other writers is an imperative. The very validity of other authors, such as Paul, turns on whether they *transgress* Jesus' teaching. As 2 John 1:9 teaches us, "Whoever goes beyond and doesn't remain in Christ's teaching, doesn't have God. He who remains in the teachings [of Jesus Christ], the same has both the Father and the Son." Jesus is the standard whether Paul is valid. If you refuse to read Jesus' meaning apart from Paul, and you are unwilling to see the differences, you are rejecting your duty to test Paul as 2 John 1:9 requires.

---

15. What is it about Colossians 3:23-24 which many believe implies salvation by faith plus works? Paul writes: "And whatsoever ye do, do it heartily, as to the Lord, and not unto men; Knowing that of the Lord ye shall receive the reward of the inheritance: for ye serve the Lord Christ. ***But he that doeth wrong*** shall receive for the wrong which he hath done: and there is no respect of persons." (Col 3:23-25) Unless parsed narrowly, this tells someone who is serving Christ that any wrong they do "shall receive for the wrong which he had done"and emphasizes you are not given any different escape than non-Christians. God has "no respect of persons." Matthew Henry sees this meaning: "There is a righteous God, who, if servants wrong their masters, will reckon with them for it, though they may conceal it from their master's notice. And ***he will be sure to punish the unjust*** as well as reward the faithful servant." The "no respect of persons" is also explained by Matthew Henry who states: "The righteous Judge of the earth will be impartial, and carry it with an ***equal hand***...not swayed by any regard to men's outward circumstances and condition of life. The one and the other will stand upon a [single] level at his tribunal."

The Salvation Message of Revelation Is Straight From the Parable of the Sower

Next, Jesus in Revelation once more states His core salvation theology. Jesus does this by reproving or commending each church by the criteria that Jesus used in the Parable of the Sower. This is done ever so subtly. Thus, many commentators miss this.

There are some who left their first love. (Rev. 2:4). They correspond to the second seed that starts with joy. This seed "believes for a while" but in time of temptation falls away. (Luke 8:13.) In Revelation, these do not "produce to completion" because of incomplete works. (Rev. 3:2.)

Then there are believers at another church who are neither hot nor cold but lukewarm. Jesus explains why: "Because thou sayest, I am rich, and have gotten riches, and have need of nothing." (Rev. 3:17.) These correspond to the third seed which was choked not only by the cares of this world, but also by "riches and pleasures" of this life. Thus, they did not produce to the end. (Luke 8:14.)

> **"So because thou art lukewarm, I will spew thee out of my mouth."**
> **Rev. 3:16**

Yet, there is one church and one seed that is viewed as on the right path. This is the church of Philadelphia which compares to the fourth seed in the Parable of the Sower. The church at Philadelphia is told "I know thy ***works***," and as a result a door is in front of them that no one can shut. (Rev. 3:8.) This church has very little "power" left, but "***did keep my word***, and did not deny my name." (Rev. 3:8.) This corresponds to the fourth seed which "in an honest and good heart, having heard the word, ***hold it fast***, and ***bring forth fruit*** with patience." (Luke 8:15.) There is an unmistakable parallelism between "keep my word" (Rev. 3:8) and "hold it fast" (Luke 8:15) as well as "thy works" (Rev. 3:8) and "bring forth fruit...." (Luke 8:15).

Thus, Jesus has made re-appear in the Book of Revelation all the criteria for assessing the saved seed versus these lost seeds from his Parable of the Sower. Why?

Precisely because there is no more difficult passage for a Paulinist to explain in the Synoptic Gospels on salvation than the Parable of the Sower. Jesus in the Book of Revelation invokes the Sower Parable obviously to rebuff Paul's message that faith alone saves, and works matter not at all. In the Sower Parable, those whose faith died, who fell in times of temptation, or whose works were incomplete were lost. Only the one who produces fruit to the end with endurance was saved in the Parable of the Sower. Ephesians 2:8-9 is thus dead on arrival when you let Jesus teach you in the Parable of the Sower. As a result, when this completely *anti-Pauline* message in the Parable of the Sower appears again in the Book of Revelation, Jesus' purpose is evident.

What About Grace?

This is doubly-evident because Jesus at the same time in Revelation ignores the word *grace*. Because Paul previously made this his most often used term to explain salvation (Rom. 3:24; 4:4, 16, 5:2, 15, 17, 20, 21; 6:1, 14, 15; 11:5-6; 12:3, 6; Gal. 1:16; 2:21; 5:4; Eph. 2:5, 8; Titus 2:11, 3:7), Jesus' *later* prophecy of Revelation has a not-so-subtle message. If Paul's doctrine were true, why does Jesus implicitly teach in Revelation that Paul's version of grace-teaching deserves no attention? Jesus' focus is to remind us of the criteria for salvation from the Parable of the Sower. His most often used exhortation to the churches in Revelation is *repent, do the same works you did at first, obey, etc.* In Revelation, *grace* is only mentioned in simple greetings by Apostle John. (Rev. 1:4; 22:21.) By its use, John merely means *mercy.*

This does not cast in doubt the canonicity of Revelation. For Jesus in His earthly ministry never once taught Paul's doctrine of grace. The word *grace* never once is uttered by Jesus in any of the four gospels! Nor did Jesus use in a theological sense the word *grace* in Revelation even though Paul enthroned that word with such great importance. Thus, it can be truly said that *grace theology,* as Paul explained it, had no place in Jesus' teachings. In Jesus' teachings on salvation, we find forgiveness and justification were always based upon repentance from sin, turning to God in faith, and staying on the path of obedience, *e.g.*, you had to thereafter forgive others. (Parable of the Publican and Pharisee; Parable of the Unmerciful Servant; Parable of the Prodigal Son. *See also*, Mark 9:42-47.)

Conclusion

Thus, it is evident in Revelation, Jesus wants us to forget about Paul's overly simplistic teaching of God's grace. He wants us to get back to Jesus' own repentance-oriented and faith-plus-works message of grace. Paul starkly stands for the opposite message. We know this stark difference all too well. Paul's doctrine has been drumb-beated into our subconscious from a thousand sermons. We must stop this brainwashing and wake up to reality: Paul abandoned Jesus' teaching of the keys to the kingdom: repentance-from-sin, obedience, and appropriation of His atonement by submitting to Him as Lord. Paul's words insisted that the obvious messages from Jesus' parables and blunt lessons, if taken seriously, were heretical. Rather than insult Jesus with the label *heretic*, Paulinists declare all of Jesus' parables are too hard to interpret. If any parable or teaching is too plain, they either ignore it or twist it unreasonably so it fits their Pauline doctrine. If that will not work, they do like Luther did with Revelation — he declared all the words of Jesus in Revelation are non-canonical. Calvin followed a similar approach — he ignored the Book of Revelation, never once providing a commentary upon it. This approach is no longer tenable.

We must break free from this constant thumping on Paul's doctrine in our churches. It is time to return to what Jesus taught not only in His parables but also in the Book of Revelation.

10 *Did Jesus Applaud the Ephesians for Exposing Paul as a False Apostle?*

Is There A Thirteenth Apostle?

It is hard to imagine that Paul's thirteen letters never came to the attention of any of the *twelve* apostles. One would expect to find some testing by the apostles of Paul's claims to be an apostle.

Jesus in Revelation 2:2 mentions a trial at Ephesus of persons who told the Ephesians they were apostles. The verdict found they were not true apostles. Jesus told the Ephesians:

> I have known thy works, and thy labour, and thy endurance, and that thou art not able to bear evil ones, and that thou hast tried those ***saying themselves to be apostles*** and are not, and hast found them ***liars.*** (Rev. 2:2. YLT)

In Revelation, Jesus did ***not*** say the same thing to any of the other six churches whom He addressed. Jesus made this remark to the only church among the seven whom we know Paul visited: the church at Ephesus. And among the seven churches, it was only the church at Ephesus whom we know Paul told that he was an apostle. (Eph. 1:1.) Paul wrote this church:

> From Paul, chosen by God to be ***an apostle of Christ Jesus***. To God's people who live in Ephesus and are faithful followers of Christ Jesus. (Ephesians 1:1 ASV.)[1]

If Paul were the object of Jesus' remarks in Rev. 2:2, it then makes sense that only the church at Ephesus would be commended for trying someone who told the Ephesians that he was an apostle. To the Ephesians, and to them alone, Jesus commends them for testing the ones who "said" they were apostles and are not, but are "liars." Now it was to the Ephesians that we likewise know Paul 'said he was an apostle....'

Was Paul *not* an apostle, thus bringing Revelation 2:2 directly to bear on Paul?

Indeed, there is no evidence for Paul being an apostle, except from Paul's own mouth. As Segal mentions, in Acts "Luke makes no reference [to the twelve accepting Paul's apostalate]."[2] Of course, the four gospel accounts have no mention of Paul, and thus offer no basis to confirm Paul as an apostle.

It is also clear from Acts that the Apostles themselves understood their number was set at *twelve*, but that this did not include Paul. Long before Revelation 2:2 was written, we know from Acts 1:21-26 that the twelfth apostle—Matthias—was chosen to replace Judas. The apostles' criteria for the replacement was that it had to be someone who was with the others from the beginning of Jesus' ministry. Luke reveals therefore that the eleven had a criteria that would likewise exclude adding Paul as an apostle.

Then Jesus in the Book of Revelation reveals *twelve is the number of apostles for all time*. The verse of Revelation 21:14 follows the mention of the twelve gates of the New Jerusalem. Each gate has a name of the twelve tribes of Israel on it. Revelation 21:14 then says:

---

1. Some of the oldest surviving manuscripts omit explicit mention of Ephesus in verse 1. Metzger argues this was due to an earlier effort to universalize the letter. Metzger concludes it probably did originally mention Ephesus. (Bruce M. Metzger, *The Canon of the New Testament: Its Origin, Development, and Significance* (Oxford: Clarendon Press, 1987) at 265.)
2. Alan F. Segal, *Paul the Convert* (New Haven: Yale University Press, 1990) at 189.

> The city was built on ***twelve*** foundation stones. On each of the stones was written the name of one of the Lamb's ***twelve apostles.*** (Rev. 21:14 CEV.)

There is a clear correspondence of one apostle for each of the twelve tribes, gates, and foundation stones. The number each time is only *twelve*. It implies there are not supposed to be more than twelve apostles. You cannot have thirteen or fourteen apostles judging the twelve tribes. Jesus made this clear during His earthly ministry as well. Jesus said the role of the *twelve* apostles was to "sit upon *twelve* thrones, judging the *twelve* tribes of Israel." (Matt. 19:28.)

The apostles understood it the same way. When Judas fell away and was lost, they added Matthias to bring their number back to twelve. (Acts 1:22-26.) When apostles were martyred later, such as Apostle James (the brother of John), mentioned in Acts 12:2, the apostles did not replace him. Had they done so, this would bring their number to thirteen in the resurrection ruling over the New Jerusalem. The apostles must have seen the mis-match which a thirteenth apostle would represent in fulfilling their role as *twelve* judges over the *twelve* tribes into eternity.

Alan Johnson in the Calvinist *Expositor's Bible Commentator* agrees the early church treated the offices of the *twelve* apostles as dying with them. They were not to be replaced. Their number of *twelve* was unique.

> As to whether the authoritative function of apostles continued after the first century, the apostolic fathers are instructive. In no case do the many references to apostles in the writings of Clement of Rome, Ignatius, Barnabas, and the Shepherd of Hermas relate to any recognized apostles other than those associated with the NT. The Fathers apparently understood ***the special apostolic function [on earth] to have ceased with the end of the apostolic era***.[3]

Luke in Acts made it evident there were only twelve apostles for all time, and this excluded Paul. ***Never does Paul claim in Acts to be an apostle of Jesus. Never do the apostles describe Paul as an apostle.*** This has been recognized by all Pauline scholars. For example, John Crossan and Jonathan Reed, in their latest work of 2004:

> [I]n all his letters, Paul sees himself as an apostle sent from God through Christ.[4] The very vocation for which Paul lives is ***denied him by Luke***. He is, to be sure, an important missionary....But ***he is not an apostle*** equal to the Twelve.[5]

Furthermore, Crossan & Reed make the point that Luke's story of how Matthias replaced Judas excludes the possibility of a thirteenth apostle such as Paul. They write:

> Luke insists in Acts 1 that, after Jesus' resurrection, there were still, ***always, and only*** 'the twelve apostles.'...For Luke, ***Paul is simply not an apostle***.[6] Without Matthias' explicit selection, one might have imagined that Luke's Paul was at least implicitly Judas' replacement as the twelfth apostle. With it, ***Luke implies that Paul was not an apostle*** and ***could never be one***....[H]e could never be the one thing Paul always insisted that he was, namely, an apostle

3. Alan Johnson, "Revelation," *Hebrews-Revelation* in *The Expositor's Bible Commentary* (Ed. F.E. Gaebelein)(Zondervan: 1981) Vol. 12 at 434.

4. *See, e.g.*,1 Cor. 1:1; 2 Cor. 1:1; Galatians 1:1; 1 Ti. 1:1. *See, viz.*, "For I am the least of the apostles, that am not meet to be called an apostle, because I persecuted the church of God." (1 Cor. 15:9, ASV) and "For I reckon that I am not a whit behind the very chiefest apostles." (2 Cor. 11:5, ASV).

5. John Crossan & Jonathan Reed, *In Search of Paul: How Jesus' Apostle Opposed Rome's Empire with God's Kingdom* (San Francisco: Harper San Francisco, 2004) at 29.

> sent by God through a revelation of the risen Lord. (*Id.*, at 29.)

Thus, the only person to say Paul is an apostle *of Jesus Christ* in the entire New Testament is Paul himself. Yet, we know that Jesus said if He alone bore witness to Himself, then His witness would be untrue. (John 5:31, "If I bear witness of myself, my witness is not true.") Jesus was extending the Law's principle, so that two witnesses were necessary to establish not only a wrong, but also anything as important as God sending someone for a special role.[7] In fact, Jesus in Revelation 2:2 clearly agrees a self-serving claim to be His apostle is insufficient.[8] Thus, Paul's claim to being an apostle thus suffers from being self-serving. By a *Biblical* standard from *Jesus* Himself, Paul's self-witness "is not true."

Thus, the identity of the person who *said* he was an apostle to the Ephesians in Revelation 2:2 but who could not be an apostle is proven from the Bible itself. Honest Pauline scholars have conceded this underlying problem to Paul's validity. His claim to apostleship is uncorroborated and thus Jesus says Paul's claim "is not true." (John 5:31.) As a result, it is obvious the person spoken of in Revelation 2:2 is Paul because the New Testament gives us a record of:

---

6. Luke does describe Paul and Barnabas as messengers from the church at Antioch. In Acts 14:4 and 14, the Greek word for *messenger* is used for them, *apostoli*. However, as the Christian historian Ben Witherington explains: "The use of the term *apostoli* in [Acts] 14:4 and 14 seems to indicate that Paul and Barnabas are being viewed as agents/apostles of the Antioch church (cf. 2 Cor. 8:23), not apostles with a capital A." (Witherington, *New Testament History* (Baker Academic: 2001) at 229.) In fact, the context clearly shows Paul was merely a messenger (*apostolos*) of the church of Antioch. Paul was not one of the *apostoli* of Jesus. Even if Luke had called Paul an apostle of Jesus, Luke does not attribute such title as coming from the twelve apostles, or from Jesus in any vision that Paul relates. Thus, it would have been Luke's remark alone. Luke never claims he himself is a prophet. Nor even if he was a prophet, we still lack the second witness. Nevertheless, Luke's meaning was *apostoli* with a small *a*. Paul was a messenger from Antioch.

- Only *one person* told the Ephesians he was an apostle who was in fact not one of the twelve apostles (*i.e.*, Paul).
- A complete record of the twelve apostles in Acts excludes Paul.
- In Acts, Paul was never recognized as an apostle by the twelve; and
- In Acts, Paul never claims to be an apostle of Jesus Christ and thus no record exists of an authoritative acceptance by the twelve of Paul as such an apostle.

---

7. Jesus was corroborated by God's Holy Spirit in the appearance of a Dove as well as the Father's voice from heaven. (Matt. 3:16-17.) Paul lacks any corroboration on his claim. The theme of corroboration by two witnesses runs throughout the Bible. The Law said that no crime could be established by a single witness. (Deut. 19:15, "any crime or any wrong"). Jesus taught in event of a dispute over a wrong, obtain witnesses so by "the mouth of two witnesses or three ***every word*** may be established." (Mat 18:16.) Why must this principle apply to would-be apostles? Because without two witnesses with *competent knowledge,* one's claim is entirely *self-serving.* If two witnesses were needed to prove a crime, how much more so to prove something far more important eternally such as one being an apostle. In this case, the Ephesians must have realized proof that someone was an apostle required more than the person's say-so that he was an apostle. Just as Jesus' witnesses were the voice of Yahweh and the Holy Spirit in the form of a dove, Paul needed two witnesses. In this case, the only valid *two* witnesses would be Jesus on one side and/or the joint decision of the twelve apostles of Jesus Christ on the other. The binding authority of the apostles required a joint decision, and not the solitary decision of a single apostle. This is precisely how Matthias was added as the twelfth. (See "Apostolic Decisions Were Binding In Heaven Only When Reached Jointly" on page 494.) However, such proof from either Jesus or the twelve is entirely lacking in the New Testament. Paul's supposed apostleship is ***never stated by Jesus*** in any of the three vision accounts in Acts. Nor is such an assertion about Paul found in any apostolic speech in Acts or letter of an apostle of Jesus Christ. Not even the pseudograph of 2 Peter says Paul is an apostle. (On its pseudograph nature, see Appendix B at page xix.)

Paul & Luke Mention A Heresy Trial of Paul at Ephesus

Is there any evidence in the Bible that the Ephesians determined Paul was not an apostle?

Yes. Paul and Luke both mention that Paul was subject to a heresy trial at Ephesus, a city of Asia (Western Turkey). Paul likewise mentions that all the churches of Asia (Western Turkey) thereafter came to reject Paul. We are puzzled by these verses and we pass over them. However, in light of Revelation 2:2, God has given us this evidence so we can apply Revelation 2:2.

Some background on Ephesus is necessary to understand the Bible passages at issue.

Ephesus was in the province of Asia. This was not near China. Rather it was a Roman province along the west coast of modern Turkey, near Greece. To differentiate this Asia from the Far East, it is sometimes called Proconsular Asia. Ephesus was Proconsular Asia's leading city. Ephesus had a population of 250,000.[9]

---

8. Revelation 2:2 specifically says the persons on trial "said" they were apostles. Yet, such a self-serving statement did not suffice. Jesus says the claimants were appropriately found to be liars. Thus, Jesus' own words in Revelation 2:2 agree that self-serving testimony cannot ever be the basis to treat someone as an apostle of Jesus Christ.
9. For background on Ephesus, see Ben Witherington, *New Testament History* (Baker Academic: 2001) at 280.

FIGURE 1. **Map of the Roman province of Proconsular Asia**

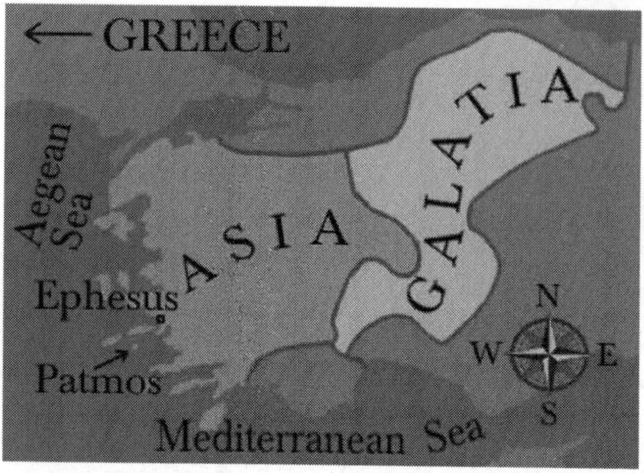

In Second Timothy, Paul talks of a trial he endured in a Christian congregation. Paul says he put up "his first defense" among them. However, Paul says "all forsook me." (2 Tim. 4:14-17.) In an exact parallel, Paul identifies in the same epistle that this trial took place in Asia—where Ephesus is the capital. Paul writes that *all the Christians of Asia defected from him*. What else other than a heresy trial at Asia's leading church of Ephesus can explain this action? In 2 Timothy 1:15, Paul writes:

> This thou knowest, that ***all that are in Asia turned away from me***; of whom are Phygelus and Hermogenes. (ASV)

Paulinists have no explanation of this verse except to deny Paul's words. Adam Clarke says Paul must be referring to Asiatic Christians at Rome. "He cannot be speaking of any general defection of the Asiatic Church...." However, *Asia* is primarily two major cities: Ephesus and Smyrna. It is not that hard to believe such a defection took place. We are not talking of a large area covering many major churches. Furthermore, Clarke has no explanation for denying Paul means what he says. It is self-evident Clarke is appealing to our respect for Paul. We cannot imagine Paul sinking so low.

Thus, even Paul's own words that "all... in Asia turned away from me..." cannot convince those devoted to Paul that what Paul says is true.

However, contrary to Clarke's spin, Luke in Acts chapter 19 records the event leading to what Paul mentioned in 2 Timothy 1:15 and 4:14-17. Luke records that the budding church of Ephesus decided at one point to have nothing further to do with Paul. In fact, Luke appears to be implying a heresy trial of Paul took place at Ephesus in Asia. Here is what Luke records in Acts 19:1, 8-9 (ASV):

> (1)...Paul...came to Ephesus....(8) And he entered into the synagogue [at Ephesus], and spake boldly for the space of three months, reasoning and persuading as to the things concerning the kingdom of God. (9) But when some were ***hardened*** and disobedient, speaking evil of the Way before the multitude, ***he departed from them*** [*i.e.*, the Ephesians].

Thus, in Luke's account, Paul no longer went to the budding church at Ephesus where he had been "persuading" them for three months. While it appears the leadership favored Paul, he encountered opposition eventually from some influential members.[10] Clearly, this event would be a muted way that a friend like Luke would record a heresy trial.

10.It is hard to imagine after three months of Paul's preaching ("reasoning and ***persuading*** concerning the kingdom of God") that this *assembly* lacked a significant support for Jesus as Messiah. Paul apparently always preached correctly the Messianic prophecies in the Law and Prophets. (Acts 28:23 *et seq.*) Thus, there could have been a significant number among the leadership who accepted Jesus as Messiah. However, then Luke says "some were hardened" at the end of this three month period. It does not appear this came at the leadership level. Apparently something Paul said at the end of three months *turned off influential members completely to Paul's version of the Way.* Thus, it appears the leadership of the assembly had previously turned to Christ, but now influential members objected to Paul's preaching there, forcing a trial to resolve the issue. Thus, this synagogue qualifies to be seen as the *assembly* mentioned in Revelation 2:2.

Yet, this parallels what Jesus spoke about twenty years later in Revelation 2:2. There was a trial at Ephesus of a person who said he was an apostle but who was not (and could not be) an apostle.

Paul in Second Corinthians again recalls this defection among Christians of Asia. He says it felt like he was under the "sentence of death." In 2 Cor. 1:8-9, Paul writes:

> (8) For we would not have you ignorant, brethren, concerning our affliction which befell us in ***Asia***, that we were weighed down exceedingly, beyond our power, insomuch that we despaired even of life: (9) yea, we ourselves have had ***the sentence of death*** within ourselves, that we should not trust in ourselves, but in God who raiseth the dead: (ASV)

Hence, Paul alludes to an affliction in Proconsular Asia—in which Ephesus was the leading city—which felt like an experience of a death-sentence. The fact Paul was not killed is proof he is speaking figuratively. A church heresy verdict in Asia would perfectly fit Paul's meaning. If Paul were the one Jesus has in mind in Revelation 2:2 (*i.e.*, someone tried as a false claimant to being an apostle), such a verdict would be like a *sentence of death.* It would be a crushing blow to Paul's evangelism.

Evidence of the Actual Verdict At Ephesus in The Writings of Tertullian in 207 A.D.

It appears in 207 A.D. that Tertullian in a work entitled *Against Marcion* memorializes the *actual verdict* at Ephesus against Paul. Tertullian is a leading member of the church of Carthage, and a prolific writer on Christian themes. He is one of the most respected of all the Christian writers who predate the Roman Catholic era which began in 325 A.D.

To understand Tertullian's words about Paul, we need to lay some background on church doctrine of that era and on Marcion.

The early church commentators in the 125-325 A.D.[11] period universally rejected almost all uniquely Pauline doctrines. Instead, in that period, almost all doctrine belonged to James' teachings.[12]

> **"The writings of Tertullian...were often on the lips of Calvin and Luther."**
> **David C. Noe, Ph.D., *Cloud of Witnesses* (2004) Bethel Presbyterian Church (Va.)**

This is never disputed by Paulinists. The first 'orthodox' post-apostolic thinker who Paulinists ever cite as holding Pauline doctrines is Augustine from the late 300s A.D. He was the first and only early Christian voice to espouse predestination as taught by Paul. He also spoke of the gift of perseverance. Augustine was a leading Roman Catholic figure whose writings date to the Fourth Century.

However, there was someone prior to Augustine who held Pauline doctrines on grace and salvation: it was Marcion. He arose around 144 A.D. (See Appendix B: *How the Canon Was Formed* at page ix.)

11. This is the period that antedates the rise of Roman Catholicism as we think of it today. While there was a bishop of Rome since apostolic times, there was no superiority of this bishop acknowledged by any others until after 325 A.D. Even after that point, this superiority was only recognized within the Roman Empire. Within its territory, the Roman government gave official sanction and exclusive legitimacy to the Roman Catholic Church. For more background, see footnote 16.

12. See "Patristic Era (125-325 A.D.) Rejected Paul's Salvation Doctrine" on page 425. See "The Patristic Era Church Also Rejected Paul's Predestination Doctrine" on page 432. See "The Patristic Era Also Blasted Paul's Doctrine on Eating Idol Meat" on page 435. See "The Eastern Orthodox Church & Paul" on page 438. See also *Paul or James' Church: Who Was The Most Successful Evangelist?*, available online exclusively at www.jesuswordsonly.com.

Despite Marcion's core doctrines agreeing with Paul, the early church in that period pursued Marcion and his followers as heretics. The Marcionites clearly held Paul's doctrines of salvation by faith alone (*i.e.* without obedience) as the true gospel. (See page 49.) Marcion insisted the twelve apostles (and their gospel narratives) were wrong on the doctrine of grace. Marcion claimed their gospel narratives were for the era of Law. Marcion opted for a narrative of Jesus' life that reads a lot like Luke's gospel. However, it is missing the first three chapters of Luke and a few other passages. Based on Paul's letter to the Galatians, Marcion claimed the Law of Moses was abrogated. We do not have to obey the God of the 'Old Testament' but only the God of the New.

To counter this movement, the issue of Paul's validity had to be resolved. It is in this context that the well-respected Christian leader, Tertullian, stood up in 207 A.D. and wrote *Against Marcion.*

Tertullian's Points About Paul

What Tertullian wrote about Paul's validity has all the earmarks of what one would expect would be a judicial decision at Ephesus involving Paul.

Tertullian makes the following sobering points about Paul:

- Jesus never made Paul an apostle from the records that we can read.
- Paul's claim to apostleship solely relies upon Paul's veracity.
- If Paul were a true apostle, he is still an inferior apostle because Paul in Acts 15 submitted his doctrine to the twelve.
- If Paul later varied from the twelve, we must regard the twelve as more authoritative than Paul because he came later.
- Paul's claim of being selected as an apostle later by Jesus seems implausible. That story asks us to believe Jesus had not planned things adequately with the twelve.

- Lastly, Jesus warned us of false prophets who would come doing miracles in His name and signs and wonders, and Paul perfectly matches that prophesied type of prophet.

This passage from Tertullian is quoted *verbatim* later in this book at page 408 *et seq.*

Tertullian's words are an echo of precisely what one would expect to hear in a sensible verdict about Paul at Ephesus. Tertullian is apparently revealing to us the findings in the Revelation 2:2 hearing. Paul is not to be regarded as an apostle on par with the twelve, if at all. Whatever Paul truly represents in God's eyes, in our finite eyes we must realize Paul is subject to the authority and *superior* teaching of the twelve. Finally, Tertullian said Paul possibly is a liar and a false prophet because he came in the name of Christ with signs and wonders and only had himself as a witness of his apostolic status. Tertullian said this meant Paul potentially fits Jesus' express warning about false prophets. (See Matt. 7:21 *et seq.*) Thus, Tertullian concluded we must quote from Paul cautiously. In other words, only if Paul's words solidly line up with Jesus' words should we follow Paul's words.

Tertullian's teachings not only reflect apparently the ruling at Ephesus, but they also *explain* why we see the early church never following most of Paul's core teachings. This pattern continued for almost two millennia until Luther revived Paulinism. In earliest Christianity, Paul must have been deemed inferior by the church at large, particularly on issues of salvation, or else the following facts make no sense:

- The early church leaders from 125-325 A.D. *universally* reject almost all of Paul's unique doctrines, *e.g.*, salvation by faith alone, total depravity, predestination, man lacks free-will, docetism, etc.[13]

---

13. See footnote 12 on page 225. On Paul's docetism, and its rejection, see "Did Paul Teach Jesus Did Not Truly Have Human Flesh?" on page 336 *et seq.*

- The Orthodox Church (now totalling 250 million members) can trace back its origins to that same early church. It existed in territories outside the Roman Empire and was free therefore to reject most of the errors later arising in Roman Catholicism (*e.g.*, extreme Mariology, etc).[14] Yet, its doctrines are identical to the early church of 125-325 A.D. To this day the Orthodox reject all of Paul's uniquely Pauline doctrines. Furthermore, in direct contravention of Paul's directive in Galatians, the Orthodox also keep the Mosaic law's command to rest on the Saturday-Sabbath. The Orthodox claim it was never abrogated. (They have always also worshipped on Sunday.)[15]
- Roman Catholicism, in the form we know it today, arose after 325 A.D.[16] Despite all its flaws, it still retained some of the core teaching of James and Jesus on salvation, claiming sin causes loss of salvation. Thus, Catholicism has always rejected Paul's faith alone and eternal security teaching. Augustine, however, misled Catholicism to adopt a Sacramental system where the church dispensed *regeneration* by baptism even to infants without faith. The Catholic church also did accept two doctrines espoused uniquely by Paul: original sin and the abrogation of the Mosaic law (*e.g.*, abrogating Saturday Sabbath for Christians). Thus, Catholicism in 363 A.D. broke the prior nearly universal tradition among Christians of keeping Saturday Sabbath. By contrast, the Orthodox—who long ago severed ties with Roman Catholicism—reject the doctrine of original sin and Mariology while they have kept the Saturday Sabbath for 2,000 years.

---

14. While the Orthodox do not engage in extreme Mariology, they do have a potentially unhealthy attention on Mary. The Orthodox "do not view Mary as a Mediator and Co-redemptrix as does the Roman Catholic church, but it does view Mary as the perpetual virgin and as an intercessor to be prayed to. Orthodox theologians are quick to deny that Mary is to be worshiped...." (Bill Crouse, *The Orthodox Church* (C.I.M.)) However, it is obvious praying to any person for supernatural assistance other than God is having another *god* before the True God. It is idol-worship. It violates the First and Second Commandments.
15. See page 438 *et seq.*

This history demonstrates that the main church, other than heretics, all rejected Paul's unique core teachings for almost two millennia. Tertullian's words show a judicious approach to Paul, as if rendered by a court. Paul can be listened to insofar as he does not contradict Jesus. But we do not

---

16.Roman Catholicism as we know it today was created after 325 A.D. After that date, the Roman Emperors authorized it to exert authority over all Christian churches in the Roman Empire. As a result, the *papacy* as we know it today arose sometime after 325 A.D. There is no denying that Peter around 47 A.D. founded a branch church at Rome. He did the same earlier at Antioch. That gave Rome a co-equal claim with the church at Antioch to apostolic origin. This gave Rome a superior claim in the West over churches outside Antioch's influence. (Sixty-six churches were under Antioch's authority.) The Roman church did become a leader among its close neighbors. (See Irenaeus, *Against Heresies*, 3:1:1 (A.D. 189); Eusebius, *History of the Church*, 6:14:1.) But was this a direct administrative control by infallible decree as we know today? No. Roman Catholic authorities try to prove the *papacy* existed in the pre-325 period from two examples. However, even by these official Catholic accounts, both times the bishop of Rome tried to exert influence outside Rome, it was not appreciated. It is resisted. The first example is from Tertullian. Tertullian ridicules the effort by the Roman bishop to be "bishop of bishops." This belies the authority was welcome or accepted. It certainly shows leaders at Carthage like Tertullian did not deem the Roman bishop's authority as infallible. The final example they cite is from Irenaeus, but it is more of the same. Rather than proving the *papacy* existed prior to 325 A.D., these two examples prove just the opposite. (See "The Pope," *The Catholic Encyclopedia*, http://www.newadvent.org/cathen/12260a.htm.) Another distinctive doctrine of the Roman Catholics is that Mary was sinless.This too materialized late. It was a doctrine rejected in the so-called *patristic* age (125-325 A.D.) As the *Catholic Encyclopedia* concedes, "in regard to the sinlessness of Mary, the older Fathers are very cautious: some of them even ***seem to be in error on the matter***." ("Immaculate Conception," *C. Enc.*, http://www.newadvent.org/cathen/07674d.htm.) Thus, what makes Roman Catholicism distinctly Catholic arose after 325 A.D. There were many later accretions that we also think of as Catholic, but they did not pre-exist 325 A.D. These include the following familiar doctrines: purgatory as doctrine (593 A.D.); prayers to Mary and dead saints (600 A.D.); celibacy of priesthood (1079 A.D.); indulgences (1190 A.D.); purgatory as dogma (1439 A.D.) etc. Thus, Roman Catholicism as we know it today arose *after* 325 A.D. It cannot trace its distinctive papal office and unique doctrines back any farther in historical records.

treat Paul as inspired, *ever*. We make no effort to bend Jesus' words to fit Paul's words. That appears to be the actual verdict at Ephesus. This explains ***why Paul's writings were allowed to be connected physically to the Lord's gospel.*** With a *proper introduction*, it was believed Paul's letters could be read for whatever worth they held. Otherwise, on any teaching at odds with Jesus, Paul had to be and was ignored.

Tertullian's comments on Paul's validity, therefore, if affixed as an introduction to Paul's letters, would allow us to sift the good from the bad. Tertullian's thoughts on Paul were forgotten or ignored by Luther and Calvin. Their emphasis on Paul's words broke every caution that Tertullian put up in 207 A.D.

Thus, the Reformation was launched in the 1520s based on Paul's writings without remembering how the church had kept Paul subordinate to the twelve. Paul was subordinate in particular to the four gospel accounts of the teachings of Jesus. This subordination apparently had been cemented in the verdict in Revelation 2:2. Paul's place in the church was decreed at Ephesus. Jesus commended the verdict in Revelation 2:2. It stood solid until the 1520s when Luther began proclaiming once again, like Marcion, the gospel of Paul.

Why Is Paul Then In the Post-Apostolic Canon Lists?

As noted above, Tertullian's view of Paul in 207 A.D. was that he was inferior to the true apostles. If this was well-known and accepted, then why was Paul added within the ensuing century to the New Testament canon? The answer primarily depends on recognition that *canon* back then did not mean what we mean by *canon* today. If we had the same concept of canon today as back then, we would be willing to include popular writers in our New Testament along with the *inspired* writers. We might attach the writings of C.S.Lewis or Billy Graham. We would know the difference. We would acknowledge both are inferior to the twelve apostles and

Jesus. But we could still read them both for edification. This was Jerome's express understanding of canon in 411 A.D. That year Jerome personally affixed the Apocrypha to his complete translation of the Bible. This Bible was known as the Latin Vulgate. Jerome clearly said he added the Apocrypha solely because it was edifying. Its connection did not signify the *Apocrypha* could be used as the basis of doctrine. In other words, it was not inspired.[17]

This was also clearly the same point Tertullian made about Paul's writings in *Against Marcion* (207 A.D.). Tertullian demonstrated a judicious approach. He affirms Paul is not a true apostle and even is possibly a false prophet. Tertullian goes on to say Paul is "my apostle." He finds edifying doctrines of Paul that are consistent with Jesus.

Tertullian was not ignoring Paul had contrary doctrine to Jesus on salvation and eternal security. Tertullian goes to great lengths to refute Paul's contrary doctrines without mentioning Paul's name.[18]

Why did Tertullian make any effort to retain Paul for edification purposes while making otherwise highly critical observations about him and his doctrines? The reason appears obvious. Tertullian is battling the Marcionites. They claim Paul alone has the true gospel. It is a gospel where obedience does not matter any more. God saves the believer and no longer judges one for disobedience.[19] The Marcionites insist the twelve apostles were legalistic. The twelve presented a Jesus who made salvation turn on obedience. The Jesus of the twelve did not present the gospel of Paul. The twelve's gospel belonged to the God of the Old Testament. Paul's gospel

17.See Footnote Number 6 on page 36.

18.See "Tertullian Criticizes Every Pauline Doctrine of Marcion" on page 421.

19.See page 49.

belonged to the God of the New Testament.[20] Tertullian was obviously struggling to find a solution to this excessive marginalization of Jesus.

What solution did Tertullian choose? It was simple. He chose good politics. We can hold onto Paul, read him for edification purposes, but we must realize he is not inspired. He is not on par with the twelve. This is what explains Paul's presence in later canon lists.

Thus, early canon lists which add Paul can only be understood in light of Marcionism. Marcionite Paul-onlyism was bravely fought off by the church. The price of peace was that Jesus' true apostles had pre-eminence, but Paul's writings could be read for edification.

Luke Even Tells Us What Were The Charges of Heresy Against Paul

Returning to the specifics of the trial at Ephesus, Luke gives us another important tid-bit. From this morsel, we can deduce what was the charge against Paul at the Ephesus church. In Acts chapter 21, Luke tells us that Jews *from Asia* at Jerusalem were saying Paul spoke against the continuing validity of the Law and against the Jewish people's position within the New Covenant. In Acts 21:28, "Jews from ***Asia***" appeal to James for help, complaining: "This is the man that teacheth all men everywhere against the people and the Law...." These Jews were likely followers of Jesus. This is apparently why they appealed to James for help. They were saying Paul was teaching against the continuing role of national Israel as covenant-partner with God and against the Law of Moses. James then takes their side in conversations with Paul, which bolsters again the fact these were Christian Jews.

20.See "Marcion's Canon (144 A.D.)." on page ix of Appendix B.

The Biblical Basis to these Charges Against Paul

> **"I will make a new covenant with the House of Israel and the House of Judah... I will put the Torah on their hearts."**
> **Jeremiah 31:31-34**

Of course, if Paul taught these things alleged in Acts 21:28, he would be contradicting God's promise of a New Covenant in Jeremiah 31:31. This promise specifically insisted it was not to replace the Mosaic Law. Nor was the New Covenant intended to forsake national Israel as God's covenant-partner. Rather, in the book of Jeremiah, God made a point of promising a "New Covenant with the House of Israel and Judah" based on *intensifying* internal knowledge of the *Law of Moses*. God would accompany this by revealing Himself more personally and offering forgiveness and mercy.[21] Thus, the Covenant of Mercy (which this New Covenant represents) was marked by making the knowledge of the terms of the Law more readily

21.Jeremiah 31:31-34 (ASV) reads: "Behold, the days come, saith Jehovah [*i.e.* Yahweh], that I will make a ***new covenant*** with the house of Israel, and with the house of Judah:...This is the covenant that I will make with the house of Israel after those days, saith Jehovah: ***I will put my Law* [Torah] *in their inward parts***, and in their heart will I write it; and I will be their God, and they shall be my people: and they shall teach no more every man his neighbor, and every man his brother, saying, Know Jehovah [*i.e.*, Yahweh]; for they shall all know me, from the least of them unto the greatest of them, saith Jehovah: for I will forgive their iniquity, and their sin will I remember no more."

known and practiced.[22] As God similarly said in Isaiah, when His Servant (Messiah) comes, God "will magnify the Law (Torah), and make it honorable." (Isaiah 42:21 KJV.)

This Jeremiah prophecy also specifically said God did not mean by a new covenant to imply he was exchanging an old partner for a new one. Immediately after the promise of the "New Covenant with the House of Israel and Judah," God declares how impossible it would be for Him to forsake the "***seed*** of Israel.... " Jeremiah chapter 31 reads:

> (35) Thus saith Jehovah, who giveth the sun for a light by day, and the ordinances of the moon and of the stars for a light by night, who stirreth up the sea, so that the waves thereof roar; Jehovah of hosts is his name: (36) ***If these ordinances depart from before me, saith Jehovah, then the seed of Israel also shall cease from being a nation before me for ever.*** (37) Thus saith Jehovah: If heaven above can be measured, and the foundations of the earth searched out beneath, then will I also cast off all the ***seed of Israel*** for all that they have done, saith Jehovah. Jeremiah 31:35-37 (ASV)

Dr. Renald Showers, in a prominent feature article on John Ankerberg's website, says this is too clear to ignore. "[I]t is evident that God intended to establish the New Covenant with the *literal* people of Israel."[23]

22. As one Jewish commentator explains Jer. 31:31 *et seq*, it "implies no rejection of the Covenant of the Torah (aka 'the Law') but rather that the Law shall be 'inscribed in hearts' of the Jewish people, *i.e.*, they will not have to study the Law, as before, but all of its details will be known 'by heart' and practiced by every Jew...." (*A Primer: Why Jews Cannot Believe in Jesus* (2003) (available online.) Indeed, how could "inscribed in their hearts" mean what Paulinists claim it means instead—the Law was *abrogated entirely?*

23. See Dr. Renald Showers, *The New Covenant*, at http://www.ankerberg.com/Articles/biblical-prophecy/BP1102W1.htm (2005).

Thus, because Paul indeed taught that God cut off Israel, abandoning her like Abraham did Hagar and Ishmael in the desert (Gal. 4:25-26) and now salvation was through another lineage (*i.e.*, Israel's father, Isaac) (Gal. 4:28), then Paul was guilty of the charge brought by the Asian Jews in Acts 21:28. The fact we know Paul taught both things charged by the "Asian Jews" heightens the probability he was convicted at Ephesus of such charges. Let's review the case.

Could A Law *Eternal for All Generations* Be Abrogated in 33 A.D.?

To prove the likelihood that Paul could be found guilty at Ephesus, let's recreate the prosecutor's probable case.

This promise of a New Covenant toward the seed of Israel in Jeremiah 31:35-37 is itself based upon the promise of God that "these ordinances" of the Law shall be "everlasting for all *generations*." (Ex. 27:21; 30:21; Lev. 6:18; 7:36; 10:9; 17:7; 23:14, 21, 41; 24:3; Num. 10:8; 15:15.)

Thus, for at least as long as humans have offspring, *i.e.*, generations, the Law remains valid. We know this period will be at least until heaven and earth pass away. This is because on the Last Day when all are resurrected (Rev. 20:13-15) appears "a new heaven and a new earth." (Rev. 21:1.) Then simultaneously the righteous are resurrected. They become like angels. They no longer get married or have offspring. (Matt. 22:30.) Thus, human generations cease on the Last Day. Thus, at least until humans no longer have generations and instead when they become like angels, the Law remains valid. It is as Jesus says:

> For verily I say unto you, Till heaven and earth pass away, one jot or one tittle shall in no wise pass away from the law, till all things be accomplished. (Matt. 5:18.)

Will the Law survive the passing of heavens and earth? We cannot know for sure. The only thing for sure we know that survives the passing of the heavens and earth are Jesus' words.

> Heaven and earth shall pass away, but my words shall not pass away. (Matt. 24:35.)

Thus, because Paul taught that a Jewish person was "released" from the Law in 33 A.D. by accepting their Messiah (Rom. 7:2), Paul was contradicting God's promise that the Law was "eternal for all generations." This may change after all the heavens and earth pass away (*i.e.*, when human generations cease), but that had not yet happened in 33 A.D. Thus, if the charges against Paul proved he said the Jewish people were released in 33 A.D. from their covenant obligation to keep the Law, Paul's Jewish-Christian opponents would have had a valid case against him.

In fact, we know Paul taught Jews were released from the Law in 33 A.D. Paul even insisted it was only because of stubbornness they continue to follow the Law. (Romans 7:1 *et seq.*; Rom. 10:21. See "Romans Chapter Seven Says the Jews Are Released From the Law" on page 80 *et seq.*; Luther, *Commentary on Galatians* 2:4-5.)

If Paul's letters did not prove these charges at Ephesus, we might doubt he was convicted there. However, because his actual writings prove the charges as true, there is a heightened probability that Paul was indeed convicted at Ephesus.

Conclusion

After Paul's death, Jesus reveals to John in Revelation some important lessons. One truth is that Jesus says there are twelve apostles. They are twelve pillars in the new heavens and earth. The number twelve is a number that is never increased in Jesus' mind, even after Paul's ministry is over. There is no thirteenth apostle. There is not a shred of evidence other than Paul's own testimony that he was an apostle.

There is never any mention in Acts or by Paul himself that the twelve apostles accepted Paul as an apostle of Jesus Christ *per se*. None in Acts. None in John's letters. Never in Paul's letters. None certainly in Revelation. Not in any apostles' letter. Nor even in the pseudograph Second Peter.[24]

Revelation 2:2 must therefore be talking about Paul. Jesus commends the Ephesians for finding someone lied when he *said* he was an apostle and *was not*. Paul was someone whom the Bible reveals told the Ephesians that he was an apostle, was not, and thus must be untruthful in this respect. Insert these facts about Paul into Revelation 2:2. One clear answer emerges: Revelation 2:2 identifies Paul. This means Jesus called Paul a *liar*. It also means Jesus commends the church for making this kind of evaluation. It proves we cannot shirk our duty to test the uncorroborated claims of Paul.

Note: Bonhoeffer — Modern Proponent of JWO

Dietrich Bonhoeffer, a Lutheran Pastor, wrote a book in 1937 entitled *Cost of Discipleship*. Bonhoeffer writes an entire book on salvation-principles that ignores Paul's doctrines. Bonhoeffer then expounds Jesus' principles on salvation and the Law. By doing so, Bonhoeffer subtly outlines what Jesus' Words Only means in terms of renovation of our doctrine: Preach and teach from Jesus' words alone.

---

24. Most Christian scholars of every stripe, including Calvin, agree Second Peter is a false addition to scripture. See "The Special Question of Second Peter" on page xix of Appendix B. Even if written by Apostle Peter, it does not help Paul's case. Second Peter does not describe him as an apostle. While Second Peter does imply Paul's writings are "Scripture," that does not mean what one might suppose. The word *Scripture* corresponds to the Hebrew for *Writings*. The Bible of that era was: Torah (Law), Prophets & Writings. The *Writings* section meant the book was not yet recognized as fully *inspired.* Thus, Daniel was kept in the *Writings* not the *Prophets* section as of Jesus' day. It was not yet recognized that Daniel's prophecies had come to pass. Thus, even if Peter implied Paul's writings were *scripture,* this does not carry with it the connotation we give the word *scripture* today.

First, Bonhoeffer concludes that Jesus has every intention that the Law (the Ten Commandments) survive in the New Testament. Bonhoeffer comments on Matthew 19:16-24. There Jesus answers on how to have eternal life by telling the young man "if you would enter life, obey the commandments." Bonhoeffer says Jesus, by quoting the Ten Commandments, has made a call "to a simple obedience to the will of God as it has been revealed." (*Cost*, *id.*, at 72.) Jesus reaffirms the Ten Commandments "as the commandments of God." (*Id.*, at 73.) Jesus is saying we must "get on with the task of obedience" and it is "high time the young man began to hear the commandment and obey it." (*Id.*)

Bonhoeffer then excoriates Christians who use Paul's attack on legalism to undermine Jesus' message:

> We are excusing ourselves from ***single-minded obedience to the words of Jesus*** [to the young rich man] on ***the pretext*** [that this endorses] ***legalism*** and a supposed preference for the obedience 'in faith.' (*Id.*, at 80.)

As to faith-and-works, Bonhoeffer ignores the dialectic of Paul. Instead, Bonhoeffer pits cheap grace against costly grace. Bonhoeffer says contemporary Christian churches which teach free grace engage in a "deliberate rejection" of Christ's teachings of the ***personal costliness*** of salvation. (*Id.* at 36.) Jesus' message of a costly grace has been overlaid with "the superstructure of... doctrinal elements" in modern preaching that destroys the cost-element Jesus demanded. (*Id.*) Bonhoeffer discusses several parables to prove obedience to the Law and repentance from sin are key.

As a result, Bonhoeffer envisioned an entire renovation of the Christian church. He believed that cheap grace had infected all our doctrine. We were a "Christianity without Christ." (*Cost of Discipleship*, *supra*, at 39.) Bonhoeffer had some even tougher words. He says of the cheap grace gospel that "Christ is misunderstood anew, and again and again put to death." (Bonhoefffer, *Christ the Center* (1960) at 35.)

11 *Was James Writing His Epistle For A Trial of Paul?*

Introduction

Scholars now recognize the Epistle of James was intended for a specific purpose: a trial. The epistle begins by explaining seating rules for a trial at a "synagogue," not at a church service.

However, there is more to support this trial theory than what the scholars have acknowledged. When one looks at James' message, one has the unmistakable sense that James is dismantling the doctrines taught by Paul. This is particularly true in James' discussion of faith and works. James explains Genesis 15:6 in a diametrically different way than Paul explained the very same verse. James tells the story of Abraham in a manner at total odds with Paul's account. James leads the reader to a diametrically opposite doctrine of justification by works and "not faith [that is] alone." There is also no mistaking that James defines salvation as crucially relying on faith and works, ***not one without the other***. He, in fact, mocks the idea that salvation depends upon doctrines you *only* mentally agree with. If mental belief *alone* were the true salvation formula, he says demons would be saved. The demons know and believe the truths about God, but they do not act upon them by pursuing God.

Finally, when you look through *all* of James, it is not just chapter two that takes Paul down a notch. It is almost every chapter and verse of James' Epistle that does so. It is as if James is spreading out Paul's letters on a table, finding flaws, and then writing messages that address those flaws.

This is precisely the kind of assistance one would expect from a leader in the early church to provide the judges in a pending trial of Paul. James' epistle would become the doctrinal reference guide for the judges.

However, did James have this role within the early church? Why would James, not Peter, provide an epistle for this special purpose if indeed that was its purpose?

It turns out that James (the brother of Jesus) was the bishop of Jerusalem. He was the first original head of Christ's church. This would make his input something to be expected at a heresy trial of Paul.

All the pieces fit that the Epistle of James was intended for a trial of Paul at a Christian-controlled synagogue. It fits the trial at Ephesus spoken about in Revelation 2:2. It fits the story of Luke in Acts chapter 19 of a budding 'synagogue'-church at Ephesus expelling Paul as a heretic.

Was It Written for A Trial At A Synagogue?

In James 2:2-4, James is discussing how a meeting at an assembly should be conducted. He discourages favoritism at this meeting. He gives rules for standing and sitting. The traditional understanding has been this was about a hypothetical gathering for worship. However, that now appears to have been a simplistic view. As Stulac mentions:

> A second and more recently advocated position is that the meeting is ***a judicial assembly of the church***, and that the rich and poor individuals are both members of the believing community who are involved in a dispute to be adjudicated.[1]

1. Stulac, *James* (1993), *supra*, at 90.

In 1969, R.B. Ward concluded James is "describing a ***judicial assembly*** rather than a worship service." (Stulac: 91.)[2] He notes there is a subsequent reference to *judges* and *courts*. (James 2:4, 2:6.) Second,

> it rather neatly resolves the questions some have had about this illustration in a worship setting. Why would Christians coming to worship need to be told where to stand or sit?... Why would some stand and others be seated? In Ward's ***judicial setting***, procedures of standing or sitting might well be unfamiliar to the participants, and clothing might be a factor that would unfairly impress the judges. (Stulac: 91.)

Nor can we overlook that this proceeding was to take place in a *synagogue*. In James 2:2-4, James uses the Greek word *synagoge* for this meeting even though in other places in the same letter (in 5:14) he refers to Christ's church as an *ecclesia*. The word *ecclesia* was typically used to mean *church*, as distinct from meetings at *synagoge*. Also, incongruously, this word *synagogue* is only used in the New Testament for a church-meeting in James 2:2-4. James intends it to be a particular gathering place for *Christians*. James' context makes it clear as to this *synagoge,* there is "Christian ownership of and authority over this assembly." (Stulac: 91.)

Thus, when we put these two facts together, we can deduce James was writing his letter in the context of an upcoming gathering at a Christian-controlled synagogue to conduct a trial. The event would involve a large crowd. Some would stand and some would sit. This is completely consistent with the idea of a *synagogue* at Ephesus at which Paul taught for three months. (Acts 19:8.) It fits the story of the synagogue at Ephesus from which Paul felt compelled to leave as recorded in Acts 19:9. It fits the place where Paul put

---

2. Stulac cites R.B. Ward, "Partiality in the Assembly: James 2:2-4," *Harvard Theological Review* 62:87-97 (1969).

on "his first defense" yet "all abandoned" him and "all in Asia abandoned" him. (2 Tim. 1:15; 4:14-17.) Ephesus was the capital city of Asia—Western Turkey. (For more discussion, see page 224 *et seq.*) James' Epistle appears to have been written for a trial of Paul. It appears it was for the trial at Ephesus which Jesus alludes to in Revelation 2:2.

James Is the Head Bishop of the Church

Why would James be giving an evaluation of Paul's teachings for purpose of a trial? Because James was the head of the church at that time. Paul indirectly alludes to this in Galatians 2:9:

> ***James*** and Cephas and John, they who were reputed to be ***pillars***...(ASV).

Cephas was the Aramaic version of Peter's name. Thus, Paul says the main supports (pillars) in Jerusalem appeared to be ***James***, Peter, and John.

Second, we find in Acts that James takes the position of the final decision-maker over and above the apostles on doctrinal issues. In Acts 15:6, the "apostles and elders were gathered together to consider" the issue whether Gentiles needed to be circumcised. After Paul and Peter speak, James gets up in Acts 15:19 and says "I judge" (Young's Literal). James then spells out exactly what is to be done and all the particulars. A letter is to be written and several specific requirements are to be demanded. Robertson's *Word Pictures* explains James uses an expression of *krino* (to judge) in the first person form. Robertson further explains that this is exactly the form used by a judicial officer. It means "I give my judgment." Robertson says the implication on James' status is clear:

> James sums up the case as President of the Conference in a masterly fashion and with that consummate wisdom for which he is noted.

The apostles including Peter were all present. Obviously, they previously had authorized James to exercise such authority on doctrine. In fact, they were evidently waiting for his final ruling.

Lastly, the proof we have that James was the head of the church at the time of his epistle comes from abundant external ancient sources. These sources say James was appointed by the twelve apostles as the head over the Jerusalem church. Because there are some in Christendom who suppose this honor belongs to Peter, we need to review the evidence in depth.

> **"[To] James alone, it was allowed to enter into the Holy of Holies because he was a Nazirite and connected to the Priesthood [through Mary and to King David through Joseph]."**
> **Epiphanius *Panarion 30***

Historical Sources For James' Role

First, Eusebius (c. 260-341) in about 325 A.D. wrote the following in *Ecclesiastical History*. Eusebius is regarded as a conservative early Church historian, having at one time himself been bishop of Caesarea in Palestine. Eusebius agrees James was the initial leader of the church after Jesus' resurrection.

> James, the brother of the Lord, to whom the episcopal seat at Jerusalem had been ***entrusted by the apostles.*** (*Ecclesiastical History*, Chapter XXIII.)

What Eusebius says, we see occurring in Acts ch. 15.

Hegesippus (c. 120?), who lived immediately after the apostles in Palestine, had written a work divided into five books called *Memoirs*. In Book V, he mentions:

> James, the brother of the Lord succeeded to the government of the Church ***in conjunction with the apostles.*** *Memoirs of Hegesippus* Book V (quoted by Eusebius).

Jerome, the famous translator of the entire Bible into the Latin Vulgate (405 A.D.), devotes chapter two of his *On Famous Men* to a biography of James the Just. This is another name for the James who is talking in Acts chapter 15. Incidentally, as you read this quote, you will see Jerome is struggling on how this person can be "the brother of Jesus" and yet Mary was a perpetual virgin. By the 400s, the Roman Catholic church was now claiming Mary remained a perpetual virgin. Jerome gives a very odd explanation of how James could be the "brother of Jesus." Jerome suggests that James is the son of a sister of Mary. (This entire effort to make Mary a perpetual virgin is unscriptural and *dangerous*.)[3] However, what is important is that Jerome cites Hegesippus for the fact that James was appointed the "bishop[4] of Jerusalem" by the "apostles." Jerome writes:

3. Roman Catholicism insists Mary remained a perpetual virgin. Yet, in Matthew 13:55-56 when the people of Nazareth are amazed at Jesus, they ask: "Is not his *brothers* ***James*** and Joseph and Simon and Judas [*i.e.*, Jude]?" Catholic authorities claim *brother* here should be understood as *cousin*. However, there is a word in Greek for cousin, *anepsios*. When ancient writers spoke of James, they called him the *brother* of Jesus. In the same context, they identified Jesus' *cousins*, using the word *anepsios*. (Eusebius, *Hist. Eccl.* 4.22.4; *see* 2.23.4 and 3.20.1 (quoting Hegesippus).) Also, Matthew 1:24-25 states Mary and Joseph had sex after Jesus was born. Once he knew of the pregnancy, Joseph "had no marital relations with her ***until she had born a son***." This is the same as saying he had sexual relations with Mary only after she had a son. Furthermore, if Mary never had sexual relations with Joseph, she would have defrauded him. (1 Cor. 7:5.) Marriage in Judaism meant having sex with God's purposes in mind: to sustain a family line. (Ben Witherington, *Woman in the Ministry of Jesus* (Cambridge: Cambridge University Press, 1984.) The notion of perpetual virginity is based on the pious but unsupportable idea that Mary has to be purer than pure sexually.

> James, who is called the brother of the Lord, surnamed the Just, the son of Joseph by another wife, as some think, but, as appears to me, the son of Mary sister of the mother of our Lord of whom John makes mention in his book, after our Lord's passion at **once ordained by the apostles bishop of Jerusalem**,... Hegesippus who lived near the apostolic age, in the fifth book of his Commentaries, writing of James. says 'After the apostles, James the brother of the Lord surnamed the Just was made ***head of the Church at Jerusalem***.'

"The Lord's brother was Holy from his birth. Everyone from the Lord's time till our time has called him the Righteous." Hegesippus (quoted in Eusebius *E.H.* 2.23)

Likewise, Epiphanius, a bishop in the late 300s, writes of James in his *Panarion* 29.3.4. He says that "James having been ordained at once the ***first*** bishop, he who is called the brother of the Lord.... [W]e find as well that he is of David's stock through being Joseph's son...."[5] To the same effect is Clement of Alexandria, who said the apostles did not pick from their own number "because the savior [already] had specifically honored them, but [instead] chose James the Just as Bishop of Jerusalem."[6]

There is thus no question that James is the original head bishop of the church of Christ. He was appointed by the twelve apostles themselves. Acts ch. 15 gives witness to this, as well as *all* ancient histor-

4. The concept of *bishop* in those days was a person whose principal function was to officiate and give a sermon at church gatherings (besides having authority over sibling churches in the *same city*). We learn this by the evidence of the *Canons of Hippolytus* (ed. Paul F. Bradshaw)(Grove Books, 1987) which discusses church offices and functions in an Egyptian church sometime between 311 and 400. Hippolytus does not mention pastors, ministers, or priests. The only other officers were elders and deacons. Deacons gave sermons sometimes.

ical sources. Thus, contrary to a popular misconception, Peter was not the bishop of the Christian church when it first began. Rather, as Acts chapter 15 depicts, in the early period Peter speaks but then everyone waits for James to decide the issue.

This is not to detract from Peter's important role either. Around 42 A.D., ten years into James' service as bishop over Jerusalem, Peter founded a church at Rome. Peter was, in effect, its first bishop.[7] (Every city in Christendom had its own bishop. Thus, Peter was *de facto* bishop at Rome even if some bishop lists omit his name.) By the same token, Peter's position at Rome ten years into James' primary position at Jerusalem does not detract from James' role.

While scholars did not initially appreciate Professor Eisenman's resurrecting these historical references about James outlined above, renown Christian scholars have now come to Eisenman's defense. They acknowledge it was James, not Peter, who *actually* first led the church from Jerusalem.[8]

---

5. Joseph was in the Davidic line, not Mary. Thus, James was born through the seed of Joseph. Epiphanius says James was picked as bishop because he shared the Davidic blood-line. Consequently ***Joseph must be the father of James***. Could Mary *not* be his physical birth-mother? It is possible but not plausible. Either Joseph must have been previously married or Mary predeceases him. The latter alternative makes no sense. When Mary is still very much alive, the townspeople ask about Jesus and his brother James. In Matthew 13:55-56, the townspeople of Nazareth ask: "Is not his brothers ***James*** and Joseph and Simon and Judas [*i.e.*, Jude]?" Thus, the only other possibility where Mary was not James' mother is if Joseph had children prior to marrying Mary. Yet, the picture of the flight to Egypt mentions only Jesus as their son at that time. Consequently, James was born of Joseph and Mary. There is no sin in Mary having sex with her husband. (See Song of Solomon.) In Jewish custom, it was virtuous and appropriate to have children. It is wrong to imply married sex is sin.
6. Clement of Alexandria, *Hypostases*, Bk. 6, cited by Eusebius, *The History of the Church* (trans. ed. G.A. Williamson) (Penguin: 1965) at 72.

The importance of this history is it proves why James was the *right person* to write a letter to Christians at Ephesus for a trial. As head bishop, he was the one to guide them on how to evaluate Paul's doctrines. James was the voice of what was *orthodox* in the church at that time.

Luther's Admission of James' Direct Conflict with Paul

The primary proof that the Epistle of James is directed at Paul is the clarity of the contradiction over faith and works. On this point, the contradiction by James of Paul is pervasive, thorough, and unmistakable. James certainly claims salvation is not by faith alone. James says that one is justified by works. He gives several examples. He uses Paul's favorite example of Abraham. James quotes and re-analyzes Genesis 15:6 to reach a contrary conclusion to that of Paul. No gloss can legitimately efface James' point. Paul clearly says the opposite. (Rom. 4:3-4; Eph. 2:8-9; Gal. 3:6 *et seq.*)

James begins his message on faith and works at James 2:14-25. James 2:17 reads: "Even so faith, if it hath not works, is dead, being alone." James asks rhetorically "can

7. Peter was crucified in Rome in 67 A.D. during the reign of Nero. Eusebius says that this was after coming to Rome twenty-five years earlier. (Eusebius, *The Chronicle.*) Peter thus arrived at Rome about 42 A.D. Several sources claim Peter was the first bishop of Rome prior to Paul's arrival. However, two more ancient Christian sources—the *Constitution of the Apostles* (ca. 200 A.D.) 7:46 and Origen (*Haer.*3.3.3)—in their lists of the bishops of Rome begin with Linus. *Constitution* says he was appointed by Paul. However, Paul did not arrive in Rome, according to Jerome, until 25 years after Jesus' resurrection. This means Paul arrived sometime after around 57 A.D. (Jerome, *Lives of Famous Men*, ch. V.) Peter apparently was acting bishop *without ordination* of the church he founded at Rome until Paul in 57 A.D. arrives. Then in Peter's absence, Paul appoints a bishop—Linus. The *Constitution* then records Peter appointed the next bishop of Rome after Linus.

such faith save?" which calls for a negative answer. Thus, faith without works (in context, ***works of charity***), James says, cannot save.

What few commentators like to note is James' words on *faith and works* are directly based on Matthew 25:30-46. In this Parable of the Sheep and the Goats, the dividing line between the saved and lost, as Jesus tells it, is whether one did works of charity to his brethren. Jesus requires the very same acts of crucial charity that James cites—provision of food, water, and clothes. (For further discussion, see page 201 *et seq.*) James then cites example after example to prove that works justify. He concludes "man is justified by works and not by faith alone" [*i.e.*, a faith that is alone]. (James 2:24.) This is discussed in more depth later on in this chapter in the topic "James on Faith and Works" on page 249.

The stark contrast between James and Paul was evident to a luminary as great as Luther. He writes of James' epistle:

> In a word, he [James] wanted to guard against those who relied ***on faith without works***, but was unequal to the task in spirit, thought, and words. He mangles the Scriptures and thereby ***opposes Paul*** and all Scripture.[9]

8. When Professor Eisenman first reminded people about James' role, the response was very hostile. Eisenman was accused of "contradicting the New Testament" which supposedly "depicts Jesus' successor as Peter." (See "Book About Brother of Jesus Stirs Up Furor," *L.A. Times* (June 14, 1997) Metro, at 4.) Other professors claimed Eisenman's views on James were "marginal." He is not even coming from "left field," but "from over the fence." *Id.* Yet, Eisenman's view is the only conclusion supported in history. Professor Eisenman now has allies willing to defend him, including the renown Christian scholar Ben Witheringon III, in *The Brother of Jesus* (N.Y.: Harper Collins, 2003) at 89-211.
9. "Preface to the Epistles of St. James and St. Jude (1522)," from the *American Edition of Luther's Works* (St. Louis: Concordia, 1963) Vol. 35 at 395-399.

Another time, Luther was even more blunt and somewhat humorous when he said:

> Many sweat hard at reconciling James with Paul... but unsuccessfully. 'Faith justifies' [Paul] stands in flat contradiction to 'Faith does not justify' [James 2:24]. If anyone can harmonize these sayings, I'll put my doctor's cap on him and let him call me a fool. [10]

Thus, indeed James is going directly after Paul's teachings on salvation. He is proving them, in his mind, to be false. The contrast is stark and blunt. There is no rational basis to imagine James intends to do something other than correct a perceived false teaching by *none other* than Paul.

What aids this conclusion is that this correction process continues throughout James' Epistle. The fact the entire epistle continues in anti-Paul directions therefore heightens the probability that James' Epistle was aimed at Paul. Before reviewing each of those smaller corrections by James of Paul, let's explore the larger conflict whether salvation can be by a *faith that lacks works*. James' points are so obviously aimed at Paul that it bespeaks this Epistle served as a road map in a trial against Paul.

James on Faith and Works

Paul teaches that one can be justified by faith without works. (Rom. 4:5; Gal. 2:16.)[11] James taught the exact opposite in James chapter two. Faith without works cannot justify and cannot save.

10.W. G. Kummel, *The New Testament: The History of the Investigation of its Problems* (Nashville/New York: Abingdon, 1972) at 26.

James is relying upon Jesus for his position. For Jesus taught the very same thing as James, using the same charitable works test. Jesus says such works were necessary to save you in Matt. 25:30-46. James says you need these identical works to add to faith to be justified. (James 2:14 *et seq*.) The works-of-charity-as-necessary-for-salvation formula is merely a repeat of Isaiah 58:5-8.[12] Thus, Jesus and James are saying nothing novel. Paul is the one staking out a novel claim that runs against the revealed word of God. Paul is claiming salvation must never turn on adding works to faith. Paul claims if you do so, you commit a heresy. You are making salvation depend on putting God in your debt—God owes you salvation. (Rom. 4:4.)

"The greatest danger zone in evangelical thinking is that most believe that because no works are required to reconcile us to God, no works are necessary to get us to heaven!" Pastor Reimar Schultze (citing the three judgment parables of Matt. 25)

11.Romans 4:5 states: "But to him that worketh not, but believeth on him that justifieth the ungodly, his faith is counted for righteousness." (KJV). This clearly says you are justified by faith even if you have no works. Paul says the same thing in Galatians 2:16: "Knowing that a man is not justified by the works of the law.... [E]en we have believed in Jesus Christ, that we might be justified by the faith of Christ, and not by the works of the law: for by the works of the law shall no flesh be justified."

12.The same message is in Isaiah 58:5-8 (NLT). God tells the people that "you humble yourselves *by going through the motions*" (v. 5) but what God wants is for "you to share your food with the hungry and welcome the poor wanderer into your homes. Give clothes to those who need them." (v. 6-7). Then quite clearly, God says: "If you do these things, ***your salvation will come like the dawn***." (v. 8.) Isaiah means mere verbal expression of faith or even humility is not enough. *Action* must follow. It is not optional or merely forensic proof of an already completed salvation. Paul's view is at odds with Isaiah whom we know was inspired.

Paul justified his conclusion based on Genesis 15:6 where God's promise in Genesis 15:5 was reckoned by Abraham as righteousness. In the Hebrew, Abraham, not God, is clearly the actor *reckoning* something as righteousness. However, Paul interpreted the verse to mean God imputed righteousness to Abraham based on faith. From this Paul deduced salvation based on Abraham's faith alone. (Gal. 3:6-9; Romans 4:3.)

Paul is thus claiming Genesis 15:6 is about Justification by Faith. As we will discuss below, however, this verse lends no support at all, just as James is asserting, to the concept of justification by faith alone. Paul was misled by an erroneous translation in the Septuagint (247 B.C.) of the Hebrew of Genesis 15:6.

Justification in Abraham's Life: James and Paul at Odds

In Young's, Genesis 15:6 reads: "And he believed [*emn*] in the Lord; and ***He*** counted it to ***him*** for righteousness." In the original Hebrew, however, this more correctly says "And he [Abram] believed the Lord, and [***he***, *i.e.*, ***Abram***] reckoned it [*i.e.*, the promise of blessing in Gen. 15:5] to Him as justice." It had nothing to do with God reckoning anything to Abraham based on faith. It was always about how Abraham viewed God's blessing in Genesis 15:5.

As the evangelical scholar Victor Hamilton points out, the Young's capitalization effort misleads you if you followed normal Hebrew syntax and ignored Paul's spin of the passage. This is because the *He* with a capital *h* is an interpolation of what is *assumed* to be present. *He* is actually missing. When the *he* is missing, under normal rules of Hebrew, the *he* that must be interpolated is borrowed from the subject of the preceding clause, namely *Abram*. Because this starts as "he [*i.e.*, Abram] believed the Lord," it must finish "he [Abram] counted it as righteousness to Him." It was wrong for the YLT to capitalize the *he* in the second part so it read "***H***e

[God] counted it to ***h***im as righteousness." Rather, it should have been "***he*** [Abram] counted it to ***H***im as righteousness/justice."

In Professor Victor P Hamilton's *New International Commentary on the Old Testament* (Eerdmans 1990), we read in Vol. I at 425:

> The second part of this verse records Yahweh's response to Abram's exercise of faith: 'he credited it to him as righteousness.' But even here there is a degree of ambiguity. Who credited whom? Of course, one may say that the NT settles the issue, for Paul expressly identifies the subject as God and the indirect object as Abram (Rom. 4:3).[13] ***If we follow normal Hebrew syntax, in which the subject of the first clause is presumed to continue into the next clause if the subject is unexpressed, then the verse's meaning is changed...*** Does *he*, therefore, continue as the logical subject of the second clause? ***The Hebrew of the verse certainly permits this interpretation***, especially when one recalls that *sedaqa* means both 'righteousness' (a theological meaning) and 'justice' (a juridical meaning). The whole verse could then be translated: "Abram put his faith in Yahweh, and ***he [Abram] considered it [the promise of seed(s)] justice***."

Thus, in the Hebrew original version of this verse, it had nothing to do with justification of Abraham *by God* based on faith. It was Abraham counting the promise of God in

13. This is implied by Paul from the Septuagint — the Greek translation of the Hebrew Scriptures circa 250 B.C. Romans 4:3 and Galatians 3:6 both have "*it* was counted unto him for righteousness." This is the Septuagint translation. Thus, Paul is reading into the ambiguity spawned by the Septuagint translation which has *it* as the subject of *counted.*

Genesis 15:5 as justice by God. Professor Hamilton was being honest despite how a true translation would upset Hamilton's own Protestant theology.[14]

Furthermore, even if *He* was the subject of *counted*, as the YLT renders it, then the *it* which is the object of *counted* would likely mean *faith*. The *faith* would be what is deemed *righteousness*, not Abraham. Abraham's faith would be deemed a righteous deed. This matches the Jewish view that faith can be described as a work.[15] Thus, it is plausible to consider that every time you trust or believe in God despite reason to doubt Him, you perform a work that pleases God.

The fact that faith (not Abraham) would be the best alternative of what is imputed to be righteousness is clearly seen by comparing Genesis 15:6 with Psalm 106:30-31. Phinehas' action of killing the wicked was "counted to him as righteousness." In Hebrew, those words in Psalm 106:30-31 are identical to Genesis 15:6. In context, Psalm 106 means the act of killing wicked people was reckoned an act of righteousness. It did not imply any kind of salvific justification of Phinehas. Thus, one should not read any salvific justification of Abraham into the identical expression in Genesis 15:6. At best, it could be Abraham's faith was a righteous deed. It would be reckoned as righteousness. Therefore, even if we viewed the *he* who is reckoning to be God, the better view would be that *faith*, not Abraham, was deemed righteous.

The Misleading Septuagint Greek Translation of 247 B.C.

In 247 B.C., the Hebrew Bible was translated into Greek, and is known as the Septuagint. Jewish scholars acknowledge "the Septuagint was translated by ***very bad***

14. Victor P. Hamilton's background is formidable. He is Professor of Bible and Theology at Asbury College. He has a B.A. from Houghton College 1963, a B.D. from Asbury Theological Seminary 1966; a Th.M. Asbury Theological Seminary 1967, an M.A., Brandeis University 1969; and a Ph.D. Brandeis University 1971. Hamilton's commentary is based on his complete translation of Genesis itself.

translators" and "very often the [Septuagint] translators ***did not even know what they were reading*** and created nonsensical sentences by translating word for word." (Nehemiah Gordon, *Hebrew Yeshua vs. Greek Jesus* (Jerusalem: 2006) at 33-34.)

Paul swallowed these errors in the Septuagint time and time again. Most important, Paul was misled by the highly ambiguous translation of Genesis 15:6 in the Septuagint Greek translation of 247 B.C. Paul quotes it twice. (Romans 4:3; Gal.3:6.)

First, the Septuagint was missing *it* altogether as the direct object of *counted* in the verse. The Septuagint error made the verse now ambiguous. What was being *counted* as righteousness? Abraham, the faith or the promise of Genesis 15:5? The Septuagint aggravates the error by a second major mistake in translation of the verse.

The Septuagint next erred by revising the verb involved. The Septuagint tense in Greek for *counted* (elogisthê) is in the third person singular aorist passive indicative. This means *was counted.* While the third person means the

15.To Jews, Abraham's faith was just another work. (C.E.B. Cranfield, *The Epistle to the Romans* (Edinburg, T. & T. Clark LTD, 1975) Vol. 1 at 229.) However, one cannot be sure this is true Biblically from the single ambiguity in Genesis 15:6. Some try to prove faith can be a work from what Jesus says in John 6:29: "This is the ***work*** of God, that ye believe on him whom he hath sent." (KJV) The translation, however, is misleading by addition of punctuation and the wrong verb tense. *Robertson's Word Pictures* points out, citing Westcott, the verse uses a present active subjunctive for *pisteuo*, meaning "that you may keep on believing" (trusting). Thus, literally Jesus says "This is the work of God that you may keep on believing on Him whom He sent." In this usage, Jesus means by *this* Himself (including His ministry) is the work of God presented so that you *may* believe. The Greek is *ho theos*, "work *of God*," not "work required by God." When the subjunctive tense *may believe* is properly revealed, it rules out the typical interpretation. For the subjunctive makes it impossible to believe God's work is that you merely only *may believe*. Rather, in context, it means Jesus is inviting them to accept Himself as "this is the work of God" which God presents so "they ***may*** keep on believing/trusting." Thus, we cannot rely upon John 6:29 to prove faith can be a work.

subject could be *he, she* or *it*, in context, the most likely subject is *it.* This is because the *passive* form of the verb *count—was counted*—reads awkwardly if any subject other than *it* is used. Thus, it makes little sense to say *he was counted to himself.* Thus, the KJV correctly reflects the Greek Septuagint, which Paul relied upon. However, if the KJV is correct, the translation flaw by the Septuagint is self-evident. **The *he* as the subject of *counted* in the original Hebrew has been erased, and now *it* is the subject**. This leaves who is doing the *counting* as ambiguous in the Septuagint. "It was counted to him...." Perhaps it is God or Abraham doing the counting. However, in the original Hebrew, as Hamilton notes, normal Hebrew syntax says it was Abraham doing the reckoning, not God.

Thus, in 247 B.C., the Septuagint launched a highly ambiguous version of Genesis 15:6, omitting the *it* as the object of *counted*, and changing the subject of *counted* from *he* to *it.* Paul got sucked into these ambiguities, like a vortex.

Post-Septuagint Commentaries within Judaism

Because of the Septuagint flaws, commentators within Judaism post-dating the Septuagint understood God was imputing a righteousness to Abraham. However, these same commentators believed it was based on Abraham's *faithful obedience*, not merely faith. This faithfulness preceded Genesis 15:6. Abraham did not suddenly *believe* in Genesis 15:6 and become *justified* for the first time.

Paul, by contrast, in Romans chapters 3-4 regarded Abraham as still a sinner who experienced his first justification by the mere *believing* recorded in Genesis 15:6.

The contrary Jewish understanding of Genesis 15:6 predating Paul is best exemplified by 1 Maccabees 2:52 (135 B.C.). This was written in Greek.[16] The following allusion to Genesis 15:6 obviously derives from the Septuagint Greek translation. Maccabees 2:52 says "Was not Abraham found faithful in temptation, and it was imputed to him for righteousness?" This has *it* as the subject of *counted*, and thus tracks the Septuagint version, not the original Hebrew. More to the point, this reading viewed the Septuagint Genesis 15:6 as teaching it was *faithful obedience* that led to an imputed righteousness. As Gathercole comments, "Here it is faithfulness under temptation that leads to his being granted a state of righteousness."[17] It was not faith that originally caused the imputation of righteousness, as Paul claimed. This must be true from a Biblical perspective as well. Otherwise, one has no explanation for all God's earlier promises and blessings on Abraham, including the promises to Abraham in Genesis 12 *et seq*.

Or must we succumb to a Pauline view that God did all this prior to Genesis 15:6 because Abraham was an unjustified sinner whom God wanted to impress to the point of *faith?* I think not. And I am in good company. The Christian scholars who address this hard question agree that Abraham had to be justified prior to Genesis 15:6.

What the Bible Teaches About Abraham's Status At This Point

The Hebrew Bible does not depict Abraham as an unjustified sinner until the believing on the Lord mentioned in Genesis 15:6. This fact has not escaped thoughtful Christian scholars. In fact, such a notion that Abraham was a lost soul until Genesis 15:6 (implied by Paul in Romans chs.3-4) is ludicrous. James B. Coffman, a conservative scholar in the Church of Christ tradition, pointed this out about Genesis 15:6 in his famous commentary on the 'Old Testament.' First, Coffman derides the view of this verse which Paul is under-

---

16.1 Maccabees was written in Greek, although it shows traces of use of Semitic (Hebrew or Aramaic) idiom. ("Books of Maccabees," *Jewish Encyclopedia* at http://www.jewishencyclopedia.com/view.jsp?artid=18&letter=M (last accessed 5-30-06).)

17.Simon J. Gathercole. *Where Is Boasting: Early Jewish Soteriology and Paul's Response in Romans 1-5.* (Wm. B. Eerdmans Publishing Company, 2002) at 51.

stood in Romans chapters 3-4 to assert. "One may only be astounded at the amount of nonsense written about this verse, which is hailed as the plan of salvation for the sinners of all ages, some even claiming that Abram was 'saved by faith only'...." Finally, Coffman concludes:

> It is absolutely impossible properly to observe this place [*i.e.*, Gen. 15:6] as the record of a new covenant. Gen. 12:1f contains the embryo of all that is given here. Therefore, this chapter has a recapitulation and further explanation of the... [promises] he received in good faith, and... ***had already demonstrated his faith by OBEDIENCE***....
>
> As Whiteside, a scholar of great discernment, exclaimed:
>
> 'One of the strangest things in all the field of Bible exegesis is the contention so generally made that this language refers to the justification of Abraham ***as an alien sinner***. It seems to be taken for granted that up to the time spoken of in this verse, Abraham was an unforgiven, condemned sinner....The facts [from Scripture] are all against such a supposition.'[18]

Thus, Paul's contrary thesis in chapters three and four of Romans that Abraham was justified by his faith alone (first experienced in Genesis 15:6) is pure nonsense. Paul wants us to see Abraham became the father of all who believe by implying he was transformed from sinner to a justified saint *only* by the step of believing. (See Rom. 3:9-10, all have sinned; Romans 4:1-5, 10-18, Abraham first justified by faith, and thus becomes father of all who believe.) However, Paul's

18.Coffman cites R. L. Whiteside, *A New Commentary on Paul's Letter to the Saints at Rome* (Fort Worth, Texas: The Manney Company, 1945) at 89-90.

notion totally contradicts what is clearly implied from Scripture, namely how Abraham must have been justified prior to Genesis 15:6.

Paul also turns a mere promise to Abram in Genesis 12:2 and 15:5 and the faith it spawned in 15:6 into a covenant that we inherit. However, this overlooks entirely the covenant God actually made with Abram was in Genesis 17:1-7, which transformed him into Abraham. The covenant was squarely conditioned on obedience.[19] Only after Abraham died did God declare Abraham had kept the covenant faithfully and then God declared He would keep His side of the covenant.[20]

Why did Paul lend support to such nonsense that Abraham was justified by faith and that Genesis 15:6 was the Abrahamic covenant we inherit? As mentioned before, the ambiguities in the Septuagint Genesis 15:6 sucked Paul in, and led him to err.

James Likewise Sees Paul's Error on Abraham's Justification

James, in his exposition of the very same verse, Genesis 15:6, still has the traditional interpretation of the Greek Septuagint in mind. God had made a new hard-to-believe promise to Abraham about offspring in his old age. (Gen. 15:5.) Yet Abraham trusted God's promise. *At that point,* this trust was simply just another good characteristic of Abraham. It merely added to the status of justification that Abraham *already* enjoyed. Because James assumed justification can be lost, to know how Abraham was justified in the sense of final

19.God said Abraham's Covenant is an "eternal covenant" for all generations (Gen. 17:7). God said He "will" create such a covenant only if Abraham would first "walk before me blamelessly." (Gen. 17:1)

20. After Abraham was dead, God declared Abraham had been obedient to all His "law, commandments and statutes," and then affirmed He was about to institute His end of the covenant with Isaac. (Gen 26:4-5.)

salvation, James must look ahead. That issue depends crucially on the final test where Abraham offered up Isaac in Genesis 22. Thus, James understood the faith of Genesis 15:6 as part of the justification process. However, if you want to know how God measured Abraham's final justification, then James implies that you look at how he did on the last test, not at the test of his *faith alone*. (James 2:21, 23.)

James starts by quoting Genesis 15:6 from the Septuagint.[21] Then James explains Genesis 15:6 opposite of what Paul sees there. James says "see that by works a man is justified and not faith alone." (James 2:23-24.) Those commentators influenced by Paul, and those who attempt to translate Genesis 15:6 to match Paul's thoughts, are left mystified. They gasp: 'How can James say this in light of what is contained in Genesis 15:6?'

However, James' understanding lines up precisely with the pre-Christian interpretation of Genesis 15:6, in particular the quote from Maccabees referenced above. To repeat, the non-canonical book of 1 Maccabees written in 135 B.C. says at 2:52: "Was not Abraham found faithful in temptation, and it was imputed to him for righteousness?"[22] This verse is precisely what James alludes to in James 2:21. James even phrased it almost identically: "Was not Abraham our father justified by works, in that he offered up Isaac his son upon the altar?"

Now combine the parallel between Maccabees and James to see what you find: 'was not Abraham found *faithful in temptation*, *i.e.*, justified by works, and that faithfulness, *i.e.*, offering up Isaac on the altar, was imputed to Abraham as righteousness?' Maccabees and James thus both say Genesis 15:6 is not the final verdict. It was an earlier step. If Abraham

21. James' epistle reads similar to the Septuagint. This Septuagint translation became the accepted version by most, and James apparently elects not to debate the translation.

22. J. W. Roberts, *The Letter of James* (Austin, Texas: Sweet Publishing Company, 1977) at 92.

had failed the test of Genesis 22, and not offered up Isaac, James is saying that then Abraham would be lost. But Abraham passed the test, and it is this later obedience which *justifies* Abraham. The earlier faith, taken *alone*, could not have saved Abraham. If he had failed in Genesis 22, then faith *alone* would have failed him as a means of final justification. *Cf.* Ezek. 33:12 *et seq*.

How could James reach this conclusion based on Genesis 15:6? He saw, like 1 Maccabees saw, that Genesis 15:6 is not actually about faith, but about faithfulness. It is not about *believing*, but justification by *faithful* obedience. This is because James was using the Hebrew concept of *faith* to construe the Greek word for *faith*. In Hebrew, *faithfulness* cannot ever be separated from *faith*, contrary to what *faith* could mean in Greek.[23] Thus, James knew the underlying Hebrew had to mean no less than that Abraham was faithful to God, and it was reckoned as righteousness.

Therefore, because Moses in writing Genesis 15:6 could not separate *faith* and *faithfulness*, a Jewish mind would understand it from a Hebrew perspective. Justification for Abraham would crucially depend on how Abraham's life finished, not how it started.

Thus, James saw the faith in Genesis 15:6 as a small step on a long road. He thus was exposing the error of how Paul was reading Genesis 15:6. James in James 2:21-24 saw *faith* as *faithfulness* in Genesis 15:6. James, like the Maccabees' interpretation, saw that the act of faith in Genesis 15:6 was good, but more important was Abraham's later faithful action of offering up Isaac in Genesis chapter 22.

Some Paulinists try to claim James is not talking about the topic of *salvific* justification, in order to avoid James' criticism of Paul's ideas. However, James is using ***justified*** in the way Paul was trying to spin Genesis 15:6. James uses the identical Greek word for "justified" that Paul used.

23.Later, at page 270, we discuss that in Hebrew, unlike Greek, *faith* could not be distinct from *faithfulness*.

He is thereby responding to Paul's interpretation of Genesis 15:6. James is saying that if you address the issue of justification that counts eternally, then Genesis 15:6 is not sufficient. Faith alone will not suffice. Nor was Abraham justified for the first time *as a person* in Genesis 15:6 by adopting a mental belief (which James derides). Abraham already had a long period of faithful obedience to God up to that point. The faith of Genesis 15:6 was just another step in what justified Abraham. However, if you want to find the moment of final justification that counts, it must come *after* faith. For Abraham, his continuing faithful obedience culminates in Genesis 22. Such faithful obedience—both before and at the moment of the offering of Isaac—is what keeps on justifying the man, not faith alone. Accordingly, James concludes that "man is justified by works and not by faith alone" [*i.e.*, a faith that is alone]. (James 2:24.)[24]

James on Paul's Idea of Faith Alone

Just as Paul's misreading of Genesis 15:6 led to a faith alone salvation (Romans 4:4-6), James' correction of how to read Genesis 15:6 led to a correction of Paul's faith alone doctrine. James says in the same context that a faith without deeds does not justify and cannot save. James says this precisely in James 2:14, at direct odds with Paul's teachings.

24.James links the lack of justification with the concept of incomplete works. (Jesus did likewise in the Parable of the Sower & his letter to the church of Sardis in Revelation chapter 2.) James does so by saying in James 2:20-24 first that Abraham's "faith was working with his works" (*synergei tois ergois*). Then James says Abraham's faith was *made complete by works*. "The verb *eteletiothe* means 'perfected' (or 'brought to maturity')." (Stulac, *James*, *supra*, at 115.) Stulac confesses that the Scriptural promise of justification that Paul ascribes to faith, James says is "to be fulfilled by works." *Id.* Thus, James says, like Jesus says, that there is no justification without faith completed by works.

Stulac explains this verse in his commentary entitled *James* (Illinois: Intervarsity Press, 1993). James makes his point plain in James 2:14 by means of the rhetorical question "can such faith [without works] save?" The question calls for a negative answer. Stulac says James means that faith without works is useless for "salvation itself." (*Id.*, at 108.) Peter Davids, another specialist on *James*, agrees. He says James means the "use [-lessness of faith without works] takes on serious consequences, for it is salvation which is at stake."[25]

Stulac explains that while James is not saying works alone without faith saves, James rejects the idea that "faith *by itself*, without the accompanying actions" can save. (*Id.* at 109.) Stulac (like others who admire James) tries to find ways to make Paul consistent with James. However, mincing words cannot work. Stulac concedes James "uses the same terms for deeds (*erga*) as Paul." (*Id.*, at 111.) The words are identical between Paul and James. However, the thoughts are at odds. There is no question that James means faith plus works justifies; faith alone does not.[26]

Luther was blunt about there being a conflict between James and Paul. He said James contradicts Paul. Luther was right. This is what further proves the Epistle of James was likely a document used to try Paul. As a matter of Biblical interpretation, the erroneous Septuagint misled Paul. As Hamilton's expert knowledge of Hebrew tells us, it was Abraham who was reckoning to God the promise of Genesis 15:5 as an act of righteousness. However, even if the Septuagint were correct, Psalm 106:30-31 likewise shows James (not

25.Peter H. Davids, *The Epistle of James: New International Greek Commentary* (Eerdmans: Grand Rapids, Michigan, 1982) at 120.

26.Paulinists try to spin James as saying works *prove* justification rather than works *justify*. This is a distortion of James. He explicitly says *works justify*. For discussion, see Richard Lusk in his *Future Justification for Doers of the Law* (2003).

Paul) was correct about Genesis 15:6.[27] The Bible never taught justification by faith alone without deeds. Paul's misinterpretation of Genesis 15:6 is a serious mistake.

What About Justification By Works in the Hebrew Scriptures?

How far off is James from the Bible itself? The Bible taught long before James that obedience to the Law (not faith alone) brings justification. Deuteronomy 6:25 clearly states:

> ***And it shall be righteousness unto us,*** if we observe to do all this commandment before Jehovah our God, as he hath commanded us. (ASV).

27.Of course, if you believe both James and Paul are inspired, you will hear attempts to reconcile the two. Stulac is an example. He contends "James is not attempting to refute Paul." (*Id.* at 114.) How so? Stulac concedes James viewed salvation apart from works as impossible. Faith and works are an integral unity in the salvation formula. (*Id.* at 110.) While most view Paul as teaching salvation by faith alone apart from any works, Stulac disagrees. He claims Paul teaches salvation cannot be by "rituals" or "acts of obedience" alone. (*Id.* at 111.) In other words, Stulac claims Paul teaches salvation is *not by works alone*. If true, then Paul and James are saying the same thing, and Stulac would be correct. However, Paul and James are diametrically apart. Stulac has ignored Paul's *actual* teachings. Paul makes it clear that if you are saved "by grace *it is no more by works*." (Romans 11:6.) This is even clearer in Rom 4:4-5: "(4) Now to him that worketh, the reward is not reckoned as of grace, but as of debt. (5) But ***to him that worketh not, but believeth on him that justifieth the ungodly, his faith is reckoned for righteousness.*** " This verse 5 clearly says that if you believe, *and have no works*, your faith alone justifies you. Hence Paul excludes the very possibility that Stulac's solution proposes to make Paul fit James. Paul teaches faith alone saves. James teaches to the contrary that faith alone without works does not save. ***If you believe Paul is an apostle, and inspired, you can see he would make a heretic out of James***. That means the twelve apostles appointed as their leader (James) a *lost* man. This is an implausible solution.

Here *righteousness* is imputed to the person if we observe all God's commands. The Protestants Keil & Delitzsch in their *Commentary on the Old Testament* agree that this verse means precisely this:

> [O]ur righteousness will consist in the observance of the law; we shall be ***regarded*** and treated ***by God as righteous***, if we are diligent in the observance of the law.

Is this obedience of which Deuteronomy speaks impossible? No. God in Deuteronomy 30:11 then assures us obedience "is not too hard for thee, neither is it far off." (ASV.) Apostle John likewise says: "And his commandments are not burdensome." (1 John 5:2-3.) As Jesus too says, "my burden is light." (Matt. 11:29-30.) It is a Pauline misconception that obedience is a task beyond our ability. (Romans 7:24.) God assures us we can do this.

Paul directly contradicts Deuteronomy 6:25 by Paul's claim that righteousness (justification) is *not* imputed from obedience. In fact, Paul tries to prove the futility of maintaining a righteousness before God by obeying the Law. Paul writes:

> [Y]et knowing that a man is not justified by the works of the law.... (Gal. 2:16) Now that no man is justified by the law before God, is evident. (Gal. 3:11).

Prior to Paul's confused analysis, the Bible gave us clear teachings on how to understand the interplay of obedience, sin, repentance, good works, and grace. The Bible teaches that once you sin, all your good works are forgotten and become as "filfthy rags." (Isaiah 64:6.) This is clearly articulated in Ezekiel 33:12. This is a passage every Christian should memorize. It explains that when the righteous transgress even one command of the Law, then all their righteousness is forgotten. However, when the sinner repents from sin, and turns to God, then all his sin is forgiven. Grace is thereby given. To him, complete righteousness is now imputed. Ezekiel 33:12 reads:

> The righteousness of the righteous shall not deliver him in the day of his transgression; and as for the wickedness of the wicked, he shall not fall thereby in the day that he turneth from his wickedness; neither shall he that is righteous be able to live thereby in the day that he sinneth. (ASV).

Imputed righteousness is caused by what? Turning from sin and going on the path of righteousness. Thus, staying on that path of righteousness, Deuteronomy 6:25 promises, will maintain an imputed righteousness before God: it "shall be righteousness unto us...."

Imputed righteousness was not by atonement. Atonement was the *payment* for sin. It did not make you righteous, *i.e.*, justify you. Rather, it made *justification* possible in God's eyes as long as His other standards are satisfied: repentance from sin and turning from sin. Jesus taught this in Matthew 5:23-24, although some translations make it more difficult to see His meaning. Jesus says that before you bring the "sacrifice"[28] (often mistranslated as 'gift') to the "sacrifice place"[29] (poorly translated as 'altar') make sure you are "reconciled to your brother" who has something against you.

---

28. The Greek word is *doron*. It can mean "gift," but its primary meaning in context is "oblation" (sacrifice) (*Interlinear Scripture Analyzer.*) To assess this word's meaning, we first look at the Hebrew equivalent. The Hebrew word for *sacrifice* is *minchah* (Hebrew Stg 4503). It came from an unused root meaning to apportion, *i.e.,* bestow; a donation; euphemism tribute; specifically a sacrificial offering (usually bloodless and voluntary). As a noun, this Hebrew word meant "gift, oblation, (meat) offering, present, sacrifice." The Greek equivalent word is *doron* (Greek Stg 1435): "a present; specially a sacrifice: gift, offering."

29. The Greek word is *thusiasterion*. It literally means "sacrifice place." (*Interlinear Scripture Analyzer.*)

Thus, Jesus said receipt of atonement had to be post-poned when there was still an unresolved sin problem between you and someone else. The rabbis always taught repentance from sin must precede your receipt of atonement.

In the Judaism of Jesus' day, there was a ten day period between the Jewish New Year and the Day of Atonement. This ten day period "was designated for seeking forgiveness between individuals."[30] The Mishnah (the Rabbinic commentary) on the Days of Ten stated that for "transgressions that are between a person and his or her neighbor, the Day of Atonement effects atonement ***only if one has first appeased his neighbor***."[31] Jesus simply made this principle a daily one. Atonement could not be pled by one who had not first appeased their neighbor to forgive them of some wrong.

Psalm 32:1, 5 repeats this principle of repentance from sin for forgiveness as the first step.

> (1) Blessed is he whose transgression is ***forgiven***, Whose sin is covered....(5) I acknowledged my sin unto thee, And mine iniquity did I not hide: I said, I will confess my transgressions unto Jehovah; And thou ***forgavest the iniquity of my sin***. Selah

Paulinists decry the promise in Deuteronomy 6:25 and 30:11. In those two verses, God promises justification based on obedience to the Law. God assures us it is not too difficult to do. Paulinism has become so entrenched that if one cites these Hebrew Scriptures as if they were valid, one supposedly not only has a wrong salvation doctrine, but also one misunderstands God. Yet the Paulinist admits this is how God taught salvation in the Law God gave Moses. If we cite this admittedly *inspired* teaching on salvation as possibly still

30.Brad H. Young, *The Parables:Jewish Tradition and Christian Interpretation* (Massachusetts: Hendrickson, 2000) at 123.

31.Quoted in *id.*, at 124.

valid, we have supposedly made God finite. We are accused of blaspheming God even though no one disagrees this was at one time God's plan of salvation.[32]

These same exponents of Paul never take this Pauline attack on Jamesian doctrine to its logical conclusion. If the Paulinists are correct, then the God of Moses was finite and Moses blasphemed God by attributing these words to God that obedience justifies.

What really is afoot is that some have made Paul's words and arguments more important than the words of God *Himself*. The danger of adding to Scripture in violation of the duty in Deuteronomy 4:2 is that God's very promises of justification by repentance and obedience are nullified. Thereby, a new conception of God takes *His* rightful place.

"How do you stay saved? What do you do to stay saved? Nothing! Absolutely nothing."
Charles Stanley
Saved and Sure
(Audiocasette AW114.)

I concur with the Paulinist that a *new God* appears depending on which side of this issue you end up teaching. If you are on James' side, you are looking at God Almighty Yahweh. You have Deuteronomy 6:25 firmly fixed in your mind. However, if you look at it from Paul's side, you have a god who barely resembles the God of Hebrew Scripture. Paul's god teaches it is far too hard to keep the Law. Paul's god says it is fruitless to try to obey the Law as a means of remaining just. Instead, as

32.The following is a common teaching among Paulinists: "***Blasphemy.*** The idea of earning anything from God by one's meritorious works is, strictly speaking, not simply a problem in *soteriology* but in *theology proper*. You are not just saying something about your works, or about sin, if the object of acquisition is salvation from the wrath to come, but you are saying something about God—or rather, about ***god***, for ***you have made him finite***. Thus, the best corrective to merit legalism is found in Paul's preaching to the pagans, not so much to the circumcision party in the Church." *See,* http://www.hornes.org/justmark/archives/2003_09.htm (accessed 2005).

Paulinist J. Vernon McGee was fond to say: "He [God] never lets go. Now sit back, relax, and enjoy your salvation."[33] Paul is the effortless way. James and Jesus provide a way that requires *agonizing effort* to enter. (Luke 13:24, Greek *agonozai*.)

What About Justification By Faith in the Hebrew Scriptures?

Paul quotes the same Psalm 32 which I quote above. (See page 266.) Paul does so to prove justification by faith without repentance. However, when Paul quotes Psalm 32:1 in Romans 4:6, Paul ***omits*** verse 5 of Psalm 32. That verse makes forgiveness contingent upon repentance from sin. Paul instead quotes Psalm 32:1-2 alone. He uses that passage to prove justification is without obedience to the Law or any action of turning in repentance. For Paul, it is solely by faith, because if anything else is required, then it makes salvation depend on a debt owed by God. (Rom. 4:4.) To prove this, Paul relies on *blatantly out-of-context quotes of Scripture!*[34]

However, Paul forgets that God made a *promise, i.e.*, a debt, that justification would result from obedience to the Law! (Deut. 6:25.) God promised it was not too difficult on our side to do! (Deut. 30:11.) Apostle John reaffirms that truth! (1 John 5:2-3.) So there is nothing contrary to God's principles of mercy (grace) if I insist justification *thereafter* is owed by God *as a debt*. God says it is a debt. He will pay the debt for that justification, *i.e.*, ultimately He will apply atonement for you. This is why it is called a Covenant!

33.McGee, *How You Can Have the Assurance of Salvation* (Pasadena: 1976) at12.

34.Paul does the same in his quotes from Psalm 36 in Romans 3. This out-of-context proclivity of Paul is discussed in S.L.Edgar, "Respect for Context in Quotations from the O.T.," *New Testament Studies* 9 (1962-63) at 56.

Paul suffers from fallacious reasoning in this regard. He argues a false dichotomy. He says if it is a debt, it is no more of grace. (Rom. 4:4.) Those are not the only two choices. Mercy (grace) only comes into play when you sin. Then forgiveness is given by unmerited favor (grace) to one who is repenting from sin. That is the doctrine of grace in Ezekiel 33:12.

Then is justification distinct and at a different point? Yes, justification is at a different point in Ezekiel 33:12. Justification *follows* repentance (and the receipt of grace). Remaining justified is by staying on the "narrow" path of obedience. God makes a promise, *i.e.*, a debt, to justify you whenever you are staying on the narrow path of obeying Him. (Deut. 6:25.) This is the Covenant promise of God!

Thus, Paul gave us a false set of choices: Paul claimed it either is debt or grace. Rather, it is ***both debt and grace***. They are not mutually exclusive. The Bible says it is debt that God owes you justification when you obey, for He honors His word in Deuteronomy 6:25. God keeps His word (*i.e.*, His covenant). However, it is grace when you disobey, and He will give you unmerited favor for true repentance in Ezekiel 33:12. Both principles of *debt* and *grace* are simultaneously true, but operative at different points.

To arrive at Paul's different conclusion, Paul quotes passages out of context. As already mentioned, in Romans 4:6, Paul quotes Psalm 32:1-2 to prove one is justified solely by faith without works of the Law (*i.e.*, obedience to the Law). Yet, Paul omits verse 5. Paul only quotes Psalm 32:1-2 which provides:

> (1) Blessed is he whose transgression is forgiven, Whose sin is covered. (2) Blessed is the man unto whom Jehovah imputeth not iniquity, And in whose spirit there is no guile. (ASV).

Paul then spins this to mean faith alone, without any obedience to the Law, brings salvation. (See Romans 4:6 *et seq.*)

However, as noted above, Paul is quoting out of context. Psalm 32 is not how faith alone leads to imputed righteousness. Such an application is frankly impossible. Rather, in Psalm 32, David has the Ezekiel 33:12 formula in mind. The verses that follow clearly prove it is repentance from sin which leads to initial forgiveness and grace. Psalm 32:3-5, which Paul omits, reads:

> (3)....my bones wasted away Through my groaning all the day long. (4)...thy hand was heavy upon me. (5) I ***acknowledged my sin unto thee***, And mine iniquity did I not hide: I said, ***I will confess my transgressions*** unto Jehovah; And ***thou forgavest the iniquity of my sin.*** Selah

Paul was wrong. James was right.

James Used 'Faith' in the Sense Genesis Used the Word

In fact, in the Hebrew Scriptures that describe Abraham's alleged justification by faith, Paul misunderstood even there the nature of *faith*. James understood it correctly.

In the Hebrew Scripture, *faith* and *obedience* were inextricably tied to one another. Abraham was not justified by faith without action. Paul was taking *believed* in Genesis 15:6 out-of-context of the entire Hebrew Scripture. In Deuteronomy 9:23, we can see clearly that obedience and faith are inextricably intertwined.

> When Yahweh sent you from Kadesh-barnea, saying, Go up and possess the land which I have given you; then ***you rebelled against the***

> ***commandment*** of Yahweh your God, and ***you didn't believe him, nor listen to his voice.***

Hebrew Scripture thus was teaching that when you disobey God, it means you do not *believe* Him. You do not *hear* Him. Thus, by a corollary, when you obey God, it means you *believe* Him and you *hear* Him. They are inextricably intertwined.

As the *Dictionary of Fundamental Theology* explains, *faith* in the Hebrew Scriptures—what it calls the 'Old Testament'—had this dual nature:

> [T]he faith of the O[ld] T[estament]...is both trust and surrender to God... it is obedience that assimilates the person....[35]

Abraham did not have faith in God that can exist apart from obeying God's voice. Mental belief apart from obedience is different from the Biblical-meaning of *faith* in the Hebrew Scripture. Works of obedience are never apart from faith, as if they are mere fruit of a tree. Rather, obedience has a synergy with mental belief. Together they form the core meaning of *believing* in Hebrew Scriptures. *Abraham's believing was inextricably intertwined with works of obedience. See* Gen. 26:4-5 ("In your seed will all the nations of the earth be blessed, because Abraham obeyed my voice, and kept my charge, my commandments, my statutes, and my laws.")

Paul, however, wanted to read Abraham's story in a new way. Paul wanted to draw a line that you could be in disobedience to God's law (in fact abandon it) but still be able to be seen as just due to *belief* mentally in two statements. These two statements were: (1) Jesus is Lord and (2) Jesus was resurrected. *See* Romans 10:9.

35.Langevin, Gilles. "Faith," *Dictionary of Fundamental Theology*. Ed. (Latourelle, Rene. New York: Crossroad Publishing Company, 1994) at 309.

To arrive at this, however, Paul was taking Genesis out-of-context. He was applying the Greek meaning of *pistis* to understand the Hebrew word for *believe* in Genesis 15:6. The Greek word *pistis* can mean a mental assent *apart* from obedience. However, in Genesis 15:6, the opposite meaning for *faith* was conveyed in the original Hebrew. The Hebrew concept of faith did not allow it to *exist* in the absence of obedience. There was no conceptual possibility that *faith* can be separated from *obedience*, as Paul saw it. Instead, *faith* in the sense of mental assent was inextricably *dependent* in Hebrew upon the necessity of a simultaneous turn toward *obedience.* (Deut. 9:23.) This is precisely what James is explaining in James chapter two.

Thus, James' statement that "faith [*i.e.*, *pistis* in Greek] without works" does not save merely was explaining the original Hebrew. James was putting back what was missing in the Greek Septuagint translation. It lacked the nuance which Hebrew implied about *faith* in the life of Abraham. Paul by contrast was explaining a Hebrew word for *believe* by a misleadingly deficient word in Greek—*pistis.* This Greek word sometimes can mean merely *mental assent*. Paul is interpreting Hebrew by a deficient and different Greek word used to translate *faith* in the Septuagint. By contrast, James is putting Gen. 15:6 back in context of the *original* Hebrew.

Accordingly, James teaches the Bible's doctrine on salvation which was at total odds with Paul. James was bringing the discussion back to the lessons of the Hebrew Scriptures. James was aware of the Septuagint translation, but urged us to use the original Hebrew meanings. Paul had relied upon an erroneous translation in the Septuagint of Genesis 15:6. James simply used the Hebrew meaning in the original passages to undermine Paul's doctrine.[36]

James' Reproof that Faith Without Endurance Saves (James 1:12)

Paul is read by almost everyone today as saying that one is saved even if they do not endure in faith. Paul in Romans 10:11 says that anyone who "trusts in Him will never be put to shame." Charles Stanley says this *trust* is a singular moment in time. Paul's doctrine implies we do not have to have an enduring faith to be saved. Rather, we need only believe in a "singular moment in time" in our enduring Lord. (Stanley, *Eternal Security, supra,* at 80-81.)

James 1:12 reproves this teaching. He says to the contrary:

> Blessed is the man that ***endureth temptation***; for when he hath been approved, he shall receive ***the crown of life***, which the Lord promised to them that love him.

James was merely repeating Jesus' words. "He who endures to the end shall be saved." (Matt. 10:22.) Jesus explained the lost ("withered away"/dead) includes those who "***believe*** for a while" but "in time of temptation fall away." (Luke 8:13.) Elsewhere, breaking faith by disobedience means one is unsaved. John 3:36 ("He who keeps on believing has eternal life, but he who keeps on *disobeying* the son, the wrath of God continues to remain on him.")

36.It is ironic but Paulinist historians recognize this contradiction, and use it to argue the Epistle of James was not written by James. "The far-reaching differences in soteriology indicate that the author of the Letter of James cannot be identical with James the Lord's brother, who according to Galatians 2.9 gave the right hand of fellowship to Paul and explicitly acknowledged his proclamation of the gospel among the Gentiles." (Udo Schnelle *The History and Theology of the New Testament Writings* (Minneapolis: Fortress Press, 1998) at 385-86.) However, this ignores Acts chapter 21 is *after the events* Paul mentions in Galatians 2:9. In Acts chapter 21, James still does not know Paul's doctrine on the Law. James asks and receives Paul's implicit reassurances that Paul is not teaching the Law's abrogation.

Habakkuk 2:4: What Does It Really Say?

How did Paul establish the contrary view to James? Besides his out-of-context quote of Psalm 32:1-2 and his mistaken view of Genesis 15:6, Paul's faith alone doctrine had one other proof text. This came from Habakkuk. Paul claimed this passage establishes a one-time faith saves, without any endurance in faithful living to the Law. Paul was quoting Habakkuk 2:4. Paul, however, quotes from the erroneous Septuagint translation. This led Paul to a completely erroneous interpretation. Paul in Romans 1:17 and Galatians 3:11 states:

> For therein is revealed a righteousness of God from faith unto faith: as it is written [in Habakkuk 2:4], But the righteous shall live by faith. (Romans 1:17) But that no man is justified by the law in the sight of God, it is evident: for, The just shall live by faith. (Gal.3:11 KJV)

Paul was apparently unaware that the Septuagint erred in its Greek translation of the Hebrew original. The key word in Habakkuk is not *faith* (*i.e.*, *pistis* in Greek), but *faithfulness* (*i.e.*, *emunah* in Hebrew). Also, Paul omits a crucial word that appears both in the Septuagint and Hebrew: it is the word *his* before *faithfulness*. Both corrections overturn Paul's intended interpretation. The restoration of these missing pieces establish the *opposite* of what Paul was trying to prove.

H. Ray Dunning, Professor of Theology at Trevecca Nazarene College in Nashville, Tennessee, did a thorough study on *emunah* and *pistis* in Habakkuk 2:4. Professor Dunning gently shows you they are diametrically different. The professor is certainly normative in his views. He does not show any sign of sympathy with my conclusions about Paul. Yet Professor Dunning is clearly showing that Paul erred in his understanding of Habakkuk 2:4. Here is the fruit of Professor Dunning's study:

> *The just shall live by his faith.* The word rendered *faith* is the Hebrew *emunah*, from a verb meaning originally "to be firm," and is used in the Old Testament in the physical sense of steadfastness (Smith, op. cit., p. 140). Thus the better rendering is "faithfulness." *Faith* is a word for which, in the New Testament active sense, ***the Hebrew has no equivalent***—though the term "believe" is derived from the same root as *emunah*.(IB, VI, 989).[37]

Professor Dunning is explaining that there is a gap in translating *faithfulness* in Hebrew into Greek. The simple concept *faith* in Greek does not work. Thus, the noun *emunah* in Hebrew does not correspond properly to the word *pistis* in Greek, despite the Septuagint making this choice. The Hebrew text therefore means the just shall live by *his faithfulness*. What does *faithfulness* mean?

Professor Dunning gives many Biblical examples of *emunah*'s meaning. He also does not shrink back from pointing out a meaning that disaffirms Paul's interpretation:

> *Emunah* is the word used to describe the uplifted hands of Moses, which were *steady* (Exod. 17:12). It is also used of men in charge of money who "dealt faithfully" (II Kings 12:15). It is closely akin, if not identical, to the English idiomatic statement "*Hold steady,*" implying that if one does not "bolt," the circumstances that surround him will alter. Lehrman's suggested meaning of the intention of this exhortation is good: "The righteous Israelite, who remains ***unswervingly loyal to the moral precepts, will endure***, although he has to suffer for his principles; whereas the wicked,

37.H. Ray Dunning, "The Divine Response, Habakkuk 2:4," *Beacon Hill Commentary* (Kansas City, Mo.: Beacon Hill Press, 1966) Vol. 5 at 277-78.

> who enjoy a temporary ascendancy through their violation of right, are in the end overthrown and humbled." (Op. cit., p. 219). (Emphasis added.)

Emunah thus means *faithfulness* with its core meaning 'holding steady, holding firm, holding true to moral precepts.' This is why for James separating faith and faithfulness made no sense.

Professor Dunning goes on to explain that Paul was led into his erroneous interpretation by relying upon the Septuagint translation of the Hebrew into Greek. The Septuagint renders *emunah* with *pistis*. The professor is thereby making an excuse for Paul's misapplication. Professor Dunning states:

> The Septuagint translated *emunah* by *pistis* (faith). It was this translation which the New Testament writers made use of and thus incorporated the vision of Habakkuk into the very heart of the Christian preaching (kerygma). Paul quotes this clause twice (Rom. 1:17; Gal. 3:11) in support of his doctrine of justification by faith. By it he "intends that ***single act*** of faith by...the sinner secures forgiveness and justification."

Hence, Professor Dunning is saying Paul has a one-time faith in mind. This fits the Septuagint's choice of *pistis*. Yet, as the professor already explained, the meaning in Hebrew requires *faithfulness,* which means in context an "unswerving loyalty...to ***endure***...."

Paul simply erred.

Thus, once more we see James 1:12, 17 is reproving Paul's entire notion that a one-time faith saves. Rather, it is the faith that endures times of temptation that will receive the "crown of life." James brushes aside Paul's contrary view with one quick jab.

James Ridicules A Faith Based on Mere Mental Assent

Paul in Romans 10:9 says that part of saving faith is "believing in your heart that God has raised Him from the dead...." The focus in Paul's salvation formula is on acknowledgment of two facts: Jesus is Lord and Jesus resurrected from the dead. However, demons surely know and believe both facts. It thus makes no sense that believing just these facts gives you a guarantee that "you shall be saved" without any repentance and obedience to follow. In modern evangelism, Paul's actual words in his sterile salvation formula in Romans 10:9 are generally ignored. Paul said you were saved if you believed Jesus is Lord and you believed in the fact of the *resurrection of Jesus*. Modern evangelists such as Stanley and Spurgeon must realize how sterile this salvation formula appears upon reflection. Thus, they change the formula to mean one has saving faith if one is "acknowledging the fact you are a *sinner* and Jesus *paid* for your *sins*." If you accept these facts as true, you are assured that you are "saved."[38] Yet, that is not Paul's *true* formula in Romans 10:9.

Whether Paul's formula or the Stanley-Spurgeon formula, modern evangelism presents this as a decision that you can do in the privacy of your own heart. You do not have to confess it out loud. Otherwise that would be a works-salvation, modern Paulinists teach. Whether we keep to Paul's for-

38. Stanley, *Eternal Security, supra*, at 33-35 (trust in Jesus' payment for sin saves you). Spurgeon's *The Warrant of Faith* (1863) typifies the modern evangelical sermon. He adds an interesting twist that tries to explain away James' point in James 2:19. Spurgeon does this by making *faith in faith* alone the *act* that James seeks beyond mere acknowledgment of facts. At first, Spurgeon appears to agree with James. After giving the Pauline gospel, he says: "The mere knowledge of these facts will not, however, save us...." What then must we *do*? Spurgeon then says we must trust in Jesus so we always accepts these facts and assure ourselves of salvation by faith alone. Spurgeon required the work of *enduring in a faith* ***in faith alone without works***. This is an obvious self-contradiction.

mula for salvation (*i.e.*, belief in the Lordship and resurrection of Jesus) or the modern formula (*i.e.*, belief in your need for Jesus and the atonement), James ridicules that salvation could be acquired by mere mental assent to facts.

James says that the "demons believe" in God, but they are not thereby saved. James says in 2:19: "Thou believest that God is one; thou doest well: the demons also believe, and shudder." James then goes on to state works are necessary to add to mental assent to make faith *complete*, as mentioned above. Faith without such works, James relates, is therefore akin to the faith which demons have. It lacks something *essential*.

James is, in fact, recalling events in the gospels themselves. These events prove mere intellectual acceptance that Jesus is divine or Messiah means nothing if they end up being alone. As Pastor Stedman, an evangelical scholar and Pauline thinker, unwittingly states:

> Remember that back in the Gospel accounts there were demons that ***acknowledged the deity of the Lord Jesus***? When he appeared before them they said, 'We know who you are, the Holy One of God.' (cf, Mark 1:24, Luke 4:34.) They ***acknowledged*** what the Jews were too blind to see, the full deity of Jesus Christ, as well as his humanity. But, though demons ***acknowledged this, they never confessed it***. They ***never trusted*** him. They did ***not commit themselves*** to him, they did not *live* by this truth.[39]

Pastor Stedman does not realize how this demonstrates Paul's invalidity. Paul said we are saved if we believe in Jesus' resurrection and that Jesus is Lord. (Romans 10:9.) The demons not only believe both facts but are personally

39. Ray C. Stedman, *When Unbelief is Right* (1967), reprinted at http://www.pbc.org/dp/stedman/1john/0161.html (last visited 2005).

knowledgeable about them. The demons pass Paul's test for salvation. Stanley and Spurgeon also say that to be saved you must believe in the atonement and that you sin. Demons likewise know Jesus died to atone for sin. *Demons would admit they sin against God and they are proud of it!* Thus, demons could be saved under either Paul's criteria (Romans 10:9) or even Stanley's or Spurgeon's criteria for salvation.

Now you can see that James 2:19 is a perfect response to Paul's teaching in Romans 10:9. James ridicules that formula by saying mere mental assent by demons to truths about God would not save them any more than it *alone* would save you. James' response in 2:19 is perfectly adapted to respond to Paul's salvation formulas. Paul emphasized *mental assent* as what saves you. James says this notion is *wrong*.

Again, the Epistle of James appears perfectly adapted to be used at a trial of Paul.

Jesus' View on Works: Forensic Test or Intrinsic Requirement?[40]

TABLE 7.

Servant, Branch, Tree	Works Intrinsically Necessary
"branch in me" (John 15:2)	"bear much fruit if remain in me...If not remain in me, it is a branch that is withered, thrown outside and is burned." (John 15:5-6.)
"his Lord" (Matt. 25:26)	"Evil and lazy slave!...It was necessary you give my money to bankers, and having come I would receive mine with interest....Throw the worthless servant into outer darkness...[where there is] weeping and gnashing of teeth." (Matt. 25:26-30.)
"Every tree" (Matt. 7:19)	"that bringeth not forth good fruit is hewn down, and thrown in the fire." (Matt. 7:19.)

James Critique of Paul's Idea That The Law Arouses Sin

In James 1:13-14 (ASV), we read:

> (13) Let no man say when he is tempted, I am tempted of God: for *God cannot* be tempted with evil, neither *tempteth he any man*: (14) But every man is tempted, when he is *drawn away of his own lust,* and enticed. (15) Then when lust hath conceived, it bringeth forth sin: and sin, when it is finished, bringeth forth death.

What is James saying here? God does not tempt anyone to sin. To say so is a blasphemy against God. When you sin, it is because you were enticed by your own desires. Right? Theologically sound? Of course.

What did Paul teach? The exact opposite. Paul says in Romans 7:7-13:

> (7) What shall we say then? Is the law sin? God forbid. Nay, I had not known sin, but by the law: ***for I had not known lust, except the law had said, Thou shalt not covet.*** (8) But sin, ***taking occasion by the commandment, wrought in me all manner of concupiscence***. For ***without the law sin was dead***. (9) For I was alive without the law once: but ***when the commandment came, sin revived***, and I died. (10) And the commandment, which was ordained to life, ***I found to be unto death***. (11) For sin, ***taking occasion by the commandment,***

40.A popular way of reconciling Paul to James is to say James merely means that works prove you were saved. This is known as the *forensic* test. The contrary says works are an *intrinsic* requirement to salvation. The intrinsic view is correct because Jesus warns Christians repeatedly to have works or perish. (Matt. 7:19, "every tree without good ***fruit*** shall be cut down and thrown in the fire").

> ***deceived me***, and by it slew me. (12) Wherefore the law is holy, and the commandment holy, and just, and good.
>
> (13) Was then that which is good made death unto me? God forbid. But sin, that it might appear sin, working death in me by that which is good; that sin by the commandment might become exceeding sinful. (ASV)

What is Paul saying? First, Paul very clearly says that he would not have known to lust after women had he not been commanded against doing so. Prior to that time, "without the law, sin was dead." (v. 8).

Paul then comes about this from the other side, making his point more shocking. Prior to the law, Paul says "I was alive without the law" (*i.e.*, spiritually alive), but then the law came, and "sin revived and I died." (v. 9) Paul is clearly saying the law brought sin to life in him. Without the law, he was living sinless and spiritually, without any temptation to sin. However, when the law came and he read its prohibition, sin, by virtue of the law's commands inciting in him to lust, occurred. Paul sinned and spiritually died.

Psalm 19:8-9 "The commandment of Yahweh is pure, **enlightening the heart.**"

James must have scratched his head reading this. How can anyone attribute to God and His law the temptation to sin? Yet, Paulinists defend and explain that is precisely what Paul means.[41]

However, Paul knows what he is saying, and knows we will object. So Paul twice does a "God forbid hand-waive." (Rom. 7:7, 13.) Paul takes what he has just said and claims "God forbid" you should think he is saying what he has otherwise clearly said. Yet, despite the *God forbid* message, Paul leaves you, the reader, with only words to support the view that the law tempted him to sin. Listen to the hand-waive in Romans 7:13:

> Was then that which is good made death unto me? ***God forbid.*** But sin, that it might appear sin, working death in me by that which is good; that sin ***by the commandment*** might become exceeding sinful. (ASV).

This quote reveals Paul senses the blasphemy of saying the law "which is good" was "made death to me." So he says, if you think that were true, *God forbid*. Yet, that is *precisely what Paul has just said,* and then *immediately repeats*. He goes back to what he was saying before, adding the post-script, "by the commandment [*i.e.,* the Law] sin became exceeding sinful." Paul was not being equivocal on that point. That is what Paul said backwards and now forwards. Paul gives himself an out from making a blasphemous statement by saying that if you think he is saying the law, which is good, "made death to me," *God forbid*. However, Paul then does ***not*** explain how

Paul Borden explains Paul "eloquently explains how the law causes us to do the very things we don't want to do...." (2005) (online sermon).

41.Paulinists admit Paul claims that reading the Law arouses sin. Paul Borden's audio online sermon *The Frustration of Doing Good* is an exposition on Romans 7. Borden, an American Baptist, introduces his sermon by saying "the apostle Paul eloquently explains how the law ***causes us*** to do the very things we don't want to do—clearly accentuating our need for grace." Borden is blunt: "Paul says the law ***caused his sin*** to 'spring to life'—***makes him want to sin***." See *Christianity Today* which hosted this sermon in 2005 at http://resources.christianity.com/ministries/christianitytoday/main/talkInfo.jhtml?id=26945 (last visited 6/2005). Incidentally, Borden's explanations later contradict Paul, claiming Paul means the Law merely incites rebellion when we are told to ***stop the sin we love***. Borden explains we like our ways prior to hearing the Law. When the Law tells us that we are sinning, we continue in our ways rebelliously. In Borden's spin, the Law did not cause the sin to start. In this manner, Borden's spin contradicts Paul. For Paul says he did not know to lust for women *until* he read the Law's command against doing so. Paul says he was previously living spiritually alive. Paulinists spin Paul to prevent exposing his blasphemy.

we are supposed to square what he previously said with his *God forbid* statement. He uses mumbo-jumbo of impenetrable words that you are somehow to think answers your concern:

> But sin, that it might appear sin, working death in me by that which is good; that *sin by the commandment might become exceeding sinful.* (Rom. 7:13.)

Those are Paul's only words to take the sting out of saying the Law tempted him to sin. Rather, it appears to be reinforcing his prior blaming his sin on the Law. He says by means of the "good" (the law) and "by the commandment" sin became exceedingly sinful. What does that mean? It appears to be repeating what Paul just said "God-forbid" you should think is what he means. Paul reduces his words into pure mumbo-jumbo. He seeks to dumbfound the reader into thinking your natural concern that Paul is uttering blasphemy has somehow been addressed. Yet, it never happens!

In response, James simply trashes the entire discussion in James 1:13-14. One quick jab, and Paul's ideas are again refuted.

James 3:17: Is It a Response to Being the Victim of Paul's Hypocrisy?

The word *hypocrite* in Greek means an actor. It is someone who pretends to be something he is not. Jesus' harshest words were reserved for *hypocrites*. (Matt. 23:13, 14, 23-28.) The Pharisees wore an actor's mask. They appeared righteous when inwardly they were full of dead men's bones. (Matt. 23:38.) Jesus used the term *hypocrite* just as we would. A hypocrite pretends to be something he is not.

James writes about hypocrisy in James 3:17:

> But the wisdom that is from above is first pure, then peaceable, gentle, easy to be entreated, full of mercy and good fruits, *without variance*, ***without hypocrisy.***

What was this supposed to address about Paul? By the time James wrote his epistle, he must have been fully aware that Paul did teach the Law was abrogated as to Jews. Paul says this clearly in Romans chapter 7 which James is apparently still reading. All James can see is the blatant hypocrisy that Paul previously committed against James in Acts 21:21 *et seq*. (For more on Paul's position on the Law, see the chapter entitled, "Did Paul Negate the Law's Further Applicability?" on page 73.)

Most of us are unaware but in Acts 21:21 Paul misleads James that he, Paul, was teaching the Law still applied to Jews who found Christ. That is why the attack on *hypocrisy* in James 3:17 is a response to Paul.

What led to this attack on hypocrisy is that James in Acts 21:21 tells Paul the following about Jews coming to Christ:

> [T]hey have been informed concerning thee, that thou teachest all the Jews who are among the Gentiles to forsake Moses, telling them not to circumcise their children neither to walk after the customs (*ethos*). (ASV)

James tells Paul that Paul can prove he is not teaching such Jews coming to Christ to forsake Moses by Paul submitting to the Nazirite vow from Numbers 6. Paul does so. Paul is thus leading James to believe that James is indeed misinformed. Paul is letting James think Paul does not advocate the Law given Moses has been abrogated even as to Jews who would accept Christ. James clearly was seeking assurance from Paul to this effect in Acts 21:21.

Yet, Paul in Romans 7:2 proudly says that by virtue of Jesus' death, under the Laws of remarriage, Jews are "loosed from the Law" (KJV) "released from the Law" (ALT) "discharged from the Law" (ASV) and "set free from the Law" (YLT). They are now free to re-marry another—a God who has no Law of Moses any longer for them. The key Greek word is *katarge*. Robertson's *Word Pictures* explains this means "to make void." Literally, Paul says the Law *becomes of none effect* for Jews any longer when Christ died. Paul uses the same expression in Ephesians 2:15 when he says the Law was "abolished." The word there is again *katagsas*—the aorist active participle in Greek of the same word in Romans 7:2. Paul's point is this principle of abolition applies to the Jews. This is why, based on Romans 7:2, some Paulinists teach Jews and Christians who follow the true Sabbath (*i.e.*, sunset-to-sunset Friday to Saturday) are "guilty of spiritual adultery."[42] The Law is so totally abolished as to Jews that a Jew (and a Christian) actually shows unfaithfulness to God by following the original command from God Himself! *Oh my!* What man cannot believe when he is at first *deceived!*

But what explains Paul letting James in Acts 21:23-26 believe erroneously that Paul taught the Law of Moses was still valid for Jewish Christians? Clearly James asks Paul to submit to the Nazirite vow to prove Paul does not in fact teach otherwise. Paul does submit to the vow. This action and Paul's silence thereby misleads James that Paul was living like a Jew not out of pretence but from a sincere belief that the Law had to be followed.

How could Paul justify such behavior? Paul gives us the answer: *he consciously practiced to make observers think he was observant of the Law* when he did not believe it was any longer valid. In 1 Corinthians chapter 6 Paul says he is "not under the Law" and in 1 Corinthians chapter 9 Paul repeats this. Paul then adds that when around Jews he acts

42. "All Sabbatarians are guilty of adultery:...Paul said that [obeying the Ten Commandments] is equal to spiritual adultery, because in order to be joined to Christ, all the old Law must be abolished." http://www.bible.ca/7-10-commandments-abolished-Romans-7-1-7.htm (last accessed 2005).

like he is under the Law (Torah). When around Gentiles who are not under the Law (Torah), he acts like one who is under no law even though he is under the Law of Christ [*i.e.*, back to Paul's "expedient" and "not be dominated" test of right and wrong in one's conscience]. Listen to Paul's open admission of such blatantly hypocritical tactics in 1 Corinthians 9:20-21:

> (20) And to the Jews I became as a Jew, that I might gain Jews; to them that are under the law, as under the law, ***not being myself under the law,*** that ***I might gain them that are under the law***; (21) to them that are without law, as without law, not being without law to God, but under law to Christ, that I might gain them that are without law. (ASV)

One Pauline pastor himself defines "without hypocrisy" in James 3:17. He unwittingly gives us a clear understanding of the problem that James saw in Paul. This pastor says James means true wisdom, if from God, involves "no attempt to play a role or pretend to be what we are not."[43] Paul blatantly admits he does this. Paul did this with James clearly in Acts 21:21 *et seq*. Therefore, James 3:17 was saying Paul cannot be a prophet from God. Paul plays the hypocrite, and teaches others to do the same. The *end justifies the means*. James says such a person does not have *true wisdom from God.*

James 3:17 on Variances (Inconsistencies)

In the balance of James chapter 3, you can sense James is still reading Paul. He finds other character flaws than merely hypocrisy which mark the fruit of a false prophet.

43. Pastor Gil Rugh (Indian Hills Community Church, New Jersey), *Wisdom From Above James 3:17,18* (1978), reprinted at http://www.biblebb.com/files/GR772.HTM (last visited 2005).

James in 3:17 says the wisdom from above is "first pure, then peaceable, gentle, easy to be entreated [*i.e.*, asked a question], full of mercy and good fruits, without ***variance***...."

The Greek word for *variance* is *adiakritos*. To be *adiakritos* means to be "unintelligible" or "undecided." (Liddell Scott Lexicon.) Thus, if you suffer from *adiakritos,* you engage in *ambiguity*. James says God's true wisdom lacks ambiguous double-speak. By contrast, muddled self-contradictory thoughts make one's teaching *ambiguous*, *hard to discern*, or *unintelligible*. James says God's wisdom is, instead, pure, single, and *unambiguous*. When two thoughts are at odds with one another, they reveal the speaker is somewhat *undecided* which direction to take. The speaker wants to please both sides of an argument. He is saying things each side wants to hear. By contrast, God's wisdom is *unwavering, direct* and not *waffling*.

How can this test apply to Paul?

James obviously saw the numerous "variances" (self-contradictions) in Paul's writings and deeds. We also saw earlier Paul's oft-repeated technique of throwing a *God-forbid hand waive* into daringly blasphemous discussions. It throws a bone to one side of an argument. Paul then goes on to emphasize a message contrary to the implication that one would assume from the *God-forbid* statement. (See page 281 *et seq.*) This methodology bespeaks intentional effort to befuddle the reader/listener with ambiguous double-speak.

Another example of Paul's self-contradiction is that Paul taught the Galatians that if they became circumcised they would be "severed from Christ." (Gal. 5:4.) Yet, in Acts 16:1-3, Paul has Timothy circumcised. Either Paul is contradicting himself or he is encouraging hypocrisy, *i.e.*, Timothy pretending to be submissive to the Law. Either way, Paul comes out as not a godly teacher, *i.e.*, either he is self-contradictory or he plays the hypocrite to deceive people.

Another example of Paul's "variances" is Paul writes: "A man is not justified by the works of the Law" (Gal. 2:16). However, to the Romans Paul wrote: "For not the hearers of the Law are just before God, but the doers of the Law shall be justified" (Rom 2:13). Which way is it?

Another time Paul says salvation is by works plus faith. In Romans 2:6-7, Paul says God "will render to every man according to his works: ***to them that by patience in well-doing seek for glory and honor and incorruption, eternal life***." The Greek words translated as 'patience in well-doing' more correctly says *endurance in good works*. Paul thus says 'to those who endure patiently in doing good works, God will render eternal life.' Paul thus contradicts his own claim that eternal life is a free gift, without works. (Eph. 2:8-9; Romans 4:4.) Which way is it?

Likewise, in Philippians 2:12-13, Paul makes a statement that is self-contradictory. First, in Philippians 2:12, Paul says "work out your own salvation with fear and trembling." Yet, in Philippians 2:13, Paul appears to negate your responsibility by saying "for it is God which worketh in you both to will and to do [His] good pleasure." The commentators have engaged in an endless struggle to match verse 12 against verse 13. Verse 12 emphasizes human responsibility while verse 13 emphasizes the 100% agency of God in your human will. Which way is it Paul? Were you unable to decide? Or did you have another purpose in speaking out of both sides of your mouth at once? James senses this problem, and says God's true wisdom lacks *variances*.

Further, Paul traps himself in a self-contradiction when he says the following:

> One of themselves, a prophet of their own said, 'Cretans are always liars, evil beasts, lazy gluttons.' ***This testimony is true*** (Titus 1:12).

Paul thereby made a self-contradictory statement. For Paul says "one of themselves" (a Cretan) made a statement that "Cretans are *always* liars," and Paul says this "is true."

However, it cannot possibly be simultaneously true that a Cretan made a true statement and Cretans are "always liars." Many scholars have poured over this to find an escape, and salvage Paul's inspiration. Christian academics have struggled to solve this logical impossibility. However, no amount of multi-dimensional analysis (which is the only solution so far that conceivably works) is a serious answer. Paul is trapped in a logical dilemma because Paul says a Cretan was telling the truth when he said "Cretans are always liars....." Paul's slur on all Cretans is a self-contradiction in terms.

James, of course, can see all these self-contradictions, just as we can easily see them. He says the true wisdom from God is **not** unintelligible, ambiguous, difficult to discern, or self-contradictory. Paul's writings cross all those boundaries.

James Faults Overbearing Rebukes

Again, James in James 3:17 notes other problems with Paul which are evident in Paul's writings.

For example, it is hard to ignore Paul's overbearing non-gentle style. Paul is not gentle with the Galatians who want to keep the Sabbath and festivals and circumcision. Paul responds to the issue by calling the Galatians "foolish" (*i.e.*, stupid) (Gal. 3:1.) To intimidate opponents further, Paul calls down curses (*anathema*, "cursed") on those who contradict him among the Galatians. (Gal. 1:8.)

How does James respond? He says one having the wisdom of God would be writing "full of mercy," not "cursing." (James 3:10.)

Are James's Remarks on Boasting Aimed for Paul?

The Epistle of James shows another earmark that it was used as Exhibit A in a trial of Paul. James writes:

> [T]he tongue is a small member, yet it ***boasts*** of great exploits. How great a forest is set ablaze by a small fire!....Who is a wise man and endued with knowledge among you? Let him show out of a ***good conversation his works,*** with the ***meekness*** of wisdom. But if you have bitter jealousy and contentiousness in your heart, ***do not boast and lie*** against the Truth. (James 2:26-3:14).[44]

James is extolling meekness in contrast to boasting. Jesus likewise promised salvation to the meek: "the meek...shall inherit the earth." (Matt. 5:3,5.) This was the quality that endeared Moses to God: "Now the man Moses was ***very meek***, above all the men that were upon the face of the earth." (Numbers 12:3.) By contrast, God does not "respect the proud." (Ps. 40:4.) Proverbs 16:5 says: "Every one that is proud in heart is an abomination to Jehovah." James makes both points simultaneously in his famous line: "God resists the ***proud***, but gives *grace* to the meek." (James 4:6.)

44.Paulinists try to save Paul from what James condemns by lifting out-of-context James 3:16. There James continues and says, "But now you are boasting in connection with your arrogance. ALL boasting *of this kind* is evil." Thus, they read James to only condemn *boasting* in *arrogance*. They insist Paul does not do this. However, *boasting* of your own exploits and background rather than God's accomplishments is likely James' meaning. The latter is appropriate "boasting in the Lord" (Jeremiah 9:23-24.) Thus, you can boast of God's accomplishments, not your own.

Paul in numerous places boasts, but the most blatant is in Second Corinthians. The KJV translation makes it difficult for you to recognize this. It changes Paul's admission that he is *boasting* into an admission he is *glorying*. Yet, Paul's Greek word is *boast* or *boasting*. Paul's admission of this behavior uses the ***same Greek word*** as used by James when he condemns such behavior in James 4:6. What the KJV incorrectly translates as *glorying* when Paul speaks, the KJV then correctly translates as *boasting* when James condemns the behavior. Oh the mysteries of Bible translation!

Regardless, Paul in Second Corinthians has a passage that is nothing but boasting. Paul admits this *boasting* behavior repeatedly in the very same context:

> Let no man think me a fool; if otherwise, yet as a fool receive me, that ***I may boast myself a little***. That which I speak, I speak it not after the Lord, but as it were foolishly, in ***this confidence of boasting***. Seeing that many glory after the flesh, I will glory also...Are they Hebrews? So am I. Are they Israelites? So am I. Are they the seed of Abraham? So am I. Are they ministers of Christ? (I speak as a fool) ***I am more***; in labors more abundant, in stripes above measure, in prisons more frequent, in deaths oft...In journeyings often, in perils of waters, in perils of robbers, in perils by my own countrymen... in perils among false brethren;.... ***in nothing am I behind the very chiefest of the apostles, though I be nothing***.... (2 Corinthians 11:16-12:19 (ASV).)

Throughout this litany of boasts, Paul confesses he is boasting. Paul appears to be admitting it is foolish to do this ("I speak as a fool"), but he does it anyway. James calls such behavior and lack of self-control a serious error:

> But now ye rejoice in your boastings: all such rejoicing is evil. (James 4:16.)

> If any man among you seems to be religious, and ***does not bridle his tongue***, but deceives his own heart, ***this man's religion is vain***. (James 1:26).

James tells you point blank, by inference, Paul's religion is "empty" and his boasts are "evil." Such a person "lies" against the truth. (James 1:26; 3:14.) If Paul knows this is foolish but cannot 'bridle his tongue,' then "this man's religion is vain." (James 1:26.) This is just the kind of information the Ephesians needed to have to try the one who "says [he is] an apostle and is not but [is a] *liar*." (Rev. 2:2.)

Conclusion

James is the head of the church in Paul's day. His epistle is intended to set up rules for attendance at a judicial assembly in a Christian-controlled synagogue. The assembly at Ephesus that pressured Paul to leave in Acts chapter 19 was in fact a *synagogue*.

Then the theological issues addressed in James' epistle all skewer Paul. It would perfectly serve as a trial brief to examine Paul's teachings for heresy if the synagogue at Ephesus requested it.

This is self-evident because James' Epistle uses all Paul's terminology, in particular the Biblical example of Abraham. James reinterprets Genesis 15:6 as having a diametrically opposite meaning from Paul's interpretation. On this and many other points, James' views are at direct odds with Paul's doctrines. It thus appears likely that James' epistle was intended for the confrontation between Paul and his detractors at the Ephesus synagogue where he had led many to Christ previously, as reflected in Acts chapter 19. With the help of James' letter, this Christian synagogue apparently found Paul not to be a true apostle of Jesus Christ. They received the highest commendation possible for doing so. A commendation from the glorious One Himself in Revelation 2:2.

12 *The Ebionite Records on the Trial of Paul*

Historical Evidence for The Trial Spoken Of In Revelation 2:2

Apart from what we reviewed so far from the Bible, are there any historical records of a trial of Paul? Yes, indeed there are.

According to Eusebius (260-340 A.D.) and Epiphanius (315?-403 A.D.), there was an early Christian group known as the Ebionites. They made findings judicial in character about Paul's background. These findings claimed both of Paul's parents were Gentile. Further, they found Paul was not circumcised until he was an adult.[1] Obviously, the implication of these findings was that Paul lied when he made claims to the contrary. (See Philippians 3:5.)

When Eusebius mentioned the Ebionites' findings, he launched attacks on the Ebionites, challenging their orthodoxy. Eusebius charged the Ebionites were heretics. They supposedly did not believe in the virgin birth.[2] They also taught the Law had not been done away with. While it is likely true that the Ebionites believed Paul erred by abolishing the Law, the question of what they taught on the virgin birth account in Luke's Gospel may have been exaggerated or inaccurately portrayed. There are no clearly recognized writings of the Ebionites on these issues which actually have survived. Therefore, we cannot validate Eusebius' accusation. Nor did Eusebius quote any records of the Ebionites that

1. For the quote, see "The Ebionite Charge Against Paul" on page 306.

could substantiate the charges. Thus, these accusations merely serve as *ad hominem* which do not resolve the claims of Paul's truthfulness about his heritage, as we shall see.

Regardless, we are obliged to re-weigh the facts. First, Eusebius in particular appeared willing to exaggerate his attacks on the Ebionites. The reason was precisely because the Ebionites wanted Paul excluded from canon. Eusebius did not want Paul discredited. What was Eusebius' motivation in

2. There is never any legitimate quote offered to prove the Ebionites denied the virgin birth. Rather, what is offered as proof by Eusebius is primarily an argument from *silence*. The original Ebionite version of the *Gospel of Matthew* in Hebrew was missing what we all today see as chapter one: the virgin birth narrative. From this absence, the charge was made that the Ebionites did not believe in a virgin birth. However, Jerome ca. 400 A.D. validated the Hebrew Matthew of the Ebionites. He cited several small variances from the Greek translation of the original Hebrew Matthew. None implied any unorthodox view. Thus, was the omission of the virgin birth narrative proof of heresy? No, because the same virgin-birth narrative is missing from Mark and John. Eusebius also tried to smear the Ebionites by claiming Symmachus, a Jewish scholar, was one of them. Symmachus disputed apparently the accuracy of the Greek Matthew's translation in Matthew chapter 1 of Isaiah 7:14 on the word *virgin*. Symmachus was correct. Therefore the fact this passage in Greek with its erroneous translation of Isaiah 7:14 is missing in the Hebrew Matthew actually heightens the validity of the Ebionite Matthew as more authentic. Regardless, Symmachus was never a Christian, and was anti-Matthew. He could not possibly be an Ebionite. The Ebionites were pro-Matthew. The impetus to bring exaggerated charges against the Ebionites was due to their position on Paul. There is no substantial evidence, pro or con, to support the Ebionites denied a virgin birth. Even if they did, because John, Mark and probably the original Matthew omit this story, how can it be a core doctrine of the church? How could denying the virgin birth make one a heretic? Jesus could still be from "everlasting" (Micah 5:2) if God occupied Jesus conceived by Mary and Joseph. In fact, one could make the case that the virgin birth account in Luke contradicts the prophecy that Jesus had to be of the lineage of David. (Jeremiah 23:6.) If there was a virgin birth, then Jesus would be, as the Epistle of Hebrews says, of the Order of Melchisedek, with no human father. How could an *adoption* by Joseph truly satisfy the prophecy of Jeremiah 23:6? This perhaps was the problem raised by the Ebionites with Luke's virgin birth account. We may never know for certain. Yet, if the Ebionites disputed the virgin birth, it could not possibly make them *real* heretics.

preventing Paul from being discredited? Was it to protect a true prophet or for political reasons? Eusebius was associated closely with Emperor Constantine. Eusebius was a promoter of the new-found powers of the bishop of Rome granted by Constantine's decrees. How would this potentially impact Eusebius' treatment of the Ebionites who attacked Paul?

The answer is obvious. After Peter founded the church of Rome and left, Paul arrived and appointed the first bishop of the church of Rome (Linus), according to *Constitution of the Apostles* (ca. 180-200 A.D.) at 7:46. That means Paul appointed the very first *pope* of Rome—although the name *pope* for the bishop of Rome was not yet in use. (Peter never apparently used the label *bishop* to identify his status at Rome.) Thus, the validity of the lineage of the Roman church depended crucially upon Paul. If Paul were discredited, it would discredit the Roman Catholic church virtually from inception.

Why No Other Ebionite Writings Survived

We do not know the Ebionites' true views because we cannot find the Ebionite works preserved in *any* library *anywhere*. Imperial Rome beginning with Theodosius' reign (379-395) outlawed any religion but that of the "bishops of Rome" (*Codex Theod.* XVI, I, 2). This was enforced by the destruction of both public and private libraries in Roman territories. If any heretical material was found, the owner suffered the death penalty. This suppression of historical works was interpreted broadly. For example, in 371, Emperor Valens ordered troops to remove from private homes at Antioch (Syria) works on liberal arts and the law, not just heretical works. "Discouraged and terrorized people all over the eastern provinces of the Empire, wishing to avoid any possible suspicion, began to burn their own libraries."[3] This grew worse under Theodosius. Then in 435 and 438, the emperors of Rome again commanded the public burning of unorthodox books throughout the empire.

So effective were these decrees, that there is not one single record written by an Ebionite that we can find preserved ***anywhere*** in ***any*** library. We know them only through the interpretation of their enemies. Our only records on the Ebionites' views are what Roman *government* authorities allowed to escape from the fire because the Ebionite's writings were quoted in the approved writings of Eusebius and Epiphanius.

Thus, it is not fair to judge the Ebionites solely from their enemies' writings. What Eusebius says needs to be taken with a grain of salt, particularly when bias can so easily enter and distort the analysis.

A Fortuitous Discovery of Ebionite Writings?

Or is that all that we now have from the Ebionites? Did the world recently discover a treasure trove of their writings from which we can objectively measure their orthodoxy? A good argument has been recently made by Professor Eisenman in *James: The Brother of Jesus* that we have recovered some of the Ebionites' writings among the Dead Sea Scrolls. How so?

Many of the sectarian works at the Dead Sea are written by a group who in Hebrew call themselves *the Ebyonim* or *Ebion—The Poor.* They even describe themselves as the "Congregation of the Poor."[4] The *Poor* of the Dead Sea Scrolls (DSS) claimed to be followers of "The Way," part of "The New Covenant" who found the "Messiah" who is called

3. Clarence A. Forbes, "Books for the Burning," *Transactions of the American Philological Society* 67 (1936) 114-25, at 125.

the "Prince of the Congregation" and "Teacher of Righteousness." He is gone, killed at the urging of the priests at Jerusalem. After the departure of the Messiah (who will return), the temporal leader who led the *Poor* was called the *Just One, i.e., Zaddik* in Hebrew.

Furthermore, their leader—the Zaddik—is in a struggle against the "Spouter of Lies" who seeks to seduce the New Covenant community from following the Law of Moses. The Poor (Ebion) reject the idea Habakkuk 2:4 means justification is by faith and insist its meaning is "justification by faithfulness." The DSS Ebion have two works called "Justification by Works" which reaffirm their rejection of the position of the "Spouter of Lies."

When we compare the Ebion of the Dead Sea Scrolls to what Eusebius describes as the Ebionites, the similarities are striking. The Christian sect of *Ebionites* seem to match the writings of the *Poor* (*Ebyonim*, *Ebion*) whose writings were found at the Dead Sea site of Qumram. These Dead Sea Scrolls (DSS) reflect ideas and thoughts that are unmistakably *Christian*.[5] The question is whether the writings of *The Poor* found at Qumram pre-date or post-date Christ.

Unfortunately, this cannot be done by carbon dating the papers found at the Dead Sea. Such dates only tell us the date of the age of the paper. Carbon dating can not tell us the date of the *writing* on the paper. Yet, we have other reliable means to identify the date of the *activity* of the people whose writings were preserved at Qumram. Fifty-seven to sixty-nine percent of all the coins in the Dead Sea caves are from the

4. The *Dead Sea Scrolls* identify the community as *The Poor* of Psalm 37 where "the ***congregation of the Poor***...shall possess the whole world as an inheritance." (Psalm 37 in *Dead Sea Scrolls* Pesher 3:10.) Their self-identification is evident repeatedly in the *Habakkuk Pesher*. The Wicked Priest who killed the *Zaddik* will be "paid back in full for his wickedness against the 'Poor' (Hebrew, *ebyonim*)." (Norman Golb, *Who Wrote the Dead Sea Scrolls?*(1995) at 85.) The verbatim original was: "The Lord will render destructive judgment [on that Wicked Priest] just as he plotted to destroy the Poor." (lQpHab 12.2.)

period 44-69 A.D.—part of the Christian era. Thus, the only way to know whether Christians or non-Christians wrote these writings is to study the words on the pages of the DSS.

Professor Eisenman finds significant proof the Dead Sea *Ebyonim* is a Christian group. For example, in the DSS, the temporal ruler of the *Ebion* who succeeds the killed Messiah (who will return) is called the *Zaddik*. Numerous ancient sources outside the DSS identify James the Just (the brother of Jesus) as *The Zaddik*. Translated, this means *Just One*. Jerome by the 400s will call him *James the Just*. In Christian writings of that era, the name of James was rarely used. He was merely called *the Zaddik* or *Just One*.[6] As we saw previously, James—the Zaddik—was the first bishop of Jerusalem after Jesus' resurrection.[7]

So is it then mere coincidence that the head of the Ebion of the Dead Sea Scrolls is called the Zaddik? Of course not. Professor Eisenman appears to have stumbled upon a major discovery.

If Professor Eisenman is correct, this means the *Ebionites* in Eusebius' writings are *the Jerusalem Church under James*. What Professor Eisenman then notes to corroborate this idea is that Paul refers twice to sending money to

5. For example, in the Dead Sea Scrolls (DSS) there is the uncanny debate over justification by works vs. faith, centering upon a discordant view of Habakkuk 2:4. The DSS writings advocate justification by works. Their "enemy" is one who espouses that the Law is no longer to be followed. "A similar vocabulary of justification was used by the [DSS]...[Paul's] invective in 2 Cor. 6:14 has close affinities with the [DSS] polemic." (Alan F. Segal, *Paul the Convert* (New Haven: Yale University Press, 1990) at 174.) Segal goes on to explain: "Paul reads Habbakuk as contradicting the notion that Torah justifies. In the [DSS] the same verse was used to prove that those who observe the Torah...will be saved." *Id.*, at 180. The DSS thus mirror uncannily the Paul v. James debate.

6. "Jame's title was 'the Just' or 'the Just One, which Epiphanius tells us was so identified with this person as to replace his very name itself." (Eisenman, *James: The Brother of Jesus*, *supra*, at 375.)

7. See "James Is the Head Bishop of the Church" on page 242.

the poor at Jerusalem. Eisenman says this just as easily could be *The Poor.* (Rom. 15:26; Gal. 2:9-10.) If we translate back Paul's words into Hebrew, he was saying *The Ebion* of Jerusalem was the name of the church under James. They were the *Congregation of the Poor*, just like we might call a church *The Lighthouse Church.* We do not see Paul's intent due to *case* size in the standard text which changes *The Poor* into *the poor.*[8]

What heightens the probability Professor Eisenman is correct is recent archaeology. The initial hypothesis was that the DSS were exclusively the writings of an Essene sect from the 200 B.C. era. This idea recently crumbled in 2004. Golb's contrary hypothesis that the DSS came from the Temple at Jerusalem between 65-70 A.D. has now been strongly confirmed by extensive archaeological digs under auspices of Israeli universities. These digs proved there was no community site of monks at Qumram. It was a clay plate factory. The initial inference of a large community of monks from the presence of a large number of plates misinterpreted the evidence. Second, we can now infer the scrolls were hidden in the mountains to protect the scrolls, and not because a large community had been involved in copying activity. In fact, archaeology now proves there was no copy center or Scriptorum, as originally claimed. None of the metal clips copyists use to guide copying were found at Qumram. A few ordinary pens and numerous coins were found. Yet, no metal clips of copyists. Not even a fragment of one!

The very nature of the scrolls likewise demonstrate that no monkish community was engaged in copying them. The Dead Sea Scrolls, it turns out, are not only an eclectic collection of sectarian materials but also a cache with numerous copies of the Bible texts. This is just what one would expect to find from the Temple Library at Jerusalem had it been secreted away in advance of the Roman troops sieging Jerusalem prior to 70 A.D. The Essenes would not be

8. Eisenman, *James the Brother of Jesus* (Penguin: 1998) at 156.

expected, by contrast, to preserve several opposing strains of sectarian writings. One such strain is the writings of *The Poor—The Ebion*. On the other hand, we would expect to find Jewish Rabbis at Jerusalem wanting to keep copies of Christian writings for informational purposes at the Library of the Temple of Jerusalem. We would expect to find records of sectarian differences maintained by such a library.

Golb's argument has now essentially been vindicated. Golb made a scholarly case that the DSS are writings that were taken from the Temple at Jerusalem during the years of the Roman siege that finally prevailed in 70 A.D. Hiding them in these caves preserved them from the torches which in the end destroyed the Temple in 70 A.D. after a long siege.[9]

Thus, recent archaeological discoveries at Qumram establish that many of the documents can be potentially prepared in the Christian-era. We no longer are forced to disregard the Christian character of certain writings merely because of the Essene hypothesis which strangled DSS studies until now. Among the newer writings in the DSS, we find some in Hebrew written by a group calling itself *The Poor—The Ebion*. This transliterates very well as *The Ebionites*.[10]

---

9. Norman Golb, *Who Wrote the Dead Sea Scrolls* (N.Y.: Scribner, 1995) at 11, 12, 30, 36. *See also* the archaeological report of 2004 by Magen & Peleg that destroyed many myths about Qumram, proving it was not an Essene settlement. *See*, AP 8/18/04; *S.F. Chronicle* (9/6/04); *Ha'aretz* (Israel), July 30, 2004. Finally, this story is now being carried in mainstream publications. See Carmichael, "Archaeology: Question in Qumram," *Newsweek* (Sept. 6, 2005), available at http://msnbc.msn.com/id/5842298/site/newsweek. *Newsweek* mentions that "Magen & Peleg set off what can only be called an academic revolution" which now corroborates "Norman Golb" who first argued what Magen & Peleg now confirm. See also, "The Dead Sea Scrolls," http://virtualreligion.net/iho/dss.html ("After 10 years of excavation Magen & Peleg conclude that the settlement at Qumran could not have been a monastery, but rather was a pottery factory which was vacated by its few inhabitants during the Jewish-Roman war.")

Do The Dead Sea Scrolls Depict A Trial of Paul?

What is highly intriguing is a further theory of Professor Eisenman about Paul. He claims the *Poor*'s writings in the DSS speak of a trial of Paul. He says James is depicted as Paul's key antagonist in a heated confrontation where Paul spoke vigorously against James. Paul's effort was viewed as an attempt to split the group. Eisenman bases this on two DSS writings. The first is the *Habakkuk Pesher*, a commentary on Habakkuk 2:4—a favorite verse of Paul. The DSS author interprets the verse, however, to require faithfulness for salvation. The *Pesher* then rejects the idea that justification is without adding works to faith.

Professor Eisenman sensibly asks us how can we credibly believe this Pesher on Habakkuk 2:4 is directed at anyone else than Paul. As we shall see next, the DSS *Poor* are up in arms about "the spouter of Lies" who opposes the *Zaddik.* Are we to believe it is merely coincidence again the *Ebion* of the DSS just so happen to want to show Habakkuk 2:4—one of Paul's favorite proof texts—does not stand for an idea that Paul alone is known to have espoused? Eisenman concludes we are clearly witnessing *deconstruction* of Paul's doctrines in the DSS *Ebion*-ite materials.

It is the next document found among the Dead Sea Scrolls which is the key document to identify Paul as the object of a trial by the *Poor* (*Ebyonim*) of the DSS. This faith-works discussion of the *Habakkuk Pesher* continues in a

---

10.Scholars other than Eisenman are beginning to realize the Dead Sea Scrolls which were written by the *Ebion* are potentially related to the group known as the *Ebionites* in Eusebius' writings. *See, e.g.,*the University of Pennsylvania DSS conference of October 19, 2004 which mentions the Pesharim document from Cave 1, stating: "Column 12 raises the question as to whether the DSS community referred to itself as 'the Poor.' ***This could be important for early Christian studies, since...the Ebionites (Hebrew for 'poor') was a name used by Jewish Christians later on***." http:// ccat. sas. upenn. edu/ rs/rak/courses/427/ minutes04.htm (last visited 2005).

work by *The Poor* entitled the *Damascus Document.* It says the contrary view on "works" justification is held by the "Spouter of Lies" who resists the "Zaddik." The "Spouter of Lies" seeks to have the "Congregation of the New Covenant" depart from the Law. A heated public confrontation occurs between the *Zaddik* and the *Spouter of Lies*. You can find this *Damascus Document* in any of the many compendiums of the DSS to verify this yourself.

Professor Eisenman claims this *Damascus Document* is too uncanny a reference to Paul and James to claim it reflects a pre-Christian debate. It appears Professor Eisenman has the better case on this point as well. The DSS scholars who initially dominated the field tried to maintain this Damascus Document is a pre-Christian document. They did so to serve their now discredited all-encompassing Essene theory.[11] They ignored the contrary internal evidence in the Damascus Document. This is one of the very few DSS documents that was found *long before* the 1950s and outside the Dead Sea area. When the Damascus Document was originally found in Egypt in the 1890s, its contents led pre-eminent historians to regard it as a Christian writing. George Margoliouth of the British Museum said in 1910 and 1911 that the Damascus Document was written around the time of the destruction of the Second Temple (*i.e.*, 70 A.D.), and was the work of the "Sadducean Christians of Damascus."[12]

11.The traditional Essene theory is that *every writing,* even copies of the Bible, were all made by an Essene community living at Qumram. The new approach, based on archaeology and textual evidence, does not deny that *some* writings were Essene *possibly*, even if such a claim is purely speculative. (The word *Essene* never once appears in the DSS.) The real mystery is how all these writings, reflecting *divergent views*, all appear at Qumram. Golb's theory is the one that best fits all the facts. It is the only explanation for *divergent views* in the DSS. The Essene *all-encompassing* theory needs serious re-evaluation.

12.G. Margoliouth, "The Sadducean Christians of Damascus," *The Athenaeum* (No. 4335) (Nov. 26, 1910) at 657-59; *The Expositor* Vol. 2 (1911) at 499-517.

Margoliouth's opinion was given long before the DSS discovery at Qumran in the 1950s. It antedated by forty years the premature fixation on Essenes of 200 B.C. as the authors of the Damascus Document. This fact proves an objective assessment of the Damascus Document would lead to a different result. One would conclude objectively it is a work of Christians known as *The Poor* who were zealous for the Law (*Zadokites=Sadducean*).

We can also see this for ourselves. The Damascus Document identifies the community as *The Poor* or *Ebion* in Hebrew. They followed the *Zaddik*, a label which independent and reliable sources prove was the moniker of James. The enemy of the *Poor* was the *Spouter of Lies*, who sought to seduce the New Covenant community from following the Law. The NT evidence strongly suggests that Paul was accused of lying about his apostleship and Paul knew this.[13] The NT evidence likewise demonstrates the Jerusalem church under James was known as *The Poor*. (Rom. 15:26; Gal. 2:9-10.) Early church evidence also demonstrates a group called *Ebionites* (which is a transliteration meaning *The Poor*) were Christians who felt Paul was seducing wrongly the Christian community from following the Law.

13.The verses which are apparently veiled criticisms of Paul in the NT always accuse him of ***lying***. Revelation 2:2 says the ones who tell the Ephesians they are apostles but are not are "***liars***." When Paul contradicts Jesus on the idol meat command, 1 John 2:4 tells us: "He that saith, I know him, and keepeth not his commandments, is a ***liar***, and the truth is not in him." When Paul says he is a Jew, and the Ebionites say they found out Paul lied, Jesus says: "them that say they are Jews, and they are not, but do **lie**." (Rev. 3:9.) Paul was apparently aware of the accusation of being a liar. He defensively insists often "I lie not." (Rom. 9:1; 2 Cor. 11:31; Gal. 1:20.) That this accusation was over his apostleship is evident in this quote from 1 Timothy 2:7: "I was appointed a preacher and an apostle (I speak the truth, ***I lie not***)."

Professor Eisenman thus has the better case on the Christian-era aspect of the *Damascus Document.* Then, if he is correct on its meaning, the DSS depiction of the *Poor—The Ebion*—perfectly and uniquely match the Ebionites of whom Eusebius spoke.

It then follows the Ebionites must be orthodox. They are to be equated with the Jerusalem church of *The Poor* under James. Eusebius must have engaged in distortion of their beliefs to serve his agenda of the 300s. Eusebius's purpose is self-evident. He wanted to discredit the Ebionites because of the centrality of Paul to the validity of the *Roman Catholic Church* (RCC). Many forget that after Peter's presumed founding of the church at Rome, it was Paul who had appointed the first bishop of Rome—Linus—of the RCC.[14] Today we call this bishop of Rome the *pope*. However, the Ebionites claimed Paul was to be ejected from canon as inconsistent with Jesus' position on the Law. If the Ebionites were right, this means the RCC was corrupted by Paul shortly after Peter founded the Roman church. Eusebius had no choice but to attack the Ebionites regardless of their high standing in the Church's recent memory. In fact, that high standing explains why Eusebius attacked them so vigorously.

Some believe it is inconceivable Eusebius could knowingly disparage the Jerusalem Church under James as legalists. However, even in our modern era, those wed to Paul make such a blatant disparagement of the Jerusalem church. Here is a quote of a fundamentalist Christian journal *The New Birth* condemning freely the Jerusalem Church of the twelve apostles and James:

> The ***gospel of the Jerusalem church became a perverted gospel*** once the Law Covenant was fulfilled and set aside as the governing covenant economy. ***And the Jerusalem church would not accept this fact, but continued***

14. See page 295 *supra*.

> ***stubbornly trying to keep the Law Covenant.*** It will be explained in this article that trying to keep both the Law Covenant along with the New Covenant perverted the gospel of Christ and annulled both covenants. It was ***necessary for the Lord to take Paul out into the wilderness apart from all the others and teach him directly the pure gospel of Christ***, because ***the gospel of the Jerusalem church was now a perverted gospel***, Gal 1:11-24.[15]

All Eusebius was doing is precisely what *The New Birth* was doing. Eusebius was putting Paul's view of the Law as the measure to test the orthodoxy of James and the Jerusalem church. Under Paul's criteria, the Jerusalem church (*The Ebion*) became the heretics. Paul's words proved to Eusebius and the *New Birth* that the apostolic church was heretical. It is thus entirely reasonable and permissible to infer Eusebius knew he was talking about the Jerusalem church of the twelve apostles when he labelled the Ebionites as heretical legalists. This is what justified Eusebius either falsely or in a misleading manner to charge the Jerusalem Church with denying the virgin birth because its Hebrew version of Matthew lacked any account of the birth narrative.

The Reliability of The Ebionites Despite the One-Sided Charges Against Them

Nevertheless, even if the Ebionites did not believe in the virgin birth as charged (see footnote 2 of this chapter for why this charge appears unfounded or does not involve true heresy), they still believed in Jesus' divinity and His resurrection. They were Jewish Christians. They simply did not regard the Law as abrogated. They still rested on the Satur-

15."Firstborn Sonship of Christ," *The New Birth* (February 2000) Vol. 25 No. 2.

day-Sabbath. For this too they were condemned by Eusebius and Jerome later. Yet, resting on Saturday-Sabbath was apostolic practice, as demonstrated by the *Constitutions of the Apostles* dating at least to the early 200s. It was only in 363 A.D. that Constantine's bishops in the Roman Empire made it heresy and *anathema* to rest on the Saturday-Sabbath. The churches that form the modern Eastern Orthodox church escaped this Roman decree. They were largely in territories that were *not* under the Roman Emperor's authority. As a result, the 250 million members of the Orthodox Church today and their members of twenty centuries past keep the Saturday-Sabbath while worshipping on Sunday.

Thus, Eusebius (who was quoting Epiphanius) presented an illogical and weak case why we should ignore the Ebionites' investigation. Eusebius clearly engaged in the fallacy of *ad hominem*. The correct response was always to examine the plausibility of the Ebionite charges against Paul from *independent evidence*. It may very well be that the Ebionites are not only orthodox in every respect, but more so than ourselves because they were led by James and the twelve apostles.

The Ebionite Charge Against Paul

Early church historians preserved the Ebionite charge against Paul even while trying to dishonor the Ebionites. This is the exact quote from Epiphanius in the 300s:

> They declare that he (Paul) was a Greek... He went up to Jerusalem, they say, and when he had spent some time there, he was seized with a passion to marry the daughter of the priest. For this reason he became a proselyte and was circumcised. Then, when he failed to get the girl, he flew into a rage and wrote against circumcision and against the sabbath and the Law. (Epiphanius, *Panarion*, 30.16. 6- 9.)

The Ebionites thus say that Paul was not a Jew, but the son of two Gentile parents. He became circumcised as an adult when he fell in love with the daughter of a priest.

How Plausible Is The Ebionite Charge Against Paul?

There is independent evidence to corroborate the Ebionite charge that Paul was not a Jew in the strict Jewish sense. It appears he was an Herodian Jew which to true Jews is *not a true Jew at all*:

- Herod and his family tried to tell Jews he was Jewish, but true Jews did not accept Herod's claims. The Herodian lineage had foreign elements in it.
- Herod the Great was a Roman collaborator ruling Judea as King prior to Jesus. He was put into power by the Romans lending him troops to subjugate Judea.
- One of his sons, Herod Antipas, succeeds him in the time of Christ to rule part of his kingdom.
- Saul/Paul in Romans 16:11 greets "Herodion, my kinsman" [*i.e.*, 'my relative'] which is a name that a member of the Herodian family would use.[16]
- Josephus, who as far as we know was not a Christian, mentions a Saulus in his work *The Antiquities of the Jews*. In book XX, chapter 9, Josephus says Saulus is a member of the family of the successor, Herod (Antipas). Josephus says this Saulus sided with the High Priest in resisting a tumult by lower order priests over temple funds going to the High Priest. Josephus records this Saulus' activity was after Jesus' movement had

"Costobarus...and ***Saulus*** did themselves get together a multitude of wicked wretches, and this because ***they were of the Royal Family***, and so they obtained favor among them because of ***their kindred to Agrippa***."
Josephus *Antiq. XX, ch, 9. sec. 4*

already begun but before we know independently that Paul joined it. (*Antiquities*, XX 9.4.). This therefore puts the Saulus of Josephus in precisely the chronological position of Saul (Paul) prior to his road to Damascus experience. Further, the Saulus of Josephus and the Saul of Acts both are collaborators of the High Priest (an appointee of Herod). So when Josephus says Saulus was of the family of Herod, this is direct evidence that Saul-Paul was of the family of Herod.

- The most important fact is that Paul says he has Roman citizenship from birth. (Acts 22:28 "I have been born a Roman citizen.") You would carry around proof on a small *Libellus*. Paul's claim was accepted in Acts. It has several implications.
- First, Roman citizenship was an honor from Rome which in the Judean region primarily only could be enjoyed by members of Herod's family or his closest allies. The list of Roman citizens was kept in Caesar's office in Rome. It was not a very long list. Most native-born Italians did not enjoy this privilege. In outlying provinces like Judea, it was dispensed to military allies and their families to give them special protection from Roman occupation forces. You could not torture or beat a Roman citizen.
- Second, Roman citizenship from birth means Saul had to be given a Roman name from birth.[17] It turns out that *Paul* is a Roman name.[18]

"I am giving [those] of the synagogue of Satan, the ones who say they are Jews and are not but are lying. Listen! I will make them so that they shall come and prostrate themselves in reverence before your feet, and they shall know that I loved you."
Jesus, Rev. 3:9

16.See discussion in Prof. Robert Eisenman, "Paul as Herodion," *JHC* (Spring 1996) at 110 *et seq*., available online at http://www.depts.drew.edu/jhc/eisenman.html (last accessed 10-05).

- How did Paul happen to have a Roman birth name if he was truly Jewish? It cannot happen. A true Jewish family would not give their child a Roman name or even accept Roman citizenship from birth. This would represent defilement. Thus, Paul had to be from birth a non-Jew. However, his parents also named him Saul, which is a Jewish name. Thus, his parents aspired to be Jewish. This fits perfectly the Herodians. They would be non-Jews and Roman citizens, but they would also aspire to be Jewish.
- Thus, in the Judea of that era, only Herodians would have a child with both a Roman and Hebrew name (*Paul Saul*) who would have Roman citizenship from birth (Acts 22:28) and who would greet a "kinsman" (*i.e.*, a relative) named Herodion. (Romans 16:11.) It thus is not a coincidence that Saul in Acts is a collaborator of the High Priest appointed by Herod. Nor is it insignificant that Saulus in Josephus is likewise a collaborator of the High Priest in precisely the time-frame of Saul-Paul prior to becoming a Christian. This then leads us to the *unequivocal* statement in Josephus that Saulus is a member of the Royal family of Herod Antipas.

In fact, Paul being an Herodian 'Jew' would explain the presence of Herod's foster brother as a member of the Christian church at Antioch. After Paul's Damascus Road experience, he went to Arabia for fourteen years. (Gal. 1:17-

17."When a foreigner received the right of citizenship, he took a new name." The *nomen* "had to be *nomen* of the person, ***always a Roman citizen***, to whom he owed his citizenship." Harold W. Johnston, *The Private Life of the Romans* (Revised by Mary Johnston) (Scott, Foresman and Company: 1932) ch. 2.

18.Most Christians assume that Jesus changed Saul's name to *Paul* in the same way Jesus changed Simon's to Peter. However, there is no mention of this in the three accounts of Paul's vision in Acts chs. 9, 22, and 26. In the middle of Acts, Luke starts referring to Saul as Paul, with no explanation. Nor does Paul explain in any of his letters why he uses the name Paul. ***It turns out that Paul is a Roman name***. *Saul* is a Hebrew name. There is an apocryphal account that Paul took his name from a Roman official Paulus whom he converted. Yet, to be a citizen from birth, one must have a *Roman* name from birth. *Paulus* must have been it.

2:1). At the end of that time, Paul emerges as a delegate from the Antioch church to go to Jerusalem for a ruling on circumcision. (Acts 14:26, 15:2.) So who previously belonged to this church at Antioch?

> And there were certain in Antioch, in the assembly there, prophets and teachers;...Manaen also—***Herod the tetrarch's foster-brother***—and Saul (Acts 13:1).

Who recruited Herod's brother? Someone had to do this. Someone of the family of Herod would be in the best position to do so. Saul-Paul, with Roman citizenship, would have the uncommon status to permit social contact with Herod's brother. If Josephus' reference to Saulus means Saul-Paul, and he was thus a member of Herod Antipas' family, then Paul likely recruited Herod's brother.

This Acts 13:1 passage underscores once more the many uncanny links between Paul and Herod. The primary ones are:

- Romans 16:11, the greeting to Paul's relative, "Herodion."
- Paul's service to the High Priest, who is appointed by Herod.
- The apparent Saulus-Paul link in Josephus where Josephus says Saulus is from the family of Herod; and
- As Acts 22:28 reveals, Paul has Roman citizenship from birth in the Judean region under Herodian control.

Paul was thus apparently an Herodian Jew, not a true Jew.

Therefore, the available evidence strongly vindicates the investigation by the Ebionites. The Ebionites could in a strict investigation prove that Paul did not have Jewish parents according to the rabbinic definition. Thus, while the Ebionites' doctrines made them want to exclude Paul because of his position on the Law, this did not apparently bias the result. It appears their claims on Paul's background are so substantial that we could conclude Paul was not a true Jew even without knowing the Ebionite claim on Paul's background.

The significance of trusting the Ebionite charge, however, is this means they were proving Paul to be untruthful. Paul claimed he was born a Jew and circumcised on the eighth day. (Phil. 3:5.) This fits right in with Rev. 2:2 where the false claimant to apostleship was proven a *liar* at Ephesus. It also fits the parallel statement by Jesus about those who "lie" and "say they are Jews but are not." (Rev. 3:9.)

Most important, the Ebionite charge has the characteristic of evidence one might bring up at a trial. It has a judicial ring to it. There is nothing polemical about it. No doctrines are involved. The charge purports to be the result of someone trying to find out more about Paul's background. Thus, it appears the Ebionites were involved in finding evidence to bring up at a trial regarding Paul.

Evidence of Peter's Testimony Against Paul in a Trial

Additional evidence of a trial of Paul comes from a sermon collection called the *Clementine Homilies* from 200 A.D. Scholars believe it contains a smaller fragment from an earlier Ebionite writing about a trial involving Paul with Peter as a star witness against Paul. This fragment is stuck inside a later story written to appear as if the opponent is someone called Simon Magus. (This was apparently done to avoid the censor's hand.) Instead scholars deduce the original fragment was certainly talking about Paul. This can be validated by comparing what Peter says to how Paul responds in statements we find in Acts chapters 22 and 26.

Homily 17 and the Trial of Paul

In this section of the *Clementine Homilies,* Peter asks Simon Magus publicly why would Jesus come to an enemy in a vision. Peter wonders why would Jesus spend years teaching the apostles to have their message supplanted by someone who merely claims to have had a vision of Jesus. These are all good questions even if the fragment were really directed at a confrontation of Peter with Simon Magus. But was it?

To answer that we need more background. This dialogue appears as Peter's testimony in a trial atmosphere. It is found in *Clementine Homilies: Homily 17.* Scholars say this fragment's original source must have been written by the Ebionites. Later, it was inserted into the *Clementine Homilies* as if directed at someone else called Simon Magus. Scholars concur that its original context was written to tell what transpired when Peter was testifying against Paul.

How do scholars deduce this? This fragment so clearly applies to Paul that it is inconceivable Simon Magus could involve all the same characteristics as Paul. As Alexander Roberts, the editor of *The Anti-Nicene Fathers,* explains: "This passage has therefore been regarded as a covert attack upon the Apostle Paul."[19] Likewise, Robert Griffin-Jones, a pro-Pauline scholar, admits Paul is the true adversary in this passage: "Paul is demonized...in a fictional dispute [in the *Clementine Homilies*] in which Peter trounces him."[20] Bart Ehrman concurs in this *Homily* that "Simon Magus in fact is a cipher for none other than Paul himself."[21]

19.The wording in *Homily 17* where Peter says his opponent claims he "stands condemned" is interpreted as a clear allusion to Paul's telling Peter he "stands condemned" in Gal. 2:11. Roberts then explains: "This passage has therefore been regarded as a covert attack upon the Apostle Paul."

20.Robin Griffith-Jones, *The Gospel According to Paul* (San Francisco: Harper Collins, 2004) at 260.

21.Ehrman, *Peter, Paul and Mary Magdalene* (Oxford: 2006) at 79.

You can decide for yourself. Here is the excerpt that has convinced scholars the target is Paul. This is Peter's statement at this trial of one who said "he became His apostle" but Peter refutes:

> If, then, our Jesus appeared to you in a vision, made Himself known to you, and spoke to you, ***it was as one who is enraged with an adversary***; and this is the reason why it was through visions and dreams, or through revelations that were from without, that He spoke to you. But can any one be ***rendered fit for instruction through apparitions***? And if you will say, 'It is possible,' then I ask, 'Why did our teacher abide and discourse a whole year to those who were awake?' And how are we to believe your word, when you tell us that He appeared to you? And how did He appear to you, when ***you entertain opinions contrary to His teaching***? But if you were seen and taught by Him, and ***became His apostle*** for a single hour, ***proclaim His utterances***, interpret His sayings, love His apostles, contend not with me who companied with Him. For in direct opposition to me, who am a firm rock, the foundation of the Church, you now stand. If you were not opposed to me, you would not accuse me, and revile the truth proclaimed by me, in order that I may not be believed when I state what I myself have heard with my own ears from the Lord, as if I were evidently a person that was condemned and in bad repute. ***But if you say that I am condemned***, you bring an accusation against God, who revealed the Christ to me, and you inveigh against Him who pronounced me blessed on account of the revelation. But if, indeed, you really wish to work in the cause of truth, ***learn first of all from us what we have learned from Him,*** and, becoming a disciple of the

> truth, become a fellow-worker with us. (*Ps-Clementine Homilies* 17,19.)[22]

Let's test the possibility that Peter did in fact deliver this speech, and Paul heard it. We will find evidence in the New Testament that Paul was aware of this charge that Peter made, as recorded in the *Clementine Homilies*. Paul's knowledge of this charge can be proven in how Paul embarrassingly changed his accounts of his vision with Jesus.

The version in Acts chapter 22 is precisely the vision that Peter is addressing in *Homily 17*, as it lacks any positive words from Jesus toward Paul. This must be what pressures Paul later to change the account into what we see in Acts chapter 26. This account reverses the Acts chapter 22 account. It puts words in Jesus' mouth for the first time that are positive toward Paul. However, by Paul changing the accounts, he demonstrates a clear contradiction with the earlier version in Acts chapter 22. Thus, the Acts chapter 26 account eliminates the point Peter raises in the *Clementine Homily 17*. However, it does so at a great price—terrible embarrassment when the later version of Acts chapter 26 is compared to Paul's earlier vision account in Acts chapter 22. Only something precisely like Peter's speech in *Homily 17* can explain such a risky reversal of the vision account. We next examine the evidence for this.

---

22. "The Clementine Apocrypha," *Anti-Nicene Fathers* (ed. Alexander Roberts, James Donaldson; rev'd A. Cleveland Coxe) Vol. VIII (Peabody, Mass.: Hendrickson Publishing Inc., 1994) at 269 *et seq*. This is available online at http://www.ccel.org/fathers2/ANF-08/anf08-61.htm#P5206_1525700. These *Clementine Homilies* were part of church history since the 200s, and even were frequently official readings in the early church. They purported to be written by Clement, the bishop at Rome around 96 A.D. Scholars of today claim these letters were written around 200, and included within them the earlier tradition of the Ebionites, such as in this passage. Because they were not apparently written by Clement, in fact, they are now labelled *The Pseudo Clementine Homilies*.

How Acts Mirrors the Clementine Homilies

Point One: Jesus Only Words Are Negative in Acts Chapter 22

The main argument in Peter's *Clementine* speech was that Paul's vision of Jesus involved Jesus only talking *negatively* to Paul. In fact, *Homily 17*, chapter 18 is devoted to Peter proving from Scripture that visions of God are how God reveals himself to enemies, not allies. In that context, Peter's point is unmistakable. Paul's vision only contains negative statements from Jesus, invalidating it as a proof of Paul's authority.

Then we will see that the account of Paul's vision given in Acts chapter 22 is exactly what Peter describes in *Clementine Homily* 17:19. In the Acts 22:7-16 account, the only positive statements come *later* from a person named Ananias. They do not come from Jesus *at all,* just as Peter says in this *Clementine Homily.* Jesus' only words are negative toward Paul, as we discuss in detail below.

Point Two: Paul Lost A Trial Before Jewish Christians.

Consider next that Paul mentions in 2 Timothy chapter 4 having had to give a "first" defense of himself from other Christians and no one came to his defense. This apparently relates to the fact that in 2 Timothy 1:15 Paul says all the Christians in Asia (*i.e.*, modern Western Turkey, which includes Ephesus) abandoned him. This defense was thus put on inside a church-setting in Asia Minor. The verdict ended up that all Christians in proconsular Asia abandoned him, according to Paul's *own words*. (2 Tim. 1:15.) Paul then mentions he still regards he somehow escaped the "mouth of the lion..." at this defense he put on. What did he mean? Paul's words at 2 Timothy 4:14-17 are:

> (14) Alexander the coppersmith did me much evil: the Lord will render to him according to his works: (15) of whom do thou also beware;

> for he greatly withstood our words. (16) ***At my first defence no one took my part, but all forsook me:*** may it not be laid to their account. (17) But... ***I was delivered out of the mouth of the lion.*** (ASV)

These statements, all read together, point to Paul admitting he was tried by fellow-Christians in Asia Minor (where Ephesus was), he lost and was then forsaken by all those in that region. Yet, then how are we to understand his words "escaped the lion"? Was it by making up the Acts chapter 26 vision account on the spot?

Point Three: The Lion represents Jewish Christians

To understand how Paul "escaped" at this trial among Christians, although he lost, we must identify the *lion* in 2 Timothy 2:17. Paul most likely meant his Jewish-Christian opponents.

While there is conjecture in Jerome's writings that Paul meant Nero when he referred to the *lion*, Jerome was relying upon an apocryphal account of a Paul-Nero encounter. Nero has no nickname as *lion*. Jerome does not explain why Paul would have used the label *lion* for Nero.[23]

The more natural reading is that *lion* represents the Tribe of Judah, *i.e.*, the Jews. This also fits the historical context. Read this way, 2 Timothy 4:17 means Paul felt he somehow escaped the Judaizing Christians. Nevertheless, the verdict in Asia Minor was a severe loss to Paul of all influence in Asia Minor among Christians there. (2 Tim. 1:15.)

23.Jerome conjectures incorrectly that Paul means that he escaped "the lion" Nero. Jerome says that in Paul's first encounter with Nero he dismissed him as harmless. Jerome says lion "clearly [is] indicating Nero as lion on account of his cruelty." (Jerome, *Lives of Famous Men*, ch. V.) However, Jerome is alluding to the Paul-Seneca correspondence as proof of the Paul-Nero encounter. However, most scholars find good reason to regard those letters as illegitimate, and this encounter as a highly improbable myth. Second, Jerome does not say Nero's nickname was lion, just that the label might fit him and be Paul's intention.

Is *lion* a symbol of Judah? Yes. The lion is historically treated as a symbol of the tribe of Judah. It comes from the Bible. In Genesis 49:9, Judah is specifically called "a lion's whelp." In Numbers 24:9, the people of Israel are likened to a "lion." This symbol for the Tribe of Judah is repeated in Revelation 5:3, 5. Thus Paul's reference to the *lion* in 2 Timothy 4:17 is likely a reference to his Jewish-Christian opponents within the church.

Point Four: Escaping With Some Legitimacy In Tact is Paul's Meaning

How can Paul escape yet lose all support? Peter's attack in the Ebionite account of a trial versus Paul goes to Paul's legitimacy. If in Paul's vision account, Jesus had no positive words for Paul, and we must rely upon Ananias (who is no prophet) to confirm Paul's legitimacy, then Paul loses *all* legitimacy. Peter's argument in the *Clementine Homilies* says Paul's authority stands on nothing positive from Jesus. If all we ever had was the Acts chapter 22 vision-account, Peter says Paul stands on *nothing* from *Jesus* to confirm Jesus ever had a positive feeling toward Paul.

However, Paul could walk away from a trial he loses on whether he is an apostle (Rev. 2:2) if he walks away with some legitimacy. If Paul was at least viewed as having met Jesus who *positively* told him he would be a *witness* (not an apostle), it would be enough for Paul to survive as a legitimate authority among Christians. This is what the vision account in Acts chapter 26 gives Paul, if the trial-judges believed Paul. Thus, at this trial, what Paul apparently means by saying he "escaped the lion" is that he was not stripped of all authority to teach and preach. He only could no longer call himself an apostle. (Rev. 2:2.) He salvaged a win on the only point that mattered to Paul up to that time. No one could disprove that Paul had seen Jesus and there were positive words for him. At least, no one could prove otherwise until Luke published Acts. There we see the vision account in Acts chapter 22 undercuts whether the Acts chapter 26 vision account *ever took place.* Let's next compare these two accounts to understand how Paul changed his accounts to save his legitimacy at a trial, but lost it for us when we critically compare the two versions.

Point Five: The Vision Account in Acts 26 Solves The Problem Posed By The Vision Account in Acts 22

First, in Acts 22:10 Paul reports that at the time of the "vision" he is criticized by Jesus and merely told to go into Damascus. There is no word of approval at all from Jesus, just as Peter says in the Peter speech above in *Homily 17*. See this for yourself by reading next Acts 22:7-16:

> (7) And I fell unto the ground, and heard a voice saying unto me, Saul, Saul, why persecutest thou me? (8) And I answered, Who art thou, Lord? And he said unto me, I am Jesus of Nazareth, ***whom thou persecutest.*** (9) And they that were with me beheld indeed the light, but they heard not the voice of him that spake to me. (10) And I said, What shall I do, Lord? And the Lord said unto me, ***Arise, and go into Damascus; and there it shall be told thee of all things which are appointed for thee to do.*** (11) And when I could not see for the glory of that light, being led by the hand of them that were with me I came into Damascus. (12) And one ***Ananias***, a devout man according to the law, well reported of by all the Jews that dwelt there, (13) came unto me, and standing by me said unto me, Brother Saul, receive thy sight. And in that very hour I looked up on him. (14) And he [Ananias] said, ***The God of our fathers hath appointed thee to know his will, and to see the Righteous One, and to hear a voice from his mouth.*** (15) For thou shalt be a witness for him unto all men of what thou hast seen and heard. (16) And now why tarriest

> thou? arise, and be baptized, and wash away thy sins, calling on his name. (ASV)

So imagine Peter has heard this same story from Paul, and only this story from Acts chapter 22. There is no word of approval from Jesus. Just condemnation. The only words ascribed to Jesus other than pure condemnation are these:

> Arise, and go into Damascus; and there it shall be told thee of all things which are appointed for thee to do. (Acts 22:10).

This Acts chapter 22 vision account gave Peter room to challenge the validity of Paul's commission from Jesus.[24] No evidence is put forth by Luke that Ananias is a prophet somehow (*i.e.*, predictive words to validate him). (Acts 9:12-17; 22:12.) Peter says in the above passage of the *Clementine Homilies* to his opponent (Paul): "If, then, our Jesus appeared to you in a vision, made Himself known to you, and spoke to you, ***it was as one who is enraged with an adversary***; and this is the reason why it was through visions and dreams...." Peter must be referring to Paul's Acts chapter 22 version of the vision account. It was a brief vision, nothing more. Jesus was adversarial in tone.

In Peter's charge, Peter has not seen or heard the next account of the vision, which we can read in Acts chapter 26. This *not only proves Paul is the intended target from the*

24.If one ignores Peter's criticism in the *Clementine Homily* and insists this Acts chapter 22 account legitimizes Paul, one must recognize the only positive remarks come from Ananias. Then this means Paul's legitimacy depends 100% on the legitimacy of Ananias. However, there is no evidence from Luke in Acts or anywhere in the New Testament that Ananias is a prophet (*i.e.*, by means of confirmed prophecy). As Gregg Bing unwittingly admits in "Useful for the Master," *Timely Messenger* (November 2004): "Ananias...was ***not an apostle, a pastor, or a prophet,*** as far as we know, but was simply what many would call an *ordinary man*." Peter in the *Homily* realizes that the validity of thinking Jesus spoke positively to Paul mistakenly ignores that Paul's *positive* commission in Acts chapter 22 solely comes from an uninspired non-prophet named Ananias.

Clementine fragment, but it also *gives* the Peter speech *immense authenticity and reliability.* Because if the Peter speech never really happened, there is little reason why Paul would go out of his way to *contradict* and put a *whole new spin* on his vision experience when we see Acts chapter 26. The purpose of Paul's switch in Acts chapter 26 is clear: it erases the criticism of Peter recorded in the *Clementine Homilies*. In Acts chapter 26, Jesus appears now to have approving words during Paul's vision experience.

To see this, we must read Paul's next account of his vision in Acts chapter 26. It is a very different account indeed. Paul, talking to Agrippa, states in Acts 26:14-18:

> (14) And when we were all fallen to the earth, I heard a voice saying unto me in the Hebrew language, Saul, Saul, why persecutest thou me? it is hard for thee to kick against the goad. (15) And I said, Who art thou, Lord? And the Lord said, I am Jesus whom thou persecutest. (16) ***But arise, and stand upon thy feet: for to this end have I appeared unto thee, to appoint thee a minister and a witness*** [Gk. *martus*] ***both of the things wherein thou hast seen me, and of the things wherein I will appear unto thee;*** (17) delivering thee from the people, and from the Gentiles, unto whom I send thee, (18) to open their eyes, that they may turn from darkness to light and from the power of Satan unto God, that they may receive remission of sins and an inheritance among them that are sanctified by faith in me. (ASV)

Do you see that verses 16-18 are *new* very positive statements by Jesus? (Also, please note, Jesus has still not once actually called Paul *an apostle.*) Do you likewise see this Acts chapter 26 version undercuts Peter's argument in the speech from the *Clementine Homilies*? Do you further see that Peter could not possibly have known of this *Acts chapter 26 version* at the time Peter confronts his opponent (obviously Paul) in the *Clementine Homilies*?

Thus, it makes the most sense that Acts chapter 26 reflects the account Paul first gave at trial in response to Peter's charge. This explains why Paul believes he "escaped" the mouth of the lion even though the result was that all Christians of Asia (Minor) abandoned Paul. (2 Tim. 1:15.) No one could disprove that Paul had some vision and there may have been positive statements by Jesus. These two vision accounts fell short of calling Paul an apostle. Paul lost the trial on that score. (Rev. 2:2.) Yet, in Paul's mind he won because he was not totally de-legitimized.

Point Six: Don't The Vision Accounts of Acts 22 & 26 Conflict?

In reflection on Paul's various vision accounts, ask yourself this: how plausible is it that the version in Acts chapter 26 just happens to allow Paul to side-step Peter's charge? Furthermore, is it really plausible that both versions (Acts 22 and 26) are true? No, it is not.

In the later version, Acts 26:16, Paul says that Jesus tells him he is appointed to be a witness (*martus*, *martyr*). However, in the earlier version of Acts 22:13-15, Jesus is harsh and then simply says Paul will be told "all" that he is to do when he gets into town. Then in town, and *only then*, Paul learns he is being appointed to be a witness. *The identical words* that Ananias' used in Acts chapter 22 are now transferred, in the next account in Acts chapter 26, into Jesus' mouth. The implausibility of both accounts being true stems from this verse in Acts chapter 22 where Jesus supposedly tells Paul:

> Arise, and go into Damascus; and there it shall be told thee of ***all things*** which are appointed for thee to do. (Acts 22:10).

In this version from Acts chapter 22, Jesus himself says it is in Damascus that Paul will learn "all" of what to do. In the Acts chapter 26 version, everything that Paul was told in the Acts chapter 22 version in Damascus (which was in Ananias' mouth) is now given by Jesus before Paul *even goes to Damascus*. Both versions simply cannot be true. This is because 100% of what Ananias said in Acts chapter 22 is given by Jesus before Jesus in the vision departs in Acts chapter 26. So how can it be true that in Damascus Paul would learn for the first time "all things which are appointed for thee to do?" In the later account of Acts chapter 26, this 100% precedes Paul's trip to Damascus, making a liar out of Jesus in the Acts chapter 22 account. There Jesus said it would be given at Damascus. If you love the Lord Jesus more than Paul, the two stories are irreconcilable.

Point Seven: Why Make A Contradictory Account of the Vision Experience?

This change between Acts chapter 22 and chapter 26 is what explains how Paul in his "first defense" was able to "escape the mouth of the lion," as he puts it in 2 Timothy 2:17. He apparently used this clever side-step. ***Paul simply made up more words of Jesus but this time words of approval before Jesus departs in the vision***. Paul thereby made it appear Jesus is now a friend, and not an adversary. This explains why Paul's "first defense" spoken about in Second Timothy succeeded to some degree in Paul's mind even though "all in... Asia abandoned me." (2 Tim. 1:15.) Paul felt he had success in holding onto some legitimacy even though the verdict was so bad that all in Asia Minor abandoned him. He must have felt his defense salvaged enough that he could believe he escaped the Jewish-Christian opponents that he faced. Thus, Paul apparently made up this Acts chapter 26 version of the Christ-vision on the spot. Paul was satisfied that in doing so he "escaped the mouth of the lion" even though he effectively lost and "all in...Asia abandoned me."

Paul's Contradictory Vision Accounts Permit Skepticism About Paul

Of course, this all depends on you having a certain skepticism about Paul. Yet, most of us evangelicals resist fervently this notion. For those of you having trouble reconsidering Paul's place in the New Testament canon, please consider the following clear-cut contradiction between Paul's first two versions of his vision.

> Acts 9:7 And the men which journeyed with him stood speechless, ***hearing a voice***, but seeing no man. (KJV)
>
> Acts 22:9 And they that were with me saw indeed the light, and were afraid; but ***they heard not the voice*** of him that spake to me. (KJV)

Square these two if you can, but the Greek is identical. The men with him in one case *heard* (Gk. *acoustica*) the voice, and in the other the men with him *did not hear* (Gk. *acoustica*) the voice. Scholars compliment Luke for his honesty, showing us the contradiction. (*Robertson's Word Pictures*.) However, these scholars are not thinking how damning this is of Paul's credibility.

The Validity of the Charges of Peter in Homily 17

Even if the Peter charges in *Homily 17* never took place at a real trial, it turns out that it still makes two arguments that are *valid.* This is interesting because it means in 200 A.D., people had already seen flaws in Paul's alleged appointment. It is not something first seen millennia later by me.

Peter's Charge That Paul Rejected the Apostles' Teachings

An important point leaps off the page of the Peter confrontation with his antagonist in the *Clementine Homilies*. John in 1 John told us, reminiscent of Revelations 2:2, to test every spirit to see whether it comes from God. There were several criteria he gave to tell the liars from the true. He said something very reminiscent of Peter's remarks in the *Clementine Homilies*:

> We belong to God, and everyone who knows God will listen to us [*i.e.*, the twelve apostles]. ***But the people who don't know God won't listen to us.*** That is how we can tell the Spirit that speaks the truth from the one that tells ***lies.*** (1 John 4:6 CEV)

Now compare this to Peter's charge against his antagonist (*i.e.*, Paul) previously quoted from the *Clementine Homilies*:

> ...love His apostles, contend not with me who companied with Him. For in direct opposition to me, who am a firm rock, the foundation of the Church, you now stand. If you were not opposed to me, you would not accuse me, and revile the truth proclaimed by me, ***in order that I may not be believed when I state what I myself have heard with my own ears from the Lord***, as if I were evidently a person that was condemned and in bad repute. But ***if you say that I am condemned, you bring an accusation against God, who revealed the Christ to me, and you inveigh against Him who pronounced me blessed on account of the revelation.*** But if, indeed, you really wish to work in the cause of truth, learn first of all from us what we have learned from Him, and, becoming a disciple of the truth, become a fellow-

> worker with us. (*Ps-Clementine Homilies* 17:19.)

Peter had the same view as John. Peter tells Paul in the *Clementine Homilies* that if you were one of us, you would listen to us, rather than make us out to be liars. John says that "the people who don't know God won't listen to us." Peter is saying, in effect, by rejecting the *twelve* apostles and their teaching, which was based on a Message delivered personally from the Lord, Paul was rejecting Christ himself.

Now where did John and Peter get that idea? Jesus in Matthew 10:14-15 said:

> (14) And whosoever ***shall not receive you, nor hear your words,*** as ye go forth out of that house or that city, shake off the dust of your feet. (15) Verily I say unto you, It shall be more tolerable for the land of Sodom and Gomorrah in the day of judgment, than for that city. (ASV)

Those who reject the *twelve* apostles were condemned by the Lord Jesus Himself. The words of the *twelve apostles,* if rejected, cause us to be at risk of the fire suffered by Sodom and Gomorrah. This is not because their words are prophetic, but because of the Message the twelve *personally* carried from Jesus. If rejected, it puts us at risk of judgment by fire.

Did Paul Admit He Rejected the Teachings of Peter?

In Paul, we see hostility toward the *twelve apostles* in many ways.[25] The twelve "imparted nothing to me," says Paul. (Gal. 2:6.)

However, let us ask whether there is anything in Paul's writings that specifically corroborates this kind of hostility between *Paul and Peter*? Peter is claiming in the *Clementine Homilies* that Paul makes up a false charge to make Peter look like a liar. Paul makes it appear Peter does not know the Lord Jesus very well. Peter calls this an opposition to an apostle of Jesus Christ. It is a major effrontery that cannot stand. Peter warns Paul in effect that Paul is in danger of the Sodom and Gomorrah warning of Jesus. Did Paul ever behave in an insulting way toward Peter from sources we all trust as true? Yes, and Paul admits it. (Actually he *boasts* about it.)

In Galatians 2:11-14, we read:

> (11) But when ***Cephas*** [*i.e.*, Peter] came to Antioch, I resisted him to the face, because he stood condemned. (12) For before that certain came from James, he ate with the Gentiles; but when they came, he drew back and separated himself, fearing them that were of the circumcision. (13) And the rest of the Jews dissembled likewise with him; insomuch that even Barnabas was carried away with their dissimulation. (14) But when I saw that they walked not uprightly according to the truth of the gospel, I said unto ***Cephas*** [*i.e.*, Peter] ***before them all***, If thou, being a Jew, livest as do the Gentiles,

25.Paul sneers at the three "so-called" leaders at Jerusalem: James, Cephas (*i.e.,* Simon Peter) and John, adding pejoratively that they "***seemed*** to be pillars" (Galatians 2:9). Paul then boasts that he believes he is at their level: "For I suppose I was not a whit behind the very chiefest apostles" (2 Corinthians 11:5). And in 2 Corinthians 12:11, Paul claims "in nothing am I behind the very chiefest apostles, though I be nothing." There is some textual and historical reasons to think Paul calls the twelve *false* apostles in 2 Cor. 11:12-23, *viz.* verse 13 "fashioning themselves into apostles of Christ." (Other than the twelve, who else claimed to be apostles other than Paul? No one that we know.) Another example of derogation involves the apostles' amazing gift of tongues (Acts 1). Paul ran down that gift, which had the effect of taking the lustre off the true apostles' gift of tongues. *See* 1 Cor 14:4-33. Finally, if the Galatians understood the twelve contradicted Paul in any way, Paul would be cursing them in Gal. 1:8-12. He warns the Galatians that even if an "angel from heaven" came with a different Gospel than Paul preached, let him be *anathema* (*cursed*). In light of Paul's comments in chapter two of Galatians, it is fair to infer he meant to warn of even a contradictory message from *the twelve and/ or James.*

> and not as do the Jews, how compellest thou the Gentiles to live as do the Jews? (ASV)

Paul boasts here of being able to condemn a true apostle of Jesus Christ. "I resisted him to the face, because he stood condemned." Then Paul says he gave Peter a dressing down "before them all." Paul did this publicly, not in private.

In doing this, Paul violates his own command to us: "Do not sharply rebuke an older man, but appeal to him as a father." (1 Tim. 5:1.) Paul also violated Jesus' command: "if your brother sins, go and reprove him ***in private***; if he listens to you, you have won your brother." (Matthew 18:15.)

Yet, who was right in this public rebuke by Paul of Peter? There is strong reason to believe *Paul was wrong*, not *Peter.*

Paul was teaching Gentiles that it was permissible to eat meat sacrificed to idols. (See page 122.) The twelve apostles tacitly approved James condemning this in Acts chapter 15. Jesus condemns it three times in the Book of Revelation.

Peter apparently discovered this practice by Paul. Peter then would have appropriately withdrawn from eating with Gentiles under Paul's influence. Peter had to be obedient to Jesus who likewise condemned what Paul was permitting.

Thus, Paul admits in Galatians that he refused to follow the example of Peter's withdrawal from eating with Gentiles. Peter was probably simply *obeying Christ*. Now you as a Christian must choose: is Peter as an apostle of Jesus Christ somehow less authoritative than Paul who Jesus never once appointed as an apostle in three vision accounts? While most commentators *assume* Paul is in the right on the withdrawal issue, on what basis? Paul's say-so? Because Paul permits eating meat sacrificed to idols but the twelve were misled in Acts chapter 15 to approve prohibiting it?

One must not be influenced by Paul's one-sided account. We can see Paul had an eating practice that made dining with Gentiles under his influence *impossible*. Jewish custom was to avoid violating food laws by simply not eating with Gentiles. This way they would not offend their host by either asking about foods presented or by refusing foods Gentiles offered. This is all that Peter was doing: being polite as well as conscientious.

Peter's Question Why Jesus Would Use Paul Aside from Apostles

Finally, Peter in the *Clementine Homilies* speech (previously quoted) asks his antagonist (Paul) a blunt question that remains valid even if *Homily 17* were fictional:

> And how did He appear to you, when you entertain opinions contrary to His teaching? But if you were seen and taught by Him, and became His apostle for a single hour, ***proclaim His utterances***, interpret His sayings, love His apostles.

Doesn't anyone else find it incongruous that not a single utterance from Jesus' teachings in the Gospel accounts are found in Paul's many letters? For Paul, Jesus is just the divine messiah who dies, resurrects and we must trust in this fact. Apart from that, Jesus' teachings are completely absent in Paul. ***Peter thinks this is a major flaw.***

What Peter brings out in the *Clementine Homilies* again can be corroborated by looking at Paul's writings. Paul admits in Galatians that after he was *converted,* he then began his work for *fourteen years* before he ever went back to Jerusalem to learn from the apostles *who knew Jesus*. (Gal. 2:1.) Paul admits that until that time, he only had a brief two week visit to Jerusalem three years after his vision. Paul emphasizes his lack of contact with the twelve by pointing out that in those two weeks he only met Peter and then briefly James, the Lord's brother. Paul adamantly insists this is his sole prior encounter with the apostles within "fourteen years" (Gal. 2:1):

> But when it pleased God, who separated me from my mother's womb... To reveal his Son in me, that I might preach him among the hea-

> then; immediately ***I conferred not with flesh and blood: Neither went I up to Jerusalem to them which were apostles before me;*** but I went into Arabia, and returned again unto Damascus. Then after ***three [more] years I went up to Jerusalem*** to see Peter, and abode with him fifteen days. But other of the apostles I saw none, save James the Lord's brother. Now the things which I write unto you, behold, before God, I lie not. Afterwards I came into the regions of Syria and Cilicia. (Galatians 1:8-21)

Peter in the *Clementine Homily 17* thus asks a very good question. If Jesus spent a year with the apostles after the resurrection teaching them, Jesus obviously did so in order that their witness would be full and superior to others. Then it was incumbent on Paul to learn from them. Yet, by Paul's own admission, Paul fails to do so *for years*. How then can Paul form the greater body of New Testament *Scripture* when his ideas are not based on Jesus' teachings? Isn't that a red flag right there? Christianity is being expounded by someone who never spent any extended time with Jesus, never trained under him, and whose writings are devoid of utterances of Jesus except a small unique aphorism and only one inaccurate quote from the Lord's supper account.[26]

Note: Peter to James, Preface to Clementine Homilies

"For some among the Gentiles have rejected my lawful preaching and have preferrred a lawless and absurd doctrine of a man who is ***my enemy***. And indeed some have attempted, while I am still alive to distort my word by interpretation of many sorts, as if I taught the dissolution of the Law ... But that may God forbid! For to do such a thing means to ***act contrary to the Law of God*** which was made to Moses and was confirmed by our Lord in its everlasting continuance. For He said: 'For heaven and earth will pass away, but not one jot or tittle shall pass away from the Law.'" *Letter of Peter to James*, 2.3-5 (presumed 92 A.D.)[a]

a. Bart D. Ehrman, *Peter, Paul & Mary Magdalene* (Oxford: 2006) at 79.

Other respected thinkers have been astonished by Paul's lack of mentioning any lessons of Jesus. Albert Schweitzer once said:

> Where possible, he (Paul) avoids quoting the teaching of Jesus, in fact even mentioning it. If we had to rely on Paul, we should not know that Jesus taught in parables, had delivered the sermon on the mount, and had taught His disciples the 'Our Father.' Even where they are specially relevant, Paul passes over the words of the Lord.[27]

"Paul created a theology of which **nothing but the vaguest warrants** can be found in the words of Christ."
Wil Durant
Caesar & Christ

A modern Christian scholar, Hans van Campenhausen, agrees this deficiency in Paul's writings is a striking and glaring problem:

> The most striking feature is that the words of the Lord, which must have been collected and handed on in the primitive community and elsewhere from the earliest days, ***played no, or at least no vital, part in Paul's basic instruction*** of his churches.[28]

Peter's point in the *Clementine Homilies* is likewise that Paul's failure to teach what Jesus teaches is the clearest proof that Paul is not following Jesus. It is a point well-taken.

---

26. Paul in 1 Corinthians 11:24-25 quotes from the Last Supper at odds with Luke's account. See Luke 22:19-20. Luke says Jesus' body is 'given' but Paul says it is 'broken.' This variance is significant. As John 19:36 mentions, Psalm 34:20 says not a bone of His shall be broken. Paul's quote is thus contradictory of Luke as well as theologically troublesome. The aphorism is 'better to give than receive.' Acts 20:35.

27. Albert Schweitzer, *Albert Schweitzer Library: The Mysticism of Paul the Apostle* (John Hopkins University Press: 1998).

28. Hans van Campenhausen, *The Formation of the Christian Bible* (J. A. Baker, trans.) (Philadelphia: Fortress Press, 1972) at 109.

13 *Did John's Epistles Identify Paul As A False Prophet?*

Introduction

John's First & Second Epistle talk in words *reminiscent* of Revelation 2:2. John speaks in his first epistle about testing those who claim to have come from God. John says you can find them to be false prophets. John writes:

> Dear friends, don't believe everyone who ***claims to have the Spirit*** of God. ***Test them all to find out if they really do come from God.*** Many ***false prophets*** have already gone out into the world (1 John 4:1 CEV).

In John's epistles, John thereafter gives us several tests that his readers can use to know whether some alleged prophet comes from God.

> His spirit [does not] say that Jesus Christ had ***truly human flesh*** (*sarx*, flesh). (1 Jn 4:2.)
>
> We belong to God, and everyone who knows God will listen to us [*i.e.*, the twelve apostles]. ***But the people who don't know God won't listen to us.*** That is how we can tell the Spirit that speaks the truth from the one that tells ***lies.*** (1 John 4:6 CEV.)
>
> These people came ***from our own group***, yet they were not part of us. If they had been part of us, they would have stayed with us. ***But they left,*** which proves that they did not belong to our group. (1 John 2:19 ASV.)

> Whoever ***transgresses*** [*i.e.*, goes beyond] and doesn't remain in ***the teachings of Christ***, doesn't have God [*i.e.*, breaks fellowship with God]. He who remains in the teachings [of Jesus Christ], the same has both the Father and the Son. (2 John 1:9 Websters.)

Thus, John gives us several criteria to identify the false prophets even if they "claim to have the Spirit" of God:

- They teach a heresy that Jesus did not come in truly human flesh (*i.e.*, his flesh just appeared to be human flesh); or
- They do not listen to the twelve apostles; or
- They became a part of the apostles' group but left the apostles' group; or
- They do not remain in the teachings by the twelve of what Jesus taught.

As hard as it may be to believe, each of these four points in First and Second John apply to Paul.

Did Paul Refuse to Listen to the Apostles?

First, Paul did not listen to the twelve apostles. Paul rails in Galatians 2:1-9 at the three "so-called" apostolic pillars of the Jerusalem church (including John) (Gal. 2:9). Paul says again they were "reputed to be something" (Gal. 2:2,6), but "whatsoever they were it makes no difference to me; God does not accept a man's person [*i.e.*, judge by their position and rank]." (Gal. 2:6.) Paul then expressly declares that he received nothing from the twelve apostles.

> I say [those] who were of repute [*i.e.*, the apostles in context] ***imparted nothing to me***, but contrariwise they saw that I was entrusted with the gospel of the uncircumcision. (Gal. 2:7.)

Paul was boasting of his failure to take any information about Jesus's teachings from the original apostles at Jerusalem. He claimed his failure to do so was positive proof his message for Gentiles came direct from God. Paul puts a spin on his behavior that he would be a lesser figure in Christendom had he learned anything about Jesus from the twelve!

Please read all the commentaries you can on those verses. They all agree on this characterization of Paul's meaning. Read the verses yourself to verify the disdain Paul was expressing toward *learning* anything *about Jesus* from the apostles or the reputed pillars of the church—Peter, John, and James.

Now listen again to what John—one of the three mentioned by Paul as "seeming pillars"—had to say about this kind of behavior. John writes:

> We belong to God, and everyone who knows God will listen to us [*i.e.*, the twelve apostles]. ***But the people who don't know God won't listen to us.*** That is how we can tell the Spirit that speaks the truth from the one that tells ***lies.*** (1 John 4:6 CEV)

John clearly would regard someone such as Paul who refused to learn from the twelve as someone who does not "know God." The fact Paul would not listen to the twelve (and was proud of it) allows us to realize Paul is one who "tells lies," if we accept John's direction.

Paul's Admission of Parting Ways With the Apostles

Paul also fits 1 John 2:19 because he left their group. Paul admits this. However, Paul claims it was because the twelve apostles decided they would ***alone*** focus on Jews and Paul ***alone*** would go to the Gentiles. Paul's explanation is implausible in the extreme. Let's follow John's directive to "test" those who claim to have the Spirit. We will see Paul's admitted split from the twelve apostles is more proof that John is speaking of Paul in veiled terms.

In Galatians 2:9, Paul tells us:

> and when they perceived the grace that was given unto me, James and Cephas and John, they who were reputed to be pillars, gave to me and Barnabas the right hands of fellowship, that ***we should go unto the Gentiles,*** and ***they unto the circumcision***;

Does Paul's account, any way you mull it over, make sense? Not only are there issues of plausibility, but, if Paul is telling the truth, it means the twelve apostles were willing to violate the Holy Spirit's guidance to the twelve that Peter was the Apostle to the Gentiles, as is clearly stated in Acts 15:7.

God Already Appointed Peter the Apostle to the Gentiles

The Holy Spirit had already showed the twelve that Peter (not Paul) was the Apostle to the Gentiles. At the Jerusalem Council, with Paul among those at his feet, Peter gets up and says he is ***the Apostle to the Gentiles*** in Acts 15:7:

> And when there had been much disputing, Peter rose up, and said unto them, Men and brethren, ye know how that a good while ago ***God made choice among us, that the Gentiles by my mouth should hear the word of the gospel,*** and believe.

Peter's statement in Acts 15:7 means God had spoken to him about his task to preach to Gentiles. We even have evidence what that included. God showed Peter visions of the unclean food so he would know to reach the Gentiles. As a result, Peter had converted Cornelius in Acts chapter 10.

If Peter sincerely believed "God made choice among us that" he was the apostle to the Gentiles in Acts 15:7, why would Peter later give this mission up to Paul? Yet, Paul in

Galatians 2:9 clearly says Peter agreed Paul would go to the Gentiles and "they [*i.e.*, Peter & the Jerusalem leaders] unto the circumcision [*i.e.*, Jews]."

What Paul claims happened makes no sense. If it happened by mutual agreement, then you would have to conclude Peter believed God changed his mind about Peter's role. This would require Peter to disregard God's choice a "good while ago" mentioned in Acts 15:7 that he be the Apostle to the Gentiles. This is completely implausible.

Thus, to believe Paul, you have to believe God would change His mind who was to go to the Gentiles. Yet, for what purpose? Wouldn't two be better than one? ***Why would God cut out Peter entirely***?

Furthermore, why would Peter diminish this Gentile ministry among the twelve that he initiated with Cornelius? Why would he put Paul ***alone*** as the leader to convert Gentiles? Moreover, there were Gentiles right in Jerusalem. How could the apostles sensibly divide up their mission field on the basis of Gentile and Jew?

The answer to all these paradoxes is quite obvious. Paul is putting a good spin on a division between himself and the home church. By claiming in a letter to Gentiles that he was still authorized to evangelize to them, they would believe him. They could not phone Jerusalem to find out the truth. Now listen to John's evaluation of what this really meant:

> These people came ***from our own group***, yet they were not part of us. If they had been part of us, they would have stayed with us. ***But they left,*** which proves that they did not belong to our group. (1 John 2:19 ASV)

Did Paul Teach Jesus Did Not Truly Have Human Flesh?

Most Christians might concede the prior points from First John *possibly* apply to Paul. What most Christians would not concede as possible is that Paul also taught Jesus did not have truly human flesh.

Before we address this point, let's distinguish this next point from what has preceded. This 'human flesh' issue is a completely independent ground to evaluate Paul. John could be talking about Paul on the issue of leaving their group (1 John 2:19) and not listening to the twelve (1 John 4:6), but not be addressing Paul on the 'human flesh issue' in 1 John 4:2. One point does not necessarily have anything to do with the other.

That said, let's investigate whether this issue of 'human flesh' in 1 John 4:2 applies to Paul as well.

To understand what teaching John is opposing when he faults as deceivers those who say "Jesus did not have human flesh," one must have a little schooling in church history. We today assume John is talking about people who say Jesus came in an imaginary way. This is not John's meaning.

The heresy that John is referring to is the claim Jesus did not have truly human flesh. Marcion's doctrine is an example of this viewpoint. Marcion came on the scene of history in approximately 144 A.D. John's epistle is written earlier, and thus is not actually directed at Marcion. Marcion helps us, however, to identify the precursor heresy that John is attacking. Marcion's doctrines are well-known. Marcion taught salvation by faith alone, the Law of Moses was abrogated, and he insisted Paul alone had the true Gospel, to the exclusion of the twelve apostles. (See Appendix B: *How the Canon Was Formed* at page ix.) Upon whom did Marcion claim his authority that Jesus only came in the appearance of human flesh? It was obviously Paul.

Marcion said, according to Tertullian's derisive quote, that Jesus "was not what he appeared to be...[saying He was] flesh and yet not flesh, man and not yet man...." (Tertullian, *On Marcion*, 3.8.)

Marcion was not denying Jesus came and looked like a man. Rather, Marcion was claiming that Jesus' flesh could not be human in our sense. Why? What did Marcion mean?

Marcion was a devout Paulinist, as mentioned before. Paul taught the doctrine that all *human* flesh inherits the *original sin* of Adam. (Romans chapter 5.) If Jesus truly had *human* flesh, Marcion must have been concerned that Jesus would have come in a human flesh which Paul taught was inherently sinful due to the taint of *original sin*. Incidentally, Paul's ideas on human flesh being inherently sinful was contrary to Hebrew Scriptures which taught all flesh was clean unless some practice or conduct made it unclean. (See, *e.g.*, Lev. 15:2 *et seq.*) In light of Paul's new doctrine, Marcion wanted to protect Jesus from being regarded as inherently sinful. Thus, Marcion was denying Jesus had truly human flesh.

Marcion's teaching on Jesus' flesh is known by scholars as *docetism.* The word *docetism* comes from a Greek work that means *appear*. Docetism says Jesus only *appeared* to come in human flesh. Docetism also became popular later among Gnostics who taught salvation by knowledge and mysteries. (Marcion taught salvation by faith in Jesus, so he is not Gnostic in the true sense.) The Gnostics were never the threat to Christianity that the Marcionites represented. Gnostics were simply writers who had no churches. The Marcionites, on the other hand, were successful in establishing a competing Paul-oriented Christian church system in most major cities that rivaled the churches founded by the twelve apostles. The Marcionites had church buildings, clergy, regular services, etc.

It was in this context that John's letter from the 90s A.D., in particular 1 John 4:2, must be understood as condemning *docetism*. John's epistle became crucial later in defeating Marcionism. This victory did not decisively happen until the 400s. Marcionite churches survived even into the eighth century A.D., but they remained weak. They later even spawned the Armenian Paulicians. This group endured into the 1200s.

However, a mystery remains. John in the 90s A.D. is writing 50 years prior to Marcion's appearance on the stage of world history.

Then of whom was John speaking? Was it Paul who Marcion claimed as his mentor in all things? Did Paul teach *docetism*?

Yes. Heretical *docetism* is found *expressly* in Paul. For Paul writes Jesus only appeared to be a man and to come in sinful human flesh. (Rom. 8:3 "likeness" or "appearance" of "sinful human flesh;"[1] see also Phil. 2:7 "appeared to be a man".)[2]

"God sending His own Son in the likeness (homomati) of sinful flesh condemned sin in the flesh." Rom. 8:3

Specialists in ancient Greek who are Christian struggle to find no heresy in Paul's words in both passages. Vincent is one of the leading Christian scholars who has done a Greek language commentary on the entire New Testament. Here is how *Vincent's Word Studies* tries to fashion an escape from Paul uttering heresy. First, Vincent explains Paul liter-

1. In Romans 8:3, Paul writes: "For what the law could not do, in that it was weak through the flesh, God, sending his own Son in the ***likeness*** [*i.e.*, appearance] of sinful flesh and for sin, condemned sin in the flesh." (ASV)

2. Of course, like Marcion, Paul does not dispute that Jesus was the Godhead who appeared in a "body" (*somatikos*). (Col. 2:9.) A *body* does not imply *human flesh.* Yet, Robertson believes that Col. 2:9 disposes with the docetic theory. Yet, Robertson describes this theory as "Jesus had no human body." This is not a precise description, at least of Marcion's docetism. Rather, docetism says the *body* in which Jesus lived *lacked human flesh*. It just appeared to be *human flesh.* Robertson's analysis thus lacks precise focus on what is *docetism.*

ally says in Romans 8:3 that Jesus came in the *likeness of the flesh of sin*. Vincent then says had Paul not used the word *likeness*, Paul would be saying Jesus had come in "*the sin of flesh*," which "would [then] have represented Him as partaking of sin." Thus, Vincent says Paul does not deny Jesus came in the *flesh* (*i.e.,* Paul is not denying Jesus' humanity), but rather Paul insists that Jesus came only in the *likeness of sinful flesh*.

My answer to Vincent is simple: you have proved my case. Vincent is conceding the Greek word *homomati* (which translates as *likeness*) means Jesus did not *truly* come in *the flesh of sin*. Vincent is intentionally ignoring what this means in Paul's theology. To Paul, all flesh is sinful. There is no such thing as *flesh* that is holy in Paul's outlook. For Paul, you are either in the Spirit or in the flesh. The latter he equates with *sin*. (Gal. 5:5,16-20.) So Paul is saying Jesus only *appeared* to come in sinful human flesh. In Paul's theology of original sin (Rom. ch. 5), this is the same thing as saying Jesus did not come in *truly human flesh.* It only appeared to be human (sinful) flesh. Paul was completely *docetic*. That is how Marcion formed his doctrine: *straight from Paul.*

Furthermore, when you compare Romans 8:3 to Philippians 2:7, there is no mistaking Paul's viewpoint. In Philippians 2:7, Paul this time says Jesus came in the "likeness (*homomati*) of men," not *flesh of sin*. Following Vincent's previous agreement on *homomati*'s meaning, this verse says Jesus did not *truly* come as a *man*. He just *appeared as if he was a man*. Vincent again struggles desperately to offer an interpretation of Philippians 2:7 that avoids Paul being a heretic. Vincent ends up conceding "*likeness of men* expresses the fact that His Mode of manifestation *resembled* what men are." When you strip away Vincent's vague words, Vincent concedes Paul teaches Jesus only appeared to be a man. Thus, he was not truly a man. This means Paul was 100% *docetic*. Listen to John's evaluation of the false prophets:

> His spirit [does not] say that Jesus Christ had a ***truly human flesh*** (*sarx*, flesh). (1 Jn 4:2.)

Was Marcion really that far from Paul? As Tertullian summarized Marcion's view, we hear the *clear echo* of Paul. Marcion taught Jesus "was not what he appeared to be...[saying He was] flesh and yet not flesh, man and not yet man...." (Tertullian, *On Marcion*, 3.8.)

John's Epistles Are Aimed At A False Teacher Once at Ephesus

The likelihood that John's epistles are veiled ways of talking about Paul gets stronger when we look at other characteristics of the heretic John is identifying in his first two epistles. Historians acknowledge that John's epistles are written of events "almost certainly in Asia Minor in or near ***Ephesus***."[3] John's concern, Ivor Davidson continues, was about someone in that region who said Jesus was "not truly a flesh-and-blood human being." To counter him, John also later wrote in his Gospel that the Word "became flesh" (John 1:14.)

Who could John be concerned about who taught *docetism* in that region of Ephesus? Again the answer is obviously Paul. For it was Paul who wrote in Romans 8:3 and Philippians 2:7 that Jesus only appeared to come as a man and in sinful human flesh. Paul must have carried the same message with himself to Ephesus. John's focus in his epistles is obviously on the same person of whom Revelation 2:2 is identifying was "a liar" to the Ephesians. John has the same person in mind in ***the same city of Ephesus***. John's intended object must be Paul.

3. Ivor J. Davidson, *The Birth of the Church: From Jesus to Constantine A.D. 30-312* (Tim Dowley Ed.) (Grand Rapids, Michigan: Baker, 2004) at 162.

Did Papias Understand John's Epistle Message Was Against Paul?

The only later figure whom we confidently can conclude knew Apostle John is Papias. He was John's pupil. Papias appears to have understood Apostle John was criticizing Paul. The surviving fragments of the writings of Papias, bishop of Hierapolis (130 A.D.) "do not contain any quotation from Paul" even while quoting John's Gospel and 1 Peter.[4] This and other evidence led Christian scholar Charles M. Nielsen to argue that Papias was writing "against a growing 'Paulinis' [*i.e.*, Paulinism] in Asia Minor *circa* 125-135 A.D., just prior to full blown Marcionism [*i.e.*, Paul-only-ism]."[5] Nielsen contends Papias' opponent was Polycarp, bishop of Smyrna, who favored Paul. (We have more to say on Polycarp in a moment.)

Thus, in Papias—a bishop of the early church and close associate of Apostle John—we find a figure who already is fighting a growing Paulinism in pre-Marcion times. This allows an inference that Apostle John shared the same concern about Paul that we identify in John's letters. Apostle John then passed on his concern to Papias. This led Papias to fight the "growing Paulinis" (*i.e.*, Paulinism) in Asia Minor—the region to which Ephesus belonged.

---

4. "Papias," *The Catholic Encyclopedia.*
5. Rev. (Lutheran) D. Richard Stuckwisch "Saint Polycarp of Smyrna: Johannine or Pauline Figure?" *Concordia Theological Quarterly* (January-April 1997)Vol. 61 at 113, 118, citing Charles M. Nielsen, "Papias: Polemicist Against Whom?" *Theological Studies* 35 (September 1974): 529-535; Charles Nielsen "Polycarp and Marcion: A Note," *Theological Studies* 47 (June 1986): 297-399; Charles Nielsen, "Polycarp, Paul and the Scriptures," *Anglican Theological Review* 47 (April 1965): 199-215.

What About Polycarp? Did He Know John Yet Accept Paul?

A word on Polycarp is necessary. Polycarp's surviving epistle holds high praise for "glorious Paul." However, it is still not Pauline in a thematic sense. There is no grace teaching in them. There is no salvation-by-faith doctrine in them. Regardless, the surviving epistle does highly praise Paul. At the same time, it is often said that Polycarp knew Apostle John. If so, and these Johannine Epistles were written by Apostle John *negatively* about Paul, as I contend above, then why does Polycarp have such high praise for Paul?

It is a good question. However, it turns out that Polycarp did not likely know Apostle John. Thus, the question becomes irrelevant. It rests on a faulty assumption that Polycarp knew Apostle John.

How did we arrive at the commonly heard notion that Polycarp was associated with Apostle John? It comes solely from Ireneaus and those quoting Ireneaus such as Tertullian. However, there is strong reason to doubt Irenaeus' claim.

Irenaeus wrote of a childhood memory listening to Polycarp tell of his familiarity with Apostle John. However, none of the surviving writings of Polycarp make any mention of his association with Apostle John. Nor is such an association mentioned in the two biographical *earlier* accounts of Polycarp contained in *Life of Polycarp* and *The Constitution of the Apostles*. Yet, these biographies predate Irenaeus and thus were closer in time to Polycarp's life. Likewise, Polycarp's own writings show no knowledge of John's Gospel. This seems extraordinarily unlikely had John been his associate late in life. As a result of the cumulative weight of evidence, most Christian scholars (including conservative ones) agree that Ireneaus' childhood memory misunderstood something Polycarp said. Perhaps Polycarp was talking of a familiarity with John the Elder rather than Apostle John.[6]

Thus, it is not likely that Polycarp knew Apostle John personally in a period after these Johannine Epistles. Also, technically speaking, we have no dates on Polycarp's epistle. Thus, we do not know if his "glorious Paul" comment came *before* or *after* John's epistles. Thus, even if there were some association between John and Polycarp, we cannot be sure whether Polycarp's positive view of Paul continued *after* that association began.

Accordingly, there is no clear case that someone associated with John after he wrote his epistles had a positive opinion of Paul. To the contrary, the only person whom we confidently can conclude knew John in this time period—Papias—was engaged in resistance to rising Paulinism, according to Christian scholars.

Thus, John's letters appear to reveal even more clearly who was being spoken about in Revelation 2:2. John's true friends (*i.e.*, Papias) had the same negative outlook on Paulinism at that time.

Conclusion

Accordingly, when John's epistles tell us the four characteristics of a false prophet and teacher who left associating with the twelve apostles, they fit Paul like a glove. Scholars agree that John is identifying a false teacher who once had been at Ephesus who taught Jesus did not come in truly human flesh. This too fits Paul like a glove. Paul expressly taught Jesus did not come in human flesh—it only appeared that way. John in his epistle is thus pointing precisely at Paul without using Paul's name.

John, in effect, tells us in 1 John 4:2-3 to regard Paul as uninspired and a liar, no matter how appealing Paul's theological arguments may sound.

6. Rev. (Lutheran) D. Richard Stuckwisch "Saint Polycarp of Smyrna: Johannine or Pauline Figure?" *Concordia Theological Quarterly* (January-April 1997) Vol. 61 at 113 *et seq.* (agrees that Polycarp did not likely know Apostle John).

Given what we find in 1 John 4:1-3, is it then really any coincidence that by the hand of the same John, Revelation 2:2 depicts someone as a liar who told the Ephesians he was an apostle but he was not? Or is it really coincidence that John's hand wrote Revelation 2:14 which refers to a Balaam figure in the apostolic New Testament era who teaches it is permissible to eat meat sacrificed to idols? Balaam, remember, was a prophet converted from evil to a Holy Spirit-filled prophet of God by his experience of seeing an angel on the Road to Moab. Yet, Balaam later apostasizes by teaching it is permissible to eat meat sacrificed to idols. Paul likewise followed the identical pattern.[7] Apostle John like ourselves can read where three times Paul says it is permissible to eat meat sacrificed to idols. John is not so unaware that he could not have known of whom Jesus was speaking when referencing an apostolic era Balaam.[8]

Accordingly, when we turn to John's epistles, we hear John talk about false prophets in terms that uniquely fit Paul:

- A recent figure at Ephesus said Jesus only appeared to have human flesh.
- A recent figure once had been part of the apostolic church but who later took a route ***exclusive*** of the twelve apostles.
- A recent figure had been at Ephesus and did not accept the teachings of Jesus from the twelve, and instead transgressed them.

John always omits names, even as John in his own Gospel never refers to himself by name. John refers to himself as the "apostle whom Jesus loved." John prefers we use deduction and context for us to deduce of whom he speaks.

7. For a full discussion on the Balaam-Paul identification, see the chapter entitled "Why Does Jesus Mention Balaam in Rev. 2:14?" on page 131 *et seq*.
8. See the chapter entitled "Paul Contradicts Jesus About Idol Meat" on page 117.

Yet, the fact Revelation 2:2, 14 and John's epistles are referring to Paul is shocking to most Christians. It is even more shocking because you can deduce Paul is being identified by relying alone on Scripture you have read for years.

"But... took upon Him the form of a servant, and was made in the likeness (homomati) of men." Phil. 2:7

Historical Note: Tertullian's Observations on Paul in 207 A.D. in *Against Marcion*

"I must with the best of reasons approach this inquiry with uneasiness when I find one affirmed to be an apostle, of whom ***in the list of the apostles in the gospel I find no trace****....* [Let's] put in evidence all the documents that attest his apostleship. ***He [i.e., Paul] himself, says Marcion, claims to be an apostle***, and that not from men nor through any man, but through Jesus Christ. Clearly ***any man can make claims for himself:*** but his claim is confirmed by another person's attestation. One person writes the document, another signs it, a third attests the signature, and a fourth enters it in the records. **No man is for himself both claimant and witness**." (See Tertullian, *Against Marcion* (207 A.D.) quoted at 418-19 *infra*.)

14 *Who is the Benjamite Wolf in Prophecy?*

Jesus' Words on the Ravening Wolf

Jesus several times mentions a wolf or wolves. He says the false prophets will be wolves dressed like sheep. This means they will claim to be followers of Christ, but "inwardly [they] are ravening wolves." The full quote is:

> Beware of false prophets, who come to you in sheep's clothing, but inwardly are *ravening wolves*. (Matt. 7:15.)

Jesus warns true Christians that they are at risk from these so-called Christians who are truly ravening wolves.

> Behold, I send you forth as sheep in the midst of *wolves*: be ye therefore wise as serpents, and harmless as doves. (Matt. 10:16)

Christian leaders who do not care for the flock will leave the average Christian at the mercy of these ravening wolves. Jesus explains:

> He that is a hireling, and not a shepherd, whose own the sheep are not, beholdeth the wolf coming, and leaveth the sheep, and fleeth, and the ***wolf snatcheth*** them, and scattereth them: (John 10:12)
>
> He fleeth because he is a hireling, and careth not for the sheep. (John 10:13)(ASV)

Is this imagery of the ravening wolf as the false prophet ever spoken about elsewhere in Scripture? Yes, in fact there is a prophecy in the book of Genesis that the tribe of Benjamin would later produce just such a "ravening wolf."

Genesis Prophecies of Messiah and His Enemy from the Tribe of Benjamin

Paul tells us in Romans 11:1, "For I also am an Israelite, of the seed of Abraham, of the tribe of *Benjamin.*" Paul repeats this in Philippians 3:5, saying he is "of the stock of Israel, of the tribe of *Benjamin.*"[1]

Keeping this in mind, Genesis has a very interesting Messianic prophecy. Modern Christians are sadly generally unaware of this prophecy. It may be ignored because the nearby passage about a Benjamite ravening wolf in the *latter days* hits too close to home. It is better to ignore a clear Messianic prophecy than to risk seeing the Bible prophesied the emergence of Paul and the error he would propagate among Christians.

In Genesis chapter 49, Jacob, also known as Israel, utters a prophecy of the *latter days.* In this prophecy, Jacob identifies the role of each son and his tribe. The passage begins:

> And Jacob called unto his sons, and said: gather yourselves together, that I may tell you that which shall befall you in the *latter days.* (Gen 49:1)

1. We discussed elsewhere the Ebionite charge that Paul was not a true Jew. Then could he still be a Benjamite? Yes, Paul could be a descendant of a tribe without being a true Jew. For example, if one of Paul's grandparents were a Benjamite, then he can be of the tribe but not a true Jew.

Then Jacob delivers a prophecy about his son Judah and the tribe of Judah for the *latter days*. It is a clear Messianic prophecy.

> The sceptre shall not depart from Judah [*i.e.*, the right to rule belongs to this tribe], Nor the ruler's staff from between his feet, ***Until Shiloh come***: And unto him shall the obedience of the peoples be. (Gen 49:10)
>
> Binding his foal unto the vine, And his ass's colt unto the choice vine; He hath ***washed his garments in wine***, And ***his vesture in the blood of grapes***. (Gen 49:11)
>
> His eyes shall be red with wine, And his teeth white with milk. (Gen 49:12) (ASV)

The root word for *Shiloh* comes from *Shalom*, meaning *peace.* Shiloh means *one who brings peace.* Shiloh comes holding the sceptre of Judah. Shilo thus is a *prince of peace.*

This passage therefore clearly depicts Messiah, the Prince of Peace, with his garments bathed in the blood of grapes. All obedience will be owed him. The Genesis-Shiloh Messiah is then presented in similar imagery as the Lamb of God in the Book of Revelation. (Rev. 19:13 "garment sprinkled with blood".)

Ancient Jewish scholars also read this Genesis passage to be a Messianic prophecy. In all three Rabbinic *Targums*, the Hebrew scholars taught *Shiloh* was the name for Messiah. This was also repeated by many ancient Jewish writers. (Gill, Gen. 49:10.)

So why is this Messianic passage so unfamiliar to Christians? Perhaps because in close proximity we find Jacob's prophecy about the tribe of Benjamin. This Benjamite prophecy follows many positive predictions for all the other eleven tribes.

Of whom does the Benjamite prophecy speak? When weighed carefully, there is very little chance that the Benjamite prophecy could be about anyone but Paul. This prophecy about Benjamin, if it was to be fulfilled and then verified, must have been fulfilled in the time of Christ. At that time, the tribes of Judah, Levi, and Benjamin still had survived. The others were the lost tribes of the Diaspora. (Gill, commentary on Gen. 49:10.) After the time of Christ, any distinguishable tribe of Benjamin soon disappeared. Thus, the prophecy about Benjamin is no longer capable of being fulfilled and confirmed. Accordingly, one must consider the possibility this verse is talking about Paul. In fact, the early Christian church, as demonstrated below, did think this was a prophecy about Paul. Somehow we lost memory of this teaching.

Let's turn now to Jacob's last prophecy about the Benjamites in the "*latter days*" when Shiloh comes. Here we read of the imagery of a *ravening wolf* that identifies the tribe of Benjamin.

> Benjamin is a *wolf that raveneth*: In the morning she shall devour the prey, And at even[ing] he shall divide the spoil. (Gen 49:27) (ASV)

Let's analyze this verse—for there is a time-sequence to the ravening wolf's activity. In the morning, he devours the prey. This means he kills his prey. In the evening, he takes the spoils left over after killing the prey. There are many metaphorical similarities to Paul. He starts as a killer of Christians or as one who approves the killing of Christians. (Acts 7:58; 8:1-3, 9:1.) However, later Paul claims a right of *division* among his earlier *prey*—he exclusively will recruit Gentiles as Christians while the twelve apostles supposedly would exclusively recruit Jews. (Galatians 2:9.)[2]

2. The unlikelihood that this was consensual from the twelve is discussed in "Paul's Admission of Parting Ways With the Apostles" on page 334.

In fact, in the early Christian church, this entire verse of Genesis 49:27 was read to be a prophecy about Paul. However, the second part was then spun favorably to Paul. An early church writer, Hippolytus (200s A.D.), said Paul fulfilled Genesis 49:27 because Paul started as a murderer of Christians, fulfilling the first part of Genesis 49:27. The second part about 'dividing the spoil' was interpreted by Hippolytus to mean Paul made Christian followers predominantly among Gentiles. However, this was read *positively.* Hippolytus believed Paul *divided the spoil* in a manner God intended. However, *dividing the spoil* means *plundered.* It does not have a positive connotation. This spin by Hippolytus on *dividing the spoil* as a *good deed* was wishful thinking. God instead was sending a prophecy of the evil that would be done by this Benjamite, not the good.

Here is the quote from the early church writer Hippolytus (estimated to be 205 A.D.) wherein he saw God prophesying of Paul in Genesis 49:27:

> 'Benjamin is a devouring wolf. In the morning, he will devour the prey, and at night he will apportion the food.' ***This thoroughly fits Paul***, who was of the tribe of Benjamin. For when he was young, he was a ravaging wolf. However, when he believed, he 'apportioned the food.' (Hippolytus, *W* 5.168.)[3]

These writings from the early church demonstrates two things: (a) early Christians were more familiar than ourselves with the Shiloh Messianic prophecy in Genesis 49:10-12; and (b) if one knew the Shiloh prophecy, one could not avoid seeing in close proximity the prophecy of a Benjamite

3. Notice incidentally that the positive spin was manufactured by Hippolytus changing the verse's meaning from *divide the spoils* to *apportion the food.*

wolf (Genesis 49:27) whereupon one would realize it is unmistakably talking about Paul. As Hippolytus says, "this thoroughly fits Paul."

What do modern Pauline Christian commentators do with the Benjamite wolf prophecy? While some admit Genesis 49:27 is about Paul, and spin the *divide the spoils* aspect of the prophecy favorably toward Paul as a *good deed*,[4] the leading commentators take an entirely different approach. Gill, for example, adopts the ancient Jewish explanation of this prophecy of the *latter days*. Because Benjamin's territory was where the Temple was located, it was said the offering of the morning and evening sacrifice fell to his lot, *i.e.*, territory.[5] Thus, this verse was supposedly intended to be talking about Benjamin's *indirect* role in the killing the sacrifice in the morning and evening. The performance of the sacrifices, of course, are positive God-serving actions if attributable to Benjamin's actions. Thus, rather than a ravening wolf being an *evil beast* who attacks innocent sheep, modern Christian commentators say Benjamin was being complimented for possessing wolf-like "fortitude, courage, and valour." (Gill.)

Gill ignores many key flaws in this application. First, the role of Benjamin's tribe in the killing was entirely passive, *i.e.*, its territory was ceded to help locate the temple where sacrifices later took place. This passive role cannot evince any kind of courage or valour. It is a poor solution.

---

4. See, *e.g.*, http://cgg.org/index.cfm/page/literature.showResource/CT/ARTB/k/1007 (last accessed 8/19/05).

5. Louis Ginzberg, *The Legends of the Jews* (1909) Vol.2 Part VIII; Gill ("the temple which stood in the lot of Benjamin"). This rationale to apply the prophecy to a role for the tribe of Benjamin in the sacrifices is extremely weak. Just because the Temple apparently occupied part of Benjamin's territory does not mean that the morning and evening sacrifice was *this tribe's* responsibility. The duty of performing the sacrifice belonged to the Levites. It is a stretch of the wildest proportions to say a Benjamite in latter days would kill an animal by the mere passive role of having its tribal land under the feet of a Levite priest.

More important, Gill ignores the context of the passage itself. The word *prey, raveneth, wolf, spoils,* etc., all are forebodings of evil acts, not courageous valor in good deeds. A ravening wolf is a wolf that is prowling and eating voraciously. Furthermore, the sacrificed animals in the temple are hardly *prey.* Also, technically, Benjamin's land-lot was used to kill the sacrifice in *both* the morning and evening. However, if *prey* means *sacrifice,* this prophecy was about killing prey *only in the morning.* Thus, it is incongruous to read this prophecy to be about Benjamin's land-lot being used in the evening and morning sacrifice.

Furthermore, Gill also overlooked the motivation behind these *Targum* explanations. The other tribes were probably mystified why their father Jacob warned them about Benjamin's tribe in the *latter days.* Gill fails to realize the Hebrew scholars who wrote the ancient *Targums* were engaged in good politics. The other eleven tribes were reassuring Benjamin that he was trusted. What else could they say to keep peace?

As a result, we are not beholden to that ancient polite resolution of this *latter days* prophecy. We now can see the clear fulfillment of this prophecy in the deeds of Paul.

Gill Also Overlooks the Bible's Portrayal Later of the Tribe of Benjamin

The Bible also gives us later an adequate depiction of the tribe of Benjamin and its members so that it is impossible to believe Genesis 49:27 was meant at all *positively.* It was a portent of gloomy evil by the Benjamites. The Bible has utterly unflattering stories about the Benjamites.

First, at the same time the tribe of Benjamin's territory served its supposedly noble role in the morning/evening sacrifice, the Benjamites were fighting a war against the other eleven tribes. In two days, the Benjamites killed 40,000 members of the other tribes. However, the Benjamites were later lured into leaving their city, and lost their war. The tribe of Benjamin was virtually annihilated. (Judges chs. 19-21). In this episode, there is a particularly distasteful event. The men of Gibeah were Benjamites who the Bible describes as "a perverse lot." They cruelly tried to abuse a visitor and then they raped an old man's concubine. (Judges 19:14, 22, 25.)

Certainly, to this point in the Bible, the Benjamites are depicted as quite evil and even as *anti-Israelites.*

The next and last Bible story of Benjamites is more of the same negative portrayal of Benjamites. This story also has uncanny parallels to Saul-Paul.

The Bible tells us King Saul was a Benjamite. (1 Sam. 9:21.) He is at one point an inspired true prophet, given a "new heart"—you could even say *born again.* (1 Sam. 10:9-10.) Yet, later King Saul pursued the man named David to kill him. Saul did so despite knowing God decided David would replace Saul as King. (1 Sam. 18:8-10; 19:10.) Saul became so depraved that he wanted to kill his own son Jonathan because of his loyalty to David. (1 Sam. 20: 30-34.) Thus, Saul is an example of a true prophet from the tribe of Benjamin who *later* turned false by virtue of defying God's anointed (*messhiach*).[6] Unfortunately, Saul also would not be the last Saul from the tribe of Benjamin to begin apparently as a true prophet but who later defied the *messhiach.*

Incidentally, it is reassuring to remember that Saul, the Benjamite, did not triumph over the house of David. Eventually David took the throne from Saul. Initially, King Saul would not yield the throne to the House of David despite Saul prophetically knowing God's will to choose David. Saul made a desperate stand to hold onto raw power even after he realized he lacked God's true blessing. Nevertheless, the *House of David* eventually triumphed anyway over the Benjamite Saul. (1 Samuel 9:1-2; 10:1; 15:10, 30, 16:1.)

6. Kings in those days were *anointed* with oil. The word anointed was *messhiach.* Thus, King David sometimes refers to himself as *messhiach—anointed one.* In Daniel, this title took on the characteristic of a future world ruler.

Thus, if Pauline Christians are the modern followers of the Benjamite wolf, then we know they are resisting following Jesus' words just like King Saul resisted letting David have the throne. Despite all their efforts to kill off Jesus' words by means of strained interpretations of various dispensations, God's anointed from the House of David will eventually triumph.

Regardless whether King Saul's story was intended to serve as such a parable, we can see in King Saul another Benjamite whose actions were evil in the last analysis. Prior to Paul's arrival, the Bible never depicts the Benjamite tribe as doing any good. Instead, the Bible portrays this tribe and its members as fighting the rest of Israel and God's anointed from the House of David. Thus, Gill's notion that Genesis 49:27 was intended to compliment the valor of the Benjamites is completely baseless. It is solely a verse portending gloomy evil by members of this tribe, of which the Bible documents every step of the way right up to the point Paul is himself helping murder Christians.

Next we shall see how to discern the wolf by his deeds. The Bible, in Ezekiel, is highly specific. There is no question that Paul in his *post-conversion* teachings fits the traits of the time of the ravening wolves depicted by Ezekiel.

Ezekiel's Warning About the Ravening Wolves

Jesus said we would know the false prophets who are ravening wolves in sheep's clothing by their "deeds." (Matt. 7:16.)

How could we know who the wolf is by *their deeds*? Does this mean their deeds are merely wicked? Or does it mean their *deeds* are precisely described elsewhere in Scripture so you could not possibly mistake who are the *wolves in sheep's clothing*? In light of Ezekiel's description of the *rav-*

ening wolves, it is likely the latter. God made a highly specific description of the *deeds* of the ravening wolves so we would "know them by their deeds." (Matt. 7:16.)

The picture in Ezekiel chapter 22 of the time of the *ravening wolves* is startling in its parallel to Paul and Pauline Christianity. This description tells us what God thinks about the descent of Christianity into church-going that disregards the true Sabbath and the Law, dismisses the teachings of Jesus as belonging to a by-gone dispensation, and instead follows Paul because he claims a vision and boldly claimed to speak in the Lord's name. Ezekiel described the time of the *ravening wolves* in an uncanny parallel to Paulinism:

> Her priests have ***done violence to my law,*** and have profaned my holy things: they have ***made no distinction between the holy and the common, neither have they caused men to discern between the unclean*** and the ***clean***, and ***have hid their eyes from my sabbaths***, and I am profaned among them. (Eze 22:26)
>
> Her princes in the midst thereof are like ***wolves ravening the prey,*** to shed blood, and to destroy souls, that they may get dishonest gain. (Eze 22:27)
>
> And ***her prophets*** have daubed for them with untempered mortar, ***seeing false visions***, and ***divining lies*** unto them, saying, Thus saith the Lord Jehovah, ***when Jehovah hath not spoken***. (Eze 22:28)
>
> The people of the land have used oppression, and exercised robbery; yea, ***they have vexed the poor*** and needy, and have oppressed the sojourner wrongfully. (Eze 22:29)
>
> And I sought for a man among them, that should build up the wall, and stand in the gap

> before me for the land, that I should not destroy it; ***but I found none***. (Eze 22:30)(ASV)

Thus, those leading the people are *ravening wolves.* They are called the *princes* (leaders) in the people's eyes. They are buttressed by those having false visions and claims to have the right to speak in the name of the Lord. Their leaders seduce the people from following the Law. They teach them they are free to ignore the true Saturday Sabbath. They say all food is pure, and none unclean. Their teaching also leads to the vexation of the poor and the foreigner. There will be a time when no one is left who stands against these principles.[7]

Now look at the parallels between these wolves and Paul.

First, Paul claimed a vision of Jesus. (Acts chapters. 9, 22, 26.) Based on this vision experience, Paul wanted us to accept that he was speaking directly from *the Lord.* (*E.g.*, 1 Cor. 14:37; 1 Tim. 2:11; 1 Cor. 2:13; 1 Thess.4:1-2,8; 1 Thess. 2:13; Eph. 4:17. *cf.* 1 Cor. 7:25, 40.)

Second, Paul's view that the Law is entirely abrogated is well-established. (2 Cor. 2:14; Gal. 5:1; Rom. 10:4; 2 Cor. 3:7; Gal. 5:1; Col. 2:14-17; Rom. 3:27; Rom. 4:15; 2 Cor. 3:9; Gal. 2:16; Gal. 3:21; Col. 2:14.)[8]

---

7. This point in 22:30 destroys the Paulinists' claim that the sovereignty of God would prevent such apostasy. Paulinists cannot imagine apostasy by ***nearly everyone*** would be tolerated by God. Thus, they reason that our last four-hundred years of emphasis on Paul is proof that God predestines such an emphasis. This assumption, however, is fed by a circular deduction from Paul's false teaching about predestination. (On proof of its falsity, see page 432 & page 504.) God repeatedly shows, however, that ***wholesale apostasy*** is ***possible***. He does nothing to stop it short of warnings in Scripture that He expects us to read!
8. "Did Paul Negate the Law's Further Applicability?" on page 73.

Third, Paul's view that we are free to ignore the Saturday Sabbath or any Sabbath-principle is undeniable. (Rom. 14:5; Col. 2:14-16.)[9] (Paul's followers typically behave like Jeroboam who offended God by moving God's set day to a "day he invented in his heart." (1 Kings 12:33 RV.))[10]

Fourth, Paul's view that we are free to eat any food we like, including eat meat sacrificed to idols, is likewise plain. (1 Tim. 4:4, 'all food is clean'; Romans 4:2.)[11] Paul taught we only refrain from eating idol meat when others are encouraged to do what they believe is wrong even though we know such food is clean. (Romans 14:21;1 Corinthians 8:4-13, and 1 Corinthians 10:19-29.)[12]

Fifth, did Paul give instructions to Christians which vex the poor? Some believe the following quote vexes the poor with a criteria for assistance *never found in the Hebrew Scriptures.*

> For even when we were with you, this we commanded you, If any will not work, neither let him eat. (2Th 3:10) (ASV)

How many people have resisted giving food to a poor person simply because they are unemployed and they do not pass a Pauline-inspired interview about their willingness to work for it? This *work* requirement sometimes will stall the urgent help that a poor person has for food. Nowhere in Hebrew Scripture is there any such barrier to God's command that you are to feed the poor. In fact, Scripture specifically intends for us to generously provide food for the poor to eat even if we have no idea whether they are willing to work.[13] Thus, Paul's principle that *if any will not work, neither let him eat* has served as a punitive vexation on poor people by

9. See page 75 *et seq.*

10.For further discussion on this passage, see page xxvi of Appendix C.

Christians who follow Paul's *dictum.* (Many Christians, of course, do not follow Paul's *dictum*, and follow instead the Bible's rule of open-handed provision of food to the poor.)

Alternatively, we also now realize the early church at Jerusalem was known as *the Poor* which would be, as an Hebraism, the name *Ebionites*. Paul was a vexing problem to

11.Some claim Jesus taught all *kosher* food laws in the Law of Moses are abrogated. They base this on the account in Mark 7:2 *et seq*. However, it is a misreading to say Jesus abrogated the laws of *kosher foods*. First, Jesus is discussing the Rabbinic *tradition* that food was unclean if you did not ritually wash your hands first. (Mark 7:2,4, 5.) Jesus' disciples ate without ritual washing of their hands. Jesus' point then is to show the Pharisees that they make up rules that (a) are not in the Bible and (b) which make of none effect what the Bible does teach. (Mark 7:7-13.) Jesus so far is tightening the reigns of the Law, not loosening them. Then Jesus says "nothing without the man that going into him can defile him." (Mark 7:15; *cf.* Matt. 15:11.) If it *defiles* you, Jesus means it makes you a sinner. This does appear to reach as far as the question of non-kosher foods. What Jesus is saying, however, is that *food laws,* even the valid *kosher laws*, are health rules of what is "clean" and "unclean." They are not rules if violated make you a sinner. Jesus was trying to give the rationale of God behind the food laws so we would know how to interpret them. The food laws are good for your health. Thus, if you violate these rules, you are not thereby a sinner. God does not want to hear prayers of repentance over violating food laws. (The idol-meat rule, however, implicates moral wrong; it was not part of the clean-unclean food laws.) Thus, a Rabbinic rule on handwashing, even if valid, could not taint you morally if you happen to violate it. What corroborates Jesus did not intend to abrogate *kosher* is that while Jesus' disciples ignored the hand-washing rule for clean foods created by Rabbis, his disciples always ate *kosher.* In Acts 10:14, when Peter in a dream is presented non-kosher foods to eat, "Peter said, Not so, Lord; for I have never eaten anything that is common and unclean." This tells us indirectly that Jesus ate *kosher.* The dream story incidentally was simply God's message to Peter to regard Gentiles as clean and disregard the *Rabbinic* teaching that Gentiles were unclean. There is not the slightest hint the *food laws* were abrogated. If either Jesus or Peter teach against the food laws, then they are implicated as apostates under Deut. 13:1-5. One must tread carefully when they try to prove Jesus or his true apostles abrogated any portion of the Law given Moses — a Law "eternal for all generations." (Ex. 27:21.)

them as well, as Acts chapter 21 clearly shows. Perhaps that is what *vexing the poor* means. It fits Paul any way you examine it.

Sixth, what about oppressing the foreigner? Did Paul and his followers do that too? Yes, in two distinct ways. By Paul saying all people born in Crete are liars, he forever slurred a whole nation of people. To be born a *Cretan* became synonymous with being born a liar, thanks to Paul. This is what Paul wrote:

> One of themselves, a prophet of their own said, "Cretans are always liars, evil beasts, lazy gluttons." *This testimony is true* (Titus 1:12).

Besides slandering all Cretans, Paul in another passage also slandered all Jews. He first labelled them as foreigners and then said they are enemies of all mankind. Let's review this with care.

One might at first think Jews cannot be viewed as foreigners in Judea. However, Paul in Galatians chapter 4 redefines Jews as foreigners in Judea. How did he do this? In our prior discussion, we saw how Paul said the Jews of Jerusalem no longer correspond to the sons of Abraham and Sarah. Instead they are now seen as Ishmael—the son of Abraham and Hagar. (Gal. 4:22-31.) Paul then says "cast out the handmaiden." This means Hagar and her children. In effect, Paul is saying the Jews in Jerusalem no longer hold the rightful

---

12.See "Paul Contradicts Jesus About Idol Meat" on page 117.

13.Exodus 23:11 says "but the seventh year thou shalt let it [your land] rest and lie fallow; ***that the poor of thy people may eat***: and what they leave the beast of the field shall eat." The field owner was also not supposed to glean the field in ordinary harvests but leave the "fallen fruit" for the "poor and sojourner." (Lev. 19:10.) Thus, Scripture always depicts food being provided to the poor without Minutemen standing at the border of the farm to be sure the poor are willing to work for the food they picked up from the orchard. The proof that Paul has affected the poor negatively is there is no custom among Christians for the last 2,000 years to comply with Exodus 23:11 or Leviticus 19:10.

position as owners of the land of Israel. They are Ishmaelites and foreigners to the covenant promise that gives them the right to the Land of Israel.

Second, after labelling Jews, in effect, as foreigners in Israel, Paul denigrates their entire race. Paul wrote "the Jews...both killed the Lord Jesus and the prophets and also drove us out. They displease God and are the enemies of the whole human race." (1 Thessalonians 2:14-16.)

The Greek in this verse means Jews oppose face-to-face every human being on earth. The various versions hold the essential meaning in tact:

> Jews...who killed the Lord Jesus and the prophets and have persecuted us. They are displeasing to God and are the ***enemies*** of all people....(1Th 2:14-15)(ISV)
>
> Jews...both killed the Lord Jesus, and their own prophets, and have persecuted us; and they please not God, and are contrary to all men: (1Th 2:14-15)(KJV)

According to James, a different group is responsible for the death of Jesus: "Go now, ye rich men, weep and howl for the miseries that shall come upon you.... Ye have condemned and killed the just [one]; and he doth not resist you." (James 5:5-6.)

Regardless of Paul's accuracy on who killed Jesus, Paul redefines Jews to be foreigners in Judea, equivalent to Ishmaelite sons of Hagar. He then denigrates Jews as the enemies of the entire human race. Paul's words of denigration aimed at Jews later inspired Martin Luther in Germany to promulgate a doctrine of harassment of the Jewish people who were by then foreigners in Germany.

The renown scholar, William Shirer, in his classic 1400 page tome *The Rise and the Fall of the Third Reich* (1960) at 236 explains what Martin Luther did. Shirer writes:

> It is difficult to understand the behavior of most German Protestants in the first Nazi years unless one is aware of two things: their history and the influence of Martin Luther. [At this point, Shirer writes in a footnote "To avoid any misunderstanding, it might be well to point out here that the author is a Protestant."] The great founder of Protestantism was both a passionate anti-Semite and a ferocious believer in absolute obedience to political authority. ***He wanted Germany rid of the Jews*** and when they were sent away he advised that they be deprived of "All their cash and jewels and silver and gold" and furthermore, "that their synagogues or schools ***be set on fire***, that their houses be broken up and destroyed... and that ***they be put under a roof or stable, like the gypsies... in misery and captivity*** as they incessantly lament and complain to God about us"—advice that was literally followed four centuries later by Hitler, Goering, and Himmler.

Paul's words about Jews, when taken literally by his pupil Martin Luther, bore their inevitable fruit: the *oppression of the foreigner* including God's special people—the Jews.

How Ezekiel's Depiction of the Deeds of Wolves Identifies Paul

Thus, we can see how the Ezekiel description of *ravening wolves* fits precisely Paul and his followers. They did violence to the Law by attributing it to angels who 'are no gods.' They taught we are free to disregard the Sabbath Law entirely. They tore away all food laws, including the laws on eating meat sacrificed to idols. They vexed the poor with *the necessity* that they must be willing to work for aid. They also oppressed the foreigners, as they defined them. This includes a slur on the people of Crete. It is a slur that has become part of our vocabulary. A *Cretan* is synonymous with a liar. Also, Paul oppressed Jews by redefining their status in Jerusalem as foreigners as well as enemies of all mankind. Centuries later

Martin Luther of Germany, inspired directly by Paul, outlined a plan of denigration of Jews. By that time, Jews were in fact *foreigners* in Germany. Pauline Christianity thereby inspired wicked men in our recent memory to follow Luther's plan to utterly oppress the Jews as foreigners.

Hence, Paul and Pauline Christianity satisfies every criteria for Ezekiel's depiction of the *ravening wolves*. So when Jesus tells us about *wolves in sheep's clothing* in Matthew 7:15 and then says we will know them by *their deeds* in Matthew 7:16, Ezekiel chapter 22 tells us precisely what deeds mark the time of the *ravening wolves*. Those deeds fit Paul like a glove.

Conclusion

Let's now pull all these Biblical references together, and see if the Bible identifies Paul as the Benjamite wolf.

TABLE 8. Who is the Benjamite Wolf?

Verse	Characteristics
Matt. 7:15	"ravening wolves" are "false prophets"
Matt. 7:15	"ravening wolves" appear as "sheep," *i.e.*, claim to be Christians.
Genesis 49:27	In *latter days*, Benjamin shall be a "ravening wolf."
Genesis 49:27	This "ravening wolf" from Benjamin's tribe first shall kill its "prey" in the morning.
Genesis 49:27	Later this "ravening wolf" from Benjamin's tribe will "divide the spoil" *i.e.*, plunder and divide its prey.
Rom. 11:1 Phil. 3:5	Paul is of the tribe of Benjamin.
Acts 7:58 8:1-3	Paul starts out participating in murders of Christians.
Gal. 2:9	Paul later divides the church along Gentile-Jew lines, reserving for himself the right to recruit Gentiles, claiming the Jerusalem church relinquished the Gentile-mission exclusively to Paul.

TABLE 8. Who is the Benjamite Wolf?

Verse	Characteristics
Ezek. 22:26-32	The "ravening wolves" will come who do "violence to the Law," and who teach the people to "hide their eyes from the Sabbath," and to no longer discern clean food from impure food, etc. These wolves are associated with those who "have false visions" and "divine" lies in the Lord's name.
Rom. 14:5; Col. 2:14-16	Paul, a Benjamite, came claiming visions of Jesus, and taught the Sabbath rule was a shadow of things to come, and no one can any longer judge another on failure to keep the Sabbath.
2 Cor. 2:14; Gal. 5:1; Rom. 7:1 *et seq*.; Rom. 10:4; 2 Cor. 3:7; Gal. 5:1; Col. 2:14-17; Rom. 3:27; Rom. 4:15; 2 Cor. 3:9; Gal. 2:16; Gal. 3:21; Col. 2:14	Paul, a Benjamite, came claiming visions of Jesus, and on that authority taught the Law was abrogated, abolished, done away with, nailed to a cross; it was against us, etc. This same Paul said Jews are released from the Law and if they follow Christ instead, He has set them free from the Law which is death and bondage. This same Paul taught the Law was given by angels who are no gods, and Paul asked 'why would anyone anyway want to submit to the weak and beggarly angels (elements)' who are no gods?
Romans 14:21;1 Corinthians 8:4-13; 1 Cor. 10:19-29; 1 Tim 4:4.	Paul, a Benjamite, came claiming visions of Jesus, and on that authority taught all foods were pure, including meat sacrificed to idols.

Thus, God prophesied a wolf from the tribe of Benjamin would emerge who would start out killing its prey but end up plundering and dividing its prey. Jesus said to look out for a wolf who would claim to be a Christian but is a false prophet. Paul repeats twice that he is of the tribe of Benjamin. Like the Genesis Benjamite wolf, Paul started out killing or participating in killing of Christians. Paul, as Jesus prophecied about the wolf, later claimed he was a Christian. Subsequently, this Benjamite Paul sought to split off the Gentiles from the main church so they would follow exclusively Paul's doctrine. God further prophesied the time of the ravening wolves would involve false prophets who would claim visions but they would be divining lies; these wolves would do violence to the Law, teaching it was permissible to disregard Sabbath and to disregard the food laws on unclean food—all of which we find precise fulfillment in the post-conversion letters of Paul.

When this mass of evidence is assembled as clearly as it is above, Paul must be the target of these prophecies. What we have done *in the name of Christ* to the teachings of Jesus in reliance on the Benjamite wolf warrant our expulsion from the kingdom. (Pray for mercy.) It is not merely that we have followed a false prophet from the tribe of Benjamin. (We should have known better because he first killed us and then divided us Gentiles from the mother-church.) Rather, what is so deplorable is we even followed the wolf's teachings when they contradicted the words of Jesus whom we claim is our Lord. It is astonishing, frankly, how we ever rationalized this behavior: claiming the name Christian but refusing to follow teachings of Jesus when we realize Jesus is incompatible with Paul such as:

> Whosoever therefore shall break one of these least commandments [of the Law of Moses], and ***shall teach men so***, shall be called least in the ***kingdom of heaven***: but whosoever ***shall do and teach them***, he shall be called ***great in the kingdom of heaven***. (Mat 5:19)

All we can do now is repent and obey.

> **"The world is filled with millions of people who think they are headed for heaven—but they are deadly wrong. Probably most people think heaven awaits them, but it doesn't. But what is especially sad, is that many of those people sit in evangelical churches misinformed."**
> **John MacArthur, *Hard to Believe* (2003) ix**

Another Prophecy Aimed At Paul?

TABLE 9. Do Not Follow The One Who Says The Time Is At Hand

Luke 21:8	Rom.13:12
"Take heed that you are not led astray; for many will come in my name, saying,... '***The time is at hand***!' [*ho kairos eggiken*] Do not go after them."	"the night is far gone, ***the day is at hand [hemera eggiken***]"

In addition to the Benjamite prophecy, it seems likely Jesus in Luke 21:8 additionally prophesied about Paul. Jesus warned us to beware of the one who would lead us astray. This deceiver would be a Christian preacher ("[he] will come in my name") who would tell you the "time is at hand." Those very words are in Paul's mouth in Romans 13:12, warning us "the day is at hand." The prophecy of a "time" is inclusive of the word *day*. Thus, Paul's phrase matches Jesus' prophecy exactly. This allows us to deduce that Paul (and Paul alone) is the Christian preacher who fits Jesus' prophecy in Luke 21:8.

To repeat, what Jesus said would be the identifying mark of the deceiver was he will say "the time is at hand." Paul precisely matches this, saying "the day is at hand," in ***exactly identical Greek***. Thereby, Jesus tells us Paul is one who comes in Jesus' name to "lead [you] astray." Jesus' warning was "do not go after them."

WILL WE OBEY JESUS?

ONE BIG SURPRISE

"In Matthew 7:21-23, the Lord described the self-deception that comes from a mere verbal profession of faith....Jesus made strong demands of those who desired to enter the kingdom that can be summed up in one word: righteousness. [Matt. 5:20, your righteousness must exceed that of the Pharisees.]...This is an important issue, because I am convinced that the visible church today is literally jammed full of people who aren't Christians but don't know it....[J]udgment is going to be one big surprise."
John MacArthur, ***Hard to Believe*** (2003) at 94-96.

15 *Does Jesus End up Marginalized To Make Room For Paul?*

Marcionism: The First Marginalization of Jesus

In 144 A.D., Marcion, a defrocked bishop, claimed that only Paul had the true gospel. Marcion insisted the twelve apostles, including Matthew and John, were legalistic. Marcion claimed they did not have the true gospel of grace of Paul. Marcion adopted as the sole correct narrative of Jesus' life an account similar to Luke's gospel. However, it omitted the first three chapters and had several other omissions. (Appendix B: *How the Gospel Was Formed* at page ix *et seq.*)

As Marcionism spread throughout the Roman Empire, and had its own churches and liturgy, the apostolic church rose up to fight Marcionism as heresy. The key spokesperson of the early church was Tertullian of Carthage, North Africa. In about 207 A.D., Tertullian wrote *Against Marcion*. He reminded everyone that Paul's authority was subordinate to the twelve apostles. Tertullian insisted Paul could not be valid if he contradicted the twelve or Jesus. Tertullian even noted that if we were being scrupulous, we must note that there is no evidence except from Paul's own mouth that Jesus made him an apostle.[1] Since nothing can depend on one witness

1. For example, not even Luke in Acts mentions Jesus ever said Paul was an apostle. See "Tertullian Questions In What Sense Paul Was An Apostle" on page 417.

(John 5:31 "If I bear witness of myself [alone], my witness is not true."), Tertullian said we cannot conclude Paul was an apostle of Jesus Christ.

Tertullian's points were designed to counter Marcion's preference for Paul. Marcion blatantly marginalized Matthew, Mark and John's Gospel to suit his preference for a Pauline Jesus. Marcion could see the contradictions between Paul and the writings of the twelve apostles. Marcion decided to choose Paul over Jesus as presented by the twelve. The early Christian Church felt compelled to rise up and brand Marcion a heretic.

For three hundred years, the apostolic church had to fight vigorously Marcion's rival church system. The Marcionites had adherents in numerous cities alongside the early church. Marcion was not battling the Roman Catholic Church (RCC). Rather, Marcion was being fought by the universal Christian church that predated the era of modern Roman Catholicism. (The RCC as we know it today did not take hold until after 325 A.D.)

Where did Marcion go wrong? Rather than re-evaluate Paul because of the contradictions with the gospel accounts, Marcion assumed Paul had the greater insight. As E.H. Broadbent in *The Pilgrim Church* concludes:

> Marcion's errors were the inevitable result of his accepting only what pleased him and rejecting the rest.[2]

Marcionism once more has crept into the church. It has done so with stealth and cunning. We must go back to Tertullian's sage advice from 207 A.D. It is Paul who must fit into the words of Christ in the Gospels. It is not the Gospel accounts which must be truncated to fit the words of Paul.

2. E.H. Broadbent, *The Pilgrim Church* (2nd ed.) (London: Pickering & Inglis, 1935) at 15.

Luther Marginalizes The Synoptic Gospels In Preference for Paul

Luther's view was that the Synoptics (*i.e.*, Matthew, Mark & Luke) did not contain the pure gospel. Paul and the Gospel of John instead were all that you needed to know about the true gospel. Luther wrote in 1522 that Paul and John's Gospel "***far surpass the other three Gospels, Matthew, Mark and Luke.***" Paul and John's Gospel are "***all that is necessary and good for you to know, even though you never see or hear any other book or doctrine.***"[3] Luther also wrote even more bluntly elsewhere that Paul had the truer gospel than what is presented in the Synoptics:

> Those Apostles who treat oftenest and highest of how faith alone justifies, are the best Evangelists. Therefore ***St. Paul's Epistles are more a Gospel than Matthew, Mark and Luke.*** For these [Matthew, Mark and Luke] do not set down much more than the works and miracles of Christ; but the grace which we receive through Christ no one so boldly extols as St. Paul, especially in his letter to the Romans.[4]

Thus, Luther like Marcion knew there was something different in the Synoptics. He did not acknowledge Jesus contradicted Paul's doctrine. Yet, if Paul's doctrine were true, then why would the Synoptics omit it? If Paul and the Synoptic-Jesus taught the same thing, then why do Luther and Marcion insist the *truer* gospel is in Paul's writings?

---

3. Martin Luther, "Preface to the New Testament [1522]," *Works of Martin Luther: The Philadelphia Edition* (trans. C.M. Jacobs) (Grand Rapids: Baker Book House, 1982) Vol. 6 at 439-444.
4. Martin Luther, quoted in G.F. Moore, *History of Religion* (Scribners: 1920) at 320. As Bainton says: "That this doctrine [*i.e.*, faith alone] is *not enunciated with equal emphasis* throughout the New Testament and appears denied in the Book of James did not escape Luther." (R. Bainton, *Here I Stand*, *supra*, at 331.)

Besides Luther's down-playing the Synoptic Gospels, Luther also rejected the Book of Revelation. He claimed it was uninspired. He dismissed it with a conclusory statement that he could not see the "Holy Spirit" in it. Luther declared it was "neither apostolic nor prophetic," and he claimed that "Christ is not taught or known in it."[5] Yet, in Revelation Jesus is talking much of the time. Also, Apostle John is certainly the human hand involved.[6]

"And if any man shall take away from the words of the book of this prophecy, God shall take away his part out of the book of life, and out of the holy city, and from the things written in this book."
Revelation 22:19, KJV

Luther's reason for rejecting the Book of Revelation is easy to deduce. Numerous Pauline thinkers have recognized the anti-Pauline emphasis on salvation by faith and works in Revelation. This is highly dangerous to their Pauline doctrine because Jesus' message was ***freshly*** delivered ***after*** Paul died. For that reason, modern Paulinists urge the rejection of Revelation as inspired canon. (See page 182 *et seq*.) It thus takes little to realize what caused Luther to reject the Book of Revelation. Christ was present in Revelation, but it is not the Christ of Paul.

5. Martin Luther, "Preface to the New Testament [1522]," *Works of Martin Luther: The Philadelphia Edition* (trans. C.M. Jacobs) (Grand Rapids: Baker Book House, 1982) Vol. 6 at 439-444 (or 1932 edition at 488-89.) See *The Canonicity of the Book of Revelation* (2005), available online at www.jesuswordsalone.com.
6. Papias (ca. 100 A.D.), Bishop of Hieropolis, is the one witness who unquestionably was an associate of Apostle John. In an ancient text, *Exposition of the Oracles of the Lord*, which Eusebius frequently cites, we learn in section VIII: "With regard to the inspiration of the book (Revelation), we deem it superfluous to add another word; for the blessed Gregory Theologus and Cyril, and even men of still older date, ***Papias***, Irenaeus, Methodius, and Hippolytus [of Rome], bore entirely satisfactory testimony to it."

This is corroborated by the fact Luther also concluded James' Epistle was uninspired. Luther freely admitted James' Epistle contradicted Paul on the same point that Jesus in Revelation contradicts Paul: James and Jesus in Revelation reject faith alone as the appropriate salvation formula.[7]

As a result of Luther's view, the Synoptics (*i.e.*, Matthew, Mark, & Luke), Revelation, and James were effectively put on the shelf by the Reformation's founder. These New Testament writings were too far afield of Paul to be given 100% validity on par with Paul.

Thus, we can see the banner of *Sola Scriptura* had quickly degraded into *Only the Scripture that Fits Paul.* Daniel Fuller correctly faults Luther's approach:

> But when he set up his understanding of justification by faith as the basis for ***suppressing such books as the Synoptic Gospels, Hebrews, and James***, he then made it impossible for these books to deepen or improve his understanding of this doctrine.[8]

Because Luther was blatantly marginalizing Jesus' words in the New Testament, the *Sola Scriptura* banner was quickly being taken down. In its place the reformed congregations re-established the banner of 'approved' church doctrine. This meant *de facto* that Paul's doctrines must triumph. Even though Jesus' words conflicted with Paul, Paul's words trumped Jesus' words every time.

This approach led eventually to an explicit abandonment of *Sola Scriptura.* The reformers quickly turned to *Catechisms* to give the right spin to things. Matthaeus Flacius (a Lutheran) said in his *Key to the Scriptures* (1567)— the first hermeneutics book to emerge from the Reformation—that:

---

7. See "Luther's Admission of James' Direct Conflict with Paul" on page 247.
8. Daniel Fuller, "Biblical Theology and the Analogy of Faith," *Unity and Diversity in N.T. Theology. Essays in Honor of George E. Ladd* (R. A. Guelich (ed.)) (Eerdmans: 1978) at 195-213.

> Every understanding and exposition of Scripture is to be in agreement with the faith. Such [agreement] is, so to speak, the norm or limit of a sound faith, that we may not be thrust over the fence into the abyss by anything, either by a storm from without or by an attack from within (Rom. 12:6). For everything that is said concerning Scripture, or on the basis of Scripture, ***must be in agreement with all that the catechism declares or that is taught by the articles of faith.***[9]

Fuller aptly criticizes this view. Flacius was urging Christians "to conform their language and thinking about a passage of scripture to an *a priori* [*i.e.*, a presupposed] understanding of what God's Word must be like."

By such illogic and violation of reformed principles of *Sola Scriptura*, marginalization of Jesus became encrusted in official reformed confessions. These writings were quickly put above Scripture. They were put above challenge even if someone were quoting Jesus' words.

The effort by Luther, Calvin and certain Protestant catechisms to marginalize Jesus' words, giving preference to Paul, have now reaped their logical conclusion. Some put it bluntly: we cannot any longer view the four gospels as truly part of the New Testament—they reflect all 'Old Testament' principles. As one sincere Paulinist, Dr. Russ Kelly, put it:

> Even though ***uninspired persons designated the four Gospels as 'New Testament' books***, most thinking Christians realize that, in reality, the New Covenant did not begin until the very moment Christ died on Calvary. The blood of Christ, the blood of the New Covenant, or testament, sealed and ratified the New Covenant and ended the Old Covenant, or Mosaic Law once for all time.

9. Kemmel, *History of Investigation*, *supra*, at 30.

Paulinists are thus so dedicated to Paul that no amount of contradiction of Paul by Jesus matters. It is all Paul, even if we must get rid of all of Jesus. They want the Jesus of the Synoptics to disappear.

Why Was John's Gospel Favored At All By the Reformers?

As mentioned elsewhere, the Synoptics (*i.e.*, Matthew, Mark & Luke) do not convey a gospel of salvation by faith alone. It is a very different gospel. See "What About Faith in the Synoptics?" on page 161.

However, Luther viewed John's gospel as consistent with Paul. If the verb tense for *believes* in John's Gospel is translated to convey a one-time faith for salvation, then John's salvation message can sound consistent with Paul. However, John's true meaning was that one who *continues to believe/trust* should have eternal life. It was not a one-time step of faith that should save, as we will soon discuss. However, Luther's conception of salvation could not easily incorporate the Greek progressive continuous tense which is in John 3:16. Why?

Because in the German language, Luther could not express the Greek *continuous* meaning. There is no German verb form equivalent to the Greek progressive tense, *i.e.*, the Greek Present Active tense. The German language "has no progressive mood."[10] Thus, due to a weakness of the German language, Luther could not even unequivocally express a progressive meaning—*continues to believe*. (The King James translators in 1611 did a similar slight of hand to *believing* in John 3:16.)[11]

However, the flaw in Luther's translation is self-evident to anyone who knows classical Greek. If John's meaning had been a one-time belief saves you, the corresponding Greek tense should have been the *aorist* for *believes*. Instead, in John 3:16 and all other Johannine salvation passages, *believe* was in the Greek form of the *present participle active*. The meaning was a faith/trust that "continues" should save, not that a one-time expression of faith saves. (For a discussion of the Greek involved, see Appendix A: *Greek Issues*.)

Yet, Luther wanted John's Gospel to fit Paul. Otherwise, there would have been no consistency whatsoever between Paul and any of the four gospel accounts. It may have been a subconscious bias. It may have been simple error. Regardless, the Greek issues involved in translating *believe* in John's Gospel are rudimentary and beyond any dispute. The Greek present participle active in John 3:16 is continuous in meaning. Had it meant a one-time faith (which fits Pauline doctrine), an *aorist* tense in Greek would have been used to convey such meaning. ***Paul used the aorist tense in Romans 10:9 to identify a faith that saves is a single step***. By contrast, John's Gospel never chose to use the *aorist* tense to identify any faith-condition for salvation. Rather, John's Gospel *always* used the continuous tense of the present participle active for *believes*. John's Gospel is not Pauline; it is *anti-Pauline*. (See "What About Faith in John's Gospel?" on page 164.) Luther's translation of John 3:16 was misleading.

10."German does not have the...progressive mood" (*i.e.*, 'is believing'). (http://io.uwinnipeg.ca/~oberle/courses/review.html#The Present Tens.) *See also*, *Simple present or present continuous?* at *http://www.lingualearn.co.uk/learners/ge/tenses.htm* ("As German ***does not have continuous tenses***, you just use the simple present for general statements, habits and future actions as well as present occurrences.") See also *German Language Course* which explains English has the "Present Progressive," *e.g.*, "are believing" but German "is able to do without the progressive forms." (See, http://www.geocities.com/CollegePark/Hall/1238/intro.html (accessed 2005). The author explains thus "I go and am going would translate the same into German." (*Id.*) Thus, in German, there is no ending that makes a verb correspond to the Greek present continuous/progressive tense. Instead, in German, the present tense can mean action in the present that continues or does not continue. Thus, unlike Greek, the German present verb tense has no endings to specify one way or the other whether action is one-time or continuous. This may have been a primary reason why Luther could convince others that John's Gospel sounded Pauline. Until *Young's Literal*, Luther's rendition has dominated all English translations.

Yet, Calvin came along and perpetuated this misleading rendering of John 3:16 that Luther first proffered. As a result, to the same degree that Luther had done, Calvin insisted John's Gospel must be viewed as the lense to read and understand Matthew, Mark and Luke. The Synoptics were of a lesser character. Calvin wrote in his *Foreword to the Book of John*:

> The doctrine which points out to us the power and the benefit of the coming Christ, ***is far more clearly exhibited by John than by the [synoptists]***. The ***three former*** [synoptic Gospels] exhibit [Christ's] body...but John exhibits his soul. On this account I am accustomed to say that this Gospel is a ***key to open the door for understanding the rest***...In reading [the four Gospels] a different order would be advantageous, which is, that when we wish to read in Matthew and others that Christ was given to us by the Father, we should first learn from John the purpose for which he was manifested.

Elimination of Synoptics in Modern Gospel Message

This perverse down-playing of Jesus' actual words in the Synoptics continues today. Even someone of Billy Graham's stature tells us that Jesus' gospel was not in the words spoken in His ministry. It was in nothing Jesus said. It was all in His death and resurrection, which is what Paul taught. If

11.The 1611 translators could have used the English Continuous Present ("is believing"). Instead, they arrived at a translation that effaced the original meaning by rendering the Greek for *is believing* in John 3:16 as *believes*. In English, this is the Simple Present tense. In this context, it implies a one-time faith saves. This would have been correct if the underlying Greek had been in the aorist tense. However, the Greek was *present participle active*. (See Appendix A: *Greek Issues*.)

you believe these two facts about Jesus (Romans 10:9), Paul taught you are saved. Here is what Billy Graham's Evangelistic Association said in 1980 in a tract entitled *The Gospel*. It says Jesus "came to do three days work, to die, be buried and raised" and that "He came ***not primarily to preach the Gospel***... but He came rather that there might be a Gospel to preach."

To say this means that Jesus' message in the Gospel accounts is not important to know about in evaluating salvation doctrine. It is far more important to believe the two simple facts about Jesus being Lord and was resurrected. (Romans 10:9.) Paul said you will be instantly saved forever if you merely acknowledge these two facts. (Romans 10:9.)

What about the validity of the Billy Graham Association's claim that Jesus did not primarily come to preach a gospel? Of course, it is impossible to reconcile these statements with Jesus' declaration "I came to preach the Gospel of the Kingdom; that is the reason why I was commissioned." (Luke 4:43.) Roy Gustafson of the Billy Graham Association explains the reasoning behind the crusade tract's opposing view:

> The word *Gospel* occurs over one hundred times in the New Testament...What then is the Gospel of the grace of God? ***Let us ask Paul***. He would point us to I Cor. 15:1-4: 'I declare to you the gospel which I preached to you...that Christ died for our sins, that he was buried, and that he rose again the third day'...***Paul never discussed the earthly life of our Lord***...The fact that the Lord Jesus died to save is one half of the Gospel! The fact that he rose from the dead...is the other half of the Gospel.

As Gustafson defines the Gospel of Jesus, it is all contained in Paul's simple message about the death and resurrection of Jesus. (1 Cor. 15:1-4.). The Gospel is not found in anything Jesus said. You won't find it in His sermons or His parables. Jesus could not be proclaiming the Gospel because had Jesus been doing so, Gustafson asks: 'why then didn't Paul ever mention anything Jesus said in that regard?' Indeed! That is precisely the question I am posing! ***Gustafson cannot see the issue right in front of his nose***. How could Paul be preaching the Gospel of Jesus if he never quotes Jesus? Furthermore, Gustafson's reasoning ignores Jesus' own statement that "I came to ***preach*** the Gospel of the Kingdom; that is the reason why I was commissioned." (Luke 4:43). Jesus and Gustafson cannot both be correct.

Gustafson's view that Jesus' words do not matter and are unimportant to comprehend how to be saved is not new. It is what Luther was saying. Calvin too.

The purpose in defining the Gospel in this way is to focus only on Paul. Its aim is to exclude Jesus' Gospel in the Synoptics. Why? Because Luther, Calvin and everyone else knows ***Jesus' Gospel in the Synoptics is a message of faith plus works, not faith alone.*** As Jesus most bluntly put it: "every tree therefore that bringeth not forth [*i.e.*, "does not keep on producing"] ***good fruit*** is hewn down, and cast into the ***fire.***" (Matt. 7:19.) The Gospel of the Synoptics is a message of the necessity of adding good fruit and repentance from sin to your faith. Jesus' Gospel is not about just belief in facts about Himself. As Jesus likewise states, His Gospel message promises "eternal life" for denying oneself, taking up one's cross and following Jesus. (Matthew 19:27-29 ("***shall*** inherit eternal life".) *See also*, Matthew 10:37-39.) The Gospel in the Synoptics contains the message of James.

What a dilemma! If Jesus' Gospel in the Synoptics is *the* Gospel, we would have to re-write all these gospel tracts. For Jesus' Gospel in the Synoptics is the *antithesis* to Paul's Gospel.

So what are these theologians like Gustafson doing? As Bonhoeffer states, "theologians...simulate concern" for Jesus but try to "avoid the encounter" with Him, and thereby "Christ is still betrayed by the kiss." (*Christ the Center* (1933 lectures) at 35.) Thus, those who deny Jesus even had a Gospel of His own so they can hold onto Paul have turned their backs on the only one who matters: Jesus.

Elimination of Jesus' Message of the Sermon on the Mount

The consequence of putting emphasis on Paul's Gospel over Jesus' Gospel is dramatic. Christians are blatantly told to dismiss Jesus' words in the Synoptics as "unimportant." For example, Jesus' Sermon on the Mount promises the kingdom to people with various characteristics. Without Paul weighing on us, Jesus would promise in the Sermon on the Mount salvation[12] for those who are humble, meek, merciful, peacemakers, and who hold their faith under pressure to disavow Christ, etc. With Paul in the mix, this must be dismissed. Walvoord is typical:

> [The Sermon on the Mount] treats ***not of salvation***, but of the character and conduct of those who belong to Christ...That it is suitable to point an unbeliever to salvation in Christ is plainly not the intention of this message...The Sermon on the Mount, as a whole, is ***not church truth precisely***...It is ***not intended*** to delineate justification by faith or ***the gospel of salvation.*** [The Sermon involves] ***unimportant truth***. (John Walvoord, *Matthew: Thy Kingdom Come* (Moody Press: 1984) at 44, 45.)

Thus, even though Jesus promises *the kingdom* to persons exhibiting certain behaviors, Walvoord insists this is not about the promise of the kingdom for persons exhibiting cer-

12. Absent pressure to distort the Sermon, Jesus is teaching salvation principles. Matthew 5:3 *et seq*. promises the receipt of the kingdom of heaven, mercy, inheriting the earth, and being children of God in return for various behaviors.

tain kinds of behaviors. This is about the kingdom being given to persons who do not necessarily have these behaviors. Why? Obviously because Paul tells us the kingdom is for those who simply believe. Because Walvoord does not want us to see the incongruity, Walvoord must direct us promptly away from the Sermon. It is "unimportant truth."

Walvoord actually leaves us puzzled. Jesus is promising the kingdom but then ties the promise to behaviors, making us doubt Paul's canonicity. Yet, that is unthinkable. So how do we cope? Walvoord's answer is that we are to abandon Jesus' words as 'unimportant' and stay on the path of following Paul. To me, ***it just doesn't make sense that we can be a Christian, treat Jesus' words as "unimportant" and prefer Paul over Jesus***. A sickening feeling should overcome any true Christian. You are being told to ignore Jesus and listen only to Paul. This is the emerging mainstream Christianity of today.

Yet, Walvoord is in line with Calvin, Luther and Billy Graham's Evangelical Association. They insist we must see Jesus' words in Matthew are *secondary* to Paul's words in his epistles. They claim we need to put Jesus' Gospel aside as "unimportant truth" when compared to Paul's Gospel.

The True Meaning of the Sermon: Reading Paul through Jesus' Words

The lesson of the Sermon on the Mount is clear but is lost on our modern ears. The best description appears from the pastor who runs *Believe*:

> Jesus concludes the sermon by setting up certain requirements that relate directly to one's being saved or lost. He divides mankind into three classes: those who (1) follow him (7:13-14, 17, 21, 24-25), (2) do not follow him (vss. 13-44, 26-27), and (3) pretend to follow him (vss. 15-20, 21-23). ***To be saved one must actually follow the teachings of the sermon,*** but

> Jesus does ***not*** say they must be ***performed perfectly***. The saved are those ***who accept and actually attempt to direct their lives by the sermon***; the lost are those who pretend to follow or who reject these teachings....Mere profession of belief, without the following, will secure Jesus' condemnation, 'I never knew you. You evildoers, depart from me' (vs. 23).[13]

What about Paul's contrary teaching? This pastor accepts Paul, but he shares my outlook. He insists we must read Paul through the lense of Jesus' words and not the other way around. He explains:

> An unfortunate feature of much post-Reformation Christianity has been ***the interpretation of Jesus in light of Paul rather than the converse***. One of the contributions of Bonhoeffer's treatment of this sermon is ***his insistence on reading Paul in light of Jesus*** and, hence, his stressing the necessity of doing the sermon. Perfection is not demanded and aid is provided, but still the true disciple is 'the who does the will of the Father' (vs. 21).

The Misleading Suggestion by Emphasizing John's Gospel Account

Also, the elevation of John's Gospel by Luther and Calvin feeds an erroneous assumption. Those unfamiliar with John's Gospel are misled to assume there is no trouble for Paul anywhere in John's Gospel. Yet, John's Gospel is filled with problems for Paul.

13.http://mb-soft.com/believe/txw/sermonmt.htm (last accessed 5-24-05).

For example, John quotes Jesus saying that those who are following Him and losing one's life in this world to serve Him do so for "life eternal." (John 12:25-26.) Not for rewards, but for eternal life.

Another example is Jesus saying: "Marvel not at this: for the hour is coming, in the which all that are in the graves shall hear his voice, And shall come forth; they that ***have done good***, unto the resurrection of life; and ***they that have done evil***, unto the resurrection of damnation." (John 5:28-29 KJV) Jesus focuses the difference between the *saved* and *lost* on who did *good* and who did *evil*. It is not a contrast between those who *believe* versus those who *do not believe*.

In fact, John 3:16 becomes another example when we reveal the subjunctive tense in the verse. It reads: "whosoever keeps on believing in Him *should* not perish but ***should*** have eternal life." There are two subjunctives in the verse—the subjunctive tense in Greek being used to show ***uncertainty*** and conditionality. (The NIV, without support in a textual variant, has it "***shall*** have eternal life.")[14] Faith alone, Jesus

14. The Greek *have* is ***echêi.*** It is in the subjunctive. However, the NIV's translation is defended because it conforms better to salvation supposedly purposed by God based on faith alone. *See,* Daniel B.Wallace, *Greek Grammar Beyond the Basics* (Zondervan: 1997) at 461, 473. Wallace claims we may vary the translation where the Divine will is involved, claiming that in such cases, "*ina* [so that] is used to express both the divine purpose and result." (*Id.* at 473.) Wallace explains: "The fact that the subjunctive is ***all but required*** after *ina* does not, of course, argue for ***uncertainty as to the fate of the believer***. This fact is obvious, ***not from this text***, but from the use of *ou mh* in John 10:28 and 11:26, as well as the ***general theological contours of the gospel of John***." What Wallace is doing is claiming *ina* creates a purpose clause that defeats the subjunctive meaning because we know from doctrine that God guarantees He will achieve His purpose of saving those who believe. (The proof he offers is utterly circular, as we shall see.) No one has ever explained why the purpose conjunction of *hina* would justify changing *should* into *shall.* In Greek, the contingency has actually a purpose of explaining the continuous tense that precedes it. Also, Wallace even concedes that there are over a dozen future indicatives after *hina* in the New Testament. (His footnote 71.) Thus, Jesus' use of the subjunctive must be deliberate in John 3:16, designed to differentiate the result from a future guaranteed result. Why is Wallace's proof circular? Because for support of the NIV translation, he cites two examples which are more of the same use of subjunctives conditioned on continuous verbs. (John 10:28 and 11:26.) Thus, to cite these two passages to support translating *should* as *shall* is simply to use the same error in the other verses as proof. That is the essence of circular proof!

implies in John, is not the sole criterion for judgment. You *should* be saved, but it is not necessarily going to be the case. Example in chief: the "believing" rulers who were too cowardly to confess Jesus. (John 12:42.) As cowards, their fate is in hell despite their *believing*. (Rev. 21:8, "cowards, unbelievers" are in hell.)(For further discussion of them, see page 450.)

Another example, assuming the NIV translation as correct, is we find in John's Gospel a competing formula for eternal life that depends on obedience. Jesus says: "Verily, verily, I say unto you, If one ***keeps my word,*** he ***shall*** never see death." (John 8:51, NIV) A better translation of *keep my word* is "***obeys*** my teaching...." (GNB.) (On page 501, we will see 3:16 and 8:15 provide a synergistic path to salvation.)

Next, John 3:36 is another very significant problem passage in John's Gospel for the Paulinist. John the Baptist (whom Jesus calls the greatest prophet) is quite clearly amplifying John 3:16 to say that a faith that *should* save is destroyed by disobedience to Jesus' commands. Thus, John 3:16 does not have Paul's meaning. John 3:16 has been quoted insufferably countless times *out-of-context* (besides being grossly mistranslated to fit Paul.) The Prophet John clearly is amplifying 3:16 in 3:36 by evoking the salvation formula of John 3:16 but modifies it. John contrasts *believing* with *disobeying* as a warning to the one-time believer about the impact of disobedience. Here is what John 3:36 says literally in a correct translation:

> He that keeps on believing/trusting on the Son keeps on having everlasting life [*cf.* the 3:16 formula], and he that keeps on ***disobeying*** [*apeitheo*] the Son shall not see life, but the wrath of God keeps on remaining on him.

This means a faith that *should* save is destroyed by disobedience. As John MacArthur says in *The Gospel According to Jesus* (Zondervan: 1994), John 3:36 teaches that salvation depends on a lasting obedience to Christ's authority, not on a one-time obedience to believe. (*Id.* at 39 fn.) A saving faith is one that "produces obedience." (*Id.* at 53.)

Hence, disobedience to Jesus' commands means God's wrath rests on you regardless of your subjective experience of a one-time *belief*. (Paulinists deflect this verse by the simple step of mistranslation.)[15]

A final example, although not the last, is Jesus in John says a branch "in me" that does not produce fruit will be cut off, and is thrown outside the vineyard. It is as a branch that is withered (died). It will be burned. (John 15:1-6.) Faith without works is dead. The branch is the Christian, not the fruit on the branch. The burning is of *you*, not some *poor fruit* (*i.e.*, defective works) as Paulinists try to spin this passage. Thus, in John 15:1-6, Jesus is explaining that works are crucial to add to one's connection to Christ, even though the connection is how one produces fruit. Otherwise, faith (connection) without fruit (works) makes you withered (dead), to be thrown "outside" to be "burned." Jesus agrees with James 2:14!

Thus, Paulinists ignore the many passages in John's Gospel that contradict Paul. They emphasize John 3:16 as if it is saying the same thing as Paul's Gospel. However, it does not. John's Gospel, correctly translated, is the antithesis to Paul's gospel.

Even C.S. Lewis Is In The Primarily-Paul Camp

One of my favorite fiction writers is C.S. Lewis. He was a brilliant author. Yet, even C.S. Lewis revealed himself to be a Paulinist who marginalized Jesus. Listen to his reasoning:

15. *Apeitheo* only has one Greek meaning: ***disobey***. (Lidell-Scott.) This is followed in ASV, RSV, NASV, WEB and GNB. *Cfr.* KJV and Luther's Bible ("not believe"). Why the difference in the KJV & Luther? Because Pauline dictionaries of ancient Greek, while admitting "not believe" is a meaning "not found outside our literature," claim the word *apeitheo* must mean *disbelieve* when used in Christian literature. (*Greek Lexicon of the New Testament* (eds. Bauer, Arndt, Gingrich, and Danker) at 82.) But why? Because unless we adopt a Pauline and idiosyncratic meaning 'just for us Christians,' then John 3:36 undermines our favorite notions about salvation by faith alone, and our favorite verse to prove it: John 3:16.

> The epistles are for the most part the earliest Christian documents we possess. The Gospels came later. They are not 'the Gospel,' the statement of the Christian belief...In that sense ***the epistles [of Paul] are*** more primitive and ***more central than the Gospels*** — though not of course than the great events which the Gospels recount. God's Act (the Incarnation, the crucifixion, and the Resurrection) comes first: the earliest theological analysis of it comes in the epistles [of Paul]: then when the generation which had heard the Lord was dying out, the Gospels were composed to provide the believers a record of the great Act and of ***some of the Lord's sayings***. (C.S. Lewis, "Introduction" to J. B. Phillips' *Letters to Young Churches* (Fontana Books n.d.) at 9, 10.)

Thus, Lewis is saying that Paul's epistles are more primary than the Gospel accounts. The key facts are the death and resurrection of Jesus. If we believe these two facts, we are saved. (Romans 10:9.) Beyond that, Lewis acknowledges we can find "some sayings" of Jesus in the gospel accounts. However, they are not the *gospel* message. Then what of Jesus' contrary claim? Jesus said: "I came to preach the Gospel of the Kingdom; that is the reason why I was commissioned." (Luke 4:43.) Lewis is confident that, to the contrary, the Gospel Jesus preached is not the Gospel we must obey. Instead, Lewis believed Paul had the Gospel we must follow.

Again, Lewis is saying nothing new. It was Luther's view. It was Calvin's view. It was or is the Billy Graham Association's view. It was Marcion's view two millennia ago. (See Appendix B: *How the Canon Was Formed* at page ix.) Yet, how can a Christ-centered life be based on de-emphasizing Jesus to accept Paul? It just doesn't make any sense.

A Better Explanation Why the Gospel Accounts Came Second

May I suggest an alternative to Lewis' view which better explains why Paul's epistles came first and then the gospels? God did not make Paul's writings come first to prove the primacy of Paul over Jesus' words. Nor did God make Paul silent on Jesus' preaching to prove how irrelevant Jesus' words were on salvation doctrine. Rather, the gospel accounts were recorded after Paul to address partly the problem of Paul's written letters. ***The gospel accounts were to correct Paul's views and give us Jesus' words lacking in Paul's writings***. Jesus thus was able to set forth the ***correct nature of salvation***. That is why Jesus' views conflict so directly with Paul. Jesus says you can go to heaven maimed or hell whole in Mark 9:42-47. Repentance from sin is crucial; belief is just one step. Jesus in the Parable of the Sheep and the Goats, Matt. 25:32 *et seq*., also said you can do works of charity for Jesus' brethren and thus go to Heaven. Alternatively, you can fail to do so and go to Hell. There is no third option of pleading a covering of Christ and skating the personal obligation. Jesus had clearly a faith-plus-works formula as the correct teaching on salvation.

Accordingly, the Gospel accounts come after Paul precisely to remind Christians of Jesus' warnings about the coming false prophets *after Jesus' crucifixion*. Jesus' warning covers the period of Paul's preaching. Jesus warned prophets would come to teach in His name but be false. (Matt. 7:15 *et seq*.) They would preach *a-nomia*, which literally means "negation of the (Mosaic) Law." Jesus says 'I will tell them on Judgment Day that I never knew you.' Jesus warns also these same preachers will do signs and wonders, and will have prophecy to deceive you into falsely trusting them. Jesus says their signs and wonders prove nothing. All that matters is that they are workers of *a-nomia*. If they are workers who seek to negate the Mosaic Law, flee from them, Jesus warned.

(For a full discussion on this passage, see the chapter "Did Jesus Warn of False Prophets Who Would Negate the Law?" on page 59.)

Thus, the sequence that Lewis is citing as proof of Paul's primacy is actually proof of the opposite. It is more likely explained by the problem of Paul. The gospel accounts were intended to correct Paul. ***Without their documentary existence, no one could expose Paul as a false apostle.*** No one could prove Paul was coming with another gospel than that of Jesus Christ Himself!

In fact, all this effort to dismiss the Synoptics by Luther, Calvin, C.S. Lewis, Billy Graham, and Walvoord ***is itself proof that Paul must have come with another gospel.*** Otherwise, why all this effort and spin to dismiss the Synoptics? If the gospel in them were the same as Paul taught, why would one have to say Paul has primacy at all over them?

The truth is one cannot make Jesus' words serve Paul's doctrines. The effect of this primacy given to Paul over the Synoptics has destroyed the integrity of commentators. As discussed next, when confronted by a contradiction of Paul by Jesus, they presuppose Jesus must fit Paul. They admit this by the most blatant illogic.

Circular Logic to Obscure Jesus' Words

The following are examples of circular logic made to force Jesus' words in the Synoptics fit Pauline interpretation. The authors insist boldly, openly but illogically that Jesus must be interpreted to fit Paul's theology. Never once does the fact of contradiction draw the commentators to question Paul's validity in canon.

> "The interpretation of the parable [of the Prodigal by Jesus] requires deduction ***compatible with known doctrine*** [*i.e.*, Paul]." (R.B. Thieme Jr., *The Prodigal Son* (1974) at 1.)

> "In other words, once [eternal] security [primarily deduced from Paul] is established, there really are 'no problem passages.' There are only Scriptures [*i.e.*, statements by Jesus apparently to the contrary] to properly interpret in light of ***an already established doctrine*** [*i.e.*, Paul's teaching.]" (*Ankerberg Theological Research Institute News Magazine* (Vol. 4 No. 7) (July 1997) at 16.)

> "In Mt. 25:34, we find that inheriting the kingdom is conditioned [by Jesus] on obedience and service to the King, ***a condition far removed from the New Testament [i.e., Pauline] teaching of justification by faith alone for entrance into heaven***. [Thus, it must mean something other than what it appears to mean.]" (Dillow, *Reign of the Servant Kings* (1992) at 72.)

These statements all share blatant illogic. The commentator interprets what Jesus is saying from the theological system of Paul. Thus, the very point of whether Paul is valid or not is avoided by rewriting Jesus' words to fit Paul. It is known as the bootstrap fallacy. Instead, the very issue raised by the contradiction is whether Paul belongs among inspired canon. Rather than face the unthinkable, bootstrap illogic is used to demand the reader accept any spin of Jesus that erases Jesus' contradiction of Paul.

Dispensational Strategy To Avoid Jesus

A more intellectual effort to displace Jesus with Paul was developed in what is called Dispensational Theology. It has given this Jesus vs. Paul division a theological basis. The fact people have had to devise a theological explanation for the division is proof that it is otherwise impossible logically to keep Jesus and Paul in the same canon. One or the other must go.

What some Christians have done, trying to be faithful to both Jesus and Paul, is take all the tension away by a theological crutch. They deem Jesus' conflicting statements as addressing the *era of Law.* All Paul's contrary teachings were addressed to the present *era of Grace*. The conflict is resolved elegantly because Paul and Jesus conflict for good reason: they are talking to different people who are subject to different covenants. These different covenants are described as different *dispensations*.

As a result, Jesus' words are deprived of any ongoing relevance. As John MacArthur says in *The Gospel According to Jesus:*

> This lamentable hermeneutic [*i.e.*, Jesus' words were for a different dispensation] is widely applied in varying degrees to much of our Lord's earthly teaching, emasculating the message of the Gospels.[16]

Any doctrine that tells us to ignore Jesus' words should raise an immediate red flag. If we take this route, we have a legitimized barrier, however well-intentioned, *against* listening any longer to Jesus on salvation issues. Jesus' words on how to be saved and have eternal life no longer interest us (unless, of course, we think they agree with Paul). Jesus' statements lose their *ongoing* validity after His death on the cross. Only Paul thereafter is left to address us on how to be saved. With this kind of reasoning, Paul trumps Jesus every time.

Yet, to the contrary, Jesus said "heaven and earth shall pass away, but my words shall not pass away." (Matt. 24:35.) Jesus was saying His words were not only valid now, but

16.John MacArthur, *The Gospel According to Jesus* (Zondervan 1994) at 33-34.

remain continuously valid in the kingdom up through the passing away of the heaven and earth. (Rev. 20:7-10.) Dispensationalism ignores this. Instead, it gives Jesus' words only a brief continuing validity on the doctrine of salvation. Once the Law was abolished at the crucifixion, as they interpret Paul's Gospel, Jesus' words on salvation became all moot. Jesus' words were meant for those under the Law. Because Jesus nailed the Law to a tree in His crucifixion, Jesus did away with the Law. Thus, all Jesus' statements no longer have any bearing on how God will deal with us who live under Grace, and who no longer are under the Law.

Can you see how the dispensational argument has an obvious logical flaw when used as a harmonization instrument? Essentially, this argument depends on the presupposition that Paul is inspired and he could define a covenant of Grace that excludes relevance of the Law (*i.e.*, repentance from sin, obedience, works, etc.) Yet, the very issue that Jesus' words raise is the legitimacy of this point of view. Only a presupposition that Paul is correct would force you to *marginalize* Jesus by claiming His words cannot possibly apply to those under a new covenant of Grace. ***Absent this bootstrapping, this conflict in salvation messages is proof itself that Paul is uninspired.*** It actually proves Paul is a false apostle. Thus, a crucial assumption of the dispensational/covenant argument is the same as its conclusion. The bootstrap is the *a priori* assumption that Paul is inspired to declare a covenant of grace that excludes repentance, obedience, and works. (Deut. 6:25.) Instead, that is the very issue at stake. This is discussed in more detail below at page 394.

Paul's Flawed Covenant Theology

Of course, there is also a Biblical flaw in Paul's presentation of a New Covenant of Grace that excludes the Law (*Torah*). It contradicts the Bible prophecy of a New Covenant. This prophecy appears in Jeremiah 31:31 *et seq*. This prediction about the New Covenant expressly says the New Covenant *continues the Torah* and *continues God's special relationship with the seed of Israel.* The New Covenant of Grace is specifically mentioned in that passage too, saying it is based on God "forgiving sins."[17] Thus, despite a New Covenant of Grace, God told us already some things will never change: the *Torah* and God's covenant partner is Israel. Please read Jeremiah 31:31 *et seq.* right now if you have any doubt. For a fuller discussion, see page 397.

Historical Background of Dispensationalism

Dispensationalism has its modern roots in the covenant theology which was first set forth in the Calvinist Westminster Confession of 1647. Prior to that date, it only appeared in Marcionism. It never appeared in any mainstream Christian writings, including those of Luther and Calvin.[18]

Gradually covenant theology gave way a hundred years ago to a method of analyzing Jesus' words called *Dispensationalism.* It is a doctrine whose most significant purpose is to resolve conflicts between Paul and Jesus.

This doctrine is quite forthright: once a verse from Jesus is deemed too difficult to reconcile with Paul, the explanation is Jesus was talking to a different dispensation. We are safe to ignore Jesus' words for we are in the dispensation of grace. Jesus' words were meant in that instance for those under the dispensation of Law (*i.e.*, the Jews). The Law after

17.See "The Biblical Basis to these Charges Against Paul" on page 233*ff.*

18.Dr. Ryrie points out: "It [covenant theology] was not the expressed doctrine of the early church. It was never taught by church leaders in the Middle Ages. It was not even mentioned by the primary leaders of the Reformation. Indeed, covenant theology as a system is only a little older than dispensationalism....Covenant theology does not appear in the writings of Luther, Zwingli, Calvin, or Melanchthon... There were no references to covenant theology in any of the great confessions of faith until the Westminster Confession in 1647...." It should be noted that Agricola was a follower of Luther who taught dispensationalism.

the cross supposedly had now become a curse and was abrogated. Therefore, Dispensationalists reason that Jesus' words at issue no longer involve any important truth for us.

For example, Dispensationalists do not ignore the inconsistencies between Jesus and Paul in the Sermon on the Mount. Jesus emphasizes works to enter the kingdom. Jesus called us to have a "righteousness that exceeds that of the Pharisees," absent which "you shall in no case enter the kingdom of heaven." (Matt. 5:20.) Jesus is making obedience a condition of entrance into heaven. This is clear from the verses that follow in the Sermon. Jesus explains what it means to have a righteousness that exceeds the Pharisees. You must not call your brother a fool (5:21-26); you must not lust after a married woman (5:27-30); you must not divorce your wife absent certain circumstances (5:31-32); you must not make false vows (5:33-37);[19] and you must not return evil for evil (5:38-48). The Pharisees obviously committed all these sins. Jesus was promising "entry...into the kingdom of heaven" (5:20) for obedience to His principles.

The Dispensationalists began their modern movement by insisting there is nothing to worry about in the Sermon on the Mount. Their leading text, still cited today, is by Clarence Larkin, *Dispensational Truth* (Philadelphia: Larkin, 1918). Based on dispensational logic, Larkin explains Jesus' teach-

19.The Greek text against *any oath-taking* is a corruption of the original Matthew. George Howard published the Hebrew Matthew which, when differences exist, often show the underlying original text. Here, the Hebrew Matthew reveals a single but crucial word was missing in the Greek translation: the word *falsely.* A Jewish scholar, Nehemiah Gordon, admires Jesus and shows Jesus' command against *any oath* would have Jesus contradict Scripture, but the command against *falsely* taking an oath would be consistent with it. He notes the significant variance in the original Hebrew Matthew that has the word *falsely.* He then explains how this makes perfect sense in what Jesus says in context about various oaths. Jesus was saying 'do not ever testify falsely in an oath, whether taken in Yahweh's name or otherwise.' The Pharisees' doctrine was that a false oath was permissible as long as not in God's name, such as if 'by the gold in the Temple.' See Nehemiah Gordon, *Hebrew Yeshua v. the Greek Jesus* (Jerusalem: 2006).

ings in the Sermon on the Mount "have no application to the Christian, but only to those who are under the Law, and therefore must apply to another Dispensation than this." (*Id.*, at 87.)

Thus, beginning in 1918, dispensationlists demonstrated how easily one could eliminate the Sermon on the Mount. Jesus was talking to Jews under the Law. Paul is talking to everyone else who exists in the 'era of grace.' The era of the Law died at the cross. Thus, this Sermon on the Mount's message died there too. Dispensationalists proclaim victory for Paul's words over Christ's words. They are not troubled in the slightest. To them, it is simply grace triumphing over Law.

As a result, for the modern Dispensationalist, the following principles of Jesus are inapplicable to us:

- Jesus' mention of the Law's ongoing validity and how crucial it is to teach every command, small and large. (Matt. 5:18-19.)
- Jesus' promise of justification for repentance from sin. (Luke 18:10 *ff.*)
- Jesus' salvation principles in the Sermon on the Mount. (Matt. 5:1 *ff.*)
- Jesus' hell-whole or heaven-maimed statement. (Mark 9:42 *ff.*)
- Jesus' emphasis on works for salvation in the Parable of the Sheep & The Goats without which one will go to hell. (Matt. 25:32 *ff.*)
- Jesus' emphasis on works in Revelation without which Jesus will spew you out of His mouth. (Rev. 3:16 *ff.*)

All such principles have been carved out of the essential values necessary for New Testament Christians. They are no longer applicable in the "Era of Grace" as defined by Paul.[20] They are wholly irrelevant.

Thus, even though Jesus said His words would remain valid even though "heaven and earth pass away" (Matt. 24:35), dispensationalism harmonizes away Jesus' teachings as invalid. They were only valid for another two years after

Jesus spoke them, *i.e.*, they expired at the crucifixion. "It is finished" for Paulinist-dispensationlists means *all of Jesus' lessons are cancelled* unless they fit Paul's doctrines.

This conclusion was driven by the necessity to harmonize Jesus with Paul. The founders of dispensationalism such as Dr. Chafer were fully aware of the tension between Jesus and Paul. Miles J. Stanford became a renown proponent from Dr. Chafer's university. He expressly recognized contradictions between Jesus and Paul.

However, this was not a problem, he claimed. Stanford insisted Paul had a different gospel from the other apostles. Thus, Stanford taught that when they do not line up, we must realize Jesus and the twelve were directed at a different dispensation—Jews under the Law. Paul was directed at humanity in the "era of grace." There is nothing therefore to reconcile when we find conflict. God just has different covenants with Jews than with the world after Jesus' ascension.[21]

20. Sometimes this is explained as an Israel vs. Christian dispensation. For example, Lewis Spencer Chafer (who founded Dallas Theological Seminary) in *He That is Spiritual* (rev. ed.)(Grand Rapids: Zondervan, 1967) claimed that the dispensation to Israel is *distinct* from the Christian church. He then contended the era of "pure law" is exclusive of our current era of "pure grace." Thus, before Christ died was the law. Now we are in grace. In the Millennial kingdom, the Law will be restored. In this manner, only Paul's teachings have current validity. The Book of Revelation, with its emphasis on repentance, has no applicability in salvation doctrine until the Millennium. Chafer is wrong on all points. First, as MacArthur says, "both law and grace are part of the program of God in every dispensation." (J. MacArthur, *The Gospel According to Jesus*, *supra*, at 31-32.) Furthermore, it is a false dichotomy to separate the church from Israel in dispensations. The New Covenant is with the "House of Judah and Israel." (Jer. 31:31.) We are the Gentiles who, if righteous sojourners, share in that covenant, but we are not the main target of Jeremiah 31:31.

21. For more on Stanford (whose doctrine harkens to Marcion), see his work *Pauline Dispensationalism* reprinted at http://withchrist.org/MJS/index.htm.

That such a theology would ever arise reflects how impossible it is to reconcile Jesus with Paul on too many points. How can Paul fit in with a 'hell-whole or heaven-maimed warning' of Jesus? In Mark chapter 9, Jesus gives no quarter to Paul: you can go to hell whole (unrepentant) or heaven-maimed (after severe repentance from sin). There is no third option of refusing to repent *from sin* and enjoy a covering of Christ based on mere belief. *Cfr.* 1 Cor. 5:5. In line with Jesus, John tells us the covering applies to a Christian *only after* confessing and repenting from sin. (1 John 1:7-9.)

Jesus and Paul are certainly at odds. Paul and Apostle John are also at odds. John thinks the covering of Christ only applies upon confession of sin. However, Paul says it permanently happens upon *belief* that Jesus is the Lord and He rose from the dead. (Romans 10:9. *See also*, Romans 8:1.)

Thus, this dispensational doctrine is necessary to *cope* with the conflict within Christianity between Paul and Jesus. Also, it is used to cope with the conflict between Paul and the other apostles' teachings. Dispensationalism is an old solution, going back to Marcion. The early church defeated Marcion's attempt to marginalize Jesus in preference for Paul. Will we?

The Circular Reasoning Involved in Dispensationalism

Dispensationalism and Covenant theology as pertains to the Jesus-Paul conflict rests upon circular reasoning. It reconciles the two by making an assumption that Paul is inspired and correct. Yet, that is precisely the challenge involved that they are hoping to resolve. The illogic involved is not evident to its proponents apparently because they never have done a logic diagram of their argument.

First, let's review some basic logic about what a conflict between Jesus and Paul *should* mean. This will help unlock rather easily the illogic of how dispensationalism and covenant theology reconcile Jesus and Paul.

Everyone knows if Jesus is inspired and Paul is inspired that they cannot contradict. If they do, either Jesus is not inspired or Paul is not inspired. Between the two, only Jesus proved to be a prophet (and more than a prophet). Paul was just a person with a vision of Jesus. So if we were forced to concede Jesus and Paul contradict, then Paul would be found *uninspired.*

Dispensationalism agrees that Jesus and Paul contradict but points out their audiences may have materially varied. Dispensationalism seizes on this point to resolve the apparent dilemma of a contradiction. Dispensational theology says Jesus was ***not*** talking to those under a covenant of grace when He taught justification by repentance from sin. Jesus aimed at Jews His Parable of the Publican and the Pharisee and His *heaven-maimed-or-hell-whole lesson* in Mark 9:42-48. Thus, Jesus was supposedly talking to Jews under their old and now expired covenant relationship which did depend on repentance. However, this notion that Jesus brought a new covenant-of-grace which excludes repentance from sin for salvation comes exclusively from Paul.[22]

Thus, the solution proposed to reconcile the conflict between Jesus and Paul is to assume the validity of Paul's teaching of the covenant of grace. Paul's doctrines (a) exclude repentance from sin as necessary for salvation and (b) exclude Jews as the principal partner. Yet, the validity of Paul as an inspired teacher to teach these two ideas is the very question at issue. To derive the dispensational solution that Jesus was talking to those under the covenant of Law and not grace, one has to assume Paul's validity. This assumption is

22. See Gal. ch. 4, the Jews now correspond to Ishmael and are cursed to follow the Law in the desert; we are children of grace, freed from bondage to the Law, etc.

the same thing as your conclusion. Paul alone teaches a break between the seed of Israel and God in forming a New Covenant people. (See Galatians 4:22 *ff.*) The Dispensational theory at issue overcomes the question of Paul's inspiration by assuming Paul is inspired despite the contradictions. The conclusion of Paul's inspiration is hidden in the discussion as a premise. Hence, dispensationalism as a tool to reconcile Jesus and Paul is based on circular logic.

You can diagram the fallacy rather easily:

- Premise #1: If Jesus and Paul would truly contradict then Paul is uninspired.
- Premise #2: Jesus and Paul addressed different audiences.
- Premise #3: Jesus and Paul have direct contradictions in talking to different audiences.
- Premise #4: **Paul is inspired** in expounding on a new covenant of grace to one audience.
- Premise #5: Jesus was inspired in expounding to a different audience who are under the covenant of Law but not under Paul's covenant of grace.
- Conclusion: Therefore both Jesus and **Paul** are **inspired.**

It is premise number 4 that contains the bootstrapped-conclusion. When one of your premises contains your conclusion, we call the conclusion a bootstrap fallacy. Thus, but for that assumption in premise number 4, you would have Jesus expounding principles of the kingdom applicable to a New Covenant member at odds with Paul. Premise number 4 marginalizes that truth, puts it in doubt, and bootstraps the conclusion. If you fallaciously contain your conclusion in a premise, you cannot help but reach the conclusion you desire. To repeat, this is known as the bootstrap fallacy.

Irreconcilable Differences in Paul's New Covenant Theology

Furthermore, there are certain contradictions between Jesus and Paul that refute the whole idea that Jesus and Paul can be reconciled on the covenant-of-grace explanation.

Jesus taught that anyone who would teach against the keeping of the least command in the Law would be least in the kingdom of heaven. Not ***until heaven and earth pass away***, Jesus says, will one little letter of the Law cease until all things are accomplished. (Matt. 5:18.) If Jesus intended that the Law would be accomplished in *toto* six months later when He died on the cross, He made an incongruous statement that the Law would continue until "heaven and earth pass away...." And Jesus would have made the further incongruous remark that a New Testament kingdom member must keep "the least command in the Law."

Obviously, Jesus sees the New Covenant precisely as Jeremiah 31:31 explained. The New Covenant continued the *Torah* (Law). And as Isaiah said, Servant-Messiah "will magnify the Law (Torah), and make it honorable." (Isaiah 42:21.) (For more discussion, see page 233 *et seq*.) The New Covenant in Jeremiah and Isaiah is thus just as Jesus sees it: the Law continues forward in the New Covenant, reinforced but never done away with until the heavens and earth pass away.

Paul clearly contradicts Jesus in this respect. Paul says the Law is nailed to a tree, abolished, etc., by Christ's death on the cross. (See chapter entitled, "Did Paul Negate the Law's Further Applicability?" on page 73.)

Also, Paul sees Israel is displaced as covenant partner. Paul says Israel now corresponds to the cursed child of Hagar, in bondage to keep the Law which cannot save. Paul insists Israel can reap no blessing from obeying the Law given Moses. Paul continues and says we under the New Covenant are free to live without the Law. We are analogized to be Isaac's children. We live instead under a covenant of grace. (Gal. 4:28 *ff.*)

However, this means Jesus and Paul contradict on one of the core premises upon which hangs the validity of the Dispensational Jesus-Paul solution.

Remember Premise #5? It said:

- Premise #5: Jesus was inspired in expounding to a different audience who are under the covenant of Law but not under Paul's covenant of grace.

Jesus would not agree that persons of the New Covenant are free to disregard the Law. Remember Jesus said the one who teaches against the validity of the least command in the Law would be *least in the kingdom of heaven.* Jesus then reiterates that not a jot will depart from the Law of Moses ***until heaven and earth pass away***. (Matt. 5:18.) Jesus is obviously warning a member of His New Covenant community to follow the Law. For Jesus, there is no such thing as a Covenant of Grace that throws out the Law two years later. Jeremiah 31:31 *et seq*. expressly promises a New Covenant of "forgiveness and mercy" in which the Law *continues* and the covenant relationship with Israel's seed *continues*. That is why there is no such thing as a dual audience of different covenant partners—one under law and one under grace—as covenant theology adopts to protect Paul's validity.

As Pastor John MacArthur says, "both law and grace are part of the program of God in every dispensation." (J. MacArthur, T*he Gospel According to Jesus*, *supra*, at 31-32.)

Thus, dispensationalism/covenant theology, in its explanation of how to reconcile Paul to Jesus, insists Paul is correct on a key premise at odds with Jesus and Jeremiah 31:31 *et seq*. and Isaiah 42:21. *See also* Isaiah 59:21.

The Consequences of Dispensational Ideas

Dispensational theory has now drastically reduced the New Testament applicable to us. Our New Testament that applies after the ascension of Jesus is, in effect, *only the words of Paul*. We have now returned 100% to the position of the early heretic Marcion of 144 A.D. He said only Paul had the message of Jesus. He rejected the salvation message of the twelve apostles. Marcion claimed their gospels were at odds with Paul. He circulated a gospel narrative that had much in common with Luke, but was much shorter. (See Appendix B: *How the Canon Was Formed.*)

It has taken almost nineteen-hundred years, but everything has come full circle back to Marcion's doctrine and his truncated gospel account. The early church branded him a heretic. Marcion was forgotten. The four gospels were later joined to canon. They appeared safely ensconced as valid until the rise of covenant theology and dispensationalism took over. By these doctrinal developments, we have come back to a Marcion heresy enveloping Christianity day by day.

These developments should disgust any *true* Christian. As John MacArthur correctly states about this aspect of Dispensationalism:

> It is no wonder that the evangelistic message growing out of such a system **differs sharply** from the gospel according to Jesus. If we begin with the **presupposition** that much of Christ's message was intended for another age, why should our gospel be the same as He preached?[23]

23. John MacArthur, *The Gospel According to Jesus* (Zondervan: 1994) at 33. MacArthur does not share my view of Paul. Instead, he tries valiantly to claim his view of Jesus' gospel is *consistent* with Paul. To do this, MacArthur argues that "repentance" (which Jesus preached) is no more a work than faith. However, because MacArthur defines repentance as "active submission" to Jesus (*id.*, at 34, 113), it just cannot wash with Paul. I tried that path myself. I found Paul is just too plain-speaking. For example, in Romans 4:4, Paul says if salvation is by *works* then it would be by a "debt." Paul then clearly says in Romans 4:5: "But to him that worketh not, but believeth on him that justifieth the ungodly, his faith is reckoned for righteousness." Clearly Paul is excluding all kinds of *effort*, including *active submission*. Paul thus eschews *repentance* from sin as part of salvation. By doing so, Paul clearly contradicts Jesus.

Dispensationalist Admits Jesus' Words Are No Longer Relevant Because of Paul

Some Christians are unfamiliar with the streak of Dispensationalism invading the churches. You have never heard this viewpoint boldly proclaimed in a sermon. Yet, its influence is growing because the contradictions between Jesus and Paul do not go away by mere spin.

Here is a very blunt but yet accurate and sincere summary of Dispensational theory. It is from a sermon by Pastor Mike Paulson of Touchet Baptist Church in Touchet, Washington. In a sermon entitled *What Would Jesus Do or What Would Paul Do?* Pastor Paulson boldly dismisses the *What Would Jesus Do* bracelets as heretical. He bases this squarely on mainstream dispensational teaching today. Pastor Paulson explains why this bracelet is heretical: it is wrong to teach anything that Jesus taught; we should instead only teach what Paul taught. Dispensational truth justifies this conclusion.

To avoid any claim that I am misleadingly taking his words out of context, I include almost all of Pastor Paulson's points. He says:

> In regards to that heretical piece of jewelry and money-making modern Christian symbol based on the mentality of modern Christianity, *What Would Jesus Do*, we should know that ***it really doesn't matter what Jesus would do in any specific situations these days***. In fact, the question is not even what Peter would do, or Mary either! The question should be, ***What Would Paul Do!....***
>
> When most people start to read their 'bible,' they usually don't get very far; in fact, most just read up to the Gospels and ignore the rest claiming they don't understand it all.
>
> ***[T]hen [they] put ***their itching ears*** to their 'modern scholarly educated Greek/Hebrew trained' pastor and let him...***teach the teachings of Jesus*** according to the Gospels

thus ***making them 'feel' like they are a good Christian following Jesus' teachings!***

Well, what's wrong with that, you ask? ***It goes against the Scriptures!!!!***

Keep in mind as you read this sermon, Acts is a transitional book. We go from Jew to Gentile; Jerusalem to Rome; Law to Grace; and Peter to Paul!

Let's remind ourselves about the proper place of Peter in today's Christianity:

According to Matthew 10:5-7, Peter, as were the rest of the twelve, was an apostle to Jews only.... ***In fact, Jesus is not even our spokesman for today!*** His 'target' was the lost sheep of Israel. Matthew 10:5,6.

Jesus' teachings in the Gospels were geared to the Jews—if they had accepted Him as their Messiah. They killed Him instead—thus the teachings in the Gospels will become the 'constitution' when He is on the earth again—however, this time He will enforce those teachings! That is what the Millennium is all about. Unfortunately, most 'modern' Christians follow those teachings today—I call them Beatitudinal Christians and a simple reading of the Sermon on the Mount should [show] them that they can NOT live that sermon completely today—no way, not at all—not even close! ***The stuff in the Sermon on the Mount actually contradicts Paul's teachings in everything from salvation to doctrinal belief!*** You would think folks would see this—but like Jesus said of them, ye err not knowing the Scriptures...

So now, let's consider the proper place of Paul in today's New Testament Christianity:

He is our one and only apostle. Jesus really came to be the Messiah to the Jews! But as they killed Him, we now are the 'target' from God....

Jesus sends us our own apostle to follow—Paul!

.... The Apostle Paul instructs us how to live as Christians. He instructs us to do those things we have learned, received, heard, and seen him do.....'Those things, which ye have both learned, and received, and heard, and seen in me, do: and the God of peace shall be with you.' Philippians 4:9.

"Whoever is ashamed of me and my words... of him shall the Son of Man be ashamed when He comes in the glory of His Father with the holy angels." Mark 8:38

If you want to understand the differences associated with the various instructions given in the scriptures (sometimes referred to as ***'contradictions')***, then we must consider what Paul says—***any instructions contradicting his writings apply to a group other than the Church***—other than the Christian today.

We shouldn't follow Peter...

We really shouldn't even follow Jesus' Millennialistic-Gospelic teachings...

We are to follow Paul!

We shouldn't care what Peter would do!

We shouldn't care what Jesus would do!....

We should only care WWPD [i.e., What Would Paul Do?]![24]

What Paulson, a Baptist Pastor, admits is that Jesus' Sermon on the Mount contradicts Paul on general doctrines as well as salvation doctrine. Rather than this being proof that Paul is a false apostle, Pastor Paulson sees this as proof that

---

24.The sermon quoted is entitled *WWJD v. WWPD*? and is reprinted at http://www.touchet1611.org/PeterPaulMary2.html (last visited 2005).

Paul alone is valid for our times. He insists all Jesus' words are invalid until the Millennium. Pastor Paulson says that it is heretical to ask 'what would Jesus do' in the era of grace. The only commands to search out are those in Paul's writings. We not only *can* ignore Jesus' words. We *must* ignore Jesus' directions and salvation theology. If we follow Jesus' words, Paulson insists we are the heretic! Oh My!

Pastor Paulson is a symptom of a much larger problem. Paulinism is taking over the churches. Jesus' words are being diminished and marginalized. The question of Paul's canonicity thus is becoming more and more urgent to resolve. If we wait too long, it may soon be regarded as heretical to teach anything Jesus taught about salvation or morality.

People's salvation is at risk. People will lose the promise that Jesus gives them that if you "kept guard" of His word you "should never taste death." (John 8:51.)

If we wait too long to re-examine Paul, John tells us that if anyone accepts any writing that *transgresses* a teaching of Jesus Christ, that Christian loses God ("doesn't have God"). John writes in 2 John 1:8-11 (Websters' Bible):

> (8) Watch yourselves, that we [*i.e.*, the twelve apostles] don't lose the things which we have accomplished, but that we receive a full reward. (9) Whoever transgresses [*i.e.*, goes beyond] and ***doesn't remain in the teaching of Christ, doesn't have God [i.e., breaks fellowship with God]***. He who ***remains in the teaching [of Jesus Christ]***, the same has both the Father and the Son.

John clearly warns that if you *go beyond* and *transgress* the teachings of Jesus Christ, you do not have God any longer. Yet, if you *remain* in the teachings of Jesus, you have both Jesus and the Father. Dispensationalism is precisely what John is warning about. Dispensationalism removes any relevancy to any teaching of Jesus. It is fundamentally misguided. It risks breaking our relationship with God upon which our salvation depends. For what benefit? Just for the opportunity to quote Paul's very different gospel from Jesus Christ? It is not worth the risk.

Conclusion

Jesus' words were marginalized by Marcion in 144 A.D. The early church recognized this as heresy. History has repeated itself. Will we recognize Marcionism of today as heresy?

We have to go back to the same solution as used in early Christianity. We could simply republish *Against Marcion* by Tertullian, and find all the lessons we need. Tertullian re-examined in what sense Paul's words could be read. Tertullian said Paul was not an inspired person, and we have no *adequate* proof he was even an apostle of Jesus Christ. Tertullian respected Paul and regarded him as edifying. But for Tertullian, his respect for Paul neither proved inspiration nor true apostleship. Can we make this leap and adopt Tertullian's 207 A.D. view of Paul is the true basis upon which Paul was placed in the New Testament? Can we dispense with our comfortable paradigms and return to the early church's view of Paul? Can we finally accept Jesus' Words Only as the *true* inspired NT canon?

16 *Long Tradition of JWO and Minimization of Paul*

Introduction

The oldest tradition in the church relied upon Jesus' Words Only (JWO) as the test of orthodoxy. In the period of 125 A.D. to 325 A.D., after the twelve apostles were gone, the church faced the crisis of Marcion (144 A.D.). He claimed only Paul had the true gospel. Marcion insisted the teachings of the twelve, particularly in the gospel of Matthew and John, did not reflect the true gospel. Marcion thus forced the early church to speak out on the issue of Paul's authority compared to the words of Christ from the twelve. Tertullian was the early church's spokesperson on Marcion. In *Against Marcion* (207 A.D.), Tertullian clarified that Paul was inferior to the twelve. Tertullian insisted Paul cannot be permitted to contradict Jesus' words in the Gospels of Matthew and John. (Tertullian put Luke's and Mark's gospels a notch below the apostolic gospels of Matthew and John.) Tertullian also said Paul's claim to being an apostle was unsupported by any corroborating witness. Tertullian's cautions about Paul were an important basis upon which the early church defeated Marcionism.

Early Church Believed in Jesus' Words Only

First, the Jesus' Words Only (JWO) perspective was the initial view of the church. JWO as a standard for orthodoxy was used long before any official canon was proposed in the late 300s. Daniel Lieuwen, a researcher-writer from the

Orthodox church tradition, explains in his work *The Emergence of the New Testament Canon* (1995): "Initially, only the life and sayings of Christ were considered of equal authority with the Old Testament scriptures."[1]

Lieuwen gives several proof texts. For example, Hegessipus in the first half of the second century said canon was only "the Law, the Prophets, and the Lord"; to this alone "a right faith must conform."[2]

The early church leaders (*e.g.,* Tertullian) simultaneously were saying that Paul's message was deemed inferior to those *Gospel* accounts of Jesus' life and teachings. Thus, orthodoxy focused on the words of Jesus from the Gospels. Jesus' words were the test of orthodoxy. The early church, through Tertullian in 207 A.D., said Paul's teachings were below these gospel accounts. In particular, Paul's words were inferior to the gospels of Matthew and John. If there was any conflict between these gospel accounts and Paul's teachings, Tertullian said we were to prefer Matthew and John over Paul. Thus, JWO has the longest support in Christendom. It also is the most common-sense position to take on determining what is orthodox. If Paul cannot be reconciled to the words of Christ, we do not bend Jesus' words to fit Paul. Rather, all of Jesus' teachings must be given precedence regardless of the impact on Pauline doctrine. Jesus must not be marginalized to fit Paul.

We shall explore the history behind JWO and its rationale in the next two sections.

---

1. This work is reprinted at http://www.orthodox.net/faq/canon.htm.
2. Hans von Campenhausen, *The Formation of the Christian Canon* (J. A. Baker, trans.) (Philadelphia: Fortress Press, 1972) at 167.

The Earliest Canon of the Ebionites Excludes Paul

The first canon list was prepared by *The Poor*, otherwise known as the Ebionites. (See *Appendix B: How the Canon Was Formed* at page ix *et seq.*)

As explained in Appendix B, sometime around 64 A.D., the Ebionites developed a canon that only included Matthew in its Hebrew original. They specifically excluded Paul's writings. As to Paul, the Ebionites made a blatant claim that Paul's words were heretically contrary to those of the Lord Jesus. Thus, Paul must be excluded, they said. We can infer their simple canon list was created around 64 A.D. because (a) Paul's writings existed and were circulating at that point and (b) the Ebionites do not comment positively or negatively on the inclusion of Mark, Luke or John's Gospel (or any other epistle, for that matter). These works date from 65 A.D. onward. Presumably these writings did not exist when the Ebionites declared the Hebrew Matthew was canon, and Paul was to be excluded.

Incidentally, the existence of this Hebrew version of Matthew comes as a surprise to some Christians. However, its existence is confirmed by numerous ancient sources, including Jerome who made a complete translation of the Hebrew Matthew which later was lost. (Jerome was the translator of the Latin Vulgate released 405 A.D.) The same ancient sources say a Hebrew version of Matthew was later translated into Greek, and it is this translation which ended up in our New Testament.[3]

In sum, the Ebionites insisted that this Hebrew Matthew was *the* canon at that time. All of Paul's writings had to be excluded as uninspired, the Ebionites claimed. (For more details, see Appendix B: *How the Canon Was Formed*. For more on the Ebionites' view of Paul, see page 306.)

Thus, the Ebionites were the first to insist Jesus' words alone were canon. They excluded Paul. In fact, the Ebionites were the first to propose a *canon*.

Tertullian (207 A.D.) Says Paul Is Inferior

In the period after the apostles from 125 to 325 A.D., Paul's views on salvation were held in very low esteem by the orthodox leaders of Christianity. It is true we can find Paul is cited as an authority by the early leaders, such as Tertullian, Origen, etc. We even can find some leaders such as Polycarp were effusive, calling Paul "glorious." Yet, they never *expressly* say Paul is a prophet. They never say Paul has specific prophecies that would put him on par with Jeremiah, Isaiah, Ezekiel or Jesus. Nor do they ever teach Paul's faith-*alone* (*i.e.*, without works) doctrine is the valid test for salvation. The early church (125-325 A.D.) always found a way to fit Paul into what Jesus says, as recorded by the twelve.

In fact, Tertullian, a well-respected Christian lawyer and apologist for the faith, wrote in 207 A.D. *Against Marcion*. This work was to attack the rising influence of Marcion. The Marcionites, beginning about 144 A.D., claimed that only Paul had the true gospel. Marcion claimed the books of Matthew, Mark, and John contradicted Paul's gospel. Marcion only accepted a shortened version of Luke's gospel as valid. As a result of Marcionism, the issue of Paul's *level* of authority had to be resolved by the apostolic churches. The apostolic church had to answer whether Marcion's emphasis on Paul was valid. (See *Appendix B: How the Canon Was Formed* at page ix *et seq.*)

3. Professor George Howard recently re-published a medieval text that has the earmarks of this Hebrew original Matthew. It was preserved ironically by a Jewish critic of Christianity as an appendix to his rebuttal work to Christianity. It reads virtually identical to our current version. Yet, its variances repair some textual errors in our Greek New Testament (*e.g.*, Jesus' ascribes the 30 pieces of silver in the Hebrew Matthew to Zechariah, but our Greek NT version ascribes this erroneously to the prophet Jeremiah). Thus, this Hebrew Matthew must be closer to the original Matthew. For more information, see the *Hebrew Matthew* at www.jesuswordsonly.com. See also, Nehemiah Gordon, *Hebrew Yeshua versus the Greek Jesus* (Jerusalem: 2006).

In response, Tertullian in 207 A.D. made several points in *Against Marcion* that clearly reduce Paul to a completely marginal figure.

First, as discussed below, Tertullian proves that Paul is inferior to the twelve apostles. Paul had to submit to their authority in Acts chapter 15. Second, Tertullian said there is no evidence other than Paul's own word that Jesus made Paul an apostle. Luke's account in Acts omits any evidence for this key claim of Paul that he was an apostle of Jesus Christ.

Lastly, one by one, Tertullian tears apart Marcion's doctrines of total depravity, predestination, salvation by faith alone, and eternal security. On this second cluster of issues, Tertullian never identifies what verses in Paul that Marcion is citing. However, we all know what they were. We can hear in Tertullian's paraphrase of Marcion's ideas the ring of Paul's doctrines. Tertullian is silent on where these specific ideas of Marcion derive, but they are all too familiar to us.

But first, let's provide a little more background on Marcion and the rival church system he founded. Here was the first *splinter* group within Christianity.

Background on Marcionism

In 144 A.D., one particular ex-bishop of the church named Marcion proclaimed three core teachings:

- Salvation-by-faith alone. "The Good [God of the NT] redeems those who *believe* in Him but He does not judge those who are *disobedient* to him." (Marcion, *Antitheses* #19.)(See page 49.)
- The Law was not given by God the Father and could be disregarded; and
- Jesus did not come in sinful human flesh but only appeared to have a body of human flesh.

Marcion relied upon Paul exclusively for doctrine. He rejected any of the Gospels written by the twelve apostles. Marcion claimed they were written solely for Jews. In a sense, he was simultaneously *Dispensational* and *Sola Scrip-*

tura. His claim that Paul alone had the correct gospel dispensation allowed Marcion to shuffle aside any of the apostles' writings as unimportant if they did not match Paul's gospel. (Appendix B: *How the Canon was Formed* at page ix.)

We have seen previously that Paul indeed taught:

- Salvation by faith alone. (Romans 4:4; Ephesians 2:8-9.) Even unrepentant disobedient Christians (committing incest) are saved. (1 Cor. 5:5, discussed at page 149.)
- The Law of Moses was given to Moses by angels who are "not gods" and no obedience to the Law was therefore necessary. (Galatians 3:17; 3:19-29, Gal. 4:8-9, discussed at "Denigration of the Law as Given by the Angels" on page 83.)
- Jesus only appeared to come in sinful human flesh (Romans 8:3) and Jesus only appeared to be a man (Philippians 2:7). (For discussion, see page 336 *et seq.*)

Yet, despite Paul teaching the three core teachings of Marcion, Marcion was rejected universally by the post-apostolic church leaders.

Marcion was a serious threat to the survival of Christianity. Marcion had created a church system, with many churches. Marcionite churches had bishops and teachers. Marcion's church was in almost every land and community. Some believe in certain cities there were more Marcionites than orthodox Christians. The *Encyclopedia Brittanica* in "Marcion" reflects this understanding:

> The Marcionite sect, highly ascetic and celibate, grew rapidly ***until it was second in strength only to the original church***; it had churches and an episcopal hierarchy and practiced the sacraments of baptism and the Eucharist... Marcion rejected the Old Testament and almost all of the New Testament... basing his teachings on ten of the Epistles of St. Paul and on an altered version of the Gospel of Luke... Marcionism flourished in the West until about the 4th century....

Thus, Tertullian was the voice of orthodoxy. He was the most prominent voice in the cause against Marcion. Tertullian's words must have been crucial to defeat Marcionism.

What was the main point of Tertullian's attack on Marcion? As we shall see, Tertullian primarily attacks Marcion for his undue reliance on Paul. Paul's apostleship is dubious, Tertullian explains. Likewise, Tertullian believed Paul was not an authority on par with the twelve apostles. If Paul contradicts the twelve, Paul's words are not to be followed. When Tertullian wants to isolate those contradictions, Tertullian is circumspect. Tertullian finds flaws in Pauline doctrines without citing Paul as the source of Marcion's wrong ideas. However, we can recognize Paul's words in Marcion's mouth.

Another major vulnerability of Marcion exploited by Tertullian was Marcion's *theological* explanation why the Law did not have to be followed. Marcion must have realized that Paul's claim that the Law was given by angels was unsound Biblically. So Marcion devised what he regarded as a better reason to prove the Law of Moses was invalid. What was this?

Marcion had a very elaborate and well-defended view why the Law was invalid, set forth in his *Antitheses.*[4] Marcion claimed that the God of the 'Old Testament' could not be the God of the New. Jesus is God, and the Father is God, but both are kindly and loving. Marcion sought to prove the creator God of the Old is a different type of God: mean, willing to do evil, sometimes unsure of His aims, repenting of plans or actions, etc.

Marcion's exposition raises 'Old Testament' verses that have perplexed many theologians to this day. Yet, Marcion's solution exposed him to the charge of polytheism. He claimed one member of the Godhead had a distinct and different nature from the other two.

4. You can find this work—patched together from various sources—at http://www.geocities.com/Athens/Ithaca/3827/antithesis.html.

Tertullian had a field day with this claim of Marcion. The Marcionites were vigorously persecuted as heretics, but not simply for this polytheistic flaw. Tertullian in *Against Marcion* relied on much more than this. Tertullian's primary defense of Christ was based on lifting up Jesus' words in the Gospels above Paul, thereby defeating the core doctrines of Marcion.

Based on Tertullian's work, the apostolic churches defeated Marcionism. The Marcionites early Paul-only-ism almost swallowed the church. Yet, the early church bravely fought back and survived. Marcionism took almost three hundred years to be defeated within Christianity.

In fact, Marcionism—despite being crippled by the 300s—had a strong fascination for centuries thereafter. Paul-only-ism lived on within the fringe of Christianity. This was because the Marcionite churches had entered Armenia early on. They re-emerged as a force in Armenia in the eighth century. Their Christian opponents labelled them Paulicians because of their adherence to Paul. Eventually they spread to Bulgaria and Turkey. The Paulicians claimed: (a) only Paul's gospel is the true gospel; (b) salvation is by faith alone; (c) the gospels Matthew, Mark and John had to be eliminated as canon; and (d) there is to be selective receipt of Luke's gospel account. This was unmistakably similar to the core doctrines of Marcion. In 844, the Paulicians took control of a state in Turkey and became a military power. In 871, they were defeated by Emperor Basil I of Byzantium. The Eastern Orthodox treated the Paulicians as heretics. Yet, the Paulicians survived into the twelfth century.[5]

5. See "Paulicians," *Catholic Encyclopedia*. It mentions they "[1]rejected the Old Testament...[2][T]o believe in him [Jesus] saves men from judgment....[3] Their Bible was a fragmentary New Testament." In N. G. Garsoïan, *The Paulician Heresy* (1968), it mentions "The sect especially valued the Gospel of Luke and the Pauline Epistles."

Thus, Marcionism remained a persistent force within Christianity from 144 A.D. to the 1200s. Yet, in all this time, they were always viewed universally as heretics.

What cannot be ignored is that in Marcionism, we have the first representatives of what today would otherwise pass as an evangelical Protestant sect. Even Marcion's view of the 'God of the Old' versus the 'God of the New' appears today in the repackaged form of *dispensational theology.* The virtue of modern dispensationalism is that it does not expose the advocate to an accusation of polytheism. Instead, it only exposes the advocate to the charge that God changes His nature in time.

Thus, Marcion forced the early church to weigh modern Pauline theology. Yet, the post-apostolic church of 125 A.D. to 325 A.D. clearly rejected Marcion and his Pauline theology.

Tertullian Demonstrates Paul is Inferior to the Other Apostles

In Book 4, chapter 2 of Tertullian's *Against Marcion* (ca. 207 A.D.), Tertullian clearly says Paul's authority is *inferior* to that of the twelve apostles. Tertullian explains Paul's gospel is only valid so long as it is consistent with Jesus and the twelve.

First, Tertullian starts out by emphasizing the priority of the gospels written by the actual twelve apostles, namely the gospels of Matthew and John. Those of Luke and Mark were inferior because they were produced merely by disciples of their teachers. Later Tertullian identifies Luke and Mark as "apostolic men," but not apostles. Tertullian writes:

> I lay it down to begin with that the documents of the ***gospel have the apostles for their authors***, and that this task of promulgating the gospel was imposed upon them by our Lord

> himself. ***If they also have for their authors apostolic men* [*i.e.*, Luke and Mark],** yet these stand not alone, ***but as companions of apostles or followers of apostles***: because the preaching of disciples [*i.e.*, Luke or Mark] might be made suspect of the desire of vainglory, unless there ***stood by it the authority of their teachers*** [*i.e.*, the twelve apostles], or rather the authority of Christ, which made the apostles teachers. In short, from among ***the apostles the faith is introduced to us by John and by Matthew***, while from among ***apostolic men Luke and Mark*** give it renewal, <all of them> beginning with the same rules <of belief>, as far as relates to the one only God, the Creator, and to his Christ, born of a virgin, the fulfillment of the law and the prophets.****Marcion seems to have singled out Luke for his mutilating process [*i.e.*, writing a gospel apparently based on Luke but altering it]. Luke, however, was **not an apostle, but only an apostolic man**; not a master, but a disciple, and ***so inferior to a master....***[6]

This unquestionably puts Luke below the other Gospels of Matthew and John. Thus, Tertullian was saying that (a) to the extent Marcion is using Luke *legitimately* then (b) Luke is still inferior to the gospel accounts of Matthew and John.

Tertullian's view of Luke's Gospel as subordinate to Matthew has *de facto* been accepted by conservative Christians today, as we must. Otherwise Luke has Jesus uttering a command to "hate your" mother and father which is contrary to prior Scripture.[7] Matthew's account of the same exchange

6. Tertullian, *Adversus Marcionem* (ed. trans.) (Oxford: Oxford University Press, 1972) at 262-63, Book 4, chapter 2. It is available online at http://www.tertullian.org/articles/evans_marc/evans_marc_10book4_eng.htm (accessed 2005).

materially differs. Jesus' command in Matthew is consistent with Scripture, saying we cannot "love more" our mother and father than Jesus. (Matt. 10:37.) Thus, today it is recognized that Luke is inferior to Matthew or John when there is a conflict, just as Tertullian teaches.[8]

The reason Tertullian is mentioning Luke is inferior to Matthew and John is that Marcion's gospel narrative of Jesus' life reads very close to the *Gospel according to Luke.* Tertullian is thus suggesting that Luke's Gospel is the source of Marcion's gospel account of Jesus' life. Tertullian is then saying that to the extent Marcion's gospel account was written by Luke, it is not as authoritative as either Matthew or John. The latter were apostles of Jesus. Luke was not.

Next, Tertullian discusses the possibility that Marcion is claiming Paul wrote this *proto-Luke gospel.* Scholars believe Tertullian was not merely hypothesizing. They believe that Marcion indeed was claiming Paul wrote *proto-Luke*. Whatever the truth, Tertullian is going to discuss what would be the authority of a gospel narrative of Jesus' life even if it were written by Paul as compared to narratives written by Matthew or John. We are going to get to a key issue: would such a gospel narrative written by Paul *be on par with a gospel written by Matthew or John*? Tertullian answers *no,* thereby demonstrating a *lower regard for Paul* than the twelve, in particular lower than the writings of *Matthew* and *John*.

7. In Luke 14:26, Luke says Jesus said, "If any man cometh unto me, and ***hateth not*** his own father, and mother, and wife, and children, and brethren, and sisters, yea, and his own life also, he cannot be my disciple."
8. Clarke realizes the contradiction between Luke & Matthew, and the terrible import of Luke's variance. He says "Matt. 10:37 expresses the true meaning" of Jesus. Gill likewise sees the problem in Luke, saying Jesus could not have uttered a command to hate, for this would be contrary "to the laws of God...and divine revelation." He says Matthew is a better "explanation" of Jesus' meaning.

Tertullian's quote below continues from the last quote above. In this next quote, Tertullian starts out by making clear that Luke is inferior to the other apostles' gospel because Luke's Master (Teacher) was Paul, and Paul was a "lesser" apostle than the twelve. Tertullian then explains Paul (a) could not come with another gospel than the twelve and (b) Paul's authority derived from the twelve and Paul was inferior to them. He cites Acts chapter 15 as proof. Tertullian explains:

> Now Luke was not an apostle but an apostolic man, not a master but a disciple, in any case less than his master [*i.e.*, Paul], and assuredly ***even more of lesser account as being the follower of a later apostle, Paul,***[9] to be sure: so that even if Marcion had introduced his gospel ***under the name of Paul in person***, that one single document would not be adequate for our faith, ***if destitute of the support of his [i.e., Paul's] predecessors [the twelve apostles].*** For we should demand the production of that gospel also which Paul found <in existence>, that to which he gave his assent, that with which shortly afterwards he was ***anxious that his own should agree***: for his intention in going up to Jerusalem to know and to consult the apostles, was lest perchance he had run in vain—that is, ***lest perchance he had not believed as they did***, or were not preaching the gospel in their manner. At length, when he [*i.e.*, Paul] had conferred with the original <apostles>, and there was agreement concerning the rule of the faith, they joined the right hands <of fellowship>....***If he [i.e., Paul] therefore who***

9. For the doubting Thomas' over this Oxford translation, the Latin original confirms this is correct. It is: "Porro Lucas non apostolus sed apostolicus, non magister sed discipulus, utique ***magistro minor***, certe tanto posterior quanto posterioris apostoli sectator, ***Pauli*** sine dubio."

> ***gave the light to Luke chose to have his predecessors' authority [i.e., the twelve]*** for his faith as well as his preaching, ***much more must I require for Luke's gospel the authority [i.e., from the twelve] which was necessary for the gospel of his master [i.e., Paul].***[10]

Tertullian could not be more clear. Paul's authority was not recognized as direct from Jesus or by revelation. It only derived from Paul's recognition by the twelve apostles. He was their disciple, and they were Paul's masters. If Paul created a gospel text, Tertullian responds that Paul's conduct in Acts chapter 15 reveals Paul's authority could not exceed the words and guidance of the twelve. Paul was not allowed to *run beyond the teaching of Christ that the twelve had.* Thus, if Paul was Luke's source for his gospel, then Luke's gospel still must be consistent with the apostolic canon of Matthew and John or otherwise it is invalid. This means that for Tertullian, Paul was not free to utter doctrines that were inconsistent with the gospels of Matthew or John.

Tertullian Questions In What Sense Paul Was An Apostle

Tertullian is not through analyzing Paul's authority within the New Testament church. Tertullian even gets to the issue in what sense Paul was an *apostle* of Jesus. Tertullian in Book 5 of *Against Marcion* remarks that there is actually no proof in the gospels of Matthew, Mark, Luke or John that Paul was made an apostle. It is solely Paul's word. Tertullian says that if we are forced to admit any contradiction between Paul and the twelve, we must abide in the words from the twelve. (Tertullian never admits a contradiction, and seeks to

10. Tertullian (ed. Evans), *Against Marcion, supra*, at 263, 265, Book IV, ch.2.

harmonize Paul, as discussed later. Thus Tertullian further on "claims him as my own," robbing Paul from Marcion.) Here is Tertullian in book 5, chapter one, of *Against Marcion:*

> I desire to hear from Marcion ***the origin of Paul the apostle***. I am a sort of new disciple, having had instruction from no other teacher. For the moment my only belief is that ***nothing ought to be believed with-out good reason***, and that is believed without good reason which is believed without knowledge of its origin: and ***I must*** with the best of reasons ***approach this inquiry with uneasiness when I find one affirmed to be an apostle, of whom in the list of the apostles in the gospel I find no trace.*** So ***when I am told that he [i.e., Paul] was subsequently promoted by our Lord, by now at rest in heaven, I find some lack of foresight in the fact that Christ did not know beforehand that he would have need of him***, but after setting in order the office of apostleship and sending them out upon their duties, considered it necessary, ***on an impulse and not by deliberation, to add another, by compulsion so to speak and not by design*** [*i.e.*, on the Road to Damascus]. So then, shipmaster out of Pontus [*i.e.*, Marcion], supposing you have never accepted into your craft any smuggled or illicit merchandise, have never appropriated or adulterated any cargo, and in the things of God are even more careful and trustworthy, will you please ***tell us under what bill of lading you accepted Paul as apostle, who had stamped him with that mark of distinction, who commended him to you, and who put him in your charge***? Only so may you with confidence disembark him [*i.e.*, Paul]: only so can he avoid being proved to belong to him who ***has put in evidence all the documents that attest his apostleship***. ***He [i.e., Paul] himself, says Mar-***

cion, claims to be an apostle, and that not from men nor through any man, but through Jesus Christ. ***Clearly any man can make claims for himself***: but his claim is ***confirmed by another person's attestation***. One person writes the document, another signs it, a third attests the signature, and a fourth enters it in the records. ***No man is for himself both claimant and witness.*** Besides this, you have found it written that ***many will come and say, I am Christ.*** If there is one that makes a false claim to be Christ, ***much more can there be one who professes that he is an apostle of Christ***. Thus far my converse has been in the guise of a disciple and an inquirer: from now on ***I propose to shatter your confidence, for you have no means of proving its validity, and to shame your presumption***, since you make claims but reject the means of establishing them. Let Christ, ***let the apostle, belong to your other god***: yet you have no proof of it except from the Creator's archives.

****[You may argue:] 'And do you then deny that Paul is an apostle?' I speak no evil against him whom I retain for myself. ***If I deny, it is to force you to prove. If I deny, it is to enforce my claim that he is mine***. Otherwise, if you have your eye on our belief, accept the evidence on which it depends. If you challenge us to adopt yours, ***tell us the facts on which it is founded.*** Either prove that the things you believe really are so: or else, ***if you have no proof***, how can you believe?[11]

11. Tertullian, *Against Marcion* (Oxford University Press, 1972) at 509, 511, reprinted online at http://www.tertullian.org/articles/evans_marc/evans_marc_12book5_eng.htm.

Tertullian is emphasizing that the story in Acts is a dubious credential for Paul, if one is objective. Why must Jesus have belatedly thought to add a thirteenth apostle? Was God pressured to pick someone who was attacking the church and could not have planned this out better? Is this the best credential that Paul can come up with? Tertullian says we would precisely suspect Paul to be a false apostle because Jesus warned us that many would come in his name but be false prophets. Tertullian refers to the "many false prophets who will come and say 'I am [of] Christ.'" (Luke 21:8.) Finally, Tertullian says Paul is basically the only witness for his own apostleship, and that is invalid. (See John 5:31.)

Tertullian then says in the quote above that he asks all these hard questions to force Marcion to prove Paul's authority apart from the twelve. Tertullian says Paul's authority is valid only to the extent it derives from the apostolic twelve and *their* teaching. There is no unique authority that Paul can ever have apart from the twelve, as Marcion was claiming.

Tertullian then goes on to prove that Paul is "his apostle" but only by Tertullian's elaborate effort to prove Paul does not contradict the twelve (*i.e.*, Matthew and John). Tertullian's arguments in the balance of Book 5 of *Against Marcion* (as well as in Book I) reveal efforts to save Paul as the source of ***edifying*** material by harmonizing him with Jesus, as we shall see in the next section.

Furthermore, elsewhere Tertullian denies that Paul had any experience in his heavenly visions that would allow him to contradict the Gospel message. Some were apparently claiming in Tertullian's day, as they do now, that Paul received ongoing revelations by being taken up into the third heaven where Paul heard "unspeakable" mysteries. Then some argued these visions give Paul a priority over the apostolic accounts of Matthew and John. Paul could give contrary principles to what Matthew or John said because Jesus gave Paul a subsequent revelation. Tertullian disagreed:

> Now, although Paul was carried away even to the third heaven, and was caught up to paradise [implied in 2 Cor. 12:4], and heard certain revelations there, ***yet these cannot possibly seem to have qualified him for (teaching) another doctrine***, seeing that their very nature [*i.e.*, they were 'unspeakable'] was such as to render them communicable to no human being.[12]

In conclusion, Tertullian's statements in *Against Marcion* and *Prescription Against Heretics* completely marginalized the status of Paul. The church was being forced to examine Paul's credentials. Tertullian found them wanting. Yet, Tertullian was not through.

Tertullian Criticizes Every Pauline Doctrine of Marcion

Tertullian throughout *Against Marcion* shows how Marcion's understanding of Paul does not square with reason, Jesus, or Paul himself. Tertullian's approach is typically "Paul says this," but 'you Marcion do not understand.' However, in a stretch of four chapters beginning at chapter 23 to chapter 27 of Book One, Tertullian does a 180 degree turn. He discusses doctrines of Marcion which come from Paul but Tertullian never mentions Paul. Then Tertullian crushes each doctrine in turn. The interesting thing is that each of these doctrines were *unquestionably Pauline.* However, Tertullian no longer could attack Marcion for taking Paul out of context or misunderstanding him. These topics that Tertullian attacked in chapters 23 through 27 were: salvation by faith alone, eternal security, predestination and total depravity.

---

12. Tertullian, *The Prescription Against Heretics*, Ch. XXIV, available online from http://www.tertullian.org/anf/anf03/anf03-24.htm, quoting entire text from *Anti-Nicene Fathers* Vol. III.

What was Tertullian's method in this regard? Instead of quoting Paul or using clearly Pauline verbiage, and then explaining his 'true meaning,' Tertullian simply destroyed the substance behind all of Paul's major doctrines. Tertullian did so with logic and reason deduced from the nature of God revealed in Scripture. Paulinists today might not accept these deductions because Tertullian does not use our modern 'citation' method to refute a point. However, the issue I am raising here is *not* to ask you to *agree with Tertullian*. Rather I ask you to acknowledge that the very early church *was proving as heresy* everything that Paulinists emphasize today as valid.

Tertullian on Predestination: Is Double Predestination Fair? Can Marcion's God Be Truly Good If He Thwarts Salvation In The Greater Part of Humanity?

- "Now, when the greater part thus perish, how can that goodness [of God] be defended as a perfect one which is inoperative in most cases, is somewhat only in few, naught in many, succumbs to perdition, and ***is a partner with destruction*** [*i.e.*, wills the lost to perdition]? And if so many shall miss salvation, it will not be with goodness, but with malignity, that the greater perfection will lie. For as it is the operation of goodness which brings salvation, ***so is it malevolence which thwarts it*** [*i.e.*, if it is goodness of God that predestines salvation, Marcion must imply it is evil in God that intentionally thwarts it]." (*Against Marcion* 1.24.)[13]

Tertullian on Total Depravity and Justification of the Ungodly Rather than the Righteous: Why Would God Capriciously Grant Salvation On Enemies Rather than Prefer Those Who Love Him and Are Righteous?

- "Now I deny that the goodness of Marcion's god is rational, on this account first, because it proceeded to the ***salvation of a human creature which was alien to him*** [*i.e.*, an enemy not seeking Him.] [I omit here T.'s discussion on limits to *love of enemies* principle.]....Since, therefore, the first step in the rea-

13. You can find this at Calvin College's online resources at http://ccel.org/fathers2/ANF-03/anf03-28.htm#P3804_1266834

sonableness of the divine goodness is that it displays itself on its ***proper object in righteousness*** [*i.e.*, a person seeking God and to please Him, not an enemy], and only at its second stage on an alien object by a redundant righteousness over and above that of scribes and Pharisees [*i.e.*, apply kindness, not salvation, to enemies], how comes it to pass that the second is attributed to him [*i.e.*, salvation for enemies] who fails in the first [*i.e.*, salvation for those who are not enemies], not having man for his proper object, and who makes his goodness on this very account defective? Moreover, how could a defective benevolence, which had no proper object whereon to expend itself, overflow on an alien one? Clear up the first step, and then vindicate the next....Suppose now the divine goodness begin at the second stage of its rational operation, that is to say, on the stranger [*i.e.*, salvation for them], this second stage will not be consistent in rationality if it be impaired in any way else. For only then will even the second stage of goodness, that which is displayed towards the stranger, be accounted rational, when it ***operates without wrong to him who has the first claim*** [*i.e.*, preference to save enemies/strangers is wrong if it neglects those who are seeking God]. It is righteousness which before everything else makes all goodness rational. It will thus be rational in its principal stage, when manifested on its proper object, if it be righteous. And thus, in like manner, it will be able to appear rational, when displayed towards the stranger, if it be not unrighteous. ***But what sort of goodness is that which is manifested in wrong, and that in behalf of an alien creature?*** For peradventure a benevolence, even when operating injuriously, might be deemed to some extent rational, if exerted for one of our own house and home. By what rule, however, can ***an unjust benevolence, displayed on behalf of a stranger, to whom not even an honest one is legitimately due, be defended as a rational one***? (Tertullian, *Against Marcion* 1.23.) [14]

Is It True If God Be In You, and You Pay Him Homage, That God Will Never Inflict Punishment? Should We Never Fear God? Didn't Jesus Threaten to Throw The Sinner Outside Mean Loss of Salvation for a Sinning Christian? (Refutation of Eternal Security.)

"[B]y the fear of the Lord men depart from evil." Prov. 16:6

- "Listen, ye sinners; and ye who have not yet come to this, hear, that you may attain to such a pass! A better god has been discovered [*n.b.*, T. is mocking Marcion], who never takes offence, is never angry, never inflicts punishment, who has prepared no fire in hell, no gnashing of teeth in the outer darkness! He is purely and simply good. He indeed forbids all delinquency, ***but only in word. He is in you, if you are willing to pay him homage....the Marcionites with such pretences, that they have no fear of their god at all.*** They say it is only a bad man who will be feared, a good man will be loved. Foolish man, do you say that he ***whom you call Lord ought not to be feared***, whilst the very title you give him indicates a power which must itself be feared? But how are you going to love, without some fear that you do not love?...Still more vainly do they act, who when asked, What is to become of ***every sinner in that great day? reply, that he is to be cast away out of sight***. Is not even this a question of judicial determination? He is adjudged to deserve rejection, and that by a sentence of condemnation; unless ***the sinner is cast away forsooth for his salvation,*** that even a leniency like this may fall inconsistently with the character of your most good and excellent god! And what will it be to be cast away, but to lose that which a man was ***in the way of obtaining***, were it not for his rejection-that is, ***his salvation***? Therefore his being cast away will involve ***the forfeiture of salvation;*** and this sentence cannot possibly be passed

14.Paul teaches we are *all* enemies of God, but God then bestowed His mercy on us while we were *yet* sinners. (Rom. 5:10.) Tertullian says this is absurd because he believes there are those who seek after God. The Lord Almighty should *pick* them to bestow His mercy. Tertullian is basing this on Jesus' clear teaching of the saved fourth seed who had prior to hearing the word been a *good and noble heart.* (Luke 8:15.) However, a Paulinist does not acknowledge *ever* that such a person exists. Yet, the Bible teaches they do exist: *e.g.*, Job 1:1, 8.

upon him, except by an angry and offended authority, who is also the punisher of sin—that is, by a judge." (Tertullian, *Against Marcion*, 1.27.)[15]

Thus, Tertullian crushed all the core teachings of Paulinism in our day. Tertullian was not alone. This was the standard viewpoint of the early post-apostolic church from 125 A.D. to 325 A.D. One can never find the slightest agreement in this period with eternal security, total depravity, predestination, bondage of the will, or salvation by faith alone (*i.e.*, repentance/works are not necessary). Instead, all were rejected *universally and expressly*, as we will next review.

Patristic Era (125-325 A.D.) Rejected Paul's Salvation Doctrine

Jesus' Words Only was the earliest post-apostolic standard of orthodoxy. The era that predates the Roman Catholic period is traditionally called the Patristic era. It spans 125 A.D. to 325 A.D. In this period, the bishop of Rome was just one of many bishops competing for influence within a loose fraternity of bishops in all major cities of the Mediterranean world. It is in that period we find church leaders, traditionally called the *fathers*, who are setting forth the earliest doctrines of churches *founded by the twelve apostles*. (This is why it is called the Patristic Era.) They thereby serve as a witness of what the twelve apostles *likely* must have been teaching. A

15. Tertullian's chapter title is interesting: "Dangerous Effects to Religion and Morality of the Doctrine of So Weak a God." He saw eternal security as a threat to morality. Tertullian repeats this attack on eternal security forcefully in his book *The Scorpion's Bite* (207 A.D.) He felt the doctrine sapped the resolve of those under persecution. Many were teaching that if you denied Christ, Christ would not deny you and you remained saved (quoting Paul in 2 Timothy). Tertullian regarded this eternal security doctrine as the *Scorpion's Bite*.

universal consensus from this early period would be a particularly compelling proof that a teaching had an origin with the twelve apostles.

What was the position of the early church leaders on salvation? Was it Pauline?

David Bercot, an attorney, has synthesized the beliefs of the church leaders in the post-apostolic era between 125 A.D. to 325 A.D. He is the author of the 703 page comprehensive *A Dictionary of Early Christian Beliefs: A Reference Guide to More than 700 Topics Discussed by the Early Church Fathers* (Peabody, Mass.: Henrickson Publishing, 1998.) Based on this extraordinary research, Bercot claims "early Christians *universally* believed that works or obedience play an essential role in our salvation."[16] This was completely contrary to Paul's teaching in Ephesians 2:8-9.

If true, then Bercot's claim causes us to ponder. Are we to believe the twelve apostle taught works were *not essential* to salvation? If we believe this, then we must also believe the church which had a diffuse organization as of 125 A.D. became heretical immediately after all the apostles died. This also had to occur simultaneously in numerous disparate congregations under different authorities. Further, as Paulinists concede, we have to believe this 'heresy' that rejected Paul's doctrines on salvation continued universally for 1400 years until Luther rediscovered the true salvation formula in 1517. If Bercot is correct, the Paulinist asks us to swallow a host of implausibilities if we assume the twelve accepted Paul's teaching on salvation.

Thus, Bercot's claim is a big one. However, it is one which Bercot backs up with thorough quotes. For example, while the early church believed you were not saved by works

16.David W. Bercot, *Will the Real Heretics Please Stand Up: A New Look at Today's Evangelical Christianity in the light of Early Christianity* (Texas: Scroll Publishing, 1999) at 57.

alone, they did not believe you were saved by faith alone. Polycarp, the bishop of Smyrna, and at one-time pro-Paul, wrote:

> He who raised Him from the dead will also raise us up—***if we do His will and walk in His commandments***, love what He loved, and keeping ourselves from all unrighteousness, covetousness, love of money, evil speaking, falsewitness;...forgive, and it shall be forgiven unto you; be merciful, that ye may obtain mercy;.....(Polycarp, *Letter to the Philippians*, ch. 2.)[17]

Hermas, whose work of about 132 A.D. was one of the favorites of that early era, wrote: "***Only*** those who fear the Lord and keep His commandments have life with God." (Hermas, *Shepherd* II. comm. 7; III sim. 10 ch. 2.)

Clement of Alexandria (150-212 A.D.), an elder of his church and whose works quote the New Testament 2,400 times,[18] wrote around 190 A.D.:

> "Even a baptized person loses the grace he has attained unless he remains innocent." Cyprian (250 A.D.) *Anti-Nicene Fathers* Vol. 5 at 542.

> Whoever obtains [the truth] and distinguishes himself in ***good works shall gain the prize of everlasting life***....Some people correctly and adequately understand how [God provides necessary power], but attaching slight importance to the ***works*** that lead to salvation, they ***fail to make the necessary preparation for attaining the objects of their hope***. (Clement, *Rich Man* chs. 1 & 2.)

17.http://www.earlychristianwritings.com/text/polycarp-roberts.html

18.Josh McDowell, *Evidence that Demands A Verdict* (San Bernardino, CA: Here's Life, 1972) at 50-52.

In response to the Marcionites' claim that salvation was by faith alone, Clement further responded:

> Let us not ***merely call Him Lord***, for that will not save us. For He says, 'Not everyone who says to me, Lord, Lord, will be saved, but he who does what is right.' Thus, brothers, ***let us acknowledge him by our actions***....This world, and the world to come are two enemies. This one means adultery, corruption, avarice, and deceit, while the other gives them up. We cannot, therefore, be friends of both. **To get the one, *we must give the other up*.** (*Second Epistle of Clement* ch. 4.)[19]

What led into this quote was Clement's explanation that a true confession of Christ is not with the lips but with the heart by *action*.

> For He himself declares, 'Whosoever shall confess me before men, him will I confess before my Father.' This, then, is our reward if we shall confess Him by whom we have been saved. But in what way shall we confess Him? ***By doing what He says, and not transgressing His commandments, and by honouring Him not with our lips only, but with all our heart and all our mind.*** For He says in Isaiah, 'This people honoureth me with their lips, but their heart is far from me.' (*Second Epistle of Clement*, ch.3.)

What if we should strive to win the crown in Christ, but commit sin *en route*? Clement is clear in the next quote below: damnation is the result for such a Christian. Clement did not acknowledge for a moment Paul's contrary teaching of eternal security in Romans 8:1 that there is now no con-

19.A reprint online from the Roberts-Donaldson translation is at http://www.earlychristianwritings.com/text/2clement-roberts.html (last accessed 2005).

demnation for those in Christ Jesus. Nor did Clement recognize we can never separate ourselves from the love of God by *sinning*, as some today read Paul's words in Romans 8:39.[20] Clement wrote instead:

> We must remember that he who strives in the corruptible contest, if ***he be found acting unfairly, is taken away and scourged, and cast forth from the lists***. What then think ye? If one does anything unseemly in the incorruptible contest, what shall he have to bear? For of ***those who do not preserve the seal*** [unbroken], [the Scripture] saith, 'Their worm shall not die, and their fire shall not be quenched, and they shall be a spectacle to all flesh.' (Second Epistle of Clement ch. 7.)

These and numerous other sources demonstrate Paul's salvation theory was not recognized. Paul's ideas were that salvation was by a one-time faith *alone*, without works, and there was no condemnation once in Christ. (Eph. 2:8-9; Rom. 8:1.). However, the only proponents who took these verses *seriously* were the Marcionites. They were branded, however, as heretics by the early post-apostolic church. Paul's salvation formulas were never accepted in the universal post-apostolic Christian church from 125 A.D. to 325 A.D. In that period, Paul, even if quoted on salvation by faith, was *always* read to line up with Christ's emphasis on the *essential* nature of works and the damning power of sin in a Christian's life.

For example, Polycarp is the ***only*** ancient 'father' to quote Ephesians 2:8-9 that we are "saved by grace, not of works." (*Epistle of Polycarp to the Philippians* 1:6.) Yet, in

20. If you go to www.earlychristianwritings.com, every time a verse is discussed in a patristic writing, it is linked. However, neither Romans 8:1 nor 8:39 are *ever once* cited by any patristic-era 'father.' *See*, http://www.earlychristianwritings.com/e-catena/romans8.html (last accessed 2005).

the very next breath in the same epistle, Polycarp has a diametrically opposed idea of how we read Ephesians 2:8-9 today. Polycarp writes:

> But He who raised Him up from the dead will raise up us also, ***if we do His will,*** and ***walk in His commandments***, and love what He loved, ***keeping ourselves from all unrighteousness***.... (*Epistle to the Philippians,* 2:13-14.)[21]

Thus, whenever tension between Paul and Jesus were apparent, our Lord Jesus was *never* interpreted to fit Paul, as is the norm today. As Bercot puts it:

> The early Christians ***didn't put Paul's letters to the Romans and Galatians up on a pedestal above the teachings of Jesus and the other apostles***. They read Paul's words about grace in conjunction with...Scriptures [where Jesus requires endurance for salvation, Matt. 24:13, doing the will of God for salvation, Matt. 7:21, the resurrected will be those who have done good, John 5:28, 29, etc.] (Bercot, *Will the Real Heretics Stand Up, supra,* at 63.)

Calvin's research corroborates Bercot's position. Calvin was the second major figure in the Reformation after Luther. Calvin cited Augustine as the only early church figure who agreed with *any* aspect of salvation in Paul's teachings. However, Augustine was *from the mid-300s*. Even here, Augustine's agreement was limited to the teaching of predestination and perserverance in good works as a gift of God's divine intervention. Augustine did believe works were necessary. However, Augustine placed that requirement outside human responsibility. If God predestined a Christian to salvation, Augustine taught God would also give the gift of perse-

21. The epistle is available online from Calvin College at http://ccel.org/fathers2/ANF-01/anf01-11.htm#P776_145896 (last accessed 2005).

verance in good works.[22] Thus, works were necessary, but God would give you the gift of doing good works if you were predestined. Accordingly, Augustine did not teach Paul's doctrine of salvation by faith alone. Regardless, the point is that Calvin like Bercot could find no one earlier who had any agreement with Paul's salvation doctrine. This is most revealing.

Thus, all the evidence strongly supports that salvation in the early post-apostolic church was never thought to be correctly stated by Paul as *faith-alone without works*. While Paul was quoted on salvation by faith, he was always put back in the context of Jesus' words. Paul was always then interpreted to line up with Jesus' emphasis on the essential nature of works for salvation, *i.e.*, obedience to Jesus' commandments, doing righteousness, charity, repentance from sin, etc. The early apostolic age emphasized *always* the damning effect of denying Christ or failing to obey Him. In the early church, salvation doctrine was dependent on Jesus' words alone.

Table: Some Reasons Why Early Church Believed Works Essential

Verse	Condition	Result
1 John 1:7	"if we walk in the light"	"the blood of Jesus, his Son, cleanses us from all sin"
Mark 13:13, Matt. 10:22	If you "stand firm to the end"	You "will be saved"
Matthew 6:12-15	"if you forgive men when they sin against you"	"your heavenly Father will also forgive you."
Matthew 12:48-50	If you do "the will of my Father in heaven"	You are "my brother, sister, etc."

22. Ironically, it was Augustine who formulated all the core problematical doctrines of Roman Catholicism too. Thus, Calvin thought Augustine was heretical on almost everything but Paul's doctrine of predestination. Why should Calvin think someone so heretical on so many doctrines could be correct about just these few points?

The Patristic Era Church Also Rejected Paul's Predestination Doctrine

Further proof of the low regard for Paul can be seen in the early church's view of predestination. The early church from 125 A.D. to 325 A.D. universally rejected Paul's teachings on predestination. Paul was not named, but they *universally* regarded his teaching as blasphemy and impiety of the worst sort. Justin Martyr died in 165 A.D. by preferring execution than to renounce his faith in Christ. He explained:

> We have learned it from the prophets, and we hold it to be true, that punishments, chastisements, and rewards are rendered according to each man's actions. Otherwise, if all things happen by fate, then nothing is in our own power. For if it is ***predestined*** that one man be good and another man evil, then the first is not deserving of praise or the other to be blamed. Unless humans have the power of avoiding evil and choosing good by free choice, they are not accountable for their actions—whatever they may be.... (Justin, *First Apology*, ch. 43.)

Clement, Archelaus, and Methodius all spoke against predestination, and in favor of free-will.[23]

The Epistle of Second Peter also reflects this early rejection of predestination. It states that God "is not ***willing*** that any should perish but that all should come to repentance." (2 Peter 3:9.) If God is not *willing* any should perish but predestination of the lost were true, then God would not be willing to have happen what He supposedly predestines to happen. God would be schizophrenic. Evidently because 2 Peter 3:9 refutes predestination, Calvin was willing to reject the entire epistle as inspired. Calvin held tightly to Pauline predestination. Calvin declared Second Peter a false addition

23.Bercot, *Will the Real Heretics Please Stand Up, supra*, at 71.

to scripture.[24] Indeed, Second Peter likely is a pseudograph. Yet, even as such, 2 Peter 3:9 is still an early fourth century reflection of church doctrine. It proves the post-apostolic age rejected predestination of the lost.

Methodius, a Christian martyr from the late 200s, likewise said predestination doctrine was an impious (blasphemous) claim. He wrote:

> Those who say that man does not have free will, but say that he is governed by the unavoidable necessities of fate, are ***guilty of impiety toward God himself***, making Him out to be the cause and author of human evils. (Methodius, *The Banquet of the Ten Virgins*, Discourse 8, ch. 6.)

Methodius was not exaggerating the meaning behind Paul's writings on predestination. Calvin in explaining Paul's writings says Paul means that God predestines all evil—God actually *directs* all evil *thoughts* with its evil *outcome*. God does not merely allow evil to happen by God's permissive will. Calvin insists Paul means God makes all evil happen.[25]

It was not until Luther that predestination resurfaced as a doctrine again. Luther went even farther than Augustine in drawing out Paul's meaning. Luther insisted Paul meant God damns the lost to hell without any free-will opportunity to accept Jesus. He said that Paul's doctrine takes great faith because God "saves so few and

> **God's Will For Lost?**
> "Have I any pleasure in the death of the wicked? sayeth the Lord Yahweh. And not rather that he should return from his way and live?... For I have no pleasure in the death of him that dies, says the Lord Yahweh. Wherefore turn yourselves and live."
> Ezek. 18:23, 32.

24.Appendix B: *How the Canon Was Formed* at page xix.

damns so many" yet we must believe God is "just" despite His own will "makes [the lost] necessarily damnable." (Martin Luther, *Bondage of the Will.*) Even though this makes God abominable, Luther skates the issue by saying "it is not lawful" to ask why God does not "change this fault of will in every man." Thus, Luther thought you proved you had great faith when you could believe Paul is correct that God is still just despite doing something so apparently unjust as damning people while depriving them of the ability of accept Him.

Neither Luther nor Calvin stopped and asked whether Paul could be inspired when Paul ascribes such incongruous impious behavior to God.

Geisler on Calvinist Predestination: "It is theologically inconsistent, philosophically insufficient, and morally repugnant." (Norman Geisler)

More important, the post-apostolic rejection of predestination from 125-325 A.D. proves that the universal church was still following Jesus' words alone. Without naming Paul specifically, they rejected every word of Paul at odds with Jesus. In particular they rejected

25.Calvin, *Institutes of the Christian Religion* Book 1, ch. XVIII. For example, Calvin writes that God "directs [Satan and his angels'] malice to whatever end he pleases, and employs their iniquities to execute his judgments." (*Institutes*, Ch. XVIII, Book 1, No. 1) Calvin says some dishonestly seek to evade this truth by claiming a distinction between God permitting evil and doing evil. But God "himself, however, openly declare[s] that he does this, [and hence God] repudiates the evasion." *Id.* Calvin means that God's word insists He does the evil. He does not merely permit it. Another example is Calvin says: "That men do nothing save at the secret instigation of God, and ***do not discuss and deliberate on anything but what he has previously decreed with himself, and brings to pass by his secret direction***, is proved by numberless clear passages of Scripture." *Id.* Later Calvin, twisting Scripture, insists: "The fiction of bare permission [of evil] is at an end," meaning it is false that God *merely permits* evil rather than directs it. *Id.* It was largely this blasphemous teaching that first led me to ever question the doctrine of the Presbyterian church I attended.

the notion that the lost were damned due to God's predetermined will. Rather, God is not *willing* that any should perish. (John 3:16; *cf.* 2 Peter 3:9.)

Calvin's writings indirectly corroborate Bercot's conclusion. Calvin could not find anyone other than Augustine from the late 300s who agreed with Paul's doctrines. And Augustine's agreement was limited only to Paul's predestination doctrine.

The Patristic Era Also Blasted Paul's Doctrine on Eating Idol Meat

We previously demonstrated that Paul three times expresses complete indifference if a Christian eats meat sacrificed to idols. Paul would prohibit it only being eaten in front of a weaker brother who thinks an idol is something. (Romans 14:21;1 Corinthians 8:4-13, and 1 Corinthians 10:19-29.) (For further discussion, see page 122 *et seq.*)

In the Patristic Era (125-325 A.D.), Paul's teaching was condemned with no thought of even discussing Paul. Irenaeus (120-202 A.D.) wrote in his *Against Heresies*, chapter XXIV, that Saturninus and Basilides were heretics because:

> He attaches no importance to [the question regarding] meats offered in sacrifice to idols, thinks them of no consequence, and ***makes use of them without any hesitation***; he holds also the use of other things, and the practice of every kind of lust, a matter of perfect indifference.

By today's standards, however, Saturninus and Basilides are not heretics on the issue of idol meat. They simply took time to read Paul's words. They got the issue straightened out by Paul's clear permission to eat such meat. However, Irenaeus' view is so clearly opposed to Paul's teaching that it reminds us *how little regard* anyone had for Paul's words back then.

However, the most intriguing quote on this issue is Irenaeus' criticism of Valentinus as a heretic. In book II of *Against Heresies*, chapter XIV, we read:

> Again, their opinion as to the indifference of [***eating of] meats*** and other actions, and as to their thinking that, from the nobility of their nature, ***they can in no degree at all contract pollution, whatever they eat*** or perform, they have derived it from the Cynics, since they do in fact belong to the same society as do these [philosophers]. They also strive to transfer to [the treatment of matters of] faith that ***hair-splitting and subtle mode of handling questions*** which is, in fact, a copying of Aristotle.

Irenaeus precisely condemned the hair-splitting quibbling with God's commands that Paul utilized himself. Paul troubles us with questions such as 'do you think an idol is *really* something?' Can't you eat it 'if you don't believe in idols'? No one back in the Patristic era showed any appreciation for Paul's teaching or methodology in how to interpret God's commands. You did not try to find hair-splitting ways to devise exceptions to commands. You simply obeyed God's word.

What Explains Almost Two Millennia of Ignoring Paul's Teachings?

As demonstrated above at page 425, all the churches founded by the apostles never taught after the apostles had died that salvation was by faith alone without works. Instead, all the apostolic churches taught salvation was by a faith that zealously seeks after God plus works. This formula was not only true in the pre-Roman Catholic era (125-325 A.D.), but in the post-Catholic era from 325 A.D. to the present within the territories that comprised the Roman empire.[26] Likewise, salvation by faith-plus-works based on Jesus' words continued on in the East where the Orthodox church flourished. For fourteen hundred post-apostolic years, no one other than Marcion, the Paulicians, and Pelagius (410 A.D.) taught salvation by faith alone without works.[27] Yet all three were regarded universally by Christendom to be heretics.

Furthermore, for fourteen hundred post-apostolic years no one taught predestination or the bondage of the will except during a small episode where it appears in Augustine's writings from the 300s. Augustine endorsed these doctrines to condemn Pelagius as a heretic. However, Augustine's ideas on predestination and free-will never became official teachings of the Roman Catholic church. Once Pelagius was found a heretic, the issue died off. The Roman church instead always has taught humans have free-will. God foreknows whom He will save, but He does not compel them to believe.[28]

Another example was that in the entire post-apostolic era, no Christian leader ever agreed with Paul's teaching that we could eat meat sacrificed to idols. Paul's indifference on the issue was soundly condemned whenever discussed in the early church.

Thus, between 125 A.D. and 1517 A.D., no church body took Paul seriously. Only Marcion did. Only Pelagius did. Only Augustine did on predestination as a temporary tool to destroy Pelagius. However, Pelagius—a pariah of Reformed theology—not only taught free-will but also Paul's

26. The Roman Catholic Church at the Council of Trent (ca. 1543), in its Sixth Session on Justification, declared as heretical two teachings in particular: (1) that "the sinner is justified by faith alone" (Canon 9) and (2) that "men are justified either by the sole imputation of the justice of Christ or by the sole remission of sins...." (Canon 11.)

doctrine of salvation by faith alone. (See footnote 27 below.) Yet, Pelagius and the Marcionites were expelled from the church in both East and West as heretics!

The Eastern Orthodox Church & Paul

We in the West often ignore there was an older and wider church than Roman Catholicism: the Orthodox. Its view on Pauline doctrine deserves great respect due to its antiquity. This original church is still going strong with ***250***

27. A little known fact about Pelagius is that he taught salvation was by faith alone. In Augustine's attacks on him as a heretic, he focused on Pelagius' belief that human free-will could, in theory, permit one to live a sinless life. Augustine never revealed what truly made Pelagius dangerous. Pelagius was resorting to Marcion's doctrine that Paul taught salvation by faith alone. Zimmer in the modern era discovered a work by Pelagius that was spared destruction. It survived because it was miscatalogued as a work of Jerome. In it, Pelagius defends that free-will allows one to live a sinless life. However, in this same book entitled *Commentary on the Epistle of St. Paul* (410 A.D.), Pelagius is a proponent of salvation by faith alone, without repentance. Pelagius even ridiculed James' doctrines. The *Catholic Encyclopedia* comments on this modern discovery, noting Pelagius taught: "By justification we are indeed cleansed of our personal sins through faith alone (loc. cit., 663, 'per solam fidem justificat Deus impium convertendum'), but this pardon (gratia remissionis) implies no interior renovation of sanctification of the soul." (Zimmer, "Realencyklopädies fur protest," *Theologie* XV, 753 (Leipzig, 1904.) The *Catholic Encyclopedia* comments: "Luther's boast of having been the first to proclaim the doctrine of abiding faith [must be re-evaluated because] Pelagius [earlier] insists expressly (loc. cit. 812), 'Ceterum sine operibus fidei, non legis, mortua est fides.' [transl. "Moreover, without the work of faith, not of law, faith is dead."] Pelagius was making fun of James by twisting his words around to sound Pauline. This raises the question whether Augustine went after Pelagius merely on the issue of capacity of free-will to avoid sin or because Pelagius rejected James' teaching in favor of Paul's on salvation. For more on this, see "Pelagius," *Catholic Encyclopedia*, reprinted at http://www.newadvent.org/cathen/11604a.htm (last visited 2005).

million members. (Protestantism represents, by comparison, only 350 million members worldwide.) We know the Orthodox today in the West as the Eastern Orthodox church.

The Orthodox church has continuously flourished from the first century in Israel, Ethiopia, Egypt, Turkey, Syria, etc. Each national church traces their roots to James as the first bishop of Jerusalem. They insist it was to him alone that the original bishops looked to for guidance. ("Eastern Orthodox Church," *Encarta*.) The Orthodox maintain an unbroken list of bishops in all its original territories (including Rome), tracing back *name-by-name* right down to the period of James and Paul. As Paul says, the Jerusalem church, in those earliest days, was regarded as the "mother of us all." (*Cf.* Gal. 4:21-26.)

But isn't the Roman Catholic Church the original church? No. This is pure myth. The original church was the one founded at Jerusalem and led by James, described in Acts chapter 15. ***Ten years later, Peter went to Rome and founded a church there.*** Peter also had founded a church at Antioch in Syria.[29] Neither the one at Rome nor at Antioch could claim superiority over the other. Each was founded by Peter.

28.In 1520, Luther attacked the doctrine of free-will. Pope Leo X condemned Luther's claims. Erasmus, a Catholic reformer, in 1524 rebutted Luther, pointing out that if man lacks a free-will ability to do good, then God is unjust to condemn man for sin. Luther's response in 1525 was to say that Paul's doctrine of grace excludes any ability of man to contribute *positively* toward his salvation. Otherwise salvation would be by works. However, Luther's response did not address the question posed by Erasmus: how can God condemn the lost if they have no free-will ability to do good? Regardless, this episode demonstrates that Paul's doctrines are used to defend the notion that man lacks free-will to do good. Paul teaches God gives man a will bound to evil unless God 'in His infinite wisdom' having nothing to do with our behavior decides to spare some. God then infuses the few with the will to believe and be saved. *Then, and only then, can man do good.* For Jesus' contrary teaching, see *Jesus' Idea of Faith* at www.jesuswordsonly.com.

29.See discussion of the Jerusalem church at 242, 295, 298, and 304.

Furthermore, prior to the 300s, the bishops throughout the Roman and non-Roman world operated as one inter-connected Christian church. There was no single head except initially James at Jerusalem. In the 300s, the Roman bishop, with the power of the Emperor behind him, began to exert direct control over churches within the Roman territories. This led to the Roman bishop (aka *the pope*) developing doctrines divergent from the bishops outside of Roman territorial control. These Orthodox Christian bishops outside the control of Rome in 1054 excommunicated the bishop of Rome (aka *the pope*). Particularly irksome to the original church of Christ was that the Roman bishop (aka *the pope*) had developed doctrines on purgatory and original sin which the Eastern bishops rejected. However, the grounds of divorce in 1054, also known as the Great Schism, rested upon the fact that the bishop of Rome (aka *the pope*) altered the Nicene Creed. Since then, the bishops outside of Roman influence have called themselves the Orthodox Church. As already noted, we in the West call them and their 250 million members the Eastern Orthodox Church.

What is the Orthodox Church's view on Paul's teachings? Despite Paul's presence in their New Testament canon, the Orthodox church's official salvation doctrine as far back as the post-apostolic records take us (125 A.D.) up through today completely ignores Paul. Not a single doctrine of Paul surfaces in the Orthodox' church doctrine. Not the doctrine of original sin from Romans chapter 5 (which the Orthodox specifically reject). Not predestination of the will. Not total depravity. Not grace alone. Not faith alone. Not one iota of anything uniquely Pauline appears in the official teachings of the Orthodox church from the earliest post-apostolic records to the present. As one Calvinist Reformed writer puts it in his critique of the Eastern Orthodox:

> Eastern Orthodox Christians reject the Reformed [*i.e.*, Pauline] teaching of the natural man's ***bondage of the will*** as well as the ***Doctrines of Grace***. They reject the Reformed view

> of ***Predestination***....They reject the doctrine of ***justification by grace alone through faith alone.*** The Orthodox reject the biblical idea (Romans 5) of ***inherited (imputed) guilt***...Orthodox hold to baptismal regeneration—no one can be saved unless he is baptized with water.[30]

For the Orthodox, only the words of Christ and His twelve apostles have influence over belief and practice. Their foremost creed was the Nicene Creed (325 A.D.). To this day, they insist it is the most accurate summary of the faith of the Church. Yet, this Creed too contains *nothing* uniquely from Paul!

So what does the Eastern Orthodox church teach about salvation? Most succinctly, it teaches you have to stay on the narrow road of following Jesus. This aims at being perfect in conduct, obeying all of Jesus' commands. We will never be perfect while on earth, but starting with baptism and following Jesus we will become more and more like God in perfection. This is called *theosis*. It means becoming like God by imitation, not like God in one's nature. For support, they rely upon Jesus' words: "whoever obeys my teaching should never ever die." (John 8:51.) When one sins, the Orthodox urge repentance and penance. Their doctrines are heavily focused therefore on Jesus' teachings. The Orthodox wholly ignore Paul's unique doctrines.

In fact, perhaps most startlingly of all, the Orthodox have an unbroken string of twenty centuries of ongoing belief in the validity of the true Saturday Sabbath. This is hardly a *Pauline* view. This was the early church's practice as well.[31]

The Orthodox' views on salvation are hard to amalgamate in our way of thinking because of our long conditioning to Paulinism. We need to mull over their ideas. They are calling for an internal transformation, not merely a verbal or

30.http://www.monergism.com/thethreshold/articles/topic (last visited 2004).

internal confession of some *knowledge about Jesus*. When we realize this is their point, it is truly closer to Christ's teaching. It completely ignores the Paulinist-inspired teachings of the Western church that focus on a mental belief change.

Regardless, what cannot be denied is the Orthodox represent a longer tradition than Roman Catholicism. Their doctrines are deeply rooted in the post-apostolic period of 125 A.D. to 325 A.D. Yet, it thoroughly rejects everything that Paul uniquely stands for. Are all 250 million Orthodox Christians lost because they emphasize Jesus' words? Whatever the answer, the history of the Orthodox church proves one thing: Paul early on and a long time thereafter was never taken seriously.

---

31. As one encyclopedia says, the "Eastern Orthodox churches distinguish between 'the sabbath' (Saturday) and 'the Lord's day' (Sunday), and both continue to play a special role for the believers...though the Lord's day with the weekly Liturgy is clearly given more emphasis. Catholics put little emphasis on that distinction and most of them, at least in colloquial language, speak of Sunday as the sabbath." (http://en.wikipedia.org/wiki/Sabbath.) Thus, the Orthodox not only reject all uniquely Pauline teachings, they also reject Paul's fright over the Galatians observing "days" (Sabbath). (Gal.4:10.) Irenaeus (130-202 A.D.) of Lyon, France gave the early rationale at total odds with Paul. "The decalogue [Ten Commandments] however was ***not cancelled by Christ***, but is always in force: men were never released from its commandments." ("Against Heresies," *Anti-Nicene Fathers*, Bk. IV, Ch. XVI, at 480.) He then explains the Sabbath must be kept on Saturday as a sign. This explains why the earliest Christian tradition followed Saturday Sabbath except at Rome and Alexandria. Socrates the Historian (b. 380 A.D.) wrote: "For although ***almost all Churches throughout the world*** celebrate the sacred mysteries [the Lord's Supper] on the Sabbath of every week, yet the Christians of Alexandria and ***Rome***, on account of some ancient tradition, refuse to do this."(Socrates, *Ecclesiastical History*, Bk 5, Ch. 22.289). Likewise Bingham summarizes numerous ancient sources: "The ancient Christians were very careful in the observation of ***Saturday***, or the seventh day... It is plain that all the ***Oriental [Eastern] churches***, and the ***greatest part of the world***, observed the Sabbath as a festival... Athanasius likewise tells us that they held religious assemblies on the Sabbath, not because they were infected with Judaism, but to worship Jesus, the Lord of the Sabbath, Epiphanius says the same." (Joseph Bingham, *Antiquities of the Christian Church* (1878) Vol. II, Bk. xx, Ch. 3, Sec. 1, 66. 1137,1136).

Protestants Agree For 1400 Years No One Had The Correct Salvation Formula

> "The truth of the New Testament church-gathering was lost for 1400 years....Luther, Calvin, and others were used of the Lord to rediscover the truth of salvation by grace at the end of the dark ages."
> *Assembly Messenger*
> Vol. 99, No. 26

Protestant historians agree. For over fourteen centuries after the death of the apostles, the Protestant story agrees that Paul was *never followed* by the *official churches, either East or West*. It was Luther who alone in this period first discovered Paul in what eventually became a large-scale movement. "But when we say Luther 'rediscovered' this [salvation] doctrine, we are implying that the doctrine had been lost or obscured *between the New Testament era and Luther's day*."[32] I will label this the Luther Rediscovery Thesis.

However, in this Luther Rediscovery Thesis, this departure from *true Christianity* includes the *post-apostolic era in both East and West*. This Luther Rediscovery Thesis brands all the churches founded by the twelve apostles as quickly having become heretical. It is not merely the Roman Bishop who strays. Rather, *all* the bishops everywhere ***all simultaneously became heretical***. This has to include what we know today as the Eastern Orthodox who *never* were under the control of the Roman Catholic Church. At the outset, the Orthodox bishops were far more numerous and territorially larger than Roman Catholicism. They grew independent from the bishop of Rome (*i.e.*, whom we today call *pope*). They even later excommunicated the Roman *pope*

32.Sermon, Dr. Michael Haykin, Grace Fellowship Church, Toronto (January 24, 2004), reprinted at http://www.gfcto.com/articles/theology/nof3.htm (last visited 2005.)

in 1054 for his innovations on the apostolic faith. These Orthodox Christians existed in Egypt, Ethiopia, Carthage, Turkey, and numerous other regions of the Middle-East.

Thus, the Luther Rediscovery Thesis insists the Orthodox—although independent from the RCC—departed *simultaneously* into heresy.

The Luther Rediscovery Thesis also teaches the early church leaders in the Western territories between 125-325 A.D. simultaneously turned heretical. This cannot be attributed to Roman Catholic corruption. There was not yet any papacy at Rome that could exert its influence as *binding* over Polycarp, Papias, Irenaeus, Origen, Justin Martyr and many others in the West. These voices are simply students of the apostles, not disciples of the bishop (pope) of Rome. In fact, none of these men knew of a Roman *papacy* as we do today. There were no Roman catechisms to which they had to conform. Such catechisms came much later—after the emperor Constantine (post-325 A.D.) and his successors gave muscle to the words of the bishop of Rome.[33] Thus, the Luther Rediscovery Thesis must also explain how in the Western pre-*papist* Roman church these early leaders from 125-325 A.D. quickly abandoned apostolic teachings if the apostles shared Paul's peculiar doctrines.

33. The first use of the title *pontiff* or *pontifex summus* for the bishop of Rome dates to the Sixth Century. This is recorded in Niermeyer's *Mediae Latinitatis Lexicon Minus,* citing the *Leonine Sacramentary* of the late sixth century. The term *papa* from which *pope* derives in English means *father*. It was used early on of *any* priest. It is impossible to say early on the title *papa* had the connotation we give it today. The notion of superiority of the bishop of Rome, justified on the successor-to-Peter principle, first was asserted in the late half of the second century. However, this attempt was "strongly criticized even by friends of Rome such as Irenaeus of Lyon." (B. Schimmelpfennig, *The Papacy* (New York: Columbia Press, 1992) at 12-14, *viz*, 12-13.) The *papacy* was not recognized until the Fourth Century but only in Roman territories.

In sum, we can see the Luther Rediscovery Thesis has a fatal problem when it comes to the validity of Paul's salvation doctrine. It suffers from the same notion that Marcion had—he claimed that he alone found the true gospel in Paul twenty to eighty years after the Twelve Apostles died.

In response to Marcion, Tertullian in 207 A.D. ridiculed this idea. Tertullian's language is even more apt for the modern claim that the church suffered 1400 years of *error of ignoring Paul* in the early *post-apostolic churches everywhere.* Tertullian skewered Marcion's similar claim, saying:

> [I insist that] no other teaching will have the right of being received as apostolic than that which is at the present day proclaimed in the churches of apostolic foundation. You will, however, find no church of apostolic origin but such as reposes its Christian faith in the Creator [being the same in the Hebrew Scriptures as in the new]. ***But if the churches shall prove to have been corrupt from the beginning, where shall the pure ones be found?*** Will it be amongst the adversaries of the Creator [*i.e.*, Marcion saying the God of the New is not the God of the Old]? Show us, then, one of your churches, ***tracing its descent from an apostle,*** and you will have gained the day. (Tertullian, *Against Marcion*, 1.23.)[34]

The same point holds true here. If one believes the Luther Rediscovery Thesis, one has to believe the very same churches founded by the twelve apostles were corrupt soon after the apostles died, missing out on Paul's teachings. You are being asked to believe this happened simultaneously among diverse churches in diverse locations even though there was no single controlling bishop after 70 A.D. The bishops in the 125-325 A.D. period did not yet know of a superior

34.http://ccel.org/fathers2/ANF-03/anf03-28.htm#P3804_1266834

council that could impose doctrine on everyone simultaneously. Yet, despite this diffuse spread of churches, run by independent bishops, we cannot find a single church tracing to one of the twelve from the Patristic Era who ever espouses Paul's core salvation doctrines. None teach his ideas of predestination. None teach his ideas of total depravity. None teach his ideas of salvation by faith alone. Instead, Paul's doctrines were universally rejected.

Tertullian rightly argues in the case of Marcion that such facts invalidate some *late* discovery previously not taught in any early apostolic church. Here, Paulinists assume there was 1400 years of darkness. Neither Paul's salvation doctrine nor most of his unique doctrines can be found in the apostolic *early church*. Instead, Paul's major doctrines were ignored for 1400 years until Luther 'rediscovered' them. Tertullian's logic is right. It is absurd to believe that the early bishops at diffuse and separate churches which had been founded by the apostles could reject Paul's doctrines unless such rejection was indeed the *orthodox* view of the *original twelve apostles themselves.*

> "Well-meaning congregations and pastors go to great lengths to steer around the teachings of Jesus that are hard to believe."
> John MacArthur (2003)

The lesson for us is we need to ***steer back*** to Jesus' words as the sole test of orthodoxy. If you cannot find justification for a doctrine in Jesus' words or the inspired Scripture that *preceded* Jesus, then you do not have to follow it. If a doctrine is proposed, whether from Paul or anyone else, that does not line up with Jesus' words or the inspired Scripture that preceded Jesus, then it is not possibly a prophetic voice. We must not fall into the same trap the Young Prophet suffered when he trusted the Old Prophet who permitted him to do what God previously prohibited. (1 Kings 13.) We must not elevate such a voice to respect as *inspired.*

17 *Does It Matter If We Rely Only Upon Jesus?*

Two Paths

In our Christian walk, what would be the difference if we had to explain salvation from Jesus' Words Only? Without using Paul? What would we say instead? How does the message change when we add Paul to the mix? If the message *substantially changes*, doesn't this raise the question of why did we ever regard Paul as inspired in the first place?

So what would salvation look like if we had Jesus' Words Alone? Then once we establish Jesus' doctrine, then we were supposed to measure whether Paul *fits* into Jesus' salvation doctrine. (2 John 1:9.) If we cannot fit Paul, we were supposed to eject Paul's words, not Jesus' words, from what we obey.

What Jesus' Words Only Means

If we quote only Jesus, we have to tell people that Jesus explains we are *justified* by repenting from sin. (Parable of the Publican and the Pharisee, Luke 18:10 *et seq*.) We have to explain Jesus gives a simple choice of two roads. You can go to heaven maimed by repenting from sin. Or you can refuse to do so and go to hell whole. (Matthew 5:29; Matthew 18:8; and Mark 9:42-46.)

> **"And if your eye ensnares you, cast it out; it is good for you to enter the kingdom of God with one eye [rather] than having two eyes to be cast into hell (Gehenna)." Mark 9:47**

We can witness to others by memorizing Jesus' steps on how to have eternal life given to the rich young man. (Matthew 19:16-26; Mark 10:17-31; Luke 18:18-26.) Jesus told him to follow the Ten Commandments,[1] deny himself (*viz.*, give away his wealth) and follow Jesus. Our Lord then explains His meaning immediately thereafter. He tells His twelve apostles that if you give up fathers, mothers, and brothers for Him, deny yourself, take up your cross, and "follow Me," you "***shall*** have eternal life." (Matthew 19:27-29.) *See also*, Matthew 10:37-39.

It was as Jesus says elsewhere. Those who are following Him and are losing their life in this world to serve Him do so for "life eternal." (John 12:25-26.)

> "I say unto you, This man went down to his house justified rather than the other. For every one that exalts himself shall be humbled but he who humbles himself shall be exalted (i.e. raised high)."
> Luke 18:14.

However, the young rich man did not respond properly to this invitation. The cost was too high for him. His work worthy of repentance that Jesus required for him to receive eternal life was giving up all his wealth and giving it to the poor. Jesus said *grace was not free*, contrary to what we are so often told. Jesus elsewhere said that you need "to count the cost" of becoming a Christian or otherwise you would not "complete" the course, but fail to continue and be destroyed. (Luke 14:28.) Thus, Jesus taught the rich young man (and ourselves) that *salvation came at a price*—a price the rich young man was unwilling to pay. It is as Jesus says in Luke 13:24: "Strive to enter in by the narrow door: for many, I say unto you, shall seek to enter in, and shall not be able [*i.e.*, lack strength]." Salvation requires a stern repentance from sin that most people *refuse* to entertain. They want eter-

1. When asked again how to have "eternal life" by a teacher of the Law, Jesus likewise told the teacher to obey the Law. (Luke 10:25-37.)

nal life but only if it comes free. Jesus expressly *rejects* such free-grace teaching, regardless of the sincerity of those who insist this doctrine belongs to Christianity.

Jesus told us vividly what the correct response should have been from the rich young man. Jesus tells us that Zaccheus did correctly understand and accept Jesus' gospel. Zaccheus is a model of what a proper response should look like. Zaccheus repents of extortion by paying back fourfold what he stole. He gives the rest of his money to the poor. Then he follows Jesus. After those works worthy of repentance, Jesus responds: "Today salvation has come to this house...." (Luke 19:9.)

Thus, if Jesus' words alone applied, we would boldly tell people that they should follow Zaccheus' example. 'Be a Zaccheus!' we would say. Zaccheus is an actual concrete example of a person whom Jesus said received salvation. What prompted that response from Jesus should be the focus of almost every salvation sermon. Alas! Today Zaccheus is a forgotten man.

If we had Jesus' words alone, what would be the meaning of the salvation promised to the thief on the cross? All the thief says is "Jesus, remember me when thou comest in thy kingdom." (Luke 23:42.) Jesus tells us the thief will be with Him that day in Paradise. Wasn't the thief saved because he "confessed me before men," declaring Jesus was the king—another way of saying He was Messiah?[2] Did not Jesus say that anyone who did this, He would then "confess him before the angels in heaven?" (Luke 12:8.)

Was this a promise of salvation for belief alone? Or is confession a step beyond mere believing? Apostle John gives us the answer in clear *unmistakable terms*. "[E]ven many of

2. The thief no doubt was Jewish and knew the Messianic prophecies. He realized that Jesus was *the king*. The prophesied figure of a king who would rule eternally was identified only one time in Hebrew Scripture as prince *Messiah*. (Dan 9:25-26.) All other references were to a king or ruler whose kingdom was universal and would endure forever. (Gen. 49:27; Numbers 24:16-19; Isaiah 9:6-7.)

the rulers ***believed*** in Him [*i.e.*, Jesus], but because of the Pharisees they were ***not confessing*** [Him] for fear they would be put out of the synagogues." (John 12:42 NASB.) Thus, confession is a courageous step beyond believing. Jesus therefore promised salvation to the thief precisely because the thief took a step beyond mere belief. Faith alone would not have saved the thief any more than it could have the *believing* rulers who were fearful and would not confess Jesus. The thief is in Paradise because he was willing to go further than *faith alone*. The thief *confessed* Jesus in front of those who would likely whip him for standing up for Jesus. Thus, we see *confession* for the thief was a means of "bear[ing] his own cross" and following Jesus despite those risks. (Matthew 19:27-29.) The thief confessed Jesus in the most unfavorable circumstances possible. He also first had to repent from sin. Originally the thief like everyone else was ridiculing Jesus. (Matt. 27:44.)[3] Without this repentance, there would be no confession.

"Neither Calvin nor Luther treated repentance as a condition for eternal salvation. Both stood firmly for ....faith alone."
Zane C. Hodges
Absolutely Free
Chapter Twelve

Without Paul in the mix, we see the thief was saved by something other than mere private mental assent of facts about Jesus. The thief is thus saved precisely because after repenting of sin he made a confession of trust in Jesus *as a king (messiah)* in public before men when the pressure surrounding him was to do otherwise. Jesus tells us this is one path to Him that saves you. (Luke 23:43.) Jesus promises He will "confess" you before the "angels in Heaven" if you "***confess me before men***." (Luke 12:8.) If on

3. As John MacArthur says of the thief: "Repentance wrought a dramatic change in his behavior, and he turned from mocking Christ to defending him." (J. MacArthur, *The Gospel According to Jesus*, *supra*, at 155 n. 1.)

the other hand, you deny Jesus, then Jesus says he will deny you—Luke 12:9, which emphasizes this confession must be *out loud* in a *pressure situation*, not just in your heart.

What does this threat by Jesus to deny those who cowardly deny Him mean? Remember the rulers who "believed" in Jesus but were "***afraid*** to confess" Him? (John 12:42.) They were moral cowards. God tells us the "cowardly" will be thrown in the "lake of burning sulfur" with "unbelievers." (Rev.21:8.) Hence, Jesus' threat to deny those who deny Him was intended to threaten actual *believers*, like the rulers were *believers*, who were "afraid to confess Him." This fact proves conclusively that the thief took a *crucial* step for salvation which belief alone could not provide. For the same reason, the belief alone of the rulers of John 12:42 will not save them. If they remained cowards to the end, God tells us such cowards will be end up in the same place as those who are unbelievers: in hell itself.

Thus, without Paul in the mix, the thief would be the perfect illustration that faith alone cannot save. What saved the thief was precisely going beyond faith and confessing Him (as Messiah-King). This is no easy step, but involves danger, and resisting cowardice. Thus, Jesus' promise to the thief of salvation is the equivalent of Jesus' promise of "eternal life" if you "deny yourself," "take up your cross," and "follow me." (Matthew 19:27-29.) Accordingly, faith alone could not therefore possibly be what saved the thief. ***He had courage, and not just belief***, and thus was saved. By contrast, the rulers in John 12:42 ***had the belief, but not the courage*** to confess Jesus and hence were lost. The cowardly but believing rulers of John 12:42 should remain a constant reminder that faith alone does not save.

Alas, with Paul in the mix, the thief is almost never remembered for anything other than to address the question whether someone is saved without water baptism.[4] And the Paulinists never try to examine how the cowardly but believing rulers of John 12:42 pin-point what saved the thief: his courageous confession.

Furthermore, if we relied upon Jesus' words alone, we would have to tell a prospective Christian whether faithfulness is necessary. We would tell our listener that Jesus assured those who "kept guard" of His word "should never taste death." (John 8:51, ASV.) He promised you "***shall*** be saved" if you "endured to the end." (Matt. 10:22.) *Cfr.* John 3:16 (if continue to believe then "should" be saved.)

In particular, if we trusted in Jesus' words alone, we would have to tell a new Christian it is imperative to be forgiving to others *post-salvation*. Jesus makes our ***post***-salvation forgiveness from God and ultimate salvation expressly conditional on our being forgiving to others. If we refuse subsequently to forgive others, God will revoke our prior forgiveness, and absent repentance, send us to hell.

For example, Jesus told us to pray daily: "Forgive us our debts, **as** we also have forgiven our debtors."(Matt. 6:12.) This makes our request for forgiveness *conditional*. We cannot make an *unconditional plea* for forgiveness that disregards our own failure to forgive.

---

4. The thief's experience is potentially relevant on the issue of baptism. Those who claim baptism is crucial to salvation cite promises of salvation if you are baptized. (Mark 16:16; Acts 2:28, 38; Acts 22:16; and 1 Peter 3:21). However, a promise is not the same as a command to be water baptized as a condition of *all paths of* salvation in Jesus. ***These promises which mention baptism among other conditions contain one element of a sure way to be saved.*** However, what is ignored by baptizers-for-salvation is that Jesus gives us similar promises without the condition of water baptism, such as publicly confessing Him (Luke 12:8). This is precisely what the thief did. ***This is equally a sure way to be saved in Jesus.*** The thief was saved without baptism. There is no valid verse saying *negatively* that whoever is not baptized is lost with the possible exception of John 3:5. It says "no one can enter the kingdom of heaven" unless they are born from Spirit and "water." However, because this does not say "born again" in this verse, it is possible "water" means the birth-waters that a baby passes through. It is plausible two births are envisioned in John 3:5, and thus water baptism is not absolutely crucial for all paths of salvation in Jesus.

Likewise, in Matthew 18:23-35, Jesus tells us that if after we are forgiven a mountain of debt which spares us from prison (hell), if we *later* are unforgiving, then our Master will be "wroth" with us. He will send us to the "jailers." These jailers are at the same prison (hell) we at first avoided by being forgiven all our debt. If you later are unforgiving, Jesus expressly says your forgiveness will be revoked and the jailers will "torment" you until you pay the entire originally forgiven debt of sin. (Matt. 18:28-35.) This means an endless imprisonment. The debt of 10,000 talents at stake in that Parable of the Unmerciful Servant is insurmountable. Hence, Jesus does not portray a Christian who later sins by being unforgiving as someone who is going to heaven. To the contrary, Jesus teaches such a Christian will be separated from God forever. Such a Christian will suffer torment in a prison which in the parable symbolizes Hell.

Furthermore, if we had Jesus' Words alone, we also would tell our friend who accepts Christ that if you deny Christ under pressure, then Jesus promises you Hell. (Luke 12:4-9.) There is no freedom to deny Christ and be faithless, and yet God will forgive you anyway. We would teach this clearly if we only had Jesus' words as the measure of orthodoxy. (Paulinists deny this threat exists for a Christian, citing Paul's assurance to the contrary in 2 Timothy 2:13.)

If we had Jesus' Words alone, we would likewise have to tell our friend that after initial salvation some 'fruit' is necessary. It is not optional, or mere proof of your saved status. John the Baptist calls for "works worthy of repentance" and then adds: "every tree therefore that bringeth not forth good fruit is hewn down, and cast into the fire." (Matt. 3:10.) Later Jesus repeats this statement in the context of warning about false prophets: "Every tree that bringeth not forth good fruit is hewn down, and cast into the fire." (Matt. 7:19.) Jesus promises hell for those who lack good fruit.

In fact, Jesus makes the most explicit link between good works and salvation in John 5:28-29: "Do not be astonished at this; for the hour is coming when all who are in their graves will hear his voice and will come out—those who have ***done good***, to the ***resurrection of life***, and those who have done evil, to the resurrection of condemnation." Gathercole comments on this verse, and acknowledges, as worded it means that "John's Jesus [says]...the criterion for whether one is punished or receives life at the *eschaton* [*i.e.*, the age to come] is the 'doing' of good or evil."[5]

Jesus repeats this principle of the necessity of *fruit* or *works* many other times. For example, in John 15:1-6, Jesus at the Last Supper, after Judas leaves (John 14:7), says "you," the apostles, are "branches" and Jesus is the Vine. They are also reassured that they are all "clean" right now. Then Jesus tells them that a branch that "keeps staying" in Him and produces fruit will be continually "cleaned." *Cf.* Deut. 6:25. This way it bears more fruit. Jesus also warns and encourages them in verses five and six that "a branch in me" that produces ***no fruit*** because it failed to "keep staying" in Jesus, will be thrown "outside" the vineyard. It is as a branch that died ("dried up"). It is gathered up into the "fire and is burned."

If our friend knows of Paul, he may not listen to Jesus' words alone from the Metaphor of the Vine which requires *works* after initial salvation. Perhaps you need to quote another passage of Jesus. In the Parable of the Unprof-

5. Simon J. Gathercole, *Where Is Boasting: Early Jewish Soteriology and Paul's Response in Romans 1-5*. (Eerdmans 2002) at 114. However, Gathercole claims that John's Jesus does not equate "doing good" with "obeying Torah" because of Jesus' answer in John 6:26-29. (*Id.*) However, Gathercole is relying on a Pauline translation of that passage, as explained at Footnote No. 15 on page 254. In fact, it stretches all credulity to think in John 5:28-29 that Jesus means by "good works" simply "belief" in Himself. To even suggest this is just another example of the Pauline mantra in contemporary Christian commentary that overshadows the literal meanings of Jesus. If Jesus had in mind those who had *belief* alone were raised, then Jesus should not have had in counterpoise that the condemned were those who have 'done evil.' He should have said those who 'did not believe' rise to condemnation. Jesus' words were well chosen to say salvation depends also upon doing good.

itable Servant, Jesus reiterates the point. Three servants are each given money — one talent, two talents, and five talents respectively. The servant given one talent hides it. The other two servants produce fruit with the money given them. When the master comes back and sees the servant given one talent still has only one talent, this servant is thrown *outside* in outer darkness. The unproductive servant suffers there weeping and gnashing of teeth. Only the two other productive servants are saved. In Matt. 25:14 *et seq*., Jesus says of the unproductive servant: "now throw this unprofitable servant into ***outer darkness*** where there will be weeping and gnashing of teeth." (Matt. 25:30, KJV).[6]

If our friend still balks at listening to Jesus alone on faith and works, we can further cement the point with the Parable of the Sower. In this parable, only the fourth seed is saved. The second seed "*believes* for a while," sprouts, but in time of temptation falls away and dies. (Luke 8:13.) The third goes further, grows substantially but is then choked by thorns—by the pleasures and riches of this life. As a result, the third seed never brings any fruit to completion. (Luke 8:14.) The fourth seed is sewn into good ground. It alone produces to the end. (Luke 8:15.) It alone is saved. Thus, Jesus again taught faith without bringing your fruit to completion does not save. Jesus expressly taught faith alone does not save. When faith is destroyed by sin, such faith is dead. Faith plus endurance in producing fruit saves, our Lord insists.[7]

---

6. Some Paulinists admit if the two productive servants are believers, there is no textual reason to believe the third servant is not a believer. (Dillow, *Reign of the Servant Kings*, *supra*, at 355.) Other Paulinists use circular logic to deny the servant with one talent was ever a saved Christian. Since he was evidently lost due to lacking works, they insist he could never have been a Christian. Yet that presupposes the very issue at stake—the validity of Paul's contrary teaching of *faith alone*.

7. For a full discussion on the Parable of the Sower, see "What The Parable of the Sower Confirms About Faith in John's Gospel" on page 171 *et seq*.

Yet, if our friend still needs convincing what Jesus says about *works*, then cite him to Jesus' Parable of the Sheep and the Goats. (Matt. 25:32 *et seq*.) Both the sheep and goats call Jesus Lord. One group serves Jesus by feeding the brethren in need, clothing them, and giving them water. The sheep in essence give charity. The other group who calls Jesus Lord fails to give any charity. Jesus calls them the goats. On Judgment Day, Jesus says he will separate the sheep from the goats. He will send the sheep to heaven but the goats to "eternal fire." It is as James says, the one who has "faith alone," lacking works of charity of feeding the brethren and giving them clothes, food, and drink, has a faith that is "dead" and "cannot save." (James 2:14-17.) As Gathercole concedes, Jesus in Matthew 25:31-46 says "***deeds*** of hospitality...are ***certainly*** the criterion for judgment."[8]

If we had Jesus' words alone, then we would have seen the identical message of faith plus works appears in the Metaphor of the Vine, the Parable of the Unprofitable Servant, the Parable of the Sower, and the Parable of the Sheep and the Goats. The productivity that Jesus implores is not optional. It is not forensic proof of some already sufficient status of being saved. Instead, if we rely on Jesus' words alone, we need to tell our friend that Jesus says productivity is ***essential*** to avoid becoming spiritually "dried up" (dead). It is ***vital*** to avoid being thrown "in outer darkness" and "outside" to be "burned." Otherwise, we will suffer "weeping and gnashing of teeth" in "eternal fire." As Jesus said, "every tree that does not bear good fruit...is cast into the fire." (Matt. 7:19.) Jesus also added that only those who have "done good" will rise to eternal life while those who have "done evil" will rise to condemnation. (John 5:28-29.) If we had Jesus' Words Only, the addition of "good fruit" (works) to faith as an *absolute condition* for salvation would never have caused a controversy at all.

---

8. Simon J. Gathercole, *Where Is Boasting: Early Jewish Soteriology and Paul's Response in Romans 1-5* (Eerdmans: 2002) at 113.

It is as Jesus says in a proper translation of Luke 13:24. Jesus literally says: "use all your strength [*agonizomai*] to be entering into the cramped door which, I tell you, [many] shall be seeking to enter [it] but they shall not *be having strength* [to do so]."[9] Jesus' words meant many will be fighting to enter because of the cramped nature of the doorway itself. But only those who strive with all their might, and are strong enough, can enter. Jesus portrays salvation as something you must use all your strength to obtain.

Yet, we must not forget that in the Metaphor of the Vine, Jesus taught that "staying in me" was the crucial means of having vital strength. The way to avoid sin that destroys the faith of the second seed in the Parable of the Sower is to "keep holding to the Root." The key is to pray every day Father "lead us from temptation." (Matt. 6:13.) We must *pray* for the strength to enter the kingdom. However, absent such strength, we will not be strong enough to enter the kingdom. The spiritually weak—those who do not pray to resist temptation—will not be able to enter. Christians whose prayer life

9. Because this runs afoul of Paulinism, this verse is often translated in a tepid manner. Yet, commentators acknowledge the true meaning. For example, Barnes agrees *agonazai* in Greek "literally [means] agonize," not *strive,* which is the common translation. (KJV.) Barnes likewise acknowledges in context it means to be "diligent...to overcome our sinful propensities." Thus, Jesus means to say salvation depends on our effort to avoid sin. Jesus thereby exhorts us in the strongest possible terms *to believe this.* In Greek, the gate here is not the same gate as in Matthew 7:13 where Jesus talks of the narrow and wide gait. Robertson explains that in Matthew 7:13, the gait is *puls*, an outside gate, while in Luke 13:24, it is *thurast*, the door to enter a house. This is important, for the emphasis here is on the *cramped* nature of the gate to enter the house. Finally, the last part of the sentence is also normally translated very tepidly. Jesus supposedly warns some "will not be able" to enter. (KJV.) However, the Greek word emphasizes they "lack being strong." The Greek word is *icxycoycin.* John 21:6 uses the same word to say the apostles were "not strong enough" to draw the net with the miraculous catch of fish. In Luke 13:24, Jesus is re-emphasizing His point that our salvation depends on our strength. Of course, that strength comes through prayer from God. Yet, Jesus intends His exhortation to stimulate such prayer.

dies, and they succumb to sin, Jesus teaches that they will not have the strength to enter the kingdom. Faith must add works or it dies and you lack the strength to enter the kingdom. Thus, Jesus exhorts we agonize to enter into salvation—we use the very last ounce of strength that an athlete uses to finish a race—or otherwise you can expect on being in the fiery furnace forever.

Paul's Different Message

However, if we preach Paul's message, we have only one simple formula to explain. Simply say with your mouth Jesus is Lord and believe "in your heart" that He rose from the dead. If you do so, then you are saved. (Romans 10:9.) It is belief plus nothing, as some say. In fact, as Paulinists explain, Paul does not mean you exert even the effort to say Jesus is Lord. Rather, the Holy Spirit entered you first and caused the words to come forth. *See* 1 Cor. 12:3 ("no man can say, Jesus is Lord, but in the Holy Spirit"). Thus, it was the *belief* given by the Holy Spirit alone that saved you. Paulinists teach salvation never depends on anything you do or initiate.

It is impossible to deny Paul teaches belief-plus-nothing saves you. And Paul teaches this belief is itself *supernaturally bestowed* with no effort on your part to even believe. When all of Paul's teachings are cross-analyzed, Paul certainly teaches salvation is a free gift at every point. (Eph. 2:8-9; Romans 4:4.) Paul teaches that if any effort beyond changing belief is required for salvation, then salvation is by works. (Rom. 4:4-6.)

This leads to a stark contradiction of Jesus. For example, if we teach repentance from sin as a condition of salvation, as Jesus in Mark 9:42-48 makes indispensable, then it is salvation by works. Based on Paul's teaching against works, the *Ryrie Study Bible* says repentance from sin is "a false addition to faith" when added as a condition of salvation.[10]

Likewise, Dr. Bob Wilkin says Paul's teaching on grace and works makes "appalling" any idea that we need to obey the repentance-from-sin principle to enter heaven. Wilkin explains how contrary Paul's teachings are to that principle: "It is gibberish to speak of a free gift which costs us everything."[11] Wilkin further cements unwittingly the stark contrast between Paul's doctrines and Jesus' teaching in Mark 9:42-48. Wilkin says a promise of heaven based on repentance from sin is a gospel "not [based upon] a free gift. It is an earned wage." (*Id.*) Exactly! As Bonhoeffer explained in the *Cost of Discipleship* (1937), Jesus said grace is costly. Paul has a different message that grace is free!

We have reached the amazing situation where R.C.Sproul can declare that "faith alone" is all there is to justification. If you reject it, you are apostate and unsaved. (R.C. Sproul, *Faith Alone: The Evangelical Doctrine of Justification* (Grand Rapids: Baker, 1995).) Any church or person that adds any requirement besides faith as a condition for salvation is lost and apostate. By Sproul's definition, Jesus is lost and apostate!

There is no doubt Jesus made repentance from sin an indispensable condition of salvation. Jesus said believers in Him must be careful not to be ensnared by sin. They must realize they can go to heaven maimed by repenting from sin. Or, if they refuse to do so, they will go to hell whole. (Matthew 5:29, Matthew 18:8, and Mark 9:42-48.) This is no doubt why Jesus warned that the road to life is "hard" and "few" find it. (Matt. 7:13, 14.) Jesus exhorts you "strive" and in Greek *agonazai*—use your very last ounce of strength you have—to enter the way that leads to life. (Luke 13:24.) With Paul in the mix, salvation relies on the *easy* step of *belief*

10.Charles Ryrie, *The Ryrie Study Bible* (Chicago: Moody Press, 1976) at 1950.

11.Dr. Bob Wilkin, *Repentance and Salvation:A Key Gospel Issue* (1988) (reprinted at http://www.faithalone.org/news/y1988/88june4.html).

alone. You never *strive* to enter into salvation. It does not depend on how much strength (*e.g.*, your prayer-life) you have. Jesus and Paul are at *total odds*.

Don't Paul & Jesus Agree on Confession with the Mouth?

What do Paulinists say about *confession of Jesus* before men? As noted earlier, Jesus promised this was one way to become saved. (Luke 12:8.) But verbal confession is more than belief (John 12:42, rulers believed but would not confess), and hence a work in the Pauline sense. What would Paulinists say about that path to salvation?

Paul in his famous *dictum* on how to be saved in Romans 10:9 said one part is "saying with the mouth" that Jesus is Lord. This appears to be an *action* beyond mere belief which even Paul endorsed. However, Paulinists stress Paul's other salvation formulas that eschew any kind of *work* as necessary for salvation. Thus, most Paulinists also dispense with *confession* with the mouth as a step in salvation. If confession were necessary in any formula, the Paulinist insists Paul would be contradicting his own teaching against *works* in Ephesians 2:8-9. In other words, the *public confession* of Jesus as Lord, if necessary for salvation, would be a work, mainstream Paulinists insist. Thus Dr. Bob Wilkin says Paul teaches against the idea that public confession is a step in any formula for salvation. He bases this upon Ephesians 2:8-9 and Romans 4:4. If a public confession were really necessary, Dr. Wilkin says such an idea "results in works salvation."[12] To keep Paul squared with Paul, Dr. Wilkin says public *confession* is the fruit of faith. *Public confession* is not what saves you despite Paul saying this is so in Romans 10:9.[13]

Yet, Jesus promised a public confession of Him "before men" would be matched by His confession of you before the Father. You will be treated like the thief on the cross. If you died that same day as your confession "before men," Jesus would promise you salvation just like He gave the thief on the cross. Jesus gave no mixed messages that a silent confession of *belief* alone had the same promise of salvation. (Luke 12:8.) Jesus told us plain and clear that confession with the mouth "before men" was one path to salvation. Jesus never cast that principle in doubt by excoriating anyone who would add *any kind action* to any salvation formula.

When previously we compared Jesus' and Paul's main salvation message, they were at direct odds at so many points. However, even when they appear consistent such as on the confession issue (Luke 12:8; Romans 10:9), the Paulinists dodge even drawing a parallel. They insist upon re-reading Paul to not line up with Jesus. They re-interpret Paul to match Paul's *faith alone* statements in Eph. 2:8-9 and Romans 4:4. They do not acknowledge that *confession with the mouth*—a clear *action*—is a necessary step to Paul's formula in Romans 10:9, even though Paul says so in this verse.

12.Bob Wilkin, *Is Confessing Christ a Condition of Salvation?* (1994) (reprinted online at http://www.faithalone.org/news/y1994/94july3.html). Ironically, Wilkin says "[s]ince the Bible [*i.e.*, Paul] is clear that eternal salvation is a free gift and that it is not of works..., this passage [*i.e.*, from Luke 12:8, 'confess me before men, and I will confess before the Father'] ***cannot be dealing with the Gospel***." Jesus' words are thereby nullified based on Paul! Wilkin is the author of such works as *Confident in Christ*. He is also the head of the Grace Evangelical Society.

13.The word translated *confess* that Paul uses is *homologeo.* (It is the same word used in Luke 12:8.) It means *to have the same word* or *agree*. Paul then says this must be in your *stoma*. This means *mouth.* Thus, in context Paul is saying *agreement with your mouth* has a promise of salvation if combined with a subjective belief in the resurrection. If an *agreement with the mouth* is truly part of the formula, then how is salvation by *faith* (belief), *not works*? (Eph. 2:8-9.) They are inconsistent. This is why most Paulinists re-read Paul in Romans 10:9 to mean *believe in your heart* Jesus is Lord. Then they see the fruit of this will be *public confession.* Thus, when you first believed in your heart, you were instantaneously saved without the *work* of a confession in public. (See prior footnote.) Thus, if you pay close attention to Paul's formulas, he is not always consistent.

Yet, it is not their fault: Paul does utter self-contradictory statements that undermine the very formula for salvation he gave in Romans 10:9. Paul's self-contradictions thus make it always impossible to line up Paul with Jesus even when Paul says the very same thing as Jesus.

What About John 3:16?

Picking just one verse from Jesus that sounds Pauline (*i.e.*, John 3:16) is not a solution. The verb tense for *believes* in John 3:16 has indeed been translated to sound Pauline. In the original Greek, it means something not only quite different, but also actually the opposite of how it reads in the KJV and NIV. It should read: "He who *continues to believe/trust* should have eternal life." This is the true meaning of the underlying Greek verbs. (See Appendix A: *Greek Issues*.) Faithfulness, not one moment of faith, is what *should* save.

Therefore, we have a choice to make. We can explain salvation based on Jesus' Words Only. Or we can use Paul's words. They are two radically different messages.

Andreas Rudolf Borenstein von Carlstadt (1480-1541). Co-leader of Reformation with Luther. Believed Jesus' words in Gospels more important than epistles for formulating doctrine.

TABLE 10. Salvation Checklist — Jesus versus Paul

Jesus	Paul
The one who repents from sin is "justified." (Parable of the Publican and the Pharisee. Luke 18:10-14.) Th son who was dead but now repents is "alive again" (born again). (Parable of the Prodigal Son, Luke 15:1-32, *viz.* v. 24.)	One is not justified nor born again by repentance from sin, but by faith alone. (Eph. 2:8-9; Rom. 4:4.) Any such addition to Paul's salvation by faith alone doctrine is the heresy of "works salvation." (Wilkin, Stanley, Hodge.)
The one who relies upon God's election to salvation and does not repent goes home unjustified. (Parable of the Publican and the Pharisee. Luke 18:10-14.)	The one who relies upon God's election alone for salvation is relying on the right thing. (Rom. 8:33.) God elects you to salvation by means of predestination, and hence without any work on your part. Faith is given to you as part of God's work in you. (Phil 1:6) (Wilkin, Stanley.)
To have eternal life, follow the Ten Commandments, deny yourself (*i.e.*, repent and do works worthy of repentance) and then follow Jesus. If you give up fathers, mothers, and brothers for Jesus, deny yourself, take up your cross, and "follow Me," you "shall have eternal life." (Matthew 19:27-29; Matthew 10:37-39; John 12:25-26.)	To have eternal life, say with your mouth that Jesus is Lord and believe He is resurrected. (Rom. 10:9.) Do not add any work. "Now to him that worketh, the reward is not reckoned as of grace, but as of debt."(Rom. 4:4.) If salvation depends on keeping the Law, then salvation by faith is made void. "[I]f they that are of the law are heirs, faith is made void..." (Rom.4:14.)
A Christian will go to hell if they deny Christ under pressure. (Luke 12:4-9.)	If we deny Jesus, He will deny us, but in the end God will still accept us because He cannot deny Himself. (Stanley.) Paul says: "if we shall deny him, he also will deny us: if we are faithless, he abideth faithful; for He cannot deny himself." (2 Tim. 2:12-13.)

TABLE 10. Salvation Checklist — Jesus versus Paul

Jesus	Paul
As part of an answer on how to have eternal life, Jesus tells a rich man to repent by giving his wealth to the poor. The man is grieved. (Matthew 19:16-26; Mark 10:17-31; Luke 18:18-26.) Jesus tells another rich man who repents and repays those he stole from that "Today salvation has come to this house...." (Luke 19:9.)	Salvation could not possibly depend on any works of repentance. Salvation is by faith alone. (Eph.2:8-9; Rom. 4:4.)
The thief on the cross, in front of a crowd hostile to Jesus, says: "Jesus, remember me when thou comest in thy kingdom."(Luke 23:42.) Jesus had said that if you "confess me before men" then he will confess you before the angels in Heaven. (Luke 12:8.) Jesus thus tells the thief "this day you will be with me in Paradise."	Salvation could never depend on a confession of Jesus before men. If it was a means of salvation, this would be works righteousness. Instead, even though Paul said that if you "say Jesus is Lord with your mouth" and believe He was resurrected, then you shall be saved (Rom. 10:9), faith is all you need to be saved. (Rom. 4:4.) Paul must mean that such confession will flow naturally from faith rather than salvation is produced by a public confession. (Wilkin.)
Salvation is based on God forgiving your sin. If you do not forgive others after you receive forgiveness, God will revoke your forgiveness and send you to hell to be tormented. (Matt. 18:28-35; *cf.* Matt. 6:12.)	Salvation is not contingent on your forgiving others. Salvation only has one condition: a one-time faith. (Romans 4:4.) If you ever once had faith (Romans 10:9), you are no longer able to be condemned. (Romans 8:1.)

TABLE 10. **Salvation Checklist — Jesus versus Paul**

Jesus	Paul
Jesus promised those who "kept guard" of His word "should never taste death." (John 8:51.) "He who continues to trust/believe should be saved." (John 3:16.) He who continues to "disobey" the Son continues to be under God's wrath. (John 3:36.)	There is no endurance in any action required. Only a one-time faith is necessary for salvation. (Romans 4:4.) One could fail to keep and guard Jesus' word and still be saved because one is eternally secure based on a one-time faith. (Romans 8:1, 10:9.)
Jesus said "a branch in me" that produces no fruit because it failed to keep staying "in me" will be thrown "outside" the vineyard. It is as a branch that died (dried up). It is gathered up into the fire and is burned. (John 15:1-6.)	If fruit or works were necessary to avoid being thrown outside God's vineyard, becoming dead and then being burned in hell, it would be a salvation by works. Instead, salvation is by faith without any works. (Romans 4:4, 14; Eph. 2:8-9.)
A servant of Jesus who produces no fruit is useless, and he will be "thrown...into outer darkness where there will be weeping and gnashing of teeth." (Matt. 25:14 *et seq.*) This place of weeping and gnashing is the "fiery furnace." (Matt. 13:42, 50.)	If fruit or works were necessary to avoid being thrown outside and be burned in hell where there is weeping and gnashing, it would be a salvation by works. Instead, salvation is by faith without any works. (Romans 4:4, 14; Eph. 2:8-9.)
If you receive the word with joy and "believe for a while," but in time of temptation, you fall away, you are lost. If you are choked by the pleasures of this world, and bring no fruit to completion, you are lost. If on the other hand, you bring forth fruit to the end, in patient endurance, you will be saved. (Luke 8:13-15.) You "shall be saved" if you "endured to the end." (Matt. 10:22.)	If you receive the word with joy and believe for a while, you are eternally saved. (Romans 8:1; 10:9.) Salvation cannot depend on you or anything you do thereafter. Otherwise, it is salvation by works. (Romans 4:4, 14; Eph. 2:8-9.) Thus, if you fall away or are choked with the pleasures of this life and have no fruit, you are still saved. There is no need to endure in faith as long as you believed once.

TABLE 10. Salvation Checklist — Jesus versus Paul

Jesus	Paul
Among the sheep and goats who both call Jesus Lord, the group who serves Jesus by feeding the brethren in need, clothing them, and giving them water, goes to heaven. The other group who calls Jesus Lord but who fails to provide such charity are, as a consequence, sent to "eternal fire." (Parable of the Sheep and the Goats. Matt. 25:32 et seq.). A faith that ignores the poor brethren is "dead" and "cannot save." (James 2:14-17.) "Every tree therefore that bringeth not forth good fruit is hewn down, and cast into the fire." (Matt. 7:19.)	Anyone who "shall call" on the name of the Lord shall be saved. (Romans 10:13.) This is permanent, and no condition subsequent can be put on this that you must be charitable or have fruit thereafter. Otherwise, it is salvation by works. (Romans 4:4, 14; Eph. 2:8-9.) Hence, it cannot be true that if the goats, in fact, ever once called on the name of the Lord that they should be sent to hell. James' statement that paraphrases the principle of Matthew 25:32 *et seq.* contradicts Paul, and we are not to believe even an angel from heaven if he should contradict Paul. (Gal. 1:8.)
"I keep telling you the one who keeps on listening to my teaching and keeps on believing in the one who sent me keeps on having eternal life and does not come into condemnation but has departed out of death into life." (John 5:24.) For the basis to this translation, see pages 167-70.	Once in Christ, there is now no condemnation. This entry is by a one-time faith. (Rom. 10:9). As a result, freedom from condemnation is not secured by any continuity in listening to Jesus' teaching or believing in God-the-Father.

Faith in the Pauline Sense?

When you abandon column one—the words of the historical Jesus—and replace His teaching with column two—the words of Paul, you have a radical separation. Yet, the one following Paul is told they are following Jesus. They label themselves a Christian. They claim they trust in Christ, and are saved. Yet, they are not following the words of Jesus Christ on *how to be saved.* Then precisely what are they doing when they follow Paul? They are following an abstract idea of what they want Jesus to be for them without a willingness to actually accept Jesus' commands and teachings. John Sobrino explains that the question comes down to:

> whether this Spirit is the Spirit of Jesus or some vague, ***abstract Spirit*** that is nothing more than the sublimated embodiment of the ***natural 'religious' person's desires and yearnings***. If it is the latter, then it is not only different from, but actually contrary to, the Spirit of Jesus.[14]

Thus, if people are asked to "accept Christ" without being told about the message of the historical Christ, how can we be sure that "Christ" is not just an abstract symbol for them? We cannot. It is a situation reminiscent of what Jesus said was happening with the Pharisees and their followers.

> (13) But woe unto you, scribes and Pharisees, hypocrites! because ye shut the kingdom of heaven against men: for ye enter not in yourselves, neither suffer ye them that are entering in to enter. (15) Woe unto you, scribes and Pharisees, hypocrites! for ye compass sea and land to make one proselyte; and when he is become so, ***ye make him twofold more a son of hell than yourselves***. (Mat 23:13, 15)(ASV)

The Pharisees were highly evangelistic. Jesus said *do not mistake this as proof they are from God.* They were blind guides. People wanted to enter the kingdom, and the Pharisees were abroad evangelizing them. Yet, the Pharisees had a false teaching that made their proselytes not enter the kingdom of God.

What did Jesus say they were falsely teaching? Jesus said the Law has two components: the weighty and less weighty. The Pharisees focused on the easy stuff. They ignored preaching the *hard stuff from the Law.* Jesus said:

14. John Sobrino, *Christology at the Crossroads* (Orbis Books: 1982) at 384.

> Woe unto you, scribes and Pharisees, hypocrites! for ye tithe mint and anise and cummin, and have ***left undone the weightier matters of the Law***, justice, and mercy, and faith: but these ye ought to have done, and ***not to have left the other undone***. (Matt. 23:23)(ASV)

The modern Pauline pastor leaves out all the *hard commands* of the Law and of Jesus, just like the Pharisees left out all the *hard commands* of the Law. Instead, the Pharisees watered down the Law to the simple stuff. Jesus was very serious about the *Law* being followed *in toto,* and called them blind guides. We have followed Paul, and stripped all the *Law* away. Paul's solution was to leave both the weighty and less weighty matters undone, replaced by the principle that "all things are lawful, but not all things are expedient."[15] No one can say this was Jesus' message. With Paul's doctrines predominating, we have reduced everything down to faith, and left the Law, justice and mercy undone. (We have retained only tithing, thus repeating virtually identically the error of the Pharisees.)[16] When those are removed, one may legitimately question whether we have even done *faith* justice.

Jesus has a warning for those who teach Paul's contrary message to what Jesus taught:

> Ye serpents, ye offspring of vipers, how shall ye escape the judgment of hell? (Mat 23:33)(ASV)

15. See "The New Morality In Its Place" on page 80 *et seq.*

16. Ironically, most Paulinist churches revive one command from the 'Old Testament'—the duty to tithe. This is the only command from the 'Old Testament' that supposedly was not abrogated. (Randy Alcorn, *Money, Possessions & Eternity* (Wheaton, Illinois: Tyndale, 2003) at 174-75, 181.) Thus, we repeat the same error as the Pharisees: we are big on tithing, but not on the *weightier matters of the Law.* This is why you will most often hear the Pharisees' wrong doctrine miscategorized as if they taught a strict adherence to *all* the Law. The commentators must distort the description of the Pharisees' error. Otherwise, Jesus would be pointing the finger of condemnation at us because we similarly reduced the Law down to tithing.

Historical Note: JWO Spurred The Reformation
Or Who Was Carlstadt & The Evangelical Brotherhood?

Carlstadt and Luther were co-lecturers at the same university. Together they launched the Protestant Reformation between 1516-1521.

A forgotten fact is the Reformation really gained momentum under Carlstadt during 1521-1522. In this period, Luther was hidden in a tower for his safety. Luther's words at the Diet of Worms were feared to make him a target of assassins. "During [Luther's] absence Professor Andreas von Carlstadt assumed leadership of the Protestant movement in Wittenberg."[17] This means the Reformation gained its early momentum largely *without* Luther's direct involvement.

By 1524, the Evangelical Brotherhood (aka "the Brethren") movement grew to the size of 250,000 people. (Schaf.) They had a Jesus' Words Only focus. They relied primarily upon Carlstadt's focus on the Lord Jesus' doctrine.

Carlstadt insisted that the Gospels about Jesus were more important than the epistles (of Paul). Carlstadt rebuffed Luther on the alleged invalidity of James' Epistle. Carlstadt argued James' Epistle cannot be shuffled aside for teaching faith and works at odds with Paul. (See page 470.) Carlstadt also insisted that Jesus reaffirmed continuation of the Law of Moses, even while Luther insisted that Paul abrogated the Law. (See page 74.) Carlstadt taught Jesus wanted the less weighty and weightier matters of the Law to be followed.[18]

How could Carlstadt insist the Law of Moses was still valid? ***Because Carlstadt had a different view of Paul's Epistles when compared to the Gospels***. As Durant notes:

17.Ross Vander Meulen, *Essay on Revolution 'The College's Role in Revolution*, talk given at Knox College's Opening Convocation on September 7, 1972, reprinted at http://www.knox.edu/x5040.xml.

> Later in the same year [1520] Carlstadt issued a little book—*De Canonicis Scripturis Libellus*— ***exalting*** the Bible over popes, councils and traditions, and ***the Gospels over Epistles***. If Luther had followed this last line, ***Protestantism might have been less Pauline***, Augustinian, and Predestinarian.[19]

Luther and Carlstadt became embittered over James' Epistle. Luther wanted the Epistle of James removed from inspired canon because it conflicted with Paul. (See page 247.) However, Carlstadt insisted that one cannot toss out James, as Luther had done, by relying upon Paul's doctrines as the criteria to determine valid canon.

> [A]s early as 1520, Luther's Wittenberg University co-reformer Bodenstein von Carlstadt...***condemned Luther's rejection of James*** and argued that one must ***appeal*** either ***to known apostolic authorship*** or to universal historical acceptance (omnium consensus) as the test of a ***book's canonicity***, not to ***internal doctrinal considerations [of a conflict with Paul]***. (Carlstadt, *De canonicis,Scripturis libellus* (Wittenberg. 1520) para, 50.)[20]

Carlstadt was saying Paul's words were not a permissible basis to close off James' words. Carlstadt resisted Paul's doctrines being used to test what is canon.

In response, Luther from his place of hiding tried demanding his old allies push out Carlstadt. The rift on the Law, James and Paul was too much. In 1521, Luther wrote a savage attack on Carlstadt entitled *The New Judas*.

---

18. Dr. Barnas Spears summarizes in *Life of Luther* (Philadelphia: 1850) at 401: "Carlstadt differed essentially from Luther in regard to the use to be made of the Old Testament. ***With him, the law of Moses was still binding***. Luther, on the contrary, had a strong aversion to what he calls a legal and Judaizing religion. Carlstadt held to the ***divine authority of the Sabbath*** from the Old Testament; Luther believed Christians were free to observe any day as a Sabbath, provided they be uniform in observing it."
19. Wil Durant, *The Reformation* (N.Y.: Simon & Schuster, 1944) at 352.
20. John Warwick Montgomery, "Lessons from Luther on the Inerrancy of Holy Writ," *God's Inerrant Word* (1974), reprinted online at http://www.mtio.com/articles/bissar37.htm.

By 1524, Luther still had not won his battle among Protestants against Carlstadt. So in 1524, Luther wrote a new pamphlet in which he strongly declared agreement with the Catholic doctrine of trans-substantiation. Luther vehemently attacked Carlstadt's position that communion was symbolic. Luther retreated from his own prior views which had said the same thing as Carlstadt about communion. Now Luther insisted, instead, that "the body of Christ... is really and substantially present in, with and under the Supper...."[21]

Why did Luther change his position on trans-substantiation and attack his old ally Carlstadt? When Luther returned from the Tower in Thuringia, Carlstadt had more followers than Luther. This apparently further embittered Luther:

> The work which he [Luther] wrote against him [Carlstadt], he entitled, 'The Book against the Celestial Prophets.' This was uncandid; for the controversy related chiefly to the ***sacrament of the supper***. In the south of Germany and in Switzerland, ***Carlstadt found more adherents than Luther.*** (Dr. Barnas Spears, *Life of Luther* (Philadelphia: 1850) at 403.)

Yet, due to Luther's pamphlets, in 1524 Carlstadt was expelled from Saxony. "[H]e [Carlstadt] was crushed by the civil power, which was on the side of Luther." (*Id.* at 400.)

Then what was Luther to do about the 250,000 Protestants who were influenced by Carlstadt's Jesus-focused doctrine? The Brethren were willing to sacrifice home and comfort to fight for religious freedom. They wanted to obey Jesus' words in all things. They did not want to pay taxes to the Catholic church any longer. It was morally offensive. They wanted to operate their own churches. (Scaff, *History of*

21."The Eucharist," *International Standard Bible Encyclopedia* reprinted online at http://bibletools.org/index.cfm/fuseaction/Def.show/RTD/ISBE/ID/5577

the Reformation, Vol. 7; Bax, *The Peasant War*, ch. 3.) Yet, they were unaware that their emphasis on the Jesus-focused doctrines taught by Carlstadt would bring them into conflict with Luther.

In 1524, Luther published a tract which told Catholic rulers to kill the Brethren as 'dogs' because they violated Paul's directive to obey rulers as God's ministers (in Romans 13:1 *et seq*.) Yet, the Brethren were all Protestants! With Luther's blessings, 100,000 of them (with women and children in significant numbers) were brutally slain in 1524-25. (Scaff.) Luther rationalized this result based on Paul, claiming "God has forbidden insurrection...."[22] But was paying tithes to a deficient church system the better choice? When faced with a force holding a civil power urging a contrary principle to God's law, Peter and the apostles said "we ought to obey God rather than men."(Acts 5:29.)

Thus, while no one can say every member of the Evangelical Brotherhood was pure, at least the cause they died for is still not lost. Their cause was the cause of Christ. The cause of the early Reformation. The cause Carlstadt was persecuted for defending. It was the cause that said Jesus' words in the Gospels are more important than Paul's words.

Fortunately, Luther came around later — denouncing in 1537 his own earlier doctrines of antinomianism. Luther insisted the Ten Commandments applies to *all* Christians. Their violation impacts salvation. (See page 106.) Luther even said this: "To abolish the Law is therefore to abolish the truth of God."[23] Leaving Paul out-to-dry, Luther said anyone who would "discard the Law would effectively put an end to our obedience to God." (*Id.* at 32.) Yet, this same Luther earlier said in 1525 Paul "abolished the Sabbath" and declared all the Law "abolished," even the moral law. (See pp. 74, 76.)

---

22. Martin Luther, *An Earnest Exhortation for all Christians, Warning Them Against Insurrection and Rebellion*, in *Luther Work*s (Philadelphia Edition)(1955) III, 201-222, quotes from 206-213, 215-16.

23. Martin Luther, *Antinomian Theses* (1537), reprinted as *Don't Tell Me That From Martin Luther's Antinomian Theses* (Minneapolis: Lutheran Press, 2004) at 33-34.

18 *Conclusion: Preach And Teach From Jesus' Words Only*

The Duty to Distinguish False Prophets Is How to Show We Love God

In Matthew 22:37-38, we read:

> (37) Jesus said to him, "'You shall love the Lord your God with all your heart, with all your soul, and with all your mind.'
>
> (38) This is the first and great commandment."

Jesus is not only quoting Deuteronomy 6:5, as most commentaries mention. Instead, Jesus is also quoting Deuteronomy 13:3. In that verse, God explains why He allows prophets with true signs and wonders to appear who yet are false prophets. It is our duty to recognize their doctrines as false because they seduce us from following God's Law. (*Cf.* Isaiah 8:20.) God explains how this is a supreme test of the command Jesus says is *the most important*:

> [Y]ou shall not listen to the words of that prophet, or to that dreamer of dreams: for Yahweh your God proves you, ***to know whether you love Yahweh your God with all your heart and with all your soul***. (Deut. 13:3, ASV.)

Thus, obedience to the command to love God with your whole heart and mind is associated with *distinguishing* true prophets from false prophets. God says He tests your love by allowing persons to come with true "signs and wonders" who you should identify as false due to their doctrine. You must disregard their signs and wonders "that come true" because their doctrine teaches you to not follow the Law. It is a privilege and a supreme duty to make this assessment.

Even a man of God, and true prophet, should be recognized as having become a false prophet when he gives you permission to do what God has previously prohibited. This is the lesson the Young Prophet from Judah learned bitterly when he was deceived by the Old Prophet in 1 Kings 13.

In a revelation-based faith, such as Judaism and Christianity, it is no wonder that God puts such a high value on making such an assessment. Distinguishing true from false prophecy is *integral* to His plan to reveal Himself through writings of prophets. If we fail to honor God's plan by obeying His command to distinguish true from false prophets, we are demonstrating a failure to love God with our whole mind, heart and soul.

Therefore, if you refuse to apply God's word to test Paul's validity, God says you do not love God with your whole heart, mind and soul. On the other hand, if you do test Paul's doctrines by God's revealed word, you are showing your supreme allegiance to God Himself, and not to any human hand that purports to speak in His name.

The conclusion follows that this is a duty from which we cannot shrink. We must make a finding no matter how unpleasant and contrary to human supposition.

The Question of Paul's Apostleship

The result concerning Paul's supposed apostleship is unavoidable from all the evidence adduced in prior chapters. Paul was a false apostle. His evidence in support is totally self-serving. Jesus said even for Himself, a self-interested statement as the sole proof He was Son of God would mean Jesus' claim was "not true." John 5:31 ("If I bear witness of Myself, my witness is not true.")[1] Tertullian in 207 A.D., speaking on behalf of apostolic Christianity, made the same point about Paul. He said the proof that Paul was an apostle of Jesus Christ was based solely on Paul's self-serving statements. Tertullian wrote in *Against Marcion.*

> I must with the best of reasons approach this inquiry with uneasiness when I find one affirmed to be an apostle, of whom ***in the list of the apostles in the gospel I find no trace****....* [Let's] put in evidence all the documents that attest his apostleship. ***He [i.e., Paul] himself, says Marcion, claims to be an apostle***, and that not from men nor through any man, but through Jesus Christ. Clearly ***any man can make claims for himself:*** but his claim is confirmed by another person's attestation. One person writes the document, another signs it, a third attests the signature, and a fourth enters it in the records. **No man is for himself both claimant and witness**. (See Tertullian, *Against Marcion* (207 A.D.) quoted at 418-19 *supra.*)

Tertullian's critical analysis is what thereafter thwarted the movement of Marcion. Why was it crucial to defeat Marcion? Because Marcion was claiming Paul's Gospel was the only true gospel. He claimed the Gospel Message presented in Matthew and John were legalistic, and no longer applied.[2] In response, universal Christianity as it existed prior to the rise of Roman Catholicism vigorously combatted Marcionism. It saw as horrifying heresy any notion that Paul had superiority over the message from Jesus carried by Matthew and John.

When the church was forced to address this crucial issue about Paul, the verdict was clear: the evidence for Paul's apostleship did not meet a Biblical standard. We have no choice but to concur. Other than Paul's own assertions, there is no proof anywhere in the New Testament writings

1. For further discussion, see page 219.
2. See "Tertullian (207 A.D.) Says Paul Is Inferior" on page 408 *et seq.*

that Paul was appointed an apostle of Jesus Christ. None in the Gospels, none in Acts, and none in any valid apostle-epistle. This is why the doctrine of the early church on salvation ignored Paul, and preached Jesus' doctrine alone.[3]

The Question of Being The Prophesied Ravening Wolf

Nor can we ignore God in the Prophecy of the Benjamite Ravening Wolf in Genesis warned us of the ravening wolf to come from the tribe of Benjamin.[4] He would come in the latter days — in the same epoch as Messiah. In Ezekiel, we learn the characteristics of ravening wolves. They would destroy the Law, cause people to no longer keep the true Sabbath, and cause the cessation of distinguishing the clean from unclean. Paul fit all these characteristics. The Benjamite Ravening Wolf Prophecy further said this Benjamite would divide his spoil. Paul did this as well, claiming the right to exclusively preach to the Gentiles. (Galatians 2:9.) Paul claimed in that verse the twelve apostles agreed to narrow their mission field to be exclusively the Jewish people. (Any notion the twelve *consented* to exclude themselves from a Gentile ministry, as Paul claimed, is ridiculous.)[5]

3. See page 425 *et seq.*
4. See "Who is the Benjamite Wolf in Prophecy?" on page 347 *et seq*
5. See page 350 *et seq.* This division in Paul's exclusive favor is dubious at best. At the Jerusalem Council in Acts 15, Peter stood up and spoke. Paul was at his feet. Peter declared He, not Paul, was *the* Apostle to the Gentiles ***by God's decree***: "God made choice among us, that the Gentiles by my mouth should hear the word of the gospel, and believe." (Acts 15:7 ASV.) Also, in the post-council era with Paul alive the Apostle Thomas was preaching the gospel in India. This is supported by Ephraem Syrus, Ambrose, Paulinus, and Jerome. ("St. Thomas The Apostle," *Catholic Encyclopedia.*) At Mylapore, not far from Madras, "tradition has it that it was here that St. Thomas laid down his life [in 72 A.D. which] is locally very strong." *Id.* If what Paul is saying were true, didn't Thomas transgress the Jewish-Gentile pact with Paul? But why would the twelve leave to one person (Paul) this important mission to reach the Gentiles? It begs all credulity to believe Paul.

Thus, even the early church writer and Roman church leader Hippolytus (170-235 A.D.) observed around 205 A.D. that the Benjamite "ravening wolf" prophecy of Genesis "thoroughly fits Paul."[6]

Jesus likewise warned of the "ravening wolf" that was coming who would be a false prophet. (Matt. 7:15.) The false prophet would have "signs and wonders," and come in Jesus' name, tell us the "time is at hand," teach eating meat sacrificed to idols was permissible, but be a worker of *anomia.*[7] *Anomia* in Greek literally means *negation* of *Nomos* — the sole and specific Greek word used to refer to the Law of Moses.[8] This ravening wolf false prophet would work the negation of the Law just as the Benjamite Ravening Wolf of the Genesis prophecy would work.

It takes enormous defiance of Jesus to ignore who is the subject of Jesus' warnings. Paul declared all the Law abolished.[9] As to Sabbath specifically, even as Luther said: "Paul [Col. 2:16]...abolish[ed] the sabbath...."[10] Paul also abolished all distinction of clean versus unclean. (1 Tim. 4:4, 'no food is to be rejected if prayed over and God is thanked'; Romans 4:2.)[11] Paul also said the "day is *at hand*" in precisely the words Jesus warned a false prophet would use, while "coming in My name." (Luke 21:8; Romans 13:12.)[12]

---

6. See page 351.
7. Matt. 7:15-23, viz., v. 22; 24:11, 24; Mark 13:22-23. See page 59 *et seq. See also,* Luke 21:8 ('time is at hand') discussed at page 366. *See*, Rev. 2: 20 (false claimant to prophecy teaches us to eat meat sacrificed to idols.)
8. See "Why Anomia Means Negator of Mosaic Law" on page 60 *et seq.*
9. See Chapter Five.
10. See page 76 *et seq.* Paul never even endorses a one-in-seven principle. Even so, God condemns keeping a mandated festival on a day different than God's appointed time. Jeroboam kept feast of tabernacles on a "day of his [own] choosing (invention)." (1 Kings 12:33.)

Paul fit Jesus' depiction of a false prophet in Revelation 2:20 who teaches it was permissible to eat meat sacrificed to idols. (*E.g.*, Corinthians 8:4-13, 1 Corinthians 10:19-29.)[13]

Finally, Paul twice unwittingly pointed at himself Jesus' warning about the "signs and wonders" prophet who would seek to "seduce the elect."[14] For Paul said twice that "signs and wonders" prove his validity. (Romans 15:19 "in the power of ***signs and wonders***... I preached the gospel"; 2 Cor. 12:12 "Truly ***the signs of an apostle*** were wrought among you in all patience, by ***signs and wonders*** and mighty works.")

Consequently, the coincidence of descriptions between the Benjamite Ravening Wolf of Genesis and the false prophet 'ravening wolf' Jesus described is too powerful to ignore. Their identical convergence on Paul is also too uncanny to deny.

Seduction From the Law As Key Biblical Test

Moreover, Jesus also left a trail of clear doctrine by which to test Paul's doctrine on the Law of Moses. Even if we balk at seeing Paul as the ravening wolf, Jesus made it impossible for us to deny there is a blatant contradiction by Paul of what Jesus (and Prophets of Old) taught on what would be the Law *even* in the *era* of the New Testament.

11.Jesus, by contrast, merely implied that if one ate unclean food, this did not make you a sinner. Jesus did not abrogate the distinction. Rather, it follows from Jesus' statement that the law of unclean food was a health rule, which we should have known anyway from the words *clean* and *unclean*. Thus, Jesus did not abrogate these rules. He just put them on a different level than other commands. See Footnote 10, page 359.

12.See "Another Prophecy Aimed At Paul?" on page 366.

13.See "Paul Contradicts Jesus About Idol Meat" on page 117 *et seq.*

14.Matt. 7:22 (miracles and prophecy); 24: 24 ("false prophets [have] signs and wonders." Jesus warns again of false prophets in Mark 13:22. He says they "shall show signs and wonders to seduce, if possible, even the elect." For further discussion, see page 59.

First, Jesus told us that anyone who teaches us not to follow the "least command (in the Law of Moses)" would be "least in the kingdom of heaven," but whoever told us to follow the "commandments (from the Law of Moses) would be the greatest in *the kingdom of heaven*." (Matt. 5:19.) God had told us likewise beforehand that the "New Covenant" was based on "inscribing the Law (Torah) on our hearts...." (Jeremiah 31:31-33.)[15] When His Servant (Messiah) comes, God "will ***magnify the Law*** (Torah), and make it ***honorable***." (Isaiah 42:21 ASV/KJV.)

Jesus fulfilled this by condemning the Pharisees for teaching traditions that "make of none effect" express commands in the Law given Moses. (Matt. 15:16.) This included Jesus' faulting the Pharisees' notion that a special korban payment could excuse honoring your parents (by supporting them if they fell in poverty). (Matt. 15:16.) This included Jesus attacking the Pharisees' emphasizing the duty to tithe to the neglect of the weightier matters of the Law of Moses. Matt. 23:23. This also included Jesus faulting the Pharisees for teaching one did no wrong engaging in adulterous lust as long as one did not follow through and commit the act of adultery. (Matt. 5:28.)[16]

Paul did not share any concern to correct the Pharisees' ***shallow*** doctrines on the Law. Paul never shared Jesus' concern that the Pharisees' traditions had made of none effect the express commands in the Law given to Moses.

To the contrary, Paul, like the Pharisees, came teaching his own tradition which did away with the Law given Moses. However, Paul went further than most Pharisees. He abrogated it down to the very last jot and tittle.

For Paul said the New Covenant "***abolished***... the Law of commandments" (Eph. 2:15). Paul likewise said the Sabbath command was "but a shadow of things to come," and

15.For further discussion, see page 233 *et seq.*

16.For discussion of this and the other faults of the Pharisees which Jesus was identifying, see page 24; page 71 *et seq.*

henceforth let no man judge you for failure to keep it, for Christ "***blotted out*** the handwriting of ordinances that was against us, which was contrary to us, and ***took it out of the way***." (Col. 2:14-17.) Paul insisted that the Law given Moses was a "ministration of death engraven on stones" because the "letter of the law kills," which now has "been ***done away***" and "is ***abolished***;" henceforth, instead, in the Lord we have "liberty." (2 Corinthians 3:6-17.) Paul defined this liberty quite clearly: "All things are ***lawful*** but not all things are necessarily ***expedient***." (1 Cor. 6:12, ASV). "All things are ***lawful*** for me." (1 Cor. 10:23.)[17]

Paul's regard for the Law reached a total low-point in Galatians with utterances which no doubt would shock our Lord. Paul says the Law given the mediator Moses was "ordained by angels." (Gal. 3:19 ASV KJV.) Anyone who wants to be in bondage to them desires to be in bondage to those who "are no gods" (Gal. 4:8) and is seeking to be "in bondage again" to "weak and beggarly elements (angels)." (Gal. 4: 9.)[18]

Paul then goes so far as to say in the same letter that even if an "angel from heaven" should come with a gospel different than Paul, such "an angel from heaven" should be "cursed." (Gal. 1:8.) In Galatians, therefore, Paul put his words expressly above the same source he ascribed as the source of the Law given Moses: angels from heaven. Paul deliberately did so in order that we would accept his word as a superior authority to the Law of Moses. This was crucial because Paul was informing us that the Law of Moses was now abolished. Such a bold declaration only had validity if the Law "ordained by angels" was given by "angels of heaven" over whom Paul was asserting a superior authority — even a right to curse them. Only by this bold contrast and curse upon such an "angel from heaven" (Gal. 1:8) could we

17.For a full discussion on how Paul applied this principle to Sabbath and eating meat sacrificed to idols, see page 80 *et seq*.

18.See "Paul Says the Law Was Ordained through Angels" on page 85 *ff.*

ever dare think a mere human could single-handedly abolish the Law given Moses. Paul's hubris had therefore reached as high as he could take it to justify his doctrine.

Paul did not limit this abolition to merely the commands in the Law applicable to Sojourners (*i.e.*, Gentiles). Paul taught this truth of abrogation also applied to all the Law's commands directed at Israel (*i.e.*, Jews/the twelve tribes). According to Paul, by the death of Christ, the Jews now experienced the death of the husband (God) who bound them to the covenant at Sinai. The legal effect of His death under the Law of Moses thereby released the wife (the Jews) to remarry a resurrected Jesus who no longer held out the Law of Moses as any sort of guidepost in the New Covenant. (Rom. 7:1-4.)

In Galatians 4:22 *ff*, Paul likewise said that the Jews of Jerusalem no longer correspond to sons of Israel, but instead to the son Ishmael of Hagar; and they continue in bondage (to the Law of Moses), and are thereby thrown out in the desert.[19] However, how could Paul be inspired by God in this when the same God said in Jeremiah 31:31 *ff* that He could never base a New Covenant other than on the Law given Moses or enter into it with any other people than the *seed* of Israel?[20] Eisenman is perhaps too kind when he says Paul's remarks in Galatians 4:22-31 contain "a series of sometimes outrageous allusions."[21]

These are all hard questions with unpleasant answers. The answers call us to trust in Jesus' words above Paul's words.

19.See page 86 *et seq.*

20.For further discussion, see page 233 *et seq.*

21.Prof. Robert Eisenman, *The New Testament Code: The Cup of the Lord, The Damascus Covenant, and the Blood of Christ* (London: Watkins Publishing, 2006) at 587.

Jesus: Our Sole Teacher

Now we are prepared to receive Jesus' doctrine on the centrality of His message. This is the meaning of *Jesus' Words Only* — it is a doctrine actually taught by Our Lord. This doctrine made His commandments the sole focus for the church. He will teach us that His commandments are necessarily diminished when we treat as inspired *every* word of any apostle (including the one we added by *tradition* as a thirteenth). Jesus clearly did not intend to impart such an authority to *every* word of any one of the individual twelve apostles merely because spoken by them. Because Jesus never extended such authority to any of the twelve, we have utterly no justification extending such authority to someone who was not even among the twelve, namely Paul.

This doctrine begins with Jesus' teaching that we have one Rabbi, one Teacher. We were not to call anyone in the church, even an apostle, a teacher. Speaking to ***both*** the apostles and the crowds, Jesus said: "Don't let anyone call you Rabbi [*i.e.,* Teacher] for you have only One Teacher, and all of you are equal as brothers and sisters." (Matt. 23:8 NLT.) "And don't let anyone call you Teacher, for you have only One Teacher, the Messiah (Christ)." (Matt. 23:10 NLT.)

Jesus was thereby admonishing the Apostles to not assume any authority above His message. As Matthew Henry explains this passage:

> The disciples ***must not assume the authority and dominion implied in those names*** [*i.e.*, teacher]; they must not domineer over their brethren, or over God's heritage, ***as if they had dominion over the faith of Christians***.

Furthermore, because Jesus was addressing both *apostles* and the *crowd*, His remark that all in attendance were "equal" as brothers has a key significance. Yet, it is often overlooked. Jesus meant all Christians are equal "brethren" with a perfectly equal authority. In this sense, no one believer is higher in position or importance than any other believer. Any sense of superiority or sense of inferiority among believers is to be avoided. None are to be masters or teachers in the church of Christ. We are all disciples of the same Master. Thereby, Jesus remains always and forever The Teacher, The Master, solely and uniquely.

Yet, as we shall see, the twelve apostles were commissioned to teach *something*. Thus, while they were to teach *something*, they still were not to be called *teachers*. In other words, they did not have the authority of a teacher apart from the message they were to teach. They held no unique superiority over anyone else merely because they had the function of teaching a certain message. Rather, the *message* that they carried from Jesus was what was *superior* to any other message. We miss this point because we do not have the immediate recognition as first century Christians would that the word *apostolos* means *messenger* in Greek. Thus, the apostles had no independent authority to teach apart from carrying the *message* of the words of Jesus.

This was in keeping with how Jesus explained the Holy Spirit would work in the New Testament church. The Holy Spirit will not say anything to us other than what the Spirit ***already*** heard from the Lord. The Spirit does not speak ***from within*** Himself *anything*! In other words, no inspired words will come *directly* from the Spirit unless the Spirit already heard it from the Lord. Please listen attentively to our Lord explaining this:

> Howbeit when he, the Spirit of truth, is come, he shall guide you into all the truth: ***for he shall not speak from himself; but what things soever he shall hear***, these shall he speak: and he shall declare unto you the things that are to come. ***He shall glorify me***: for he shall take of mine, and shall declare it unto you. (John 16:13-14 ASV.)

Clarke says this bolded language means "He shall teach *nothing contrary* to what I have taught you."

Thus, the Holy Spirit would do three things: (a) guide them in all truth; (b) provide prophecy of future events, as John later received in Revelation; (c) but otherwise, only repeat what the Spirit already heard from the Lord Himself (thus never contradicting Jesus' words). Jesus tells us why! Because this would *glorify* Jesus.

Later, Jesus gave a contrast in John 7:18: "He that speaketh from himself seeketh his own glory." Thus, if anyone spoke new principles different than what Jesus already said, they actually were speaking for themselves alone. Their words would be to "seek their own glory."

Jesus helps us understand this in another passage. He says to the twelve that the Holy Spirit will bring "remembrance" of Jesus' words and "teach you all things."

> But the Comforter, even the Holy Spirit, whom the Father will send in my name, he shall teach you all things, and ***bring to your remembrance all that I said unto you***. Joh 14:26 ASV

Thus, combining John 14:26 and 16:13-14, it means the Holy Spirit "shall...bring to your remembrance all that I said to you." But the Holy Spirit will not cause a recollection of any words contrary to what Jesus said in the hearing of the twelve. This is so because the Holy Spirit does not speak of itself. Clarke explains John 14:26 thusly: "Here Christ promises them that inspiration of the Holy Spirit which enabled them not only to give a true history of his life and death, but also gave them the most perfect recollection of all the words which he had spoken to them...."

But what about the Holy Spirit's *teaching* and *guiding* in all things? What does this mean? Because the Holy Spirit would not speak from itself, and not speak anything other than what Jesus already said, we know the *teaching* and *guiding* would itself not involve distinct *new* commands or doctrine. Rather, to keep the glory of God focused on Jesus, its teachings would be solely explanation. It would be *teaching* the meaning of Jesus' words. As Gill explains: the Holy Spirit would "explain all things which ***Christ had said*** to them; to make them more plain and easy to their understandings."

Moreover, we know Jesus was not implying this teaching operation of the Holy Spirit effected an instantaneous infallible understanding in the apostles, let alone anyone else who enjoys the Holy Spirit. Why is this?

First, because the function of *teaching* and *guiding* has always been a work of the Holy Spirit in all who have received it. As MacDonald comments on this part of the verse: "But it is, of course, true in all ages that the Spirit guides God's people into all the truth." (MacDonald, *Believer's Bible Commentary*.)

And the Holy Spirit did not uniquely belong to the apostles in the New Testament era.[22] Peter says the "Holy Spirit God has given to them that ***obey*** Him." (Acts 5:32.) Peter said the Holy Spirit would be received by a crowd of 3,000 if they "***repented*** and [were] baptized" in the name of Jesus. (Acts 2:38.)[23]

Thus, if the Holy Spirit did not uniquely belong to the Apostles, then Jesus could not possibly mean the teaching and guidance of the Holy Spirit implied instantaneous infallible understanding. If instead He did mean this, then all who

---

22.As Wesley comments on John 14:26, Jesus' promise of a teaching ministry of the Holy Spirit applied to "the apostles, and their *successors* in the faith...."

23.Jesus tells us how to receive the Holy Spirit. He does so in a story about the persistent widow. Jesus says we should follow her example, and persistently ask God to give us the Holy Spirit. Luke 11:10-13. Using the continuous present tense verb, Jesus says, "everyone who ***keeps on*** asking receives...." (Luke 11:10.) Then Jesus says "how much moreso shall your heavenly Father ***give the Holy Spirit*** to them that ask him?" (Luke 11:13.) Thus, it appears our "repentance" unto salvation and receipt of the Holy Spirit (Acts 2:38) is not necessarily a quick process. Yet, we are promised by Jesus if we are persistent, God will answer, forgive, and give us His Holy Spirit.

"obey Him" and have "repented and been baptized" would have infallible identical understandings of church doctrine. Alas, no such miracle has yet happened.

Furthermore, Jesus' choice of words appears intended to confirm there is no infallible result guaranteed by this work of the Holy Spirit: "He (the Holy Spirit) shall ***guide*** you into all the truth...." (John 16:13.) When you are *guided* to something, it means you can be at the wrong point of understanding along the way. The *Guide* here is *never* wrong. Yet, the *guidee* might be. As Clarke says, Jesus' terminology is "as a father leads ***a child*** by the hand." The Holy Spirit is teaching you the path; you are a child; your understanding may be imperfect along the path even as you hear and try to apprehend your teacher. Your teacher is infallible; you are not.

In similar fashion, Jesus compares the Spirit's guiding role to that of a teacher. "He shall teach you all things...." (John 14:26.) Again this does not guarantee that the student will correctly get every lesson. The *Teacher* here is *never* wrong. But Jesus did not say the student will always correctly understand the teacher. The student can be wrong or growing in his or her understanding. Thus, all who have the Holy Spirit will be guided and taught by the Holy Spirit, but it does not mean any Christian can affirm they have an *infallible* understanding. This is true whether they are an apostle or the corner grocer.

Thus, the metaphors of *guiding* and *teaching* that Jesus used when the Holy Spirit operated in them was different than how Jesus described the Holy Spirit's work in the apostles which He said will assuredly "bring to your remembrance" the words of Jesus. Their remembrance was guaranteed to be accurate. However, whether they (or any Holy Spirit-filled Christian) would understand the Spirit's teaching or guidance infallibly was not guaranteed. This understanding was to grow from the Holy Spirit's *guiding* and *teaching* assistance in understanding the infallibly-recollected words of Jesus.

What confirms that *teachings* had to be measured for accuracy against the words of Jesus is that Apostle John understood it this way. He is the one writing these words in John chapters 14 and 16. Therefore, his personal understanding speaks volumes. John said anyone whose teachings "go beyond" or "overstep" the "***teachings*** of [Jesus] Christ doesn't have God." (2 John 1:8-11.) This means the Holy Spirit is not present (note the verb is *has, have*) in anyone when such a person insists the church follow doctrine that goes beyond or oversteps the teachings of Jesus.

John's lesson paralleled precisely Jesus' lesson that the Holy Spirit would not go beyond what Jesus ever said to the apostles: "for he [the Spirit] shall ***not speak from himself***; but what things soever he shall hear." (John 16:13-14.) Thus, anyone who comes with a teaching that goes beyond Jesus' teaching is speaking "from himself" and not for Jesus' glory, and hence without the Holy Spirit. Such a speaker does not *have God* at that moment or in those teachings. Their teaching can and must be ignored.

Thus, whether one's teaching really reflects the teachings of the Holy Spirit depends crucially upon whether one's words are truly *compatible* with the words of the Lord Jesus (both given to the twelve apostles and the prophets that preceded them).

If, however, anyone insists Jesus intended instead that the apostles could each be individual oracles of God on every teaching they uttered, and this was beyond testing by the words of Jesus or the Law and the Prophets, Jesus would Himself become a false prophet. He would be giving the apostles an authority that God previously said no prophet can have. Even a true prophet, like Balaam and the Old Prophet of 1 Kings 13, had to be tested by their consistency with what had been revealed first to Moses and then by the words delivered to every *verified* prophet thereafter. Balaam and the Old Prophet failed the test later. Jesus cannot establish a new group of super prophets whose words we are not permitted to test for consistency with what preceded without Jesus Himself contradicting the word before Him. Thus, Jesus could never have intended any such class of super prophets.

Accordingly, we know instead that Jesus was telling us about the limited speaking authority of the Holy Spirit so we would know the *legitimate* and *limited* sources for church doctrine. It starts and finishes with Jesus' words. The Holy Spirit will help teach their meaning. But the Holy Spirit is not going to add as inspired canon *anything* apart from Jesus' words *any more*. The only other thing the Holy Spirit will do (and did do in Revelation) is give a message about things that are to come to pass.

In fact, the Book of Revelation is a perfect picture of how the Spirit was operating in this *self-limited* way after the Ascension. This book John calls the "Revelation of Jesus Christ." (Rev. 1:1.) John summarizes up front what His sources are: he "bare record of the word of God, the testimony of Jesus and all things that he saw." Nothing is spoken doctrinally that does not come from Jesus. The Lord Jesus is present throughout, talking to John directly just before the visions and just after they finish. (Rev. 1:8,11,17-20; 2:1-29; 3:1-22; 21:5-8; 22:12-13,16.) The angel explains the context of the various visions with Jesus present at all times. This is similar to what happened with the Prophet Daniel: the Son of Man (Jesus) tells the angel Gabriel to make Daniel understand the visions. (Dan. 8:15-16.)

Thus, here we see the Holy Spirit is giving all glory to Jesus. Apostle John hears nothing but Jesus' words and things to come. Otherwise, the Holy Spirit is relaying visions to John while Jesus is present observing everything. This tracks the Holy Spirit's role that Jesus explained in John 16:13-14.

The Importance of John The Baptist's Actions

John the Baptist is placed in the New Testament by God partly to demonstrate to us the sharp break off of the work of the Holy Spirit once Jesus' ministry began. As we all know, John the Baptist was the "greatest prophet" of all the prophets (Matt. 11:11). John had been preaching and teaching prior to Jesus' ministry. Yet, John saw that once Jesus arrived on the scene, John's prophetic ministry had to recede away. The Teacher and The Prophet had arrived. John then only gave a message that insisted everyone turn to Jesus to hear His doctrine. John's *independent* message was to decrease. John explained why:

> ***He must increase***, but ***I must decrease***. He that cometh from above is above all: he that is of the earth is of the earth, and of the earth he speaketh: ***he that cometh from heaven is above all***. John 3:30-31 ASV.

John knew if he continued his own message distinct from that of Jesus, John would necessarily *diminish* from the centrality of the message Jesus was now bringing. To allow emphasis and allegiance to switch to Jesus and His doctrine, John the Baptist was willing to let the focus on himself decrease. In the above speech, John the Baptist gives a long explanation of why Jesus is now the focus. Had John lived past the ascension of Jesus, no doubt John would still have had a ministry that focused now on the centrality of Jesus and His words. That's why John the Baptist preached in John 3:36 that "all who keep on ***disobeying*** the Son, the wrath of God continues to remain on him."[24] John understood the gospel very well and repeated it. Teaching the nations to "obey all that [Jesus] commanded" (Matt. 28:20) was all that now mattered.

24. This is the literal Greek, reflecting correctly each present participle as a continuous tense. For an explanation, see Appendix A.

Jesus' Warning Of Treating An Apostle On Par With Him

Jesus likewise warned us to not let any apostle's importance grow to the point the apostle's words were on par or greater than words from Jesus. Jesus said this plainly enough in John 13:16 but this is obscured in the KJV translation. Jesus said:

> I tell you the truth, slaves are not greater than their master. ***Nor is the Apostolos (messenger) more important than the One who sends the message***. (John 13:16 NLT with Greek *Apostolos* revealed.)[25]

Thus, if we put greater emphasis upon the words of an *apostolos* than Jesus' words, we commit the error identified in John 13:16. For example, if we dismiss Jesus' words as applicable only to a supposedly defunct dispensation, preferring some competing doctrine we like in a presumed apostle's letter, we would violate John 13:16. Yet, this is what a large segment of modern evangelical Christianity has opted to do in the doctrine of Dispensationalism. This doctrine gives a current validity to Paul's teachings while blatantly claiming any of Jesus' teachings to the contrary are defunct.[26]

However, to give any equal or superior authority as a teacher to any of the apostles when they were not quoting Jesus would be to allow the apostle to assume a role exceeding the bounds of their apostleship — their role as *messengers*. To allow an individual apostle to assume such a role in the church would permit focus on that apostle's doctrine apart from the lessons of Jesus. The Lord wanted us to have one Master, one Teacher: Himself. This was to protect His glory.

25.This is a paraphrase of Isaiah 6:8. Notice the difference in the King James of John 13:16. It has the effect of obscuring needlessly Jesus' message is about *apostles*. The KJV reads: "The servant is not greater than his lord; ***neither he that is sent*** greater than he that sent him." However, 'he that is sent' is wholly incorrect. It is a noun nominative singular masculine, *apostolos*. How can this be read "he that is sent"?

26.See "Dispensational Strategy To Avoid Jesus" on page 387 *et seq.*

Thus, Jesus intended His message was what gave the apostles any cause to be a teacher. They were not authorized to be teachers in their own right, with their own unique doctrines. This is why the fact Paul barely mentions even one sentence from Jesus,[27] and paraphrases very few of Jesus' words, makes his doctrine completely his own.

As a result, we must reject Paul's statement in 2 Thessalonians 2:15 that we are to "stand fast and hold the traditions you were taught... by our epistle." Such a doctrine makes Paul's epistles on par with Jesus' words. If Paul were construing Jesus' words, it would not be so serious a problem. But Paul never mentions any *specific* doctrine of Jesus (except the smallest snippet).[28] And Paul has doctrines so contrary to Jesus that most evangelicals have made up the fiction of separate dispensations containing contrary salvation principles to rationalize the differences.[29] Thus, when Paul invites us to elevate tradition, including Paul's own epistles, to the point we should remain "steadfast" in them, we must reject that idea. Only Jesus' doctrine is something to remain steadfast in.

27.See page 328 *et seq.*

28.It is a unique attribution of words to Jesus: "it is better to give than receive." Acts 20:35. Other than this, no attribution of words from Jesus on *doctrine* are ever given by Paul.

29.The Dispensationalists concede the Covenant of Moses did require obedience for imputed justification. (Deut. 6:25.) However, we are supposedly in a new dispensation. We are told by Paul we are justified by faith apart from any need to obey. (Eph. 2:8-9; Romans 4:3-5.) However, it is never explained why Deuteronomy 6:25 is abrogated when God declared repeatedly the Law given Moses was "eternal for all generations." *See* Ex. 27:21; 30:21; Lev. 6:18; 7:36; 10:9; 17:7; 23:14, 21, 41; 24:3; Num. 10:8; 15:15.

Unwarranted Catholic Tradition Expanded Apostolic 'Binding' Authority

Then what did Jesus mean by saying that "whatever" the apostles bound or loosed on earth was bound or loosed in heaven? (Matt. 16:19.)[30] The simple answer is the judicial function of adjudicating cases. It did not authorize them to make up new laws or doctrine not already given by God/ Jesus. There are several clear proofs this was Jesus' meaning.

First, Jesus' terminology of 'binding-and-loosing' clearly was a reference to what a first century Christian knew was a function of a judge. In that day and consistently up until only a century ago, a judge would "bind" or "loose" a prisoner with a leather strap.[31] Jesus was merely alluding to what Jesus repeatedly told the twelve early in His ministry: they were going to be the "twelve judges" who were judging the "twelve tribes of Israel."[32] Such judicial authority did not make them individually or corporately oracles of God or some new Moses-like law-givers from God. Such judicial authority merely allowed their decision on judicial matters to be bound in heaven.

30.It is true this statement was actually spoken to Peter alone upon his being the first to confess Jesus was Messiah. However, as this discussion progresses, we shall see in John 20:21-23, Jesus will give all the apostles the Holy Spirit, and extend this power to all of them.

31.Gill (a Protestant commentator) insists the Talmud shows "times without number" this means the ability to declare what is "lawful and unlawful..." and God would have to accept such decrees in heaven. However, Gill is speaking too broadly. There is an important distinction. It is a judge's function to declare *in the particular* what is lawful/ unlawful, reasoning from a *general* law. Such a role of the judges of Israel was not an authority to make up ***new laws*** or ***principles***. Jesus refuted continually they had an authority to do so. When religious authorities do so, Jesus said then the people end up worshipping God with their lips, but their worship is empty. (Matt. 15:9.) For a full discussion of that passage, see page 71 *et seq.*

32.See page 14 *et seq.*

Second, Jesus explained a judicial authority is intended in Matthew 16:19 (binding/loosing) by means of an exactly parallel statement in John 20:21-23 where we read:

> (22) And when he had said this, he breathed on them, and saith unto them, Receive ye the Holy Spirit: (23) ***whose soever sins ye forgive, they are forgiven unto them; whose soever sins ye retain, they are retained***. John 20:22-23 ASV.

Thus, the authority the apostles enjoyed was the power to bind their decisions on guilt or forgiveness in heaven as on earth.

It was a later Roman Catholic innovation to make this apostolic authority into more than it really was. The Catholic church claimed this 'binding' and 'loosing' meant an oracle-like power. This was to their advantage because they taught this power belonged to each individual pope who became the bishop of Rome in the footsteps of Peter. Each pope was thereby an 'infallible' oracle of God.[33] Whatever the pope taught was *de facto* on par with what Jesus *ever* said.

Pauline Protestants have proven equally anxious to have the twelve apostles have such demi-god status. Such Protestants unhesitatingly ascribe the same infallibility to each of the twelve based on this "binding and loosing" verse.[34] This way we evangelicals have been able to extend

33.The *Catholic Encyclopedia* defines *infallibility* of the pope as: "it means exemption from the possibility of error." (http://www.newadvent.org/cathen/07790a.htm (accessed 1/17/07).) Yet, the Catholic church will insist this does not mean the pope is *inspired*. Rather, the *Holy Spirit* supposedly gives the pope an infallible decision on *doctrine*. The distinction is one without a difference.

34.Clarke is a Protestant example of how to read Matthew 16:19. "The disciples of our Lord, from having the keys, *i.e.* the true knowledge of the doctrine of the kingdom of heaven, should be able at all times to... pronounce ***infallible judgment***; and this binding and loosing... should be considered as ***proceeding immediately from heaven***, and consequently ***as Divinely ratified***."

this mantle of infallibility to Paul. We do so on the presumption that Paul's claim to being an apostle is valid. However, Paul was not one of the twelve apostles and did not enjoy whatever power Jesus was giving the twelve. Regardless, such an interpretation of Jesus' remarks is a Roman Catholic anachronism which needs to be finally recognized as such.

We must eject all Catholic traditions that do not have a warrant in the Bible itself. The notion of apostolic authority as binding in delivery of unique new doctrines, rather than when issuing a judicial decision or with inspiration relaying Jesus' words, is wholly unwarranted. This was a self-serving expansion of apostolic authority by the Catholic church. It is connived at by Pauline Protestants who find such doctrine conducive to giving an elevated importance to Paul's words.

Apostolic Decisions Were Binding In Heaven Only When Reached Jointly

An example of the Apostles acting as judges over a case is when they decided to add Matthias as the twelfth apostle. This was their remedy for the transgression they found Judas had committed.[35] (Acts chapter one.)

Peter did not assume a superiority, and declare Matthias an apostle. It was a joint decision. Why did the apostles act this way on such a matter?

Because Jesus made it quite clear that the apostles, if they wanted their judicial decision to be binding in heaven, had to act jointly, and not in solitary fashion. (Matt. 20:26-27.) With regard to the question of a twelfth apostle, the apostles recognized this was the kind of decision they wanted bound in heaven, and not just on earth. That's why the apostles acted jointly.

35. A judge's authority extends to remedies for transgression, even if sometimes third parties must fulfill the vow of another.

This is the true import of Jesus' lesson to the apostles in Matthew 20:26-27. Unfortunately, the translators do not assist us. They leave the meaning obscure. The correct translation is:

> (25) But Jesus called them unto him, and said, Ye know that the ***supreme magistrates*** (***archon***, plural) of the Gentiles lord against them, and their great ones exercise a full privilege over them. (26) Not so shall it be among you: but whosoever would become ***first*** (*protos*) among you shall be your servant (*diakonos*, deacon); (27) and whosoever would be ***first*** (*protos*) among you shall be your slave (*doulos*). (Matt.20:26-27.)

Jesus is talking to twelve new judges who shall be supreme over Israel. He is contrasting how *supreme judges* operate among the Gentiles. He wants the apostles to be sure not to copy how an *archon* operated among the Gentiles. An *archon* acted as the *first* over and above other magistrates, as a supreme solitary magistrate. An *archon* did so in his jurisdiction, thereby lording it over the people.

How do we know this was Jesus' intention? First, because in context, Jesus is speaking to *twelve judges* he just gave such similar supreme judicial power *over* Israel. Second, Jesus was being disparaging of acting *first* among other judges, which is something we will in a moment discuss was the *archon* practice. Lastly, Jesus used the word *archon* to precisely mean such a supreme magistrate in Luke 12:58. When the Luke passage is translated, *archon* is always translated as *magistrate*. Somewhat perplexingly, in Matthew 20:26-27, its plural is always translated as *rulers*.

Vine's New Testament explains what *archon* meant in Luke 12:58. It says that

> *archon*, a 'ruler,' denotes, in Luke 12:58 'a local authority, a magistrate,' acting in the capacity of one who received complaints, and possess-

> ing higher authority than the judge, to whom the 'magistrate' remits the case.

Thus, when Jesus speaks of an *archon* in Luke 12:58, Jesus is talking about someone whose role included acting as a supreme court justice who acted alone. *Archons* in that judicial role did not function in a council to apply existing law to new cases. They acted as *first* among judges who were beneath them, reviewing cases sent them by lower level judges.

Why was Jesus concerned the apostles might copy the Gentile *archon* approach and behave as *first* over other judges, and thereby lord it over the church of Christ?

Jesus' intent is obvious when you compare the *binding* authority among judges under Jewish law of that era.

In Jewish legal tradition as of the first century, supreme judicial authority was always held by a joint committee. It was never held by a solitary individual. Jewish law required judicial decisions at the supreme level of the Sanhedrin to be done by joint votes. (*Tractate Sanhedrin*, Herbert Danby trans. (1919) at 68.)

This ancient text *Tractate Sanhedrin* then explained the ***binding*** nature of joint decisions:

> If in a case, the ***majority decreed a thing*** to be unclean, it was unclean; if clean, it was clean. Thence did the legal decision go forth and spread abroad in Israel.

As John Gill notes, time and time again these judicial rulings of the Sanhedrin were said in the Talmud to be binding in heaven as on earth.[36] Thus, when Jesus gives the twelve a similar power to bind/find guilt or loose/forgive sin, they knew He meant such authority was to be exercised jointly. Consequently, when Jesus condemns the Gentile *archon* practice of operating as the *first* among what should be equals, we know Jesus is extolling the Jewish format of

---

36.See Footnote 31, page 492.

joint *judicial* decision-making. Just as the Sanhedrin believed their joint council rulings were bound throughout Israel, the apostles were being told similar joint action by themselves on judicial matters would be binding on heaven as on earth.

Roman Catholic authorities ignore this background because they wanted to invest the solitary pope with a supreme authority acting as *first* among all officers of the church. Their entire theory of papal infallibility was on the presumption that Peter could be deduced to be *first* among the twelve. Not only did Jesus fault the apostles when they started to speculate who was the most important among them (Mark 9:33-34), but here in Matthew 20:26-27, Jesus gave clear direction against this principle. There is to be no *first* apostle among apostles on judicial matters. Jesus uses the word *first* twice to disparage the superiority principle among apostles on judicial issues. Jesus warned that such a unilateral approach can potentially lead to abuse of judicial power. It was not in Roman Catholicism's interest to bring out Jesus' meaning. Thus, they buried it.

Yet, since the same approach serves treating the solitary-speaking Paul, assumed to be a true apostle, as a solitary binding oracle, Paulinist Protestants leave in place the Roman Catholic tradition. No one faults the idea that a single apostle could act just like an *archon*. Jesus, in truth, abhorred this idea.

Thus, even if Paul were a valid thirteenth apostle, and even supposing Jesus meant a binding decision could extend to more than judicial decisions, Paul could *not* act in this regard on his own say-so.

Yet, in Scripture, the only evidence of a joint apostolic judicial decision is in Acts 1:23-24. To remedy Judas' transgression, the twelve put forth two candidates for a twelfth to replace him. Then they let the lot decide. Interestingly, there is no evidence in scripture of a joint decision by the apostles over doctrine.[37]

This means there was never any judicial decision by the twelve apostles confirming Paul was an apostle or a prophet. Paul thus never enjoyed a finding by the apostles about himself that was *binding* in heaven by the twelve which would ever give us justification to treat Paul's words as *binding* over Christ's church.

Violating JWO By Having A Second Master

Accordingly, if we treat someone like Paul as an inspired voice who makes the criteria for salvation even in the ***slightest*** any different than what Jesus announced, we have a problem. We have created a risk of Two Teachers and Two Masters. However, Jesus told us what happens when you have two masters (teachers) competing for control of doctrine:

> No man can serve two masters (*kurios*); for either he will hate the one, and love the other; or else he will ***hold to one***, and ***despise the other***. (Matt. 6:24 ASV.)

Despite this warning, many hold to one Master (Paul) while despising the words of Jesus. This is most obvious in how they treat Jesus' words defining the Gospel.

---

37. The decision in Acts 15 on whether Gentiles were to be circumcised was a decision over doctrine. No individual was on trial. Who decided this? Not the twelve. The twelve obviously did not regard their judicial authority was involved and only engaged in the discussion. In that case the twelve submitted to the superior authority of James, the Lord's brother and non-apostle, who made the final decision. James apparently had their consent, but there is no indication the twelve voted on the issue. Thus, the twelve must not have regarded their superior judicial authority extended into issues of doctrine. There, James as city-bishop, had authority to decide doctrine.

For indeed, Jesus' doctrine of salvation is not hard to discern. His Gospel was reflected right within the Great Commission itself. Jesus told the apostles to make disciples of all the nations, "teaching them to ***obey*** [*tereo*] everything I commanded you." (Matt. 28:19-20.) Why were these commandments to be taught and obeyed by the nations? Because Jesus explained in John 8:51: "I tell you the truth, anyone who ***obeys*** [*tereo*] My teaching will never die!"[38] To be more accurate, "obeys" is "*should* have kept on obeying" and "will never" is actually "*should* never."[39] Thus, it says, "all those who *should* have kept on obeying My Teaching *should* never ever die."[40]

Well then, to whom does Jesus affix the *absolute promise* of salvation? It is to only ***one*** type of person. In Matthew 10:22, Jesus says "the one who has endured (aorist active) to the end ***shall*** be saved (future indicative)."

Jesus said likewise in the Parable of the Sower. From among the four seeds, even the seed which sprouted and thus "***believed*** for a while" (Luke 8:13) but fell in time of tempta-

38.*New Living Translation.*The King James renders "obey" in this verse as "kept guard." In Greek, the literal meaning is "to attend to carefully" or "guard." Metaphorically it means *obey*, *observe*, etc. Here, the NLT's *obey* is the more contextually accurate meaning.

39.The word for *obey* and *have* are both active aorist subjunctives. The habit of the NIV and KJV is to translate any verse on salvation with *shall* rather than *should* to serve doctrine. This is because ordinarily the active verb which precedes is *believe*, *e.g.*, John 11:26. Thus, due to this habit, they translate John 8:51 with *shall*, which no doubt they prefer not doing, since now Jesus links obedience to salvation. However, we cannot ignore the subjunctive. For why the verb *obey* and *have* should be translated as subjunctives, see Footnote 15, page 383.

40.This is exactly comparable to John 3:16 and 11:26 in proper translation. "All those who *keep on* believing *should* not perish but *should* have eternal life." (John 3:16.) Likewise, John 11:26 should read: "whoever *keeps on* living and *keeps on* believing in me *should* never ever perish." For discussion on how the subjunctive tense is often ignored to serve doctrinal biases, see Footnote 15, page 383.

tion, Jesus said only one was saved. Jesus said it was the fourth seed. It was the only seed which 'brought forth fruit with patient ***endurance*** to the end.'[41]

Thus, whenever the Great Commission is fulfilled by teaching obedience to Jesus' commands, including the necessity to *endure* successfully in them, the Gospel that saves is spread.

This is the same message in Jesus' parable about the one who builds on sand. "And every one that heareth these words of mine, and ***doeth them not***, shall be likened unto a foolish man, who built his house upon the sand [whose end is destruction]." Matt. 7:26-27 ASV.

So what are these commandments which lead to life if obeyed in patient endurance, or hell if disobeyed? Here is a small sampling of verses from just the early chapters of Apostle Matthew's Gospel. None are parabolic. Hence, there is no mystery involved. All threaten damnation if certain principles are disobeyed. Or they promise eternal life if certain principles are obeyed:

- "One who is ***angry*** with his brother shall be in ***danger of judgment***." Matt. 5:22.
- "Whosoever shall ***say 'Fool'*** shall be in ***danger of Hell fire***." Matt. 5:22.
- "Every tree that ***bringeth not forth good fruit*** is hewn down, and ***cast into the fire***." Matt. 7:19 ASV.
- "[B]ut I say unto you, that every one that ***looketh on a [married] woman to lust*** after her hath committed adultery with her already in his heart. And if thy right eye causeth thee to stumble, ***pluck it out,*** and cast it from thee: for it is profitable for thee that one of thy members should perish, and not thy whole body be ***cast into hell***." Matt. 5:28-29.
- "[B]ut I say unto you, ***love your enemies***, and pray for them that persecute you; that you may be ***sons of your Father*** who is in heaven." Matt. 5:44-45.

41.See page 171 *et seq.*

- "And be not afraid of them that kill the body, but are not able to kill the soul: but rather ***fear him who is able to destroy both soul and body in hell***...But ***whosoever shall deny me*** before men, him will I also deny before my Father who is in heaven...He that ***findeth his life shall lose it***; and ***he that loseth his life for my sake shall find it***." Matt. 10:28, 33, 39 ASV.
- "And behold, one came to him and said, Teacher, what good thing shall I do, that I may have ***eternal life***? And he said unto him,... '[I]f thou wouldest ***enter into life***, ***keep the commandments***. He saith unto him, Which? And Jesus said, Thou ***shalt not kill***, Thou shalt ***not commit adultery,*** Thou shalt not steal, Thou shalt ***not bear false witness***, ***Honor thy father and mother***; and, Thou shalt ***love thy neighbor*** as thyself.'" Matt. 19:16-19 ASV.

Yet, despite the clarity of Jesus' Gospel, how many evangelicals would teach obedience to the commands in these verses *actually* are crucial for salvation? Each verse expressly says so. Each verse points us away from thinking that John 3:16 means that faith *alone* should save. (John 3:16.) Now we realize that with equal force, Jesus says in John 8:51 that obedience *should* save. Jesus obviously intends us to read both John 3:16 and 8:51 together. When both verses are combined, it is *faith* and *obedience* that Jesus simultaneously says *should* save.[42] Where have we heard that before? In James' Epistle! James says when faith is working together with obedience (works) in *synergy*, one is justified. (James 2:20-24.)[43] Jesus then assures us the result after a lifetime of patient endurance in both principles is that we "***shall*** be saved." (Matthew 10:22.)

Thus, we cannot emphasize for salvation the importance of faith that neglects obedience. Nor can we emphasize obedience for salvation that neglects faith. They are working

42. On the *should* versus *shall* issue in both John 3:16 and 8:51, *see* Footnote 50, page 506.

43. See Footnote 24, page 261.

together to justify one who calls on the name of the Lord. Jesus only gives *assurance of salvation* when both principles are operative.[44]

However, we all know that *no evangelical teaches the necessity of obedience to any of Jesus' commands* quoted above for *salvation-sake* itself, whether in patient endurance or otherwise.

Why is this?

There is no secret here. Most of us evangelical Christians claim that teaching that our salvation depends on any kind of obedience to any *Law*, whether from Jesus or Moses, is the heresy of works. For this proposition, we rely upon Paul. (Romans 4:3-5.) In fact, most evangelicals will mock anyone who dares teach the necessity to obey these commandments of Jesus to spare ourselves from damnation. More to the point, the Modern Pauline Gospel teaches us emphatically that we are saved without having "kept guard" or "obeyed" Jesus' teaching, despite Jesus saying the opposite in John 8:51. This implies that anyone who teaches what Jesus teaches in John 8:51 is, in fact, *lost*. Thus, to most evangelicals, anyone who teaches the literal meaning of what Jesus taught in John 8:51 or any of the numerous verses quoted above is damned!

The Evangelical Rationale

What is the rationale that explains away Jesus' contrary statements? The evangelical position is that the only command we must obey from Jesus is *faith*. That supposedly

44.Jesus said if we "keep on *listening* and keep on *following*" Jesus "we should not perish" and "***shall*** not be snatched from my hand." (John 10:27-28.) Notice the verbs are no longer about *believing* or *obeying*. They are now *listening* and *following*. Assurance has a different source than the specific principles of faith and obedience which *should save*. The terms Jesus focuses on are, instead, principles of *endurance:* listening and following. On the correct translation of this verse, see Appendix A: Greek Issues page ii for discussion of John 10:27-28.

answers all these other commands with a 'not guilty' declaration! Atonement applies across the board now and for every future sin as long as I said I believe in Jesus and trust in His work on the cross. That's the only superficially-satisfactory explanation that has ever been offered on how to square these demanding words from Jesus with Paul's doctrine.[45]

But no one cares that Jesus refuted that idea Himself. Jesus was emphatic that the atonement sacrifice does you no good if you have not *first* appeased the one you had sinned against. Jesus commands you to leave your sacrifice at the sacrifice-place (Jesus' true words), and be *first* reconciled to the one you offended. Then come with the atoning sacrifice to the sacrifice place. Matthew 5:23-24.[46]

Jesus was saying nothing new. The Prophets of old always said that it was an abuse of the atonement-offerings for an unrepentant person to expect forgiveness from God by such offerings. Unless one already had repented from sin and turned from evil, the atonement had no application to you.[47]

Furthermore, no one seems to care that this inflated significance to atonement directly discourages taking seriously the numerous warnings of Jesus to believers. Where Jesus sows doubt, this argument sows assurance. Where Jesus wants believers to fear damnation, this argument sows the unalterable promise of heaven. Where Jesus exhorts the

---

45. The Dispensationalists give up on the attempt to square everything from Jesus with Paul. They admit most of these passages contradict Paul's Gospel. Their solution to the conflict is to toss all these verses from Jesus in the dust-bin of a supposedly defunct dispensation between God and Moses. For extended discussion, see page 387 *et seq.*

46. See page 265 *et seq.* for further discussion.

47. "The Prophets disparaged sacrifices that were offered without a regeneration of the heart, *i.e.,* a determined turning from sin and returning to God by striving after righteousness." ("Korban," *Wikipedia Encyclopedia.*) Some of the many such verses are: Micah 6:6-8, Joel 2:13, Hosea 14:1-2; and Malachi 1:10, 3:3-4. *Cf.* Isaiah 27:9.

sternest self-control to enter heaven *albeit maimed* (Mark 9:42-47), this view tells you to "relax, sit back" (J. Vernon McGee) and rely on the atonement alone.

When these incongruities were finally faced, the most absurd solution of all was offered. Calvinism teaches that Jesus uses these warnings to sow fear and ***lack of assurance*** to fulfill God's supposed ***absolute assurance*** that God will never allow us to fall from His predestined will that we will be saved.[48] (This reasoning is compelled by Paul's doctrine of predestination.) However, this makes God deliver a two-faced message. For God would be using warnings that are premised upon attacking assurance to accomplish the very assurance of predestination that Calvinists insist (based upon Paul) is the ***real*** truth. If predestination were true, then a believer would have every right instead to believe he has *total assurance* based on predestination. He thus would be free to disregard the *insecurity for his own salvation* that Jesus taught. Unless God wants us to accept He can lie to us, Jesus cannot utter threats which negate the very assurance that God supposedly wants us to know we have in the doctrine of predestination. In other words, if Jesus threatens an assurance of a believer, but it is false that any believer has any grounds to doubt his assurance (based on Paul), wouldn't Jesus have to be a liar in uttering the threat in the first place? Of course, He would. The correct solution is to reject any doctrine of Calvinists (and Paul) that would make Jesus into a liar. One of these doctrines is predestination. If you assume Paul is telling the truth, then Jesus is the liar. If Jesus is telling the *real* truth that our salvation is at risk for certain misbehavior, then

48. In 1878, the famous Robert Dabney put forth the Calvinist argument "The ***certainty*** that he will ***not [apostasize]*** arises... from God's secret...purpose.... Among those appropriate motives [***God uses*** in man] are these ***very warnings*** of danger and wholesale ***fears*** about apostasy....They are part of that plan by which ***God ensures that he shall not***." (Robert L. Dabney, *Lectures in Systematic Theology* (Grand Rapids, Mi., Eerdmans, 1971 reprint) at 697.)

Paul's teaching that no such risk exists is false doctrine. I prefer to accept Paul has the false doctrine than swallow the idea that Jesus was deceptive, misleading, or worse.

These Pauline rationalizations are just more proof that much of Christianity has come to despise Jesus' words in preference for another Master: Paul. For what else could explain why anyone would take Jesus' threats and promises which hinge salvation on obedience, in part, and which are clearly *directed* at us, and yet claim they are really all resolved by Jesus' atonement? Under this Pauline view, all Jesus' warnings were really pointless. All He had to do is tell us about atonement and faith, and leave out all these troublesome threats and promises. What is really afoot is many have decided that rather than ***let go of Paul and hold onto Jesus***, they prefer ***letting go of Jesus*** and ***holding onto Paul***.

Bonhoeffer saw through these mental twists and turns. In his famous book entitled *The Cost of Discipleship* (1937), Bonhoeffer preached Jesus' words alone. He ignored Paul's doctrines. Bonhoeffer saw clearly that Jesus' doctrine of salvation turns on costly obedience to the Law, in particular the Ten Commandments in addition to faith. Bonhoeffer was blunt. He mocked the Modern Gospel as cheap grace. That Modern Gospel ignored Jesus' dominant theme of a personal costliness to receive eternal life. Bonhoeffer says the cheap grace gospel clearly is denying the words of Jesus. Bonhoeffer boldly calls this a "Christianity without Christ." (*Cost of Discipleship* (1937) at 39.)

Despising Jesus' Words Via Translation

Thus, it is clear that much of modern Christianity has come to despise our True Master in preference for another Master. If this really is not what is going on, then why would many in the church consent to translators not properly reflecting "*keep on* believing" is the real language of John 3:16, preferring instead to make it appear a one-time faith ("believes") is at issue?[49] What else explains why translators would change "*should* have eternal life" improperly into "*shall* have eternal life" in John 3:16?[50]

If the Modern Gospel has not led to the disdain for Jesus' words, then why else would translators make it appear God's wrath remains on those who "disbelieve the Son" in John 3:36 rather than what the verse actually says — God's wrath rests on those who "*disobey* the Son"?[51]

If Christians have not become lax in loyalty to their Lord, why else would there be no anger about the twisting of our Lord's words to Moses in Genesis 15:6? For the Lord told Moses that "he (Abram) reckoned it (the promise of 15:5) to Him (God) as righteousness." Premier evangelical scholars of Hebrew concur this is what the Hebrew means if we did not have Paul's words to deal with.[52] God was not reckoning anything to Abraham. It was the reverse: Abraham was reckoning God's promise of Genesis 15:5 as a righteous deed. This is because the *he* we see in most translations before *reckoned* is not actually present in the Hebrew. It is an interpolation. So without interpolating the addition of this *he*, its meaning is unmistakable in both English and Hebrew syntax: "He (Abram) believed the Lord and reckoned it to Him for righteousness." Hebrew's syntax here is identical to English. The correct meaning for the subject of *reckoned* was the *he* from the earlier clause: Abram. (Later his name was changed by God to Abraham.) Therefore, this verse never had anything to do with the idea of justification by faith, contrary to how Paul construed it.

49.See page 373 *et seq. See also,* Appendix A: Greek Issues.

50.The KJV preserves the correct tense of the subjunctive in John 3:16 although you have to interpolate it. "That whosoever believeth in him ***should*** not perish, but [*should*] have eternal life." However, the NIV renders it "shall" have eternal life. For the rationalization of using Paul's faith-alone doctrine to do so, see page 381.

51.See page 382 *et seq.*

52.See page 251 *et seq.*

Consequently, but for a primary allegiance to Paul, why would anyone tolerate any more the modern translations of Genesis 15:6 which even as they translate word-for-word correctly, mislead us by (a) interpolating the second *he* without bracketing it [*e.g.*, [he]) and (b) then capitalizing it. Watch how these two alterations trick your mind: "And he believed in the LORD; and ***He*** counted it to ***him*** for righteousness." (NASB YLT.)[53] But in Hebrew, the meaning is the reverse: "[***he***] (*i.e.*, Abram) counted it to ***Him*** for righteousness." Same words, but a totally opposite meaning!

But for transferring part of our allegiance from our Lord to Paul, why would anyone tolerate Paul's translation of Habakkuk 2:4? It is no excuse that Paul relied upon the erroneous Greek translation of the Septuagint. Instead, to this very day, we know that Habakkuk 2:4 in Hebrew stands for the *opposite* of what Paul thought it said! Its true meaning in the original Hebrew is: "The just shall live by his ***faithfulness***," which in Hebrew means ***obedient living***.[54] The verse thus had actually the opposite meaning from what Paul deduced. The obedient (faithful) are just. One is not justified by faith that is alone! Paul was simply using a wrong translation — a defect which was pointed out two millennia ago in the Dead Sea Scroll *Habakkuk Pesher.*

---

53. The King James, NIV, and ASV correctly translate Genesis 15:6, including omitting any capitalization to the second-clause *he*. Yet, they do add the second-clause *he* without indicating it is an interpolation. Some publishers of the KJV do capitalize the second-clause *he*. Yet, the following versions *officially* capitalize the second-clause *he* (and fail to bracket it to indicate it is an interpolation): NASB and YLT. Some even blatantly change the *he* to the *Lord*: GWT.

54. See "Habakkuk 2:4: What Does It Really Say?" on page 274 *et seq*. Only a few translations are correct: "by his ***steadfastness*** liveth" (YLT); "faithfulness" (God's Word); "faithful to God" (GNB). The Hebrew word *emunah* here is derived from *aman,* "to be firm, last." When used as a personal attribute of man, it means fidelity in word and deed (Jer.7:28; Jer. 9:2; Psalm 37:3.) It is solely a Pauline re-interpretation to replace its sense here by the solitary concept of a mere belief in some truth about God/Jesus/the atonement, etc.

What did this ancient commentary on *Habakkuk* say? It said Habakkuk 2:4 did not imply *faith* (as used in the Greek Septuagint) made one just, but rather *faithfulness* which in the Hebrew meant *obedient living* did so and made one "saved."[55]

Thus, Habakkuk 2:4 has always stood for the exact opposite of how Paul understood the verse! However, due to Paul's competing understanding, evangelicals refuse to see that Habakkuk 2:4's view on obedience is the Gospel that the Lord Jesus repeats in the Great Commission, John 8:51, Matthew 10:22, His parables, and numerous other verses.

Yes, much of modern Christianity has come to accept a competing Master. As a result, it has despised the Lord's words. It has added to and diminished from the Lord's words in violation of Deuteronomy 4:2. The reason is that Paul's doctrines are treated on par with Jesus' words (whether Jesus expressed them in the New Testament or through the Prophets). This approach has made Paul a competing Master. This preference for Paul is what is used to rationalize skewing Jesus' words in John 3:16 and elsewhere to fit Paul's words. People criticize the cults (and rightly so) for translating passages to fit their doctrine. Before we evangelicals can take the speck out of their eye, however, we need to take the beam out of our own!

A Clear Example of Suppression of Jesus' Words

People ask me for proof that they can more easily recognize that we have indeed killed off Jesus' words in preference for Paul. They do not know enough classical Greek to uncover the mysteries of John's Gospel. They do not know enough Hebrew to decipher the issues in Habakkuk 2:4 or Genesis 15:6.

55. See page 297 *et seq.*

Thus, here is one of the clearest examples of the mental gymnastics used to suppress Jesus' words in preference for Paul's doctrines. It comes from Charles Stanley. No one needs training in classical Greek or in Hebrew to see this.

Charles Stanley is the head of the eighteen million member Baptist church. Stanley comments on Jesus' many parables that discuss "weeping and gnashing of teeth" which servants of His in the parables will suffer typically "outside in darkness." These servants' errors were:

- not having interest on their talents given by God. Matt. 25:14 *ff.*
- abusing fellow Christian servants. Luke 12:41 *ff.* Matt.24:48 *ff.*
- failing to have charity to the brothers. Matt. 25:31 *ff.*
- being once virgins who later let their oil burn out. Matt. 25:1 *ff.*
- being once a "friend" who accepts the "call" and is even seated at the great banquet but when the time for examination comes they lack a "proper robe." Matt. 22:2 *ff.*

Stanley confesses it is too obvious to deny that Jesus is warning Christians of this place of weeping and gnashing for misbehavior. So isn't Jesus warning Christians ***hell*** (weeping and gnashing outside in darkness) if they have the failings of the "unprofitable servant"? If they are an "abusive servant"? If they are "goats" who call Him Lord but do not provide food, clothing and water to the brethren? Etc.

Stanley says *no*. Charles Stanley insists this "weeping and gnashing" which is "outside in darkness" is in *heaven*, not hell: "It certainly ***does not mean hell***...It clearly refers to being thrown ***outside*** a building into the ***dark***. There is no mention of pain, fire or worms."[56]

In arriving at such conclusion, Stanley never discusses His true Master's words in Matthew 13:42. Jesus calls the place of "weeping and gnashing" in Matthew 13:42 the "***fiery furnace***" where the angels at the time of final judgment throw those who were "ensnared" in sin.[57] If Stanley

56.Charles Stanley, *Eternal Security: Can You Be Sure*, *supra*, at 125.

discussed that verse, Jesus would no longer fit Paul. Losing Paul is too horrible a consideration. Thus, Jesus and His meaning are sacrificed. As Bonhoeffer said of the modern cheap grace gospel: "Jesus is misunderstood anew, and again and again ***put to death***." (Bonhoeffer, *Christ the Center* (1960) at 39.)

The Dilemma of Two Masters

How did such serious and prominent Christian leaders succumb to positions that hold tightly to Paul, while blatantly disregarding Jesus' words? It is simple. When you have two masters, you have a dilemma. These Christian leaders solved their dilemma by choosing Paul on certain issues. Jesus says when you so choose Paul, then you will love Paul on those issues. Jesus told us the consequence: you will despise your true Master (Jesus) when He speaks on the same issues. Jesus, however, said we cannot live like this. We must choose one over the other. Yet, it is not an acceptable choice to choose Paul over Jesus. Jesus told us to have an allegiance for Him greater than any family or personal ties. (Matt. 10:37.)

Thus, if Jesus and Paul conflict, we *must* choose Jesus' clear meaning over giving the slightest weight to a contrary teaching from Paul.

However, this approach has not been followed. Modern Christianity in large part has, instead, left Jesus' doctrine in shambles. As Bonhoeffer said of the cheap grace gospel, it is a Christianity without Christ. It denies the costliness of grace. The root cause of this desolation of Jesus' doctrine is the Paul-Jesus division. Jesus explained the eternal principle at work:

> Every kingdom ***divided against itself is brought to desolation***; and every city or house

---

57.Stanley's claim also disregards God's consistent message that in heaven there is "no more sorrow, nor crying." (Rev. 21:4; *see also*, Isaiah 25:8 "God will wipe away tears from all faces"; Rev. 7:17.)

> divided against itself shall not stand.
> Matt. 12:25.

Regrettably, mainstream Protestantism remains highly divided. The divide is typically drawn on lines that directly trace back to the Paul versus Jesus division. Lutherans who adhere to the mature Luther's *Catechisms* (like Bonhoeffer),[58] Methodists and Pentecostals along with Messianics tend to stress Jesus' words on salvation and the Law. On the other side are the Baptists, Reformed (conservative) Presbyterians and Evangelicals who accept Luther's youthful emphasis on Paul's doctrines. This Pauline side has several main sub-splinters based upon whether one believes something Paul said deserves greater emphasis than what other churches emphasize. For example, Predestination is highly important in Presbyterianism but is either sometimes ignored or sometimes rejected by certain Baptist scholars and evangelicals. See Dillow's *Reign of the Servant Kings*. Within this pro-Paul splinter, there are sub-groups who preach Law mixed with Pauline salvation doctrines. For example, some Baptist groups teach restoration of the Sabbath day. What we find then is there are sub-divisions even among Pauline Christians which sometimes lay partial emphasis on something Jesus taught to the detriment of accepting competing doctrine from Paul.

From these conflicts, however, a miracle recently emerged from the Paulinist side. This miracle shows Jesus is drawing the two sides closer together to accept one master both in faith and doctrine: Jesus Christ.

What was this miracle of God? It is John MacArthur's conversion to Jesus' Gospel. MacArthur first announced this in the 1990s. Since then, he has become progressively more centered upon Jesus' Gospel up through his latest work of

58. Lutherans comprise 70 million of the approximately 350 million Protestant Christians. On how Luther's mature writings come close to *Jesus' Words Only*, see page 106 *et seq*.

2003.[59] MacArthur's writings hold clear earmarks of influence from Dietrich Bonhoeffer's *The Cost of Discipleship* (1937). MacArthur's 2003 work *Hard to Believe* even has a subtitle drawn from Bonhoeffer: *The High Cost and Infinite Value of Following Jesus*. MacArthur has thus bravely weathered the charge of heretic as he holds dearly to the true salvation doctrine of Jesus. Yet, simultaneously, he avows his belief in the Paulinist-Calvinist doctrine of the 'sovereignty of God'[60] and the "faith alone doctrine."

How does MacArthur reconcile Paul's doctrine to Jesus' Gospel? MacArthur insists that we can simultaneously hold onto Paul and Jesus' true gospel if we just squeeze repentance and obedience to the Law under the meaning of *faith* alone.[61] MacArthur constantly is trying to thread a needle. He wants to keep all Paul's jargon but re-interpret its meaning in the hope of preserving Jesus' Gospel.[62] It is a valiant effort by a sincere but utterly conflicted man.

Yet, MacArthur represents an extraordinary movement of the Spirit bringing the Calvinist and Lutheran sides closer together on doctrine. MacArthur is speaking from the Calvinist side tilting in favor of JWO on salvation. Bonhoeffer speaks likewise from the Lutheran side in favor of JWO.

59.See, *e.g.*, "One Big Surprise" on page 366.

60.The 'sovereignty-of-God' doctrine is a euphemism for the doctrine that God directs and ordains evil thoughts and objectives yet supposedly remains untainted by such direction. See page 433. For MacArthur's defense of the 'sovereignty-of-God' doctrine, see MacArthur, *Hard to Believe* (Nelson: 2003) at 34-35. He admits evangelicals call this doctrine 'dreadful,' 'blasphemy,' 'God-dishonoring.' 'incongruous,'and 'the most twisted thing I have ever read.' Citing only Paul, MacArthur insists it is true. To deny it, MacArthur puts us in a box: it only can be denied if one is willing to deny Paul's validity. That's the step that MacArthur thought was unthinkable. However, it is that step which God's honor demands we consider. What John MacArthur supposed was unthinkable is the correct question rather than accepting a teaching so dreadful and God-dishonoring as what Calvinists euphemistically refer to as the 'sovereignty-of-God doctrine.'

61.See Footnote 23, page 399.

Thus, MacArthur and Bonhoeffer must reflect what is going on inside the hearts and minds of many believers. God is moving. God wants us to know there is no need any longer to live with such internal tension between two competing doctrines. Instead, there is one obvious solution. It will erase all this confusion and division. What if within Christianity, we all simultaneously agreed Jesus' words were the ***sole inspired source*** to formulate church doctrine? Jesus prayed that "they all may be one...." (John 17:21.) Jesus wanted this unity so *His* message would be unified and a *better* witness. What more sensible and better way to obey Jesus' intentions than to unite on the *single-source* of Jesus' words to formulate doctrine? It's the obvious solution to this nagging disunity. Unless we take this brave step, our witness for Christ is marred. And we will continue to defy our Lord's wishes of unity for us.

62. To see MacArthur's conflicting reasonings in just one book, see John MacArthur, *The Gospel According to the Apostles* (Nelson: 2000). He condemns once saved always saved. (*Id.* at 158-159.) He then affirms perserverance of the saints. (*Id.*) MacArthur doctrine teaches salvation depends on repentance from sin and submission. (*Id.* at 7.) Yet, salvation is by grace through faith. (*Id.* at 8.) Jesus supposedly said little about justification. (*Id.* at 78.) While the Law can never justify, yet the true believer will persevere in obedience. (*Id.* at 9, 83.) But to what end is perserverance? Then MacArthur says that no-Lordship doctrine that prevails in evangelical churches is killing the church. It teaches salvation even if does not "continue believing" or turns into "hostile unbelief." (*Id.* at 33.) No-lordship wrongly teaches faith in "a message," not in Jesus *per se*. (*Id.* at 34.) True faith "necessarily impacts behavior." (*Id.* at 35.) MacArthur then tries to un-entwine faith and works so works is never a condition of salvation. (*Id.* at 36.) Yet, then he says that "faith that remains idle is no better than the faith that demons display." (*Id.* at 37.) One can see a valiant effort to hold onto Jesus' gospel despite the agonizing pressure to conform to Paul's gospel. It is a brave but ultimately unavailing effort.

Final Thoughts

We can now finish the battle that the Reformers courageously began for Christ. However, we no longer can permit ourselves to turn a blind eye to the error in the Roman Catholic tradition that sees Paul too as an apostle of Jesus Christ. This was not the view of the earliest church when the question was squarely faced in 207 A.D. We can also now see Jesus gave us significant warnings of the "ravening wolf" from the tribe of Benjamin, not only through Moses and Ezekiel but also during His earthly ministry.

We must no longer be distracted from following our Lord's teachings. We can now take the first step to a thorough-going reformation. This one will examine all doctrine in the exclusive light of Jesus' words. Even doctrines that solely rely upon Paul.

When the Reformation started in 1517, there was a great advantage in using Paul to strike a blow at the Catholic doctrine of indulgences. Clearly, the Catholic church was selling a ***work*** of obedience as a means of salvation. An indulgence was a payment by a loved one to obtain a papal certificate for a deceased relative, whereupon the deceased was supposedly released from purgatory. They were now free to enter heaven. Certainly, such a doctrine violated Paul's teaching that works of obedience can never contribute toward salvation. (Eph. 2:8-9; Romans 4:3-5.)

However, Luther overlooked that an indulgence was a work not required by Jesus. It was a *tradition*. Moreover, unlike Jesus' doctrine of salvation, the indulgence doctrine taught salvation was achieved ***without any personal repentance*** of the person allegedly in purgatory. The indulgence doctrine negated Jesus' salvation Gospel. His Gospel emphasized the centrality of repentance from sin. (Mark 9:42-47.) The Catholic doctrine of indulgences also depended on belief in a place called purgatory. However, it nowhere appears in Jesus' words or any inspired Scripture. It too only had support in Catholic tradition based on the Apocrypha.

Thus, the young Luther overlooked a better strategy than relying upon Paul. Luther could have instead relied upon the Jesus' Words Only doctrine. With it, Luther would have easily blasted as unwarranted such traditions of the Roman Catholic church, including the notions of purgatory, indulgences, and countless other innovations. Luther did not realize he had a better weapon in hand than Paul. He had the weapon of the Exclusive Authority of Jesus over His church that neither popes, priests, nor ministers can claim to hold.

Unfortunately, Luther's emphasis on Paul and failure to use Jesus' Words Only to attack indulgences has had a terrible consequence. It has led to a teaching even more horrible than the doctrine of indulgences. We have taken any of Jesus' doctrine which does not comport with Paul, and found ways to ignore it and suppress it. When that would not work, we altogether dismissed such conflicting doctrine from Jesus as belonging to a supposedly defunct dispensation.[63] We have thereby drained Christianity of Christ's teachings. We have consequently arrived at a "Christianity without Christ" to borrow Bonhoeffer's expression.

However, I now look forward to the renovation which Bonhoeffer first let us glimpse. Not a word of Paul influenced him to depart from his loyalty to the words of Christ. Every word of *The Cost of Discipleship* (1937) is a testament to a man convicted by God of the verity of the Jesus' Words Only proposition. He did so bravely. Bonhoeffer died a hero as well as a martyr, suffering being murdered by the Nazis. Thus, let Christ be victorious for you as well, as He was in the end for Bonhoefffer. MacArthur likewise gives us hope that evangelicals and Calvinists will realize that Christ is the *Way,* the *Truth* and the *Life*, and "no man comes to the Father but through me." (John 14:6.) Soon I trust we will no longer

63.See "Does Jesus End up Marginalized To Make Room For Paul?" on page 367 *et seq*.

teach the lost about a pathway to Christ other than what Christ Himself taught. All who come up by a different path than what Jesus taught are "thieves and robbers." (John 10:1.)

This change in our pathway to God, based on what Jesus alone taught, can never possibly end up with a dangerous doctrine of salvation. This is because we are solely relying upon what Jesus said was required for salvation. We are still saved and justified solely by grace. But God's conditions for grace is not solely a one-time faith. Rather, as Bonhoeffer clearly explained, Jesus insisted upon a costly grace. Jesus rejected any notion of a cheap grace.

But when will we know we have a tangible victory for Christ based on Jesus' Words only? When no Christian during devotions treats Paul as a director of doctrine, but relies instead upon Our Lord's words alone. Then this battle is won. When no Christian would think of buying a Bible any longer that contains the words of a false apostle and false prophet, we will have grasped a victory for our Lord. When Paul is treated just like the Apocrypha, which Christians pressured the King James Bible in 1825 to drop from canon, we will have seen a tangible result. When all Christians relinquish every doctrine not of Jesus Christ, we know the Church has finally given glory where the glory belongs.

Is making this change all that hard? Tony Coffey in *Once A Catholic* made an interesting statement. In appealing to Catholics to focus on Jesus, and jettison Catholic traditions, he said he had a "heart filled with the conviction that if we follow Jesus Christ, we will never be lost."[64]

I wholeheartedly agree. If Protestants can tell a Catholic this is true for the Catholic about their traditions, then Protestants should agree it is true about their own traditions. A Protestant should agree there is nothing dangerous in following Jesus' words alone. There is, in fact, only danger in not doing so.

64.Tony Coffey, *Once A Catholic: What You Need to Know About Roman Catholicism* (Eugene, Oregon: Harvest House, 1984) at 15.

Appendix A: Greek Issues

Calvinists Admit Continuity Is Intended Meaning

Calvinists have always cited the Book of John to argue a one-time coming to Jesus guarantees salvation. Jesus will never thereafter cast you out. This is cited in support of their doctrine of perseverance of the saints. However, now even leading Calvinists concede the KJV mistranslated the verb for *come* as well as *believe* in the Book of John.

One of the leading advocates of Calvinist predestination is Dr. James White. He is the author of *Drawn by the Father: A Summary of John 6:35-45* (1999). He explains that the present tense for "come" in John 6:37 as well as "believe," "see" and "hear" in other verses in John's Gospel (such as John 3:16) signifies in Greek *continuing* action. He says:

> Throughout this passage an important truth is presented that again might be ***missed by many English translations***. When Jesus describes the one who *comes* to him and who *believes* in him (3:16, 5:24, 6:35, 37, 40, 47, etc.), he uses the present tense to describe this coming, believing, or, in other passages, hearing or seeing. The ***present tense refers to a continuous, on-going action***. The Greek ***contrasts this kind of action against the aorist tense***, which is a point action, ***a single action in time that is not on-going***.... The wonderful promises that are provided by Christ are ***not for those who do not truly and continuously believe***. The faith that saves is a living faith, a faith that always looks to Christ as Lord and Savior. (White, *id.*, at 10-11)(emphasis added).

Please note Dr. White realizes "many English translations" erroneously translate Jesus' words in John's Gospel. (In fact, in English, only the *Young's Literal* translates the verbs in John's Gospel correctly.) Please also note that Dr. White concedes that a correct translation of Jesus' words in John's Gospel would mean a "***continuous ongoing*** action" is necessary to be saved. Jesus' true meaning is that if you "don't truly and ***continuously*** believe" you will not be saved. Jesus' true words are salvation depends on "***always*** looking to Christ as our Lord and Savior." So when Jesus tells us if we "believe for a while" but later sin—"fall into temptation"—that we are deemed "withered" (*i.e.*, dead) (Luke 8:13), we must regard obedience to God/Jesus as necessary to salvation. *Cf.* John 3:36, 8:51 (ASV).

Dr. White's recognition of Jesus' true meaning shows even Calvinists are beginning to acknowledge the Greek present active tense radically changes the picture. When will we change our doctrines? When will we say that a faith that endures saves (Matt. 10:22) while those who "continue to believe for a while" but in time of temptation sin and "fall away" are not saved? (Luke 8:13.) When will Jesus' words have such priority that we no longer listen to any tradition which might teach otherwise?

Experts Explain How the Book of John's Meaning Changes On Salvation Doctrine

The dramatic impact of a correct translation of the Greek present participle active in John's Gospel is explained by an expert on Greek, Professor Dale Moody. He was a pastor and then for forty years Professor of Christian Theology at Southern Baptist Theological Seminary. In *The Word of Truth* (Grand Rapids: Eerdmans, 1981), Professor Moody at page 357 explains what John 10:27-29 really means in the original Greek. In doing so, Professor Moody explains how a proper translation of the Greek present participles overturns the popular notion that a one-time coming to Christ eternally secures your salvation.

> John 10:28 is frequently used as a security blanket by those who ignore many of the New Testament warnings about going back or falling away, but a literal translation of John 10:27-28... hardly needs explanation... 'My sheep ***keep on hearing my voice***, and I ***keep on knowing them***, and ***they keep on following me***: and ***I keep on giving them eternal life***, and ***they shall never perish***, and no one shall snatch them out of my hand.' Some read the passage as if it says: 'My sheep ***heard my voice***, and I knew them, and ***they followed me***, and I gave to them eternal life.' [But] ***[t]he verbs are present linear, indicating continuous action by the sheep*** and by the Shepherd, ***not the punctiliar fallacy*** of the past tense.

Those who should be secure in verses 28-29 are those sheep in verse 27 who *keep on listening* and *keep on following*. You are not secure based upon one-time having followed Jesus or one-time having listened to Jesus.

Now we can understand that John 3:16 is promising those who "keep on trusting" in Jesus *should* be saved. The meaning of John 3:16 is therefore likewise reversed when its grammar is properly reflected. This verse is talking about salvation by *endurance* in trust, not salvation by a one-time faith.

Likewise consider John 5:24. In our KJV this verse reads, "whoever *hears* my word and *believes* him who sent me has eternal life and will not be condemned; he has crossed over from death to life." In English, this means that if you once heard the word and just once believed it, you have crossed into the saved list. Right? But in the original Greek, the verbs for *hears* and *believes* are both *present participles active*. (See *Interlinear Scripture Analyzer*.) (Also, the "will not be condemned" is in the present middle passive deponent, not the future tense.) So what does this verse really say? It really should be translated: "whoever *keeps listening* to my word and *continues to trust* Him who sent me *keeps on having* eternal life and is not coming into judgment; he has stepped out of death into life." (See *Interlinear Scripture Analyzer.*)

When we translate accurately John 10:27-29 and John 5:24, there is a dramatic reversal of meaning from what we all assumed Jesus was saying in John's Gospel. Yet it is a truth that was always there. It was simply obscured for hundreds of years by its mistranslation in the KJV in 1611. (The Latin Vulgate which predominated prior to the KJV conveys the correct Greek meaning. Latin verb tenses have an identical correspondence to Greek verbs in their function.) It was also hidden by all other modern English translations that were not willing or courageous enough to repair the KJV error. Young's Literal Translation is a notable exception, translating the verb tenses accurately.

Grammar experts below will explain in depth what Mr. White conceded. They will concur unanimously that what Professor Moody taught is the only proper understanding of the Greek involved. This issue deserves serious unbiased consideration in light of the significant impact it has on doctrine.

Grammar Pros on Greek Present Tense

What is the present tense in Greek? One Greek grammar text explains the present tense and its meaning as follows:

> The present tense is basically linear or durative, ongoing in its kind of action. The durative notion may be expressed graphically by an unbroken line (—), since the action is simply *continuous.* This is known as the progressive present. Refinements of this general rule will be encountered; however, the fundamental distinction will not be negated.[1]

Dana and Mantey in their *A Manual Grammar of the Greek New Testament* likewise explain the Greek present tense has a primary meaning of action in progress. Dana and Mantey explain the present progressive (active) tense thusly:

> The fundamental significance of the ***present*** tense is the idea of ***progress***. It is the linear tense... the progressive force of the present tense should ***always*** be considered ***as primary***, especially with reference to the potential moods, which in the nature of the case do not need any 'present ***punctiliar***' tense...
>
> There are three varieties of the present tense in which its fundamental idea of progress is especially patent. Under the ***Progressive Present***...[t]his use is manifestly nearest the root idea of the tense. It signifies action in progress, or state of ***persistence***....

Rydberg likewise explains:

> Present. The present tense denotes an action in the present time with ***continuing*** aspect.[2]

Rydberg is saying the present tense in Greek signifies a continuing sense.

Within the Greek present tense are two distinct active forms. These two are the *present indicative active* and the *present participle active*. There is a slight difference as to the latter which is always to be translated with a continuing sense. The *Syntax Reference Guide* (Quick Verse 6.0) provides this further explanation, starting first with the *present indicative*:

1. James Hewitt, *New Testament Greek* (Hedrickson Publishers: 1986) at 13.
2. See "Jeffrey Rydberg Cox Overview of Greek Syntax," *WH Greek New Testament* (Tuft's University on-line).

> ***Present.*** Definition-Present tense in the *indicative* mood represents current action, as opposed to past or future action. In moods *other than the indicative mood,* it refers ***only*** to ***continuous*** *or* ***repeated*** *action.*

Thus, this means the *present participle active* (as in John 3:16) falls in the category of a mood "other than the indicative." It thus signifies "***only...continuous*** or ***repeated*** action."

Contrast the Aorist Tense

What makes it clear that the Greek present active tense is continuous is that in Greek grammar we have the aorist tense.

The aorist tense signifies a punctiliar meaning. That is, it indicates a single point in time. Actually, it is such a singular point in time that it is without regard to past, present or future.

Some explain the aorist incorrectly as always translated into English with a past tense. Rather, to repeat, the aorist indicates a verb activity is one time and completed. It does not mean simply a past action. Such descriptions of the aorist miss the point that Greeks did not think so much in terms of past and present, like we do. They thought more in terms of continuous or one-time events.

For example, when Jesus says in Matthew 10:22 that he who has kept on enduring to the end shall be *saved*, the word for *saved* is the aorist future of *sozo*. (*Word Studies of the New Testament.*) Jesus means that he who kept on enduring to the end shall be saved (*aorist future*) enjoys this in a completed one-time sense in the future. The completion of your salvation is aorist *punctiliar* (single point-in-time) in the future.

So you can have the aorist tense even in the future. It is not always a past event. It is, instead, a completed one-time event.

Thus, for Greeks, their thinking was always "is this continuous, linear, and durative," or, rather, is this "one-time, punctiliar, and not enduring"?

There is total consensus among non-Christian professionals on the proper manner of translating these Greek tenses. The *Vroma Project* on-line is an association of classic language scholars. They are un-attached to any Christian viewpoint. They are sponsored by the National Endowment for the Humanities. *Vroma* explains:

> You know that the *present indicative* indicates *continuous action* in the present time and the future indicative indicates future time. (It is important to remember that what we call 'present' represents *continuous action* in Greek. In the indicative form only it represents *continuous* action in the present time.)
>
> The verb *epai-deuse* is an example of the aorist. The Greek *aorist* indicates punctual action. In the *indicative only,* the aorist represents punctual action in the past.[3]

3. http://www.vroma.org/~abarker/tschapelevtwelve.html (last visited 1-2006).

Latin is similar. This helps explain why salvation doctrine did not take our modern twists and turns until the KJV in 1611 changed John's Gospel via translation. The rules in Latin are:

> Verbs in non-indicative moods use the present to describe actions that are *continuous* or repeated; they use the *aorist* to describe actions that are *single* or finite.[4]

Thus, none of our ancient forefathers for fifteen centuries who relied upon the Latin translation ever heard the familiar idea of salvation by a one-time faith that we read every day in John 3:16. No wonder their doctrine differed.

Precision Available To Say Whether A One-Time Faith Saves

The presence of the Greek aorist tense is deadly to those who defend translating John 3:16 to imply faith is a one-time event. If John 3:16 had this meaning, the underlying verb should have been in the Greek *aorist* instead of the *present participle active.* The very existence of the Greek aorist is dispositive proof that if a one-time faith saves, the aorist tense would have been used to convey such meaning in John 3:16. Its absence in John 3:16 thus prohibits using the equivalent of the aorist in English—*believes.* A correct translation should have used the English Continuous Present ("is believing") or a closer-to-original translation of "keeps on believing/ trusting." The KJV mistranslated John 3:16. This has had a devastatingly misleading effect on our perception of what is entailed in salvation.

The unvarnished truth is that John's Gospel uses the Greek *present participle active* in John 3:16. It does not use the aorist for *believes.*

Now compare this with the aorist active participle when used in a salvation passage. In Matthew 10:22, this aorist conveys a completed condition of endurance as what saves. Jesus says: "he who endured (aorist active participle) to the end shall be saved." A single-momentary faith is not promised salvation here. Only a lifetime of endurance is promised salvation. Thus, we see the Gospel writers knew how to use the aorist in relation to salvation in such a manner compatible with the ***true*** translation of John 3:16.

Accordingly, every way you slice it, salvation is based on enduring to the end and not on a one time believing (trusting) in Jesus. A one time faith that has failed never can save and never will. The idea that a one-time faith means you are saved eternally is based on a fiction born from English defective translation.

The NIV Half-Step

English simple present tense, as Stanley unwittingly proves in *Eternal Security: Can You Be Sure?,* is a leaking tense. Stanley says *believes* means in English a one-time belief. Stanley proves this from many examples of the usage of the English simple present. (Stanley, *Eternal Security, supra,* at 95). For example, Stanley points out that if I say "I live in Atlanta" that may be true today but it does not have to continue. It can become a one-time event and exist only in the past. So

4. See http://www.latin-uk-online.com/heuix/aspect.html (last visited 2005).

English simple present has a leaking meaning of a one-time event. Stanley did not realize the English-meaning corresponds to the Greek aorist present tense. "I live at this moment in Atlanta" in Greek aorist present can be translated into English as "I live in Atlanta." Therefore, even as Stanley unwittingly admits, English simple present can convey the Greek aorist meaning.

English also has a tense known as the English Continuous Present. This is rendered "I am living" in Atlanta. So this emphasizes the action is ongoing and continuing. This is approximately what the meaning is for a Greek present active tense.

The Greek present active tense means in fact the action will continue and progress in the same direction. This is true unless an adverb signals it is to last for "a while" or end at a certain time.

So when translating the Greek present active tense, translation experts often prefer adding "keeps on" or "continue to" in front of the English verb root. Thus, in the NIV, in 1 John 3:5 we find the two uses of the Greek present active tense of *to sin* translated once as "keep on sinning" and another time as "continue to sin."

In fact, the NIV's frequent approach was to translate the Greek present active tenses using "keeps on" or "continues to" with the verb root plus *ing*. However, if the correct translation of the verb would affect the doctrines of faith alone or of eternal security, the NIV reverted to the KJV erroneous use of English simple present tense to translate Greek present active tenses.

For example, in 1 John 3:5, as just mentioned, the NIV twice correctly renders the present active (indicative) for the verb *to sin* by adding "keep on" once and "continues to" on the second occasion.

While the NIV made this correction over seventeen times to present active tenses, the KJV consistently did not correctly translate the Greek active (continuous) tenses. The KJV routinely erred by using English simple present tense. These seventeen corrected verses in the NIV include Matt. 24:42 (*paim* "keep watch" v. KJV "Watch");[5] Matt. 25:13 (*paim* "Keep watch" v. KJV "watch); John 15:20 (*paim* "keep in mind" v. KJV "know" v. literally "keep on understanding"); Acts 18:9 (*paim* "keep on speaking" v. KJV "speak"); Romans 7:19 (*paind* "I keep on doing" v. KJV "I do"); Romans 12:11 (*ppa* "keep your spiritual fervor" v. KJV "fervent" v. literally "continuing to be fervent"); Galatians 5:15 (*paind* "keep on biting" v. KJV "bite"); Galatians 5:25 (*pasubj* "keep in step" v. KJV "walk" v. literally "to Spirit also should keep on observing"); 1 Tim. 3:9 (*ppa* "they must keep hold" v. KJV "holding"v. literally "continuing to hold"); 2 Tim. 2:14 (*paim* "keep reminding" v. KJV "put in remembrance"); Heb. 10:26 (*ppa* "if we keep on sinning" v. KJV "if we sin").

In six other places, the NIV uses "continue" to render the Greek active tenses. For example, Galatians 2:10 (*pasubj* "we should continue to remember" v. KJV "we should remember"); Col. 2:6 (*paimp* "continue to live" v. KJV "walk"); Heb. 6:10 (*ppa* "you continue to help" v. KJV "do minister"); 3 John 1:3 (*paind* "you continue to walk" v. KJV "thou walkest"). See also, 1 John 3:5 (*paind* "keep on sinning" and "continue to sin" v. KJV "sin" and "sin").

5. The abbreviations are: *pap* = present participle active; *paind* = present active indicative; *paimp* = present active imperative; and *pasubj* = present active subjunctive.

All these verses, however, have one thing in common. Their correction by the NIV editors did not upset the Pauline doctrine of a one-time faith saves you. You can readily see this inconsistency. In fact, what makes it obvious is that four times above you can see that the same *present participle active* used in John 3:16 is translated in a continuous tense, but not in John 3:16. What explains this different treatment? We already saw that Greek does not mandate this difference. Rather, ancient Greek mandates there should be no difference in John 3:16 than in those four instances where the NIV rendered it with a *continuous* sense. Wherever we find a present participle active, it should be rendered with a continuous meaning. This leaves doctrinal considerations as the most likely culprit to explain the difference.

Whatever their explanation, it is a fact the NIV translators never fixed the present active tenses in any verse that would flip it from Pauline-salvation formulas to Jesus' message of an enduring faith that saves. Thus, the NIV leaves alone the pivotal verse for so many: John 3:16. This verse really says all those who "keep on believing/trusting" should not perish but *should* have eternal life.[6] The NIV left it "who believes." In English, *believes* can mean a one-time faith, as Charles Stanley abundantly proved in *Eternal Security*, *supra*, at 95. The NIV version thereby left intact doctrine that had become encrusted in reliance on the KJV defective translation. The simple fact is the Greeks had the aorist tense if a one-time faith was what Jesus intended to endorse as a predicate for what *should* make you saved. Yet any notion that a one-time faith is the true predicate is emphatically erased by the use in John 3:16 of the present participle active of *believes*, meaning "he who keeps on believing" (or "trusting") should be saved.

6. It is *should* have eternal life, as the KJV has it, not *shall* as the NIV renders it. See Footnote 14 on page 381.

Appendix B: How The Canon Was Formed

First Written Canon (64-70 A.D.)

The first written Christian canon was proposed by the Ebionites. They said it was only the book of Matthew in Hebrew. As explained in the main text, the Ebionites knew of Paul, but excluded Paul as a false apostle because he rejected the Law of Moses.[1] There is no indication that they knew of Luke's or Mark's gospels. Nor is there any evidence they heard of John's Gospel or Revelation. Therefore, we can deduce this simple canon list of the Ebionites was developed around 64 A.D. At that point, Paul's writings were in circulation, but neither Mark, Luke, John nor Revelation had yet been written. Since the original Ebionites apparently disappear upon the fall of Jerusalem in 70 A.D., it is safe to say their canon list was no later than 70 A.D.

This is often overlooked because mention is made of another group of Ebionites. However, they existed in the second century and are not necessarily to be linked *organically* to the first Ebionites. According to Origen writing in about 200 A.D., another group calling themselves Ebionites came along after the earlier Ebionites disappeared.[2] Some historians lack this perspective, and thus do not date the Ebionite canon to the 64-70 A.D. period. However, it is more reasonable to infer that the original Ebionites existed as of 64 A.D. and then disappeared because of the fall of Jerusalem in 70 A.D. This would explain why they mention only Paul and the Hebrew Matthew, and fail to mention any other NT writing. Thus, the original Ebionites must date to about 64 A.D. when Paul's writings & the Hebrew Matthew existed but nothing else was yet written for our NT.

Furthermore, as mentioned earlier, it is likely the earliest Ebionites are the Jerusalem Church under James which we see operating in Acts chapter 15. After James died, it dispersed by 70 A.D. when the Romans razed Jerusalem.[3]

Marcion's Canon (144 A.D.).

In about 144 A.D., Marcion (85-160 A.D.) publicly declared the only apostle who had the true message of Jesus was Paul. Marcion said the twelve apostles were misled to mix Judaism (the Law) with the gospel of Jesus. Marcion's canon primarily consisted of Paul's epistles.[4] Marcion also added his own Gospel narrative

1. See page 306 *et seq.*
2. "Origen is the first (C. Cels., V, lxi) to mark a distinction between two classes of Ebionites, a distinction which Eusebius also gives (*Hist. Eccl.,* III, xxvii)." ("Ebionites," *Catholic Encyclopedia* http://www.newadvent.org/cathen/05242c.htm) (last accessed 2005).
3. For an explanation, see Chapter Twelve.

of Jesus' life. In it, the narrative of Jesus' life appears almost identical to Luke's gospel. Marcion, however, omitted portions that detract from Pauline theology such as Jesus' emphasis on Law-keeping.[5]

Marcion also rejected the continuing validity of the Hebrew Scriptures, *i.e.*, 'the Old Testament.' Marcion did so claiming reliance upon Paul's chapter 4 of Galatians. Marcion claimed the God who delivered the Hebrew Scriptures was a different God than God, the Father of Jesus. Paul said in Galatians ch. 4 that if we submit to the Law of Moses, we are submitting to those who "are no gods." The Law rather was given by angels. This created a lesser-greater revelation distinction. This fed Marcion's lesser-greater God theory. Marcion also believed the gospel of Grace was so much about love and mercy that it excluded the God of Hebrew Scriptures. Yahweh of the 'Old Testament' was at odds with Grace. He clearly wanted obedience to the Law. Marcion in his work *Antitheses* tried demonstrating from the Bible how the God of the New (relying on Paul) was different from the God of the Old. The Old would only save the obedient, while the God of the New would save all who believed even if they became disobedient. (Marcion, *Antitheses* # 19 (quoted at 49 *supra*.))

John Knox (not the reformer) summarizes Marcion:

> (1) The Creator of the world, although a real God, must be distinguished from the ***higher god***, unknown except as he was revealed in Christ; (2) The Creator of the world is a just God, but sever[e] and harsh; the God whom Christ revealed is a Father, ***a God of love***; (3) judgment is the prerogative of the Creator; redemption is the ***free gift*** of the God of love; (4) the Jewish Scriptures represent a true revelation of the Creator, but they do not speak of or for the God whom alone Christians ought to worship and ***from whom alone salvation from the present wicked world is to be received***; (5) the revelation in Christ was intended not merely to supplement or 'fulfil' Judaism but ***entirely to displace it***—the ***one had no connection with the other***; (6) the Son of the Father did ***not***

4. Of note, Marcion's version of Romans is missing chapters 9 through 11 and 15 & 16. (Origen, *Commentary on Romans*, xvi: 25.) One explanation is that Marcion rejected the grafting in concept in chapters 9-11. Others suggest these four chapters were a later addition fifty years after Paul was dead. I believe the former is true; these ideas are all true to Paul. Marcion is also missing 1 & 2 Timothy and Titus. (http://www.bible-researcher.com/canon3.html.)
5. Charles B. Waite, "The Gospel of Marcion and the Gospel of Luke Compared," *The History of the Christian Religion to the Year Two-Hundred* (Chicago, C.V. Waite & Co., 1900) at 287-303, reprinted at http://www.geocities.com/Athens/Ithaca/3827/wait2.htm. The early heretic hunters of the church accused Marcion of mutilating Luke. However, conservative Christian scholars today generally agree Marcion did not know of Luke's gospel. He simply had received or developed himself what was a source for Luke. Marcion gave no name to the writer of the gospel he put forth. In fact, Tertullian excoriated Marcion for not identifying the human author. (Tertullian, *Adv. Marc.* 4.2) Merely because the early heretic hunters such as Irenaeus saw the evident similarities to Luke does not mean Marcion mutilated Luke. He may or may not have done so. If he did not, then Marcion relied upon what is called the proto-Luke gospel. There is no trouble for the validity of Luke's gospel if Luke relied on the same text. Luke after all does not claim inspiration; he claims perspiration of research. (Luke 1:1-4.) It appears possible then Marcion either had Luke as his source or Luke added to an old source which scholars call the *proto-Luke*.

> ***actually take sinful flesh but only appeared to do so***; (7) there is no resurrection of the flesh [i.e., only of the spirit]; and (8) ***Paul was the only true apostle, to whom Christ committed his gospel*** [of salvation by faith alone]—***the other 'apostles' were false and had misled the church*** [i.e., by teaching works were also necessary].[6]

Thus, the second canon proposed about 144 A.D. was exclusively Paul and a truncated Gospel narrative that suited Marcion. This narrative is similar to Luke's gospel. The major difference is that the first three chapters of Luke are absent.[7]

Marcion's proposition was at odds with the Ebionite view. The Ebionites had insisted the canon was only about Jesus, based exclusively upon the Hebrew version of Matthew. Marcion implicitly rejected this. Accordingly, it was predictable that the next canon lists were compromises between these two diametrically opposed views.

The Muratorian Fragment (170 A.D.? 350 A.D.?)

The Muratorian fragment was discovered in the 1700s in a Catholic monastery. The actual document is from the seventh or eighth century. The source from which it comes from has no easy means of identifying its date.

Initially, the Muratorian fragment was estimated to be from 170 A.D. For tradition-sake, it is placed at this juncture in the canon story. However, in 1992, an Oxford scholar put forth what appears to be a better reasoned case which dates it to the Fourth Century. It matches several canons in the East from that period. Geofrey Hahneman thus says the early dating would represent "an extraordinary anomaly on numerous counts."[8] I concur. If you simply read it without knowing the date ascribed, it has the clear scent of later Roman Catholic terminology.

Regardless of its dating, the *Muratorian Fragment* starts mid-sentence. It starts with an apparent list of approved reading materials. It starts saying Luke is the "third" gospel. It is fair to assume Matthew and Mark were first mentioned. Then it continues its list:

> John, Acts, the Epistles of Paul (Corinthians (2), Galatians, Romans, Ephesians, Philippians, Colossians, Thessalonians (2), Philemon, Titus, Timothy (2)), John's Apocalypse, Jude,

6. John Knox, *Marcion and the New Testament* (Chicago: University of Chicago Press, 1942) at 7.
7. See *Marcion: Gospel of the Lord and Other Writings* at http://www.gnosis.org/library/marcionsection.htm (2005). For more original material on Marcion, see *Fragments of Marcion* at http://www.earlychristianwritings.com/marcion.html.
8. Geoffrey Mark Hahneman, *The Muratorian Fragment and the Development of Canon* (Oxford Theological Monographs)(Oxford: Clarendon Press, 1992) at 131. This is critiqued in C.E. Hill, "The Debate Over the Muratorian Fragment and the Development of Canon," *Westminster Theological Journal* 57:2 (Fall 1995) at 437 *ff.* The only support for an early date is the Muratorian Fragment refers to the Shepherd as writing in "our time." This amorphous language is hardly compelling given the many valid problems that Hahneman raises with the early dating hypothesis.

> John's epistles (2) [N.B. not 3], the Apocalypse of Peter [although] some of us are not willing [it] be read in church. [9]

This omits all of the epistles of Peter and James. It drops Third John. Hebrews is not mentioned.

If this the Muratorian Fragment (MF) identifies canon as of 170 A.D., please note how early that John's *Apocalypse* (today known as *Revelation*) was accepted. Its subject matter alone is what created controversy one-hundred and fifty years later.

The MF lacks any clear mention that inspiration is the criteria for each book listed as canon. It speaks of 'receiving' works. It does not ever suggest *inspiration* is the sole criteria for *receiving*.

In fact, in reference to Paul, the Muratorian Fragment describes Paul's works in a flat manner. It reads: "As to the epistles of Paul, again, to those who will understand the matter, they indicate of themselves what they are, and from what place or with what object they were directed."[10] There is no excitement that we have here *inspired* works. It is described in utter blandness. Then, slightly with more excitement, the MF refers to Paul's epistles to Timothy as follows: "[There are] two [epistles] to Timothy, in simple personal affection and love indeed; but yet these are ***hallowed in the esteem*** of the Catholic Church, and in the regulation of ecclesiastical discipline." This says clearly these two Pauline epistles were held as esteemed guides on how to institute discipline in the church. Otherwise, there is nothing more to imply about inspiration.

The MF also speaks of canon as including the Gospel of Luke but yet holding it in less than 100% certainty of its inspiration. As to Luke's Gospel, the MF says Luke is one who was "studious" and who "himself [never] saw the Lord in the flesh." Then it says Luke "according as he was able to accomplish it" wrote the nativity of John the Baptist. There *human historical* research, not inspiration, is ascribed to Luke. (This was precisely Tertullian's assessment of Luke's gospel as well in *Against Marcion.*) Since the MF regarded Luke as canon, but MF had an understanding it was included because it was *reliable* rather than *inspired*, one can recognize a test is at work other than *inspiration.* Canon was formed due to *esteem* or *high regard* or *trust*, not because each and every work was deemed *inspired.*

Origen's List (240 A.D.)

Origen said there were four Gospels. He mentions that Matthew was "composed as it was in the Hebrew language..." just as the Ebionites had claimed.

9. The source of this list, and all the subsequent lists, you will find at *New Testament Canon and Ancient Canon Texts* quoted in full at http://www.bible-researcher.com/canon8.html (last visited 8/26/05).
10. The entire MF text is at http://www.scrollpublishing.com/store/Muratorian-Canon.html (last accessed 1/7/07).

A Word About the Hebrew Matthew

Origen is the first mention of the Hebrew Matthew in the early lists outside the list of the Ebionites. Some people are surprised to learn Matthew was written originally in Hebrew, as the Ebionites earlier claimed. However, Eusebius in 325 A.D. agreed, and said the version we have today is a Greek ***translation*** of the Hebrew Matthew.[11] Irenaeus too in 125 A.D. knew of the Hebrew Matthew which later became the Greek Matthew. As the *Catholic Encyclopedia* relates, "Irenæus...wrote about A.D. 125 [and] he speaks of Hebrew... Sayings of Christ, composed by St. Matthew, which there is reason to believe ***formed the basis*** of the canonical Gospel of that name."[12] The Hebrew Matthew was also said to have been brought to India by the Apostle Bartholomew. Pantaenus, visiting India late in the second century, reported that "he found on his own arrival anticipated by some... to whom Bartholomew, one of the apostles, had preached, and had left them the Gospel of Matthew in Hebrew." (Eusebius quoted by H.J. Schonfield. *The History of Jewish Christianity* (London: Duckworth, 1936) at 66.)[13]

Incidentally, for some inexplicable reason, the early existence of the Hebrew Matthew is ignored in the scholarly analysis of the dating of the gospels as well as the order of their writing. This is apparently so because its very existence puts in doubt many pet theories to attack the gospels, such as the Marcan priority claim. Many scholars, typically liberal ones, argue that Matthew relied upon Mark. If true, this casts in doubt that Matthew, an apostle, wrote from an understanding he was *inspired* by the Holy Spirit. This Marcan priority claim, while not having a shred of evidence to support it,[14] has become modern dogma. It runs against the grain of the history we do have. Irenaeus in 125 A.D. and Origen in 240 A.D. both say Matthew

11. Eusebius, *Hist. Eccl.* iii. 39; Irenaeus, *Against Heresies,* Bk III, ch. 1; Jerome, *Lives of Illustrious Men,* ch. III; Jerome, *Commentary on Matthew* [12:13]. The only significant difference mentioned in ancient works between the Hebrew Matthew and the Greek is that the Hebrew Matthew is missing chapter one that is present in the Greek. (Epiphanius, *Panarion* 30.13.1-30.22.4). This means the Hebrew is lacking some serious errors that appear in the Greek. This first chapter in Greek contains the genealogy and virgin birth account. The genealogy is clearly flawed. Honest evangelical Christian scholars admit the Greek Matthew's genealogy has several errors. (Ben Witherington, *New Testament in History: A Narrative Account* (Baker 2001) at 70.) Also, other flaws in the Greek text disappear when we look at the Hebrew Matthew recovered recently from a medieval text. A modern translation of it can be found in the work of George Howard (Professor of Religion, University of Georgia) entitled *Hebrew Gospel of Matthew* (Mercer University Press, 1995). The original Hebrew Matthew that Howard recovered shows Jesus correctly saying the prophecy of the 30 pieces of silver is in *Zechariah* (11:10-13), but our Greek version from which our English translations derive has Jesus Himself incorrectly saying it was in *Jeremiah.* (Matt. 27:9.) Thus, the Hebrew Matthew is indeed the more authentic version. Whether by fortuity or God's design, it was preserved and we can all enjoy it now in Mr. Howard's scholarly book.
12. http://www.newadvent.org/cathen/03274a.htm (accessed 8/27/05).
13. Thomas is typically regarded as the main apostle to the people of India. The traditional date of Thomas'martyrdom is 72 A.D. in Mylapore, India. See "History of Christian Missions," *Wikipedia.*
14. The Marcan priority claim rests on an unproven assumption: if Mark wrote after Matthew, he would have relied upon Matthew. Based on that assumption, then it is allegedly hard to explain why Mark omits the Sermon on the Mount. However, if Mark was relying primarily upon Peter's recollections, as was Origen's claim, then Mark has no need to read Matthew. The assumption at stake that Mark would rely upon Matthew is an unfounded supposition.

came first. (*Against Heresies* 3.1.1. and Origen in Eusebius' *Eccl. Hist.*6.25.3-6.) Likewise, Augustine, writing in the 300s, said the evangelists "have written in this order: first Matthew, then Mark, third Luke, and last John." (*De Consensu Evangelistarum* I.3.)

The Marcan priority claim crumbles if the Hebrew Matthew is acknowledged to exist and pre-exist the Greek version. For if Matthew came first in Hebrew, this explains perfectly why Mark—who as a Gentile at Rome evidently did not understand Hebrew—would not have included the Sermon on the Mount which is present in Matthew. Mark could not read Hebrew! Mark did not omit the Sermon on the Mount because of the frequently heard argument that the Gospel of Matthew *did not exist yet.* This omission of the Sermon by Mark—the main support for the Marcan priority claim—therefore vanishes as relevant evidence. No wonder no scholar wants to discuss the existence of the Hebrew Matthew. They fear their pet theory will evaporate. Conventional thinking has taken over.

Furthermore, the Hebrew Matthew affects dating issues as well. The Ebionites' reference to it appears to predate 70 A.D. The first Ebionites disappear at about that time, which supports their canon list predates 70 A.D., as explained above. Also, their canon list does not mention Mark, Luke, John or any other NT writing except Paul, whom they reject. Their canon list thus spans as early as 45 A.D. to 65 A.D., but not beyond. (See page ix *supra.*) Thus, the Hebrew Matthew must have been written in that approximate time frame.

This matches the textual clues in the Gospel of Matthew itself. John A.T. Robinson in his book *Redating the New Testament* (SCM Press: 1976) rejects the modern dogma that Matthew was written in 85 A.D. He redates Matthew to 40-50 A.D. Robinson argues that because Matthew does not mention the fall of Jerusalem, which took place in 70 A.D., and Matthew includes Jesus' prophecy of its fall, then likely the fall had not yet happened when Matthew wrote his gospel. Thus, it was written pre-70 A.D. This is a reasonable position because Matthew had a penchant for citing all the fulfilled prophecies he could find. Matthew would not omit mention of the fulfillment of Jesus' prophecy of the fall of Jerusalem had he been writing post-70 A.D.

However, most skeptical modern scholars merely assume true prophecy is impossible, and put Matthew necessarily after the events of 70 A.D. Based on that logic, they date him to 85 A.D.

There is no justification for such skepticism. The prophecy of the fall of the temple after the Prince Messiah was cut-off is clearly in Daniel 9:25-26. This writing is traditionally dated by Jews and Christians to 600 ***B.C.***! Would these same scholars, who assume prophecy is impossible, redate Daniel 9:25-26 to 85 A.D. too? Of course not. There is no more reason to redate Matthew to post 70 A.D. than there is to redate the book of Daniel to post 70 A.D. As long as you put aside the supposition that the temple destruction prophecy could not possibly be uttered pre-70 A.D., all the evidence points to a pre-70 A.D. date for the original Hebrew Matthew. Of course, these same scholars are partially correct about the dating of the *Greek* Matthew. It would be true that the Greek translation of Matthew came later — possibly in 85 A.D. Then it is true the Greek Mark comes *before* the Greek Matthew. This would then explain perfectly why Mark does not have the Sermon on the Mount which is in the Greek Matthew. This also perfectly explains why Luke has parts of the Sermon on the Mount. His gospel account comes *after* the Greek Matthew.

Continuing With Origen's List

As to Mark's Gospel, Origen says Mark "composed it in accordance with the instructions of Peter." Then Origen mentions the gospels of Luke and John.

Origen continues his list by simply saying "Paul," without listing the individual epistles.

Origen next mentions Peter who "left one acknowledged epistle; possibly also a second, but this is disputed." Origen means Second Peter was disputed as not genuinely written by Peter.

Origen next mentions Revelation: "[John] wrote also the Apocalypse." Again please note that in the *Muratorian Fragment* of 170 A.D.(?) and now again in the Origen list of 240 A.D., John's Apocalypse (what we call Revelation) was clearly accepted.

Origen next adds 1 John and raises dispute with 2 John and 3 John. "[John] has left also an epistle of a very few lines; and, it may be, a second and a third; for not all say that these are genuine but the two of them are not a hundred lines long."

As to the Epistles of James and Jude, Origen is sometimes firm of their inclusion and other times waffling. *James* is an "epistle in circulation under the name of James...." This seems waffling. As to Jude, he likewise says: "And if indeed one were to accept the epistle of Jude...." However, in Origen's *Homilies on Joshua*, viii. 1, Origen is firm that they are both authentic canon:

> So too our Lord, whose advent was typified by the son of Nun, when he came sent his apostles as priests bearing well-wrought trumpets. Matthew first sounded the priestly trumpet in his Gospel. Mark also, Luke and John, each gave forth a strain on their priestly trumpets. Peter moreover sounds loudly on the twofold trumpet of his epistles; and so also ***James and Jude***.

As to *Hebrews*, Origen says its writing style is certainly not Paul's. Yet the thoughts are admirable and on par with Paul's thoughts. Thus, it is commendable to attribute it to Paul, although Origen 'concedes' the author's identity is unknown.

Eusebius' List (324 A.D.)

Eusebius acknowledges the four Gospels, Acts, and Paul. For Paul, he counts 14 epistles. This apparently means he was including Hebrews as a work of Paul's. Then Eusebius mentions Hebrews was disputed by the Roman Bishop. "[I]t is controverted by the church of Rome as not being Paul's."

Eusebius next acknowledges 1John and 1Peter.

Then as to John's Revelation, Eusebius is the first published source in church history to raise any doubt. He says:

> After these must be put, if it really seems right, the Apocalypse of John, concerning which we shall give the different opinions at the proper time (Concerning the Apocalypse men's opinions even now are generally divided). These, then, are among the recognized books.

Please note the test Eusebius utilized was recognition, with no mention of inspiration.

Eusebius then repeats about Revelation: "This last, as I said, is rejected by some, but others count it among the recognized books." Eusebius then goes on, and becomes the loudest voice against the book of Revelation. He raised as many points as possible to undermine its validity. He did not appreciate its content, apparently because it contained anti-Roman millenialism. Because Roman rulers now embraced Christianity, the prophecies in Revelation were embarrassing to the church. Eusebius thus did everything he could to support doubts about the Book of Revelation.[15]

Then Eusebius discusses James and Jude and 2 Peter. He says:

> Of the disputed books, which are nevertheless familiar to the majority, there are extant the epistle of James, as it is called; and that of Jude; and the second epistle of Peter (that which is circulated as his second epistle ***we have received to be uncanonical***; still as it appeared useful to many it has been diligently read with the other scriptures).

Please note he affirms strongly here that Second Peter is non-canonical.

What was the dispute over the Epistle of James? Eusebius writes that it was supposedly not frequently cited by the 'ancients':

> These things are recorded in regard to James, who is said to be the author of the first of the so-called Catholic epistles. But it is to be observed that it is disputed; at least, ***not many of the ancients have mentioned it***, as is the case likewise with the epistle that bears the name of Jude, which is also one of the seven so-called Catholic epistles. Nevertheless we know that these also, with the rest, ***have been read publicly*** in very many churches.

We now know that James was cited by several of the 'ancients' very early on.[16] Eusebius was either unaware of this or was unimpressed.

As to 2 and 3 John, Eusebius wrote:

> I recognize one epistle only as genuine and acknowledged by the ancient presbyters, and those that are called the Second and Third of John (these two remaining epistles are disputed), whether they belong to the evangelist or to another person of the same name.

It is interesting to see that early on up through Eusebius' day that 3 John was always disputed.

15. For proof that Revelation is authentic, see *Canonicity of the Book of Revelation* at www.jesuswordsonly.com.

16. See www.earlychristianwritings.com/james.html and under *e-catena* it shows James was cited earliest by 1 Clement (80-140 A.D.), the Epistle of Barnabas (80-120 A.D.) and Justin (150-160 A.D.)

Please also note that Eusebius is concerned whether the source is genuine rather than whether it is inspired. His list does not purport to list inspired texts. He lists only works which are genuinely written by the author to whom it purports to belong.

Council of Laodicea (363 A.D.)

This council is estimated to have taken place in 363 A.D. It was under the influence of the Roman Catholic Church (RCC). The council rulings clearly reflect RCC practices. In canon 60 of the council decrees, it has a list of both approved Hebrew Scriptures and New Testament books. The only omission from the New Testament at odds with our present usage is the Book of Revelation. The only significant omission from the 'Old Testament' which Christians previously had accepted was the Book of Enoch. These two books would be politically incorrect to the Roman emperors.

Some claim the materials proving this list ever existed are inaccurate and unreliable.[17] This criticism, however, is weak. The disputed Canon 60 appears in the oldest records. However, it does not appear in a work written in 544 A.D. In that year, a Roman Catholic historian Dionysius Exiguus omits Canon 60 from his version of the council decrees. Likewise, in 610 John of Antioch, a monk in Orthodox territory, omits it.

These later omissions are unimportant. What is ignored is why later Roman Catholic historians would omit canon 60 and want to rewrite history. It is fairly obvious. The Pope in the Council of Rome of 382 re-issued a new NT list. This list restored Revelation to approved reading material in the church. This rejoining Revelation to NT canon was repeated by Pope Innocent I in 405 A.D.

So why would Dionysius Exiguus in 544 A.D. omit canon 60 in his summary of the Laodicean decrees of 363 A.D.? The Roman Catholic church would not want to admit popes and councils make mistakes. If Dionysius repeated the significant deletion of the Book of Revelation in 363 which appears in the earliest reliable texts from the Council of Laodicea, it would embarrass the church. It would also promote uncertainty about the Book of Revelation, which the Roman Catholic church now was willing to endorse. These realities destroy our ability to rely upon Dionysius. John of Antioch apparently used Dionysius uncritically as his source. Thus, one biased presentation leads to a later unwitting repetition of that same bias.

Furthermore, the omission of Revelation in the Council of Laodicea was combined with deletion of the Book of Enoch in 363 A.D. This twin deletion completely matches the political-religious feelings at that time. It matches the thoughts and ideas of Eusebius in *Ecclesiastical History* written sometime after 325 A.D. Eusebius was Emperor Constantine's favorite bishop. Eusebius strongly disliked the Book of Revelation, and spoke vigorously against its inclusion in canon. Political issues explain his outlook. The Roman Catholic Church (RCC) was in the early 300s well on the way to becoming the official religion of the Roman empire. (This officially took place in 380 A.D.) The Roman bishop came to dominate all other churches within the empire. Previously, the Christian church was a loose confedera-

17. *History of the Canon of the New Testament* (4th Ed.) III at 428, excerpted at http://www.ccel.org/fathers/NPNF2-14/2ancyra/Laocn60.htm (accessed 2005).

tion of bishops. That original confederation traces directly to what we know today as the Orthodox church. It does not trace to Roman Catholicism, contrary to RCC myth. The Orthodox church of that earliest era was centered in Jerusalem. What could undermine this shift from the Orthodox council to a Rome-dominated church was precisely the Book of Revelation. Revelation was in turn a continuation of the Book of Enoch from the pre-Christian era. Thus, Constantine's imperative would be to erase the Book of Revelation and Enoch. He naturally feared how Christians would interpret end-time literature that made the "city on seven hills" (Rome) into the seat of the Great Whore/Beast/Anti-Christ. (Rev. 17:9.)

Thus, this list at Laodicea appears to be historically accurate, even though, for dubious reasons, it is not recognized.

Athanasius' List (367 A.D.)

Athanasius, bishop of Alexandria (Egypt), published the following list of approved reading sources in church in his *Easter Letter of 367 A.D.*:

> Matthew, Mark, Luke, John, Acts, James, Peter (2), John epistles (3), Paul, 14 epistles total (naming Romans, Corinthians (2), Galatians, Ephesians, Philippians, Colossians, Thessalonians (2), Hebrews, Timothy (2), Titus, Philemon), and the Revelation of John.

It therefore omits Jude.

The Syrian Apostolic Canons (380 A.D.)

The Syrian book of church order includes on its list of approved reading sources a book entitled *The Constitutions of the Apostles*. It purports to be first person statements by Peter, John, Andrew and other apostles. It is a blatant imposture. No scholar seriously contends otherwise today. However, it contains a list of approved NT-era reading sources as of 380 A.D.

The list includes Matthew, Mark, Luke, and John. Also Paul, 14 epistles (which means it includes Hebrews), Peter (2), John (3), James, Jude, Acts, Clement's Epistles, and lastly the Constitutions of the Apostles. The latter two are no longer in our NT.

Rufinus List (380 A.D.)

Rufinus, an elder at Aquileia in northeastern Italy, prepared a list in 380 A.D.

His list includes Matthew, Mark, Luke & John. Also Acts, Paul, 14 epistles (which means he includes Hebrews), James, Jude, John [3], and Revelation. He totally excludes the two epistles of Peter.

Augustine & Council of Carthage (397 A.D.)

Augustine, the famous bishop of Hippo (West Africa) who was the principle formulator of Roman Catholic doctrine, made up a list in 397 A.D. This list was identically adopted by three other African Bishops at the regional Council of Carthage. It is the same as our modern New Testament list.

The Carthage ruling provides us little context to deduce upon what criteria inclusion or exclusion was based. Its decree was:

> The books of the New Testament: the Gospels, four books; the Acts of the Apostles, one book; the epistles of the apostle Paul, thirteen; of the same to the Hebrews, one epistle; of Peter, two; of John the apostle, three; of James, one; of Jude, one; the Revelation of John. Concerning the confirmation of this canon, the Church across the sea [*i.e.*, Rome] shall be consulted. On the anniversaries of martyrs, their acts shall also be read.

Thus, even this list was uncertain. It needed confirmation and input from the church at Rome. No one knows if such confirmation was ever obtained.

How We Arrived At Our Modern Canon

The foregoing history is the sole tradition of how our current list of New Testament books were formed prior to the modern era.

In 1522, Luther assembled a New Testament based on the 397 A.D. list. However, in his *Preface* to the NT, Luther specifically declared the Epistle of James and the Book of Revelation were uninspired and should not be viewed as scripture.

As a response to Luther, in 1543 the Roman Catholic Church at the Council of Trent created an identical list to our current New Testament canon. The council decreed that the basis of this list was its traditional acceptance, not whether there was prophecy that justified inclusion of any specific book.

Then later in the 1500s, Calvin declared Second Peter should not be regarded as a valid part of scripture, as discussed next.

After Calvin's statement, credible challenges to canon by sincere Christians have ceased.

The Special Question of Second Peter

As the history detailed above shows, the only consistently rejected document (until 367 A.D. but dropped again in 380 A.D.) in our current New Testament canon is Second Peter. This bespeaks forgery. It should now be finally eliminated. The word of God is too precious to permit tradition to justify inclusion.

This recommendation is not the product of radical liberal insight. The flaws of Second Peter are so self-evident that even Calvin provides support for it being a pseudograph. As Metzger explains:

> Calvin applies philological tests as to authorship of various books...The style of 2 Peter differs from that of 1 Peter and

> was therefore probably not written by the apostle himself....[18]

Furthermore, Eusebius thought it a pseudograph in 325 A.D.[19] Eusebius wrote that among the disputed books are "the second epistle of Peter." One of his reasons was how few early church leaders cited Second Peter. Especially troublesome was that those who knew of First Peter did not know of Second Peter. Polycarp and Irenaeus, for example, only reveal knowledge of First Peter. One can verify this by visiting the computerized cross-reference of every verse of First and Second Peter to the writings of the early Church leaders. You can find this resource at Peter Kirby's excellent website: www.earlychristianwritings.com/2peter.html.

However, as Peter Kirby explains, there are many other reasons to believe Second Peter is a pseudograph. One telling internal evidence is a reference by "Peter" to Paul's writings as if they already had been collected and assembled in "Scripture." (2 Peter 3:16.) Such an event did not occur until well after Peter's death. Peter Kirby then explains: "Accordingly, we find ourselves without doubt far beyond the time of Peter and into the epoch of 'early Catholicism.'" *Id.* The pseudograph nature of Second Peter is now "widely acknowledged." *Id.*

---

18. Bruce M. Metzger, *The Canon of the New Testament: Its Origin, Development, and Significance* (Oxford: Clarendon Press, 1987) at 245.
19. See "The Canon of Eusebius," *Lost Scriptures: Books That Did Not Make It Into the New Testament* (ed. Bart D. Ehrman) (Oxford University Press: 2003) at 337-38.

Appendix C: The Easter Error

Jesus' Command Of A Passover Remembrance

The Hebrew word for Passover is *Pesach.* The King James Bible translates the word for *Passover* in Greek (*Pascha*) with the word *Easter* in Acts 12:4. The King James translators thus believed *Easter* was synonymous with *Passover.* Why was this? To find the answer, we need to go back to what early Christians understood (and everyone but English-speaking Christians still understand) was the *context* in which Jesus intended the communion command to be fulfilled.

We English-speaking Protestants are generally ignorant of Jesus' intention behind the "remembrance of me" command at the Passover dinner before He was crucified. (Luke 22:19.) As explained below,[1] the command from Jesus was supposed to be part of the Passover service that his Jewish apostles were to keep and celebrate annually. When Jesus said "do this in remembrance of me," He did not envision a new ceremony called Communion. When He did likewise with the cup of wine, Jesus was not envisioning a new second step to what we call Communion. Rather, Jesus was saying when you "do this," that is, recite remembrances as the head of the table shares the unleavened bread and as each table-participant drinks from the Cup of Redemption in the Passover Dinner, the participants were henceforth to now do this in remembrance of Jesus. The story of Jesus' sacrifice for our sins would now be added as a remembrance at these two junctures of the Passover Dinner.

This explains why the early church practiced Passover. The Bishop of Smyrna, Polycarp (died 155 A.D.), asserted Passover observance was ***directly handed to him by the apostles***. Polycarp also said he was taught by them to keep it on 14 Nissan, exactly as prescribed as the day for Passover in the Law given Moses.[2]

It may surprise an English-speaking evangelical to learn this, but it was this apostolic practice which explains why the Catholics and Orthodox ***still keep Passover each year.*** We find the Catholics in Italy call it *Pasqua*. In the Orthodox church, *Pascha*. Among Catholics it is an eight day period.[3]

---

1. See "Jesus' Intention to Transform the Passover Dinner" on page xxiii.
2. Of this there can be no doubt. Polycarp (martyred 155 A.D.) spoke of Christians keeping Passover at 14 Nissan, which he claimed he learned from Apostle John (whom he claimed to know as a child) and other apostles. Eusebius records that Polycarp went to Rome to convince the bishop of Rome to change back to apostolic practice. Eusebius says the bishop of Rome could not "persuade Polycarp not to observe what he had always observed with John, the disciple of our Lord, and the other apostles with whom he associated." (Eusebius, *Ecclessiastical History*, Ch. XXIII.) Likewise, passover for Christians on 14 Nissan was recorded in the *Apostolic Constitution* which dates somewhere between 220 A.D. and the late 300s.
3. "In the Roman Catholic Church, Easter is actually an eight-day feast called the Octave of Easter." ("Easter," *Wikipedia*, at http://en.wikipedia.org/wiki/Easter (last accessed 1/7/07).)

In fact, even in the ***evangelical Protestant church*** outside English-speaking lands, the celebration week ending with Resurrection Sunday still retains its correct name of ***Passover***, *e.g.*, *Pascua* in Spanish; *Paschen* in Dutch, *Pâques* in French, etc. I first learned this by living abroad in Costa Rica. I was puzzled why Protestant Christians there called Easter *Pascua*. That's how I stumbled across this issue.

The Law of Passover

The Passover Season was comprised of two parts: a Passover dinner and a week-long Feast of Unleavened Bread. The Passover dinner was celebrated at a dining-room table in a house (Exodus 12:46) besides at the Temple (Deut. 16:2). The home-observance was typically led by the head of a family. The house had to be cleaned of all scraps of unleavened bread in preparation for passover and the feast of unleavened bread. The sojourner (Gentile sharing community with the Jews) was enjoined ***only*** not to eat unleavened bread in this season. Exodus 12:19. Otherwise, the sojourner did not have to keep the Passover dinner or celebrate the Feast of Unleavened Bread. Yet, if the sojourner chose to keep the Passover dinner, he had to be circumcised first. Exodus 12:49. Thus, it was an honor that a sojourner could share in, but it was not a requirement to do so.

How the Timing Was Changed From 14 Nissan

Why does Passover in the Catholic, Orthodox, and Evangelical Protestant communities no longer coincide with the Jewish day of observance of Passover?[4] Why in particular is this true even if they retain the name *Passover* as the festival-season they celebrate?

At the Council of Nicea in 325, Passover's day of celebration was changed at the urging of the Emperor of Rome. He specifically demanded it be a different day other than 14 Nissan so as to *spite the Jews*. Emperor Constantine's ostensible reasons were all blatantly grounded on a virulent anti-semitical tirade![5]

However, there were actually some other competing considerations not specifically mentioned in the records from the Council of Nicea. The true Passover could fall in March. However, the new chronology guaranteed Passover would land in April. Why was this important? Because in that era, the English and Germanic name for April was *Eostremonat* or *Ostaramonath* respectively. What did this name mean? In April, the pagans celebrated the festival of Osiris. It was her month. In Britain, her name was *Eastre*. There is no dispute this is the origin of the name for *Easter.* In the Eighth century, a Christian monk and historian, Bede, explained why

4. For reasons too complex to narrate, the Orthodox do not agree with the Catholic date for Passover.
5. Emperor Constantine at the Council of Nicea in 325 A.D. stated the ostensible rationale for the change. He thought it imperative Passover ***not be held on the same day*** as Jews keep Passover. Constantine stated victoriously at the Council: "It was, in the first place, declared improper to follow the custom of the Jews in the celebration of this holy festival....Let us, then, have ***nothing in common*** with the Jews, who are our adversaries.... avoiding all contact with that evil way.... Therefore, this ***irregularity*** must be corrected, in order that we may ***no more have any thing in common*** with those parricides and the murderers of our Lord.... ***no single point in common*** with the perjury of the Jews." (*Theodoret's Ecclesiastical History*.)

English-speaking lands persisted in calling the Passover by the name *Easter*. He explained: "Eosturmonath, which is now interpreted as the paschal month, was formerly named after the goddess Eostre, and has given its name to the festival [Passover in Britain]."[6]

Thus, there was a more compromising rationale and purpose to Constantine's change. He desired to appease pagan citizens. This is why Constantine would not tolerate those who wanted to retain the apostolic practice of keeping Passover on 14 Nissan. These were known as *Quatordecimans, i.e.*, ***14-ers*** in Latin. Like we call the gold-rush enthusiasts *49ers*, these adherents were called the *14ers*. Because Constantine was able to heavily influence doctrine, the Roman Catholic church now inflicted excommunication on all Quatordecimans. This resulted in all kinds of civil penalties, *e.g.*, inability to inherit, etc.[7] This is how the true apostolic practice of observing 14 Nissan as the true day for Passover was wiped out in the Roman territories. Yet, the name *Passover* continued to be used. This is why the feast is still called *Passover* in all of Christendom except in English-speaking lands.

Thus, it was the British who solely refused to observe Passover under any name other than that of their goddess *Eastre.* She would have a priority over *Passover.* The Catholic church tolerated this in Britain. This was simply inherited by the Protestant English Church without any re-examination. As a result, Protestants in English-speaking lands came to completely forget the very context in which the drama of the Resurrection was to be recreated each year: it was the PASSOVER week, which starts with the Passover Dinner and continues in what is called the Feast of Unleavened Bread.

Jesus' Intention to Transform the Passover Dinner

But why did the early apostolic church follow Passover? Because Jesus commanded a change within the Passover Dinner. (Luke 22:19.) It was not something new called Communion. Jesus instead was adding a memorial to step four of the traditional Passover Seder where the unleavened bread is broken. He added another memorial at a later juncture where the Cup of Redemption was drunk. At each point, the bread and wine are shared by the head of the table with a recitation of certain traditional remembrances. Thus, the early church had to know this was the true nature of Jesus' command regarding Communion. This is why the *apostles* kept Passover, as Polycarp affirmed.

How do we know this was Jesus' meaning? First, the Passover ceremony had been standardized for millennia prior to Jesus Christ. It had fifteen clearly defined steps. We have Gospel-confirmation there had been no significant change in the fifteen steps by Jesus' day. The record in the Gospels shows Jesus followed six of the fifteen steps in exactly identical order. The only thing not mentioned are the steps involving the meal itself in the middle. While those steps are not mentioned, the six steps mentioned in the Gospels do not vary in the slightest from the traditional Pass-

6. He wrote in Latin: "Eosturmonath, qui nunc paschalis mensis interpretatur, quondam a dea illorum quae Eostre vocabatur et cui in illo festa celebrabant nomen habuit." (*Venerable Bede: The Reckoning of Time* Faith Wallis (trans.) (Liverpool University Press, 1999) at 54.)

over seder even as it is kept to this very day by Jews.[8] The dinner's outline was never enacted as a law in the Bible or otherwise, yet one can see Jesus went through it step-by-step in the First Century A.D.

Therefore, we know that Jesus was first saying at step four, we need to change something. This is when we eat the unleavened bread. It was at that point that Jesus *commanded* we were to "***do this*** in remembrance of me." (Luke 22:19.) Next, Jesus clearly henceforth was associating the Passover Cup of Redemption with Himself: "this is the cup of the New Covenant in my blood, which is poured out for you." (Luke 22:20.) Our Redemption was now from His blood, symbolized by that cup.

What else confirms Jesus' intent to modify the Passover Seder? His *remembrance* terminology in Luke 22:19 also fits in with the nature of the Passover Seder. The head of the table leads the participants in a series of remembrances of the work of God with the people of Israel. It includes not only the Passover but the bitter herbs the people of Israel ate in the desert. There is a remembrance too that Elijah will come back before Messiah, and so on. All Jesus was saying was He wanted to *add one more work* of God to the list of remembrances which were already being recounted at every Passover.

Now hopefully you can understand why it was so imperative to retain Passover within the early church. This is why Roman Catholicism and the Orthodox Church continued the observance of Passover all these centuries. To rid ourselves of Passover's observance completely would be to rid ourselves of the very context in which at least a Jewish Christian was to obey the commandment of Jesus to "do this in remembrance of me." (Luke 22:19.) If our intent is to enjoy the privilege of Passover, then our persistent use of the word *Easter* for *Passover* has a negative effect. It

---

7. The Quatordecimans were vigorously routed out by Roman Catholicism which deemed them heretics for refusal to move Passover to a day of man's choosing. See "Quatordecimanism," http://en.wikipedia.org/wiki/Quartodeciman (last accessed 1/7/07). A subsidiary issue was that Catholics insisted that the Resurrection celebration ***must always coincide with a Sunday***. The Quatordecimans disagreed. If you kept 14 Nissan as Passover as a memorial each year, the celebration of the Resurrection does not always fall on a Sunday. Why? Because 14 Nissan is not always a Thursday in our solar calendar as it was in the year Jesus was crucified. (The Jews used a lunar calendar which is why variances will creep in from year-to-year.) There is no doubt this was the day of Passover in the year of Jesus' crucifixion. The Passover Sabbath falls on 15 Nissan regardless of the day that the weekly Sabbath may fall. (Exodus 12:16; Lev 23:7; Num 28:16-18.) The Gospels say Jesus was crucified and died just before the Passover Sabbath. This is called the "day of preparation." (Matt. 27:62.) This was a reference to just before the beginning of 15 Nissan. Thus, when Jesus resurrected Sunday, Jesus would be ***three days and three nights in the grave***, as He predicted. (Matt. 12:40.) But if you accept a memorial of Passover as 14 Nissan, but tolerate the Catholic idea of always celebrating the Resurrection on a Sunday, then because of the variance in the solar versus lunar calendars involved, sometimes Sunday will be ***less than three days and more than three days*** from 14 Nissan. Anyone knowing Jesus' prophecy will suspect Jesus was a liar. (Sometimes atheists spot the inconsistency, and they hurl this back as proof that Jesus was a liar.) Thus, the Quatordecimans were additionally trying to argue Sunday was an inappropriate day to celebrate the Resurrection in a week in which you were observing the Passover correctly on 14 Nissan. Such Sunday-observance combined with Passover on 14 Nissan would leave the faith open to attack by making Jesus appear to be a liar. The Quatordecimans had a compromise solution. They suggested, to simplify things, that the resurrection should be celebrated on 14 Nissan (with the Passover) even though technically the Resurrection did not fall on Passover. Look at the validity of the Quatordecimans' concerns even among Protestants. We Protestants like Catholics persist in calling the Friday before Easter Sunday the "Good Friday." Good Friday commemorates the crucifixion. Now do the math! Three ***days*** and three ***nights*** later is Monday, not Sunday.

has led to ignorance. What else explains an otherwise brilliant and famous commentator like Gill actually saying: "the passover was... abolished, and not to be observed by Christians." (Commentary on Acts 20:6.) Due to the *Easter* moniker for Passover, no one within English-speaking Christianity has any footing to even begin to suspect Gill is wrong. At least for the Jewish-Christian, Jesus intended they "do this in remembrance of me," *i.e.*, share the bread and wine at Passover with a remembrance of Jesus' work on the cross. For the Gentile Christian who exercises the privilege to keep Passover, then he must follow Jesus' revision to that dinner celebration.

The Orthodox Confront English-speaking "Easter" Terminology

This background now allows you to understand why the Orthodox Church in English countries cannot fathom the practice of calling this feast *Easter.* As Michael Harper, an Orthodox 'father,' notes: "This is a much more important subject than a mere dispute about words." Harper acknowledges that virtually no one realizes the original pagan goddess worshipped in April was named *Easter.* Yet, it is this very meaninglessness of the name *Easter* which effectuated a loss of the real meaning of the season. This is how we lost the content of what we were trying to *do* — amend the Passover service to remember Jesus while we simultaneously remembered all the other works of God which were part of the Passover dinner. Harper explains the Orthodox' Church's viewpoint on this phenomenon among English-speakers:

> [There is a] constant temptation to drop the word *Pascha* and for clarity (and sometimes charity) use the western word *Easter.* But perhaps the ***time has come for us to make a stand against this***. In our increasingly secular and pagan society the use of a pagan word, of which ***no one knows the meaning***, is hardly suitable to describe the greatest day in the Christian year. When most people knew ***the Christian meaning of the word Easter [as Passover]*** one could perhaps make out a case for using the word. But not today![9]

In other words, if we did retain the substance of Passover practice within our Easter-observance, perhaps you could say using *Easter* as a name is harmless. But now the word *Easter* obscures rather than highlights what we are trying to celebrate to honor Jesus' command to revise the Passover ceremony.

8. There are fifteen points covered in a standard Passover Seder. When you correlate John, Matthew and Luke, steps one through four are mentioned in exact parallel; steps five through twelve (*i.e.*, the particulars of the meal) are omitted; and then steps thirteen and fourteen are repeated again in identical parallel to the standard service. (See http://home.earthlink.net/~lionlamb/PassoverSeder.html.) What Jesus was saying *in context* was He wanted step four (the bread) and step thirteen (the wine) to now be done "in remembrance of Me."
9. See Michael Harper, *It IS Pascha not Easter!* http://www.antiochian-orthodox.co.uk/pascha.htm (accessed 1/5/2007).

Any Imperative To Reform?

There is absolutely no dispute factually that the early apostolic church kept Passover. There is no dispute that universal non-English speaking Christianity has always kept Passover, whether Protestant, Orthodox or Catholic. There is no dispute that it was only in 325 A.D. that this observance was moved from 14 Nissan to a date that coincides instead always with a date in April. (This is because the Christian Passover-Easter is measured in relation to the vernal equinox.) There is no dispute that the current date does not coincide with the Passover in God's Law. There is no dispute that the only reason English-speaking Christianity lost the memory of the Passover festival was due to the stubborness of Englishmen. By the time of the Eighth Century, as recorded by Bede, the British Christians preferred to worship under their pagan goddess' name of *Eastre*.

With these indisputable facts, what should a Christian do? First, assuming Passover is something still to be observed, it is impermissible to move the timing.

When King Jeroboam moved the feast of tabernacles by one month from the time specified in the Law, the way this is described shows God's displeasure. (1 Kings 12:33.)[10] The Spanish Reina Valera is the closest to the correct translation. Jeroboam selected a "month he ***invented*** in his heart." (Reina Valera.) The Hebrew is *bada*, which means "to invent." (Strong's #908.) *Cf.* "devised in his own heart" (ASV KJV); "fixed by him at his pleasure" (BBE); "of his own choosing" (CEV).

What did Jesus likewise teach when we ***invent*** our own traditions in place of God's commands?

> (6) And ye have made ***void the word of God because of your tradition***. (7) Ye hypocrites, well did Isaiah prophesy of you, saying, (8) This people honoreth me with their lips; But their heart is far from me. (9) But ***in vain do they worship me***, Teaching as their doctrines the precepts of men. (Matt. 15:6-9 ASV.)

Thus, moving Passover, if we observe it, to anything other than 14 Nissan is vain (empty) worship, so says the Lord Jesus Christ. It is moved solely by tradition. Jesus says God does not accept vain worship. Jesus was alluding to the second commandment which says "do not use the Lord's name in vain."

Nor can one ignore that Daniel says what will mark "another" who "puts down three rulers" (Dan. 7:24) is that he "shall wear out the saints of the Most High; and he shall think to ***change the times*** and ***the Law***; and they shall be given into his hand until a time and times and half a time." Dan 7:25. Thus, God gives us an idea

10. Keil & Delitzsch explain this was an "arbitrary alteration of the Law." They explain: "Jeroboam also transferred to the eighth month the feast which ought to have been kept in the seventh month (the feast of tabernacles, Lev 23:34.)."

that this "other" acts wrongly by changing the "times and the Law."[11] If this is so, then how can moving the date for Passover as provided in the Law given Moses be correct? As the Psalmist says, "Your royal laws cannot be changed." (Ps. 93:5.)

The remaining question, and the most important, is whether Jesus intended the apostles to keep Passover.

First, in broad terms, it is undisputed that the command to keep the Passover applied to Jews. It was optional for sojourners (Gentiles), but if they elected to keep it, they had to be circumcised. Thus, only if God abrogated the Law as to Jews can one say Jesus did not intend the apostles to keep Passover.

There are some fundamentally difficult passages to overcome if we contend God intended to abrogate the Law (Torah) in the New Testament. The New Testament was prophesied to "inscribe the Law (Torah) on our hearts." (Jeremiah 31:31-33.) When a Redeemer is sent to Israel to create a new covenant, God promises that "***these words*** that ***I have given you***" (the Law) "will be on your lips and on the lips of your children and your children's children ***forever***." (Isaiah 59:21 NLT.)[12] When His Servant (Messiah) comes, God "will ***magnify the Law*** (Torah), and make it honorable." (Isaiah 42:21 ASV/KJV.) Jesus, for His part, did everything possible to put the Law given Moses on our lips and in our hearts forever. Jesus said immediately after just referring to the "Law (given Moses) and the Prophets" (Matt. 5:17):

> Whosoever therefore shall break ***one of these least commandments, and shall teach men so***, he shall be called the least in the kingdom of heaven: but whosoever ***shall do and teach them***, the same shall be called ***great in the kingdom of heaven***. (Matt. 5:19 KJV)

In an identical spirit, Jesus excoriated the Pharisees for a shallow teaching of the "less weighty matters of the Law," but leaving the "weightier matters of the Law undone." Matt. 23:23. Jesus attacked the Pharisees' oral traditions which made of none effect the written commandments of God given Moses. Matt. 15:6-9 (the Pharisees taught that a special korban payment which they invented would excuse later having to honor one's parents if they fell into poverty — in violation of one of the Ten Commandments.) Jesus did everything He could to elevate obedience to the Law given Moses. Jesus' critiques all reveal the Pharisees had a *shallow* defective Law-negating doctrine. The people merely assumed the Pharisees were teaching the Law because the people were told by the Pharisees what the Law was. Bible-texts were not ubiquitous as they are now. But Jesus said this supposition about the Pharisees was untrue.

---

11. Daniel shows this *other*'s activity is viewed negatively by saying in Daniel 7:26 "But the judgment shall be set, and they ***shall take away his dominion***, to consume and to destroy it unto the end." Then in turn the kingdom taken from him "shall be given to the people of the saints of the Most High: His kingdom is an everlasting kingdom, and all dominions shall serve and obey him." (Dan. 7:27.)

12. All commentators agree Isaiah 59:21 is a promise of the New Covenant. Barnes says "these words" or "my words" means God's truth previously given "for the guidance and instruction of the church." Clarke says this means the "words of Jesus." But this overlooks the tense, which is a *past* tense. "These words" are words given prior to the coming of the Redeemer. Keil & Delitzsch concur, but they try to claim the prior "words" are the words of a covenant given to Abraham in Genesis 17:1 *et seq.* No one wants to accept the simplest solution: Isaiah is saying the same thing as Jeremiah. God intended the Law is on the lips and in the hearts of all those who belong to the New Covenant.

Moreover, if the New Testament somehow abrogates the Law, including the Law of Passover, this would contradict God's repeated emphasis that "these ordinances" of the Law shall be "everlasting for all generations." (Ex. 27:21; 30:21; Lev. 6:18; 7:36; 10:9; 17:7; 23:14, 21, 41; 24:3; Num. 10:8; 15:15.)

Luther reculctantly came to accept Jesus intended the Law given Moses remains the rule of life for the Christian. While Luther originally subscribed to an anti-Law position in his *Commentary on Galatians*, Luther eventually made an about face. He insisted the Law, in particular the Ten Commandments, applies to Christians. (*Shorter/Longer Catechisms* (1531-32); *Antinomian Theses* (1537); *cfr. Commentary on Galatians* (1531).)[13]

Thus, it would appear that Jesus at least intended His Jewish apostles to keep Passover. It remained an honor for a Gentile to keep it.

What confirms this is that Polycarp, Bishop of Smyrna, said the apostles themselves *personally* taught him to keep Passover. If Polycarp were lying, it makes no sense that there is such a strong universal memory (other than in English-speaking lands) that the festival we call Easter is everywhere else called Passover, and is universally kept.

Finally, Jesus' command to "do this in remembrance of Me" during the Passover dinner has one obvious meaning. Jesus gave two remembrances that would be spoken of when the apostles "do this"— distribute the unleavened bread and share the Cup of Redemption at Passover. The context defines what *do this* meant. The later tradition of what we do on Sunday in Communion does not define what Jesus meant by *do this.* To think Jesus meant "do this" in a vacuum of a Sunday church communion service which observance is itself nowhere commanded in Scripture is replacing tradition for what is the import of Jesus' command. He clearly assumed that the apostles would keep the Passover dinner, as the Law mandated upon a Jew. It is within this context the apostles would fulfill His remembrance-commands of the communion cup and wine. To use tradition to avoid the import of Jesus' command would be "empty" worship. Jesus specifically said worship is vain when *tradition* replaces *commandments of God.* (Matt. 15:6-9.) This includes commandments from Our Lord to remember Him when we 'do this' (*i.e.*, keep passover sharing of the bread and wine).

Thus, we should re-examine our own practice of Easter: do you know it is Passover that we are attempting to celebrate? If not, that is the first sign of an *empty* and *vain* worship. Do we know we are being told to exchange unleavened bread and a Cup of Redemption as remembrances at a Passover dinner *at home* if we are electing to keep the Passover season as a Christian? If not, that is a second sign of an *empty* and *vain* worship. Finally, are we troubled in the slightest that we are worshipping Christ under the name of a pagan goddess albeit a long forgotten association? If not, then that is a final sign that our worship has become so *empty* and so *vain* that even the clear historical taint of idol-worship does not concern us.

13. See page 102 *et seq., viz.*, at 106. See also page 472.

Appendix D: The Abrahamic Covenant

Most Christians are unaware that Paul also overthrew the true Abrahamic Covenant. Paul's arguments create a *de-facto* new Abrahamic covenant from Genesis 15:5-6, which he insisted had priority over the true Abrahamic covenant which is recorded in Genesis 17:1-7. Paul says the alleged promise in Genesis 15:6 of justification by faith is inherited by the offspring of Abraham, including believers in Christ (Gal. 3:6, 26). However, Genesis 15:5-6 does not say any such thing. In making this claim, Paul makes of none effect the terms of the true Abrahamic Covenant of Genesis 17:1-7. How so?

First, Paul tries to claim the promise of Genesis 15:6 created faith alone as a basis of Abraham being right with God. Gal. 3:6. (As discussed elsewhere, this verse had nothing to do with imputed righteousness.)[1] Then Paul says we inherit the promise of Genesis 15:5 (blessing of offspring as the number of stars) by the sheer step of faith that supposedly justified Abraham in Genesis 15:6. (Gal. 3:26.) The problem is that Paul has utterly ignored that there is no covenant offered with either Abraham or with any offspring in Genesis 15:5-6. A covenant with Abraham is only offered in Genesis 17:1-7, specifically mentioning it runs in favor of Abraham's offspring: "And I ***will*** establish my covenant between me and thee and ***thy seed*** after thee in ***their generations*** for an ***everlasting covenant***, to be a God unto thee, and to thy seed after thee." (Gen 17:7.)[2] Please also note it was an *eternal covenant*. Its terms would never expire.

Furthermore, the condition of the Abrahamic covenant is not faith, but the obedience of Abraham: "walk before me, and be thou blameless and[3] I ***will*** make my covenant between me and thee, and will multiply thee exceedingly." (Gen 17:1-2.) Consequently, Abraham and his "seed after

1. See pages 251-53, 495, and 507.

you" had a duty in turn to "keep my covenant." (Gen. 17:3.) God repeats this in Genesis 18:8-9, saying that the covenant promise of God is ***contingent*** on the Abraham obeying and teaching his children to obey God's commands.[4] Then, after Abraham's death, God affirmed to Isaac that Abraham had obeyed all God's law, which now justified God keeping His side of the covenant to Abraham's seed, namely Isaac:

> (1)... And Isaac went... unto Gerar. (2) And Jehovah appeared unto him, and said, Go not down into Egypt. Dwell in the land which I shall tell thee of. (3) Sojourn in this land, and I will be with thee, and will bless thee. For unto thee, and unto thy seed, I will give all these lands, and ***I will establish the oath*** which I sware unto Abraham thy father. (4) And I will multiply thy seed as the stars of heaven, and will give unto thy seed all these lands. And in thy seed shall all the nations of the earth be blessed. (5) ***Because*** that Abraham ***obeyed my***

---

2. Pauline-biased scholars try to assert the covenant was put in place fourteen years earlier than Genesis 17:1-7. They claim it really was instituted when we read the promise in Genesis 15:5-6. (*Keil & Delitzsch.*) However, that is not testing Paul by God's word for *consistency*, is it? That is backward reading into a passage to vindicate Paul. However, there is nothing in Genesis 17:1-7 to suggest any covenant was previously in place. In fact, as worded in Genesis 17:1-7, a covenant is still only a plan of God in the future, dependent on Abraham's obedience which had to be proven, ***not assumed***. Genesis 17 reads: "And when Abram was ninety years old and nine, Jehovah appeared to Abram, and said unto him, I am God Almighty; ***walk before me, and be thou blameless*** [a]nd I ***will*** make my covenant between me and thee, and will multiply thee exceedingly." (Gen 17:1-2 NAS.)
3. Some break these two clauses by putting a period before *and.* The apparent rationale is to weaken the embarrassing conditionality of obedience to God's adoption of the Abrahamic Covenant. The correct translation has no *period*, such as in the Geneva Study Bible, Latin Vulgate, Websters, Young's Literal, Italian Riveduta, Contemporary English Version, etc. The period punctuation appears in the KJV, NAS and the German Luther Bible. Yet, even with a period before *and*, the conditionality remains.

> ***voice, and kept my charge, my commandments, my statutes, and my laws.*** Gen 26:1-5 (ASV)

Thus, Paul turned a mere promise to Abraham *alone* in Genesis 15:5-6 into something it was never intended to be. Paul made it a distinct covenant of righteousness by faith that belonged to Abraham's offspring. Paul has caused generations of Christians to ignore the ***true covenant*** made between Abraham and God that was inheritable. It was clearly one premised on Abraham "walking with me blamelessly" in which case God "***will***" later enter into a covenant with Abraham. Gen. 17:1-2. We know from Genesis 26:1-5 that Abraham did obey God's commandments, and that God did assume His obligation under the covenant. God at that juncture brought a blessing on offspring of Abraham. The blessing was obtained by a covenant of obedience, not one upon faith alone.

Indeed, thereafter the terms of the true Abrahamic Covenant remained "eternal," just as God said. (Gen. 17:7.) This is ignored by Pauline Christians for it would overthrow Paul's Gospel if ever accepted.

For the ***same terms*** of the Abrahamic Covenant were then repeated by Moses in the Law in Deuteronomy 6:25: "And it shall be righteousness unto us, if we observe to do all this commandment before Jehovah our God, as he hath commanded us." Mercy is always possible for transgression if you turn from evil (Deut.13:17), but righteousness was only to be imputed again if repentance ensued. (Ezekiel 33:12-14.)

This is why the Prophet Daniel likewise repeated the obedience-requirement for covenant promises to be kept: "And I prayed unto Jehovah my God, and made confession,

4. "For I have known him [Abraham], ***to the end*** that he may ***command his children*** and his household after him, that they ***may keep the way of Jehovah***, to do [*work*] ***righteousness*** and justice; ***to the end*** that Jehovah ***may bring*** upon Abraham that which he hath spoken of him." (Gen. 18:19 ASV.)

and said, Oh, Lord, the great and dreadful God, who ***keepeth covenant*** and lovingkindness ***with them*** that love him and ***keep his commandments***..." Dan 9:4.

Then of course Jesus put the same emphasis on "obeying" all "my teaching" for eternal life in John 8:51. Then, of course, if you fail to obey but you repent from sin and turn back to obedience, you are once more "justified" with God. (Luke 18:10 *ff.*) But those who "keep on disobeying the son continue to have the wrath of God reside on them." (John 3:36 ASV.)

Thus, we see all three covenants have identical principles on obedience and justification. They are a ***continuum of an identical message***. God's promise of salvation is upon those who obey all His commands, statutes and ordinances. Atonement under such a system only applied to those who fled the altar first to be reconciled to the one they knew they had sinned against, as Jesus Himself said. (Matthew 5:23-24.)[5] As Jesus repeatedly said, if you violate the commandments, you must engage in severe repentance (figuratively cut off offending body parts) to avoid being sent to hell. (Matthew 5:29, Matthew 18:8, and Mark 9:42-48.) Thus, all three covenants match each other with the same salvation doctrine.

This explains why God could say the Abrahamic covenant was "an ***everlasting covenant***" (Gen 17:7) just as God could say "these ordinances" given Moses in the Law shall be "everlasting for all generations." (Ex. 27:21; 30:21; Lev. 6:18; 7:36; 10:9; 17:7; 23:14, 21, 41; 24:3; Num. 10:8.)

But if obedience to the Law creates justification (Deut. 6:25) this never meant it does so without faith, as Paul assumed. A command to have faith is not absent in the Law. Jesus said the "weightier matters of the Law" include not only Justice and Mercy, but also Faith. (Matt. 23:23.) A command to have faith/trust is found numerous times in the Law and Prophets, *e.g.*, Deut. 31:6; Isaiah 26:4; and Jer. 17:7.

5. For a full discussion on this passage, and the clear reference to the Days of Ten, see page 265 *et seq.*

Bibliographical References

___. "The Canon of Eusebius," *Lost Scriptures: Books That Did Not Make It Into the New Testament* (ed. Bart D. Ehrman) (Oxford University Press: 2003).

___. "Pelagius,"*Catholic Encyclopedia,* available at http://www.newadvent.org/cathen/11604a.htm (last visited 2005)

___. *Hebrew Scriptures* (*OT*), online interlinear at http://www.scripture4all.org/OnlineInterlinear/Hebrew_Index.htm. (Sources: Biblia Hebraica Stuttgartensia with Concordant Hebrew-English Sublinear. © Copyright 2004 Menno Haaijman).

___. *Interlinear Scripture Analyzer* available from http://www.scripture4all.org (English-Greek New Testament interlinear).

___. *Luther's Catechism* (Produced by Board for Parish Services, Wisconsin Evangelical Lutheran Synod) (Northwestern Publishing House, 1998).

___. *The Message:Attitudes of Faith* (Boston Christian Bible Study Resources: 2004) at http://www.bcbsr.com/topics/fj7.html (last accessed 2005).

___. *New Testament Canon* and *Ancient Canon Texts Quoted in Full* at http://www.bible-researcher.com.

Bercot, David W. *A Dictionary of Early Christian Beliefs* (Bercot ed.)(1998).

Bercot, David W. *Will the Real Heretics Please Stand Up: A New Look at Today's Evangelical Christianity in the light of Early Christianity* (Texas: Scroll Publishing, 1999).

Bonhoeffer, Dietrich. *The Cost of Discipleship* (orig. ed. 1937) (Touchstone: 1995).

Bonhoeffer, Dietrich. *Christ the Center* (Harper's: 1978). (These are lectures given in 1933.)

Borden, Paul. *The Frustration of Doing Good* (audio sermon) (availabe online from *Christianity Today* 6-19-05 at http ://resources.christianity.com/ ministries/ christianity-today/ main/ talkInfo.jhtml? id= 26945) (last accessed 2005).

Calvin, John. *Institutes of the Christian Religion* (Trans. Henry Beveridge) (Grand Rapids: Eerdmans, 1983).

Campenhausen, Hans van. *The Formation of the Christian Bible* (J. A. Baker, trans.) (Philadelphia: Fortress Press, 1972).

Coffey, Tony. *Once A Catholic: What You Need to Know About Roman Catholicism* (Eugene, Oregon: Harvest House, 1984).

Crossan, John. *In Search of Paul: How Jesus' Apostle Opposed Rome's Empire with God's Kingdom* (San Francisco, Harper San Francisco, 2004).

Dillow, Joseph. *Reign of the Servant Kings* (2d ed.)(Schoettle Publishing,1992).

Dunning, H. Ray. "The Divine Response, Habakkuk 2:4," *Beacon Hill Commentary* (Kansas City, Mo.: Beacon Hill Press, 1966) Vol. 5 at 277 *et seq.*

Ehrman, Bart D. *The Orthodox Corruption of Scripture: The Effect of Early Christological Controversies on the Text of the New Testament* (N.Y.: Oxford University Press, 1993).

Ehrman, Bart D. *Peter, Paul & Mary Magdalene* (Oxford: Oxford University Press, 2006).

Eisenman, Robert. *James, The Brother of Jesus: The Key to Unlocking the Secrets of Early Christianity and the Dead Sea Scrolls* (Penguin, 1998).

Eisenman, Robert. *The New Testament Code: The Cup of the Lord, The Damascus Covenant, and the Blood of Christ* (London: Watkins Publishing, 2006).

Eusebius, *The History of the Church* (Trans. ed. G.A. Williamson) (Penguin: 1965).

Friedman, Richard Elliott. *Commentary on the Torah with a New English Translation and the Hebrew Text* (N.Y., Harper Collins, 2001).

Fuller, Daniel. "Biblical Theology and the Analogy of Faith," *Unity and Diversity in N.T. Theology. Essays in Honor of George E. Ladd* (R. A. Guelich (ed.)) (Eerdmans: 1978) at 195-213, available at http://www.fuller.edu/ministry/berean/analogy.htm.

Gaebelin, Frank E. *Expositor's Bible Commentary* (Ed. Gaebelin) (Grand Rapids, Michigan: 1967 & 1989).

Geisler, Norman. "The Canonicity of the Bible, Part One," *Baker Encyclopedia of Christian Apologetics* (Baker Book House, 1999).

George, Bob. *People to People* (Radio Talk Show, 11/16/93).

Golb, Norman. *Who Wrote the Dead Sea Scrolls* (N.Y.: Scribner, 1995).

Gordon, Nehemiah. *The Hebrew Yeshua vs. The Greek Jesus* (Jerusalem: Hilkiah Press, 2006).

Griffith-Jones, Robin. *The Gospel According to Paul* (San Francisco: Harper Collins, 2004).

Hamilton, Victor P. *New International Commentary on the Old Testament* (Eerdmans 1990) Vol. 1.

Jastrow Jr., Robert, "Balaam," *Encyclopedia of Judaism* available online at http://www.jewishencyclopedia.com/view.jsp?artid=161&letter=B&search=balaam.

Jepperson, Knudd. (D.D., University Lecturer.) *On False And True Prophets in the Old Testament* (2005) at http://www.theonet.dk/spirituality/spirit95-6/prophesy.html.

Johnson, Alan. "Revelation," *Hebrews-Revelation* in *The Expositor's Bible Commentary* (Ed. F.E.Gaebelein) Vol. 12 at 434. (Zondervan, 1981).

Keil & Delitzsch. *Commentary on the Old Testament* (10 Vols.) (Hendrickson, 1996).

Knox, John. *Marcion and the New Testament* (Chicago: University of Chicago Press, 1942).

Langevin, Gilles. "Faith," *Dictionary of Fundamental Theology* (Ed. Latourelle, Rene). (New York: Crossroad Publishing Company, 1994) at 309.

Larkin, Clarence. *Dispensational Truth* (Philadelphia: Larkin, 1918).

Liddell, Henry George & Scott, Robert. *A Greek-English Lexicon* (1940) (available online http://www.perseus.tufts.edu/cgi-bin/ptext?doc=Perseus%3Atext%3A1999.01.0155&layout=&loc=Matthew+7.1) (last visited 2005).

Lieuwen, Daniel. *The Emergence of the New Testament Canon* (1995) available at http://www.orthodox.net/faq/canon.htm (last visited 2005).

Loy, Jr., Kenneth. *My Body His Temple: The Prophet Daniel's Guide to Nutrition* (Aroh Publishing, 2001).

Lusk, Richard. *Future Justification for Doers of the Law* (2003) at http://www.hornes.org/theologia/content/ rich_lusk/future _ justification _to _ the _ doers_of_the_law.htm (last visited 2005).

Luther, Martin. *Antinomian Theses (1537),* reprinted as *Don't Tell Me That From Martin Luther's Antinomian Theses* (Minneapolis: Lutheran Press, 2004). The *Antinomian Thesis* is also available online at http://www.truecovenanter.com/truelutheran / luther_ against_ the_ antinomians.html#note01.

Luther, Martin. *Epistle on Galatians* (1535), available at http://www.biblehelpsonline.com/martinluther/galatians/galatians4.htm (last accessed 2005).

Luther, Martin. "Epistle August 1, 1521," *Luther's Works: American Edition* (ed. J. Pelikan & H. Lehman)(St. Louis: Concordia Publishing & Philadelphia: Fortress Press) (1955-1986).

Luther, Martin. "How Christians Should Regard Moses [given August 27, 1525]," *Luther's Works: Word and Sacrament I* (Philadelphia: Muhlenberg Press, 1960) Vol. 35 at 161-174.

Luther, Martin. "The Christian in Society IV," *Luther's Works* (Philadelphia: Fortress Press, 1971) Vol. 47 at 268-293.

Luther, Martin. "Preface to the Epistles of St. James and St. Jude (1522)," from the *American edition of Luther's Works* (St. Louis: Concordia, 1963) Vol. 35 at 395-399.

Luther, Martin. "Preface to the New Testament [1522]," *Works of Martin Luther:The Philadelphia Edition* (trans. C.M. Jacobs) (Grand Rapids: Baker Book House, 1982) Vol. 6 at 439-444.

Luther, Martin. "The Parable of the Sower," *The Precious and Sacred Writings of Martin Luther* (Minneapolis, MN: Lutherans in All Lands, 1906) Vol. 11 reprinted as *The Sermons of Martin Luther* (Grand Rapids, Michigan: Baker Book House) (1983) Vol. II at 113 *et seq.*

Luther, Martin. "Yohannine 3:16," *Luther's Bible in German* (1545), available at http://bible.gospelcom.net/passage/?search=John+3:16-21&version=10.

MacArthur, John. *Back to Basics: The Presentation of My Life: Sacrifice* at http://www.biblebb.com/files/MAC/1390.htm (last visited 2005).

MacArthur, John. *Christ Displays His Glory: A Preview of the Second Coming, Part 2* at http://www.biblebb.com/files (last visited 2005).

MacArthur, John. *Hard to Believe: The High Cost and Infinite Value of Following Jesus* (2003).

MacArthur, John. *The Gospel According to the Apostles* (Nelson: 2000).

MacArthur, John. *Liberty in Christ* at http://www.biblebb.com/files/MAC/sg1669.htm (last visited 2005).

MacArthur, John. *The Gospel According to Jesus.* (Zondervan, 1994).

MacArthur, John. *Hard to Believe: The High Cost and Infinite Value of Following Jesus* (Nelson Books: 2003).

Marcion. *Marcion: Gospel of the Lord and Other Writings* at http://www.gnosis.org/library/marcionsection.htm (last visited 2005).

Marcion. *Fragments of Marcion* at http://www.earlychristianwritings.com/marcion.html (last visited 2005).

Marcion. *Antithesis* at http://www.geocities.com/Athens/Ithaca/3827/antithesis.html (last visited 2005).

Margoliouth, G. "The Sadducean Christians of Damascus," *The Athenaeum* (No. 4335) 26 November 1910 at 657-59.

Margoliouth, G. *The Expositor* Vol. 2 (1911) at 499-517.

Mathison, Keith A. *Dispensationalism: Rightly Dividing The People of God?* (New Jersey: Presbyterian & Reformed Publishing, 1995).

Metzger, Bruce M. *The Canon of the New Testament: Its Origin, Development, and Significance* (New York: Abingdon, 1965) and (Oxford: Clarendon Press, 1987).

Moody, Dale. *The Word of Truth* (Grand Rapids: Eerdmans, 1981).

Muncaster, Ralph O. *The Bible Prophecy Miracles: Investigation of the Evidence* (Mission Viejo: Strong Basis to Believe, 1996).

Paulson, Mike (Pastor Touchet Baptist Church). *What Would Jesus Do or What Would Paul Do?* available at http://www.touchet1611.org/PeterPaulMary2.html (last visited 2005).

Roberts, Alexander et al. "The Clementine Apocrypha," *Anti-Nicene Fathers* (ed. Alexander Roberts & James Donaldson; revised A. Cleveland Coxe) (Peabody, Mass.: Hendrickson Publishing, 1994)(available online at http://www.ccel.org/fathers2/ANF-08/anf08-61.htm#P5206_1525700)(last visited 2005).

Segal, Alan F. *Paul the Convert* (New Haven: Yale University Press, 1990).

Shirer, William L. *The Rise and Fall of the Third Reich* (N.Y.: Simon & Schuster 1960).

Spears, Dr. Barnas. *Life of Luther* (Philadelphia: 1850).

Swindol, Chuck. *The Problem of Defection* (audiotape YYP.6A).

Standford, Miles J. *Pauline Dispensationalism* at http://withchrist.org/MJS/index.htm (last visited 2005).

Stanley, Charles. *Eternal Security: Can You Be Sure?* (Nelson, 1990).

Stedman, Ray. *When Unbelief is Right* (1967), available at http://www.pbc.org/dp/stedman/1john/0161.html (last visited 2005).

Stuckwisch, Rev. (Lutheran) D. Richard. "Saint Polycarp of Smyrna: Johannine or Pauline Figure?" *Concordia Theological Quarterly* (January-April 1997) Vol. 61 at 113.

Stulac, George M. *James* (Illinois: Intervarsity Press,1993).

Tertullian, *Libellus Adversus Omnes Haereses,* available at http://www.thelatinlibrary.com (last visited 2005).

Tertullian, *Adversus Marcionem* (ed. trans.) (Oxford: Oxford University Press, 1972) at 262-63, Book 4, chapter 2, available at http://www.tertullian.org/articles/evans_marc/evans_marc_10book4_eng.htm (last visited 2005).

Throckmorton, Jr., Burton H. *Gospel Parallels* (5th Ed.). (Nelson, 1992).

Wallace, Daniel B. *Greek Grammar Beyond the Basics* (Zondervan: 1997).

Weakley, Jr., Clare G. *Why the Book of Revelation is Heresy*, http://www.christian-community.org/library/revelheresy.html (last visited 2005).

White, Dr. James. *Drawn by the Father: A Summary of John 6:35-45* (Reformation Press: 1999).

Wilkin, Bob. *Is Confessing Christ a Condition of Salvation?* (1994) available at http://www.faithalone.org/news/y1994/94july3.html (last visited 2005).

Wilkin, Bob. *Repentance and Salvation: A Key Gospel Issue* (1988) available at http://www.faithalone.org/news/y1988/88june4.html (last visited 2005).

Willard, Dallas. *The Great Omission* (2005).

Willard, Dallas. *The Spirit of the Disciplines* (San Francisco: Harper Collins, 1988).

Software-Resources

E-Sword and its modules were also used in preparing this book. This software is free and can be downloaded at http://www.e-sword.net. The resource modules relied upon from within E-Sword were: various Bibles (GNB, ASV, KJV, YLT, RV, JPS, Webster's, Vulgate, GB) and Commentaries (Gill, Henry, Wesley, Vincent Word Studies, Barnes, Clarke, Keil & Delitzsch, JFB, Geneva Notes.)

Topics

D

E

Made in the USA
Las Vegas, NV
21 December 2022

63792893R10315